In the Trenches at Petersburg

CIVIL WAR AMERICA  *Gary W. Gallagher, editor*

# *In the Trenches at Petersburg*

FIELD FORTIFICATIONS

& CONFEDERATE DEFEAT

Earl J. Hess

THE UNIVERSITY OF
NORTH CAROLINA PRESS
*Chapel Hill*

This book was published with the assistance of the Fred W. Morrison Fund for Southern Studies of the University of North Carolina Press.

© 2009 THE UNIVERSITY OF NORTH CAROLINA PRESS
ALL RIGHTS RESERVED

Designed by Courtney Leigh Baker
Set in Minion by Tseng Information Systems, Inc.
Manufactured in the United States of America

The paper in this book meets the guidelines for permanence and durability of the Committee on Production Guidelines for Book Longevity of the Council on Library Resources.

The University of North Carolina Press has been a member of the Green Press Initiative since 2003.

Library of Congress Cataloging-in-Publication Data
Hess, Earl J.
In the trenches at Petersburg : field fortifications and Confederate defeat / by Earl J. Hess.
    p. cm. — (Civil War America)
Includes bibliographical references and index.
ISBN 978-0-8078-3282-0 (cloth : alk. paper)
    1. Petersburg (Va.)—History—Siege, 1864–1865. 2. Virginia—History—Civil War, 1861–1865—Trench warfare. 3. United States—History—Civil War, 1861–1865—Trench warfare. 4. Fortification—Virginia—Petersburg—History. 5. Fortification, Field—History—19th century. 6. United States—Defenses—History—19th century. 7. Confederate States of America—Defenses—History. I. Title.
E476.93.H47 2009
973.7′455—dc22
2008053307

CLOTH   13 12 11 10 09   5 4 3 2 1

FOR JULIE & PRATIBHA
*with love*

CONTENTS

*Preface* {xiii}

CHAPTER ONE
*Engineers and War* {1}

CHAPTER TWO
*Crossing the James River* {9}

CHAPTER THREE
*Three Days in June* {21}

CHAPTER FOUR
*Searching for a Solution* {38}

CHAPTER FIVE
*Digging In* {50}

CHAPTER SIX
*Soldiering in the Trenches* {65}

CHAPTER SEVEN
*The Third Offensive* {78}

CHAPTER EIGHT
*The Crater* {90}

CHAPTER NINE
*August* {107}

CHAPTER TEN
 The Fourth Offensive {124}

CHAPTER ELEVEN
 September {142}

CHAPTER TWELVE
 The Fifth Offensive {160}

CHAPTER THIRTEEN
 October and the Sixth Offensive {182}

CHAPTER FOURTEEN
 November, December, and January {199}

CHAPTER FIFTEEN
 Winter {215}

CHAPTER SIXTEEN
 The Seventh Offensive, February, and March {229}

CHAPTER SEVENTEEN
 Fort Stedman and the Eighth Offensive {245}

CHAPTER EIGHTEEN
 The Ninth Offensive, April 2 {264}

Conclusion {280}

APPENDIX ONE
 Artifacts of War {287}

APPENDIX TWO
 The Richmond-Petersburg Line {295}

Notes {317}

Bibliography {377}

Index {399}

ILLUSTRATIONS

McKnight's 12th New York Battery at Confederate
   Battery No. 8, Dimmock Line {31}
Dimmock Line, U.S.-made artillery emplacement
   next to Confederate ditch {54}
Covered way from Fort Rice to Fort Meikel {56}
Confederate works, view of interior of parapet {62}
Entrance to a bombproof {66}
Possible entrance to Confederate countermine {113}
Entrance to countermine {114}
Possible Federal countermine shaft {117}
Arched ceiling in gallery of Confederate
   countermine, Jerusalem Plank Road {122}
Western bastion at Fort Sedgwick {149}
Fort Burnham {171}
Fort Brady {171}
Wooden banquette at Elliott's Salient {177}
Ditch at Fort Johnson {177}
Modern view of ditch at Fort Johnson {178}
Gabion revetment of rear line at Fort Sedgwick {200}
Gracie's Salient {205}
Headquarters bombproof at Fort Sedgwick {209}
Casemates at Fort Burnham {236}
Interior of Fort Stedman {249}

Fort Stedman, 1939 {252}
Artillery emplacements and traverses at Fort Mahone {266}
Federals standing on traverses at Fort Mahone {267}
Interior of Fort Mahone {268}
Covered way linking Fort Mahone to
    Confederate main line {270}
Right end of main battery at Fort Sedgwick {297}
Front of Federal Battery No. 21 {300}
Traverses of main battery at Fort Sedgwick {300}
Bombproofs at Fort Sedgwick {301}
Left end of main battery at Fort Sedgwick {302}
Artillery emplacement at Fort Sedgwick {303}

## MAPS

Defenses of Petersburg, 1862–1864, and Grant's Crossing
    of the James River, June 11–18, 1864 {13}
Petersburg, June 15–18, 1864 {22}
Digging In at Petersburg, June 19–July 30, 1864 {52}
First Deep Bottom, July 26–29, 1864 {80}
Pegram's Salient, July 30, 1864 {84}
Crater Battlefield, July 30, 1864 {93}
Confederate Countermines, July–December 1864 {116}
The Fourth Offensive, August 14–25, 1864 {126}
Federal Works from Jerusalem Plank Road to Weldon and
    Petersburg Railroad, August 22–September 28, 1864 {143}
City Point Defenses and Harrison's Landing,
    September–October 1864 {148}

Confederate Countermine at Squirrel Level Road,
　　September 15–November 1864 {155}
The Fifth Offensive, September 29–October 2,
　　1864 {162}
Federal Works West of Weldon and Petersburg
　　Railroad, October 3–26, 1864 {167}
Federal Works North of the James River,
　　October 3–26, 1864 {170}
Confederate Works North of the James River,
　　October 3–26, 1864 {176}
Confederate Countermine at City Point Road,
　　October 1864 {185}
The Sixth Offensive, October 27, 1864 {191}
Hatcher's Run, February 5–7, 1865 {230}
Fort Stedman, March 25, 1865 {247}
The Eighth Offensive, March 29–April 1, 1865 {256}
The Ninth Offensive, April 2, 1865 {265}
Fort Sedgwick, April 3, 1865 {299}
Federal and Confederate Works at Bermuda
　　Hundred, April 3, 1865 {307}
Fort Harrison, 1863, and Fort Burnham, April 3, 1865 {311}
Federal Line from Fort Burnham to Fort Brady,
　　April 3, 1865 {312}
Confederate Line from Fort Maury to
　　New Market Road, April 3, 1865 {314}
Confederate Line from Fort Johnson to Fort Gilmer,
　　April 3, 1865 {315}

PREFACE

Petersburg was the longest, the most complex, and perhaps the most important campaign of the Civil War. Gen. Robert E. Lee staked the fate of his Army of Northern Virginia on the outcome of this campaign, which lasted from June 15, 1864, to April 2, 1865. He had lost the strategic initiative to Lt. Gen. Ulysses S. Grant in the Overland campaign that preceded the confrontation at Petersburg and was fighting to save both his army and the Confederate capital. Even with the important triumphs achieved by Federal troops in the West, the Confederates were still holed up in what a recent historian has called their "last citadel," the lines that defended Richmond and Petersburg. In fact, Maj. Gen. William T. Sherman's grand march from Atlanta to the sea and through the Carolinas was primarily a movement to bring 60,000 western veterans to help Grant reduce that last Rebel stronghold.

Field fortifications played a pivotal role in the operations of both armies at Petersburg. In fact, no other campaign of the Civil War saw such heavy reliance on earthworks to promote the grand tactical goals of opposing field armies. After 292 days of continuous contact, the trenches stretched for some thirty-five miles from a point southeast of Richmond to the area west of Petersburg, crossing two rivers, two rail lines, and several major roads. At several points along those lines, engineers had designed defenses in depth, and all along the front of the trenches were extensive fields of obstructions to trip up and delay an attacker. The obstructions included a minefield that stretched 2,266 yards before a section of the Confederate works. Dams across creeks created water barriers, and extensive countermines guarded against an underground approach by the enemy. Aboveground, thousands of soldiers manned the works, enduring months of broiling sunshine, drenching rain, snow, and wind. Union and Confederate soldiers spent many days in uncomfortable but usually safe underground shelters and learned how to endure hours on fortified picket lines, exposed to a sudden rush by the enemy.

The grim fighting of the Overland campaign preceded the confrontation at Petersburg. From May 4 to June 12, 1864, Grant tried to use the Army of the Potomac to smash the Army of Northern Virginia or to drive it to Richmond. Although Lee's Confederate army remained unbroken, the Federals succeeded in pushing it sixty miles in five weeks of heavy fighting, from the Rapidan River to a point only nine miles east of Richmond near Cold Harbor.

Along the way, both armies developed the habit of digging in whenever opportunity presented itself. Union and Confederate troops had used field fortifications from the start of the conflict in 1861; now, however, both armies remained within striking distance of each other for weeks on end. Lee's men quickly learned the value of fieldworks in repelling massed attacks and in offering protection against sharpshooters, harassing artillery fire, and skirmishing between assaults. The Federals were forced to dig in also, although Lee rarely sallied forth to strike at Grant. Northern commanders relied on fieldworks to hold their position within striking range of the enemy before launching another flanking maneuver. But at Cold Harbor, after the failure of the June 3 attack, the Unionists changed that pattern by digging in only a few yards from the Rebels and beginning parallels and a mine. Grant experimented with siege approaches for only a few days, however, before opting for a sweeping move that would take his forces across the James River. Until then, the Federals remained locked in complex trench systems opposite their equally well fortified enemy for nearly two weeks at Cold Harbor, where the tactical situation resembled what was soon to come at Petersburg.

DESPITE THE IMPORTANCE of what happened at Petersburg, there is no book that covers the use of field fortifications during the campaign, even though historians and readers alike are aware that fieldworks played a key role in it. This book is an attempt to fill the need for a detailed study of field fortifications, and engineering in general, during the Petersburg campaign. It is the third volume in my series of books on the use of fieldworks by the major armies of the East and follows through with the themes, research, and goals established for the series. While the first volume (*Field Armies and Fortifications in the Civil War: The Eastern Campaigns, 1861–1864*) covered the eastern campaigns from the beginning of the war to April 1864, the second volume (*Trench Warfare under Grant and Lee: Field Fortifications in the Overland Campaign*) dealt with the Overland campaign. I consulted a wide variety of sources for this book on Petersburg, from published and unpublished personal accounts to official reports, unit histories, relevant secondary works, archaeological reports, tour guides, and historical photographs. The remnants of earthworks at Petersburg constituted some of the most important resources for this study. A number of other topics important to understanding the campaign, including logistics, intelligence gathering, and the life of the common soldier, are covered in this book because they are tied to the employment of field fortifications.

CONTRARY TO PREVAILING scholarly interpretation, the huge increase in the use of field fortifications in May 1864 did not come about through the widespread adoption of the rifle musket. Grant's insistence on continuous contact, keeping the Federals within striking distance of the Confederates for months on end, caused the deepening of reliance on extemporized field defense. It is not a coincidence that the heaviest use of fieldworks took place during the campaigns that witnessed the most intense employment of continuous contact, in both the East and the West. Petersburg saw the longest period of close contact of any campaign in the Civil War and produced the longest, most sophisticated system of field defense as well.

In fact, the armies seemed stuck in the trenches at Petersburg so long that some characteristics of a siege began to develop. Petersburg was one phase in a highly mobile campaign that took the Army of the Potomac and the Army of Northern Virginia from the Rapidan River in early May 1864 to Appomattox Court House, 160 miles away, by early April 1865. The Federals conducted several offensives to extricate themselves from the static position at Petersburg rather than rely on traditional siege approaches to capture the town. They eventually succeeded in extending the fortified line until Grant was able to simultaneously outflank the opposing line and break through its front, bringing the campaign to an end and restoring mobility to operations in Virginia.

Petersburg was less of a siege than it was a traditional field campaign with some limited aspects of siege warfare. While a number of contemporaries used the terminology of sieges when referring to operations at Petersburg, engineer Nathaniel Michler asserted that "no regular siege was intended." It was impossible for Grant to invest the town with the number of men available, and the strength of Confederate defenses prevented a successful frontal attack, at least until Grant's movements extended Lee's line to the breaking point. "The new era in field-works," continued Michler, "has so changed their character as in fact to render them almost as strong as permanent ones, and the facility with which new and successive lines of works can be constructed (so well proven throughout the whole campaign just terminated) renders it almost useless to attempt a regular siege."[1]

The use of fieldworks was so intensive and extensive at Petersburg that they came to play an important role in determining the outcome of the campaign. Engineering design and a great deal of hard work by Union soldiers aided grand tactics in prying a stubborn enemy out of a seemingly impregnable position. Field fortifications helped to bring about final Confederate defeat in the Civil War.

UNTIL TWENTY-FIVE YEARS AGO, there was only one book about the important campaign of Petersburg. Maj. Gen. Andrew Atkinson Humphreys, chief of staff of the Army of the Potomac for much of the campaign until he took control of the Second Corps, also covered the operations from the Wilderness to Cold Harbor in *The Virginia Campaign of '64 and '65*. As a topographical engineer, Humphreys paid a lot of attention to terrain as well as to grand tactics, but his book is thin and based on very little research. Published in 1883, it has long since been outdated and is more useful as a primary than a secondary source.

Nearly 100 years later, historian Richard J. Sommers published a book that still towers among Civil War campaign studies. It was the first detailed, tactical book about a battle or offensive within the Petersburg campaign. Exhaustively researched and told with a critical eye for detail, *Richmond Redeemed* definitively covers Grant's Fifth Offensive in late September and early October 1864. Sommers's book, which appeared in 1981, also set the pace for a number of other historians who began to write detailed battle and campaign studies of the Civil War, developing a new trend in operational histories. While not necessarily appreciated by all historians, this trend represents the highest mark of excellence in the genre of battle and campaign studies.

A. Wilson Greene published the only other detailed tactical study of a segment of the Petersburg campaign, *Breaking the Backbone of the Rebellion*, in 2000. It grew out of his job as executive director of Pamplin Historical Park and the National Museum of the Civil War Soldier. The park preserves a key bit of ground where the Sixth Corps broke through Lee's Petersburg line on the morning of April 2, 1865. In detailing the story of this breakthrough, Greene provides a great deal of coverage for all of Grant's efforts to extend beyond Lee's right from March 26 to April 2, but the most complete coverage is given to the Sixth Corps attack and the subsequent fight for Fort Gregg by the Twenty-Fourth Corps. Other aspects of the April 2 battle, such as the attack by the Ninth Corps along Jerusalem Plank Road, are not covered in similar detail, but Greene's discussion of Sixth Corps operations is definitive.

H. E. Howard, formerly of Lynchburg and currently of Appomattox Court House, has spent nearly twenty years publishing short books on the Civil War history of Virginia. Included in that list are four books on various aspects of the Petersburg campaign. Thomas J. Howe authored a volume on the failed Union attacks of June 15–18 (*Wasted Valor: June 15–18, 1864*); Michael A. Cavanaugh and William Marvel wrote another volume on the Crater (*The Battle of the Crater: "The Horrid Pit"*); John Horn wrote a book on the three battles (First Deep Bottom, Globe Tavern, and Reams's Station) associated with the Fourth Offensive (*The Destruction of the Weldon Railroad*); and Ed Bearss and Chris Calkins covered Five Forks in another volume (*Battle of Five Forks*). All of the Howard books have something valuable to say about their subjects, but their impact on the historiography is limited by the length of each book in the series. Nevertheless, the Howard studies offer a first step for anyone interested in learning about four of the major events within the campaign.

Besides Humphreys, there are yet only two general studies of Petersburg. Noah Andre Trudeau wrote *The Last Citadel* in 1991. Based on good but not exhaustive research, Trudeau's book also fails to clarify some important aspects, such as the sequence of attacks on June 16–18. With caution, it will serve as an introduction for the novice. John Horn's *The Petersburg Campaign*, published initially in 1993, is a short overview of the subject. It later appeared as part of the Great Campaigns Series issued by Combined Publishing. The book covers all major military movements of the campaign, although it is based on limited research and takes up less than 300 pages. It can profitably be combined with Trudeau's book to allow for a wider understanding of the campaign.

To date, there is no general history of Petersburg that combines all desirable qualities—thorough research, full and detailed coverage of grand tactics as well as strategy, and new interpretations of the events associated with the campaign. This study is an attempt to fill that gap, even though the difficulties of covering a long, complex campaign such as Petersburg in one volume are enormous.

Finally, a road map to make sense of the campaign around Petersburg seems necessary. Inspired by an idea proposed by Richard Sommers, I have divided the operations around Petersburg into nine Union offensives, two cavalry or infantry raids to tear up rail lines into the city, and three Confederate offensives.

First Union Offensive: June 15–18, 1864, the first round of fighting at Petersburg, in which elements of the Eighteenth Corps achieved limited gains by capturing a section of the Confederate Dimmock Line. Subsequent attacks on June 16–18 by units of the Army of the Potomac also failed to win important success.

Second Union Offensive: June 22–23, 1864, in which Grant sent the Second

Corps and Sixth Corps into a poorly prepared strike west of Jerusalem Plank Road, the farthest extent of the Union line at that time. Troubled by unknown terrain and losing connection with each other, the two corps floundered until a smartly planned counterattack by William Mahone's division sent the Second Corps reeling in retreat and left the Sixth Corps alone and vulnerable. It reached the Weldon and Petersburg Railroad but was driven back.

Wilson-Kautz Raid: June 22–29, 1864, in which two divisions of Union cavalry tore up sections of the South Side Railroad and the Richmond and Danville Railroad west and southwest of Petersburg. Energetic movements and hard fighting by Confederate cavalry prevented the Federals from doing irreparable damage and resulted in several pitched battles. The Union horsemen were nearly trapped and captured, but many managed to fight their way back to Meade's army.

First Confederate Offensive: June 24, 1864, in which the Confederates launched a poorly coordinated effort to turn and roll up the right flank of the Union line just south of the Appomattox River. The Federals easily repulsed them.

Third Union Offensive: July 26–30, 1864, a complex operation involving a double approach. Winfield S. Hancock's Second Corps crossed the James River and tried to advance beyond Bailey's Creek near Deep Bottom, supporting Philip Sheridan's cavalry, which was supposed to raid the Virginia Central Railroad north of Richmond. Hancock had orders to advance into Richmond if opportunity presented. Both efforts failed due to stiff Confederate resistance. The other punch was the digging of a mine gallery toward a shallow angle in the Confederate line south of the Appomattox River and blowing up eight tons of powder. The hole blasted in the Confederate line was an open door that the Ninth Corps could not exploit due to a mix-up of orders by the lead division commander, the physical obstruction offered by the jumble of Confederate earthworks in the salient, and stiff Confederate resistance. The resulting catastrophe represented a sad and bloody day for the Army of the Potomac.

Fourth Union Offensive: August 14–25, 1864, in which Grant tried to operate at both flanks simultaneously. Hancock and the cavalry again failed to break through at Deep Bottom, even though they tried with more troops and for a longer time, but Gouverneur Warren's Fifth Corps grabbed a section of the Weldon and Petersburg Railroad west of Jerusalem Plank Road and held it against three days of Confederate counterattacks in what was termed the battle of Globe Tavern. Hancock tried to extend Union control of the railroad farther south but was severely defeated in the battle of Reams's Station. Yet Warren's success pointed the way to future, effective efforts to force Lee out of his entrenchments.

Fifth Union Offensive: September 29–October 2, 1864, in which Grant again tried to work at both flanks and made significant progress. The Army of the James attacked with maximum force and captured New Market Heights and a section of the Confederate Outer Line defending Richmond (most significantly the area around Fort Harrison), greatly enlarging the area under Union control north of the James River. The Federals also repelled a Confederate counterattack on September 30 that was designed to retake Fort Harrison. The Fifth and Ninth Corps succeeded in advancing the Union left to the area of Peebles's Farm, even though a Confederate counterattack on September 30 prevented them from extending even farther. A feeble Rebel counterattack the next day on the right of Warren's corps was easily repelled, and a large but poorly led effort to extend the Union flank on October 2 was easily stopped by Confederate defensive measures.

Second Confederate Offensive: October 7, 1864, in which the Rebels tried to roll up the right flank of the Army of the James north of the James River. After some initial success, they were stopped before achieving that goal. The Federals launched a reconnaissance in force on October 13, 1864, based on reports that the Rebels were building a new line of works near the Union right flank, but were easily repulsed.

Sixth Union Offensive: October 27, 1864, in which Hancock's Second Corps was sent to gain Boydton Plank Road and then to push on to cut the South Side Railroad leading into Petersburg from the west. Hancock made it to Boydton Plank Road, but supporting troops could not connect with him; the Confederates mounted a counterattack that was repulsed, but Hancock withdrew anyway, in what came to be known as the battle of Burgess's Mill. To support Hancock's move, the Army of the James tried to find and go around the Confederate left flank north of the James River, but it failed.

Warren's Raid on the Weldon and Petersburg Railroad: December 7–12, 1864, more popularly known as the Applejack Raid because of Union foraging efforts along the way. It was not a serious effort to grab and hold territory, but an attempt to tear up miles of track. The Confederates had been using the line from Weldon, North Carolina, unloading supplies at Stony Creek Station and transporting them by wagons along Boydton Plank Road. Warren tore up the rail line down to the crossing of Meherrin River and then returned before the Confederates could maneuver units to trap him.

Seventh Union Offensive: February 5–7, 1865, in which Grant initially attempted a massive raid on the Weldon and Petersburg Railroad but changed his objective when the Second Corps succeeded in seizing and holding a crossing of Hatcher's Run at Armstrong's Mill on February 5. This convinced Grant to redirect his forces to seize the Vaughan Road crossing of the Run, intending to use both crossings to support a push west, around the southern end of the Confederate fortifications along Boydton Plank Road, and to reach the South Side Railroad. Efforts by the Fifth Corps to do so were stalled in fierce fighting near Dabney's Saw Mill on February 6 and 7, but the Federals still held both crossings of Hatcher's Run and retained the opportunity to use them to bypass the Confederate works in the future.

Third Confederate Offensive: March 25, 1865, in which Lee attacked Fort Stedman, ostensibly to disrupt the Federals so they could not respond to his planned evacuation of the Richmond-Petersburg lines. The carefully organized attack by the Confederate Second Corps quickly captured this earthwork and contiguous entrenchments, but the offensive foundered in the face of a layered Union defensive plan that prevented the Confederates from exploiting their success.

Eighth Union Offensive: March 29–April 1, 1865, a major Union effort to exploit the advantages won in the Seventh Offensive by pushing four divisions of cavalry under Philip Sheridan, supported by the Fifth Corps, in a wide flanking movement around Lee's right. This resulted in a small fight at Lewis's Farm between elements of the Fifth Corps and Confederate infantry on March 29, and a major attack by the Rebels against the Fifth Corps called the battle of the White Oak Road on March 31. On the same day, other Confederate troops attacked Sheridan's cavalry in the Battle of Dinwiddie Court House. Both Federal forces were driven back some distance but counterattacked and recovered lost ground. On April 1, the combined Union forces attacked an outnumbered Rebel force at Five Forks and decisively whipped it, finally outflanking Lee's fortified line many miles west of Petersburg.

Ninth Union Offensive: April 2, 1865, which ended the Petersburg campaign with a bloody drama. The Ninth Corps attacked along Jerusalem Plank Road and achieved a hard-won lodgment in the layered Confederate defenses after costly fighting. The Sixth Corps achieved a decisive breakthrough that collapsed Confederate defensive arrangements west of the city, even though last-ditch efforts to defend Fort Gregg exacted a heavy cost in Union casualties. Union Second Corps operations resulted in the battle of Sutherland Station, which delayed Federal efforts to exploit their success. Lee evacuated both Petersburg and Richmond that night.

This division of the component military moves during the Petersburg campaign varies from that proposed by Sommers, who considers the Confederate attack north of the James on October 7 as the First Battle of the Darbytown Road and the Union strike on October 13 as the Second Battle of the Darbytown Road. He places both actions as part of the Fifth Offensive. John Horn followed Sommers's outline in his study of the Petersburg campaign and called the entire series of moves from March 29 to April 2, 1865, the Ninth Offensive. I prefer to divide that series into two offensives, for the operations from March 29 to April 1, culminating in the battle of Five Forks, were designed to outflank the Confederate line. The assaults of April 2 were mostly launched against Lee's front. Although set up by the successful effort to flank Lee, the April 2 attacks were a separate set of moves designed to punish the Confederates before they evacuated the line.[2]

The very fact that historians disagree on such a basic thing as designating the order of events indicates that the Petersburg campaign is not only complex but understudied. To a degree, this book necessarily has to be a general history of the campaign to set the proper context for understanding fortifications and engineering operations.

I WISH TO THANK Harry L. Jackson for his eagerness to help in fleshing out my knowledge of Confederate countermining operations at Petersburg. I especially appreciate his diligence in finding a rare sketch map of the Confederate countermine complex at Jerusalem Plank Road that was essential to my understanding of that project.

Chris Calkins, historian at Petersburg National Battlefield, also was very helpful in sharing information in his files and from his personal knowledge about the fieldworks and the mining operations at Petersburg.

Kevin M. Levin helped in gathering material for this book, and Laura Willoughby and Michael Cavanaugh provided copies of material as well, for which I am grateful.

I also wish to heartily thank A. Wilson Greene, David Lowe, and Richard Sommers for their careful reading of this manuscript and their willingness to offer advice that greatly improved it. No one knows more detail about the operations around Petersburg than Richard, and his expertise especially helped me to avoid many errors. I wish to thank the two reviewers who read the manuscript for the University of North Carolina Press as well, and to Gary Gallagher and David Perry, I offer my thanks for their support of this project.

Most of all, my love and gratitude to my wife, Pratibha, for all she does for me.

In the Trenches at Petersburg

CHAPTER ONE

# *Engineers and War*

The engineering resources of both Union and Confederates armies were vital to operations in the Petersburg campaign. Engineer officers and troops provided technical expertise in the design and construction of the complex aspects of fortifications, such as embrasures and platforms in artillery emplacements, the revetting of infantry parapets, and a variety of obstacles in front of the works. Perhaps the most complex engineering operation at Petersburg was mining and countermining, while transportation facilities ranging from corduroyed roads to bridges to river docks demanded a great deal of work. Engineer officers also managed large working parties of infantrymen detailed from line units, which provided the bulk of unskilled labor performed on the thirty-five miles of field fortifications at Richmond and Petersburg.

## UNION ENGINEERING RESOURCES

Maj. James Chatham Duane, a New York–born West Pointer, served as chief engineer of the Army of the Potomac. He had commanded the army's only prewar company of engineer troops and had led the U.S. Engineer Battalion during the Peninsula campaign. Duane was George B. McClellan's chief engineer during the Maryland campaign and served for a time on the Georgia and South Carolina coast before resuming his former role in the Army of the Potomac on July 15, 1863, under George G. Meade. He held that position for the rest of the war. In late August 1864 Duane suffered from sunstroke, which led to an extended sick leave.

Nathaniel Michler filled in for Duane while he was gone. Born in Pennsylvania, Michler had graduated from West Point in the class of 1848 and entered the topographical engineers. He served in Texas and helped to survey a possible canal route across Panama in the 1850s. He served with Don Carlos Buell and William S. Rosecrans in the West. Meade requested his assignment to the Army of the Potomac as chief topographical engineer in 1864.

"The silent and arduous labors of the engineer, upon which depends to such a great extent the success of a campaign, are too apt to be forgotten and overshadowed by the brilliancy of the noble and brave deeds of other arms of the service," Michler noted in an official report. Army regulations kept the number and rank of engineer officers painfully low, and about the only way to reward them for distinguished service was by bestowing honorable rank. Both Duane and Michler ended the war as brevet brigadier generals.[1]

Meade had an efficient force of engineer troops, including Capt. George H. Mendell's U.S. Engineer Battalion, consisting of four companies. Brig. Gen. Henry W. Benham's Volunteer Engineer Brigade, like the regular battalion, had served with the Army of the Potomac since late 1861. It was a fine unit of volunteers, originally consisting of the 15th and 50th New York Engineer regiments. Soon after Chancellorsville, the 15th New York was mostly mustered out of service, and its few remaining companies were detailed to behind-the-lines duty; but the 50th New York remained with the Army of the Potomac throughout the war. Benham and most of the 15th were at the Engineer Depot in Washington, D.C., during the Overland campaign. He transferred the 15th and his headquarters to City Point when that place became the forward supply base for Grant's operations at Petersburg.

Lt. Col. Ira Spaulding's 50th New York Engineers was the mainstay of Meade's engineer force. Spaulding had bypassed Benham and reported directly to Duane during the Overland campaign. For several months after Benham moved to City Point, Spaulding once again reported to him but came back under Duane's control by early October. Benham's responsibilities were restricted to safeguarding City Point and supplying the engineer equipment needed by the army. The different battalions of the 50th New York Engineers had been parceled out to operate with the different corps of Meade's army during the Overland campaign, but when the army became stationary, the regiment was reunited under Spaulding's control by mid-July.[2]

The regiment's duties included making gabions and fascines, constructing embrasures and traverses, corduroying roads, and setting up obstructions like abatis, palisades, and wire entanglements. In addition, the engineer troops plugged gaps in the line while operations took place at other points on several occasions during the Petersburg campaign. Spaulding's regiment served in the trenches five times, the 15th New York performed this duty twice, and the regular engineers did so three times during the Petersburg campaign.[3]

The only corps not allocated engineer troops at the start of the Overland campaign was Ambrose Burnside's Ninth Corps, because it was not initially incorporated into the Army of the Potomac's administrative structure. Burnside's chief engineer, Maj. James St. Clair Morton, detached good line regiments for engineer duty. Although Grant incorporated the Ninth Corps into the Army of the Potomac's command structure on May 24, 1864, Morton pushed on with his project.

The 35th Massachusetts was designated as the engineer regiment of the First Division on May 26. The rank and file took to their new work well, but the regimental commander had to report to both Morton and his brigade leader at the same time. One solution was to have brigaded the engineer regiments under Morton's command, but that would have severely weakened the parent brigades. The uneasy relationship continued after Morton was killed on June 17, with the 35th Massachusetts participating in all but one battle fought by its brigade, in addition to performing a great deal of engineering work. A reluctance to lose the services of too many men led Brig. Gen. Robert B. Potter to replace the 51st New York with the 7th Rhode Island, which was only half as large as the New York unit, as his designated engineer regiment.[4]

Pioneer units replaced the Ninth Corps engineer regiments and allowed them to return to their brigades in September. Meade apparently did not have a consistent pioneer organization for his entire army during either the Overland or Petersburg campaigns. The Ninth Corps formed pioneer companies in all brigades, led by a lieutenant selected by brigade commanders. Officers selected one man out of fifty to fill the ranks of the company, and a first lieutenant or captain was to command the two pioneer companies in each division. The men retained their weapons but were excused from picket duty, while pack mules carried their axes, shovels, and picks. Lt. Richard C. Phillips of the 43rd U.S. Colored Troops (USCT) was chosen from among six men to command his brigade's pioneer company. He supervised forty-two soldiers (and eighteen axes, two shovels, and six picks) and messed with the brigade leader and his staff.[5]

Maj. Gen. Benjamin F. Butler's Army of the James cooperated with Meade at Petersburg. This was a field force newly created for the Overland campaign, consisting of the Tenth and Eighteenth Corps. Its regiments had been in service a long time but had seen only scattered action. The army had failed to take advantage of Confederate weakness in early May when it tentatively advanced into the area between Petersburg and Richmond. After Beauregard's counterattack forced Butler back to his base at the tip of Bermuda Hundred on May 16, both sides fortified across that wedge of land between the Appomattox and James rivers, making the Bermuda Hundred Line the longest occupied segment of what would soon become the Richmond-Petersburg lines.

Initially, Lt. Francis U. Farquhar served as chief engineer of the Army of the James. Born in Pennsylvania and a graduate of the West Point class of 1861, the young officer had participated in the Peninsula campaign. He became chief engineer of the Department of Virginia and North Carolina and then of Butler's field army. Poor health caused him to take a leave of absence the day after Butler's repulse at Drewry's Bluff.

Butler called on his protégé, Brig. Gen. Godfrey Weitzel, to fill in. Born in Ohio of German immigrant parents, he had graduated from West Point in 1855 and then entered the Corps of Engineers. Weitzel had served as Butler's chief engineer during the occupation of New Orleans and commanded a division in the Port Hudson campaign. He also commanded a division in the Eighteenth Corps during the Bermuda Hundred campaign. The army commander also asked him to act as his chief of staff in early July. Weitzel then assigned Lt. Peter Smith Michie to act as chief engineer of the Army of the James, with Farquhar becoming chief engineer of the Eighteenth Corps when he returned to duty.

Michie had been born in Scotland and immigrated with his family to the United States at age four. He completed a high school education in Cincinnati, Ohio, and went on to graduate second in the class of 1863 at West Point. Michie participated in the reduction of Battery Wagner on Morris Island in the summer of 1863 and later on the staff of Maj. Gen. Quincy A. Gillmore, commander of the Tenth Corps. Beginning in July 1864, he served as chief engineer of the Army of the James for the rest of the war. Michie's rank and pay were so low that he considered an appointment as assistant inspector-general of the Twenty-Fifth Corps in March 1865 to support his family. The current commander of the Army of the James, Maj. Gen. Edward O. C. Ord, thought Michie was "worth his weight in gold as an engineer." Grant advised Michie to accept the position and urged Ord to retain him as chief engineer by placing him on detached duty from the Twenty-Fifth Corps.[6]

Butler's engineer troops consisted of eight companies of the 1st New York Engineers, commanded by Col. Edward W. Serrell. The other four companies of the regiment remained on duty at various points along the Carolina coast. The Army of the James apparently had a weak pioneer organization as well. Michie often had to borrow engineer troops from the Army of the Potomac. He had only 565 engineer troops present for duty in March, and his suggestion that a good infantry regiment be dedicated to engineer duty came to naught.[7]

Grant appointed an engineer to his staff on June 5, 1864, when the armies were mired in stalemate at Cold Harbor. Brig. Gen. John G. Barnard was born in Massachusetts in 1815 and had graduated second in the 1833 class at West Point. An inherited hearing problem had not prevented him from pursuing a full career in coastal fortifications before the war. Barnard served as chief engineer of the Army of the Potomac from August 1861 to August 1862 and had been responsible for supervising the construction of the defenses of Washington, D.C. He also saw extensive service in the Peninsula campaign before devoting most of his time to continued work on the Washington defenses. Grant appointed him "chief engineer of the armies operating against Richmond" to give Barnard an opportunity to return to field duty. He had no real need for an engineer officer on his staff but allowed Barnard to offer suggestions and manage paperwork. Barnard began to collect weekly reports on the progress of fortifications along the Richmond-Petersburg lines, monthly reports on engineer equipment and supplies in stock, and any requests for engineering material needed by either army.

Grant could rely on Cyrus Ballou Comstock, his senior aide-de-camp, for engineering advice. Born in Massachusetts, he had graduated first in the class of 1855 at West Point, was very active during the Peninsula campaign, and served as chief engineer of the Army of the Potomac from November 1862 to March 1863. Transferred west, he served as chief engineer of Grant's Army of the Tennessee, and Grant brought him east again in early 1864.[8]

### CONFEDERATE ENGINEERING RESOURCES

Maj. Gen. Martin Luther Smith served as chief engineer of the Army of Northern Virginia during the Overland campaign and for the first month of the Petersburg operation. A New Yorker by birth, Smith had served in the topographical engineers after graduation from West Point in 1842. He married a woman from Athens, Georgia, and decided to support the Confederacy. Smith received an appointment in the Corps of Engineers, commanded a Louisiana regiment for a time, and then was promoted to the volunteer rank of major general in November 1862. He performed engineering duties at New Orleans and Vicksburg and became Lee's chief engineer on April 6, 1864. Smith had an eye for terrain, which led to the effective placement of Lee's heavily fortified line at the North Anna River. Smith was transferred to Georgia on July 20, at the request of Gen. John Bell Hood, to serve as chief engineer of the Army of Tennessee.[9]

Col. Walter Husted Stevens served as Lee's chief engineer for the rest of the war. Also a New Yorker, he worked at various coastal forts after graduation from West Point in 1848. Commissioned in the Confederate Corps of Engineers, he served on P. G. T. Beauregard's staff at Manassas Junction; later he was chief engineer for Joseph E. Johnston and for Lee until assigned to oversee construction of the Richmond defenses in July 1862. This remained his primary responsibility for the next two years. Promoted to brigadier general one month after becoming Lee's chief engineer for the second time, Stevens was baptized at St. Paul's Church with Lee as his witness on September 25. Lee later paid Stevens a high compliment. After thoroughly looking at his fortifications, the army commander told him, "'Well, sir, I have gone around all your lines—and have yet to see a dead space.'"[10]

Lee's Army of Northern Virginia cooperated with the troops of Beauregard's Department of Virginia and North Carolina. Beauregard's chief engineer, David Bullock Harris, was born in Louisa County, Virginia, in 1814 and had graduated from West Point in 1833. Prof. Dennis Hart Mahan was so impressed with his engineering drawings that he used them as teaching aids. Harris taught engineering at the academy, but his father urged him to resign from the army, believing it offered no opportunities for fame as long as the country remained at peace. Harris engaged in a variety of business pursuits in the United States and Europe, married an Englishwoman, and grew tobacco with his brother in Louisa County.

Harris served entirely on Beauregard's staff during the war. He rose to the rank of colonel, playing a big role in planning and building fortifications for Beauregard at Manassas Junction, Vicksburg, and Charleston. Harris was primarily responsible for laying out the defensive line that Beauregard's outnumbered troops fell back to on the night of June 17, 1864, and which they defended the next day. Beauregard complimented Harris by identifying him as "the only officer in his command who never made a mistake." Harris died of yellow fever in South Carolina on October 10, 1864.[11]

The Confederates organized engineer troops in 1863, and the 1st Confederate Engineers was ready for service in Lee's army by the start of the Overland campaign. Two companies of the 2nd Confederate Engineers were organized for service with Lee in the fall of 1864, while the other companies of the 2nd Engineers and the 3rd Confederate Engineers were scattered across the southeastern states and the West.

Col. Thomas Mann Randolph Talcott commanded the 1st Confederate Engineers. T. M. R. Talcott had served as an engineer on Lee's staff before the army leader recommended him for the regimental command. The unit was armed with modified Enfield rifle muskets (with a shortened barrel) and with sword bayonets that were useful mainly for cutting brush.

All companies of engineer troops were recruited from among existing infantry regiments. The 1st Engineers came from Lee's divisions, while Company G and H of the 2nd Engineers came from Beauregard's troops. Harris recommended the subordinate officers in the two companies, which were slowly organized from August to October 1864. They had not yet received their guns by December.[12]

The Confederate engineer troops repaired railroad tracks damaged by Union cavalry raids and countermined along the Petersburg lines, digging a total of two and a half miles of galleries. They also constructed gabions and chevaux-de-frise. Company F of the 1st Regiment made material for countermining operations at the Engineer Depot in Petersburg. The troops rushed into the trenches to serve as infantry on occasion, most notably for thirty-six hours on October 27 and on February 5.[13]

Manpower shortages presented an ongoing problem for the engineer companies. When the Confederates learned that the Federals were mining Pegram's Salient in early July, they pressed forward with rapid countermining there and at two other salients nearby. Talcott needed more men, so Stephen Elliott's South Carolina brigade and Archibald Gracie's Alabama brigade detailed fifty-two soldiers. These men were later incorporated into Company H of the 2nd Engineers. One of the Alabamans, James H. Lee, was mildly pleased with his new responsibilities. "It is some better than lieing in the ditches all the time," he informed his wife.[14]

Charles W. Trueheart became assistant surgeon of the 1st Engineers late in 1864, after having served in the 8th Alabama. He liked the change a great deal, enjoying more comfortable quarters and the opportunity to associate with educated and intelligent men. He was also responsible for black laborers and thus had more variety in his medical practice. Trueheart tried to convince his brother Henry, who was fighting somewhere as a partisan, to seek a commission with the engineers. "With your business habits practical good sense, and readiness at calculations, etc., and even limited acquaintance with land surveying, and the use of the compass, you would be an acquisition to the Engineer Corps." Charles thought the corps needed "men of good sense, intelligence, reliability, enterprise, etc." All these inducements failed; Henry refused, apparently believing the engineer service was too safe. Charles assured him that it was "not as bomb-proof as you seem to imagine."[15]

Col. John J. Clarke, an engineer officer at Charleston, South Carolina, proposed using blacks as engineers in late January 1865, when there was growing support for enlisting blacks as troops. Lee thought well of Clarke's plan. "It is necessary to act cautiously in the matter," wrote Lee's assistant adjutant general, "in consideration of the prejudices of the people, or a part of them, but as such discipline as you propose will render the Negroes far more efficient as Engineer soldiers, there can be no objection to it." The proposal was never implemented, however, despite Lee's strong support for it.[16]

The Army of Northern Virginia dissolved its pioneer organization in October 1864, replacing it with temporary details of workers. This was probably done because of the need for those men in the ranks. The primary duty of pioneer companies had always been to repair roads and bridges during marches, and therefore their services were more easily dispensed with while the army was locked in the trenches.[17]

Engineer officers and troops provided the technical expertise and the skilled labor for building fortifications on both sides of no-man's-land at Petersburg,

*Engineers and War* { 7 }

but infantrymen provided most of the unskilled labor. They dug trenches, piled dirt into parapets, and cut trees and brush in front of the line. In addition to doing most of the fighting, infantrymen also were an important engineering asset, vital for the construction and maintenance of the Union and Confederate works that fronted Petersburg and Richmond.

## GEOGRAPHY

Petersburg nestles in the valley of the Appomattox River twenty-three miles south of Richmond. It is located at the falls of the Appomattox, which demark the upper reaches of ship navigation from the ocean as well as the geographic boundary between the coastal plain and the piedmont. The flat, sandy land of the coastal plain, formerly part of the ocean floor, has a soil with a mixture of sand and clay. While the river lies essentially at sea level up to the falls, the ground east and south of town lies at elevations of 120 to 170 feet. Because of its location, Union and Confederate soldiers found generally sandy soil to dig in around Petersburg, making the task of fortifying much easier.[18]

The piedmont, an intermediate zone between the coastal plain and the mountains, offers a greater diversity of trees, better water, and more varied terrain than the coastal plain. But there is no sharp break in the landscape between the two zones; Lee's men, during their retreat from Petersburg to Appomattox, headed west for many miles before seeing rolling hills, grassy valleys, and clear streams.

CHAPTER TWO

# *Crossing the James River*

Grant's crossing of the James River in mid-June 1864 was a complex operation. It involved disengaging the Army of the Potomac and the Eighteenth Corps from the tangled system of trenches at Cold Harbor, moving them southward more than twenty miles, and building the longest pontoon bridge ever used in the Civil War. Union engineers needed to locate and plan four different lines of fieldworks to protect the movement. Grant hoped to accomplish this without tipping off Lee as to his intentions and then to attack and capture Petersburg, a city that had been fortified for almost two years. The fortifications of Richmond, older and more complex than those of Petersburg, also played a role in the movement. The Confederate Howlett Line that stretched from the James to the Appomattox served as a link between the defenses of both cities.

## THE DEFENSES OF RICHMOND

While scouting the terrain to Lee's rear on May 29, Martin L. Smith caught a glimpse of the Richmond defenses. The armies were still maneuvering north and northwest of Cold Harbor at that time, but Smith knew that if Grant continued his attempts to outflank Lee, the time would soon come when "these fortifications must form part of our lines."[1]

Starting soon after the firing on Fort Sumter, the Confederates built concentric rings of fieldworks on both sides of the James River. The Inner Line was the first, laid out and constructed by Virginia state engineers as a series of batteries that covered the eastern approaches to the city. Confederate authorities later deemed it too close to Richmond but did not begin work on a more forward line until McClellan's Peninsula campaign threatened to bring the Army of the Potomac near the city. They pushed the completion of the Inner Line and the construction of the Intermediate Line beginning in March 1862. The latter was anchored on both ends at the James River and stretched along the eastern, northern, and western sides of the capital. An extension of it also covered about half of the southern approaches to Richmond. After Lee took command of the Army of Northern Virginia early in June, he initiated the construction of the Outer Line, a third defense, to protect the city while he massed troops for the Seven Days offensive. The most important purpose of this line was to shield the eastern approaches to the capital, from the James River at Chaffin's Bluff to the Chickahominy River at New Bridge. The Outer Line continued westward past Richmond and then angled south to hit the James upstream from the city. The Outer Line was the most important of the three, and in a sense it made the previous two defenses redundant. Located about five miles from the city, and twenty-six miles in length, the Outer Line was the only one of the three Richmond defenses that Grant tested in the Petersburg campaign.[2]

The Confederates had anchored the Outer Line at Chaffin's Bluff on the James River, where river batteries held seventeen heavy guns aimed to fire on Union boat traffic. They had lavished a great deal of labor on the network of lines that stretched north and northeast from Chaffin's to form the Outer Line in 1862, and they performed additional work on it the following year.[3]

A newspaper correspondent for the *Montgomery Daily Mail* conducted an inspection of the Richmond fortifications in the spring of 1864. He noted that a telegraph line thirty miles long ran along the defenses. Military roads connected the concentric rings and "negroes were swarming thick as bees" on the Outer Line, while abatis fronted the redoubts. In fact, the writer noted, the "destruction of timber for abattis, fuel, houses, and to afford play for the guns, has been enormous." The Engineer Bureau of the Confederate War Department had been trying to help Walter Husted Stevens to find laborers to push the defenses to completion since early May. It had relied on pressing slaves and free blacks for the past two years to work on the capital fortifications, with ambivalent results. Stevens wanted at least 1,500 workers, but Secretary of War James A. Seddon refused to call up large numbers of slaves because their masters needed them for spring planting.[4]

### THE DEFENSES OF PETERSBURG

The defenses of Petersburg covered all approaches to the city south of the Appomattox River. When Butler approached Petersburg from the north during the Bermuda Hundred campaign in May, the Confederates built a temporary set of fieldworks along the south bank of Swift Creek that effectively blocked the Yankees.

Untouched by direct enemy action, Petersburg had a prewar population of more than 18,000 residents. Railroad connections made it an important point. Called the Cockade City because of a compliment President James Madison paid to the town's volunteers in the War of 1812, it also was an industrial city with cotton and flour mills, tobacco factories, and iron-casting shops. Five railroads met there. The Richmond and Petersburg line stretched north to the capital, twenty-three miles away. The City Point Branch of the South Side Railroad (usually referred to as the City Point Railroad) led east to a prominent bluff on the south bank of the James River. The Norfolk and Petersburg Railroad stretched off to the southeast, where it connected with Suffolk, while the South Side Railroad connected the city with Lynchburg. Finally, the Weldon and Petersburg Railroad linked the city with the important blockade-running port of Wilmington, North Carolina. In addition to the rail lines, six major wagon roads connected Petersburg with the outside world.[5]

The Confederates began fortifying Petersburg in the summer of 1862. Daniel Harvey Hill pushed forward with construction immediately after taking command of the Department of North Carolina on July 17. Lee sent Stevens and Jeremy F. Gilmer to plan the defenses in early August. Hill also assigned Capt. Charles H. Dimmock, a prewar civil engineer, to supervise construction, using three brigades of available troops and more than 1,200 slaves from Virginia and North Carolina. Stevens selected the ground where the line was built east of Jerusalem Plank Road but merely "pointed out" to Dimmock where he should construct the works west of the road before he and Gilmer returned to their usual duties near Richmond.

When George B. McClellan's Army of the Potomac evacuated the Peninsula in August 1862, the urgency to finish the defenses of Petersburg waned. Troops were shifted elsewhere, severely reducing the number of available workers, and local slaveowners grew more reluctant to allow their property to work for the government. Dimmock and Samuel G. French, the new department commander, convinced the Petersburg city council to hire slaves and free blacks to work on the fortifications, but it was an uncertain and expensive source of labor. The city defenses were not complete until the spring of 1864.[6]

What came to be known as the Dimmock Line ran for ten miles, with both flanks anchored on the Appomattox River, and included fifty-five batteries that were open to the rear. The works consisted of large parapets, deep ditches, and a sharp profile. The infantry parapet between the batteries was 20 feet thick at the base and 6 feet wide at the top, while the ditch measured 15 feet wide and 6 feet deep. Slight works had been constructed for skirmishers in the form of a gently descending plane dug into the earth for 12 feet before some parts of the line. When this excavating resulted in a perpendicular wall 3 feet deep, the diggers stopped. An admiring Federal officer who saw these skirmish shelters called them "French rifle pits." The Confederates had cut all the timber for half a mile in front of the line and constructed an abatis. By June 1864, most of this obstruction had been removed, and it no longer proved much of an obstacle.

The cleared space also had begun to grow back with scattered underbrush between the stumps. A military road stretched at least from Jerusalem Plank Road to Battery No. 5, which formed a prominent salient in the line on the far left, protecting the approach along the City Point Railroad.[7]

The Federals directly threatened Petersburg for the first time on June 9, 1864. Butler sent 1,800 Tenth Corps infantrymen, part of Edward W. Hincks's black division of the Eighteenth Corps, and his cavalry division under August V. Kautz. The force totaled no more than 4,500 men under the general command of Quincy Gillmore. It split into two columns on the way to Petersburg, with Gillmore leading the infantry to the Dimmock Line near the City Point Railroad. Kautz took his cavalrymen south of town to Jerusalem Plank Road. Both commanders had authority to attack if they felt there was a prospect of breaking through the Confederate defenses.

The operation proved to be a failure, even though the Confederates held Petersburg with a meager force. Local reserve troops supplemented Henry A. Wise's Virginia brigade, with most of the men positioned to confront Gillmore. Maj. Fletcher Anderson's Reserve Battalion, bolstered by two guns, confronted Kautz. The German-born cavalry officer cautiously advanced his skirmish line twice and was repulsed each time, but his main advance succeeded with artillery support. The dismounted troops approached the Confederate works through ravines without being seen until they were only fifty yards away. As soon as they began to spill into Battery No. 26, the Confederate position became untenable. Raleigh E. Colston, who had come on the scene in time to take command of the Confederates, ordered a retreat to Reservoir Hill some distance to the rear and near the outskirts of town.

This could have led to the fall of Petersburg, but Kautz ended his pursuit when Confederate field artillery took position on Reservoir Hill and opened fire. James Dearing's cavalry brigade also arrived in time to block further progress, and Kautz withdrew from the Dimmock Line. Gillmore pushed his skirmishers forward along City Point Road, but they stopped as soon as they made contact with the Confederates. Receiving no word from Kautz, he left the vicinity of Petersburg at 1:30 P.M.[8]

Congratulations on the successful defense of Petersburg were muted by criticism of the Dimmock Line. Colston later claimed that the works were not complete along Jerusalem Plank Road. "With the exception of a few lunettes and redoubts at the most commanding positions, they were barely marked out, and a horseman could ride over them without the least difficulty almost anywhere." Colston remembered that the parapets at Batteries No. 27 and 28 were only waist high. P. G. T. Beauregard, responsible for defending the area south of the James River, was unhappy with the design of the works. "Affair of

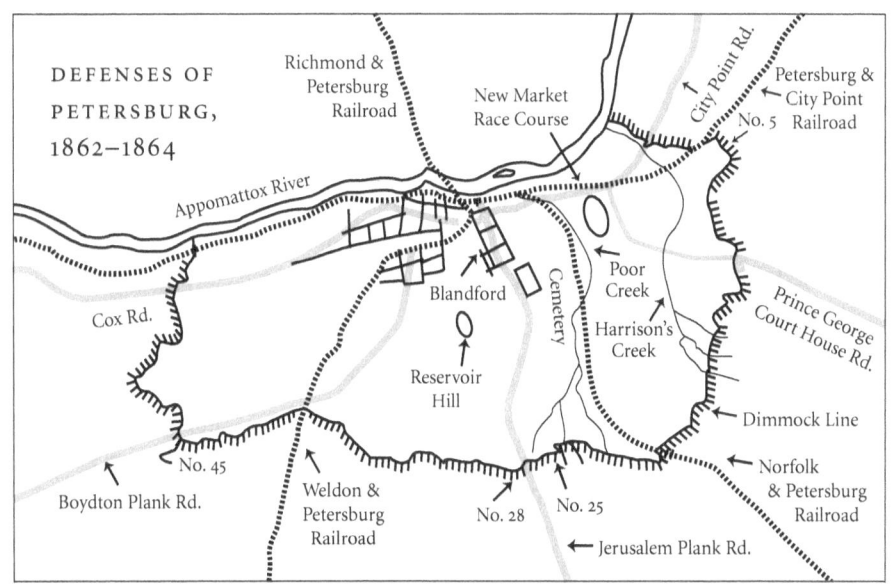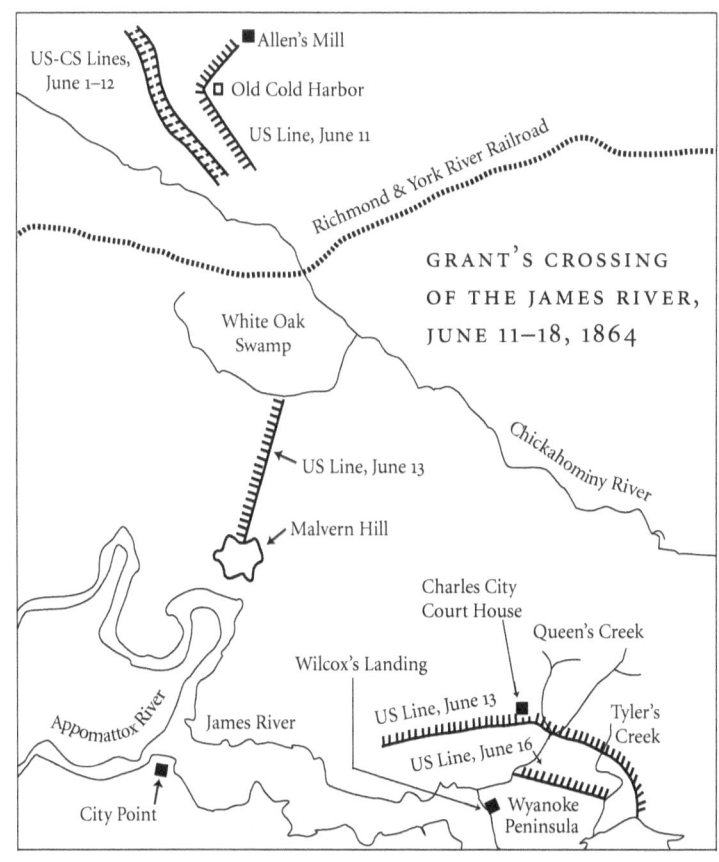

yesterday demonstrates fully bad system of defensive works constructed for Petersburg," he wrote. "When will our engineers adopt strong detached inclosed works in preference to elongated and weak continuous lines requiring a large army to hold them?" He felt that enclosed forts, even if unconnected by infantry trenches, could be defended even by small forces. Beauregard ordered hasty work on the Dimmock Line, and a Confederate artillery officer reported on June 10 that it was "still weak; but, much improved." When Beauregard inspected the line the next day, "his presence inspired all with confidence that all that could be done *would* be."[9]

## OVER THE JAMES

Grant began to prepare for crossing the James on June 8 by sending Barnard to scout for a new defensive line that could be held by two divisions as a covering force. He wanted it placed a bit to the rear of the present line. Barnard, James Duane, and Nathaniel Michler anchored the right of the new position at Allen's Mill on the Matadequin Creek, a tributary of the Pamunkey River. The line bent forward to include Old Cold Harbor junction as a salient in the center and continued to Elder Swamp near the Chickahominy River. Details from the Second and Sixth Corps began digging this seven-mile-long fortification on the morning of June 10. Two engineer officers, Capt. George L. Gillespie and Lt. William H. H. Benyaurd, divided the line into halves and supervised the infantrymen. Horatio G. Wright's Sixth Corps provided 1,720 men for this work, including 150 men of the U.S. Engineer Battalion, using 1,400 spades, 500 picks, and 100 axes. The work details completed digging at dawn of June 11 and cut military roads from the present line back to the new one the next day. Apparently Lee also considered preparing a smaller, well-fortified position to his rear in case he might need to disengage from the Cold Harbor lines. Martin L. Smith scouted around for a good position for an "Entrenched Camp. With Chickahominy for our side," on June 12.[10]

Grant informed Butler on June 11 that he was ready to move the next day. William F. Smith received instructions to ship his Eighteenth Corps back to Bermuda Hundred and then to immediately move out as the point of the Union offensive. Grant also instructed Butler to collect bridging material to facilitate Meade's crossing of the James.[11]

The Federals pulled out of the Cold Harbor lines soon after dusk on June 12. Smith's corps marched to White House Landing, where it boarded boats and headed for Bermuda Hundred. Winfield S. Hancock's Second Corps and Wright's Sixth Corps occupied the newly constructed line to the rear as the rest of Meade's army disengaged from the battlefield. They evacuated the new defensive line later on the night of June 12, having used it only a few hours, and the entire Army of the Potomac moved southward across the Chickahominy River. Another new defensive position was needed for the next phase of the movement. Gouverneur K. Warren, commander of the Fifth Corps, apparently directed the laying out of this line. It stretched from White Oak Swamp, a tributary of the Chickahominy River, to Malvern Hill near the James River. Fifth Corps infantry and James H. Wilson's cavalry division dug this five-mile-long line and held it as the other three corps of Meade's army neared the James River on the evening of June 13.[12]

The Confederates realized their enemy was gone from Cold Harbor early on the morning of the 13th, and Lee pulled his men out of their fetid trenches to find out where Grant was heading. Richard H. Anderson's First Corps and A. P. Hill's Third Corps moved south across the Chickahominy and came up against Warren's and Wilson's position between White Oak Swamp and Malvern Hill. In contrast, Lee sent Jubal Early's Second Corps away from the army to save Lynchburg from a Union column under David Hunter, who was advancing up the nearly defenseless Shenandoah Valley.[13]

Lee's problem lay not in being surprised at Grant's move but in being uncertain as to its ultimate objectives. Beauregard had suggested to Bragg as early as June 7 that Grant would likely cross the James and strike at Richmond from Bermuda Hundred, and the *Richmond Examiner* had also predicted the Federal maneuver the same day. Daniel Harvey Hill, who was in charge of the fortifications along the Howlett Line, thought Grant would strike at Petersburg rather than the capital. Warren and Wilson had blocked the Confederate advance so Lee could not send his cavalry to reconnoiter. He had to wait until sizable numbers of Federal troops appeared somewhere before he could determine Grant's objective. Lee considered the possibility that Meade would cross the Chickahominy but remain north of the James and advance toward Richmond in conjunction with Butler on the south side of the river.[14]

Lee's willingness to wait played into Grant's hands. On June 13, Nathaniel Michler received instructions to lay out a line near Charles City Court House to demark a fortified bridgehead covering the crossing of the James. The left of Michler's line rested on Herring Creek, the center skirted Charles City Court House, and the right neared the James River downstream. The line covered the approach to Wyanoke Peninsula, formed by a jog of the river southward as it flowed to Chesapeake Bay. About twenty miles southeast of Richmond, Michler traced out a curved line that stretched for eight miles.

The Second Corps reached Wilcox's Landing, upstream from Wyanoke Peninsula but within the confines of Michler's proposed bridgehead, on the evening of June 13. The entire corps deployed along the left wing of Michler's line and started to dig in by dusk. Daniel Chisholm of the 116th Pennsylvania reported that "we are all busy carrying Rails, boards, logs and everything that will stop a bullet," completing work "by the light of the moon." Wright's Sixth Corps arrived on the morning of June 14 and deployed in the center, while Burnside's Ninth Corps marched in later that day and constructed the right wing of the line. Warren evacuated his covering position between White Oak Swamp and Malvern Hill early on the morning of June 14, leaving Wilson's cavalry in place. He marched to the bridgehead, where his men relieved Hancock's command on the left of the line. The Second Corps then prepared to be the first of Meade's army to cross the river. By the evening of June 14, the entire Army of the Potomac, except Sheridan's cavalry and the army trains, was safely inside the bridgehead.[15]

Meanwhile, Butler's part of the program became more apparent. The Eighteenth Corps had made good progress after boarding the boats at White House Landing, steaming down the Pamunkey and the Chickahominy and then up the James River past Wyanoke Peninsula and Wilcox's Landing. Smith arrived at Bermuda Hundred at 9:00 P.M. on June 14. That was also the day that Grant held a conference with Butler to acquaint him with his plans. He wanted the Eighteenth Corps to strike for Petersburg, aided by Hincks's division of black troops that had earlier been detached from the corps. Kautz's cavalry division would go along. Smith had instructions to cross the Appomattox River on pontoons at Point of Rocks, and Grant intended to hurry the Second Corps along to support him as soon as possible. Smith commanded up to 14,000 men while Hancock brought some 20,000 reinforcements.[16]

Lee continued to hold his position between White Oak Swamp and Malvern Hill with 29,000 men, most of his available force, on June 14. Despite conflicting reports, he received enough information to conclude that Grant had established a base on the north bank of the James River, and Lee was inclined to believe that Grant meant to operate against Petersburg. But uncertainty plagued Lee's thinking. A few Yankee stragglers claimed that Grant was heading for Harrison's Landing, McClellan's old base on the north bank of the James. Lee knew the strong Federal works there were intact. "I do not think it would be advantageous to attack him in that position," he confided to President Davis. Grant could use Harrison's Landing as a base for either crossing the river or advancing up its northern side.[17]

The grand movement across the river began on the morning of June 14, when Hancock's corps boarded boats at Wilcox's Landing. The pontoon bridge at the head of Wyanoke Peninsula was not yet ready, and Hancock could not afford to wait. A number of steamers began to ferry his corps over the wide river.

Peter Michie had scouted for the best spot to lay the pontoon bridge on June

12 and 13. He recommended three places, and his superiors chose the end of Wyanoke Peninsula, where the water was 80 to 90 feet deep and rose 3 or 4 feet when the tide came in. The James was 1,992 feet wide here, and the approaches to the bridge site needed grading. Grant approved of all these arrangements on the afternoon of June 13, and the engineer troops finished work on the approaches the next morning, with George H. Mendell's regular engineers building the approach to the bridge site across 150 feet of slimy tidal mud.

The pontoons reached the end of Wyanoke Peninsula by noon of June 14, and James Duane took charge of the project. He relied on 200 regular engineers and 220 men of the 50th New York Engineers to construct the bridge. They lay heavy wooden pontoons of the French type from both banks of the river, placing anchors both upstream and downstream to secure the boats, as the tidal action caused the current to flow alternately in both directions. The water was so deep in the main river channel that Godfrey Weitzel placed three schooners upstream and three downstream from the bridge to add stability, as the anchor ropes were stretched to their limit. Over the course of five hours, the engineers deployed 101 pontoons to make a bridge nearly 2,000 feet long and 10 feet wide. The crossing was delayed several hours to allow Smith's Eighteenth Corps to steam through a removable section spanning the main river channel on its way to attack Petersburg.

A nearly constant stream of men, horses, wagons, and artillery crossed the pontoon bridge on June 15–16. While the Second Corps and Fifth Corps consumed sixty-two hours in crossing by boat from Wilcox's Landing, the rest of the army and its artillery crossed in only forty-six hours over the bridge. Fifth Corps artillery chief Charles Wainwright was very impressed by the structure. It was "really a wonderful piece of pontooning," he wrote, "equal I suspect to anything of the sort ever before done." Wainwright found it to be "very steady in crossing, nor has there been the slightest trouble so far as I can learn."

As the troops flowed across the James, Michler located the position for a smaller bridgehead on the north side of the river. He staked it out on June 15, and the Sixth Corps dug it the next day. This fourth and last line to protect Grant's crossing of the James River stretched from Tyler's Creek on the right to Queen's Creek on the left, about three miles, and lay from half a mile to one and a half miles south of the larger bridgehead line. It protected less ground, uncovering Wilcox's Landing upstream, but still screened the approach to Wyanoke Peninsula and the pontoon bridge.[18]

"Since Sunday we have been engaged in one of the most perilous movements ever executed by a large army," Grant informed his wife on June 15. The crossing greatly uplifted the spirits of the men, who were out of the horrid trenches at Cold Harbor and enjoying the beautiful vistas along the river.

"Where is Grant agoing to elbow us again?" called out a Confederate picket to his Union counterpart.[19]

## JUNE 15

Lee continued to hesitate on June 15, the first day of fighting outside Petersburg. Beauregard assured him that he could hold the Howlett Line and protect Petersburg, but the Creole general wanted "his original force" back. Therefore, Lee sent Robert F. Hoke's division to his aid. Lee had started the day intending to move Anderson and Hill back to the Outer Line of the Richmond defenses; but Federal cavalry movements created uncertainty, and he decided to remain in place. He ordered another pontoon bridge laid across the James River one mile downstream from Chaffin's Bluff, making a total of three usable bridges across that stream ready for rapid movement as soon as Grant's target became clear.[20]

Grant's planning had enabled William F. Smith to reach Petersburg with an overwhelming advantage in numbers. His 14,000 men opposed a mere 2,200 Confederates, who were supported by about 2,000 militiamen. Smith concentrated his force at City Point and then approached Petersburg, receiving artillery fire from the Dimmock Line at midafternoon on June 15.[21]

Henry Wise, the crusty commander of a Virginia brigade that had seen long service in the Richmond-Petersburg area, distributed his men from Battery No. 1 to a point on the Dimmock Line near Butterworth's Bridge. To his right the rest of the Dimmock Line was essentially empty. Wise received evidence that trouble was coming, for Dearing's cavalry brigade skirmished with Smith's cavalry advance all day.[22]

Smith's approach to Petersburg brought him up against a pronounced salient in the Dimmock Line, formed by Batteries No. 4, 5, 6, and 7. Battery No. 5, the key to this bulge, was located south of the City Point Railroad. Planted atop Jordan's Hill, Battery No. 5 was 600 yards forward of the rest of the line. This part of the Dimmock defenses lay just east of Harrison's Creek and about two miles outside town. The creek valley is about twenty feet deep but has wide, gentle slopes. Observers described the works here as well constructed, and the ground was still open in the front.[23]

Smith expected weak defenses at Petersburg because of the relative ease with which Kautz had penetrated the Dimmock Line on June 9, but he was surprised when he saw Dimmock's handiwork. A topographical engineer by training, and naturally cautious when he felt the weight of responsibility, Smith spent two hours scouting the position. Satisfied that he knew what to do, Smith then waited an additional two hours for his infantry to get into position. He would have to go in alone, for Hancock could not get his Second Corps up before dark.

Four hours had slipped by, giving Hoke an important opportunity to march toward Petersburg.[24]

The Federals finally went in at 7:00 P.M., supported by a short artillery bombardment. Smith had seen on his scout that a ravine between Batteries No. 6 and 7 could be used to gain access to the rear of the Rebel works. The Federals cracked open the Dimmock Line with astonishing ease. Louis Bell's brigade got into the unenclosed rear of Batteries No. 5 and 6 as men from Hiram Burnham's brigade approached Battery No. 5 from the front. Burnham's people got into the ditch and scaled the outer slope of the parapet by sticking bayonets into the dirt, digging their heels into it, or pulling themselves up by grabbing weeds and grass that had grown on the long-unused works.

As Batteries No. 5 and 6 fell, regiments of Hincks's division took Battery No. 7 by striking at its rear and front simultaneously. Part of John H. Martindale's division took Battery No. 3 as well. Battery No. 8 fell to the 1st and 22nd USCT, and the Confederates evacuated Battery No. 9 when No. 8 fell. The 4th USCT took Battery No. 10 near the Dunn House, and the defenders evacuated Battery No. 11 without a fight. Within a few minutes, all batteries from No. 3 to No. 11 were in Federal hands. The Rebels continued to hold Batteries No. 1 and 2 on the far left, but everything that Smith tried to take had fallen. The amazing thing is that most of this was accomplished by a reinforced skirmish line. Smith had noticed while scouting that the works were lightly held; but he feared casualties from artillery fire, so beefed up his skirmish line rather than expose the battle line too freely. Confederate casualties totaled 378, but Smith never reported his light losses.[25]

Dusk and the timely arrival of Hoke's division robbed the Federals of an opportunity to exploit their success. Johnson Hagood's South Carolina brigade led the division into Petersburg. At first, David B. Harris directed Hagood to take position in the Dimmock Line near Jerusalem Plank Road. But then word arrived of Smith's attack, and Hagood rushed out along City Point Road to throw his men in Smith's way.

The Carolinians encountered a stream of Wise's men retreating from the Federals. Halting his command, Hagood took two staff members forward to scout the terrain in the growing darkness. Harris then sent out a map of the area, along with a candle and some matches, and Alfred H. Colquitt's Georgia brigade of Hoke's division showed up as well. Colquitt and Hagood consulted and decided to establish a new line west of Harrison's Creek. Hagood placed his own brigade on the far left, resting on the Appomattox, and relieved Wise's men who still held Batteries No. 1 and 2. The South Carolinians dug in, using bayonets and tin plates, in a position where they had good command across the wide valley of the creek. What came to be known as the Hagood Line filled out with Colquitt's brigade to Hagood's right, then James G. Martin's and Thomas L. Clingman's North Carolina brigades before dawn. Wise's brigade held the far right, which joined the Dimmock Line somewhere near Battery No. 15. The Confederates still held Batteries No. 12, 13, and 14, which now were forward of the new Rebel line.[26]

The arrival of Hoke's 5,000 men was the turning point in the campaign for Petersburg. The Yankees failed to capitalize on their chance to demolish Wise's outnumbered command on June 15. Smith used four hours to scout and prepare his command so that when he achieved an easy penetration of the bulge in the Dimmock Line, darkness was already setting in. Even then he was content to wait until dawn to exploit his success. Claiming that the Dimmock Line was "a stronger position than Missionary Ridge," Smith told Hincks to reverse the captured works and hold what he had gained.[27]

The van of Hancock's Second Corps reached the battlefield at 9:00 P.M., relieving Hincks's division on Smith's left and extending the Federal line. Beauregard thought that Petersburg was still at Smith's mercy and prepared for the worst all night of June 15–16. He issued orders for Bushrod R. Johnson's division to abandon the Howlett Line, hastily informing Lee of his action. Johnson's men left pickets and some campfires burning and then hastened toward Petersburg. Still outnumbered, Beauregard nevertheless assembled a sizable force for the defense of the Cockade City by dawn. What might have been a Federal walkover was developing into a fierce battle.[28]

CHAPTER THREE

## *Three Days in June*

Even after June 15, the Federals maintained the advantage of momentum — they continued to move troops south of the Appomattox faster than the Confederates. But whether they could overcome the problems of troop exhaustion, lack of information, and the defensive potential of even modest earthworks remained to be seen.

When Lee received word in the early morning hours of June 16 that Beauregard planned to abandon the Howlett Line, he hurried George E. Pickett's division from its position near Glendale, on the old Frayser's Farm battlefield. Lee also sent Anderson to take charge of the Howlett Line and asked Beauregard to leave his pickets behind until the relieving force arrived. But it soon became apparent that the pickets were gone and some Federals had already occupied the Howlett works. Lee dispatched two other divisions to help Pickett retake them. The army commander had thus far repositioned his force so that about half his available troops were south of the James River.[1]

### JUNE 16

Beauregard was too busy at Petersburg to worry about the Bermuda Hundred line. Johnson's division arrived at 10:00 A.M., giving Beauregard a total of 10,000 men to defend the city. Johnson placed his troops to Wise's right, extending the Confederate position east and southeast of town. Even though the Second and Eighteenth Corps were in place and could have moved forward at any time, Meade ordered Hancock and Smith to wait until Burnside arrived before they launched another attack. The two corps already had around 30,000 men on the battlefield, outnumbering Beauregard three to one, but they were idle nearly all day. Hancock's and Smith's commands joined at the Friend House, near Battery No. 8, while Hancock's left wing extended nearly to the Norfolk and Petersburg Railroad.[2]

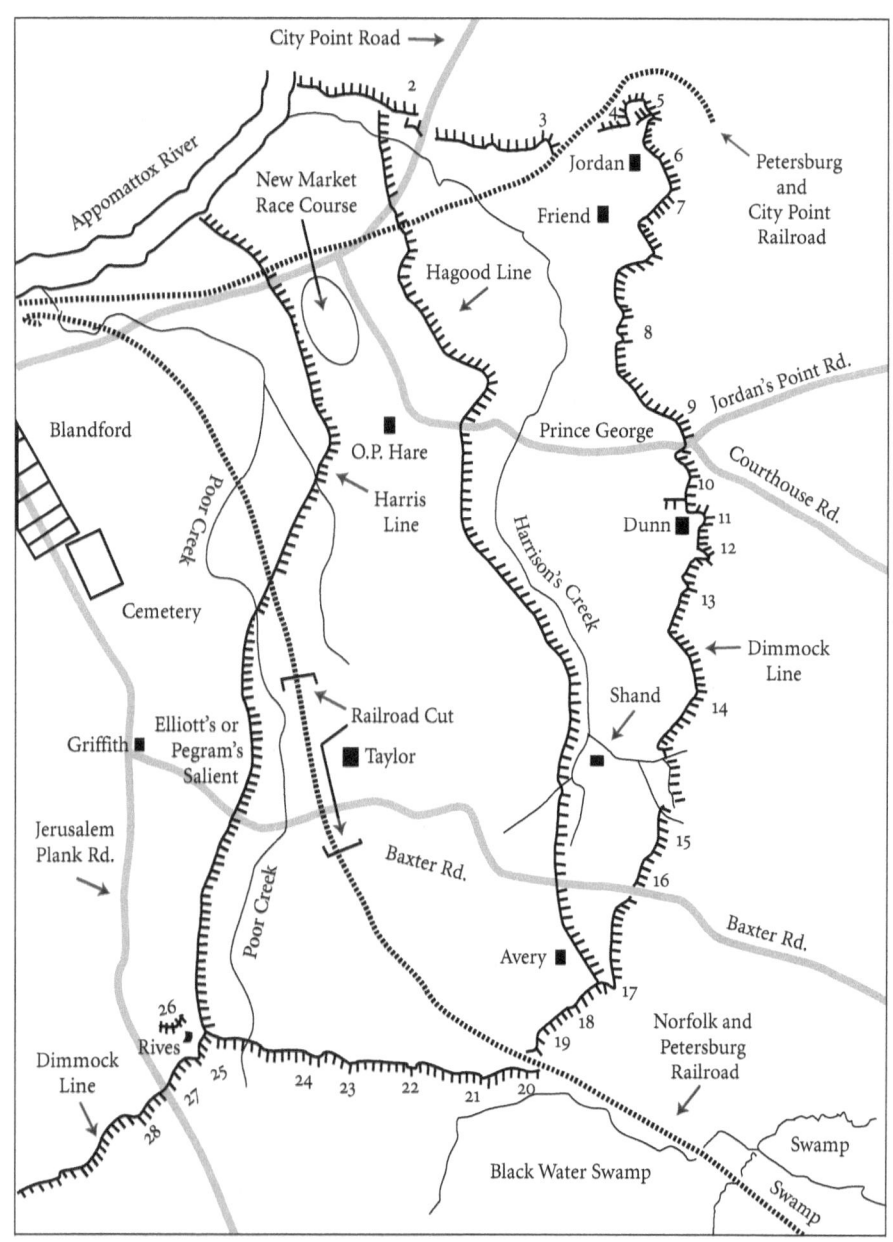

Petersburg, June 15–18, 1864

By the end of the day, Beauregard decided that Hagood's line was not strong enough. He ordered David B. Harris to lay out a new position on more advantageous ground to the rear and informed Lee that he would fall back to it as soon as possible.[3]

As the armies waited, a seesaw struggle for control of the Howlett Line took place at Bermuda Hundred. Butler became aware that Beauregard had given up the strong work on the morning of June 16. He advanced the Tenth Corps and a portion of the Eighteenth Corps to take possession of the works and tear up the Richmond and Petersburg Railroad. The Yankees occupied the entire line, even Battery Dantzler, the northern anchor, by early afternoon. Grant was greatly encouraged by this news and arranged for two divisions of the Sixth Corps to help Butler.[4]

Instead of pushing out to permanently sever the lines of communication between Richmond and Petersburg, or to move on Petersburg from the north, Butler's men busied themselves with minor and shortsighted tasks. Weitzel put 1,200 men to work shoveling away the Confederate parapet and cutting trees that stood between the lines, for they had served as cover for Confederate sharpshooters during the past month. Weitzel tried to make a "rapid survey" of the Rebel works and looked for suitable ground for advanced redoubts between the lines. From Butler down to the lowest private, no one seemed to think this was a unique opportunity that had to be exploited. Instead, housekeeping chores occupied everyone's attention.[5]

This gave Anderson a chance to reclaim the Howlett Line. He deployed Pickett's and Charles W. Field's divisions and pushed back Federal pickets on the Richmond and Petersburg Turnpike. These pickets warned Alfred H. Terry, temporarily commanding the Tenth Corps, that all of Lee's army was advancing, and he ordered a retreat. The Confederates reoccupied most of the Howlett Line by 6:00 P.M. Field advanced to an unfinished Confederate extension that diverged from the original Howlett Line about halfway between the two rivers. It angled off to the southwest and connected with the Appomattox about a mile upstream from the southern terminus of the original line. The Federals still held that southern half of the original works, but darkness prevented the Rebels from pushing on.[6]

Lee still could not make sense of Grant's intentions on June 16, even though he had allowed his army to straddle the James River in an effort to make up for Beauregard's need to shift troops to Petersburg. Word that the Second and Eighteenth Corps fronted Beauregard did not clarify the situation; it could mean that Grant intended to advance on both sides of the river. Lee waited a little longer while shifting the minimum force necessary to help Beauregard.[7]

Grant, on the other hand, possessed the strategic initiative. He and Meade were already on the battlefield outside Petersburg by midday on June 16. The van of the Ninth Corps had also arrived at 10:00 A.M., and two of its divisions were in line by early afternoon. The Fifth Corps was then crossing the James River, and the Sixth Corps was preparing to cross too. But when Grant and Meade took in the situation, they decided that the Ninth Corps was too exhausted and scattered to play a significant role in the day's attack—the last division did not arrive until 6:00 P.M. The assault would have to be made by the troops already in position.[8]

Hancock commanded both corps that day, but his initiative had been stifled by Meade's order to wait. A reconnaissance in force by Col. Thomas W. Egan's brigade of Birney's division led to the capture of Battery No. 12, one of the works now located forward of the right wing of the Hagood Line. Ransom's brigade, however, prevented Egan from advancing any farther. The Federals dug in at a right angle to the Dimmock Line facing north and waited for further orders.[9]

Grant told Meade to attack, and it took the army leader two hours to plan what to do. Barnard and Comstock of Grant's staff reconnoitered the terrain but could not determine where the Rebels were strong or weak. Barnard nevertheless recommended an attack by one division on Hancock's left, which led Francis C. Barlow and Meade's chief of staff, Andrew A. Humphreys, to scout that area. Meanwhile, Meade devised an order of attack in which Barlow was to strike at the area around the Avery and Shand houses, supported by two brigades of the Ninth Corps. David B. Birney's division was to strike at the area around the Hare House, supported by John Gibbon's division. The Eighteenth Corps was to demonstrate to Hancock's right.[10]

Barlow went in vigorously at 6:00 P.M. and happened to approach a flaw in the Confederate position. When Johnson's division took post to Wise's right that morning, Johnson had allowed a ravine to create a gap a quarter-mile wide between the two commands. Wise told Johnson of this weakness, and the latter agreed to fill the gap with a brigade, but this had not been done before Barlow's men went in.

The Federals captured Batteries No. 13 and 14, which also were forward of the Hagood Line, and they dented the main Confederate position. Col. John S. Fulton's Tennessee brigade of Johnson's division fell back a short distance under the pressure. This exposed Wise's flank, and he dispatched troops to help Fulton stabilize the line. As a result, even though Burnside sent in a brigade to support Barlow's left, the Federals achieved no breakthrough on Beauregard's right wing.[11]

Birney had little more luck than Barlow. His division struck out from the captured portion of the Dimmock Line near the Dunn House and mostly hit

Clingman's brigade of Hoke's division. Birney's troops made a temporary and limited lodgment in the Rebel trench, but they could not exploit it before the Confederates pushed them back. Gibbon tried to support Birney to the north. Here, Martin's brigade of Hoke's division was positioned east of the Hare House, fronted by a wide open field. As soon as Col. John Ramsey's brigade of Gibbon's division emerged from the tree cover on the opposite side of the field, the Confederates subjected it to a storm of artillery and small arms fire. Some of Ramsey's men got within thirty yards of the Confederate parapet, but most fell back to the edge of the woods and dug in. To Hancock's right, Smith's Eighteenth Corps pushed to within seventy-five yards of Hagood's brigade before they gave up and retired.[12]

By 9:00 P.M., after three hours of sporadic fighting, the Union advance came to a halt. Meade failed to utilize his three-to-one numerical superiority over Beauregard and started too late in the day to allow the Federals an opportunity to exploit success. All in all, June 16 was yet another day of deliverance for the Confederates.[13]

Warren's Fifth Corps began arriving on the battlefield late that evening, but the Confederates did not remain idle in the dark. Their skirmishers opened fire on the Yankees who were digging in close to the Hagood Line. This lasted until 4:00 in the morning of June 17 and destroyed the sleep of everyone involved; it also failed to prevent the Federals from fortifying deeply enough to afford some shelter by dawn.[14]

## JUNE 17

Unlike the previous two days, fighting began at daybreak on June 17 with an attack by the Ninth Corps. Robert B. Potter's division, on the far left, faced a Confederate position that had significant weaknesses. A network of ravines, forming the headwaters of Harrison's Creek, separated Potter from the Rebels, with the Shand House on high ground in the middle of this network and in front of the Confederate line. There was a shallow salient there as the extreme right of the Hagood Line extended forward, toward the Federals, in order to connect with Battery No. 15 southeast of the Shand House. The Rebel guns in the battery were able to partially fire down the length of the main ravine that Potter had to cross. The Confederate infantry, however, was stretched very thin. Clingman's North Carolina brigade had been inserted between Wise's command and Fulton's Tennesseans, but a gap of 100 yards still existed between Fulton's right and the battery. There still was a gap of some distance between Fulton and Clingman.

Potter carefully planned his attack, placing his two brigades in the main ravine at about 3:00 A.M. They moved out before Confederate gunners could catch sight of them in the daylight. The Federals pushed back Fulton's skirmish line, located on the western edge of the ravine system, and smashed into the main line. Fulton's troubled brigade, which had formerly been commanded by Johnson himself, folded in the early dawn. Potter captured 600 men along with the flag of the 44th Tennessee, and the 48th Pennsylvania took Battery No. 15 with two Rebel guns.

Unfortunately, no one came up to help Potter exploit his success. James H. Ledlie's division started out but was slowed by the ravines and brush and could not bring any weight to bear. Barlow's division of the Second Corps also failed to support Potter's right. As a result, Stephen Elliott's South Carolina brigade of Johnson's division was able to establish a new line several hundred yards west of Potter's breakthrough, and the Ninth Corps troops busied themselves with consolidating their position. Meade's artillery chief, Henry J. Hunt, placed two batteries near Battery No. 15 and ordered that the open gorge of the captured work be closed with a new parapet after dark.[15]

Another Ninth Corps effort was postponed until 2:00 P.M., when Orlando B. Willcox's division sallied forth against the Hagood Line north of the Shand House. Willcox formed his two brigades partly in the ravine and partly on its western crest, but the advance was marred by confusion. The guide unit, the 2nd Michigan, got its directions mixed up and veered sharply to the right, causing the whole of John F. Hartranft's brigade to follow. The Confederates poured enfilade fire into its exposed left flank, completely breaking the momentum of the assault. The situation was made worse for Willcox by the absence of artillery support and by the dust kicked up by his men as they struggled across a cornfield that fronted the Rebel line, which here was held primarily by Wise's brigade.

Burnside's engineer officer, James St. Clair Morton, was killed by the explosion of a shell in this attack. His loss affected many in Burnside's corps. Willcox suffered 840 casualties out of only 1,890 men engaged in his division and accomplished nothing for the loss. The survivors dug in wherever they could for the rest of what one Federal called "a hard fighting day." Nelson A. Miles's brigade of Barlow's division advanced to the north of Willcox as support, but it made no headway.[16]

By the time Willcox's men accepted their repulse, Lee finally became convinced that Grant was making his main effort south of the Appomattox. Beauregard relayed further information about the units confronting him, which prompted Lee to order Hill's Third Corps to Drewry's Bluff so he could push it south if further developments warranted. Beauregard also informed Lee that he intended to fall back to his new line that night. If worst came to worst, the Creole general intended to evacuate Petersburg, cross the Appomattox, and secure his men behind Swift Creek. This ominous warning reached Lee at 10:00 P.M. Twenty minutes later, word arrived from his cavalry that the Army of the Potomac had definitely crossed the James. At 11:00 P.M., Lee finally ordered Hill to cross the Appomattox.[17]

Long before that order reached Hill, more fighting took place on both sides of the Appomattox. Lee spent some time that afternoon at Bermuda Hundred, helping Anderson manage the recapture of the Howlett Line. The question was whether the Confederates should risk an attack to secure the southern segment of the original line, still held by Butler's men. At first Lee authorized an advance to begin at 5:00 P.M., but at the last minute he sent Anderson and some engineer officers to see if the new line, which angled southwest from the center of the Howlett works, would do just as well as the old one. The group quickly surveyed the trench and decided not to risk any more lives in an attack. Field was riding with Anderson and quickly sent word to his division to cancel the assault, but Pickett was with his command and never got the word. The Virginia division advanced as planned. When he learned of this, Field threw in a brigade of his own as support. The Army of the James offered scant resistance, and the Rebels reclaimed all of the original Howlett Line.[18]

About the time that Pickett and Field completed their restoration of the Howlett Line, Ledlie's division launched a spirited attack against Petersburg. Moved up to command the division a short time before, Ledlie took shelter in a ravine as his division moved forward under Col. Jacob P. Gould at 6:00 P.M. It started from the same ravine north of the Shand House that Willcox had used as his jump-off point earlier in the day. Rather than veer northwest, Gould angled the division toward the southwest as soon as it started.

Three Confederate brigades got mixed up in the coming fight: the right wing of Clingman, much of Wise, and part of Elliott. John Forrest-Robinson of the 23rd South Carolina was not happy with the works Elliott defended. They were "of slight protection, only about waist deep and no ditch in front." Suddenly Forrest-Robinson heard the Federals shout "Forward" in the ravine. Then he saw first their regimental flags appear over the crest and then their gun barrels and their heads. The Confederates waited until the whole man appeared, then opened fire. Gould's command advanced with vigor and broke into the Confederate works, driving three Rebel regiments from the field and forcing the two on both sides of the breach to refuse their lines. A quarter-mile segment of the Hagood Line fell into Federal hands; but Gould had no reserves to widen the breach, and counterthrusts by the Confederates kept his troops off balance. Yet it was not until 11:00 P.M. that Ransom's and Gracie's brigades mounted a strong counterattack that finally sealed the breach.[19]

Warren's Fifth Corps began to reach the field by midmorning of June 17 and deployed to the left of the Ninth Corps, stretching the Union line a bit beyond Beauregard's flank. Meade feared a Rebel attack might slice into his unprotected left, so he deployed Warren in a defensive posture. Lysander Cutler took position south of Baxter Road, but Samuel W. Crawford and Romeyn B. Ayres deployed to Burnside's rear. Charles Griffin remained in reserve close by. For the rest of the day Warren scouted and became familiar with the terrain but made no effort to bypass the Confederate flank. On the far Union right, a similar sort of inactivity prevailed on June 17 as Smith's Eighteenth Corps remained quiet all day.[20]

Meanwhile, David B. Harris and Hilary P. Jones, Beauregard's artillery chief, laid out a new line to the rear of the Hagood position that would become known as the Harris Line. The two officers worked all day of June 17 to drive stakes from the Appomattox River to Baxter Road. Then they showed the line to various staff officers of Hoke's and Johnson's divisions before dark so they could pass on detailed information about where each regiment should be posted. Brigade commanders received orders to fall back to this new position at night.[21]

Darkness settled on the battlefield as the Confederates began to light campfires and post pickets. Then they quietly evacuated the Hagood Line at 12:30 A.M. Units took up their assigned positions on Harris's line and started to entrench. In some areas, a little digging had already been done. Members of the 34th Virginia found a group of black laborers fortifying near Baxter Road. They pitched in with cups and bayonets to speed the work. Nearby, the 49th North Carolina discovered a trench that already was two feet deep and began to improve it. Troops along the line complained there were not enough entrenching tools, and they were forced to use anything handy, "in fact, every utensil that could be found." As a result, some units, such as Ransom's 56th North Carolina, constructed only meager works before dawn.[22]

Hagood also found the crude beginnings of a trench when he pulled his brigade back to the Harris Line, which was some 800 yards behind his former position. At some spots, the trench was two feet deep. At others, "not a spade had been put in the ground—the line had been merely marked out by the engineers." His South Carolinians settled in by 1:30 A.M., with the left resting on the Appomattox and the brigade stretched to the breaking point across the City Point Railroad all the way to Hare House Hill. New Market Race Course, a large oval of cleared land, lay in front of his right wing. Hagood's men started trenches where none existed and improved trenches already begun.[23]

Capt. Richard G. Pegram's Virginia battery pulled out of the Howlett Line on June 16 and took position on the Harris Line opposite the Taylor House before nightfall on June 17. Pegram failed to notice the stakes that Harris had planted, which marked the exact position for the guns. Instead, the captain put his pieces a few yards forward and began to dig detached, one-gun emplacements with semicircular parapets. Harris was surprised when he rode up at 11:00 P.M., and he told Pegram of his mistake. The stakes behind his guns indicated what Pegram later called a heavily fortified battery position, "with traverses of such thickness as would require a large force to complete it in a day." Harris, however, warned him not to expect any infantrymen to construct the work, as they had their hands full on the rest of the line. Pegram knew his men were too tired to dig the emplacement that Harris contemplated. "I was compelled to hold on to the position I had already taken," he later recalled. As the infantry fell back to either side of him, they were also compelled to align with his forward position. A shallow bulge in the line, later called Pegram's or Elliott's Salient, was thus created. Pegram's men constructed only "slight earthworks" by dawn. When Union artillery opened at 10:00 A.M. of June 18, several projectiles plowed through the thin parapets.[24]

Despite this weak sector, the Harris Line was stronger than the Hagood Line. It stretched from the Appomattox River to Battery No. 25 just east of Jerusalem Plank Road and was located 500 to 1,000 yards behind Hagood's position and about a mile behind the left wing of the Dimmock Line. Although it had some shallow angles, Harris's line took advantage of high ground between ravines and creeks. There were several open fields in front of the position, most notably at the New Market Race Course, around Hare House Hill, and between Taylor's Farm and Pegram's Salient. Harris's position eliminated the huge bulge created by the placement of the Dimmock Line from Battery No. 1 to 24.[25]

## JUNE 18

In the early morning hours of June 18, an officer from Beauregard's headquarters brought information that finally convinced Lee that Grant was completely across the James River. He had hesitated for days before committing his own army to that area. Now Lee sent orders for Kershaw, Field, and Hill to march for Petersburg. Only Pickett and half of Wilcox's divisions continued to hold the Howlett Line, and no appreciable number of Confederate troops remained north of the James.[26]

But it took many hours for these units to reach the battlefield. Meanwhile, the Federals enjoyed a four-to-one numerical advantage over Beauregard. Fourteen Union divisions were on the field, totaling 80,000 men. The Army of the Potomac advanced at 4:30 A.M. to find the Hagood Line empty. Judging from reports, Meade believed the new Confederate position was not well fortified, so he ordered a general attack. Smith planned to make the main effort of the Eighteenth Corps with John H. Martindale's division, and Thomas H. Neill's division of the Sixth Corps in support. Gibbon's and Birney's divisions, the latter commanded by Gershom Mott because Birney had to take charge of the Second Corps from the ailing Hancock, would attack in the center. Mott faced the Hare House Hill sector and a salient held by Alfred H. Colquitt's Georgians. Burnside crunched his command into a narrow one-division front, with Willcox leading the way and Potter and Ledlie behind as support. Warren rearranged his corps as well, with Crawford's division extending the Union line left of Burnside, then Cutler's division to his left, as he held Ayres's and Griffin's divisions in reserve.[27]

The Second Corps was the first to come to grips with the new Rebel position. McAllister's brigade of Mott's division advanced at 11:00 A.M., crossing a sunken portion of the Prince George Court House Road. His troops managed to get only 100 yards beyond the road before withering fire brought them to a halt. "Our ranks melted away," McAllister frankly admitted to his family, "and we could not advance further." His brigade remained here until midafternoon, when it fell back and reformed. Before that withdrawal, and after McAllister's advance, Gibbon went forward to his right at about noon. Two of his brigades, led by Byron R. Pierce and John Ramsey, were torn apart by the same kind of devastating fire that had stopped Mott. Gibbon was only feebly supported by the tentative advance of Martindale's division to the north.

When Pierce and Ramsey stopped and fell back, Gibbon sent Thomas A. Smyth's brigade in to Pierce's right. George D. Bowen noted that the sunken section of the Prince George Court House Road made a superb defensive feature, as it was four feet deep and bordered by a fence three or four boards high. But between it and the Rebel line was an open cornfield, the tender stalks only a foot tall. He could see the Confederate works on the other side, 400 to 500 yards away. They "appeared to be very strong," crammed with guns and men. Smyth advanced but made little headway.[28]

Some of the hardest fighting occurred farther to the Union left on the Ninth Corps sector of the line. Willcox advanced across an oat field and drove Confederate skirmishers from Taylor's Farm about noon. As his men approached the deep cut of the Norfolk and Petersburg Railroad, they found telegraph wire stretched between stumps and partially hidden by grass. It caused momentary confusion and milling about. Eventually, Willcox's men spilled into the cut, where they found some degree of safety. Crawford's division and part of Griffin's division, to Willcox's left, also advanced about this time. Many of Warren's troops got into the cut where the Federal advance stalled.

McKnight's 12th New York Battery at Confederate Battery No. 8, Dimmock Line. (Massachusetts Commandery, Military Order of the Loyal Legion and the U.S. Army Military History Institute)

The cut was both a shelter and an obstacle for the Unionists. Its sides were up to thirty-five feet tall and nearly vertical on the Confederate side, forcing the Yankees to cut steps to reach the top. Willcox had pushed the Rebel skirmishers to the valley of Poor Creek, but the main Confederate line, anchored by Pegram's battery, lay just west of the stream. The Harris Line crossed both Poor Creek and the railroad grade to the north of the cut, allowing Confederate troops and artillery to hit Willcox's right flank with enfilade fire. Some of Hartranft's men ripped up ties and rails and threw together an improvised breastwork.[29]

Matt W. Ransom's Tar Heels were positioned just south of Elliott's brigade and within sight of the railroad cut. W. A. Day of the 49th North Carolina managed to raise the small parapet he found on Harris's line a foot before the Federal attack started. As soon as it stalled in the cut, Day's comrades grabbed whatever improvised tools they could find and furiously dug some more. "Then we made the dirt fly," he remembered after the war; "we worked in a hurry."

Ransom's units deployed in a single rank and suffered from the usual shortage of entrenching tools, but they managed to construct a parapet at least shoulder high by evening.[30]

By midday on June 18, Federal commanders on all segments of the battlefield had more detailed information about the terrain fronting the new Rebel line, and many had a vivid demonstration of its strength. Yet Meade began to send desperate messages urging his corps commanders to push on with no further delay.[31]

This led to another round of attacks by 2:00 P.M., when Martindale advanced George J. Stannard's and Griffin A. Stedman's brigades between the Appomattox River and City Point Road. The attack was stopped by only three regiments of Hagood's brigade before the Yankees got closer than 300 yards from the parapet. Stannard's and Stedman's men dug in where they halted, which was only about fifty yards from their starting point. Some of them incorporated the bodies of their dead comrades into the parapet, piling dirt over them. South of City Point Road, Neill sent out Frank Wheaton's brigade from his Sixth Corps division. It did not push the attack vigorously, and Hagood's two remaining regiments had no difficulty convincing Wheaton's men to halt. All efforts to make headway north of the Hare property ended by 3:30 P.M.[32]

By the time things settled on the Sixth and Eighteenth Corps front, elements of Lee's army had reached the battlefield. Kershaw and Field were now in place to the right of Beauregard's beleaguered command, extending the Confederate line beyond Jerusalem Plank Road. Warren's Fifth Corps, which had not yet been engaged at Petersburg, mounted an extensive effort to push through. Warren was responsible for the left of the army, stretching west from the railroad cut. Much of his line took shelter along the rail bed before going in. Warren held Ayres's division in reserve on his far left as he advanced the rest of his line. The men soon discovered that Poor Creek Valley lay in the way, while the extreme right of Elliott's brigade, all of Ransom's brigade, and all of Kershaw's division lay beyond.

The Confederates swept the open, broken landscape between the lines with fire. Crawford never got close to the Rebel position, but elements of Griffin's division made greater progress. Joshua L. Chamberlain's brigade of Pennsylvania troops rolled into Poor Creek Valley, although Chamberlain was severely wounded on the way, and managed to claw its way up the opposite slope to within a few yards of the enemy parapet before stopping. Cutler failed to close with the Rebel line, while Ayres never conducted an attack at all. He ordered his men to advance into the open as a diversion but then halted them partway. Ayres's men dug in for shelter. "We gradually sunk ourselves in the sandy soil by a regular *hen scratching* with our hands & got so low as to feel middling safe," reported Charles Bowen of the 12th U.S. Infantry. Heavy artillery fire tore into Ayres's division, taking out 160 men in J. Howard Kitching's heavy artillery brigade. The men dug with spoons, sticks, hands, and bayonets until spades arrived at dusk; then they constructed a regular parapet nine feet thick and four feet tall. "We can laugh at our shot & shell now," crowed Bowen.[33]

Artillery officer Charles Wainwright did not think his corps pressed its attack. "I cannot say that our men went in well, or at all as if they meant to carry the works. In five minutes they were coming back." Wainwright tried to rally several hundred men of Cutler's division who had fallen back to his guns, taking shelter behind a shallow ridge. Even though he offered to lead them personally, only two dozen or so responded.[34]

On the other side of this contested field, the Confederates had little difficulty holding the Harris Line. In fact, Rebel accounts of this day say very little about the fighting. Pvt. John Alvis Parker of the 56th North Carolina, however, won distinction by saving his comrades from a Yankee shell that landed in his trench. He quickly scooped it up with a shovel and yelled, "Get out of here," while throwing it away. The projectile exploded just after clearing the parapet, but it injured no one.[35]

On the Ninth Corps front, Willcox's division and one brigade of Potter's division went forward at about the same time as Crawford's division to the left. Members of Hartranft's brigade dug holes in the side of the railroad cut with their bayonets to climb out. They received a terrible hail of small arms and artillery fire as soon as they became visible above the lip of the cut, but they managed to drive the Confederate skirmishers across Poor Creek Valley. Many kept going up the western side of the valley, but they had little momentum left. About 1,000 men, all that were left of Hartranft's brigade, dug in 125 yards short of Pegram's battery. The attack on the Confederate right ended with a portion of Burnside's corps closer to the Rebels than any other Union force.[36]

Even before Willcox's men drove to their limit near Taylor's House, the Second Corps had resumed its advance. It would be more appropriate to say it attempted to resume the attack, for several units of Hancock's command refused to obey orders to go in. This was the most visible instance of a refusal to fight among Union soldiers in the Civil War, and it demonstrated that some troops in the Army of the Potomac neared the end of their endurance.

In response to Meade's repeated order to assault without reference to the movements of troops to either side, Gibbon ordered Smyth's brigade to attack at about 3:00 P.M. Company commander George D. Bowen recorded how the men responded. "The officers jumped up, waved their swords and gave the order to charge. The men did not stir. The more I saw they were going to refuse to go the more urgent I became. I was so afraid they would go [I] did not know what to do. The men knew what they could or could not do; they had decided that they could not take this line. They had had experience. The whole Brigade acted the same way; not a man started."

Commanders accepted this behavior, as Bowen's own actions demonstrated. The troops of John Fraser's brigade of Gibbon's division received orders to attack. "They looked the ground over, and they refused to attempt it," Bowen recorded. Then Byron R. Pierce's brigade of the same division received the order. "They, officers and men, positively refused." This unprecedented chain of events was followed by a try with the Third Brigade of Mott's division. It had formerly been commanded by Mott and then by Robert McAllister; now it was led by Col. Daniel Chaplin of the 1st Maine Heavy Artillery. The brigade consisted mostly of veteran units; the Maine regiment, previously inexperienced in battle, had but recently joined it.[37]

Before Chaplin advanced, McAllister told Mott, "It is a death trap. . . . A brigade can't live in there for five minutes." Before Mott could reply, an aide rode up and confirmed the order to attack. Mott felt compelled to obey. He issued the final word, and Chaplin's command started on an epic charge.[38]

The charge was epic not because of what it accomplished but because of the horrible losses Chaplin's men suffered. Yet, one need only mention the 1st Maine Heavy Artillery in this regard, for the rest of the brigade refused to go in with their green comrades. When Chaplin started at about 4:30 P.M., only his old regiment responded. It was led by Maj. Russell B. Shepherd and formed in three lines in the sunken portion of Prince George Court House Road. Advancing between the New Market Race Course and the Hare House, the Maine Heavies struck for the right wing of Colquitt's Georgia brigade, with the 41st Alabama of Gracie's brigade in support.

George D. Bowen watched as the Maine soldiers tore down some fencing along the sunken roadbed. Then they "climbed out of the road, dressed their lines," and stepped off. A torrent of fire immediately fell on them, but the brave artillerymen marched steadily across the open, ascending cornfield. "The nearer they approached . . . the thinner their line became," Bowen reported. He estimated the surviving members of the regiment made it about two-thirds of the way across the field before the momentum of the advance was broken. In all, the attack lasted about ten minutes. Of 900 men engaged, the 1st Maine Heavy Artillery lost 632, the highest loss of a single regiment in either army during the war. In contrast, the 41st Alabama reported the loss of only 1 man killed and 24 wounded on June 18.

Shepherd's regiment went in essentially unsupported. Mott had been able to prod Henry J. Madill's brigade forward a short distance to Shepherd's left, but it stopped too soon to be of any assistance. The rest of Chaplin's brigade took cover in the sunken road while his former regiment was slaughtered. "It was a sickening sight to see men cut down as they were," admitted Bowen, "we looking on knowing it was but a chance that we were not out there ourselves."[39]

This was one of the most dismal days of fighting by the Army of the Potomac during the war, characterized by equal parts of bravery, foolishness, and understandable reluctance to obey orders. Under pressure from Grant, Meade sent his army into piecemeal assaults without developing an overall plan, probing for weak points, organizing supporting units, or looking for ways to bypass Beauregard's position altogether and cross the undefended sector of the Dimmock Line. "I had positive information the enemy had not occupied [the Harris Line] more than twelve hours, and that no digging had been done on the lines prior to their occupation," Meade explained. Yet he believed the failure of the attacks was due mostly to "the moral condition of the army; for I am satisfied, had these assaults been made on the 5th and 6th of May, we should have succeeded with half the loss we met."[40]

Grant supported his subordinate fully. "I am perfectly satisfied that all has been done that could be done and that the assaults today were called for by all the appearances and information that could be obtained. Now we will rest the men and use the shade for their protection u[ntil] a new vein can be [s]truck."[41]

Wainwright pinpointed one problem. "The attack this afternoon was a fiasco of the worse kind," he wrote of the fighting. "I trust it will be the last attempt at this most absurd way of attacking entrenchments by a general advance in line. It has been tried so often now and with such fearful losses that even the stupidest private now knows that it cannot succeed, and the natural consequence follows: the men will not try it. The very sight of a bank of fresh earth now brings them to a dead halt."[42]

The Federals were not only exhausted in body, but many were demoralized. The problem was worse in some units than in others. The Second Corps suffered the most from this malaise. Four of its brigades refused orders to attack that afternoon. Frank Wilkeson, a New York gunner, spoke with members of William R. Brewster's brigade of Mott's division late on the afternoon of June 18. "'Going in to the charge, men?'" he asked of them. About ten infantrymen replied, "'No, we are not going to charge. We are going to run towards the Confederate earthworks, and then we are going to run back. We have had enough of assaulting earthworks. We are hungry and tired, and we want to rest and to eat.'" Wilkeson heard similar comments from other troops when he went to the rear later that evening for more ammunition.[43]

With the ending of the day, both sides settled in for what became a tour of duty along these lines lasting until April 2, 1865. The accumulation of Second

Corps units at the sunken section of Prince George Court House Road broke up that evening. Only Smyth's brigade stayed behind to hold the road. He sent out a skirmish line and kept half his men awake all night. The bright moonlight helped in the recovery of wounded Federals between the lines, except those close to the Rebels. Farther to the west, Richard G. Pegram finally got some infantrymen to help him with his earthworks. Bushrod Johnson sent a detail of men with spades to improve his parapet that night, under constant sniping from Willcox's men 125 yards away.[44]

The rest of Lee's army trickled into Petersburg throughout the day. Kershaw and Field had been the first to arrive that morning to guard Beauregard's flank, unengaged all day. Hill's Third Corps arrived about 6:00 P.M. and also was not engaged. Beauregard had 20,000 men available on June 18, but the troops of his own department saved Petersburg in the fighting.[45]

Lee reached Petersburg with his headquarters staff by 11:30 A.M. on June 18, but he allowed Beauregard to conduct the defense of the city. The two cooperated well enough in the essentials, but Lee would not allow Beauregard to set overall strategy. The Creole general tried to persuade Lee to adopt the offensive by attacking on the afternoon of June 19 before the Yankees could dig in. Lee firmly declined, citing the need to rest his men and to continue the defensive policy he had adopted since Spotsylvania. Beauregard argued that the Federals had to be just as tired and, moreover, did not know the local area, but Lee would not budge.

The two agreed on one matter: the Harris Line was a secure defensive position. Beauregard took Lee to the top of Reservoir Hill at about 1:30 on the afternoon of June 19 to show him the topography around Petersburg. He defended Harris's decision to place most of the line down from the highest crest, especially at Pegram's Salient, by noting that it offered the Confederates a better opportunity to lay down fire on the opposite slope occupied by the enemy. This might lessen the chances that the Yankees could start siege approaches. The Harris Line became the left wing of Lee's position at Petersburg for the next nine and a half months. The Confederates positioned guns on the higher crest to the rear, but they never built a second line of works behind the Harris Line except at a few isolated locations.[46]

The Harris Line was a stronger position than either the Hagood Line or the left wing of the Dimmock Line. The easy rupture of the latter on the evening of June 15 came to haunt Charles H. Dimmock after the war. Local talk spread the idea that Smith's victory had been the result of a flaw in the design of the earthworks, and to a considerable degree that was true. The batteries were open at the rear, and Dimmock had allowed an uncovered ravine to lie close to the line. Harris had more time to lay out his line than had Hagood, and of course more troops were available to defend it on June 18 than to hold Hagood's line during the previous two days.[47]

### AN END AND A BEGINNING

The Federals lost heavily, about 10,600 men, in the fighting of June 15–18. Their losses included sixteen regimental commanders and fourteen brigade leaders. Estimates of Confederate losses range from 2,970 to 4,700 men. Given the size of the contending forces, the Confederates lost a much higher proportion of their available manpower than did the Yankees.[48]

Despite the brilliant crossing of the James River, the Federals could not capitalize on their advantages. The Confederates were able to construct new works hastily to contain the initial rupture of the Dimmock Line on the night of June 15. As the enemy erected more fortifications and ably manned them, the willingness of some Federals and the opportunity of their comrades to take them declined. John Gibbon recalled after the war that "it became a recognized fact amongst the men themselves that when the enemy had occupied a position six or eight hours ahead of us, it was useless to attempt to take it. This feeling became so marked that when troops under these circumstances were ordered forward, they went a certain distance and then lay down and opened fire. It became a saying in the army that when the old troops got as far forward as they thought they ought to go 'they sat down and made coffee!'" Theodore Lyman, Meade's staff member, thought the results of the June 18 attacks reinforced this tendency. "Put a man in a hole and a good battery on a hill behind him, and he will beat off three times his number, even if he is not a very good soldier." Meade felt bad about the results of the fighting on June 18. "*I* should have taken Petersburg," he admitted to Lyman in late August, as the stalemate outside the city seemed to lengthen. "I had reason to calculate on success. The enemy had no defences but what they had thrown up in a few hours."[49]

The men of both armies settled in for a long stay in trenches that soon grew in depth, length, and complexity around Petersburg. Enoch Alexander McNair, a soldier in the 49th North Carolina, had often been under fire during the several days of battle that inaugurated the Petersburg campaign. He received two letters, one of which was from his father. "I lay in the works and Read them by moon shine while the shell was falling and bursting all round us," he told his family. Like the doughty Tar Heel, thousands of blue and gray soldiers learned to live as well as fight in their trenches, which became their homes for months to come.[50]

CHAPTER FOUR

## *Searching for a Solution*

Despite the failure of June 15–18, Grant quickly organized an effort to rest his left wing on the Appomattox upstream from Petersburg. This would enable the Federals to invest the city south of the river. In addition, Grant authorized the Army of the James to create a bridgehead on the north side of the James at Deep Bottom, which could be useful if he decided to operate north of the river. Ironically, the Confederates also prepared to take the offensive by attacking the Union works south of the Appomattox. The period of June 20–24, therefore, represented a brief mobile phase of the Petersburg campaign.

### GRANT'S SECOND OFFENSIVE, JUNE 22–23

The area west of Jerusalem Plank Road, which demarked the left flank of Meade's army, was largely unknown to the Federals. It was covered with dense thickets and lined with a system of roads that stretched from Petersburg to the south and southwest. The Federals assumed that the Dimmock Line continued all the way to the Appomattox, but Grant did not want the Second or Sixth Corps to attack strong fortifications. He merely aimed to stop the flow of supplies into Petersburg by way of the Weldon and Petersburg Railroad, Boydton Plank Road, and the South Side Railroad. The Fifth, Ninth, and Eighteenth Corps would hold the developing line of fortifications east of Jerusalem Plank Road. At the same time, James H. Wilson planned to hit the railroads at points much farther from the infantry's line of approach with two cavalry divisions.[1]

What transpired constituted Grant's Second Offensive at Petersburg, a hastily prepared effort to achieve quick gain. The Second and Sixth Corps were too weak to cover the entire swath of territory to the Appomattox. Birney continued to command the Second Corps while Hancock recuperated from the flare-up of his Gettysburg wound. The corps was to cross Jerusalem Plank Road in line of battle and pivot north to extend the line of the Fifth Corps west of the road. Wright's Sixth Corps had a more difficult role to play. It was to

{ 38 }

march westward, trying to keep connection with Birney's left, and wheel north through the woods so as to extend the Second Corps line.

The offensive began early on the morning of June 22. Two of Birney's divisions, Gibbon's on the right and Mott's in the center, had no difficulty crossing Jerusalem Plank Road and digging in so as to prolong the Fifth Corps line, but Barlow's division on the left lost connection with Wright in the thicket. Barlow placed one of his brigades to extend Mott's left, but he refused his other two brigades so as to face west and protect Birney's left flank. Wright continued westward and soon became isolated from the Second Corps.

Lee reacted quickly to Grant's movement. Brig. Gen. William Mahone, who led a division in Hill's Third Corps, knew the Petersburg area well from his prewar residence in the city. He recalled a ravine that stretched north and south about one and a half miles west of Jerusalem Plank Road and offered an avenue of approach into the heart of the Union position. Lee authorized him to take three of his brigades. They were ready to hit the Federals about 3:00 P.M.

Mahone caught the Federals completely by surprise when he assaulted Birney's left flank. Barlow's division initially held firm but then fell apart, followed by Mott's division and a portion of Gibbon's. When he heard a description of the attack, Charles Wainwright accurately wrote that Birney's line "was just eaten up like flame travels up a slip of paper." Four guns of Capt. George F. McKnight's 12th New York Battery fell into Rebel hands as the entire Second Corps retired east of Jerusalem Plank Road.

Wright escaped most of the action; only Maj. Gen. Cadmus M. Wilcox's division of Hill's Corps opposed his advance. The Sixth Corps remained west of the plank road and advanced to the Weldon and Petersburg Railroad on June 23. Mahone again foiled Union plans by hitting Wright's left wing and driving the corps away. Federal casualties amounted to nearly 3,000, all but 600 suffered by the Second Corps. "The affair was a stampede and surprise to both parties and ought to have been turned in our favor," Grant sadly wrote. The fighting involved little in the way of field fortification.[2]

### DEEP BOTTOM, JUNE 20–21

With Confederate pickets only 400 yards away, Godfrey Weitzel and Peter Michie scouted the area north of the James River at a place called Deep Bottom on June 20. The river made a graceful curve to the north at this location and scarred out a section of river bottom that was unusually deep. Weitzel pointed out where the fortified bridgehead should be built and put Michie in charge of the details. That night, 1,400 men of Col. Harris M. Plaisted's brigade of the Tenth Corps crossed the river in pontoons and established the position, sending the boats back to the south bank so the pontoniers could begin laying a bridge. One of Plaisted's regiments established a picket line to screen the workers as hundreds of shovels, axes, and picks came into play. The pontoniers finished the bridge and its approaches well before dawn, but the earthworks took more time because of the "hard, white soil" that broke into small lumps when disturbed. Several companies of the 1st New York Engineers lent a hand on June 21, and infantrymen cut trees in front of the line for several more days. Brig. Gen. Robert S. Foster took command of Plaisted's brigade on July 1 and pushed the works to completion by mid-July.

Lee understood the potential danger of Grant's foothold. "I do not like the continuance of the enemy on the north side of the James River," he complained to Lt. Gen. Richard S. Ewell, who was in charge of troops on that side of the stream. Lee hoped Ewell could find some way to eliminate the bridgehead, but the latter general had far too few resources to attempt it.[3]

### FIRST CONFEDERATE OFFENSIVE, JUNE 24

The day after Mahone drove Birney's Second Corps back across Jerusalem Plank Road, the Confederates laid plans for an offensive of their own. Lee and Beauregard targeted the incomplete Federal works that stretched from the Appomattox River to the City Point Railroad, held by units of the Eighteenth Corps. There yet was no abatis in front of the earthworks, and the Confederates could enfilade the line with guns placed north of the river. Beauregard wrote the operational order, which involved a thirty-minute artillery bombardment followed by Hoke's attempt to smash through the Federal line far enough to roll it up southward at least as far as the Hare House. Field's division was available to help.

The intention became garbled as details of the plan filtered down the chain of command. Hoke assumed he was only supposed to take the Union picket line and designated three regiments of Hagood's South Carolina brigade for the attack. Then, according to Hoke, Field would penetrate the main Union line. Field correctly believed he was to wait until Hoke had taken both Northern lines before putting his men into action.

After the artillery fired for forty minutes, Hagood's men set out at 7:42 A.M., crossing 400 yards of neutral ground between the lines with 400 men acting as skirmishers and 550 serving in the battle line. The Carolinians captured 30 Federal skirmishers, but Field's men did not appear to strike the Yankees in their main trench. Col. Guy V. Henry's Eighteenth Corps brigade mounted a counterattack that swept Hagood halfway across the oat field that separated the two lines, where they fell down for protection and waited until after dark to retire. Hagood lost one-third of his attacking force, while Henry lost only 11 men killed and wounded, plus the 30 skirmishers who were captured.

This failure demonstrated what the Federals had long since learned: attacking even poorly made earthworks well-manned by veteran troops was unlikely to succeed. "I do not know if it is intended to renew the attempt," reported Henry I. Greer of Hagood's brigade, but "[I] hope not, as I am opposed to charging Batteries."[4]

### WHAT NEXT?

Grant reacted to the failure of his Second Offensive by carefully weighing all his options for nearly a month. He could afford to wait, allowing the men to dig in as he sorted through several possible plans. Grant initially liked the idea of duplicating Butler's line of advance in early May, striking out of the fortified portion of the Bermuda Hundred peninsula. Such a move could place Union troops on the railroad and turnpike that linked Petersburg with Richmond. But reports from an observation tower indicated that the Confederates had constructed a new line of works from Port Walthall Station to Swift Creek, blocking this line of attack.

Alternatively, Grant suggested swinging the entire Army of the Potomac around the Confederate right, temporarily cutting communications with City Point. This would allow Meade to cross the Appomattox upstream from Petersburg and advance eastward between the two cities. Warren proposed a less ambitious version of this plan, shifting the army onto the Weldon and Petersburg Railroad and digging in. Meade pointed out that Lee could then advance eastward between his army and City Point, and that little would be gained if the two sides traded supply lines.[5]

John G. Barnard proposed an attack where the Ninth Corps joined the Fifth Corps. He believed the ground favored a concentration of Federal artillery to enfilade the enemy line fronting Burnside's troops and the Eighteenth Corps. Barnard argued that the crest of the slight ridge behind the Rebel works was the key to Petersburg. Jerusalem Plank Road ran along that crest and through the suburb of Blandford, with its prominent cemetery. Control of this high ground would allow the Federals to so dominate Petersburg that Lee would have to give up the town. Grant liked the idea. It better suited his hope for a "bold and decisive attack" that could end the campaign in one stroke, and he asked Meade to investigate whether it could be done. If not, he leaned toward moving a massive force completely around Lee's right, but he despaired of doing so until the arrival of the Nineteenth Corps from Louisiana.

Meade consulted his corps commanders, and Warren quickly said no. Burnside, on the other hand, was optimistic. He had already been working on a mine designed to blow up the Rebel guns at Pegram's Salient. Lt. Col. Henry Pleasants Jr., commander of the 48th Pennsylvania, developed the idea. A civil engineer commanding a unit that originally had many coal miners, Pleasants received permission from division commander Potter, and eventually from Burnside, to push forward with the project. Meade had no doubt that the mine would work, but he despaired of decisively breaking through the shallow angle at Pegram's Salient with a follow-up infantry attack. Nevertheless, he allowed the work to continue.

Meade sent Duane and artillery chief Henry J. Hunt to examine the prospects for a frontal attack at Pegram's Salient. Hunt was no stranger to the mining operation. He had known of it from the day after Pleasants started digging and had already examined the gallery. In fact, Hunt had submitted Burnside's request for 12,000 pounds of powder and 1,000 yards of safety fuse, to be used in priming and exploding the mine, on June 29.

Even before waiting for Duane and Hunt to report, Meade told Grant that he thought an attack was not practicable, suggesting regular siege approaches instead. Burnside's mine was one such approach already under way, but Meade also envisioned surface approaches in the form of parallels and saps. In short, while the Pennsylvanians tunneled under no-man's-land, other troops would dig trenches in zigzag designs to inch their way across the surface of that disputed ground. Meade was leery of any effort to turn Lee's right flank and had anticipated siege operations ever since June 17, when he wrote his wife that "it looks very much as if we will have to go through a siege of Petersburg before entering on the siege of Richmond."

Duane and Hunt essentially came to the same conclusion as their commander. Neither felt enthusiastic about a frontal attack or a flank movement, and both thought the best prospect for siege approaches lay on the Fifth Corps front, where the Harris Line joined the Dimmock Line to form an angle. The Gregory House lay behind the angle, so the two officers used it as a reference point when explaining their views. The only prospect on the Ninth Corps front was the mine, which they recommended should be continued and somehow incorporated into offensive plans.[6]

By July 5, Grant received the views of several men on his own staff that a decisive breakthrough of the Confederate works could not be achieved by direct attack. He was, at least temporarily, resigned to Meade's view. "The best we can do now is to strengthen our present line on Burnside's and Warren's front and advance by gradual approaches as you propose." This must have pleased the commander of the Army of the Potomac. He had been privately critical of Grant's frontal attacks during the Overland campaign and at times was even jealous of Grant's reputation. Now he had managed to shape his superior's thinking about grand tactics toward a safer but slower course of action. Reinforced by Duane and Hunt, Meade proposed that Warren and Burnside push siege operations simultaneously. The sappers could work their way along the slightly higher ground on which Jerusalem Plank Road crossed no-man's-land to reduce the Rebel position near Gregory's House. This had to be accomplished before following up the explosion of Pleasants's mine with an infantry attack at Pegram's Salient because Rebel artillery near Gregory's House could rake the left flank of an attacking column at Pegram's.[7]

Meade designated Hunt as commander of siege operations on July 9. He and Duane began to measure no-man's-land, essential for starting siege approaches. In addition, a surveying party started triangulating so as to map the opposing lines, using the spires and other prominent buildings in Petersburg as reference points. The U.S. Coast Survey also forwarded a map that proved useful. Hunt and Duane wanted Warren to advance his line closer to the objective before he started siege approaches, and those approaches had to be well under way before Burnside sprung his mine. After the explosion, if Burnside could not gain the crest of the ridge behind Confederate lines, he needed to dig in as far forward as possible and commence siege approaches to reach the high ground. All of this accorded with Meade's thinking.[8]

But by now Grant had second thoughts. He had never felt comfortable with the slow, uncertain prospects of a siege, but he could not determine which option for movement had a chance of success. He made it clear to Meade that if "the approaches are made it will be with the view of ultimately making an assault on the enemy's lines." While Grant deliberated, Cyrus Comstock urged him to move onto the railroads or to swing out beyond Lee's flank rather than rely on siege approaches. Despite his engineering training, Comstock advocated troop movement rather than engineering as the solution to the grand tactical problem at Petersburg.[9]

As long as he had the luxury of time, Grant allowed Meade, Duane, and Hunt to prepare for a siege. But circumstances forced him to make a decision. Jubal Early had been operating in the Shenandoah Valley with the Second Corps of Lee's army since mid-June, and there were disturbing signs of a Rebel movement down the valley and across the Potomac. Grant instructed Meade to send a division of the Sixth Corps, which arrived at Baltimore by July 8, soon to be followed by the rest of Wright's command. Grant had counted on the Nineteenth Corps to make up for the Army of the Potomac's losses during the past two months, but now he was compelled to divert it to the Washington area, too.

Grant felt pressured to attempt something quickly that might get his troops into Petersburg before all of them were forced to go north. This ended any attempt to initiate siege operations. The first shipment of siege material, some of it procured by the U.S. Engineer Department's purchasing agent in New York

City, reached the army on July 15, but Meade reported that he needed another week to begin approaching the Confederate works near the Gregory House. There was no more talk of siege operations after that. It had always been the least attractive option on Grant's list.[10]

While the generals debated, the rank and file assumed a siege was likely to take place. Everyone was aware of Grant's Vicksburg campaign and assumed he would "try and dig them out of their holes." Staff officer Hazard Stevens welcomed the rest and advised his mother to "expect a second siege of Yorktown. Slow tedious operations, but little loss of life."[11]

The Confederates also assumed siege operations would start any day. Col. E. P. Alexander, artillery chief of the First Corps, carefully observed Yankee digging to detect any signs of saps. Infantry commanders reported that Union siege approaches were starting to take shape in their front, and engineer officers raced to the trenches only to report false alarms.[12]

Nevertheless, at least one siege approach appeared on the Eighteenth Corps front when Francis Farquhar started a sap to place sharpshooters in a more advanced position. He used a sap roller that was six feet in diameter, made of wood, and filled with tamped earth. Following the sapping procedure outlined in James C. Duane's engineer manual, the diggers lined gabions and sandbags along the approach trench to provide more protection. The Federals used this approach to harass the Confederates. On July 19, an officer of the 13th Indiana went to the far end of the sap and tossed twenty hand grenades at the Rebel skirmish pits, which were no more than twenty yards away.

Another grenade attack took place on July 22, causing the local commander, Brig. Gen. Archibald Gracie, to suggest planting torpedoes along his front and pushing forward countermines to intercept the Federal sap. He also requested some sort of incendiary device to set fire to the sap roller and placed heavy abatis in the path of the roller. Confederate mortar fire proved effective; gunners heard groans after bombarding the head of the sap on July 27. The Confederates had grenades in their arsenal, but there is no proof that they ever used them during the Petersburg campaign.[13]

Beauregard was surprised that Grant did not rely on siege approaches to take Petersburg. He identified the ground along City Point Road and Jerusalem Plank Road as the best prospects for sapping. "We might have resisted a few weeks," he commented after the war, but Grant "would surely have gotten into Petersburg at the end of that time." Federal engineers were more realistic in their evaluations. Farquhar pointed out that "the enemy can fortify to the rear as fast as we can approach." Even Duane admitted this, cautioning Meade's chief of staff that siege operations would be long, uncertain, difficult, and costly. Michler was much more emphatic, believing it "almost useless to attempt a regular siege."[14]

## THE MINE

As Grant considered and then rejected siege approaches, a group of volunteer soldiers dug the most famous mine gallery of the Civil War. Only 103 original members of the 48th Pennsylvania were left by the summer of 1864, but enough of them were professional miners to constitute a corps of experienced diggers. Pleasants developed the idea as early as June 21 and discussed it with Farquhar, his prewar friend. Potter liked the idea, and Burnside was captivated by the project; it seemed to stoke a new fire in him when consulting with Potter and Pleasants on the night of June 24. When Burnside informed Meade, the army leader reminded him that only Grant could authorize siege operations, but he allowed Burnside's men to go ahead.[15]

The Pennsylvanians started at noon on June 25, digging a horizontal gallery into the bank of Poor Creek to avoid having to sink a vertical shaft. This meant, however, that they had to run the gallery through several layers of sediments. On July 2, they encountered "extremely wet ground" that wrecked the wooden framing that supported the gallery walls and roof. After repairing the damage, the Pennsylvanians struck a layer of marl. It had a consistency like "putty," according to Pleasants, who inclined the gallery a bit to avoid the clay. His men took chunks of marl out of the mine, dried them in the sun, and carved hundreds of pipes, corps badges, and other souvenirs.[16]

Pleasants put Sgt. Henry Reese, a professional miner from Wales, in charge of the project. Reese literally lived at the mine, using only members of the 48th Pennsylvania, handpicked for their mining skills, to do the most important jobs in the gallery. The rest of Pleasants's men performed less specialized chores. The normal shift was two and a half hours, with a whiskey ration at the end of each shift. Working around the clock, the Pennsylvanians averaged forty feet per day. They used empty cracker boxes to deposit the dirt in low places behind the lines, cutting brush to cover the piles. Details from Ferrero's black regiments also carried dirt out of the gallery in sacks and manhandled timber up to the mine.[17]

The Federals used timbers from small bridges on the Norfolk and Petersburg Railroad, sawing boards at a mill six miles away, to provide wood for the gallery frame. They nailed it together in sections outside the mine, carried it in, and quietly positioned the frame without hammering, adding boards only if the soil was too loose to hold naturally. For light, the miners attached candles or lanterns to the frame every ten feet inside the gallery.[18]

At first, Pleasants ventilated the gallery with a square wooden tube that took gases emanating from the soil and the exhalation of the miners to a vertical shaft, where he burned a fire to create a column of heated air that drew the gases up the hole. As the gallery lengthened, Pleasants reversed the flow of current to bring fresh air from the mouth of the gallery to the head through the wooden tube. Then the foul air was drawn back through the gallery to the vertical shaft. This was possible because a partition with a door was installed just outside the base of the shaft.[19]

Pleasants could not get the proper instruments from army headquarters to measure distance, so Burnside obtained "an old-fashioned theodolite" from a depot in Washington, D.C. The Pennsylvanian conducted five different triangulations from the Union line. When compared with accurate tape measurements of the gallery's length, he could determine how far the men yet needed to dig.[20]

On July 17, as the head of the gallery neared Pegram's Battery, the miners heard the Rebels working on the surface. That morning, three deserters from the 49th North Carolina told the Federals that their former comrades knew what was going on and had been countermining for a week. Burnside reasoned that the Federals were digging so deeply the Rebels would never find the gallery, but Pleasants was worried. He went to the head of the excavation at midnight and lay down while all work ceased in the gallery. After half an hour of silence, he concluded the project was safe for the time being. Pleasants then reported the gallery was finished at a length of 510.8 feet.[21]

Now it was time to break out on both sides, to dig branches along the Confederate line. Reese's miners finished the left branch by midnight of July 22, at thirty-seven feet in length, and the right branch by the evening of July 23, at thirty-eight feet in length. Pleasants frequently stopped the work to listen for countermining. He came to believe the Confederates were close, and he angled the right branch a bit to avoid the spot he suspected. "It did not move out of line much," Pleasants later reported.[22]

Army headquarters had little to do with the mine project. Meade held little hope that a follow-through attack could succeed, given the terrain behind Pegram's Salient and the shallow angle of the Confederate line. Duane tried to keep Burnside staffed with an engineer officer; but Capt. Franklin Harwood seemed lazy, and the corps commander asked that he be replaced. Lt. William H. H. Benyaurd was willing to work, but Burnside kept him busy on the corps fortifications. Duane hoped that a regular engineer officer could take over the mine project, but Meade told him not to interfere. There were no hard feelings. In late July, Pleasants gave Benyaurd, Ira Spaulding, and Nathaniel Michler an extensive tour of the mine, and Michler "found it fascinating."[23]

Burnside wanted the mine to remain an exclusive Ninth Corps project, and that opened it up to some degree of ridicule. Many officers and men in the army disliked him because of the fiasco at Fredericksburg in December 1862, and they often criticized his performance during the Overland campaign. "Burnside somehow is never up to the mark when the tug comes," commented Charles Wainwright. As the mine became known, it was "generally much laughed at." Even Confederate pickets began "asking after its welfare."[24]

The Confederates assumed Pegram's Salient was a likely target of Union siege approaches. E. P. Alexander called it "the weakest part of our whole line, a piece of bad location with a great dead space in front." That "dead space" was the valley of Poor Creek, about 250 yards in front of Pegram's guns. The valley was wide and deep enough to hide hundreds of troops. On the other side of the valley lay the homestead of William Byrd Taylor, whose brick house burned to its foundation at the start of the campaign. Burnside constructed many artillery emplacements near the house to form a secondary line. Pegram's four 12-pounder Napoleons were secure behind his parapet, but the ascending ground to the rear meant that gunners, infantrymen, and staff could approach only through a ravine that drained toward the Federals and which was several hundred yards to the left. The Confederates dug a covered way down the length of this ravine to protect the flow of men to and from the line.[25]

Alexander noticed that more sharpshooting took place at Pegram's than anywhere else along the line, and he expected every day to see a Union sap roller inching its way up the slope. He ordered the placement of more guns to the right, left, and rear to help Pegram. On June 30, while Alexander was gazing at the Union lines, the thought came to him that the Federals might be mining. He decided to tell Lee personally but was hit in the shoulder along the way. The next day, he stopped at army headquarters on his way home to recover. Lee was not available, but Alexander warned Col. Charles Venable of the mine danger.[26]

Nothing was done until July 9, when Martin L. Smith ordered Capt. Hugh Thomas Douglas's Company F, 1st Confederate Engineers, to report for countermining duty. The Virginia-born officer had served in an artillery battery before he was detailed to engineer duty, receiving a commission in the Engineer Corps of the Provisional Army of the Confederacy. He proposed the creation of a specialized company for bridge and road construction in 1862 and commanded one of the early companies of the 1st Confederate Engineers. Although he was inexperienced in mining and had no professional training as a military engineer, Douglas was widely praised as "an intelligent active and practical man."[27]

Douglas established a camp at Blandford and began work on July 10. He found that a vertical shaft had already been dug six feet deep at Pegram's Salient and another shaft had been started at Colquitt's Salient, opposite the Union position at the Hare House. The first task was to finish both shafts and then start horizontal galleries toward the Union line. By July 13, the gallery at Pegram's was already more than seven feet long, six feet tall, and three feet, three inches wide. Douglas's first lieutenant, Edwin N. Wise, started a second shaft at Pegram's 250 feet from the first. Designated Shaft No. 2, it was fourteen feet below the surface, while Shaft No. 1 was eighteen feet deep. As Wise started another gallery from the second shaft, Douglas planned to advance both galleries some distance in front of the salient and connect them to screen the entire battery position.[28]

The Engineer Bureau in Richmond sent large numbers of sperm candles to illuminate the galleries. Douglas also requested ten pounds of leather to make knee pads for his men. In addition to these items, the miners needed much timber and lumber to shore up the galleries.[29]

With details from Clingman's and McAfee's North Carolina brigades and Goode's Virginia brigade, Douglas worked around the clock. On July 16 the miners pushed one gallery more than twenty-three feet. Two days later, additional men arrived from Gracie's Alabama brigade and Elliott's South Carolina brigade. Douglas issued whiskey, sugar, and coffee every day to the miners to sustain their heavy labor.[30]

Douglas organized the men in two detachments, one for each shaft, with fourteen men and one noncommissioned officer in each detachment. Two men dug, two shoveled, two carried dirt to the bottom of the shaft, and two worked the windlass to haul it to the surface. Two more men carried the dirt to appropriate places, and two spread it out. Each shift lasted twelve hours. Douglas constructed a berm of earth around the entrance to each shaft to deflect rainwater and dug a two-foot-deep well at the bottom to pool any water that did fall in. The miners framed each gallery, allowing no more than two feet of unshored tunnel at any time. They dug the galleries level for twenty feet, but then Douglas declined them at the rate of one foot for every ten feet to account for the descending slope of the surface above. The diggers at the forward edge of the galleries stopped every fifteen minutes to listen for sounds of Federal mining.[31]

Douglas considered the Yankee threat to be more serious at Colquitt's Salient and decided not to push the galleries at Pegram's to completion. He intended to use Gallery No. 2 as a listening post. Even if he had completed and connected the galleries, Douglas would not have intercepted the Yankees because Pleasants's mine was several feet deeper. From about July 15, Douglas pushed the gallery at Colquitt's fifty-six feet from the shaft and about six feet under the

Confederate picket line. An officer in the gallery thought he heard digging on the night of July 21, and Douglas decided to run a branch to the left toward the sound. Whatever the officer heard, it certainly was not Union mining. False alarms, which were inevitable in underground warfare, diverted Douglas's attention from the real threat at Pegram's. Moreover, Gracie pleaded for a gallery at his salient between Colquitt's and Pegram's, compelling Douglas to start a shaft there on July 22.[32]

The heaviest rain yet during the campaign fell on the night of July 24, putting a temporary halt to mining because the berms could not keep rainwater out of the shafts. The Confederates undoubtedly welcomed the opportunity to rest that night and all next day, unaware that Pleasants had already won the underground race with Douglas. His mine was finished and ready for priming.[33]

The Federals also countermined on a limited basis between the Appomattox River and the City Point Railroad during July. Reports of enemy offensive mining toward Batteries No. 4 and 5 on the Eighteenth Corps sector led Farquhar to sink a shaft on July 23. He found that the nature of the soil and the presence of water prevented the digging of galleries. Two days later, he began to sink a twelve-foot-deep shaft close to Battery No. 8 and ran listening galleries from it in front of Batteries No. 6 and 7. Sticky clay and water hampered digging, but the listening gallery was forty feet long by the end of July.[34]

After becoming aware of Pleasants's mine, Grant hesitated for three weeks before committing himself to a plan of action against Lee. Only when word arrived that the Pennsylvanians had finished the gallery and branches did he decide, on the rainy night of July 24, to incorporate the mine into plans for a major offensive.[35]

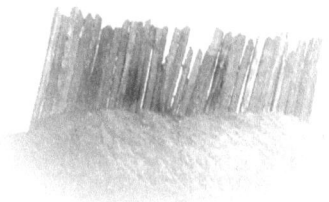

CHAPTER FIVE

# *Digging In*

While Grant and his subordinates debated grand tactics, their men secured the Union position from the Appomattox to Jerusalem Plank Road with heavy earthworks. Despite fatigue and worsening heat, the Federals dug steadily. One Ninth Corps soldier marveled as the fortifications "sprung into existence as if by magic."[1]

### FEDERAL WORKS

The men typically piled logs and rails in a line up to four feet tall and then dug a trench behind it, throwing the dirt on top. They made a parapet that often was eight feet thick at the base and three feet wide at the top, tall enough so that their heads were safely covered. Seventy-five yards in front of their earthwork, Sixth Corps troops positioned abatis consisting of "tree tops with the butts sunk in the ground and the limbs cut off a distance from the main trunk and all sharpened."[2]

On the Eighteenth Corps sector, Farquhar directed the construction of traverses for artillery and infantry and a covered way to link battery emplacements. The infantrymen improvised loopholes on top of the parapet with layers of sandbags and old shelter tents converted into bags. Confederate artillery fire from the north side of the Appomattox prompted an Eighteenth Corps officer to construct a roof over his deep trench, making a bombproof shelter rather than a fighting position. As staff officer Thomas L. Livermore put it, "The trench was only attacked by ridicule." Accustomed to digging, an Indiana soldier in Smith's corps humorously wrote that "if ever I get home I will run a line of breastworks around the yard."[3]

Hancock's men literally ran their line across the yard of Otway P. Hare's beautiful house. McAllister's brigade dug a trench through the flowerbeds and among the trees. His troops also dug covered ways six feet deep and twelve feet wide up to the homestead. The gunners of the 10th Massachusetts Battery dug in near the Norfolk and Petersburg Railroad cut, placing mantlets across their deep embrasures.[4]

Farther to the left, other Second Corps troops advanced their line to more advantageous ground east of Jerusalem Plank Road under cover of darkness. Erasmus C. Gilreath, an officer of the 20th Indiana, led his men forward in single file and placed them on the new position three feet apart. Every fifth man held a pick, while the rest used shovels. The detail finished by dawn. "I found on my next visit that I got it fairly straight," Gilreath proudly recalled. "The irregularities were easily corrected."[5]

Grant instructed Meade to tear down most of the Dimmock Line that was in Union hands to prevent the enemy from using it in case they recaptured lost ground. Grant exempted any portions that had already been reversed for use by Federal batteries and any portions in full view of Confederate artillery. Details from the U.S. Engineer Battalion had surveyed these works on June 23 to prepare for this work. Federal opinions on the quality of the Dimmock Line differed widely. Gilbert Thompson of the Engineer Battalion noted that the guns were mounted en barbette, exposing crews behind a three-foot-tall parapet. Some of the connecting infantry lines had no revetment to support the parapet. Nathaniel Michler, however, thought Dimmock's work "beautifully planned and constructed," while the site "was a most magnificent and commanding one, the natural lay of the open fields in front forming a most perfect glacis."[6]

Meade ordered Hancock's men to demolish the Confederate works, which had been hardened by months of settling. Barlow's and Birney's divisions began working on the night of July 14 with 10,000 men, probably the largest detail ever mustered on a fortification project in the war. Quartermasters used eighteen wagons to haul enough tools for the men. Mott's division reinforced the laborers as nearly the entire Second Corps worked feverishly for several days, discovering it was harder to tear down an earthwork than to build one.[7]

Ninth Corps troops dug in securely because they were very close to the enemy. The 56th Massachusetts constructed a banquette, or firing step, to allow the trench bottom to be low enough so they could walk through it without exposure. Officers located their quarters in holes to the rear of the line, covered with roofs made of logs and earth. The rank and file placed traverses every twenty feet, forming bays with protection on three sides. Stephen Minot Weld dug a covered way parallel to the rear of his regimental line with covered ways leading from it to each bay.[8]

Burnside's troops used many sandbags for revetting, and the men scrambled to find enough of them. Col. Henry Larcom Abbot, commander of the siege train, thought he could spare a few even though he needed 5,000 bags for each

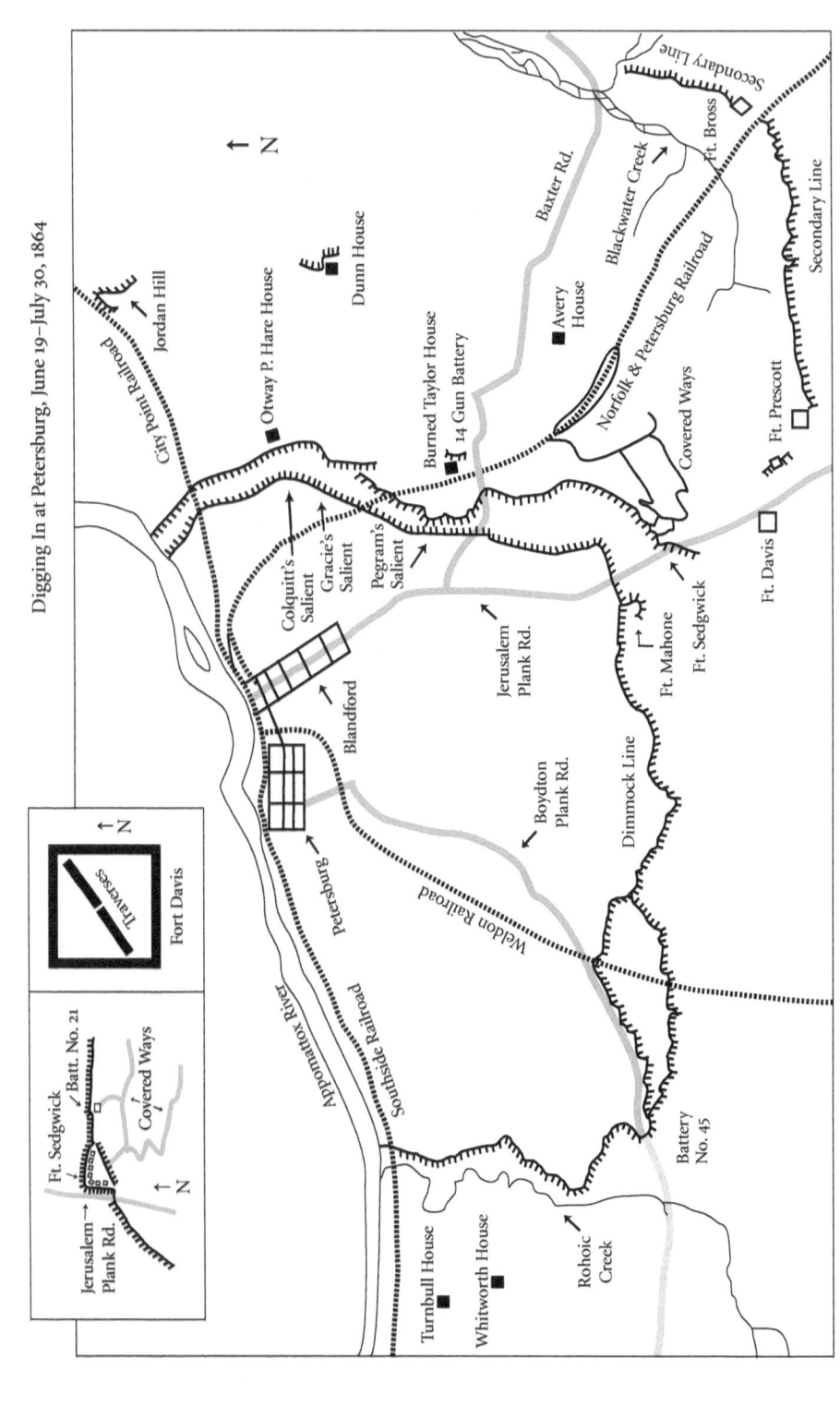

of his own gun emplacements. Ledlie noticed that the Confederates used sandbags to make loopholes for their sharpshooters, and he urged corps headquarters to do the same. Until proper sandbags became available, the Federals used empty grain sacks. They employed 150 to 300 bags on each regimental front and replaced them regularly because rain and bullets weakened or tore the fabric. The men came to realize that sandbags, smaller and more easily handled, served their purposes better than grain sacks.[9]

Burnside assigned brigade and division commanders to serve as general of the trenches for the Ninth Corps, rotating them in twelve-hour shifts. These officers inspected the works and found banquettes that were too low for the men to use or too narrow for them to stand firmly while firing. Ledlie recommended that the top of the parapet be at least seven feet above the bottom of the trench and that the trench should be at least six feet wide. Some traverses were torn down to make more room because of these reports.[10]

Covered ways became important avenues of movement to and from the works, given the comparatively flat nature of the landscape around Petersburg. The Ninth Corps constructed them in stages, beginning with a trench six feet deep and wide enough for men to move in single file. When opportunity appeared, they widened the trench up to ten feet, with the dirt piled up in berms on each side. The men often gouged out small holes in the walls of these covered ways for protection against artillery and mortar fire. William Benyaurd directed work details from Company A, U.S. Engineer Battalion, as they dug 300 yards of covered ways linking the forward line west of Poor Creek with the rest of Burnside's corps. These covered ways served as avenues of attack following the mine explosion.[11]

Burnside's men turned the Avery House and its grounds into a shambles when they stretched their line east of the Norfolk and Petersburg Railroad. Infantrymen and gunners constructed an emplacement for Durell's Battery D, Independent Pennsylvania Artillery, cutting down an apple orchard and a grove of old trees and using the limbs to make an abatis. One tree fell the wrong way and landed on the house. The Federals also burned slave cabins to clear a field of fire for the guns and slashed the pine trees nearby to make an obstacle in front of the position. They called the emplacement Fort Durell, later renamed Battery No. 17. It eventually sported eighteen guns and a ditch twelve feet wide. Engineer troops constructed a magazine inside the fort.[12]

The major fort on the Ninth Corps line was called the Fourteen Gun Battery, or the Taylor House Battery, but was later designated Fort Morton. Its parapets stood seven feet tall and were nearly ten feet thick. Much of the interior was sunken three feet deep. Work crews used logs and gabions as revetment and

cut embrasures for fourteen cannon into the parapet. They placed traverses and dug two magazines, each one twelve feet by six feet in dimension and four feet deep. The covered way connecting Fort Morton to the rear was 600 yards long.[13]

Members of the regular engineer battalion taught Burnside's designated engineer regiments how to make gabions and fascines. The 35th Massachusetts soon made 150 gabions each day. The designated engineers then constructed artillery emplacements, placed abatis, cut embrasures, and built traverses and bridges. The historian of the 35th Massachusetts wrote that "it took a cool head and steady hand to stand upon the parapet of our earthworks, unsheltered from the cross fire, and cut embrasures for guns, drive the poles and make the necessary hurdle work or wattling to support the earth at the sides."[14]

Ferrero's black division became a source of labor for the defenses. The commander of the U.S. Engineer Battalion declared bluntly that a "negro is worth two, if not three, white men to dig." Warren suggested that the entire division be dedicated to engineer duty. While Ferrero's men sometimes held the trenches, they more often cut abatis, made gabions, and dug works on various parts of the army's line. When placing abatis before the line, the black troops often took a sharpened branch and moved across the parapet after dark. They secured the branches with stakes and tied them together with telegraph wire under scattered skirmish fire. Capt. Warren H. Hurd of the 23rd USCT discovered that his men were expected to work on a battery emplacement all day and night without food, because the engineer officer wanted "to get all he could out

Dimmock Line, U.S.-made artillery emplacement next to Confederate ditch. (Library of Congress, LC-DIG-CWPB-00500)

of the d—— niggers." Hurd complained so loudly that the officer relented and brought food and another work party up soon after dark.[15]

Warren took charge of fortification work as his Fifth Corps secured the army's left flank at Jerusalem Plank Road. "I have made myself general of trenches," he reported to Meade, and he visited the works every day. His staff also played an active role in directing and advising earthwork construction.[16]

Volunteer officers in the Fifth Corps improvised effective methods of fortifying in dangerous spots. Maj. Ellis Spear of the 20th Maine staked out a new line to be dug forward of his current position with "green sassafras sticks," after peeling off the bark to better expose them in the dark. These substituted for the white stakes normally used. While some men stood picket, the rest stuck their bayoneted muskets into the ground for use in case of trouble and quietly dug the line, cutting the sticks with their tools and filling the air with the smell of sassafras.[17]

The 13th Massachusetts had quite a different experience when it fortified soon after the failed attack of June 18. The men positioned some of the bodies that still littered the ground in a line and piled dirt on them, both to quickly inter the dead and to increase the size of their fortification.[18]

The Fifth Corps raised many earthworks for artillery and covered ways six feet deep and twelve feet wide. A detail of up to 4,000 infantrymen worked on one covered way that was 4,100 feet long. Warren's men placed head logs on some parts of the line, squaring them to ten inches by ten inches and placing them on top of the parapet at night.[19]

*Digging In* { 55 }

Covered way from Fort Rice to Fort Meikel. (Library of Congress, LC-DIG-CWPB-01323)

The Norfolk and Petersburg Railroad cut demarked the boundary between Warren's right and Burnside's left. It was one-third of a mile long across the ridge that served as the watershed between Blackwater Creek to the south and Poor Creek to the north. The Avery House stood on this ridge about 200 yards from the cut, which was thirty-five feet at its deepest. Fifth Corps troops laid out a work, which later was designated Battery No. 19, opposite Burnside's Fort Durell. Warren helped to lay it out and to position one of the 4.5-inch Rodman guns. Afraid the piece might recoil too far, he told the men to narrow the embrasure with more gabions and raise the rear of the platform. Other Fifth Corps troops tore up the rails and ties inside the cut, built a barricade at its entrance, and placed two field pieces to sweep its length. A covered way four feet deep, with a berm another four feet tall, led to this area from the rear.[20]

Meade's left flank demanded more attention than any other part of the Fifth Corps line. Artillery chief Hunt scouted the terrain and recommended that a large fort be constructed west of Jerusalem Plank Road to protect the flank and counter Confederate guns near Gregory's House. Officers of the Engineer Battalion laid out the work in early July, calling it Fort Warren (later renamed Fort Davis). Heavy details from the Fifth Corps and troops from Ferrero's division dug the fort, the latter "doing more in one day than the whites in two," according to topographical draftsman Charles W. Reed. The Confederates frequently lobbed shells at the Federals even though they erected brush screens to hide their work. The fort was 200 feet square with parapets 10 feet thick and 8 feet tall. The Federals clear-cut trees outside the fort but left several pines inside to provide shade for the garrison. The work details constructed the log-and-post revetment before piling up the parapet against it and extended cross ties from the revetment into the parapet to bind it more securely. Warren's troops erected a frame of light poles to provide an outline for the profile of the parapet, as recommended in fortification manuals. Fort Warren had a wide banquette but no head logs. The Federals constructed a large traverse in the middle, made of logs laid horizontally as revetment on all four sides and cross logs extending through the middle to bind the four walls tightly. Then they filled the interior space with earth.[21]

While still working on Fort Warren, Fifth Corps troops began another strong work east of Jerusalem Plank Road and about 1,200 yards northeast of the earlier work on July 6. They located it as far forward as possible and therefore exposed it to Confederate fire from Gregory's House. Maj. Washington Roebling, an engineer serving on Warren's staff, took charge of the project and used details from Griffin's division and the Second Corps. Initially called Roebling's Redoubt, it later was named Fort Sedgwick. The fort consisted of eighteen embrasured gun emplacements and a smaller redan to its right for four guns. The Engineer Battalion did much of the detailed work at Fort Sedgwick, including numerous traverses held up by gabion revetments. The Federals enclosed the gorge with a stockade, placed abatis in front, and slashed timber in front of the work.[22]

Col. William S. Tilton's Pennsylvania brigade provided up to 400 men at a time to help engineer Capt. Franklin Harwood make magazines and traverses at Fort Sedgwick, while the regular engineers constructed gun platforms. Tilton bypassed Harwood and received Warren's permission to dig a deep ditch and use the fill to form a glacis in front of it. The embrasures of Fort Sedgwick were revetted with gabions. Tilton also detailed his pioneer squad to build a small work (termed a caponier), extending from the parapet so as to sweep the ditch with fire. Hancock's men dug a covered way from near the Avery House to Fort Sedgwick that was twelve feet wide and four feet deep, with enough logs and dirt banked on the sides to provide eight feet of cover. Fort Sedgwick was almost complete after three weeks of hard work.[23]

The Federals constructed a third work on the Union left, 1,350 yards southeast of Fort Davis and more than a mile from Fort Sedgwick, and later named it Fort Prescott. Located immediately east of the plank road, it was 400 feet square and had emplacements for ten guns. Between Prescott and Fort Davis, the Federals built a small emplacement for field guns with an attached infantry parapet.²⁴

Warren could not resist issuing directives for completing Fifth Corps fortifications. He lectured officers who had not properly carried out his detailed instructions and argued that corps works would have been erected more efficiently if they had done so. Yet, Warren reported that his fieldworks were nearly complete in late July. He believed he could hold the line with minimal strength and mass troops for an offensive west of Jerusalem Plank Road, but there were yet no plans to attempt such a move.²⁵

To further strengthen the left flank, Meade instructed Michler to lay out a refused, secondary line stretching east from Jerusalem Plank Road on July 10. He wanted the line to extend to the headwaters of Blackwater Creek, which flowed northeastward behind the center of the Union position. Essentially a swamp, Blackwater Creek extended the protection afforded by this proposed line farther to the northwest. Michler started the line at Fort Prescott and planted a redoubt later named Fort Bross about two-thirds of the way to the creek. It measured 200 feet square and had embrasures for fourteen guns and barbette emplacements for six more cannon. Eight hundred soldiers constructed Fort Bross as 1,200 troops from Ferrero's division dug the infantry line between Prescott and Bross on July 13. Regular engineer troops built a stockade with a heavy wooden gate to protect the entrance to Bross. Michler also added Batteries No. 41 and 42 to the refused line.²⁶

Meade's worry for the security of his left flank stemmed from the result of Mahone's attack on June 22 and the reports of Confederate deserters that a turning movement seemed imminent. The result was a refused line about two and a quarter miles long and just as strong in its construction and artillery platforms as the main line. Meade insisted on adding to this rear-facing line when his army extended west of Jerusalem Plank Road in late August.²⁷

Butler's men busied themselves with perfecting their defenses between the James and the Appomattox. Those works were essentially like those fronting Petersburg, but Butler's engineers adopted a different strategy to deal with a sudden Confederate attack. They placed small, detached redoubts, each one sporting four field pieces and a small garrison, about 300 to 400 yards in front of the main line. The Confederates could not ignore these strong points and would be forced to delay their advance while trying to deal with them.²⁸

Henry L. Abbot had organized a siege train in April 1864 and now was commanding the heavy artillery of Butler's army. He took charge of the siege train when it arrived from Washington on June 22, placing the heavy guns and mortars where needed and allowing artillery officers to design emplacements when engineers were not available. Capt. William G. Pride of the 1st

Connecticut Heavy Artillery took command of the ordnance in Mortar Battery No. 12, between Fort Stedman and Fort Haskell on the Eighteenth Corps sector. He placed the mortars in pairs, with traverses between each pair, and built a splinterproof shelter on each side of the traverse. Pride also designed a covered lookout post on top of a traverse to protect spotters. Few men were hit in this battery even though it received enemy fire that "tore up the platforms and marked the mortars with fragments."[29]

By late July, the Federals built a continuous line 3.3 miles long from the Appomattox to Jerusalem Plank Road. The southward-facing secondary line stretched for an additional 2.75 miles from Fort Prescott to Blackwater Swamp. The U.S. Engineer Battalion alone constructed more than three miles of covered ways leading to various parts of the line, averaging nine feet wide and three and a half feet deep. Members of the 50th New York Engineers cut a supply road more than nine miles long from Meade's headquarters. The Petersburg line and its attendant road system was the largest fieldwork yet constructed by the Army of the Potomac.[30]

The earthwork that was later named Fort Sedgwick acquired a popular and colorful designation as early as July 21. The constant artillery and skirmish fire the Confederates offered those who constructed it led the Federals to begin calling the work Fort Hell. Yet there were stories that the name derived from various officers—Henry J. Hunt and William F. Smith were mentioned—who yelled "Fort Hell!" when told the work had a name they did not think appropriate.[31]

Construction of the Union defenses at Petersburg drained the Federals of energy exactly when they needed to rest, following the Overland campaign and the first round of fighting outside town. John Haley reported that his comrades "did just as little work as possible, for we have no strength," as they worked on the covered way to Fort Sedgwick from the Avery House area. Even fresh soldiers often found ways to avoid labor. W. S. Weed of the 130th Ohio, a new regiment that reached Bermuda Hundred on June 14, had little interest in digging earthworks. On his first night duty, Weed worked for only two hours and then foraged for food. He "loafed around until the officer came after us" and put him back to work until morning.[32]

A shortage of tools also hampered the construction of Union earthworks. Mendell complained that he had only ninety axes for his engineer battalion, "and those in bad condition." The Engineer Department in Washington shipped 7,000 axes in late July to compensate for this shortage, but soldiers tended to be careless with government property. They also kept axes for use in performing camp chores. Quartermasters expended a great deal of time and effort transporting entrenching tools from field depots to work details. Hancock tried to streamline logistics by assigning a wagon filled with 150 shovels, 150 axes, and 50 picks to each division of the Second Corps. Division leaders were then responsible for them, aided by an enlisted man detailed from the U.S. Engineer Battalion. Hancock insisted on issuing written orders to allow the tools to be distributed to work details every day.[33]

A better solution was to design a shovel small enough for each soldier to carry as part of his equipment. Henry W. Benham designed a "picket" shovel, inspired by "a child's garden spade or scoop." He thought it would be useful for skirmishers who had to dig in under fire. With a leather strap so it could be attached to the knapsack, the tool was a "light, serviceable implement" that could be issued to all soldiers. Meade endorsed the concept and authorized the manufacture of 2,000 experimental tools.[34]

The First Division of the Ninth Corps issued 250 picket shovels to each brigade in November. They apparently worked, for authorities placed orders for a total of 21,000 additional picket shovels with the Engineer Department by February 1865. The contractor encountered difficulty in meeting the specifications because the implements required "new models and tools." He managed to produce only 324 by late March 1865. The Engineer Department canceled all outstanding orders in April, but nearly all of the tools had already been made by then. They probably were sold at bargain prices when the Engineer Department reduced the inventory in its Washington depot later that year. Benham's picket shovel was the forerunner of the modern entrenching tool, but no specimens of it have survived.[35]

The engineers assembled a wide variety of revetting material. Benham arranged for the purchase of 100,000 sandbags in mid-July, although a large portion of one lot proved to be rotten and therefore useless in the field. Other revetting had to be made out of readily available material. Skillful engineers wove vines or supple branches into matting to form panels that could be carried to the site, but they more commonly used gabions and fascines. Spaulding's 50th New York Engineers made 10,000 of the former and 1,200 of the latter in five weeks. They worked at a steady pace of one gabion per man per day and made fascines at the rate of ten per day for each fifteen-man squad.[36]

Benham's engineer troops made hundreds of sections of chevaux-de-frise, each section typically sixteen feet long. The central log had holes drilled every twelve to sixteen inches along two different lines, with stakes seven feet long and sharpened at each end shoved through the holes. One observer thought the device "looked like the head of a revolving horse-rake with two sets of teeth." They were placed at night about 100 yards in front of the line and wired together.[37]

Artillerymen preferred to place mantlets across the embrasures of their gun emplacements for protection. Chief Engineer Richard Delafield, who had been responsible for making a number of mantlets for McClellan's use at Yorktown in the spring of 1862, authorized the shipment of about fifty of those old coverings from storage at Suffolk. Some had been made of rope, while others consisted of wood or boiler iron. Henry Abbot conducted experiments to see if they worked. He found that a Springfield musket ball penetrated only three inches of the rope mantlet, even at a range of twenty paces, while the blast from a 12-pounder howitzer demolished the iron and wood mantlets. Abbot therefore requested 100 new rope mantlets for his guns.[38]

The Engineer Department sent 500-pound rope mantlets that were four and a half feet by five feet in dimension and six inches thick. Later, an improved version was reduced to four inches thick. It was more tightly woven than the previous mantlet, but sometimes a musket ball managed to pass through between the ropes. The gunners draped them from poles supported by forked stands to cover the embrasure. It was important for the mantlet to swing when hit, as that greatly slowed the velocity of bullets and artillery rounds.[39]

The Engineer Department also supplied technical information to the armies at Petersburg. Barnard wanted a copy of the French report of siege operations at Sebastopol, and Delafield authorized his agent in New York City to purchase a copy or borrow it from the military academy library at West Point. Barnard passed it on to Michler when he finished reading it.[40]

### CONFEDERATE WORKS

The Confederates had a head start on the Federals in fortifying their positions outside Petersburg, building on the Harris Line and what was left of Dimmock's works in their possession, but they also faced a daunting task to make these beginnings into an effective line. On Hagood's sector, there was no exterior ditch because of the danger involved in exposing oneself to dig it. For a long while some sectors of the Harris Line had no abatis, palisades, or other obstructions in front of the parapet. Eventually, infantrymen improved the profile of the parapet, drained the trenches, and built traverses and covered ways.[41]

The Dimmock Line from Battery No. 25 to a point about a mile west of Jerusalem Plank Road needed improvements, for it had been designed as a simple ditch and parapet. There were no traverses or covered ways, and the abatis had long since disappeared. Martin L. Smith examined the line for several days in late June only to conclude it was "badly laid off and in some instances badly located." Smith plotted the course of a new line west of Boydton Plank Road through the Whitworth and Turnbull farms, all the way to the Appomattox. This new line lay west of Indian Town Creek (also known as Old Town Creek or Rohoic Creek). It was located about three-fourths of a mile forward of the

Confederate works, view of interior of parapet. The location is unknown. (Library of Congress, LC-DIG-CWPB-02624)

Dimmock works that lay east of the creek. Work on the new line proceeded slowly because this area was inactive for a long time. Fort Gregg and Fort Whitworth eventually took shape and would play roles in the heavy fighting that ended the Petersburg campaign on April 2, 1865.[42]

While this line west of Indian Town Creek was the only new work the Confederates initiated, Smith improved the rest of Dimmock's line. He planned to strengthen Battery No. 45, where the line crossed Boydton Plank Road, and worked with David Harris to select ground for a possible second line of defense behind the Harris Line. Smith also plotted the location of possible new works to anchor the southern portion of the Howlett Line at Bermuda Hundred.[43]

Lee involved himself in engineering matters to a limited degree. He wanted information from his First Corps commander about whether the Federals were using siege approaches and what was being done to provide for the comfort of his troops in the works. Anderson's chief engineer directed the construction of traverses, covered ways, and artillery emplacements, recommending that a double line of palisades and abatis be emplaced wherever possible. The First Corps used hundreds of sandbags as well. In general, the Confederates favored wide but shallow trenches. J. B. Polley of the Texas brigade in Anderson's Corps estimated his section of trench to be eight feet wide and four feet deep. Anderson felt that his artillery was not sufficiently protected and urged officers to thicken their parapets. He advised them to use their gunners, for the infantry had their hands full improving their own defenses.[44]

On Beauregard's sector, division leader Johnson erected palisades and sandbag embrasures for sharpshooters. Gracie and McAfee constructed covered ways to connect their brigade picket lines with the main lines, running them under the parapet through tunnels. McAfee's Tar Heels dug their trench eleven feet wide and four feet deep, with a two-foot-high banquette, carrying timber into the works by hand to use it as revetment for traverses. Pegram's battery on Elliott's front received a hail of close-range sniper fire that tore up the gabion revetment of its embrasures. The gunners replaced the smashed gabions and shoveled the loose dirt out of the embrasures before putting the pieces back in action. Johnson had lost twenty to twenty-eight men per day during the last two weeks of June. By mid-July, with his works in better shape, the loss rate dropped to four to fifteen men per day.[45]

Johnson wanted to dig a series of artillery works with short infantry trenches behind the line so that reserve troops could be close to the scene of a surprise attack. He thought this would "give a sense of strength and security to our front line which would render it invincible." Johnson made it clear that he did not mean to have "a line to fall back on. I think our troops should fully understand that the present line has to be held." He managed to put one regiment of each brigade in reserve for one to two days at a time.[46]

Confederate engineers constructed defense in depth behind the angles in the line. They built a cavalier, a parapet taller than that in the main line, so infantrymen could command the entire area around Pegram's Salient. Work details from Goode's Virginia brigade and Elliott's South Carolina brigade began digging it as early as June 29. Other troops began building a similar work behind Colquitt's Salient, although it progressed slowly because of the "constant firing of the enemy on the working parties." A number of small emplacements for mortars and guns and short trenches for infantrymen dotted the ascending slope behind some portions of the Harris Line all the way up to Jerusalem Plank Road.[47]

The Confederates encountered more difficulty than the Federals in their efforts to supply the tools and material necessary to fight at Petersburg. The Engineer Bureau in Richmond could send only small shipments of shovels, picks, and axes at a time. Raiding Union cavalrymen had burned 500 spades at a depot in Burkeville, west of Petersburg, late in June, and the bureau tried to hire people who could make new handles for them. Lee's and Beauregard's men placed chevaux-de-frise (spelled "shevade friezes" in the correspondence of one Tar Heel) before some parts of their line. The Confederates also used small rope mantlets that fitted tightly around the tube of the artillery piece. Sometimes they merely hung "pieces of gunny sack" across the embrasures when not using the weapons.[48]

CHAPTER SIX

## *Soldiering in the Trenches*

As the earthworks rose outside Petersburg, they made victims of nearly all trees and bushes in the immediate vicinity. The wood was useful for revetting and obstructions, and clear fields of fire were necessary for defense. Moreover, thousands of soldiers needed wood for cooking their meals. The bare earth around the works reflected the sun and made the trenches "terribly hot," reported a man in the 4th New Hampshire. He enjoyed some "cool nice air" only in the evenings. Other men put shelter tent halves and blankets across poles that they laid over the trenches, but this did not always provide relief. Capt. Will Biggs of the 17th North Carolina reported that "the heat and dust will in some manner get to us . . . , we are almost burnt up." Men in Elliott's brigade started to sicken from the "hot sun and confinement" of the trenches, and J. Warren Pursley reported to his sister that the men "is giting verry tired and ware out."[1]

The dry weather and digging created a "peculiar dust, fine and sticky," that lay two inches deep on the ground like "an impalpable powder." It rose in clouds, "filling everything, covering everything," each time someone walked by or a wagon rolled past. "Our boys look as though there was a heavy frost on their hair & whiskers," mused James M. Snook, while the chaplain of the 102nd Pennsylvania reported, "You see nothing but dust, you smell dust, you eat dust, you drink dust. Your clothes, blanket, food, drink, are all permeated with dust."[2]

Imagine, then, what happened when a few rain showers descended on this dirty environment. The night of July 24 proved to be not only wet but cold. "The boys shivered with their blankets around them," noted James Snook, while the trenches became creeks and shelters turned into mud holes with the rain. A portion of the Union picket line flooded, but the opposing Confederates did not have the heart to fire on the Yankees when they jumped out and plodded across a muddy field to their main line. Even after the rainwater drained away, the trench floors retained a deposit of mud sometimes knee deep. On the Fifth

Entrance to a bombproof. While a note on the image indicates this is a Confederate shelter, it is more likely a Union bombproof at Fort Sedgwick. (Library of Congress, LC-DIG-CWPB-02630)

Corps front, the men constructed traverses to funnel water away from artillery positions and into the main trench.[3]

### SHELTERS

The areas around and in the trenches were potted with small holes, some merely two feet deep and large enough for a single individual. A shelter tent half served as a roof. Soldiers in the Tenth Corps called these excavations "rat holes," while men in the Eighteenth Corps thought they resembled caves. They were deeper where the soil consisted of heavy clay, but if rain soaked the ground, the walls could collapse. Daniel W. Sawtelle heard about several men who died this way.[4]

Many Rebels cut holes in the sides of their trenches where they slept and built fires. Soldiers in the 5th Florida dug a large space into the rear of their trench, twenty feet long, to make "a kind of little back yard." They covered it with brush and shelter tent halves. Here they could "walk about, lie down, [and] cook" in relative safety.[5]

The larger Federal bombproofs demanded a great deal of labor. The first difficulty was finding enough timber to revet the walls and cover the top. If a nearby battery was willing, the infantrymen borrowed its horses to pull logs as close to the rear of the line as possible and then carried them through the covered ways. One brigade of the Ninth Corps accumulated sixty logs up to twelve feet long, to be used in the construction of bombproofs and traverses.[6]

Members of the 118th Pennsylvania made bombproofs fourteen by sixteen feet, which they considered large enough for a dozen men. The Pennsylvanians covered the pine log roof with leaves and piled more than two feet of dirt on top. Another Fifth Corps regiment built its bombproof six feet square and six feet deep, with a door on the side opposite the enemy.[7]

These structures, which were little more than cellars, were generally safe but hardly comfortable. The men lived "low and damp," according to a soldier in the 17th Maine, and were constantly afraid of cave-ins. When candles flickered through the openings late at night, Robert Goldthwaite Carter thought "of the old-time concert or basement saloon in New York or Boston, with their cellars ablaze." During the day, Carter thought "the whole ground, thrown up in heaps, resembled an immense prairie dog village." In photographs taken soon after the campaign ended, these bombproofs appear as large mounds of dirt with dark openings.[8]

The Confederates also dug a few bombproofs. A unit of artillerymen in Hill's Third Corps fashioned one that was twelve feet square and seven feet deep. They placed layers of pine logs in crisscross fashion to make a roof and covered them with five feet of earth. This shelter protected them from Union artillery fire.[9]

#### FOOD, WATER, AND SANITATION

Union officers usually did not allow their men to build fires in the narrow trenches. This led the Yankees to find a convenient ravine as close to the rear as possible and carry food and coffee into the works at dawn. A Fifth Corps regiment fortified its cookhouse with a horseshoe-shaped parapet linked to the main line with a covered way.[10]

The quality of rations and their preparation often were inadequate. The medical inspector of the Fifth Corps saw men frying their food in greasy skillets, broiling it on sticks over fires, or boiling it in tip cups. The end result, in his opinion, was that they wasted part of their rations and wound up with miserable fare. The lack of fresh vegetables hurt John Haley the most. "We live mostly on *promises* of potatoes and 'desecrated' vegetables," he complained on July 17. "But each of us gets so little of these that it is only an aggravation." Haley saw many men who were sick because of inadequate diets and admitted that hundreds, himself included, "amble around on legs as raw as a piece of meat." The United States Sanitary Commission garnered much praise for shipping tons of vegetables to Grant's men in July. The shipments included pickled cucumbers, pickled onions, and dried apples, as well as fresh onions and lemons. Commission agents estimated that it would take 1,500 barrels of fresh potatoes to offer just one meal to every Federal along the Petersburg line, but they were able to send only 54 barrels.[11]

The story was much the same on the Confederate side. A Georgian reported that his comrades received just enough food "to keep sole and Boddy to gether." Southerners learned to find substitutes for vegetables among various weeds and grasses. G. H. Dorman of Florida hated the sight of "old-time yard [parsley]" cooking over a fire; it reminded him of a "pot of earth worms boiled up." He preferred lamb's quarter, pepper grass, and poke leaves. Virginian J. T. Binford added watermelon vines to this list, "and a good many sorts of things that I never thought a cow would eat." Richmond bureaucrats recognized the hardships of trench duty by adding coffee and sugar to the normal issue of bread and meat.[12]

It was also difficult to find a cup of good drinking water along the trench lines. Lewis Bissell of the 2nd Connecticut Heavy Artillery informed his father that the water was white with various minerals. Left to settle in a cup overnight, they formed up to half an inch of mud on the bottom. But Bissell mixed the relatively clear part with plenty of coffee and sugar and found it tasted "very good." The Yankees began to sink wells as much as thirty feet deep because the surface water tended to be filthy. The ground was "alive with vermin," and "maggots washed down from the hillsides abound in the runs and springs," recalled Howard Aston in the Ninth Corps. Federal commissaries issued whiskey to those who labored on the fortifications. It amounted to half a gill per day in the Ninth Corps, but the men had to drink it in the presence of a commissioned officer.[13]

Sanitation became a more severe problem as time passed. On the Ninth Corps sector, the men "lie in the pitts [sic] and suffer rather than visit [the latrines] in the day time, at night they get behind some big tree, in preference." As a result, the ground just behind the trench was littered with what Civil War officers called "nuisances." In places there was so much human waste that Confederate sharpshooters targeted the few paths that allowed the Yankees to walk through this muck. Officers of the day recommended the digging of many more latrines with fortifications to protect them, linked with the trenches by covered ways. Signs of improvement soon appeared. "There is but little offensive matter visible," reported an officer of the day. "Some old clothing carelessly thrown away was the worst feature." In the Second Corps, officers allowed their men to dirty the works for a long while but issued orders to clean them up when the filth became intolerable.[14]

## ENTERTAINMENT

The only break in the monotony of trench duty lay in whatever diversion the soldiers could manufacture. The regimental band of the 16th Maine often played just behind the works, its music attracting listeners across no-man's-land. On Sunday evenings, the Maine soldiers assembled to sing "Old Hundredth" and other religious hymns.[15]

More common than band music were the jokes that enlivened the daily lives of all soldiers. W. A. Day of the 49th North Carolina enjoyed hosting civilian visitors to the trenches; the men often stooped half over when giving them tours and enjoyed seeing them stoop too. Day also amused himself by throwing stones into the Federal picket line only a few yards away. Soon an irritated Yankee yelled out, "'Johnny, you quit throwing rocks over here.'"[16]

Members of the 4th Texas played a more elaborate joke in the trenches. J. C. Jordan and Levi S. Pogue allowed themselves to be objects of attention any time someone needed to laugh. Jordan was a superb shot and preferred to wait until many of his comrades called his name before he demonstrated how coolly he could aim across the parapet and find something to shoot at. Pogue was a nervous fellow who, "with a great show of alacrity and desire to please," stuck the barrel of his musket tentatively out of the trench. "Lower the muzzle of your gun, Po[g]ue," yelled the onlookers, "for you will hit nothing but a quartermaster or commissary that way, and they ain't worth killing." He screwed up his courage, nervously bobbed up and down until he caught a fleeting glimpse of the opposing line, and fired. Then the warrior "sinks back, exhausted, pale, and perspiring, into the arms of his friends," wrote J. B. Polley, "ready to receive their laughing congratulations."[17]

## TRUCES

On the morning of July 10, some soldiers in the 11th New Hampshire stuck a newspaper on a stick and exposed it above the parapet on the Ninth Corps sector. White handkerchiefs began to flutter above the Confederate line, and a Federal took his newspaper into no-man's-land as sporadic firing ceased for a few minutes. The Southerner who came out to meet him had nothing to trade. He dashed back, found a newspaper, and returned. The trade consummated, both men returned to their holes and resumed firing.[18]

This was the first informal truce in Potter's division at Petersburg, but similar scenes were common enough along other parts of the line to raise concern among officers. Truces represented a welcome break in the monotony of trench life, and they had a humanizing effect, for soldiers could see their enemy and realize they shared a common danger. Officers also saw truces as opportunities to glean information from the enemy or as a chance to examine the condition of their defenses. But what was an opportunity for one side was an opportunity for the other, so officers more often wanted to stop truces than to initiate them.

In the Fifth Corps sector, a stream between the lines often held enough water to tempt thirsty soldiers on both sides. All one had to do was hold up a canteen, and a truce held sway for some time. Division leader Samuel Crawford stood openly during one such truce, gazing at the Confederate line with an opera glass. Soon a Confederate threw a rock with a piece of paper wrapped around it into the Union picket line. "'Tell the fellow with the spy-glass to clear out, or we shall have to shoot him.'" During another day's truce, a Rebel soldier discharged his musket either by accident or through ignorance of protocol. The Federals took cover until their counterparts yelled, "'Don't shoot; you'll see how we'll fix him!'" They disarmed the man and forced him to carry a rail while walking back and forth in front of the trench.[19]

### INTELLIGENCE

The Federals detected much activity in the Confederate lines by stationing signal officers in trees and towers. Isaac S. Lyon saw the enemy working inside one corner of the redoubt near Gregory's House as they cut new embrasures and erected a platform for a gun.[20]

Gracie sometimes sent a man out to exchange newspapers and report on what he could see of the Union works on the way. He also used the occasion of a local burial truce that the Federals requested on July 15 to closely examine enemy defenses. Federal officers normally cut out the most important items from newspapers before allowing their men to exchange them.[21]

Scouting remained a valuable way to obtain information, even though the armies were locked only a few hundred yards from each other. Johnson instructed a brigade commander to "send some intelligent men to crawl out two or three times every night" to see if the Federals were trying to dig fortifications in a ravine in advance of his picket line. Union officers also relied on the more daring of their men to crawl into no-man's-land at night and listen to Rebel conversations.[22]

Engineer Stevens was nearly shot when he held up a mirror at Pegram's Salient to spy on the Federals. He was careful to expose only one end of it while crouching behind the parapet, but very soon a Yankee sharpshooter found his mark and shattered the glass. "'Set it up again, Johnny!'" he yelled at Stevens.[23]

Deserters sometimes proved to be valuable sources of intelligence for both armies, although their stories could not always be taken at face value. The Federals routinely questioned them at the picket line first, then at division headquarters, and then at corps headquarters. "By comparing each of these talks," recalled an officer, "it was thot [sic] the truth might be arrived at."[24]

### MANNING THE WORKS

Every Federal unit worked out a system to man its works and relieve troops on a regular basis. In the Eighteenth Corps, each brigade rested half its manpower in rear of the defenses. These men exchanged places with the other half every forty-eight hours. Resting in the rear actually meant holding a secondary position 200 yards behind the first. The men were still exposed to enemy fire, but they had opportunities "to wash up and rest." In the Ninth Corps, one of the two brigades in each division held the division front for a four-day shift. While holding the rear line, the brigade not on duty was allowed to send half its men at a time to rest for one day in "some safe and convenient spot" farther to the rear. Here the Ninth Corps veterans could "unloosen their clothes at night," sleep better, and only have to worry about some artillery fire.[25]

Returning to duty in an unfamiliar part of the front line, the men often had trouble finding their way through the complicated system of trenches. The works in places "formed each a labyrinth [such] that only those that were in them daily were able to find their way to the front," according to Erasmus Gilreath. Second Corps troops set up signboards to direct newcomers where to go. Moreover, the change from the relatively safe rear area to the front caused Edmund J. Cleveland to not sleep at all during his first night of each rotation in the trenches.[26]

The Confederates rarely rotated units, for they barely had enough manpower to hold the line. Everyone in Hagood's South Carolina brigade stood in the trenches ready for action thirty minutes before and thirty minutes after sunset. During the night, half the men stayed awake while the other half slept on the trench floor, "disturbed by the frequent passage of inspecting officers or fatigue parties blundering along in the dark." No one was allowed to leave the trench during the day. Company officers endured the same routine as their men. Brigade staff and field officers had relatively comfortable pits six feet to the rear of the trench, but they were not allowed to use them while the men stood to.[27]

Colquitt insisted that his superiors work out a system of relieving troops, such as keeping one brigade of each division in reserve while the others spread out and held the works more thinly, believing it would reduce sickness and fatigue. In Hagood's brigade, "Diarrhoea, & dysentery & hard work have used up the men terribly," reported Sgt. Henry Greer.[28]

Officers blamed extended service in the trenches for the high number of votes cast for William Holden, the antiwar gubernatorial candidate in North Carolina. The Holden vote was stronger among infantrymen who served in the trenches than it was among artillerymen and cavalrymen who had less demanding stations. A "more tiresome and exhausting service cannot well be imagined," thought D. M. Carter, a Third Corps staff officer, "nor one better calculated to disgust a man with war.... The devil always whispers his evil suggestions in the ear of a man who is out of temper, morose and miserable."[29]

Desertions began to increase in Lee's army in July because of the hard conditions. One evening, a Rebel waving a newspaper began to cross no-man's-land on the Eighteenth Corps sector, but then he suddenly ran forward and jumped into the Union trench. He told the Yankees "it was better to exchange himself than newspapers." Some cases of self-inflicted wounds also began to appear. When a man in the 11th Georgia reported a gunshot wound in his hand, his comrades believed that "he did it a purpose." John A. Everett thought that "if he did[,] it out to of bin his head in stid of his hand."[30]

Johnson worked out a system of relieving his men for short times. McAfee's brigade sent one company of each regiment to the rear every day to rest and clean up. When Gracie's brigade returned to the works on July 9 after a short rest to the rear, Lewellyn Shaver had difficulty adjusting to the confusing maze of trenches in the night. It "was, probably, as unpleasant as groping in the darkness of the midnight hour, among a chaos of chairs, cradles, and other *domestic accoutrements*, in search of the paregoric bottle, in response to the plaintive appeal of an aggrieved and weeping infant."[31]

## SHARPSHOOTING

"There is not a day passes when at least one member of our number is not struck with a minnie ball," recorded George Bowen of the 12th New Jersey. "This picking us off one at a time gets on one's nerves." A Jersey artilleryman in the Second Corps wrote to a friend that if "you dare to show your head above the rifle pits you are a gone goose." Burnside reported losing 480 men in the Ninth Corps to sniping and artillery fire during a ten-day period.[32]

Sharpshooting became a science by early July. The Ninth Corps organized details of its best marksmen, excused them from fatigue and picket duty, and told them to target Confederate sharpshooters first, artillerymen second, and then anyone who exposed himself. Eighteenth Corps snipers took position on July 19, making loopholes out of sandbags. They developed all sorts of stratagems, such as raising a hat on a ramrod to draw fire and then shooting at the powder smoke. Other snipers sighted their guns on exposed parts of the Rebel lines during the day and erected forked sticks at the exact height to rest their trigger guards. This enabled them to fire blindly and with some degree of accuracy at night. Soldiers on the Ninth Corps sector learned never to step in front of a loophole in the morning, for the sun was then to their back and Rebel snipers fired every time the hole darkened.[33]

Tired of taking punishment, Ellis Spear formed a detail of sharpshooters from the 20th Maine. He obtained telescopic sights for at least a few of his men and compelled the Confederates to arrange a truce after only one day of firing. Gracie's brigade detailed two men from each company who were told to fire every five minutes, amounting to forty rounds from each regiment every ten minutes, yet this failed to keep the Yankees from doing their best to kill the Alabamans.[34]

On any given part of the line, sniping took a toll of both blue and gray casualties. Clarion Miltmore of the 37th Wisconsin tried to pen a letter to his mother from the trenches. While he wrote, "three men were shot dead within the reach of my arm & another may sign, Seal, & direct this for me, from a similar cause." On the other side of no-man's-land, Joab Goodson of the 44th Alabama lost his brother Rufe to a Yankee sharpshooter. Rufe raised his head a bit to find some sugar in a haversack that hung on the trench wall when a bullet glanced against the top of the parapet and hit his head, killing him instantly. Joab grieved with all his heart. "I wept as I never wept before. I bent over the dear boy, and called him back, but in vain." He kept Rufe's body in the trench for the rest of the day, unable to remove him until dark.[35]

## PICKET DUTY

Both sides established picket lines before their works to guard against sudden attack and to keep the enemy as far from the main line as possible. Where the main trenches were too close, pickets went out only under cover of darkness and sheltered in pits for the night, returning to the main line before dawn.[36]

The pickets often engaged in struggles for possession of advantageous ground. In the Fifth Corps sector, Spear advanced his 20th Maine skirmishers into an unoccupied ravine to secure possession of a spring. Each man carried a spade and began to dig in. The Rebel pickets quickly approached to lodge a protest, but a Federal sergeant yelled, "'Can't help it, we were ordered out here.'" The Confederates did not want to come to blows, so they threw a few dirt clods at the Yankees and left.[37]

Although the infantry worked out agreements for peace on many parts of the line, artillerymen reserved the right to fire on any target that appeared. Confederate pickets apologized for this by explaining that the gunners "never had to go on picket, and did not know the difficulty and the danger attendant upon that duty."[38]

## ALARMS

With the opposing armies locked in place within sight of each other, rumors of impending attacks circulated freely among the troops. Independence Day seemed to be a perfect time for the Yankees to advance, but the holiday came and went quietly.[39]

The Federals developed "Fire Balls" to light up the night in case of trouble. These devices were small frames made of tarred cording material, eight inches in diameter, and filled with "the most combustible materials science has been able to invent." They had the capacity to burn "for some time with an intensely brilliant flame which lights up objects for a great distance around." The Confederates apparently did not have them at Petersburg, although members of the Army of Tennessee used similar devices at Kennesaw Mountain in late June. For that matter, there is no recorded instance of their use by the Federals at Petersburg.[40]

Troops on the main line often engaged in outbursts of nervous firing caused by unexplained noise in the enemy works. Some men fired their muskets behind the Ninth Corps line to empty old cartridges, and the Confederates thought it was the beginning of an attack. They opened fire, and the spirit of resistance spread to comrades right and left. Such incidents could last a few minutes or extend for hours, and they often prompted commanders to send puzzled dispatches to their subordinates inquiring about the cause of all the noise.[41]

## ARTILLERY FIRE

Artillery fire was a constant part of life in the trenches because officers normally gave free rein to their gunners to fire at will. In the Eighteenth Corps, this discretion extended to battery commanders, although it was given with an admonition not to waste ammunition or unnecessarily expose their locations. Superior officers told their battery leaders to "have the elevations and directions fixed for night firing" as well.[42]

Whether someone became a casualty of artillery fire often depended on chance. Seven men of the 8th Maine were sleeping in the trench when a solid shot happened to fall directly onto them, killing every one. On the Eighteenth Corps line, a New York man had the brawn and presence of mind to throw a lighted shell out of the works before it exploded, saving himself and many others. When a Confederate shell landed only four feet from a Union infantryman who was preparing his dinner, "he looked at it a second, very coolly picked up the [skillet,] crawled into his hole, and as soon as the shell exploded came out and commenced his cooking."[43]

## MORTARS

The extended stay at Petersburg allowed for the heavy deployment of mortars. The smallest was the Coehorn, a portable weapon carried by four men into the trenches. Developed by the Dutch engineer Baron Menno van Coehoorn and first used by him in 1673, it had seen service during the colonial era of American history as well as during the Mexican War. There had been no opportunity to use it in the eastern campaigns until Spotsylvania and Cold Harbor. The Coehorn mortar could fire a seventeen-pound shell anywhere from 25 to 1,200 yards. Hunt began ordering them for use as early as June 17, and Meade's army had forty Coehorns in service by the end of the campaign. Engineer troops usually constructed battery emplacements for the heavier mortars that were also deployed along the line. Until the ordnance became available, some field artillerists tried to simulate mortar fire by rigging their guns to fire at high angles.[44]

The Dictator, the most famous mortar at Petersburg, was a monster 13-inch weapon mounted on a railroad car. It was the only mortar of its size in use during the campaign, although a few had been deployed at Yorktown in 1862. Members of the 1st Connecticut Heavy Artillery fired only five rounds before the platform broke. After repairs, they resumed firing two weeks later. All told, the gunners chalked up 218 rounds before removing the Dictator to City Point for storage.[45]

It was possible to deploy the Dictator because the Federals rebuilt the City Point branch of the South Side Railroad to supply Meade's army. Charles L. McAlpine and a civilian crew began work on June 18, repairing more than two miles of disrupted track and re-laying undisturbed track to allow narrow-gauge Northern engines to use it. McAlpine also replaced the outdated U-rail of the prewar South with the improved T-rail. The crews finished the track and all bridges for seven miles out of City Point and established four stations along the route. It was officially designated the City Point and Army Line, and 24 locomotives and 275 cars shuttled supplies out to the troops and brought back the wounded.[46]

The Confederates also deployed mortars along the line. Alexander received his first shipment of twelve mortars on June 24 and placed them to fire on the Federals opposite Pegram's Salient. Hagood experimented with a field piece deployed as a mortar and found it worked well with small charges. Confederate artillerists soon placed eight Coehorn mortars near his line.[47]

Mortar rounds "were a continual torment to us for we could never tell where they would drop and we could not tell when or where they would burst," recalled a Union infantryman. They made "a swishing noise" as they flew through the air, caused by the burning fuse as the ball lazily rolled in flight. "The boys said they were whispering and talking to themselves, saying, 'Which one? Which one?'" Because of this effect, the Confederates called them "'Demoralizers.'"[48]

If the gunners cut the fuse improperly, the projectile could bury itself before exploding, creating a huge hole. A mortar shell burrowed into the earth only six feet from Edward King Wightman, splattering mud all around but hurting no one. John Malachi Bowden of the 2nd Georgia calculated correctly that a mortar shell heading his way would overshoot the trench, but he remembered that the fuse might have been cut too short. The round exploded only fifteen feet above his head. "The concussion was awful, and as I was in the act of lying down, it drove me against the bottom of the ditch with tremendous force. A piece of the shell as large as a man's fist brushed my ear and went twelve or fifteen miles into the ground."[49]

## SHELLING PETERSBURG

The residents of Petersburg shared the dangers of artillery fire. The first Federal rounds sailed into the town on June 16 when gunners of the 10th Massachusetts Battery opened fire from a point near the Hare House. Lee wanted to move 3,000 sick and wounded soldiers in the town's hospitals westward along the South Side Railroad, but Surgeon John Herbert Claiborne argued that the logistical difficulties and the danger to the more severely wounded were too great. Lee's staff officers investigated and recommended that Claiborne be allowed to decide the best course of action. Two wounded men had already died in transit, and many others preferred to take their chances with the shells. Claiborne shifted patients to less exposed sections of town and closed some hospitals.[50]

The shelling continued sporadically for several weeks, at first causing some level of panic among citizens who fled the town. It set fire to a number of buildings and killed people now and then. At least three civilians died due to Federal shelling during June. The bombardment intensified in early July, leading to another wave of evacuation, until one resident estimated that two out of three Petersburg residents had abandoned their homes. Then the shelling eased off in late July. As historian Will Greene has put it, the Federal shelling of Petersburg, unlike the Union shelling of Atlanta, "would never reach the level of a formal tactical operation" but was "a form of terror and a source of disruption."[51]

Petersburg's residents reacted in different ways to the shelling. While some panicked and fled, others dug bombproofs in their backyards and covered them with timber and earth similar to how soldiers constructed their shelters. Some civilians also used basements as bombproofs, while sandbags and cotton bales proved to be effective in shielding the facades of houses. Some residents set up tents on the western outskirts of Petersburg, where they intended to wait until the campaign ended. Even though some parts of town were "almost knocked to pieces," those residents who stayed adjusted to the shelling and carried on with their lives. The most exposed streets were hit hard, but only a block away, life appeared normal to visiting soldiers.[52]

CHAPTER SEVEN

# *The Third Offensive*

By about July 10, Early's raid into Maryland compelled Grant to send the Sixth Corps and eventually plan to divert the Nineteenth Corps to protect Washington, D.C. He also worried that Early's rapid movements might compel him to send even more troops from Petersburg. This led Grant to abandon all thought of conducting siege approaches. When Early skirmished outside the forts around Washington on July 11–12 and then retired across the Potomac, Grant was relieved of an immediate need to attack.

Grant learned that Burnside was nearly ready to charge his mine by July 23. He also received alarming reports of heavy fighting in Georgia, where Gen. John Bell Hood's Confederate Army of Tennessee took the offensive against Maj. Gen. William T. Sherman's army group. On July 20, Hood struck the Army of the Cumberland north of Atlanta, catching it by surprise while it crossed Peachtree Creek. Although repulsed, the Confederates demonstrated a boldness not yet seen in the Atlanta campaign. On July 22, Hood outflanked Sherman's left wing east of Atlanta by striking the Army of the Tennessee. Through luck and hard fighting, the Federals saved the situation and repulsed Hood again, but there was every prospect of another Confederate attack.[1]

These events produced a strong desire at Grant's headquarters to prevent Lee from sending reinforcements to Georgia. Grant asked Meade's opinion on the feasibility of attacking after Burnside sprung his mine. Meade agreed with Duane that Burnside could take Pegram's Salient, but Confederate artillery might tear into the flanks of the Ninth Corps advance unless Warren also advanced toward the Gregory House. They also feared that the Confederates had a second line on the crest of the ridge behind Pegram's Salient. While Meade recommended against an attack, he admitted the need for action and was ready to try it.[2]

Grant told Meade that if the attack took place, it would have to be done with maximum force and penetrate as deeply as possible, but the men should promptly retreat if they could not break through all Confederate defenses. The Eighteenth Corps and a division of the Tenth Corps could support Burnside. Grant intended to sleep on it before making a decision, but he wanted Burnside to spring his mine in any case. If nothing else, Meade could also raid the Weldon and Petersburg Railroad.[3]

A heavy rain descended on the night of July 24, filling trenches and bombproofs, but Grant rode out the storm thinking of his next move. After a month of waiting, he decided to launch a complex operation that incorporated Burnside's mine in a multilayered plan filled with options. He would use the bridgehead on the north bank of the James River at Deep Bottom to push large numbers of troops around Lee's left flank. If that did not work, a massive infantry attack following the mine explosion might break the Confederate line near its center. Grant could decide whether to make his major effort north or south of the river at the last minute.[4]

The next day, Grant told Meade to start loading Burnside's mine but to wait until ordered to spring it. Encouraging reports from a new signal station, confirmed by interviews with deserters and captured Rebels, indicated that the Confederates had a series of detached artillery and mortar emplacements rather than a continuous line of defenses along Jerusalem Plank Road. Meade asked Burnside for a detailed plan of attack and received it on July 26. It seemed possible that all the elements of this complex operation could be brought together in time to make it work.[5]

### FIRST DEEP BOTTOM, JULY 26-29

Grant organized the Third Offensive as a two-phased operation. First, Hancock's Second Corps and two divisions of cavalry under Maj. Gen. Philip Sheridan would advance from the fortified bridgehead at Deep Bottom. Sheridan would ride northwest and tear up the Virginia Central Railroad north of Richmond, burning the bridges across the Chickahominy and the South Anna. Hancock would advance toward Chaffin's Bluff, the anchor of Richmond's Outer Line, to support the cavalry. There was a remote possibility that Sheridan could enter Richmond; if so, Hancock was to help him as much as possible, or he should cover Sheridan's retreat if necessary.[6]

Foster's brigade of 2,000 men had held the fortified bridgehead at Deep Bottom since the night of June 20. Lee had wanted to eliminate it, but local commanders had too few troops and artillery. Capt. Archibald Graham's First Rockbridge Virginia Battery opened fire on the night of June 28 from works at the foot of New Market Heights, but at a range of 2,000 yards it did little harm to Foster or to Federal shipping. On the night of June 29, Graham moved a bit

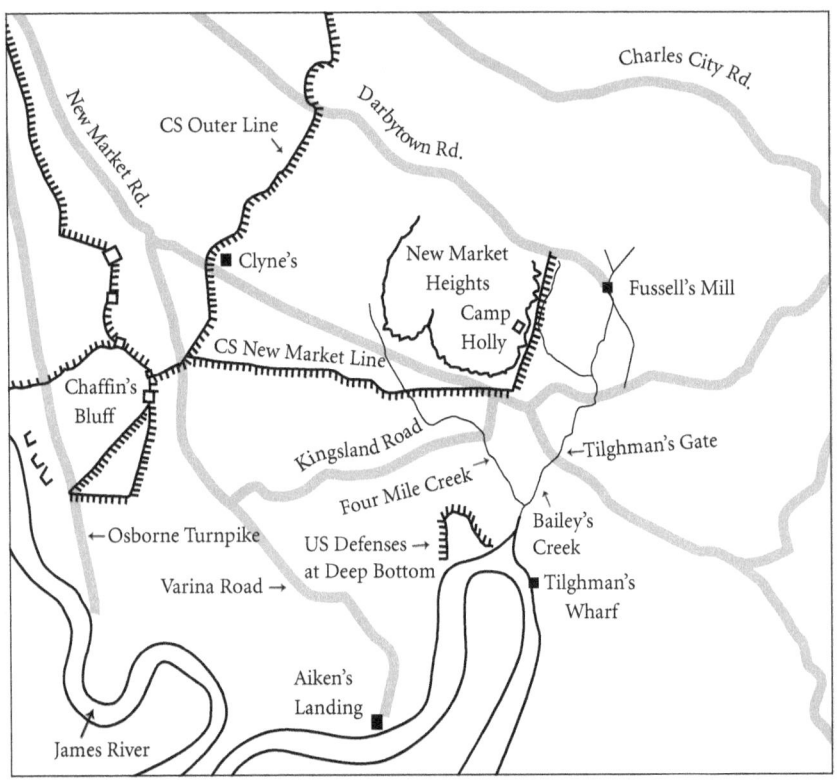

First Deep Bottom, July 26–29, 1864

closer, to Tilghman's Gate, where the New Market Road crossed Bailey's Creek, with no better results.[7]

Lee shifted Lane's North Carolina brigade and McGowan's South Carolina brigade north of the river to Chaffin's Bluff, where they joined the Richmond City Battalion and a few reserve battalions on June 30, but he could not find any heavy artillery. Graham's field guns annoyed Foster, almost hitting the pontoon bridge that linked him with the south side of the river and damaging some ships. Grant and Butler visited Deep Bottom on July 16 and had to leave under a hail of artillery fire. Grant therefore shipped Currie's brigade of the Nineteenth Corps to Curl's Neck, located on the north side of the river downstream from Deep Bottom, and Butler instructed Foster to establish a picket line at Tilghman's Gate.[8]

These Federal moves prompted Lee to send Kershaw's division north of the James on July 23. Kershaw moved from Chaffin's Bluff to New Market Heights with Lane's and McGowan's commands in tow, taking charge of the whole force. Alarmed at reports that the Yankees were digging in at Tilghman's Gate,

Lee wanted Kershaw to crush the Union bridgehead. "We cannot afford to sit down in front of the enemy and allow him to intrench himself wherever he pleases," he lectured Lt. Gen. Richard S. Ewell, commander of the Department of Richmond. Kershaw sent Henagan's South Carolina brigade east of Bailey's Creek to hit Foster's picket line at Tilghman's Gate just before midnight of July 25. This line was held by the 11th Maine, which retreated to the fortifications at Deep Bottom. Foster advanced the 10th Connecticut and 11th Maine on the morning of July 26, covered by fire from the gunboats, but they could not retake the position. The two regiments established a new post within small-arms range of New Market Road. Kershaw was unable to do more because of Hancock's and Sheridan's advance on July 27.[9]

By late July, the Confederates had dug a long line of works from the Chaffin's Bluff defenses between New Market Road and Kingsland Road to New Market Heights, about four miles away. Here the line made a right turn northward and extended six miles toward the Chickahominy River, crossing Darbytown Road and Charles City Road. Due to manpower shortages, the Confederates dug little more than a shallow trench, but it was well suited to the terrain. Hancock and Sheridan would threaten the stretch that ran northward from the angle at New Market Heights. It faced east and was located 1,000 yards west of Bailey's Creek. The Confederates cut down trees and erected abatis between the line and the stream, while Bailey's Creek served as an effective obstacle to an infantry attack. The Rebels had not dug the trench north of Fussell's Mill, located where Darbytown Road crossed the upper reaches of the creek.[10]

Hancock started the Second Corps toward Deep Bottom on the afternoon of July 26, reaching the river at 2:00 the next morning. Grant wanted Hancock to cross on a newly laid pontoon bridge upstream from the mouth of Bailey's Creek and take a more direct route toward Chaffin's Bluff, but Foster told Hancock about the newly constructed New Market Line. Meade approved Hancock's request to use the old pontoon bridge farther downstream so as to outflank the new Confederate line, although Hancock had no idea how far north it extended.[11]

Kershaw placed three of his brigades in the works at the base of New Market Heights while putting two of them at Tilghman's Gate. Humphreys's Mississippi brigade and Henagan's South Carolina brigade deployed along New Market Road facing south, the right of the Confederate line resting near Bailey's Creek. Graham placed his four 20-pounder Parrotts between the two brigades and behind meager earthworks — a parapet consisting of irregular mounds of dirt and unrevetted embrasures. It is unclear whether the infantry had any works at all. The Confederate line held 2,400 men and four guns in a line stretching west to east with Gary's cavalry brigade in reserve. Hancock deployed Barlow's division on his left, Mott's division on his right, and Gibbon in reserve.[12]

As the Federals advanced, Henagan shifted his brigade a bit and created a fifty-yard gap near the guns. The Yankees exploited this gap to capture Graham's battery and drive the gray infantry from the field. Hancock soon discovered that the Rebels had a strong, fortified position west of the creek, so he wheeled the Second Corps to the left as it advanced. Gibbon deployed on the left; Barlow, in the center; and Mott, on the right. When finished, the corps faced west but remained on the east side of Bailey's Creek. Sheridan then deployed his two cavalry divisions to Hancock's right, between Darbytown Road and Charles City Road, and north of the head of Bailey's Creek. Only Gary's cavalry blocked Sheridan, while Ewell spread the Richmond City Battalion and some artillery in a thin line between Chaffin's Bluff and New Market Heights.[13]

Grant arrived at Deep Bottom by midafternoon of July 27 and quickly concluded that Hancock needed to drive Kershaw all the way to Chaffin's Bluff to insure that Sheridan could conduct his raid. Reluctant to engage in attacks on fortified lines, he instructed Hancock to wait until the following day to see if the situation changed. After returning to his headquarters at City Point that evening, Grant received reports that Lee was shifting more troops to the north side of the James. He then urged Hancock to turn Kershaw's left flank but cautioned him not to attack strong fortifications. Grant also sent Birge's Nineteenth Corps brigade to support Hancock and instructed Foster to demonstrate out of his Deep Bottom entrenchments to draw Confederate attention.[14]

Lee shifted Heth's infantry division and two cavalry divisions north of the James on the night of July 27 and sent First Corps commander Anderson to take overall command of the troops at New Market Heights. While Heth and two of Kershaw's brigades held the New Market Line, four brigades assembled for an attack against Sheridan's cavalry north of Darbytown Road on July 28. Only three brigades—Henagan's, Lane's, and McGowan's—went into action. They advanced across unfamiliar terrain that broke their formations. The brigades lost contact with each other and hit the Union cavalry at different times, allowing the troopers to obtain crossfires. Although some Federal units fell back 300 yards, all of them dismounted and held their ground. Sheridan counterattacked and drove the Confederates almost a mile, taking 200 prisoners while losing only 200 of his men. No fortifications were involved in this fight.[15]

Hancock made a feeble attempt to outflank the Confederate line on July 28 until Grant called off operations north of the James. He still wanted to maintain a presence there to compel Lee to shift more troops from Petersburg, so Hancock sent one division south of the river but kept the rest and Sheridan's cavalry near Deep Bottom.[16]

Just after noon on July 28, Grant ordered Meade to finish preparations for the mine attack. Hunt needed to plant more heavy guns and mortars, and Meade had to reposition troops—dawn of July 30 was the earliest Burnside could go. Meanwhile, Grant's scheme seemed to be working. Hours after Mott's division left Deep Bottom to relieve the Eighteenth Corps, Lee shifted Field's division from the south to the north early on July 29. That left only three divisions (Hoke's, Johnson's, and Mahone's) to secure nine miles of line at Petersburg usually held by six divisions. Grant informed Meade that the Confederates were "piling everything, except a very thin line in your front, to the north side of the river." The prospects for Burnside's mine attack seemed bright.[17]

Hancock's two divisions and Sheridan's cavalry remained north of the James on July 29. When the Second Corps troops received orders to dig fieldworks, the men made "a pretense of so doing, throwing the dirt down hill, so that they could not be used against us should we ever come here again," wrote George Bowen.[18]

The Federals evacuated most of their remaining troops from Deep Bottom on the evening of July 29. Hancock's two divisions headed for the scene of Burnside's attack, and Sheridan headed for Meade's left flank. Foster continued to hold the bridgehead at Deep Bottom, leaving nearly 17,000 Confederate troops north of the James River. The Federals lost 488 men out of more than 28,000 engaged at First Deep Bottom, and the Confederates lost 635. Although imperfectly dug, the Confederate New Market Line stymied the first punch of Grant's offensive. Hancock and Sheridan failed to take it or to outflank the Confederates, but they forced Lee to shift a large proportion of his troops north of the James, inviting Burnside to try his mine with a follow-up attack that held some promise of success.[19]

### THE MINE

Preparations for the second phase of the Third Offensive continued as Hancock and Sheridan conducted their futile operations north of the James. Pleasants and his subordinates finished excavating the mine by July 27, draining excess water and putting up the frame inside the two branches. They also constructed eight magazines, wooden bins shaped like a funnel to hold the powder. While this work proceeded, Burnside feared that the left branch might cave in due to the weight of Pegram's field guns overhead. Extra framing solved this problem. When finished, the gallery was 510 feet long, and each branch was nearly 40 feet long. Pleasants estimated his men had removed 18,000 cubic feet of dirt from the mine.[20]

Hugh Thomas Douglas countermined to the bitter end. He never had time to connect the two galleries that extended on either side of Pegram's guns, but

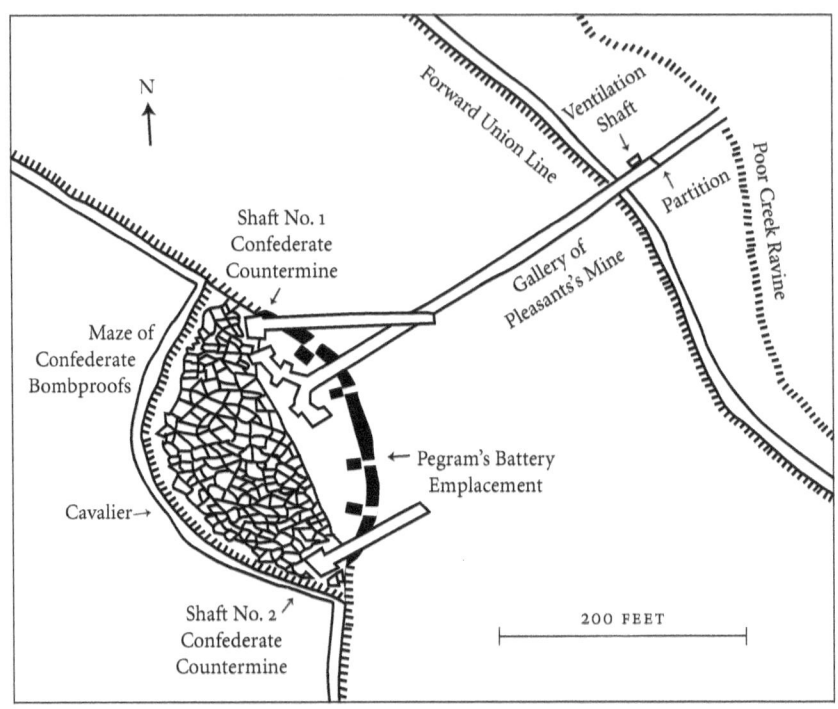

Pegram's Salient, July 30, 1864

his galleries were too shallow to intercept the Federals anyway. While Pleasants's gallery was about twenty-five feet below the surface, the roof of Douglas's gallery at Shaft No. 2 was only seven feet deep. The Federal mine crossed about seven feet below the Confederate countermine at an angle.[21]

Douglas pushed ahead, digging an additional 25 feet in both galleries until the one attached to Shaft No. 1 totaled 107 feet and the gallery of Shaft No. 2 was 96 feet long. Douglas was also in charge of four galleries at Colquitt's Salient and two at Gracie's Salient. By July 29, he had dug a total of 368 feet in eight galleries at three locations, but the Federals had still outmaneuvered him in the underground war. Pleasants used about 400 men to dig one gallery, while Douglas divided 220 men among three sites.[22]

Pleasants began to place his powder charge on the afternoon of July 27. The Federals carried 8,000 pounds of powder into the gallery in small barrels, two per man, held in a sling draped across the shoulders. Each hopperlike magazine was connected to its neighbor by a wooden trough half-filled with powder; the troughs then extended out of the branches and met at the forward end of the gallery. From here, two pine troughs six inches square ran along the floor of the gallery for thirty-four feet. Three "common blasting" fuses, cut into ten-foot-long sections, ran from the two troughs for another ninety-eight feet. When the fuse lines were finished, the delicate job of tamping the mine began. If the gallery was not sealed tight, the blast would funnel out of the mine gallery into the ravine rather than upward through solid earth. Pleasants's men carefully positioned logs and sandbags so as not to disturb the magazines or the fuses, filling the first ten feet of each branch and thirty-four feet of the gallery by the evening of July 28. After thirty-four days of hard work, Pleasants and the 48th Pennsylvania were ready to blow a hole in the Confederate line.[23]

The entire Ninth Corps—four divisions—prepared to attack. One division of the Tenth Corps and one of the Eighteenth Corps stood ready to help, and Warren made available one division and a portion of another as a reserve force. Moreover, Warren could use the rest of his corps if needed. Mott's division of the Second Corps replaced the Eighteenth Corps so it could relieve Burnside's troops in the line. Hancock planned to assemble the rest of his corps near the area of attack as a final reserve. Altogether most of the Federal troops south of the Appomattox were deployed to either take part in or support the attack. Burnside crammed the Ninth Corps into trenches as close to the salient as possible, moving them into position after nightfall of July 29. The two covered ways that connected the forward and rear Union lines opposite the salient now were more important than ever. They ran from the rear areas behind the Fourteen Gun Battery about 1,000 yards forward to the valley of Poor Creek and then continued to the advanced Union line only 130 yards from the Rebels. The covered ways extended through ravines that drained into the creek.[24]

Meade wanted all obstacles removed from in front of the works, and the forward Union trench prepared in some manner to allow the Ninth Corps to cross. Burnside did not worry about the obstructions, for most of the Federal abatis had already been "shot away." Duane confirmed that the Confederate abatis consisted of loose limbs thrown across the parapet, unsecured to the ground. Burnside also feared that any effort to remove obstructions would alert the enemy, but orders went out to fill up the forward trench with sandbags for 200 yards to allow one regiment to advance in line of battle at a time. Instead, due to a shortage of bags, the Federals filled in only about ten feet of trench, forcing regiments to advance by the flank or to find some other means of getting out of the trench. By July 29, Hunt had placed 110 guns and 54 mortars to support the advance.[25]

While Douglas labored in vain underground, the Confederates were improving their defenses at Pegram's Salient. Pegram later recalled that his battery was in a "decidedly uncomfortable" position. Constant Union sniping deprived him of manpower and deteriorated his four embrasures. A Ninth Corps officer later remembered that the Confederates covered these embrasures with mantlets, but Pegram only mentioned using gabions to shore them up. Elliott's South Carolina troops made loopholes by placing three cotton sacks, each holding a bushel of dirt, in an arrangement on top of the parapet. This technique was soon noted and copied by the Federals, who often shot the Rebel sacks to shreds. Elliott's men endured a steady shelling each day from about 8:00 to 10:00 A.M. and for another two hours in the evening.[26]

Most Rebels gained access to the salient and all the line north of it through a covered way dug from Jerusalem Plank Road down a ravine, 700 yards to the Confederate line. This covered way ended 300 yards north of the salient, but a branch of it angled off toward Pegram's position. Four or five traverses, each one twenty yards long, lay just north of the salient to protect infantrymen from enfilade fire. To the rear of the semicircular line of the salient, both gunners and infantrymen had dug a series of short ditches with sleep holes cut in the sides. "Every man needed a little bombproof to sleep in at night, & to dodge into in the day," recalled Alexander. "They soon honeycombed the rear side of the trenches with all sorts of little caves & cellars in which all sorts of individual ingenuity was displayed." At Pegram's Salient, they dug a maze of ditches and holes covering an area seventy-five feet behind the guns. There was no order to this digging, except that all ditches eventually led to the rear.[27]

The Confederates began to dig a second line behind Pegram's Salient on June 29. It was called a cavalier because the parapet was higher than the forward line to give those manning it greater opportunity to command the area with their fire. The second line consisted of a "wide ditch" with the dirt forming an "irregular and ungraded embankment," and both ends joined the main line to either side of Pegram's battery. The Confederates finished and manned the cavalier with two infantry companies by July 9.[28]

Alexander placed the first installment of nine mortars along Jerusalem Plank Road on June 25, the very day that Pleasants began digging his gallery. Capt. James Nelson Lamkin's Virginia Light Artillery, which left its field guns behind in South Carolina when it was transferred to Petersburg in early May, manned many of the mortars that continued to be placed around Pegram's Salient. Joseph William Eggleston later recalled that his two mortars were put in an emplacement dug for field guns, which was too large for his ordnance. The men suffered from Federal shelling, and the wooden platforms were too weak for mortar firing. Eggleston rebuilt the platforms and asked division commander Johnson to detail men to construct bombproofs. Eggleston fixed the range and direction of all Union guns within his purview by firing test shots during the day and "nailing cleets on the solid platform on which the mortar bed rested and numbering them. These numbers were recorded in the gunner's book together with the amount of powder and length of fuse." In addition to Lamkin's men, Maj. John C. Haskell's artillery battalion in the First Corps provided gunners for sixteen mortars near Pegram's Salient. Six of the pieces were planted along Jerusalem Plank Road, and the rest were secreted in ravines between the road and the salient.[29]

In addition to Pegram's guns, the Confederates had three batteries in place to fire directly on the Ninth Corps as it advanced. Capt. Samuel T. Wright's Virginia Battery, belonging to Beauregard's command, was positioned to the left of the salient and 100 yards behind McAfee's North Carolina brigade. It was in a superb position to cover the entire salient area, 555 yards away. Capt. George S. Davidson's Battery C, 13th Virginia Light Artillery, belonging to Hill's Third Corps (and commanded by Lt. James C. Otey) had two 12-pounder Napoleons 373 yards south of the salient near Baxter Road. The left gun also was in a superb position to rake the left flank of the Ninth Corps advance. Finally, Capt. Henry G. Flanner's Battery F, 13th Battalion North Carolina Artillery, had six 12-pounder Napoleons located near the junction of Jerusalem Plank Road and Baxter Road.[30]

The prime objective of the Union attack was to punch through these defenses and take possession of the ridge crest 533 yards to the rear of Pegram's guns. In their way stood Elliott's brigade, 15 field guns, and about 20 mortars. Grant had managed to assemble 9½ divisions, 110 guns, and 54 mortars to oppose them.[31]

The first problem in this otherwise promising arrangement occurred on July 28 when Meade informed Burnside that his attack plan was unacceptable. Burnside had decided as early as July 10 that his black division should lead the assault. He was among the few high-ranking officers who had faith in the black troops. The nine regiments that constituted Ferrero's Fourth Division had been organized only during the winter of 1863–64. They had been used to guard the army's trains during the Overland campaign and were employed in earthwork construction and routine trench duty at Petersburg. Burnside hoped that enthusiasm would compensate for their lack of combat experience. Ferrero worked out a plan to maneuver his two brigades through the gap to be blown in the Confederate line, sending some troops to the right and others to the left to widen the breach while the rest headed straight for the ridge crest. If all went well, the black troops could also enter Petersburg. Burnside rated the chances of success as "more than even."[32]

Meade considered this plan for two days before telling Burnside that he objected to the use of the black troops. He had no faith in their ability to spearhead such an important operation, but there is no evidence that racial prejudice lay at the root of his opinion. Meade knew that green troops did not have the steadiness of veterans when opposed by tough obstacles. As Grant later explained it, Meade was afraid that the odds for success were far less than even and the public would say "we were shoving those people ahead to get killed because we did not care anything about them." Meade also believed that the plan called for Burnside's troops to consume too much time in widening the breach. He believed that rushing all available men to the crest as quickly as possible was the best thing to do.[33]

Burnside fought for his plan. He argued with Meade on July 28 and talked the army commander into consulting Grant before making a final decision. He did not hear from Meade that evening and assumed his plan was approved, but Meade appeared at his headquarters the next morning and told him that Grant agreed with Meade's judgment. Again Burnside argued, but Meade would not be moved. Burnside had to change his attack plan less than eighteen hours before the mine was scheduled to go up. Not until midafternoon did he assemble the leaders of his three white divisions and tell them the news. He thought Ledlie's men were relatively the most rested, but he suggested drawing lots. Ledlie "won" the drawing.[34]

A worse commander could not have been chosen by design. James Hewett Ledlie was a civil engineer, educated at Union College in Utica, New York, with long but undistinguished service on the regimental level in eastern North Carolina. Through attrition, he rose to brigade command in the Ninth Corps by late May 1864 and replaced Maj. Gen. Thomas L. Crittenden, a washed-up corps commander from the Army of the Cumberland, who let the division run down before asking to be relieved of command on June 8. Ledlie had been drunk at North Anna and had ordered his brigade into an unnecessary charge on May 24, which cost more than 100 casualties. Even though Ledlie's staff had no sympathy for him, they protected the reputation of their division by concealing all they knew. Thus Burnside apparently had no information about Ledlie's incompetence.[35]

Ledlie proved he was incapable of understanding and communicating the division's role in the attack. Burnside passed on clear instructions to his division leaders that evening. Not only would the black division be held back, but all troops were to head for the ridge crest and let other corps worry about widening the gap in the Confederate line. The mine would be sprung at 3:30 A.M., July 30; Ledlie was to go to the crest and then take possession of Blandford Cemetery. Willcox was to follow and veer left to take possession of Jerusalem Plank Road as Potter was to veer right for the same purpose. Ferrero would enter Petersburg if possible. Potter and, to an extent, Willcox understood these instructions and passed them down to their brigade leaders. Ledlie later reported that he did the same, but staff and regimental officers told a different story. After the war, at least one brigade-level staff officer indicated that Ledlie had given completely wrong instructions to his brigade commanders, telling them to take and hold the crater and adjoining Confederate works to right and left. It is quite possible, as Burnside's biographer William Marvel has suggested, that Ledlie was drunk or otherwise impaired during the conference with Burnside and did not understand what he was supposed to do. In fairness to Ledlie, it should be noted that his drinking problem stemmed from his use of alcohol to deal with a serious and chronic problem of malarial poisoning.[36]

After this ill-fated conference, the difficult task of pulling Ninth Corps units from their trenches and assembling them for the attack began. It consumed the entire night and was barely finished when the mine exploded. Several of Burnside's units had to delay their movements while waiting for Ord's Eighteenth Corps to replace them because Ord had to wait until Mott's division relieved his men. Under cover of darkness, Ledlie positioned his division just behind the forward Union line on the west side of Poor Creek. Willcox moved one brigade into the valley of Poor Creek as the other brigade crowded into the left covered way on the east side of the stream. Ord's Third Division replaced Potter, and his Second Division (commanded by Brig. Gen. Adelbert Ames) took position as a ready reserve for Burnside's advance. Brig. Gen. John W. Turner's Second Division of the Tenth Corps placed itself near the right covered way, east of Poor Creek, ready to advance when ordered.[37]

CHAPTER EIGHT

## *The Crater*

The most extensive preparation for any Union offensive at Petersburg was finally over as dawn approached on Saturday, July 30. Pleasants entered the gallery, lit the fuse at 3:15 A.M., and calmly walked out. He kept an eye on his watch, but 3:30 came and went with no explosion. Lt. Col. Byron M. Cutcheon of the 20th Michigan also watched from the position of Willcox's division, 225 yards away. He began to see Pegram's Salient in the first hint of daylight; the sky was completely clear, and Confederate soldiers began to stir. Meade worried at the delay, sending four notes of inquiry to Burnside's temporary headquarters at the Fourteen Gun Battery. The army commander, who temporarily used Burnside's old headquarters site as his own, decided to attack even if the mine did not work. Burnside delayed giving that order until Pleasants had more time to sort out the problem.[1]

The Pennsylvania miner waited until 4:15 A.M. to give the charge an hour to blow, then two men volunteered to investigate. Sgt. Henry Reese, who had managed the workforce that dug the gallery, and Lt. Jacob Douty of the 48th Pennsylvania found that all three fuses had gone out at a splice. The two men fixed the problem and rushed out.[2]

Soon after, at exactly 4:44 A.M., the mine went up with spectacular results. "There flashed out a lily-shaped fountain of dark red and yellow fire, with brown spots and streaks in it," recalled Capt. Thomas W. Clarke, a staff officer serving with Marshall's brigade. Clarke turned to Marshall and said, "'Colonel, was anything ever so beautiful as that?'" To a man in Bartlett's brigade the ascending cone of earth "seemed to stand still when it reached its height and fell as a shower from a fountain." For those who looked more closely, it was apparent that the clay and sand were mixed with camp equipment, artillery accoutrements, and men, "the red explosions of powder glowing in the horrid mass." The geyser of dirt ascended to about 200 feet before beginning to fall back to earth in a rain of debris. The explosion itself had lifted many men of Ledlie's division off their stomachs as they lay on the ground behind the forward Union line. Other troops of Ledlie's command instinctively recoiled when it looked as if the debris might fall on them, but Stephen M. Weld insisted that this caused only "momentary" disorder.[3]

The mine blasted an irregular hole in the earth 125 feet long, 50 feet wide, and 30 feet deep. One hundred thousand cubic feet of dirt were taken out of the ground, and the resulting crater was shaped like "a long Irish potato, the sides of loose pulverized sand piled up precipitately, from which projected huge blocks of clay." After everything settled, the rim around the crater's edge stood 12 feet above the natural level of the earth. Clods of clayish soil "of all sizes from that of a small house down to that of one's fist," lay scattered around the crater.[4]

Richard Pegram happened to be away on the morning of July 30 and thus survived the blast, but nineteen of his men were killed and two were injured. The rightmost thirty yards of his emplacement and two of his guns were intact, although the pieces were partially buried by dirt. The other two guns were blown twenty yards and forty yards forward into no-man's-land. Elliott's infantrymen suffered tremendously. There were 650 men serving in the 18th and 22nd South Carolina, which held the lines closest to the explosion. The two regiments lost 278, or 42.7 percent, of them. Most of those casualties were buried alive, many as they slept.[5]

Douglas's counterminers were very lucky. Sgt. A. H. Smyth was leading a detachment of eight men digging in the gallery of Shaft No. 2 when the mine went up. The shock of the explosion threw him off his feet as the ground "heaved and waved." He got all but one of his men out of the shaft to see that the works all around were destroyed. Shaft No. 1 and its gallery were "blown to atoms."[6]

### THE FEDERAL ATTACK

Hunt's artillery and mortars opened fire as soon as the mine exploded. Ledlie's infantrymen hesitated a few minutes, disoriented by the blast and falling debris, but both Bartlett and Marshall pushed their troops across the forward Union line within ten minutes of the explosion. It proved too time-consuming for all to advance by the flank across the bridge of sandbagged trench line, so many Federals tried to climb out of the eight-foot-deep trench by sticking bayonets into the revetment, either at hip or shoulder height. Some men volunteered to hold the other end of the bayonet as their comrades stepped up and out of the trench. What was left of the Union obstructions in front of the line proved to be no obstacle to the advance.[7]

As Ledlie's men streamed into the jagged crater, confusion began to dominate the battlefield. Assuming they were merely to hold the hole, Bartlett and

Marshall made little effort to advance beyond it, and they also found that the crater was not a good place to form regular lines. The men had to assemble any way they could along the rim and were distracted by partially buried Confederates who called for help. Ledlie was nowhere to be seen, and Confederate fire began to sweep the area outside the hole.[8]

A portion of Potter's division advanced simultaneously with Ledlie's command. Griffin's Second Brigade crossed the forward Union line just to the right of Ledlie's position and advanced against elements of Elliott's brigade that still held the line north of the crater. Elliott's fire, and the confusion produced by lingering smoke and dust from the explosion, caused Griffin's men to veer left. Several of his regiments entered the hole and mixed with Ledlie's troops. Regimental commanders in both divisions tried to advance northward along the Confederate trench line but encountered substantial resistance. McAfee sent the 49th North Carolina to help. It left its position in the trench and moved across open ground to the rear of the Rebel line, then reentered the trench near the crater. The Tar Heels encountered retiring elements of Elliott's 17th South Carolina, then opened fire at the Yankees in and north of the hole. "Our men aimed steadily and true," recalled Thomas R. Roulhac, "and as each rifle became too hot to be used another gun was at work by one who took the place of the first, or supplied him with rifles which could be handled." This prevented the Unionists from advancing more than 200 yards north of the crater before they stalled.[9]

Any units that tumbled into the crater became engulfed by confusion. With all or parts of three brigades stuffed in, the crater was already "full to suffocation," in the words of Maj. William H. Powell of Ledlie's staff. "Every organization melted away, as soon as it entered this hole in the ground, into a mass of human beings clinging by toes and heels to the almost perpendicular sides. If a man was shot on the crest he fell and rolled to the bottom of the pit." Many men in the crater, like Don E. Scott of Griffin's brigade, were fascinated by the Confederates who were "half buried alive ... some with their heads downwards & their feet & legs protruding—others with their feet down & buried to their waists & even shoulders with one arm out, and some with neither."[10]

A portion of Willcox's division went in immediately after Ledlie. Three regiments of Hartranft's brigade piled into the crater and got stuck while two more halted temporarily in no-man's-land until room could be found for them. Hartranft and the lead regiments crowded into ninety feet of intact gun emplacement, where Hartranft discovered the two partially buried but workable cannon of Pegram's battery. He helped Sgt. Wesley Stanley of the 14th New York Heavy Artillery, of Marshall's brigade, to dig them out. Stanley also found and dug out Pegram's magazine, assigned members of the 14th to the guns, and

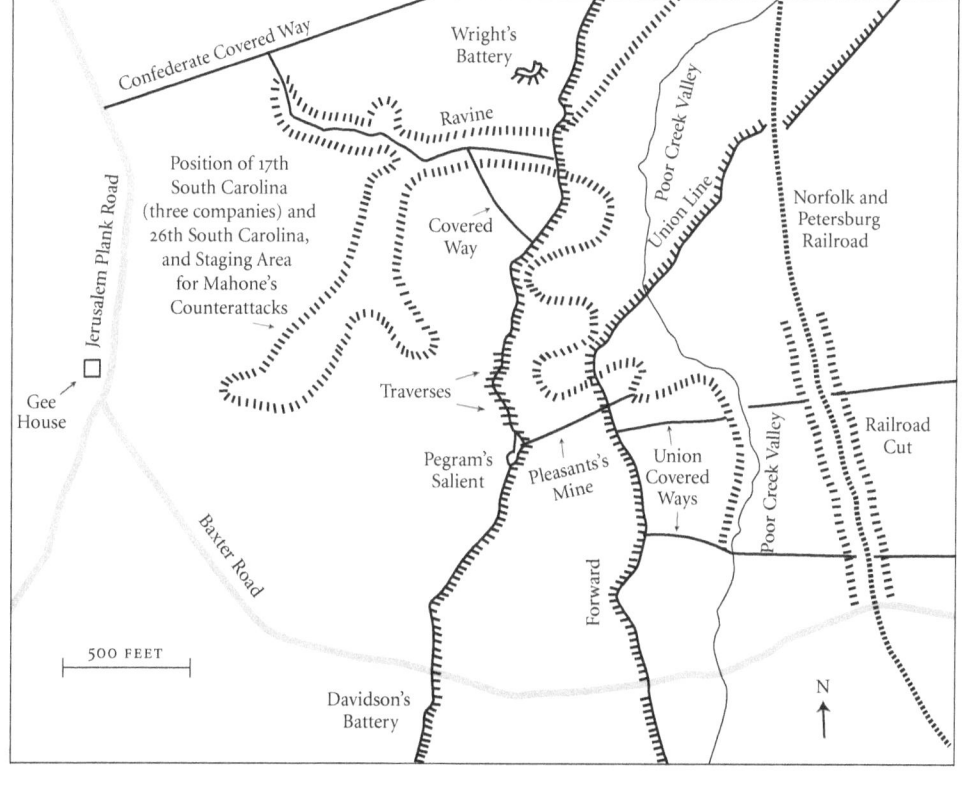

Crater Battlefield, July 30, 1864
(based on T. F. Rives Map, 1892, in Bernard, *War Talks*, 320–21)

opened fire at targets south of the crater. Some members of Hartranft's brigade also found the entrance to Shaft No. 1. The crowding in Hartranft's section of the Confederate emplacement eased, and his other three regiments advanced across no-man's-land, when his lead unit, the 27th Michigan, pushed south of the crater against Goode's brigade. It had a tough time, for the 26th and 59th Virginia, helped by fragments of Elliott's 22nd and 23rd South Carolina, put up stiff resistance.[11]

By 6:00 A.M., the first wave of the Federal attack had advanced into the breach. Four Ninth Corps brigades filled it to capacity. Meade's impatience and frustration grew with each passing minute. "Our chance is now," he telegraphed Burnside; "push your men forward at all hazards (white and black) and don't lose time in making formations, but rush for the crest." Burnside issued directives to all division leaders to "push forward at once," but it was practically impossible. Lt. Col. Charles G. Loring, his assistant inspector general, went into the crater and reported that Ledlie's men could not be moved forward. Unfortunately, he sent the note to Burnside's old headquarters site instead of to the Fourteen Gun Battery, and it fell into Meade's hands. The army commander became furious that he found out such important news by accident and sent a message to Burnside to use the 5th and 18th Corps as well as his own troops.[12]

On the Confederate side of the battlefield, a great deal of confusion, even panic, emerged among some portions of Elliott's brigade. For about fifteen minutes after the explosion, some of his men ran down the trench line to escape the blast and falling debris. They were "covered with earth and wild with fright," according to one observer. But that passed quickly enough, and what was left of the South Carolina brigade grimly fought to hold its ground. For nearly four hours, and with support from McAfee to the north and Goode to the south, Elliott's men were all that stood in Burnside's way.[13]

Elliott took in the situation and organized a counterattack a little after 6:00 A.M. He tried to form his men outside the works and advance across the open, as the captured trenches were packed with Yankees, but he was shot as soon as he stepped out of the trench. Fifty men, mostly of the 26th South Carolina, also fell within seconds of starting out. Col. Fitz William McMaster of the 17th South Carolina now took command of the brigade and devised a more workable scheme. He sent what was left of Col. Alexander D. Smith's 26th South Carolina and Capt. E. A. Crawford with three companies of the 17th South Carolina, about 200 men, to a shallow ravine due west of the crater. The troops moved through the trench and the covered way, for the ravine drained into the covered way itself. Once in position, these few Confederates could fire into any Union attempt to advance directly toward Jerusalem Plank Road. The rest of the 17th and what was left of the 18th South Carolina remained north of the crater, the only Rebels between it and McAfee's brigade. The Tar Heels extended farther south to meet these remnants.[14]

The few troops who stood in Burnside's way could not have held without the fewer Confederate gunners and mortar men who poured fire into the crater area. To the north, Wright's gunners kept up a steady and effective fire throughout the entire battle. Flanner's men also did their duty. The only instance of wavering among Rebel gunners took place in Davidson's Battery to the south. Lt. Otey and some of his men were so shocked by the explosion that they abandoned their guns. His battalion commander, Maj. Wade Hampton Gibbs, personally took charge of the emplacement. Aided by three men from Alexander's staff and some volunteers from Goode's brigade, Gibbs directed the fire of the one gun that was ideally sited to aim at the crater.[15]

Lee learned of the mine explosion at 6:10 A.M. and immediately sent a staff member, Col. Charles Venable, to get two brigades of Mahone's division.

Mahone held the Dimmock Line west of Jerusalem Plank Road, the rightmost Confederate unit at Petersburg. He was not fronted by any Union troops; no other division south of the Appomattox could spare sizable numbers of troops to help Johnson's command. After dispatching Venable and checking in at Beauregard's and Johnson's headquarters, Lee went to the Gee House on Jerusalem Plank Road, only 500 yards from the crater, where he found Beauregard already watching the flow of events.[16]

Federal signal officers noticed the movement of Mahone's two brigades toward the battlefield, and Meade thought it might be an opportunity for Warren to attack west of the plank road. The Fifth Corps commander could have used Crawford's division, which held the extreme left of the Army of the Potomac, but Meade insisted that Crawford conduct a reconnaissance before he ordered a full-scale attack. Crawford gingerly sent out troops to see what lay ahead a bit after 8:00 A.M. and reported that an attack would be difficult; he had a long distance to move before hitting the Dimmock Line. After digesting this information, Meade authorized Warren to use Ayres's division instead, since it already was in supporting position just to Burnside's left, and to aim at Davidson's gun emplacement to eliminate its fire on the Ninth Corps. By the time all this was worked out, Mahone attacked Burnside's troops in the crater area, and Meade called off all offensive movements. Burnside received no help from the Fifth Corps.[17]

With repeated urgings from army headquarters, and becoming desperate at the loss of time and opportunity, Burnside sent in the rest of his corps and some supporting troops beginning about 7:00 A.M. This second wave in the Union offensive merely compounded the problem of crowding in the breach.

Bliss's brigade of Potter's division advanced toward the position defended by McAfee's Tar Heels near the mouth of the ravine. Bliss divided his brigade, dispatching the 51st New York and 2nd New York Mounted Rifles (dismounted) to approach the ravine mouth directly across no-man's-land, while the other three advanced along and cleared the Confederate line toward that objective. His plans immediately changed when an order arrived from corps headquarters to push all troops through the existing gap in the enemy line and head for the crest without delay. Three of Bliss's units tried to do so, but the two New York regiments continued on their separate way, engaged McAfee, and made no headway.[18]

Burnside sent in his Fourth Division, which advanced with spirit and widened the crack in the Confederate works. Sigfried's brigade went forward by the flank through the covered way, with the 43rd USCT in the van. It reached the edge of the crater but fortunately did not go into it. The men moved north in front of the Confederate line and just before the abatis, until they overlapped the Rebel troops. Then they stopped, turned west, and pushed forward. Some Confederates ran immediately while others fought, only to be shot or bayoneted in the trench. The 43rd USCT reportedly captured 200 prisoners and a flag, but Confederate sources admit only 28 lost as prisoners. Nevertheless, two companies of the 17th South Carolina were forced back to another traverse north of the crater, where they put up a wall of sandbags across the trench. The 43rd was lodged only a dozen yards from the sandbag wall.[19]

Thomas's brigade advanced out of the covered way immediately after Sigfried and shouldered its way into the packed works. Two of Thomas's regiments got into the crater and became useless for further operations. The rest were separated from Sigfried's position by three regiments of Bliss's brigade, to their right. On their left, the black units became intermingled with Griffin's regiments. It took some time for Thomas to get an appreciable number of his men disentangled from this mess so he could attempt to move forward into contested territory.[20]

Willcox sent Humphrey's brigade to hit the Confederate line south of the crater, immediately after Ferrero attacked. Humphrey's three right regiments captured 150 yards of trench, forcing the 26th Virginia and the South Carolinians from a traverse where they had earlier stopped the 27th Michigan of Hartranft's brigade. Humphrey also captured forty prisoners. The breach probably could have been widened even more, but the 46th New York hesitated just after it left the forward Union line and lost connection with the regiment to its right. The New Yorkers lost their nerve, broke, and ran back, carrying the other three regiments of the brigade with them.[21]

Turner's Tenth Corps division was next in the lineup. Turner had earlier made his way into the crater, viewed the crowded conditions, and reported to Ord, who was with Burnside at the Fourteen Gun Battery. The Eighteenth Corps commander temporarily was in charge of Turner's division and instructed him to advance to the right. Turner sent in Bell's brigade and reported that it captured 100 yards of Confederate trench, but there is no supporting evidence for this. Bell reached a point just outside the captured Confederate line north of the crater before Mahone's counterattack stopped his further progress at 9:00 A.M. Coan's brigade advanced toward the mouth of the ravine, the same target that two of Bliss's regiments had tried to take, and was halfway across the valley of Poor Creek when Mahone advanced. Curtis's brigade moved through the covered way and took up a reserve position in the forward Union line. Turner's men started too late to accomplish anything.[22]

Despite the dispatch of six brigades in the second wave, no appreciable advance from the captured Confederate line appeared imminent. Frustrations at Ninth Corps and army headquarters reached a breaking point. When Meade learned of the continued stalemate, he demanded a full report of conditions in the crater, implying that Burnside had deliberately kept him in the dark. "I wish to know the truth, and desire an immediate answer," the army commander testily wrote. Burnside's patience snapped. He replied that Meade's message was "unofficerlike and ungentlemanly." It was already 7:30 A.M., nearly three hours after the mine explosion.[23]

This exchange was the last straw in a brewing confrontation between Meade and Burnside. It was made worse by the fact that Burnside's chief of staff, Maj. Gen. John G. Parke, was absent on sick leave. Brig. Gen. Julius White replaced him just before midnight of July 29. Parke had diplomatically soothed relations between the two generals, but White sent only one message to Meade all day of July 30, contributing to an atmosphere of misunderstanding and distrust at army headquarters.[24]

Ledlie also failed to help Burnside that day. After giving the order for his division to advance, he wandered around the Union works for a half-hour before taking refuge in a bombproof where Surgeon Orville P. Chubb of the 20th Michigan had set up an aid station. Ledlie claimed he was hit by a spent ball and was suffering from malarial poisoning. He used both excuses to explain why he was unable to go into the crater, and he asked for something to drink. Surgeon H. E. Smith of the 27th Michigan gave him some rum. When a staff officer brought word that Burnside wanted all troops to advance to the ridge behind Pegram's Salient, Ledlie told him to spread the word and remained in the bombproof.[25]

By 9:00 A.M., the Federals occupied 320 yards of the Confederate main line north of the crater and about 150 yards south of it. While nearly 500 yards north to south, the breach was very narrow east to west, and all or part of eight Union brigades huddled in it. The 35th Massachusetts, Ledlie's engineer regiment, tried to dig a covered way to link the hole with the forward Union line. This would have incorporated the captured segment into the Federal defenses, but the ground was "hard baked" and difficult to break open even with picks. Moreover, stragglers gathered for shelter behind the crater and got in the way. The Massachusetts men worked very hard at first, then weakened when "nervous prostration" affected their actions.[26]

The real problem lay not in linking the crater to the Union line but in the failure to push men out of the breach and into the open ground so they could advance to Jerusalem Plank Road. The Federals controlled the maze of Confederate bombproofs that extended 100 feet behind Pegram's gun emplacements and the cavalier that ringed the western edge of the maze. After pushing his men into the warren of holes, brigade commander Thomas was impressed by their complexity. "These pits were different from any in our lines," he later recalled, "a labyrinth of bomb-proofs and magazines, with passages between." They were an effective obstacle to a further Union advance.[27]

The black troops took the lead in trying to reach Jerusalem Plank Road. Thomas managed to bring out some of his men, before the white troops to either side of his fragmented command were ready to support him, and they received such heavy fire that the attack faltered before it started. Sigfried's brigade then launched an effort. While two of his regiments could not advance because of entanglement with white units, the 30th and 43rd USCT worked free. Delevan Bates led his regiment forward, his black troops yelling "'Remember Fort Pillow!'" and the South Carolinians shouting back "'Kill 'em! Shoot 'em! Kill the damned niggers!'" Bates was shot in the face but survived his ugly wound, while his men were repulsed.[28]

Thomas mounted another effort. Lt. Col. John A. Bross of the 29th USCT assembled 300 men of his regiment and the 31st USCT. Bross cut a magnificent figure, clearly visible from Confederate positions, as he stepped into the open ground and began to form his men.[29]

### THE CONFEDERATE COUNTERATTACK

Bross's appearance, more than four hours after the mine explosion, marked the high point of Union efforts on July 30. The appearance of Mahone's division soon after that completely changed the flow of events around the crater. The Confederates went on the counteroffensive and, after three brigade-level attacks and bloody fighting that extended over four hours, restored their broken line.

Mahone decided to lead his two brigades to the battlefield personally. The men slipped out of their position west of Jerusalem Plank Road singly and in small groups, so as not to arouse Federal attention. He then led Weisiger's Virginia brigade, his old command, and Hall's Georgia brigade toward the scene of action. Mahone went ahead and reached Johnson's headquarters at 8:15 A.M., not long after Fererro's division advanced into the breach. Johnson appeared ready to eat his breakfast and was happy to let Mahone take charge of the Confederate effort, including the use of his own troops. Mahone pumped Johnson for information on the size of the Union front and then followed one of Johnson's aides, who guided him down the covered way and pointed out the shallow ravine as the best place to assemble his troops.[30]

Mahone entered the ravine and looked toward the crater. "For the moment I could scarcely take in the reality," he later wrote, for the breach was jammed with thousands of Federal soldiers and more than a dozen flags. Mahone could see that the Yankees were "greatly disorganized." He sent word for Sanders's

Alabama brigade to join him and began to place the first two units that were just then arriving on the field.[31]

Weisiger crossed Jerusalem Plank Road after a march of two and a half miles. His men entered the covered way, which had several zigzags at which the Rebels were exposed to the view of those Federals who occupied the crater. Weisiger told his men to run past these places in single file, which slowed his advance a bit. They also met several stragglers from Elliott's brigade, who told them that the Federals were using black troops. This was the first time that Lee's infantry confronted African American soldiers, and the news angered them. "I never felt more like fighting in my life," recalled Lt. Col. William H. Stewart of the 61st Virginia. Mahone stood at the junction of the ravine and the covered way as Weisiger directed his column into the ravine. The Virginians found Elliott's 200 men, who had manfully held the Federals in place for a long time, sheltering behind a line of meager works, apparently dug that morning with bayonets.[32]

Bross and his men stepped out of the captured Confederate works and began to assemble for a charge. Some of Weisiger's Virginians took potshots at them as Mahone quickly ordered a charge of his own. It was then about 9:00 A.M.; 800 Virginians stepped out of the ravine and started to cross 200 yards of open space. All or most of Smith's South Carolinians—the 26th and three companies of the 17th—participated in the attack.[33]

This charge had an instantaneous effect on the course of the battle. Bross and several of his men were shot down, and the rest jumped back into the captured Confederate works. Many black soldiers in the maze completely lost their nerve and fled in panic. Others fired a volley at Weisiger when the Confederates neared the captured works, but the Confederates plunged into the warren of bombproofs.[34]

As these opponents struggled in the maze, hundreds of black and white Federals stampeded out of the breach and back to Union lines. Retreating members of Sigfried's brigade ran into Bell's Tenth Corps brigade; they wounded some of Bell's troops by carelessly handling their bayoneted muskets, scattering the white troops and taking them to the rear. Curtis's brigade of Turner's division was just then trying to advance through the covered way and was met by the retreating Federals. A member of the 112th New York recalled that the blacks were "crowding, swearing, yelling, making frantic endeavors to get through; some were down and others treading over them; and those in front were pushed on by the dense mass behind." The New Yorkers had to jump out of the covered way and advance across the open ground, losing fourteen men to Confederate fire in the process. Lt. Freeman Bowley of the 30th USCT wrote that many of the "blacks were brave in their charge, but, as a body, wholly unmanageable, and totally demoralized in their defeat."[35]

Weisiger's Virginians and a collection of black and white Federals fought a vicious hand-to-hand combat inside the maze of bombproofs. Weisiger's brigade had veered left in its advance, due to a hail of fire coming from the crater, and its right wing took shelter in the maze behind a traverse that extended rearward from the main Confederate trench. It was located forty yards north of the crater. Hand-to-hand combat took place between this traverse and the ravine to the north.[36]

"Our men would drive the bayonet into one man," remembered a Virginia officer, "pull it out, turn the butt and knock the brains out of another, and so on until the ditch ran with blood of the dead and dying." A captain of Griffin's brigade heard the Rebels shout, "Save the white men but kill the damn niggers." Another Virginian "saw men slam their bayonets in the Enemy and fire the guns off in them, then I also saw them knock the enemy on the heads with the but of their guns, & others Cut them with swords." It took twenty minutes of such work for Weisiger's troops to clear all Federals from the captured works north of the traverse. By then, the floors of the trenches were carpeted with bodies, and pools of blood collected in the lower parts. Stewart recalled that the red mud was "shoe-sole deep" in places. In the lull that followed, Rebel officers detailed men "to pile up the dead on the side of the ditch to make room so we could reinforce to the right or left, as occasion might require."[37]

Weisiger's attack did not reclaim all of the captured Rebel works. The Unionists who evacuated the trenches north of the crater retreated into the hole itself. About 600 Federals jammed into the crater; some took position along the rim and fired at the enemy. When hit in the head, they "rolled down the steep sides to the bottom, and in places they were piled up four and five deep." Bartlett told Freeman Bowley to build a barricade across the trench that entered the north side of the crater. His men used dirt clods at first and then piled bodies of both white and black men across the opening.[38]

The Federals also evacuated their holdings south of the crater. Hartranft pulled the Michigan units that held the trench back to the intact segment of Pegram's Salient, where Stanley still fired two Rebel guns. By about 9:30 A.M. the crater and this intact segment were the only part of the breach under Union control.[39]

Even before Weisiger attacked, Grant and Meade had come to the conclusion that the attack was a failure and ought to be called off. They delayed issuing the order upon receiving reports that the black troops were making headway, but Mahone's counteroffensive convinced them to call off the operation. They agreed that there was no need to hold what Burnside had gained.[40]

The Ninth Corps commander received two orders to retire between 9:30 and 10:00 A.M., but he was reluctant to do so. He rode to army headquarters with Ord and tried to convince Meade to keep trying. Meade refused, and tempers grew hot—Burnside's desperate effort to save his offensive fell on deaf ears, and even Ord refused to support his plea. Meade allowed him to postpone the withdrawal until nightfall. Burnside rode back to the Fourteen Gun Battery and issued a directive to his subordinates in the crater at 12:20 P.M., leaving it up to them to decide when and how to pull out.[41]

Mahone had no intention of allowing the Federals to determine their own fate. He told Hall to take his Georgia brigade into action, hit the area south of the traverse that marked the extent of reclaimed ground, and drive the Yankees out of the crater. The Georgians tried at about 11:00 A.M. but failed. They veered left to avoid heavy fire coming out of the crater, bringing the brigade exactly behind Weisiger's Virginians, who were sheltering in the maze of Confederate bombproofs. Mahone could only hope that Sanders's brigade arrived soon. Johnson appeared on the battlefield and offered to help coordinate the next attack. While Goode's brigade and remnants of Elliott's command advanced toward the crater from the south, Mahone would send Sanders directly toward the hole from the ravine. They fixed 1:00 P.M. as the time for action. Meanwhile, John C. Haskell advanced two Coehorn mortars that were in the ravine into the reclaimed Confederate works, only a few yards away from the crater, and began to lob shells into the chasm. Lamkin's gunners fired the pieces with very small charges.[42]

For some two and a half hours, as the Confederates waited for Sanders, conditions worsened inside the crater. It was a particularly hot day, with temperatures rising from 80 degrees at 6:00 A.M. to 99 degrees by noon, as the sun baked the raw, upturned clay. William Powell noted that the heat caused "waves of moisture produced by the exhalation from this mass to rise above the crater." Charles H. Houghton of the 14th New York Heavy Artillery was sickened by the sight of "dead and dying all around us; blood was streaming down the sides of the crater to the bottom, where it gathered in pools for a time before being absorbed by the hard red clay."[43]

Many of Lamkin's mortar shells burrowed into the ground and did no harm, but a lot of them burst in the air with frightful effect. One hit an officer of a Maine regiment and exploded at the same time, disintegrating his head and upper body. His remains fell "sloping downwards, and the blood rushed out as from an overturned bucket," according to Freeman Bowley. Thirst, heat, fear, and the awful sight of mangled bodies took their toll on morale. Gradually, more Federals along the crater rim lost heart and stopped firing. They simply turned around and braced themselves on the sloping sides of the hole, and no encouragement by officers could induce them to do otherwise. Several Ottawa Indians serving in Company K, 1st Michigan Sharpshooters, "pulled their blouses over their faces and chanted a death song."[44]

When the brigade leaders received Burnside's order to retire, they agreed it was too dangerous to attempt it in daylight. Yet they needed artillery support, tools, sandbags, and ammunition to hold out in the crater until dusk. Cutcheon went back to the forward Union line to inform Burnside of these needs; he barely escaped with his life while dodging the hail of Confederate fire across no-man's-land.[45]

All these preparations for an orderly retreat became futile when Sanders attacked at 1:00 P.M. with about 630 men. The 61st North Carolina, sent from Clingman's brigade of Hoke's division, participated in the charge, while the 23rd South Carolina and part of the 22nd South Carolina of Elliott's brigade advanced along the Confederate main line south of the crater.[46]

Sanders guided his men directly toward the crater because most of the Federals had given up their firing positions along the rim. William H. Randall of the 1st Michigan Sharpshooters noted that many Unionists "could not be drove to take a part in the action." The Alabamians advanced to the foot of the crater rim but then stopped, uncertain how to cross the twelve-foot-tall berm. For a while they threw dirt clods, shell fragments, and bayoneted muskets across. A few of the braver Confederates crawled to the top of the rim and stuck their muskets over to fire into the crater. Capt. William B. Young, who served on Sanders's staff, received a message from Mahone asking why the brigade did not close in and finish the job. Young personally sought the division commander and explained to him, "'General they are so thick in there that if men jumped over they would jump into a bayonet and the men know it.'" Mahone advised recruiting volunteers to lead the way. The men themselves worked out a scheme before Young could act on Mahone's suggestion. They put hats on their bayonets and lifted them to draw Yankee fire, then crossed the rim in a rush.[47]

Once inside the hole, Sanders's men shot and stabbed blacks even after the Yankees gave up. While some Confederate officers encouraged this, others tried to stop it. The brigade had never fought black soldiers before, and the men "seemed particularly incensed against them," recalled a member of the 9th Alabama.[48]

The close-range combat in this crowded hole was terrible, and even some Union officers apparently killed black enlisted men "in order to preserve the whites from Confederate vengeance." A Georgia rebel named James Paul Verdery who witnessed the fighting reported to his sister the next day, "The Bayonet was plunged through their hearts & the muzzle of our guns was put on their temple & their brains blown out." After a half-hour of such unequal combat, the crater was in Confederate hands. Sanders captured about 500 Federals and three flags.[49]

## THE AFTERMATH

The battle of the crater ended about 1:45 P.M., but neither Grant nor Meade fully realized it for many hours. Burnside was so stunned by the events of the day, and so angry with Meade, that he failed to inform army headquarters. Grant spent the rest of July 30 contemplating further action. Since Lee apparently was not yet shifting troops to the south side of the Appomattox, Grant wanted to send an infantry corps and some cavalry to tear up twenty miles of the Weldon and Petersburg Railroad the next day. Meade was willing and suggested using the Eighteenth Corps. When signal officers reported Confederate movement across the river, Grant canceled the raid and began to warn Meade that Lee might attempt a counterattack late on July 31 or early on August 1. He also wanted the heavy artillery that had supported Burnside's attack to be removed to a safe depot on the Appomattox River. Grant sent final orders for Butler to dispatch those brigades of the Nineteenth Corps that were serving with the Army of the James to Washington, D.C., and further instructed Meade to strip the trenches and sally out to meet the Confederates in the open if they tried to turn his left flank. This was enough to send Meade into a frenzy of preparation for an attack that Lee never contemplated. Henry L. Abbot removed fifty-two pieces of heavy artillery and mortars eight miles to Broadway Landing in record time on the night of July 30. He left thirty-three guns and mortars on the Bermuda Hundred Line and twenty-nine on the Petersburg Line, in addition to the field batteries under Hunt's control.[50]

The first task for the Confederates after the fighting ended was to clear out the works. This was a gruesome job, for the crater, the trenches north and south, and the maze of bombproofs were littered with bodies. One observer noted a spot in the crater where the dead were eight deep. "The bottom was layered with mangled men," recalled William H. Stewart; "the dead trimmed the sides. . . . It was a veritable inferno filled with sounds of suffering and paved with the rigid dead."[51]

Lt. Thomas Smith of the 16th Virginia superintended the burial of the dead inside the crater. He counted 177 bodies; about 20 percent were blacks, and the rest were equally divided between white Unionists and Confederates. The Confederates rolled the dead down the sides to the bottom and shoveled dirt onto them from the walls. When those who died in the mine explosion were added, estimates of the number of men buried in the crater varied from 200 to 300. Black prisoners were forced to dig a burial trench just to the rear of the crater to inter the dead lying in the rest of the recaptured works.[52]

By dusk of July 30, the men of Weisiger's and Sanders's brigades had "dug with our bayonets a foothold" along the crater rim to serve as firing positions. They had to do much more work in the coming weeks to restore the defenses of Pegram's Salient. The dead remained buried at the bottom of the crater, walked on by hundreds of Confederates who held the chasm for the rest of the campaign. The smell of those Federals who died in no-man's-land was so strong that Stewart's Virginians were unable to consume their rations, even though they had not eaten for twenty-four hours.[53]

Grant lost 3,798 men in this fiasco, 1,413 of whom were captured or missing. Burnside suffered all but 300 of those losses, and Ferrero's division accounted for more than one-third of all Union casualties. The black troops made up 41 percent of the Federals killed, even though they accounted for only 20 percent of the men engaged. The Confederates lost from 1,100 to 1,600 men. Mahone's men captured more than 900 Yankees and twelve to twenty flags. Two Union brigade leaders—Bartlett and Marshall—were taken captive, while Griffin and Hartranft managed to escape with some of their men when Sanders launched the final Confederate attack.[54]

Willcox thought that about fifty wounded Federals lay between the lines after the battle. Potter's men dug a sap under the parapet of their forward trench and extended it far enough on the night of July 30 to recover six of them, but the rest could not be reached. They shared this narrow strip of ground with up to 300 dead, and the air was foul all around. Weisiger's troops finally grew accustomed to the smell so that they were able to eat breakfast on the morning of July 31, "a day of hot sunshine and sickening odors," as William Stewart recalled.[55]

Meade wanted Burnside to arrange an informal truce to recover the remaining wounded and bury the dead, but the Confederates insisted on protocol. Meade addressed a letter requesting a truce to Lee, who forwarded it to Beauregard because the latter's departmental command was responsible for holding this sector. By the time the request went through proper channels, it was too late in the day. Officers arranged it for 5:00 A.M. of August 1, and local commanders worked out the details. They established a picket line down the middle of no-man's-land. The Confederates moved dead and wounded Yankees up to that line and delivered them into Union hands, while the Federals ranged freely on their side of the line. Thousands of Union and Confederate troops crowded the parapets of the opposing works to watch. "It was our first chance to stand up and look over since the beginning of the siege," commented a man in the 49th North Carolina. The Federals recovered only about twenty wounded who were still alive, and they buried at least 220 dead by 11:00 A.M. Many of the latter were so mangled by artillery fire that they literally lay in fragments. The burning sun had turned other bodies into "a swollen and putrifying mass, unrecognizable." Blacks were buried with whites, and the Confederates found twelve of their comrades lying dead between the lines, probably prisoners who had been caught in the crossfire while trying to reach Union lines.[56]

Grant himself led the way in characterizing the attack as a "miserable failure," the "saddest affair I have witnessed in the war." "So fair an opportunity will probably never occur again for carrying fortifications," he told Meade. "Our experience of to-day proves that fortifications come near holding themselves without troops," he continued with little exaggeration. "With a reasonable amount of artillery and one infantryman to six feet I am confident either party could hold their lines against a direct attack of the other."[57]

Meade's subordinates fully agreed. "The affair proved a fiasco, a most miserable fizzle," commented Charles Wainwright. Burnside's troops felt the humiliation and the frustration most keenly. Cutcheon, who barely escaped from the crater, wrote in his autobiography that the attack "was botched and bungled and bedeviled from the beginning." Charging earthworks was "one of the follies of modern warfare, provided the works are only half manned," reasoned William Taylor of the 100th Pennsylvania.[58]

Many factors contributed to the failure of this Union offensive, among them Ledlie's inability to give proper instructions to his brigade commanders. Bartlett and Marshall were good leaders who would have tried to go through the crater and advance toward Jerusalem Plank Road if they had known that was their assignment. Instead, their brigades effectively plugged the breach in the Confederate line. The Union guns failed to play a decisive role in the battle, even though they fired more than 10,000 rounds. In contrast, Wright's gray-clad gunners fired only 600 rounds with telling effect.[59]

While the Confederates rejoiced at their deliverance, the editor of the *Richmond Enquirer* saw reason for alarm. He was loath to criticize Rebel engineers but pointed out that they could have avoided the near-catastrophe of July 30 if they had intercepted Pleasants's gallery. The editor went on to use the mine as an example of Yankee technical superiority. "The mechanical skill of these people was shown in the facility with which they have intrenched themselves in the field, and the formidable earthworks which they erect to cover their cowardly Dutch and negroes. It has been signally shown by the perseverance of Grant before Vicksburg, and by the recent mine before Petersburg, and, indeed, by works which dot and deface the whole South."[60]

There was no cause for rejoicing on the Union side of no-man's-land, despite the validity of the Richmond editor's viewpoint. Burnside suggested trying the mine again, reporting that the gallery was intact up to the tamping. He proposed starting two branches twenty-five feet from the tamping and extending them to both sides of the crater to reach the Confederate line, believing it would take only "a few days" to dig them. Meade ignored the suggestion. In fact, the army commander had every intention of getting rid of Burnside. Grant authorized Meade to grant the Ninth Corps commander a leave of absence on August 13, assigning Parke to replace him. The leave became permanent a few months later. Ledlie was granted a sick leave on August 4, which was later converted into an indefinite leave of absence. He resigned in January 1865.[61]

Meade separated these officers from his army and convinced Grant to authorize a court of inquiry into the cause of the fiasco. Headed by Hancock, the court was packed with men Meade could rely on to see things his way. It began meeting on August 6 and interviewed thirty-two people. Most of them stated that they had no faith in the operation and criticized many details of the preparation. Both Meade and Burnside offered lengthy testimony. After seventeen days of hearings, the court filed a report that leaned heavily on Burnside as the chief cause of the disaster. The court identified faulty troop formations, the halt of Ledlie's men inside the crater, poor use of engineer officers and troops, and poor leadership by many Ninth Corps officers as additional causes.[62]

Burnside and his supporters eagerly cooperated when the Joint Congressional Committee on the Conduct of the War held its own investigation. This committee had a long-standing antipathy toward Meade, and its members gave Burnside opportunities to present his case in a more favorable light. It interviewed several officers the court of inquiry had ignored, as well as many who had testified before Hancock's panel. The committee gathered testimony in December 1864, and its report cited Meade's interference with Burnside's plan as the chief cause of the failure. Yet the committee members were careful to blame Burnside as well. As a result, the congressmen issued a more fair and balanced report than the army officers.[63]

CHAPTER NINE

## *August*

The trenches at Petersburg became filthy by August. Officers tried to enforce cleanliness, but the men always dropped bits of food on the floor. "Vermin abounded," recalled the inspector of Hagood's staff, "and diseases of various kinds showed themselves. The digestive organs became impaired by the rations issued and the manner in which they were prepared. Diarrhoea and dysentery were universal; the legs and feet of the men swelled until they could not wear their shoes, and the filth of their persons from the scarcity of water was almost unbearable." Thomas Jackson Strayhorn of the 27th North Carolina enjoyed a short rest outside the works, but the thought of returning to "those dirty ditches" haunted him. "I hope we will not have to go into those trenches any more; they are so dirty and hot you can get no air at all scarcely."[1]

Insects of all kinds increased in number as the summer progressed, but worst of all were the flies. Their population exploded with the accumulation of horse dung, offal from slaughtered cattle, and the bodily filth of the troops. "They seem to fairly spring out of the ground when you move," noted Henry E. Taintor. "They run your face and hands so that it is impossible to keep *still* an instant." A Fifth Corps soldier was impressed by their appetite, often mistaking their bite for the sting of a bee. "We have to keep constantly in motion as their capacity is so great that they can scarcely be driven away from one[;] they drive the horses and mules perfectly crazy."[2]

Living amid freshly turned dirt caused the men's clothes to become "packed full of dust" and their skin to be "caked with dirt." Most soldiers along the Petersburg lines suffered to some degree with what William R. Ray of the Iron Brigade called the "ground itch." A few days out of the trenches and a good wash took care of such complaints, but soap was in short supply in Lee's army. The quartermasters had issued it three times since early May, but only enough each time for three days' use. "The great want of cleanliness which is a necessary consequence of these very limited issues is now producing sickness among the men in the trenches, and must effect their self respect & morale," Lee reported on August 9. He urged President Davis to purchase soap at any cost, but the authorities failed to solve the problem.³

Continual duty in the works wore the men down physically and emotionally. L. S. Wright of the 56th North Carolina noted how his comrades were "giting mity pore and pale and look very bad." Wright was so exhausted that he found it difficult to write a letter home, "my mind is so confused." The trenches became a kind of prison for him, as the Yankees "kill sum of our men and I am allway in a dred . . . to cum out of they brest[works] for fear of being kild."⁴

Material shortages continued to plague the Confederates. An inspection of Pickett's division on the Howlett Line indicated that 27 percent of the men present for duty did not have jackets, 29 percent had inadequate trousers, 25 percent had poor or no shirts, 29 percent were without underwear, 28 percent needed shoes, and 36 percent had no socks. There were lesser shortages of many other pieces of clothing and equipment, but nearly everyone had weapons and gun accoutrements. Some Confederates in other divisions who did have shirts, like Younger Longest of the 26th Virginia, wore the same one for four weeks before they had an opportunity to give it a wash.⁵

The Federals never suffered material shortages as severe as those of their counterparts, but they endured onerous duty in the works. Ord instructed his brigade commanders to mix quinine with the daily whiskey ration to combat disease, and officers received orders to provide shade for reserve troops. Tenth Corps brigade commander Louis Bell applied for a leave of absence, explaining to his wife that "what has chiefly used me up is the constant anxiety and watchfulness required in the front, want of sleep, and weary care."⁶

The weather continued hot and dry for most of August, but it rained a lot in mid-month. An especially hard shower fell on August 15 and created havoc with the earthworks and the men's living quarters. The storm flooded trenches and collapsed 100 yards of parapet on the Ninth Corps front, almost burying many soldiers. Corps headquarters issued orders to be ready in case the enemy tried to take advantage of the situation. In the batteries, the storm flooded magazines, forcing the gunners to empty them and cover the ordnance with tarpaulins. Many Federals had to walk out in the open to avoid flooded covered ways, but fortunately the Confederates were too busy dealing with the rain to shoot them. Rebel trenches were so filled with water that they "ran like a creek," and infantrymen were forced to sit and lie in several inches of fresh mud. A deep ravine behind the Eighteenth Corps line, filled with headquarters personnel and the camp of a sharpshooter battalion, was washed out by a flood that killed some men and destroyed a lot of personal belongings and equipment.⁷

Wet weather continued for several days after this heavy storm. "The trenches were almost knee deep in mud and it was still raining," recalled W. A. Day of the 49th North Carolina. "Our clothes were covered with mud and soaked with rain, no place to sleep and nothing much to eat, and sixty-four pound mortar shells bursting all around."[8]

Lee understood that worsening conditions in the trenches led to a rise in desertion rates by mid-August. Ord also noted the lowered morale among Confederate deserters and informed his wife that "they and our men *are tired of being killed.*"[9]

The men repaired the works, and the sun dried up the mud and lifted spirits. Rotating units in and out of the trenches also helped to maintain morale. John R. Cooke's North Carolina brigade was lucky to stay in the trenches only eight days and nights before resting in a "deep hollow" to the rear for a week. Hagood's South Carolinians suffered a great deal by being on duty for sixty-five days without a break, and they were pulled out only to take part in the hard-fought battle of Globe Tavern on August 21.[10]

Firing continued sporadically on most parts of the line during August; but it remained hot and persistent along the Ninth Corps front, and some of it spilled over into the Eighteenth Corps sector. The close proximity of the opposing lines accounted for this. Pickets and artillerymen fired "as if they ware carrying on a battle all the time day and night," as Benjamin Mason put it. Some of Parke's regiments lost up to ten men each day, while Johnson's division lost an average of nine men each day during the first half of August. "The siege had now settled down to the arithmetical process of killing us off little by little," thought Alexander.[11]

### MAINTENANCE AND IMPROVEMENT

Most of the repair work during August centered on the Ninth Corps defenses. "Much labor will be required to repair the breast-works and abatis" following the mine attack, reported Willcox. Regimental commanders were responsible for defenses in their sector and were expected to do the work with their own men. When refurbished, the forward Union parapet was revetted with horizontal layers of logs and laced with loopholes fashioned from two rows of sandbags. Members of the 50th New York Engineers erected chevaux-de-frise opposite Pegram's Salient. Working at night and using "Movable breast works" made of three-inch lumber to shield the crew, twelve engineers drove stakes into the ground under fire. Then others placed the sections of chevaux-de-frise and nailed them together. The screens worked pretty well, although bullets penetrated them now and then. In addition to rebuilding parapets, the Ninth Corps constructed more traverses and drained, deepened, and widened covered ways. The infantrymen also tried to clean up the awful mess left by men who were "in the practice of using the unoccupied works as sinks." Perhaps they did this because some of the latrines were in "shamefully bad" condition.[12]

Elements of the U.S. Engineer Battalion and the 50th New York Engineers also renovated the Fourteen Gun Battery. They razed one covered way and began digging a new one, protecting themselves from the fire of Rebel sharpshooters by erecting a line of dirt-filled gabions. The engineers cut new embrasures and replaced rotting gabions on the fort's traverses. They also constructed a new, much smaller artillery work called the Taylor Battery, located 100 yards in front of and on lower ground than the Fourteen Gun Battery. It was sited to fire down the length of Poor Creek valley. Captain Hudson of the 35th Massachusetts laid out the work using "narrow bandages for a tape line to measure by; so inadequately provided with equipment for engineering were the troops at the front." Three men of Company B, U.S. Engineer Battalion, laid out a new covered way linking it with the railroad.[13]

Warren busied himself with repairs and new engineering work on the Fifth Corps front. He wanted to connect five covered ways with a line of infantry trench which could serve as a rear line of defense. Tilton made a shorter rear line of defense on his brigade front, sending an officer and 200 men to dig a covered way parallel to his main line and construct a parapet four feet, three inches high along its edge, "so that musketry fire can be delivered from it." Warren's men built a new covered way west of Jerusalem Plank Road to connect Fort Sedgwick with Fort Davis and added banquettes to some batteries originally built only to accommodate artillery.[14]

Much of this work came from a high-level directive to improve the existing trenches so they could be held by a small number of troops, allowing Grant to assemble a strike force for future operations. Hot weather and the need to work mostly at night slowed the pace. On the Tenth Corps sector, details constructed new loopholes along the line because Rebel sharpshooters had zeroed in on those already in place and made them dangerous to use. The Engineer Department in Washington, D.C., contributed to this effort by dispatching 100,000 sandbags as well as thirty rope mantlets to Butler's army. Tenth Corps troops also slashed more trees to create larger fields of fire.[15]

Early in August, Herbert E. Valentine, a clerk at division headquarters, took a stroll through the works occupied by the Eighteenth Corps. He "followed the narrow trench winding in & out, almost making one dizzy. At intervals on our left would be little trenches leading to the rear, and plenty of gopher holes dug out of the dirt to sleep in." Valentine saw lookouts peering through sandbagged loopholes, and he noted that the banquette had a drainage ditch to its rear. Some infantrymen slept on the banquette itself while others cooked their rations in the trench.[16]

The Confederates were no less busy after the crater battle. In addition to improving their defenses at Pegram's Salient, they built a cavalier behind Gracie's Salient in case it might be the next target of Federal mining. Goode's brigade added a number of traverses to its line, having learned how useful they were on July 30.[17]

By late summer, the Confederates were making more chevaux-de-frise than abatis to serve as their main obstruction in front of the line. Troops made them at the engineer depot near Blandford and lowered them across the works at night where the opposing lines were close. Robert Richard Bragg, a noncommissioned officer of the 59th Virginia, took charge of putting the "Shiver de freze" out along Goode's line.[18]

Pendleton recommended the construction of "a covered way along the rear line of works and guns," between Pegram's Salient and Jerusalem Plank Road, that would be useful in moving troops back and forth in case the Federals sprung more mines. It could also serve as a second line of defense. Although Alexander and Stevens supported the idea, it was never acted on due to labor shortages.[19]

### COUNTERMINING

The crater battle greatly increased the pace and intensity of countermining at Petersburg. "This was something so new and so terrible that a profound impression was produced," recalled engineer officer W. W. Blackford, "and nothing else was talked about. Every man in the trenches was sure there were a hundred kegs of powder right under him. Not a card could be seen, and everybody was reading his Bible." Virginia artilleryman John Walters confessed to his diary, "Though I do not show it, yet I am becoming terribly demoralized at the thought of finding myself going up some fine morning or other." Walters worried about slowly suffocating "while the panorama of my last life passed before my eyes in all its startling hideousness, this thought is terrible and almost unmans me."[20]

Blackford was placed in overall charge of countermining along the Richmond-Petersburg lines. Born at Fredericksburg, he attended the University of Virginia and worked as a railroad engineer and businessman before the war. Blackford served as an engineer officer on J. E. B. Stuart's staff and received a commission as lieutenant colonel of Lee's engineer regiment in April 1864. Blackford expanded countermining efforts to eight sites by adding works where City Point Road, Jerusalem Plank Road, and Squirrel Level Road crossed the defenses. Cooke's Salient, located somewhere between Pegram's Salient and Jerusalem Plank Road, and Elliott's Salient north of the James River were the other locations.[21]

A large quantity of supplies and specialized equipment began to flow toward these work sites. Hundreds of feet of rope; dozens of sperm, tallow, and wax candles; a variety of carpenter tools; thousands of sandbags; boxes of matches; 3,300 feet of one-inch plank; and quantities of sheet iron were requisitioned and shipped. The diggers used oil-burning miner's lamps at the head of the galleries, while candles illuminated the rest of the excavation.[22]

It was difficult to find ventilating equipment. The Engineer Bureau in Richmond tried to purchase "six good second hand blacksmith bellows" to pump air, but they were not available. Instead, Alfred L. Rives suggested that Lee's engineer troops construct fans "to force in the air through wooden box tubes, connected by canvas covered with pitch." This was similar to the improvised method that Pleasants used. The Engineer Bureau found several water pumps and shipped large amounts of iron, wood, and lead pipe. The Confederates hired a civilian plumber to connect the pipes, using the softer lead variety to join sections of wood and iron piping, "thus making a flexible joint."[23]

The miners needed augers to bore forward through the undisturbed earth at the head of each gallery when near a suspected Union mine. The augers came in 4- and 8-inch widths, and iron extensions enabled the operator to work the device while many feet away. Some of the augers were made from damaged circular saws. An inventive soldier, Pvt. Thomas Fowler of the 41st Alabama in Gracie's brigade, developed an auger for use aboveground. It consisted of a hollow cylinder of iron, 3 inches wide and 10 inches long, "slightly flared

Possible entrance to Confederate countermine. While there is an indication that it was located at Union Fort McGilvery, that seems very unlikely. (Library of Congress, LC-DIG-CWPB-00521)

at the end," and attached to a 10-foot wooden pole. It could be rammed into the ground and twisted, then drawn out to bring up dirt that was knocked or pushed out of the cylinder. A man reportedly could dig 10 feet in 15 minutes (although Blackford later claimed a rate of only 20 feet in half a day). Gracie admitted that the tool was quite noisy, but he was enthusiastic about it. Walter Stevens sent a pattern of the borer to the Tredegar Iron Works in Richmond and ordered 100 for immediate delivery. He distributed them to the troops, who eagerly dug holes in the trench floors 30 feet apart and later dug more holes at 2-foot intervals. After digging some 20 feet (using rope attached to the wooden handle), the men poured water into the hole, knowing the red clay would hold the liquid in place for a long time. If a Federal mine hit it, the water would fall out as a danger signal to the anxious Rebels. Blackford admitted after the war that this really did not make the salients more secure, but it eased the minds of the infantrymen.[24]

The purpose of countermining was to detect the underground enemy long before he reached a point directly beneath the main line, and that could be done only by digging galleries well forward of the position. The top priority was Pegram's Salient; the engineers had to find the Union gallery before Burnside used it for another attack. Douglas and Wise examined the crater after 5:00 P.M. on July 30 but found too many bodies yet unburied to allow them to discover anything. They continued the next morning with a crew of twenty men (some of whom were black Union prisoners), digging three new shafts in the

Entrance to countermine. While there is an indication that it was located at Fort Mahone, it was more likely at Jerusalem Plank Road or Squirrel Level Road. (Library of Congress, LC-DIG-CWPB-02576)

north, south, and center of the crater near its rim. Over the next two days, they discovered what seemed to be evidence of the Union branches in the northern shaft, and they stopped work at the other two spots.[25]

Blackford wanted to enter the shaft to examine the evidence, but by then the air inside had become foul with the stench of decaying bodies. Some 300 Union and Confederate soldiers were buried only a few feet away in the center of the crater, and gases seeped through the underground fissures created by the mine explosion. Blackford tied a rope around his shoulders and went down; his head started to swim, and subordinates pulled him out. The smell was "villainous beyond description." The engineers acquired a fan used to blow chaff away when wheat was thrown in front of it, and they rigged a pipe made of grain bags, sticking one end into the shaft and attaching the other end to the fan. A Federal mortar shell destroyed the fan one day, but the Confederates replaced it and cleared the air inside. They continued to use the apparatus to cool off workers in the shaft.[26]

Unable to locate the Union gallery, Blackford, Douglas, and Wise shifted their attention to other locations. At Colquitt's Salient, Company H, 1st Confederate Engineers, extended the gallery more than eighty-three feet toward the Hare House and carved out three branches before stopping work on August 3.[27]

Lt. William Alexander Gordon of Talcott's regiment took charge of the countermining at Cooke's Salient, employing his Company G and 100 infantrymen. With advice from more experienced miners, Gordon sank shafts at both wings and in the middle of the salient. The shafts were 4 feet square and went to a depth of 26 feet through hard clay. Galleries extended forward from each shaft, 43 feet long on the wings and 50 feet in the center. Then Gordon's men dug a connecting gallery that was 1,116 yards long at the forward ends to connect all three shafts. The design was exactly like that of Douglas's countermine at Pegram's Salient, although it presented a much wider front. Gordon finished the countermine in late September and placed guards in it twenty-four hours a day to listen for signs of enemy mining.[28]

Although Blackford was in overall charge, Douglas continued to supervise the daily work details at each site. He organized the men much as he had done before the mine attack, with two detachments responsible for a single shaft. Douglas was always on the lookout for experienced miners among the infantry units. Matthew Venable, a seventeen-year-old student at Hampden-Sidney College before he enlisted in Company H, 1st Confederate Engineers, recalled that the shifts dug for six hours at a time while other engineers and detailed infantrymen framed the gallery. They used wheelbarrows to transport the dirt back to the shaft, where it was lifted out by windlass. The quality of soil varied from "sand and soft clay" to "compact brown clay."[29]

The pace of Federal countermining quickened after July 30 as well. The Yankees had worked only two locations before the mine attack, before Batteries No. 4 and No. 5 and in front of Batteries No. 6, No. 7, and No. 8, all on the Eighteenth Corps front. They started countermines at four more locations in the first week of August: at Fort Sedgwick, at Fort Stedman, on the right of Willcox's Ninth Corps division line, and at Fort Morton.

The impetus for these Federal projects lay in fear that the Confederates might try an offensive mine. When sounds of underground digging could be heard at Fort Sedgwick on the morning of August 1, troops from Bartlett's Fifth Corps brigade started to dig two shafts, one in the ditch of the work and another just inside the parapet. They sunk these shafts fifteen and twenty-one feet before troops from the U.S. Engineer Battalion and Company M, 50th New York Engineers, arrived to take over. Warren visited Fort Sedgwick on the morning of August 2, stood for some time in the magazine, and could hear at least three picks at work. He ordered Bartlett to evacuate the fort, and the engineers pushed the shafts as rapidly as possible. Warren also ordered a

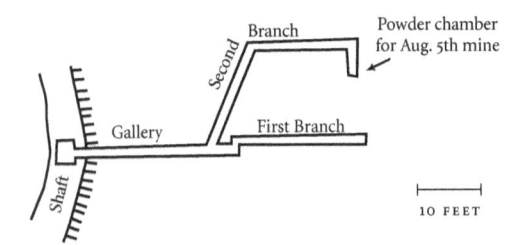

GRACIE'S SALIENT

July 22 to August 5, 1864, based on Hugh T. Douglas to Thomas M. R. Talcott, August 2, 1864, OR 42(2): 1158

COLQUITT'S SALIENT

July 10 to August 3, 1864, based on Hugh T. Douglas to Thomas M. R. Talcott, August 2 & 5, 1864, OR 42(2):1158–59, 1163

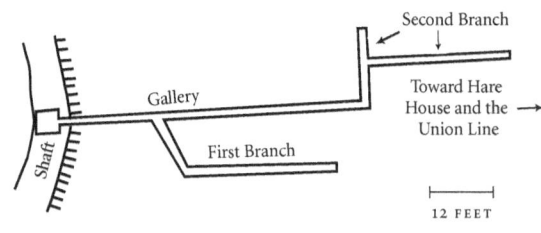

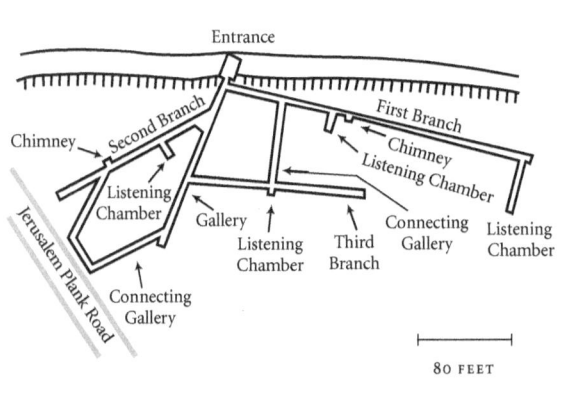

JERUSALEM PLANK ROAD

August 12 to December 1864, based on Carter R. Bishop and Willie E. Wells, "Confederate Tunnels at Pine Gardens, Prince George County, Virginia," courtesy of Harry Jackson

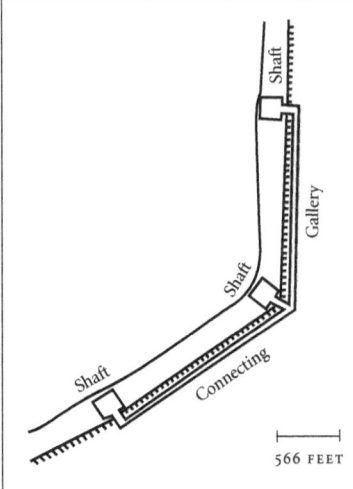

COOKE'S SALIENT

July 31 to late September 1864, based on William Alexander Gordon Memoirs, 147–49, WLU

Confederate Countermines, July–December 1864

Possible Federal countermine shaft. It was possibly located at Fort Sedgwick. (Library of Congress, LC-DIG-CWPB-02843)

secondary line constructed to the rear of the fort. He contemplated letting the Confederates explode their mine so he could follow up with a counterattack, with Meade's approval.[30]

Gilbert Thompson of the U.S. Engineer Battalion led six men into the shafts at Fort Sedgwick on the evening of August 3. His first descent into the earth "aroused . . . queer and lonesome sensations." He could hear pick work, apparently close by. "A ramrod was driven at different places and held between the teeth to detect the direction of the mining, but without any definite result." Thompson devised a clever way to determine what was going on. He stationed a man at the mouth of the shaft with orders to give a signal whenever he heard a shot from the picket line. In this way, Thompson reported that the "pick" noise was simply the echo of distant sharpshooting.[31]

Ironically, the Confederates did begin to countermine opposite Fort Sedgwick sometime in August, but they had no intention of running an approach toward the Union position. The Federals had no way of knowing their enemy's plans and began to dig a more extensive countermine system in front of Sedgwick on August 4. It was to consist of three new shafts with forward galleries connected by a cross gallery, but the diggers encountered so much water fifteen feet down that they temporarily stopped their work.[32]

Rumors of Confederate mining on the Eighteenth Corps front worried Ord. Rebel deserters fed him reports that their former comrades were extending the mine at Colquitt's Salient toward the Hare House with the intention of blowing up the work later named Fort Stedman. Ord requested help, and engineers soon started digging a listening shaft at the fort.[33]

Unknown to Ord, the Confederates fully intended to spring a mine on his front, but at Gracie's Salient instead of Colquitt's. Walter Stevens ordered it on July 31, based on apparent evidence that the Federals were mining from the head of the sap they had dug in July. The powder arrived on the evening of July 31, and Douglas supervised its placement all night. Mr. Blunt and Mr. Black, two civilian miners, provided technical assistance. They placed four barrels of powder, totaling 450 pounds, in two chambers. Douglas hoped to spring the mine with lanyards, but they were not available. Instead, he used four strands of safety fuse, each one stretched from a powder barrel to a single powder train that reached the mouth of the gallery. The tamping consisted of sandbags and dirt. All was ready by 9:15 on the morning of August 1, but then Douglas was informed that he could not spring the mine while the burial truce was in effect at Pegram's Salient 600 yards south. When it ended at 11:00 A.M., Gracie gave the signal, and Black lit the powder train.[34]

Douglas and his crew waited forty-five minutes, but nothing happened. Black then went into the gallery and found that three pieces of the fuse had burned out and the fourth piece was "burning slowly." He cut off the fourth piece, believing the slow burn would produce a poor detonation, and brought it out for examination. It was found to be "very defective and perfectly valueless," in Douglas's words. The frustrated engineer decided to postpone the explosion and extend the mine closer to the Federals.[35]

Douglas's men removed the tamping and powder, shoveled out mud, and pumped water on the night of August 1. The gallery had two branches, both of which had been started before July 31, but the second one seemed to be headed more directly toward the sap. Douglas decided to clear out the debris and leftover sandbags from this second branch and extend it as far as possible. A new shipment of shovels and picks arrived, and Douglas's men worked around the clock. By August 4, they had gone as far as Douglas dared and began to dig a powder chamber to the side and at the head of the branch. It was only four and a half feet long.[36]

That night, Douglas directed the placement of eight barrels of powder, totaling 850 pounds. He put half of them in the powder chamber and the rest apparently in the head of the branch. Douglas tamped only up to the top of the powder barrels rather than all the way to the ceiling of the branch. He again used safety fuses and constructed cotton tubing to hold the powder train encased inside a long wooden box.[37]

All was ready by the evening of August 5, and Wise fired the mine at 6:30 P.M. The Federals were taken by surprise as a mass of earth 30 feet in diameter suddenly rose 100 feet into the sky, "the centre portion being elevated considerably above the sides." Fortunately for the Yankees, the mine exploded 40 yards short of the saphead. The main Union line was so far away that no debris fell into it. Federal sharpshooters in the sap did not even feel it was necessary to evacuate their positions.[38]

Ord was inspecting his line at a spot fairly near the explosion when he felt the earth jar and saw "a cloud of dust and smoke rising high in the air." He ordered reserve troops up to the line as a hail of Rebel artillery and musket fire followed the explosion. Union casualties were slight but included one of Ord's best brigade commanders. Col. Griffin Stedman and Ames, his division leader, were leaning against the side of a trench in conversation when a bullet smacked into Stedman's chest. The brigade leader began to walk away, but weakness overcame him; he died the next morning.[39]

The Confederates lost a few men in the exchange of fire, which lasted at least half an hour after the explosion. When everything became quiet again, Farquhar examined the crater from the head of the sap and assumed the Confederates had intended to destroy the position but made a mistake. Meade did not believe Lee's engineers would miss their target by forty yards. He suggested that they intended to use the crater as an advanced infantry position to attack the Eighteenth Corps at night. Ord did not support this view, asserting that the crater was "not in a place likely to be occupied by them."[40]

While Beauregard tried to put the best face on the explosion, calling it an "experimental mine" that "much alarmed" the enemy, all other Confederates recognized it as a failure. Bushrod Johnson thought it was badly tamped and therefore the "effect was slight. Not a gabion or sap roller displaced, nor much of a crater formed." The explosion collapsed the branch and the gallery back to the shaft and dropped debris on the Confederate picket line.[41]

This was the second failed countermining effort by Douglas, and it ruined his military career. Douglas was out of his element, and for some reason, Blunt and Black were not available to offer assistance on August 5. Talcott had ordered him to fire the mine at noon that day, but he hesitated, saying "'that he was not a miner.'" Behind schedule, he apparently tamped the charge only halfway, which led to a less effective explosion and the destruction of the branch and gallery. Talcott placed him under arrest. Douglas admitted to "a grave error" and offered to resign his commission. He cited his age (somewhat more than forty-five years) and "other reasons, not deemed necessary to mention." Stevens and Lee approved the resignation, but Jeremy Gilmer demanded to know the "other reasons." This compelled Talcott to file formal court-martial charges on September 1, further humiliating Douglas.⁴²

Meanwhile, Douglas turned over piles of equipment and supplies to Wise, the new commander of Company F. The Confederates had accumulated 1,150 barrels of cannon powder, 500 feet of safety fuse, and 10 pounds of fine rifle powder for countermine use. Despite Talcott's filing of charges, Gilmer failed to approve Douglas's resignation, but Douglas sent in another letter of resignation that was accepted on September 28. He finished the war as a civilian engineer employed by the Confederate army.⁴³

The Confederates were a step behind the Federals in underground engineering at Petersburg. In stopping forty yards short of the saphead and improperly tamping the mine, Douglas made two basic mistakes. It is possible that his age, combined with fatigue and perhaps depression over his failure to stop Pleasants's mine, led to these errors. The strands of safety fuse Douglas used on August 1 happened to be defective, but those employed on August 5 worked perfectly. The Confederates acquired 458 feet of powder hose in late August, a premanufactured powder train consisting of a "tube of strong linen." Often called a Gomez fuse, it was to be put in a wooden casing and filled with the aid of a tin funnel.⁴⁴

Countermining continued under Blackford's supervision after August 5. Usually, the Confederates located their shafts inside the trench itself and penetrated as much as thirty feet into the earth. They built a floor five feet from the bottom and started the gallery at that level. The cavity left at the bottom of the shaft, beneath the floor, collected water that drained from the gallery, which was dug at a slight incline. Now and then, the collected water had to be bailed out with buckets. Inside the listening galleries, the engineers bored a series of four-inch auger holes forward as well as upward, and sentries paced back and forth around the clock. Blackford claimed they were armed with a device to release smoke inside a Union gallery through the auger holes, if the enemy ever dug close enough.⁴⁵

Blackford also asserted that all Confederate countermines at Petersburg were designed alike, with two galleries extending forward connected by a listening gallery at their heads. Actually this was planned for Pegram's Salient and finished only at Cooke's Salient. The other six countermines consisted of galleries and a series of branches extending from them, all generally pointing toward the enemy. Alexander was convinced that the design attempted at Pegram's contributed to the failure to detect Pleasants's mine. He preferred extending a single gallery from the center of the salient as quickly as possible until the enemy could be located.⁴⁶

All the galleries needed to be framed to prevent cave-ins, but the Confederates built minimal structures to save time, labor, and material. They constructed the frames in sections, using four inch by four inch timber, and then carried them into the gallery. A one-inch plank connected each section and provided rigidity. Planks laid on timber runners made up the floor of the galleries and provided a smooth runway for wheelbarrows. Blackford constructed a bombproof near each shaft where the men could keep their hats and coats while underground. Alert officers began to have beeswax mixed into the tallow used to make candles for the galleries. They noticed that the diggers sometimes ate the pure tallow candles, which consisted of animal fat.⁴⁷

Blackford discovered the source of one ventilating problem and fixed it with a simple solution. He noticed that infantrymen sleeping in the trench exhaled "carbonic acid gas," which settled on the trench floor and seeped down the shafts. There already was a short wooden border around the mouth of the shaft to keep anyone from falling in. He simply raised this three feet above the ground, and that was enough to keep the gas out.⁴⁸

Matthew Venable recalled encountering different soils in the length of each gallery. The diggers often found "very compact, pure clay of a grayish brown color so tenacious that the picks had to be made with short blades, with widened chisel-like edges and short handles, and we had to chip the material out by inches." This type of clay could be molded into pipes and other objects. Red clay proved easier to dig through, and sand required extra planking on the gallery frame.⁴⁹

Almost every noise made on the surface could be heard underground, and it seemed to come from every direction. Blackford developed a routine; when a report came in, he waited for a second report before proceeding to the spot. Sometimes he had to devise ways to clear up the ambiguity in order to calm nervous infantry officers. One day a reliable man reported that the Yankees were using picks only ten yards away for more than an hour. Blackford found that the noise could be heard the entire length of the gallery, and it was impossible to determine the direction from which it came. So he sent two men along the trench line to stop everyone who was working and then to give a signal with their own picks when all was clear. The noises completely stopped a few minutes later when his "sound patrol" quieted fifty yards of the trench.⁵⁰

The Confederates began a new countermine near Jerusalem Plank Road by August 12, and it was the most extensive at Petersburg. When finished, the complex totaled 1,088 feet of galleries and branches. The main gallery extended

Arched ceiling in gallery of Confederate countermine, Jerusalem Plank Road. The arched ceiling was probably made in the 1920s by the tourist developers. (Petersburg National Battlefield)

more than 146 feet southwest toward Jerusalem Plank Road, with a network of three branches and two connecting galleries between the branches. The Confederates built two chimneys for ventilation and four short listening chambers at key locations. Unlike most of the other Confederate countermines, this one did not have a shaft but was started in a ravine, like Pleasants's mine.[51]

The Federals learned of the Rebel countermine at Jerusalem Plank Road from a deserter on August 12 and assumed it was an offensive mine. On more than one occasion, they evacuated Fort Sedgwick for a few hours until the current warning of its imminent destruction proved false. Countermining began at Fort Stedman sometime in early August as well. The shaft was sunk in the ditch of the work, its dimensions were 7 feet by 10 feet, and the hole was 12 feet deep. By the end of the Petersburg campaign, Stedman was protected by a network of galleries and branches that totaled 200 feet in length. A detail from the U.S. Engineer Battalion started a countermine at Fort Morton on August 21 as information about enemy digging continued to flow in.[52]

Grant saw an opportunity in a Confederate mine attack. He advised Meade to let them come, prepare a secondary line opposite the point of attack, and repel them as Burnside had been stopped on July 30. He assumed Ord's Eighteenth Corps front was the most likely place for Rebel mining efforts and believed any assault could be "repulsed with great slaughter."[53]

## DUTCH GAP CANAL

As the First Battle of Deep Bottom was unfolding, Butler proposed to Grant that a massive engineering project might enable the Federal gunboats to bypass the batteries at the Howlett House and ascend the James River. Howlett's was located on a huge bend of the stream, and it seemed possible to cut a canal across the neck of land formed by that bend. The area was called Dutch Gap because of a failed prewar effort by a Dutch engineer to dig a canal there. Such a canal would save nearly five miles of travel on the river and avoid obstructions placed by the Federals at Trent's Reach to block Confederate boats from descending the river. Grant waited until the Third Offensive had run its course and then gave Butler his approval. He had approved a similar effort at Vicksburg the previous year, although it failed to provide a suitable alternate route for his river fleet to bypass the heavily fortified town.[54]

Peter Michie surveyed the neck of land and reported that the canal would be 166 yards long, 15 feet deep, 85 feet wide at top, and 40 feet wide at bottom. Because of the uneven lay of the land, the troops had to dig much deeper than 15 feet to place the canal at water level, and they contended with a mixture of hardened clay, sand, and gravel, the latter the size of paving stones. Digging began on August 9 as heavy plows broke the topsoil. Initially, Michie planned to dig the entire canal while leaving bulkheads at each end to keep the water out, and then he would blow the bulkheads with mines. He put a steam dredging machine to work digging out a 30-foot hole underwater next to the bulkhead for the debris to fall into without blocking the entrance to the canal. Michie used up to 1,000 men, drawn from both black and white units in Butler's army. Civilian operators of the dredges moved only 7,000 of the 48,000 cubic yards of material involved in the project because their equipment was "old and almost worn out."[55]

Unlike mining operations, it was impossible to keep the canal project secret. Confederate land-based artillery and river gunboats began firing on the workers by August 13. The next day, this fire killed and wounded thirty diggers and later damaged the steam dredge, also driving away the civilian operators. The Confederates continued to lay down harassing fire, often at night and normally at intervals of fifteen minutes during the day. This fire never stopped the Federals, who constructed bombproofs in the walls of the canal and continued digging.[56]

CHAPTER TEN

# *The Fourth Offensive*

By August 12, after nearly two weeks of idleness following the Crater battle, Grant was ready to begin another offensive. He hoped that Lee had diverted enough troops to the Shenandoah Valley to give a Federal strike some hope of success. Initially, Grant thought of holding the lines only with black troops, perhaps supplemented by the white soldiers of the Tenth Corps. He estimated that placing one man every six feet in the trenches would be enough to hold the Bermuda Hundred line, and one man for every four feet could secure the Petersburg defenses. Backed up by a reserve force, this "thin skirmish line" would free maximum strength for offensive operations. Grant wanted Hancock to once again spearhead the drive north of the James River by way of Deep Bottom. He held open the possibility of organizing a complementary strike south of the Appomattox River if circumstances warranted. The operation might force the Confederates to recall troops that were reportedly marching from Petersburg to the Shenandoah Valley.[1]

Plans called for Hancock to embark his corps on steamers at City Point and pretend to head for Washington, D.C., but the boats would actually steam up the James River at dark and deposit the troops just downstream from Deep Bottom. Two divisions of Birney's Tenth Corps and Gregg's cavalry division were earmarked to cross the James over a pontoon bridge to be laid just upstream from Deep Bottom. This was the same location where the engineers had placed the second pontoon bridge for the Third Offensive the previous month. All or parts of the Fifth and Ninth Corps could sally forth if Hancock, Birney, and Gregg could force Lee to weaken the Petersburg defenses.[2]

### SECOND DEEP BOTTOM

Initially, Birney and Hancock operated on separate lines of advance. Terry's division and two brigades of Turner's division crossed the newly laid pontoon bridge as sixteen boats carried the Second Corps from City Point up the James

River on the night of August 13. While Birney was to attack the southward-facing Confederate line defending New Market Heights, Hancock was to attack the east-facing line.[3]

More Confederates waited than they expected. Field commanded seven brigades at or near Deep Bottom: five were his own, and two were detailed from Wilcox's division. A small cavalry brigade covered his left, for a total of 8,220 men. In addition to these troops, Ewell commanded about 2,900 infantry and artillery. Against this force of 11,120, the Federals brought 29,000 infantry and cavalry.[4]

The Union offensive got off to a rocky start. Tilghman's Wharf, located half a mile downstream from Deep Bottom, had been destroyed by the Confederates and was not yet repaired. Many boats could not extend their gangplanks to the river bluff. The troops had to unload onto the decks of light draft vessels anchored closer to shore while labor details tried to patch together the docks. It took more than five hours for Hancock's lead division under Mott to get onshore, while the rest of the corps disembarked by 9:00 A.M. of August 14.[5]

Birney was ahead of Hancock, crossing the pontoon bridge at Jones's Neck at 5:00 A.M. on August 14. He then advanced northward and captured Field's picket line, but he halted when confronted by the main line of works at the foot of New Market Heights. Grant later confirmed Birney's decision not to attack when he learned how strong the Confederate position appeared to be. When Birney slowly shifted his command eastward across Bailey's Creek to connect with Hancock, Terry's men surprised and captured four eight-inch howitzers in an exposed position.[6]

Hancock's advance from Tilghman's Wharf fared little better. He pushed northward in two columns, with Mott's division turning left onto New Market Road and advancing toward Tilghman's Gate. Mott pushed Confederate skirmishers back but halted before a redoubt filled with artillery. Barlow's and Gibbon's divisions (the latter temporarily under Smyth) advanced to the north along Darbytown Road. They initially met only Gary's cavalry brigade. Barlow mishandled the advance and delayed his movement to Bailey's Creek long enough for Field to send two infantry brigades to the scene. As in July, Hancock's advance was stymied on the east side of the creek.[7]

Hancock hoped Birney's command could flank Field's left during the night. He believed the Confederate line ended somewhere near Fussell's Mill, which lay on Bailey's Creek about four miles north of the James River. Many delays beset Birney, who did not reach the area of Fussell's Mill until 1:00 P.M. on August 15. He consumed more hours in scouting the terrain and positioning troops until reporting himself ready at 6:40 P.M. By then, Hancock had decided to postpone the attack until the next day.[8]

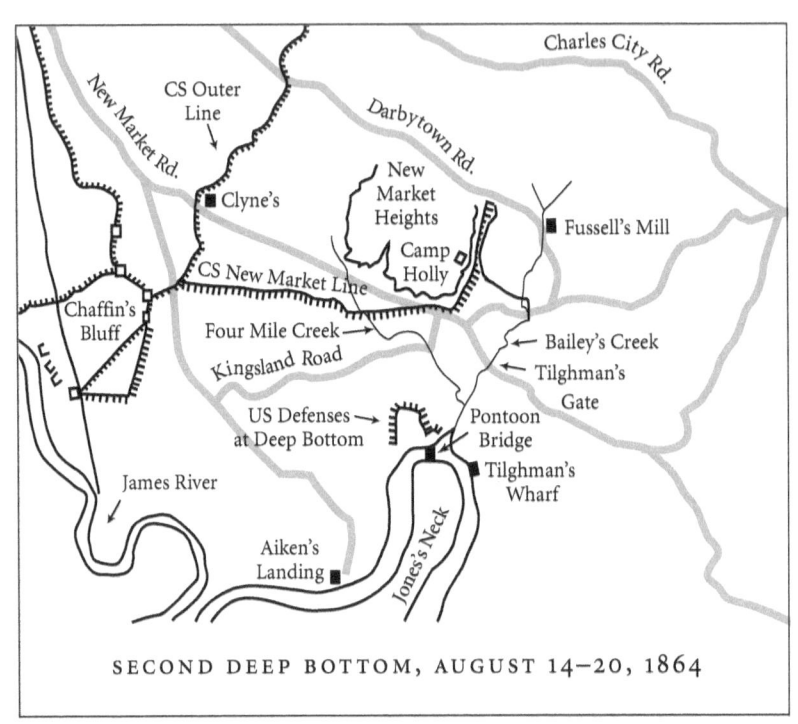

SECOND DEEP BOTTOM, AUGUST 14–20, 1864

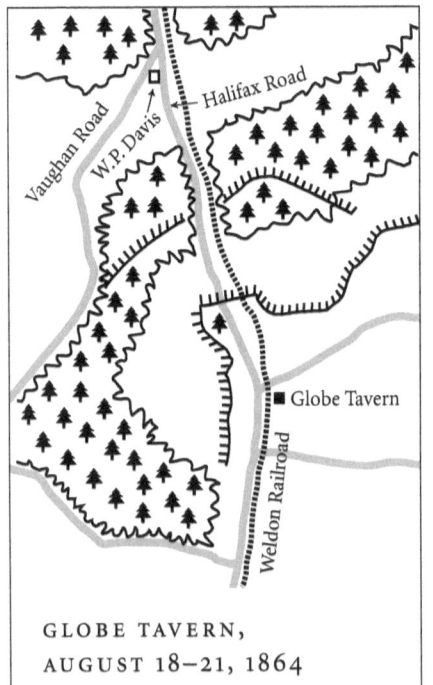

GLOBE TAVERN,
AUGUST 18–21, 1864

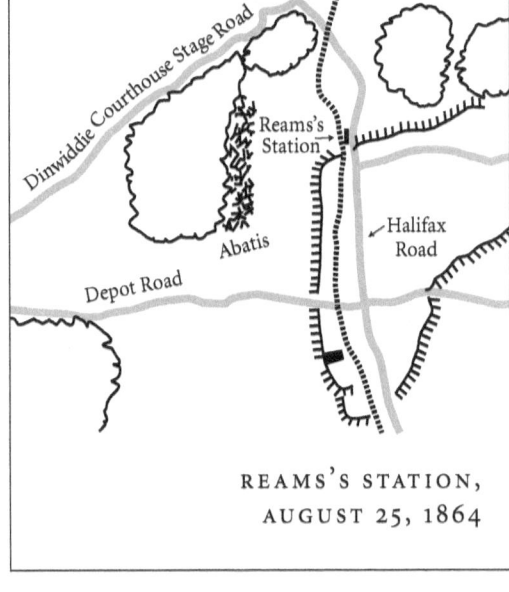

REAMS'S STATION,
AUGUST 25, 1864

The Fourth Offensive, August 14–25, 1864

Field also shifted troops during the night of August 14. Paying little attention to the small holding force that Birney left south of New Market Heights, he moved most of his command to face east, extending the Confederate line to Fussell's Mill. Lee also sent two brigades from Mahone's division, which prolonged Field's line to a point well north of the mill. Rooney Lee's cavalry division screened Field's left. There were now 17,000 Confederates holding the line along Bailey's Creek.[9]

Hancock hoped to deliver two strikes by dawn of August 16. While Birney advanced against Fussell's Mill, Gregg's cavalry, supported by Miles's brigade of Barlow's division, was to advance farther northward along Charles City Road. If neither achieved a breakthrough, perhaps Field would be forced to shift enough troops northward to allow Mott to advance at Tilghman's Gate. Gregg and Miles attacked at 6:00 A.M. to fulfill their part of the plan, but little came of it. They struck Chambliss's cavalry brigade, killed Chambliss himself, and forced the Rebel horsemen to retire some distance west of Fussell's Mill; but Rooney Lee sent reinforcements that drove the Federals back to their starting point.[10]

Birney delayed his attack seven hours due to ignorance of the terrain around Fussell's Mill. Darbytown Road crossed Bailey's Creek on the mill dam; not only was this a narrow line of approach, but Confederate trenches commanded the road. He then shifted three-quarters of a mile northward where two ravines drained toward the south to form the headwaters of Bailey's Creek. Birney carefully advanced into this unknown sector, taking a fortified picket line on the east side of the first ravine and later capturing an entrenched skirmish line on the east side of the second ravine. This was merely a preliminary to the main attack by three brigades (Craig's brigade from Mott's division on the right, Pond's Tenth Corps brigade in the center, and Foster's Tenth Corps brigade on the left), with Hawley's brigade as a reserve. Birney lined up twenty guns to provide fire support. Brig. Gen. Victor J. B. Girardey's Georgia brigade of Mahone's division, which had been led by Matthew Hall during the crater battle, opposed this Union force. The Federals hoped to break the Confederate line and then wheel left to outflank the rest of Field's command.[11]

Girardey's 825 men were vulnerable. There were two other Confederate brigades half a mile north of his position, but to the south, the low ridge he occupied was separated from the rest of Field's position by a ravine. Sanders's Alabama brigade occupied a bluff higher than Girardey's position, with a refused left flank. This would enable the Alabamians to fire into Girardey's trench if the enemy should capture it. The Georgia brigade was almost in the position of a sacrificial lamb, but if Birney smashed it, at least Sanders could prevent a larger catastrophe from taking place.[12]

The Tenth Corps attack, the heaviest at Second Deep Bottom, finally started about noon on August 16. Pond's brigade crossed the ravine and struggled through a slashing of felled timber, all the while under heavy fire. It overwhelmed the 2nd Georgia Battalion and 10th Georgia Battalion, taking a section of the line. The Federals then began to outflank the 64th Georgia. Girardey was killed while trying to rally the latter regiment. Pond, Craig, and Hawley occupied most of Girardey's position, but on the Union left, Foster could not dislodge Sanders's men from their stronger position on the bluff. As Birney tried to exploit his advantage, his other brigades became entangled in the rough terrain of the ravine that separated Girardey from Sanders, and the Alabamians also delivered commanding fire into the ravine to cause casualties and more confusion.[13]

Reinforcements arrived to save the Confederate flank. Col. William C. Oates led the 15th Alabama and 48th Alabama in a counterattack, receiving a severe wound in the arm. Tough fighting ensued as Birney's men took shelter in Girardey's trench, then DuBose's Georgia brigade managed to turn their right flank. The Federals gave up the ridge that had once been Girardey's position and returned to the east side of Bailey's Creek. They suffered more than 1,500 casualties out of 7,258 men engaged, while the Rebels lost 917 men out of 6,414.[14]

Nothing more was attempted that day as Grant accepted the fact that Hancock's effort north of the James River had fizzled. But, Grant asserted on August 17, it might be possible to shift a corps onto the Weldon and Petersburg Railroad to cut one of Lee's supply lines. Warren's command was conveniently placed to do this. "I do not want him to fight any unequal battles," Grant lectured Meade, "nor to assault fortifications. His movement should be more a reconnaisance [sic] in force with instructions to take advantage of any weakness of the enemy he may discover." Thinking of the larger strategic picture, Grant hoped Lee might be induced to recall some of his troops from the Shenandoah Valley to allow Sheridan to take the offensive there.[15]

Although Deep Bottom had become an inactive sector, Grant wanted Hancock to hold on a bit longer to draw Confederate attention from Warren's movement. Both sides skirmished, and the Rebels strengthened their works on August 17. The next day, before dawn, Warren began his advance toward the Weldon and Petersburg Railroad, easily made a lodgment on it, and began to dig in. Lee, meanwhile, planned a major counterattack against Hancock at Deep Bottom. While Rebel cavalry hit Gregg along Charles City Road, infantry units were to strike Birney around Fussell's Mill. The advance began at 5:00 P.M. on August 18, delayed by a mix-up of orders, and it accomplished nothing save to drive in the Union picket line.[16]

It was now time to shift Hancock and Birney to the south side of James

River. Hancock sent Mott's division at 8:00 P.M., August 18, with orders to relieve the Ninth Corps so Parke could help Warren on the railroad. Lee also sent Rooney Lee's cavalry division away from Deep Bottom to other duties on August 18. The next day, Grant could not resist the urge to push Hancock to exploit any advantage in the Rebel position west of Bailey's Creek. After careful consideration, the Second Corps commander organized an attack on the center with Barlow's division, led by Miles (who took command of the division when Barlow had to leave for health reasons). The center of Field's line hardly presented a clear advantage for an assault, and when informed of the details, Grant ordered Hancock to cancel it. The opponents quietly observed each other from opposite sides of Bailey's Creek for the rest of August 19 and all day of August 20. Hancock began to pull out that night under a heavy rain, crossing the pontoon bridge at Jones's Neck. His Second Corps was back at Petersburg by dawn as Birney's Tenth Corps troops resumed their former post at Bermuda Hundred.[17]

After six days, Hancock and Birney had only proved it was nearly impossible to trick Lee into fatally weakening any sector to protect the approach to Richmond by way of Deep Bottom. The Rebel earthworks south of New Market Heights and west of Bailey's Creek proved strong enough, when adequately manned, to foil even a heavy infantry attack. The Federals lost 2,901 men, compared to Confederate losses of about 1,500.[18]

## GLOBE TAVERN

Grant had limited hopes for Warren's success, based on the outcome of the Second and Sixth Corps advance in that region the previous June, and on his assessment of Warren as a field commander. Hancock, who retained Grant's good opinion, would be available to support Warren as soon as his Second Corps returned to the Petersburg side of the Appomattox River.[19]

Warren had pulled his men out of the trenches on the night of August 14 as Ninth Corps units shifted left to fill the space vacated. Now Parke held the sector from the crater to Jerusalem Plank Road, and the Eighteenth Corps held the line from the crater to the river. Meade instructed Warren to move out early on the morning of August 18, secure a position on the railroad, but not to attack fortifications.[20]

An extension of the Union line west of Jerusalem Plank Road thrust Warren into the flat land south of the junction of Vaughan Road and Halifax Road. It was a mix of open fields and dense patches of trees, primarily pines with minimal undergrowth. Globe Tavern, also known as the Yellow House, was the most prominent landmark. A country inn situated one and a half miles south of the junction of Vaughan and Halifax roads, and a short distance east of the

Weldon and Petersburg Railroad, it became the focal point of Warren's new position.[21]

The Fifth Corps set out at 5:00 A.M. of August 18 and easily grabbed the railroad near Globe Tavern four hours later. While some units advanced a third of a mile northward to establish a defensive position, using railroad ties and fence rails as the base of their parapet, others began tearing up track. The Federal position lay within a large cleared area that straddled the railroad and extended north of Globe Tavern for half a mile. A belt of trees 500 yards deep bordered the north side of this clearing. Ayres's division advanced northward to the west of the railroad while Crawford's division kept pace east of the track. Their skirmish lines penetrated this belt and crossed another open area containing a cornfield and the W. P. Davis House located at the junction of Vaughan Road and Halifax Road. The skirmishers stopped near the house, close to the southern edge of another belt of trees north of the junction, while Ayres's and Crawford's main lines took position just inside the southern edge of the first belt of trees, which lay between the Davis House and Globe Tavern.[22]

The Confederates responded immediately with only two brigades, but this meager force took Warren's corps by surprise. Heth conducted Davis's Mississippi brigade and Walker's Virginia brigade (led by Col. Robert M. Mayo) to a point just north of the W. P. Davis House. The Mississippians were west of the railroad, facing Ayres, while Mayo's Virginians opposed Crawford east of the track. The Confederates had no difficulty driving back the Union skirmishers and were fortunate to discover a gap of about 150 yards between Crawford's leftmost unit, the 16th Maine, and the railroad. Col. Peter Lyle, the brigade leader, had become confused while advancing through the woods and veered east. The Rebels drove both Ayres and Crawford back three-quarters of a mile, even though they were outnumbered three to one. Warren dispatched reinforcements and stopped Heth by 2:30 P.M. The Federals constructed temporary defenses where they halted, digging a shallow ditch and slashing trees. They lost 900 men that day, while inflicting only 350 casualties on the Confederates.[23]

The Federals were delayed in their effort to send reinforcements to Warren. Mott's division, which left Deep Bottom on the evening of August 18, did not arrive quickly enough to relieve Ninth Corps troops, so Grant decided to use the reserve units of Ord's Eighteenth Corps to relieve Willcox's division at 3:00 A.M. of August 18. Willcox began a rather slow, halting advance toward the west.[24]

The next day, three more Confederate brigades, under Mahone's direction, advanced on Warren in a more serious effort to dislodge him from the railroad. Mahone used the same ravine that had allowed him access to the open area of the Johnson farm in his attack against the Second Corps on June 22.

This time, instead of attacking east from the farm, he intended to head west into Warren's right flank. Colquitt's Georgia brigade occupied Mahone's left, Clingman's North Carolina brigade was on his right, and Weisiger's Virginia brigade acted as a reserve. At the same time, Heth again advanced from the north with Davis's brigade west of the track and Walker's brigade (now led by Col. William S. Christian) to the east.[25]

Warren's men made a mistake that almost proved fatal. They entrenched a line through the belt of woods that lay between Globe Tavern and the W. P. Davis House, advancing their skirmish line up to the northern edge of the belt, on the night of August 18. Instead of angling the skirmish line east by northeast, as Warren wanted it, subordinate commanders slanted it southeast. This allowed Mahone to advance closer to the main position without detection.[26]

Friday, August 19, was a "nasty, rainy, drizzling day," ill suited for operations, but the Confederates could not afford to wait while Warren consolidated his position on the railroad. Davis and Christian plunged into the belt of woods at about 4:00 P.M., easily pushed back the Union skirmishers, and became engaged in a confused fight with Warren's main line. The earthworks and Wainwright's artillery fire were the keys to blunting this attack.[27]

Mahone came close to duplicating his success on June 22, taking the Union picket line completely by surprise and easily driving it away. Bragg's brigade, which was stretched out in a thin line in an attempt to connect Warren's position with the Ninth Corps's left near Jerusalem Plank Road, was forced to run for the rear. Bragg's men held temporarily wherever they found shelter—at a fence with a drainage ditch on both sides of it, or in a barn—until they reached Globe Tavern itself. The right wing of Colquitt's brigade managed to reach the Weldon and Petersburg Railroad, well to the rear of those Fifth Corps troops who had just repulsed Davis and Christian.[28]

Willcox's division of the Ninth Corps now came to the rescue. It had finally reached Globe Tavern at 7:30 that morning and rested east of the building in the rain. Firing broke out just as the men were about to receive their ration of salted mackerel. While Humphrey's brigade advanced north and helped to repulse Christian, Hartranft's brigade advanced and blunted Mahone's drive with the help of Fifth Corps troops. White's division of the Ninth Corps now arrived and took position to Willcox's right. The fighting lasted until dusk, and some of Weisiger's men nearly ran out of ammunition while holding their position on the battlefield. Having failed to shatter the Union position on the Weldon and Petersburg Railroad, Mahone withdrew his brigades.[29]

It had been a close call for Warren. Federal losses totaled 3,000, of whom 2,700 were taken prisoner. The Confederates lost 600 men, half of them taken captive. But the Yankee grip on the railroad remained secure. The rain poured down that night, filling the trenches with two inches of mud and water, but Grant was eager to make more of the army's success. "I want now principally the enemy so occupied that he cannot send off any of his forces" to the Shenandoah, he informed his subordinates. If Lee wanted to attack Warren again, he should have to pay for it by a corresponding Union attack. "There must be a weak point somewhere," Grant concluded.[30]

The Confederates were determined to try again. Mahone formulated a new plan to hit Warren with six brigades from the west, instead of the east, while Heth attacked from the north with three brigades. Far more complex, in that Mahone's force would have to make a wide flanking march away from supporting troops, the attack had to be postponed until August 21.[31]

Meanwhile, Warren was determined to strengthen his position on the railroad by digging in more securely. Grant did not necessarily want the Fifth Corps to stay forever. "I am not so particular about holding the Weldon Road permanently as I am to destroy it effectually & to force the Enemy to attack us with advantages on our side," he informed Meade. As tactical commander on the battlefield, Warren correctly saw that coming to grips with the roving Rebel brigades in this tangled environment was difficult. Far better it was to protect his men behind strong fieldworks and make permanent possession of the track the measure of success in the Fourth Offensive.[32]

First, Warren closed the gap between his corps and Jerusalem Plank Road that Mahone had exploited on August 19. His engineer officers laid out a new line from a point on the railroad north of Globe Tavern, extending it eastward to the plank road, on the morning of August 20. They also extended it west of the Weldon Railroad and then angled the line south, parallel to and a quarter-mile from the track. All day, Fifth Corps troops dug in along this line as Wainwright planted his guns. In the evening, all units gave up their forward positions and retired to the new line. Ayres's division partially demolished its trench in the south edge of the belt of woods, 700 yards forward of Warren's new line. His men constructed abatis and strung telegraph wire among the stumps near the southern edge of the belt. The new line was largely in the open area around Globe Tavern but located on a gentle rise of ground.[33]

Under Warren's personal guidance, the Fifth Corps constructed works that would defy any Confederate attempt to retake the railroad. The Federals did so in the worst weather imaginable. The rain "came down in sheets," recorded James P. Sullivan of the 6th Wisconsin, "everything soaking wet; no fires; no coffee; lived on condensed milk and hardtack." The food shortage arose from the weather, too, for the rain had so damaged the roads that supply trains were stuck.[34]

The suffering soldiers found relief the next morning, which dawned "clear and bright." Warren explained to Meade that his new position was only a temporary expedient, even though very strong, to hold against any attacks that may occur in the immediate future. The landscape between Globe Tavern and Jerusalem Plank Road was too wooded to allow his engineer officers to quickly see where to place the permanent extension of the Union line. His entire corps was ensconced in an area no more than one mile square. Warren suggested that Hancock's Second Corps assume a similar, compact position somewhere between the Tavern and the plank road, and then he and Hancock could extend out to connect with each other. Grant, however, thought only in terms of offense. He suggested to Meade that Warren should advance and cut off any Confederate force that tried to march around his left flank, separating it from Petersburg. Meade wisely allowed Warren to make his own dispositions, knowing that Grant had limited knowledge of the situation at Globe Tavern.[35]

The Confederates prepared all day of August 20 and part of the next day for their biggest strike at Warren. Heth replaced Davis and Christian with fresh brigades, Cooke's and MacRae's Tar Heels, and added McAfee's North Carolina brigade (commanded by Lt. Col. John L. Harris). MacRae took position west of the railroad, with Harris to the east and Cooke in support behind Harris.[36]

Heth's three brigades set out when the artillery opened to signal the attack on August 21. MacRae outpaced Harris, having slightly less tangled vegetation to traverse. His men made their way through the maze of wired stumps and scattered abatis and then charged across the open space fronting Warren's new line. Sergeant Sullivan of the 6th Wisconsin noted that the Tar Heels came on "with their heads down and arms at a trail," but Wainwright's artillery fire stopped them halfway to the works. MacRae's skirmishers took shelter in a convenient ravine, but the rest of the command retired to the belt of woods and positioned itself behind the partially razed Union line.[37]

Harris and Cooke had a great deal of difficulty burrowing through the tangled woods east of the railroad and emerged at the southern edge of the trees after MacRae's repulse. The abatis and wire apparently was thicker here than west of the track, for neither brigade managed to break through the entanglements. The color-bearer of the 49th North Carolina "was up in the tree tops with the flag in one hand and fighting his way through the limbs with the other," recalled W. A. Day. Harris's men received heavy artillery fire both from the Federals and, inadvertently, from their own gunners, so officers ordered their men back into the woods. They took shelter behind the partially razed Union line until dusk, when all three of Heth's brigades retired.[38]

All Confederate hopes now rested on Mahone's flank attack. He moved six brigades around Warren's left without detection and lined them up straddling the Vaughan Wagon Road. Mahone's command faced northeast because, according to latest intelligence, the Union line angled toward the southwest after it crossed Weldon Railroad, and he planned to hit it squarely on the flank. But this was Warren's old line, abandoned as soon as his new, heavily entrenched position was finished on the evening of August 20. Mahone was surprised during the course of his advance to discover that the Federals had fallen back several hundred yards and were now facing due west. He adjusted his formation slightly toward the east to confront this new line head-on and sent Hagood's South Carolina brigade from his far right to find Warren's flank.[39]

Struggling through "thick and tangled woods and swamps," Finegan's Florida brigade retreated "in confusion and disorder" upon closing with the new line. Harris's Mississippi brigade, led by Col. Joseph M. Jayne, double-quicked through Finegan's broken remnants. Some of Jayne's men, members of the 12th and 16th Mississippi, managed to break into the works but were repulsed as the rest of the brigade retired. To the left, Sanders's Alabama brigade also reached a point close to the works but had to fall back. Behind the entrenchments, Ellis Spear of the 20th Maine marveled at the novelty of repelling attacks from a fortified position. Many of his men became so excited they crossed the parapet and gathered up dozens of prisoners.[40]

Hagood nearly lost his whole brigade while advancing toward the Union position. He took the fortified Yankee skirmish line, which was placed 250 yards before the main line, but found upon approaching it that he had failed to turn the Union flank. Moreover, Federal artillery to his right, placed in a pronounced bastion of the line, had a clear shot at his men, and he had no connection to the rest of Mahone's command to the left. Nevertheless, the Confederates advanced against Hofmann's brigade of Cutler's division. Hagood's left wing became separated from the right by a ravine, and it also became entangled in the abatis thickly placed in front of the line. The works here were five feet tall, and the ditch in front was ten feet wide.[41]

Hagood's right wing also came close to the Union line and then stalled. Much to everyone's surprise, a lone Union officer, Dennis B. Daley of Cutler's staff, rode out with a white flag, demanding that the Rebels surrender. Some men dropped their guns, while others stopped firing but held on to their weapons. The Yankee put on such a show of confidence that no one seemed to know how to react. Finally, Hagood demanded that the officer surrender. When he refused, Hagood shot him, took his horse, and led his men in a fighting retreat through encircling Federals to the rear. He saved his command but lost 449 out of 740 men engaged.[42]

Mahone failed to reclaim the railroad, and Lee authorized no more attempts. The battle of Globe Tavern, August 18–21, resulted in 4,300 Federal casualties and 2,300 Confederate losses. Warren was jubilant, claiming credit for his earthworks and the effective fire of his artillery, while the Confederates were stunned at their bloody failure. "I heard some say, they were not going to charge breastworks, like they had been doing," reported a band member in MacRae's brigade. "I don't blame them either." Hagood also was appalled by the results of his near-catastrophe on August 21, becoming "sensitive to even a suspicion of recklessly wielding a blade so highly tempered and uselessly hacking it against impossibilities."[43]

## REAMS'S STATION

When the Second Corps became available to support operations along the Weldon and Petersburg Railroad, Grant decided not to post it at an intermediate point between Globe Tavern and Jerusalem Plank Road, as Warren had suggested. Instead, it made a second, detached lodgment on the railroad several miles south of the Fifth Corps. Grant probably wanted to lure the Confederates into another attack, hoping the outcome would duplicate the drubbing they received at Globe Tavern. "I never before saw Grant so intensely anxious *to do something*," reported staff member George K. Leet. "He appears determined to try every possible expedient. His plans are good but the great difficulty is that *our troops cannot be relied on*. The failure to take advantage of opportunities pain and chafe him beyond anything that I have ever before known him to manifest."[44]

Miles's division reached Reams's Station by early afternoon, August 23, after tearing up track for some distance north of that point. His men continued to destroy the railroad three miles south, as far as Malone's Crossing, while Gibbon's division reached the area by midmorning of August 24. Hancock was supposed to tear up track down to the crossing of Rowanty Creek, eight miles south of Reams's Station; but Meade sent a report that thousands of Confederate troops were moving around Warren toward Reams's, and the Second Corps consolidated its position at the station. Hancock had only two divisions, consisting of 6,000 infantrymen, plus 2,000 cavalrymen and sixteen field guns. Mott's division remained in the Petersburg lines, but Warren held three divisions of the Ninth Corps near Globe Tavern that were available as support.[45]

Unfortunately, Hancock did little to prepare for an attack. He failed to call up the Ninth Corps supports, ignored the yawning gap between his command and the Fifth Corps, and did not properly fortify his position. Hancock seems to have assumed that the old fieldworks already in place at Reams's Station were good enough for his purpose. Sixth Corps troops had constructed them the previous June when sent to support the return of Wilson's and Kautz's cavalry from their raid on the South Side Railroad and the Richmond and Danville Railroad. Kautz's division initiated the fieldwork construction on June 29, and

Sixth Corps infantrymen continued it. They also tore up much of the track and burned the station.[46]

Lt. George K. Dauchy of the 12th New York Independent Battery thought the fieldworks at Reams's Station "were hurriedly thrown up, badly constructed, and poorly located." Rather than use the railroad embankment, the Sixth Corps troops had placed the line twenty to thirty yards west of it, nearly parallel to the track. This line ran about 700 yards north and south. The railroad embankment, which had a cut on the right thirteen feet deep and a fill on the left six feet high, impeded the flow of ammunition from the caissons east of the railroad to the guns in the works, and it also impeded the movement of infantrymen to and from the trench. Depot Road ran through the center of this line; a lone traverse extended to the rear halfway between it and the southern end of the trench. A connecting line extended eastward across the track for 1,000 yards at the northern end of the line. The two lines were not connected; a twenty-yard gap existed at the angle, and a patch of woods lay only about fifteen feet in front of the northward-facing line.[47]

Placed on a foundation of fence rails, the parapet was not revetted and had eroded until it was no more than three feet high in many places. The parapet was stronger between the traverse and the southern end of the westward-facing line, but very low north of the traverse. Overall, no one was impressed by the fortifications. Daniel Chisholm of the 116th Pennsylvania called them "very poor works," while Francis Walker of Hancock's staff referred to them as "this most unfortunate line." Charles Wainwright rode south to visit the Second Corps and spent an hour at Hancock's headquarters. "His lines struck me as very badly laid out and quite untenable in case of a strong attack." Yet little was done to improve the position beyond cutting some timber in front of the westward-facing line and making an abatis. Walker contended that Hancock had no idea of being attacked, but the corps commander had a responsibility to prepare for anything. If his men had taken a position that had no previously constructed works, they likely would have taken the time to fortify it properly, but everyone seemed to be easily lured into thinking that these eroded parapets would do in a pinch.[48]

Hancock was so unaware of impending danger that he sent Gibbon's division to tear up more track south of Reams's Station on the morning of August 25. The Confederates attacked the cavalrymen who screened his work, forcing Gibbon to come to their aid. Then orders arrived to return to Reams's Station. Gibbon's men heard the sound of heavy firing as they approached.[49]

The Confederates had already launched their first attack on Hancock's position. Wade Hampton had reported that the Federals were vulnerable and urged an assault, which Lee quickly approved. A. P. Hill took eight brigades in a roundabout circuit to bypass Warren at Globe Tavern. Suffering from poor health, Hill charged Wilcox with managing the attack. Wilcox placed three brigades north of Depot Road and one south of it and ordered them forward at about 2:00 P.M., before the rest of Hill's strike force reached the field. They drove back the Union skirmish line, but the three brigades north of Depot Road were stopped by infantry and artillery fire in the open field that fronted the westward-facing line. McGowan's South Carolina brigade, south of Depot Road, received orders to hold its position within sight of the earthworks to draw Yankee attention. This gave McGowan's sharpshooter battalion the opportunity to begin picking off everyone who exposed his head above the meager parapet. South of Reams's Station, Hampton's cavalry followed up Gibbon's withdrawal and also heard the attack. The troopers hastily threw together logs and brush to make a breastwork and tried to dig in as best they could.[50]

Soon after the first Confederate assault, Hancock received a message from Meade authorizing him to pull away from Reams's Station and connect with Warren. If this message had arrived earlier, he might have acted on it, but Francis Walker later commented that his commander stubbornly refused to leave the field after battle was joined. Moreover, a lot of battery horses were already being shot by the Rebel skirmishers, and it would not be easy to disengage from such awkwardly constructed defenses under fire. He informed Meade of his intention to stay until dark, prompting the army commander to position Willcox's division east of Reams's Station so Hancock could call on it for help if needed.[51]

While these arrangements were under way, Heth brought two more brigades of Hill's strike force to the battlefield. Weisiger's and Sanders's brigades arrived even later that day. Heth took over management of affairs from Wilcox, arranging four brigades north of Depot Road. Cooke's and Lane's North Carolina brigades (the latter under James Conner) were in the center, with only the right half of Cooke's command in the open and the rest, along with Conner, in thick woods. Scales's North Carolina brigade took position to the left rear of Conner, and MacRae's North Carolina brigade was to the right rear of Cooke. While abatis stood in Conner's and Cooke's way, in the edge of the woods, MacRae was in the open and 300 yards from the Federals.[52]

Confederate sharpshooters continued to harass the Federals while the infantry took position. Every man in McGowan's battalion fired 160 rounds over the course of five hours. At first, the Federals responded vigorously, but then they slacked off until there was virtually no return fire. Confederate marksmen targeted artillery horses, shooting nearly all in the 10th Massachusetts Battery, and some were "riddled by a dozen balls." The Confederate skirmishers also made several dashes to get closer and further unnerve the Yankees. Heth arranged for a twenty-minute artillery barrage by eight guns beginning at 5:20 P.M.[53]

Twenty minutes later, Heth ordered 1,750 men forward. All of Conner's brigade and the left wing of Cooke's struggled through dense woods and emerged to find at least thirty yards of abatis skirting the eastern edge of the trees. It took at least ten minutes for the men to claw their way through this entanglement under artillery fire, only to find that the open field was too hotly covered by the Yankees. Conner's brigade, if not Cooke's left, then retired to its starting point.[54]

Cooke's right wing stalled, waiting for the left to emerge from the trees, but this frustrated MacRae, who was eager to press home the attack. His patience snapped and he pushed forward his brigade, ignoring the movements of his comrades to the left. MacRae had prepared his men for this moment, telling them he wanted the brigade to move swiftly across the open field without halting to fire a shot. It straddled Depot Road, aiming at a sector of the Union parapet held by the left wing of Byron's Consolidated Brigade (north of the road) and the right wing of Broady's brigade (south of the road). Byron's men had become demoralized by the Confederate sharpshooting and offered weak resistance, enabling most of MacRae's troops to enter the line. On his right, however, the 66th New York of Broady's command fired heavily into his rightmost regiment, the 47th North Carolina, which was forced to stop in the open and trade fire. The New Yorkers weakened when it became apparent that the enemy had breached the line north of Depot Road, enabling the 47th to cross the parapet.[55]

This was the turning point of the battle of Reams's Station. There would be plenty of hard, confused fighting to come, but MacRae's limited penetration of Hancock's position altered the character of the battle. The Tar Heels found it impossible to continue advancing eastward. The Federals who gave up their sector of the line merely retired to the rear and took shelter behind the railroad embankment. So MacRae extended the breach by advancing southward along the trench, opening up a wide hole for support troops to enter. He organized three columns—one to advance in the trench, one in front of the line, and the third atop the parapet. The latter course indicates that few Federals behind the railroad embankment were firing at the Confederates. MacRae's men ejected one Yankee unit after another, capturing Sleeper's 10th Massachusetts Battery in a hand-to-hand fight. The Tar Heels stopped at the traverse, where the 4th New York Heavy Artillery was sheltered, but McGowan now came into play. He ordered his South Carolinians forward and smashed into the line south of the traverse, capturing hundreds of New Yorkers.[56]

McGowan's attack also harassed the right wing of Gibbon's division, which had taken position to screen Reams's Station from the south only a short time before. Upon reaching the area after the repulse of the first Confederate attack, Gibbon placed his men from the southern end of the westward-facing line across the railroad and Halifax Road, extending his line toward the northeast. This created a shallow angle on his right that could easily be caught in a cross fire. Moreover, his men were able to construct only minimal earthworks. George D. Bowen of the 12th New Jersey pulled up sorghum canes as a substitute for logs and piled dirt over them. Without tools, the men scooped up the sandy soil with their hands, plates, and cups. When McGowan attacked, the extreme right of Gibbon's line received fire to its rear, forcing the Federals there to jump their meager parapet and take shelter in front of the line. Then they received fire from Hampton's skirmish line south of their position and were compelled to return to the proper side of the earthwork.[57]

MacRae's success inspired other Confederates to renewed efforts. Conner and Cooke tried another push through the woods and abatis. The 37th North Carolina of Conner's brigade penetrated the works between Byron's Consolidated Brigade and Lynch's brigade to its right. Miles tried to push forward his second line from behind the railroad embankment to seal the breach, but the men refused even though the Confederates were only twenty or thirty yards away. Lt. Col. Arthur Russell Curtis of the 20th Massachusetts claimed that his comrades were taken by surprise. They could not see across the embankment and had no idea the Confederates had penetrated the works until they were nearly surrounded.[58]

Frantic efforts to save the position followed. Gibbon received orders to help Miles restore his line, but his attempt to do so was a failure. Most units of the Second Division left their parapet and slogged north by northwest, with no clear idea what they were up against. When the troops on Gibbon's left received enfilade fire from those Rebels who now held the westward-facing line, they quickly retired to the southern line. A portion of his center, elements of Smyth's brigade, advanced all the way to the northern face and cooperated with Miles in a counterattack that confined the Rebels to the narrow space between the western line and the railroad embankment. Meanwhile, Hancock patched together a new line about 300 yards east of the railroad.[59]

Heth sent in more troops to help Conner, Cooke, MacRae, and McGowan. Scales advanced to the left of Conner, and Sanders's and Weisiger's brigades came up behind the three original brigades to fill the space between the Union west face and the railroad with more men.[60]

Hampton's dismounted troopers launched the final Confederate attack at Reams's Station, against Gibbon's division. "Never marched men over worse ground than we on this occasion," reported G. W. Beale of the 9th Virginia Cavalry. "For fifty yards at times my feet did not touch the ground. We had to walk over felled trees or crouch down to get through them." Yet Hampton's left wing crossed the minor parapet because Gibbon's rightmost unit had evacuated the line due to McGowan's capture of the angle. Hampton's right initially encountered stiff resistance, but the Federal position collapsed when the men realized their flank was in the air. "The whole division seemed suddenly to go to pieces," recalled Gibbon. "It is too pitiful a subject to dwell upon," admitted Francis Walker years after the war. Gibbon managed to reassemble most of his men some distance north of the line as Hampton's cavalrymen halted in the works.[61]

During the lull that followed, Hancock held a consultation with his division leaders. Everyone talked stubbornly of counterattacking and regaining lost ground, but Gibbon stated that his division was at the end of its rope and could not be relied on. Hancock decided to hold east of the railroad and wait until dark offered a chance to withdraw. A short time later, his two divisions marched east to make contact with Willcox and use the comparatively fresh troops of the Ninth Corps to cover their retreat.[62]

The Second Corps lost 600 killed and wounded, and 2,000 were taken prisoner; it also lost nine guns and twelve regimental flags, on August 25. Hill's command suffered only 720 casualties. Hancock was deeply humiliated, losing much of his confidence in the corps. Three major factors account for the defeat. First, the ranks were filled by a lot of newly inducted men with little experience and less will to fight. Many of them refused to expose themselves above the parapet and gave up by the hundreds as soon as the Confederates appeared inside the defenses. Second, MacRae's fierce determination to lead his Tar Heels into the Union position at any cost was a watershed in the course of the battle, and then he opened the way for other Confederate brigades to enter the Federal position. Third, the field defenses at Reams's Station failed to serve Hancock's needs.[63]

As Hampton's cavalrymen buried the dead on the field, using trenches as ready-made graves, everyone began to feel the effects of Reams's Station. Charles Wainwright correctly guessed that the battle would inspire the Confederates following their thrashing at Globe Tavern. James Conner informed his sister that it was "the first time in this campaign that we have taken breastworks, and our troops had begun to believe that they could not take them. They regarded storming works as belonging to an early period of the War and played out now." Grant gave up plans to send more troops farther south along the Weldon and Petersburg Railroad and warned Meade to prepare the Fifth

Corps for a possible attack from the south. That attack never materialized, for Lee called off further counteroffensive operations.[64]

The Fourth Offensive was a mixed bag of results that greatly favored the Federals. Lee had relied on improvised responses to Union moves, and in two of the three engagements of this offensive, that tactic continued to work. By shifting heavy forces north of the James, he was able to neutralize Hancock's second attempt to use Deep Bottom as a springboard to wreck the Virginia Central Railroad and to crash through the defenses near Chaffin's Bluff. The improvised counteroffensive at Reams's Station worked spectacularly, with the same results that followed Mahone's June 22–23 counteroffensive and his handling of the crater battle.

But those same tactics utterly failed at Globe Tavern, and Warren has never received the credit he deserves from either his contemporaries or historians for making this part of the Fourth Offensive a success. The key here was Warren's obsession with defensive tactics bolstered by heavy fieldworks. Luck helped him, too, in that Mahone failed to fully exploit the disposition of the Union picket line on August 19 and did not know of the new, heavily fortified line on August 21. But luck had nothing to do with the fact that Warren foresaw the need to thoroughly prepare his position with fortifications, shielded in places by wire entanglements, and Hancock ignored this need at Reams's Station.

Warren transformed a complete Union failure into a limited but important success. Grant paid attention to its lesson. On June 22, he had tried to accomplish too much in one movement with inadequate resources. Hancock's efforts to use Deep Bottom to operate from the right flank proved a failure on two occasions, and Burnside's attempt to smash through the Confederate center on July 30 proved disastrous. Warren now pointed the way for future operations: make short movements to the left to extend the line in stages, something the Army of the Potomac was fully capable of doing. Ironically, Grant had always envisioned Warren's lodgment on the Weldon and Petersburg Railroad to be temporary, to serve as a lure to draw the Rebels out of their trenches and to destroy track. He would have been content if Warren had evacuated his position at Globe Tavern. Warren was the officer who initiated efforts to ensure a permanent lodgment there and to extend the existing Union line east of Jerusalem Plank Road to meet it. To his credit, Grant accepted this initiative and continued Warren's line of operations for the rest of the campaign. After two months of futile experiments, the Federals at last hit upon an ultimately winning tactic at Petersburg.

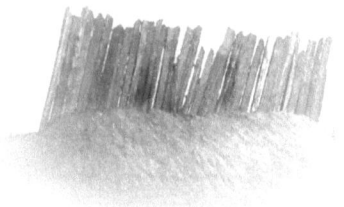

CHAPTER ELEVEN

## *September*

As early as August 22, the day after Mahone's last attack, Warren felt that the ground his men occupied at Globe Tavern was as good as any for a permanent line. He proposed the construction of a large fort and a strong curtain connecting it to Jerusalem Plank Road. If Grant wanted further offensive operations, Warren could fill the fort with a garrison and take the rest of the Fifth Corps toward the Richmond and Danville Railroad to draw Lee's men out of their works. Grant mulled it over and decided by August 25 to call off the Fourth Offensive. "I desire to hold the Weldon railroad as long as possible," he informed Meade. "Redoubts should be constructed on Warrens [sic] left and the line generally strengthened."[1]

### FEDERAL EARTHWORK CONSTRUCTION

Even before Grant's decision, Warren pulled his men "a few rods" to the rear on August 23 and started to dig a permanent line, leveling the works they had defended two days earlier. "This looks like staying here," thought William Ray of the 7th Wisconsin. "We will soon have [the defenses] as strong as those in front of Petersburg."[2]

Many units slashed the trees for a couple of hundred yards before their new position. Second-growth pine about six inches in diameter fronted Gwyn's brigade of Griffin's division. Each regiment sent out many men who were poorly skilled with the ax. They felled trees in every direction imaginable, yelling "'look out'" every few seconds and making everyone nervous. Trunks often fell against standing trees, creating a further hazard. But Ellis Spear of the 20th Maine had just received 100 recruits from eastern Maine who knew how to work timber. They chopped all the trees nearly through and then finished cutting those closest to the Union position. These fell and knocked the rest down in one swoop, all pointing in the right direction.[3]

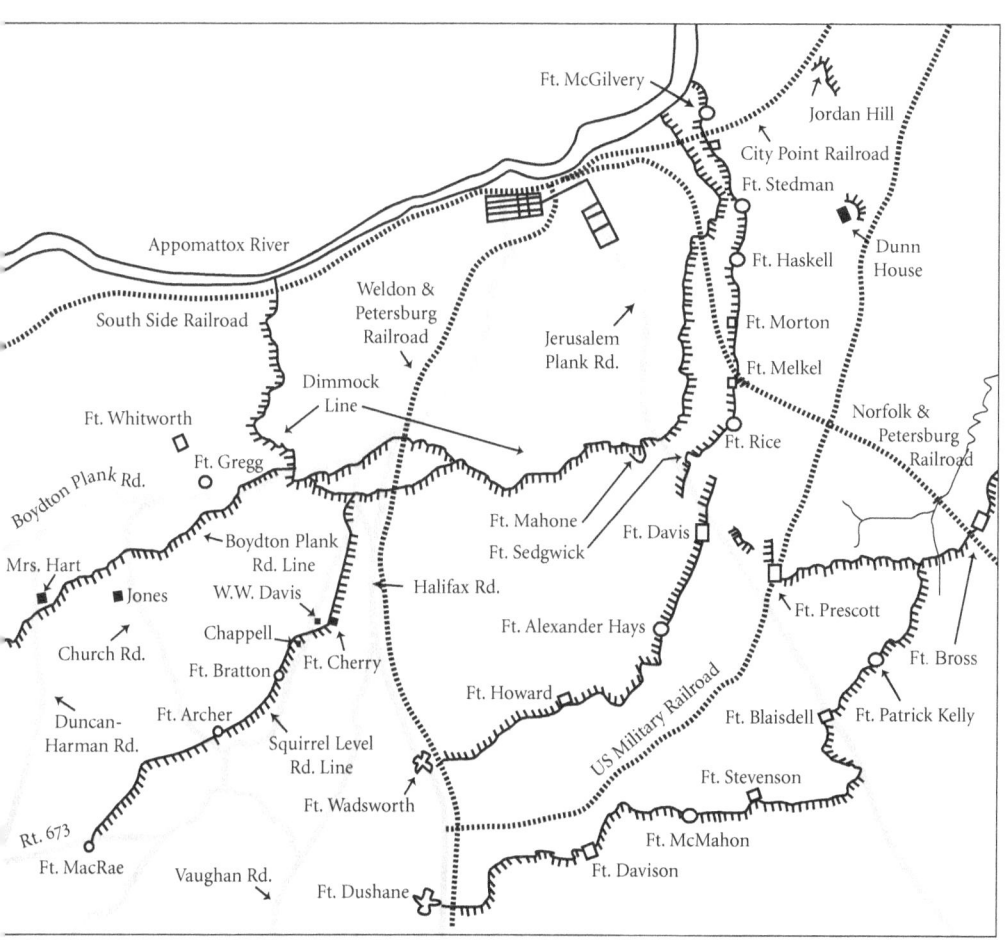

Federal Works from Jerusalem Plank Road to Weldon and
Petersburg Railroad, August 22–September 28, 1864

The construction of the line itself began with the major enclosed works. William Benyaurd and Charles Lydecker laid out the large fort Warren wanted, later designated Fort Wadsworth, on August 26. Company B, U.S. Engineer Battalion, broke ground the next day, but details from Crawford's division dug most of the work. Fort Wadsworth straddled both the Halifax Road and the Weldon and Petersburg Railroad. It had four bastions with a ditch eighteen feet deep and fifteen feet wide, and embrasures for sixteen guns. Warren complained to Duane that Benyaurd and Lydecker had laid it out in a way that "diminishes the interior space . . . increases the length of the parapet and labor of construction without benefit, and increases the dead spaces in front of the curtain. Your west front was so far from meeting flanking principles that I remodeled it myself." A company of the 50th New York Engineers revetted the parapets and traverses and made platforms, bombproofs, and magazines, as well as the abatis and wire entanglements in front of the work. The engineers essentially completed Fort Wadsworth by September 24.[4]

Parke's Ninth Corps filled most of the four-mile space between Warren's corps at Globe Tavern and Hancock's command at Jerusalem Plank Road. His men also fell back a short distance before starting to dig in. They began by slashing timber in front and then digging a curtain studded with small, mostly enclosed works. Officers placed pickets well forward of the new line to protect the labor crews, and they positioned artillery to the rear to fire over their heads if needed. The soldiers paced themselves by working a half-hour and resting for thirty minutes. They also leveled the temporary works in their front.[5]

Hancock's Second Corps extended the line from Fort Davis toward the vicinity of the Strong House, about one-third of the way from Jerusalem Plank Road to Globe Tavern. Engineers started a large work, later designated Fort Alexander Hays, about 250 yards north of the house. Mott's division provided as many as 1,300 men to dig the connecting line between the fort and the plank road. Fort Alexander Hays was nearly done by late September. It had a bombproof and magazine, two traverses, and sandbag parapets to protect the guns mounted en barbette.[6]

Warren started another work, later designated Fort Dushane, at a spot west of the railroad and south of Fort Wadsworth. Company B, U.S. Engineer Battalion, and elements of the 50th New York Engineers started the skilled work on August 30, while 1,000 infantrymen performed the unskilled labor. Within four weeks, they constructed the defenses and built a bombproof capable of holding 600 men, in addition to eight traverses (half of which also had a magazine built into them). The engineers used iron rails from the Weldon and Petersburg Railroad to clad the outer walls of the magazines and traverses, placing abatis and a wire entanglement by September 17.[7]

Meade extended the southward-facing secondary line west of Jerusalem Plank Road to prevent the enemy from turning Warren's flank. Michler staked out a line from Fort Dushane to the Williams House, which lay just west of Jerusalem Plank Road and one and a half miles south of the west end of the current Secondary Line at Fort Prescott. From the Williams House, the new line angled northeast to intersect the old Secondary Line halfway between the plank road and Blackwater Swamp. The U.S. Engineer Battalion began to lay out five enclosed works along this extension of the Secondary Line by September 1.[8]

Three days later, an intelligence report reached army headquarters that increased Meade's fear of a turning movement. A scout who had ridden to Gordonsville, many miles northwest of Richmond, reported that Early's entire command was moving from the Shenandoah Valley to rejoin Lee. Early seemed "likely [to] make an attack on or near the Jerusalem plank road." Grant saw this as an opportunity. He wanted the lines stripped of men to throw as many troops as possible into an open field fight with Early, leaving only 2,000 men per mile in the trenches east of the plank road and only the garrisons of enclosed works west of it.[9]

Grant also wanted the new Secondary Line pushed to completion in case the plan to intercept Early failed. The forts were laid out but not yet constructed; engineer officers quickly staked the connecting infantry line between Fort Dushane and the Williams House on September 5 so that Willcox's division of the Ninth Corps could start digging it. Willcox postponed work on his northward-facing line and shifted most of his resources to the Secondary Line. The black division of the Ninth Corps was assigned in whole to this project. The men slashed trees in front of the Secondary Line, and thirty wagonloads of logs provided the regular engineers with material to make revetments at Fort Stevenson. Hancock assumed the responsibility of constructing the works near the Williams House and all the way to the old Secondary Line.[10]

On September 6, deserters from several Confederate divisions told Union officers that Early had turned Warren's left the night before. Warren did not believe it, but the Federals prepared for action. Hancock issued a circular to his divisions urging the men to greater exertions. "A few hours more of such labor as has been performed during the past twenty-four hours will have put the line in a state of defense to render it easy to repulse any attack of the enemy." But such an attack never came because Early had never left the Shenandoah.[11]

The Second, Fifth, and Ninth Corps completed the Secondary Line after Early's threat evaporated. They nearly finished the enclosed works by September 24. The engineer troops placed three magazines in Fort Stevenson, one of the largest works on the Secondary Line, and used 300 gabions along with logs to revet the parapet.[12]

The Secondary Line was an impressive piece of work. William Ray commented that those defenses on the northward-facing line were "poor by the side of them." The enclosed works along the Secondary Line were large because the Federals wanted to hold the position with these garrisons alone in case of emergency. While most of the emplacements in these enclosed works were embrasured, a minority of them (for example, one of five at Fort Patrick Kelly and two of six at Battery No. 40) were en barbette.[13]

When finished, the new entrenchments inspired confidence among the Federals. "If General *Lee* could see these works," mused a man in the 50th New

York Engineers, "he would bid good bye to any hopes, if he has any, of ever taking this line." The northward-facing line and the Secondary Line essentially formed a fortified camp one mile deep, north to south, offering protection against attack from all directions. Combined with what had already been constructed east of Jerusalem Plank Road and south of the Appomattox River, the Federals now had close to ten miles of earthworks at Petersburg. Seven forts and batteries constituted the northward-facing line, while nineteen works made up the flank protection and the southward-facing line. The Yankees constructed 6,700 feet of bridges and corduroyed 2,000 yards of roads and one-third of their covered ways within this fortified camp.[14]

Hancock and Warren recommended that army headquarters assign names to the forts early in September, and Hancock further suggested that a sign be placed inside every work with its name prominently shown. Meade responded by requiring each corps commander to recommend the names of officers who had fallen in Virginia since May 5, 1864. Army headquarters issued a circular on September 21 naming all the works from the Appomattox River to the Weldon and Petersburg Railroad and designating numbers of artillery pieces and soldiers as permanent garrisons. There were 41 batteries, with 4 to 6 embrasures in each, all designated with numbers. There were also 20 redoubts, lettered A to T, and all additionally designated with the names of fallen officers. Two of the redoubts were called bastion forts (Wadsworth and Dushane), and one was designated as a fort (Sedgwick). Most of the redoubts had 6 to 10 embrasures, although Sedgwick had 25, Stevenson had 27, and Bross had 20. Michler produced a complete map of the lines and prepared plans and profiles of the major forts, as well as overseeing the painting of signboards.[15]

Meade supported his new position west of Jerusalem Plank Road by extending the Army Line to Globe Tavern. Grant readily approved. "I do not want to give up the Weldon road, if it can be avoided, until we get Richmond. That may be months yet." The engineers laid nine miles of track during the first ten days of September, with five new stations (Birney, Meade, Hancock, Parke, and Warren). A half-mile section was exposed to Confederate view because the Federals wanted to save time by not placing it farther south. The engineers sank the track five feet and built a protective berm to give the trains eleven feet of coverage. The line from City Point to Warren's position was fourteen and a half miles long. The first trains reached Warren Station, only 100 yards south of Globe Tavern, on September 11.[16]

In addition to the labor expended on the extension of the Union line west of Jerusalem Plank Road, Grant wanted to protect the army's logistical support system. He ordered new defenses built at Harrison's Landing on the north bank of the James River, four miles downstream from City Point. Barnard laid out the line on August 30 for a garrison of two infantry companies, a section of artillery, and a cavalry squadron. Eighteenth Corps troops dug the works by late September, consisting of a small redoubt north of the Berkeley mansion and connecting infantry lines from both flanks back to the river. The line totaled 1,412 yards with a parapet only four and a half feet tall.[17]

Grant feared for the safety of City Point when Wade Hampton conducted a daring raid behind Union lines and stole a herd of cattle from the Yankees. The Beefsteak Raid of September 14–17 involved a circuitous ride from the Petersburg line along Boydton Plank Road, then across country to Stony Creek Station on the Weldon and Petersburg Railroad, well south of Globe Tavern. Hampton pushed on northeastward, crossing Blackwater Swamp and making his way to Prince George Court House. Here he was only four miles to the rear of the Union line at Petersburg and six miles due south of City Point. Hampton rode to the Federal cattle corral, located four miles east of City Point near the south bank of the James River. He stole 2,486 head of beef while losing only sixty-one men by the time he herded the cattle back to Petersburg.[18]

Hampton's raid dramatized the fact that City Point was inadequately fortified. A redoubt and a short connecting line located relatively close to the wharves had been built in early May, but nothing guarded against an approach from the east, between Blackwater Swamp and the James River. To close this gap, Meade sent Michler to reconnoiter the country and plan a defensive line with the help of Harwood and Lydecker. They started with the keystone of the new line, a redoubt and battery near Prince George Court House, but postponed work to consult with Benham about erecting another, longer line to cover the western approaches to City Point. This proposed line would have to connect with the one Michler's subordinates were building. Benham scouted the location for his part of the project on September 19, placing it two miles from the wharves at City Point to allow room for expanding the logistical complex. In consultation with the other engineer officers, Benham recommended that the two lines intersect at Bailey's Creek, near Old Court House. Benham's line would head northwestward from there to the Appomattox River, while Michler's line would go due north to the James River, fitting City Point snugly within a fortified pocket. Harwood and Lydecker resumed work on Michler's line by September 27, employing Company C, U.S. Engineer Battalion, but Benham delayed for weeks before shaping up his line.[19]

Engineers and infantrymen alike scurried to build these new earthworks, yet they also had to repair and improve the preexisting works. Labor parties drained the ditch and constructed new magazines, embrasures, and gun platforms at Fort Davis. They also constructed fresh abatis and a new row of pointed stakes, connected with "iron wire," at the work.[20]

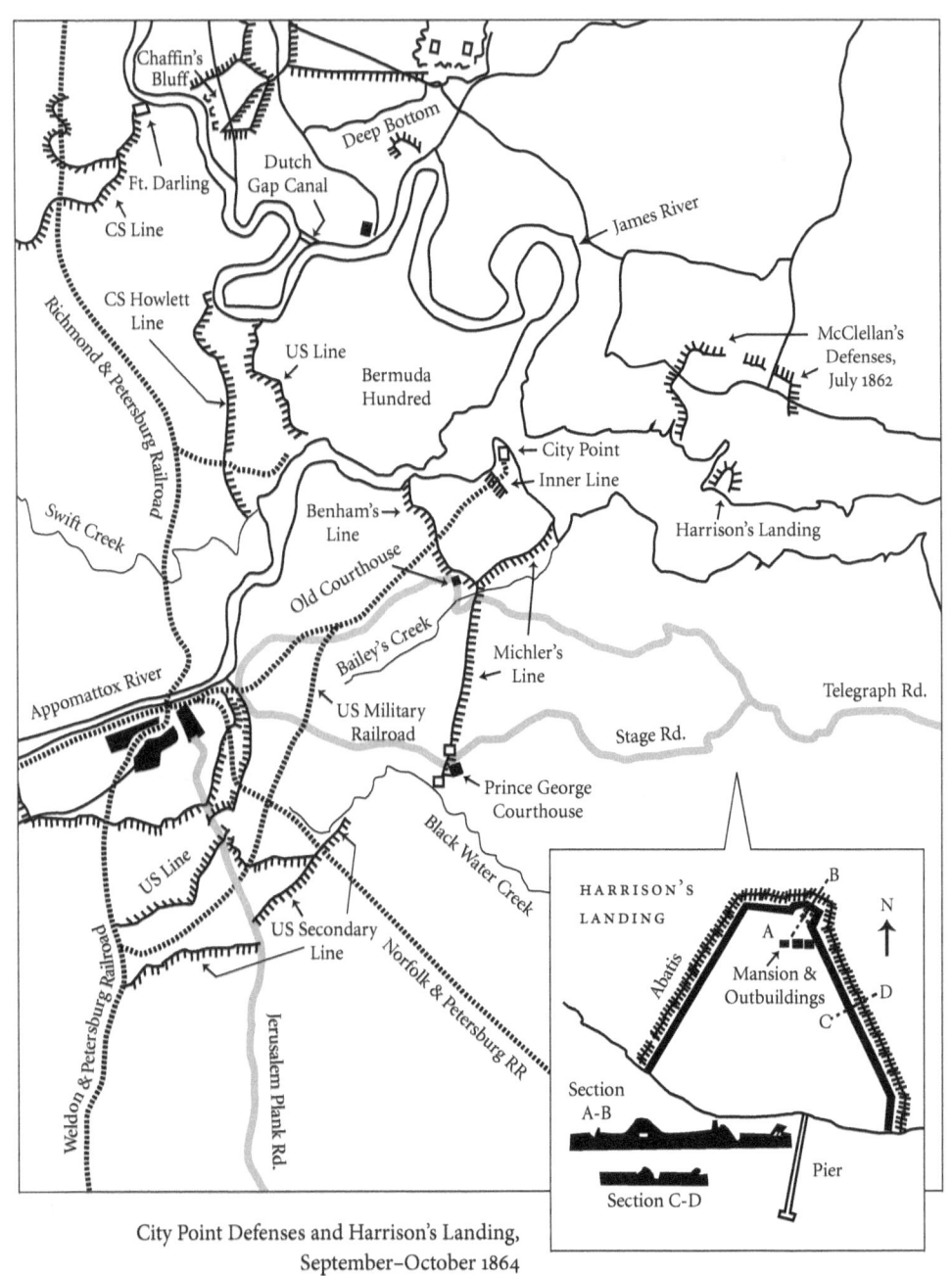

City Point Defenses and Harrison's Landing,
September–October 1864

Western bastion at Fort Sedgwick. Taken from atop the parapet of the left wing of the fort's main battery, looking west. (Library of Congress, LC-DIG-CWPB-02604)

At Fort Sedgwick, "a lively artillery duel" that resulted from Federal efforts to dislodge Rebel sharpshooters from two barns between the lines damaged several embrasures on September 22. Members of Company D, U.S. Engineer Battalion, built a wall of sandbags in front of each embrasure to protect themselves from Rebel sharpshooters, then tore up the old revetment and replaced it with gabions and fascines, working on their knees in the dark. With the gunners' help, they then took down the sandbag wall and tamped the floor of the embrasure. Additional work at Fort Sedgwick included placing a fraise of sharpened stakes to supplement the abatis and wire entanglement already in place.[21]

Hancock suggested leveling the connecting line to the left of Fort Sedgwick and rebuilding it as a return to the rear so that fire from Fort Davis to the south could sweep the front of the new line. He therefore created a reinforced angle just west of Jerusalem Plank Road for ten guns and supporting infantry. Michler thought that Fort Davis itself should have been built in an entirely different spot much farther north to handle this same problem, but that was not practical.[22]

Mott's division expended a great deal of work improving its defenses. The troops placed brush to screen as much of the parapet from Rebel view as possible and created a street between their tents and the rear of the line for easy movement of units. They also cleared streets through the camps so units could move from the rear up to the works and back again without hindrance. Three companies of the 50th New York Engineers planted new abatis from Fort Sedgwick to Fort Haskell and cleared foot passages through it for the pickets to take post farther out. On September 6, Hancock detailed 1,000 men of his corps to finish the abatis and wire entanglement in front of Mott's division and to drain the covered ways to the rear. Although they used every form of obstacle, the Federals tended to prefer abatis, which the soldiers called "gut rippers," to impede an enemy attack on their line.[23]

Farther to Mott's right, at Battery No. 14 near Fort Morton, the engineers preferred to erect a fraise. Placed five yards in front of the ditch, it consisted of "large, pointed stakes set firmly in the ground about six inches or more apart," and leaning about thirty degrees forward so the points would be chest high. The Federals tied them together with telegraph wire. Rope mantlets covered the embrasures at Battery No. 14, with holes small enough to let the muzzles of the field guns poke through. Engineer troops placed traverses between each gun emplacement. The picket line in front was well fortified and connected to the main line by covered ways. To the rear, additional covered ways allowed the Federals to gain access to a nearby ravine. Everything to the rear for at least one mile was fortified—sutler's stores, stables, tents—everything had a mound of dirt covering the side that faced toward the Rebels.[24]

A company of the 50th New York Engineers added two huge bombproofs to Fort Morton, each one ten feet by eighty-four feet in dimension. Other engineers constructed a new Battery No. 11, made a new connecting line between Battery No. 10 and Fort Stedman, and added a row of fraise between Fort Stedman and Battery No. 11 and between Fort Haskell and Battery No. 13. Benyaurd directed the razing of some older batteries and curtains left standing in front of the main line, oversaw the tracing and building of Battery No. 19, and finished the construction of Battery No. 18 near the Norfolk and Petersburg Railroad. The Federals enhanced communications with the rear by constructing additional covered ways and laying corduroy, "properly secured with side rails, and covered with earth."[25]

The Tenth Corps took position from the Appomattox River to the crater area in September and found some parts of the line "in a very filthy condition." The men built covered ways to latrines located behind the line to alleviate the problem, and additional covered ways linked the main line with reserve positions to the rear and with the picket line to the front. Rebuilding abatis and strengthening the parapet became a daily routine. Peter Michie recommended shortening a stretch of the line on the far right by building a new trench connecting Batteries No. 3 and 5, which isolated No. 4. Fort McGilvery was constructed on this new line as Battery No. 4 was incorporated into the picket line. This shortened the main line by 100 yards and made lateral troop movement easier.[26]

The Confederates began to advance one to four saps near the Hare House, toward Pond's brigade of Terry's division, in early September. Birney thought it either an offensive move against his line or merely an attempt to connect their main line with the pickets. The latter alternative proved to be the case, and nothing was done except to harass the diggers with artillery fire. Birney's artillery chief requested 10,000 feet of good rope to make mantlets, for many of his batteries were "very much exposed to the fire of the enemy's sharpshooters."[27]

Hancock complained that his First and Second Divisions had detailed 2,700 men each day to work on fortifications by late September. This allowed no time to drill the recruits, and inspectors could not determine what equipment they needed. The Federals had no time to clean their weapons, police their camps, or bathe. "The men have, in fact, become day laborers," Hancock reported, "and suffer in their proper character as soldiers. The effect on the morale of the troops I believe to be unfortunate." Warren made the same complaint about the Fifth Corps.[28]

## CONFEDERATE EARTHWORK CONSTRUCTION

The Fourth Offensive shocked the Confederates into changing their grand tactics at Petersburg. Previously, they had relied on the old Dimmock Line as their primary defense and had stationed troops no more than a mile or so west of Jerusalem Plank Road, using them to strike at Union attempts to extend westward. This tactic had failed, and Lee now ordered a new defense line constructed away from the Dimmock Line, toward the southwest, to protect Boydton Plank Road and the South Side Railroad. The Confederates started not one but two lines and finished neither before Grant launched his Fifth Offensive in late September.

On September 16, Heth sent two brigades and Field sent three to construct a line from Battery No. 45, located a few hundred yards east of the road. It extended two miles and ended a bit past Duncan-Harman Road. The infantrymen barely etched out a rude work, what a modern historian has called "no more than primitive logworks barely covered with earth," in four days.[29]

While Hampton detailed some cavalrymen to continue working on the Boydton Plank Road Line, the five infantry brigades moved eastward to Squirrel Level Road to begin the second, more forward line on September 20. Whether this was pre-planned or a belated decision, it prevented the infantrymen from finishing either earthwork. The line hugged the east side of Squirrel

Level Road, then crossed the roadbed near W. W. Davis's house about one and a half miles from the Dimmock Line. Here the Confederates constructed Fort Cherry, and they built Fort Bratton half a mile farther southwest on Chappell's Farm. Three-quarters of a mile farther out from Fort Bratton, they constructed an enclosed work called Fort Archer just north of Church Road. The line then traversed Peebles's Farm and Arthur's Swamp before reaching modern Route 673, where Fort MacRae was constructed. At this point the line was a mile west of Squirrel Level Road and a total of three miles long. After ten days of work, the Confederates were far from finished. Fort Archer had a ditch fourteen feet wide and ten feet deep, but barely a connecting line on either side of it. The parapets were no more than three feet tall in some places along the infantry line, and the only obstacle was a fraise 100 yards in front of Fort Archer. In the words of Richard Sommers, the Squirrel Level Road Line was "little more than an elementary trench."[30]

The Confederates engaged in construction projects north of the James River as well. To support an attack on Dutch Gap Canal scheduled for October 6, they constructed a new line from New Market Heights southwest toward Signal Hill. This eminence was about three-quarters of a mile forward of the Rebel defenses at Chaffin's Bluff and just north of the James. It also was about one mile upriver from the canal. Pemberton had some guns on the hill capable of firing on the canal diggers. Richard S. Ewell thought this Signal Hill Line had natural strength, for it ran along a ridge that commanded Aiken's Landing on the north bank of the river, but the defenses were not "worked sufficiently" to make it a strong position before Grant launched the Fifth Offensive. Ewell thought that another week of labor would have made the line impregnable. It was four miles long and crossed Varina Road, but Ewell could only spare 1,500 men to hold it.[31]

From New Market Heights, the Confederates tried to extend their defenses north to White Oak Swamp. The line remained unfinished by late September due to lack of manpower. Between White Oak Swamp and the Chickahominy River, engineers managed to stake out the proposed line, but not a spadeful of dirt had been turned by the time of the Fifth Offensive.[32]

All of the defenses that extended north, west, and southwest from New Market Heights were well forward of the Exterior Line of works guarding Richmond. All of them had been improvised since the beginning of the Petersburg campaign, yet they had aided in the repulse of two Union offensives coming out of Deep Bottom. The Confederates also strengthened the main Richmond defenses in September. Two hundred convicts from the state penitentiary, 300 black laborers, and all the available men of the 17th Georgia tried to plant abatis in front of Fort Harrison on the Chaffin's Bluff position when the Fifth

Offensive began. On the far left of the line that extended from Chaffin's Bluff, the Confederates had no effective flank protection. They relied on preexisting trenches dug during the spring of 1862 in the seven-mile stretch of ground that lay between New Market Road and the Chickahominy River. These old works were "much washed by rains, destitute even of gun platforms, & of abattis & of any garrison except a picket line," reported Alexander.[33]

The majority of Lee's available manpower was tied down manning the trench lines at Petersburg, where preexisting earthworks demanded repair and improvement. The Confederates worked hard on the vulnerable salient that Burnside had attacked on July 30. One hundred of Johnson's men dug three saps forward to recover the two guns blown into no-man's-land by the Union mine. They excavated each sap seven feet deep and five feet wide under cover of darkness. The guns were repaired and emplaced near the Gee House. The Confederates then dug an entrenched picket line as close as twenty yards from the crater. Modern archaeologists have discovered two hearths on the bottom of this trench, built by the pickets to keep warm, and the remnants of five head-logs with ninety-six Union bullets embedded in them.[34]

Johnson wanted to connect individual rifle pits and make a continuous trench along the picket line of his entire position. He also wanted abatis ten paces in front of the pickets and suggested that the rear of their trench remain exposed so that troops in the main line could fire at the Federals if they captured it. On Hoke's division front, the objective was to make substantial bombproofs, but the logs had to be hauled all the way from Dunlop's Farm north of the Appomattox River by railroad cars.[35]

John Hampden Chamberlayne, the new commander of Davidson's Battery, received orders to construct a work for two guns 250 yards to the rear of the main line. Although inexperienced at earthwork construction, he managed to design it himself and was very proud when Alexander told him to design a second one as well, "saying he would not bother me by any instructions or by setting any engineers after me." Chamberlayne's gunners built both works. Artillery chief Pendleton ordered all battalion commanders in the Army of Northern Virginia to cover exposed embrasures with mantlets and to build "lookout loop-holes" on each side of every gun, so that observers could view no-man's-land from a protected position.[36]

Lee tried to mobilize additional manpower to supplement the labor of his troops. He needed 5,000 blacks to work on the defenses of Richmond and Petersburg, along the James River, at Danville, and along the South Side and Danville railroads. "Much of the work is to be performed at places where there are few or no troops at present, but where it is deemed proper to prepare for possible future operations." According to a congressional act passed the previous February, the Confederate government had no right to press slaves who were engaged in raising food, but local commanders possessed emergency authority to do so. Lee, however, had no mechanism to round up the laborers, so Secretary of War Seddon instructed the Bureau of Conscription to help him. Slaveowners in forty-one counties, plus the cities of Richmond and Danville, received orders to send slaves between eighteen and fifty years old who were not domestic servants. Lee had authority to press no more than one out of five slaves on every farm or plantation.[37]

### MINING

The underground war continued during September, highlighted by the Confederate discovery of Pleasants's gallery. Major Blackford sunk a shaft as deep as possible, knowing his men could dig branches upward in search of it. They discovered the abandoned gallery on September 25 and explored it for about ninety yards before finding that the Federals had blocked it up. They thought of employing the gallery to "give the enemy a lift," but Lee said no. According to Blackford, the army commander "was not in a position to follow it up, and it would be a useless sacrifice of life."[38]

The Confederates dug yet another countermine in September, located west of Jerusalem Plank Road and extended from a forward extension of the Dimmock Line between Batteries No. 39 and 45. Scales's North Carolina brigade did most of the work. They sank the gallery only ten feet below the surface and extended it 323 yards, ending at an abandoned house owned by Dr. Duval. The house was on ground about forty feet higher than the Confederate line, and the Rebels did not want to see a Yankee battery planted there. They dug chambers for a powder charge and were ready to place the explosive if needed. The Tar Heels were digging this countermine, nearly double the length of Pleasants's gallery, by September 15, and they finished it in November. Deserters from the North Carolina brigade told the Federals about the mine by November 20.[39]

Most Southern countermining was finished by late September, but rumors continued to circulate about the enemy in their subterranean haunts. Infantry officers often reported enemy mining, but Meade discounted most of them unless they were "accompanied by some very specific details." Nevertheless, Birney resumed work on the old countermine at the Hare House by mid-September.[40]

### TRENCH LIFE

September brought relief to the men of both armies as cool weather made living in the works more bearable. The Confederates received coffee and sugar to help them through the chilly mornings, but Johnson noticed "many cases of

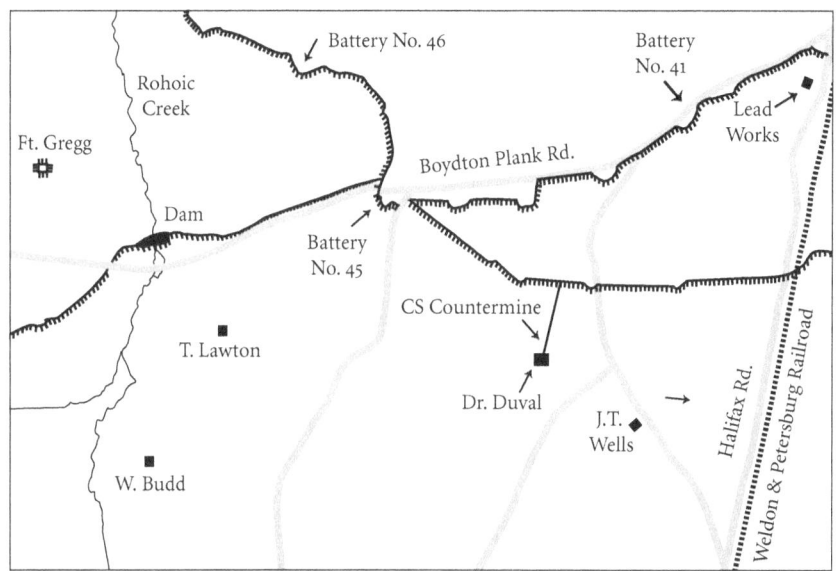

Confederate Countermine at Squirrel Level Road, September 15–November 1864

incipient scurvey" in his division and recommended an issue of vinegar as the cure. For entertainment, Fred Fleet of the 26th Virginia listened to the Yankee bands. He did not mind "Hail Columbia," the "Star Spangled Banner," and "When This Cruel War Is Over" because he thought the Federals played better than the Confederates.[41]

Gracie frequently ordered his men to exchange newspapers with the Yankees as part of the intelligence war. Someone only had to tie a newspaper to the end of a musket and wave it above the parapet. For ten or fifteen minutes all firing ceased, and everyone stretched above the works, gazing at the enemy. When finished, a cry of "Get in your holes" brought everyone back to harsh reality. Artilleryman James W. Albright had a different method of exchanging newspapers. His comrades tied a paper to the leather string that wedged the fuse plug of mortar shells, dangled it outside the barrel so it would not scorch, and attached a note asking for a paper in return. Surprisingly, the Yankees reciprocated.[42]

Where the lines were close, as at the crater, soldiers often engaged in playful banter. "Where is Hood?" a Federal would shout, or "What has become of Early?" A Confederate might counter by asking if they ever got any beef for dinner, an oblique reference to Hampton's Raid. When a Rebel officer ordered his men not to communicate with the enemy, the Yankees were puzzled by the silence and called out to see "if we were mad with them." One night when there were no questions or catcalls from Federal lines, the Confederates guessed their friends in blue were replaced by black soldiers.[43]

Members of Goode's brigade had a party with the enemy on the night of September 15. Under cover of darkness, dozens of men from both sides freely mingled in a "very sociable" manner from 3:00 A.M. until dawn. Their conversation sometimes turned to "sharp language," but that failed to break up the gathering. "All on both sides were gay and merry, singing, talking, and laughing all night," noted William Russell.[44]

More rain fell in September than during the summer months. "The soil is composed of clay and a sort of quick-sand," reported a Union battery officer, "and the roads are horrible after a heavy rain." The medical inspector of Warren's corps issued whiskey and quinine to keep sickness down, for the corps occupied low ground that was "saturated with moisture." Trenches were always muddy because water oozed into them from the surface soil, and the camps became filthy because the men were too busy digging earthworks to police them. They failed to cover latrines for long periods of time, but deep wells provided relatively clean water.[45]

Many officers and men became dull after weeks of duty in the trenches. When William W. Kirkland took command of Martin's North Carolina brigade in Hoke's division, he instructed officers to be punctual about relieving pickets, making sure that at least 10 percent of their men were on the picket line and that pickets remained awake all night. Regimental commanders were to keep one-third of their men in the works at all times, ready to fight, and everyone was to be awake by 4:00 A.M. Kirkland issued orders to shoot anyone trying to exchange newspapers or talk to the enemy.[46]

Similarly lax conditions prevailed in many artillery units. Johnson blamed the constant rotation of gunners who seemed uninterested in learning information about ranges, often neglected to post sentinels, and failed to fire when they had easy targets. Johnson felt they were only concerned about "serving out their tour and returning to repose, or perhaps idle pleasures in rear." William Nelson Pendleton issued a long set of instructions to Beauregard's acting chief of artillery that was designed to correct these problems. He added that the artillerymen tended to rely too heavily on the infantry to construct and improve defensive works for the guns.[47]

Pendleton also noted that men were killed and injured while collecting unexploded shells. The Ordnance Department offered bounties for such projectiles, and many infantrymen gathered them while not on duty. Pendleton advised officers to detail experienced artillerymen to do this to avoid accidents.[48]

On the Federal side, Birney's Tenth Corps took over the line held by Ord's Eighteenth Corps from the Appomattox River to the Norfolk and Petersburg

Railroad in late August. Ord had reported losing 1,000 men a month, according to Birney, and he tried to restrict firing as a way to entice the Rebels to also remain quiet. It seemed to work. "I think it will be found that less ammunition has been expended during my command than during same time preceding," Birney reported to Meade, "and troops have had more rest and done double the fatigue duty." The firing on Hancock's line also was heavy. Amory K. Allen sent five men of his company each evening to the detached rifle pits that constituted his picket line, each of them with 100 to 150 rounds of ammunition. If they fired all of those rounds, that totaled 3,750 shots from each regiment during one tour of picket duty.[49]

Hancock's First and Second Divisions relieved Birney's Tenth Corps from the Appomattox River to the Norfolk and Petersburg Railroad on the night of September 24, reconnecting with Mott's Third Division already in place to the left of the railroad. The first step was to issue orders detailing exactly which sections of the line were assigned to each division, with special attention to the size of garrisons for the major forts and the new location of corps headquarters.[50]

The men took up their positions and surveyed the landscape before them at dawn. George Bowen noticed that the picket line consisted of a continuous trench with a parapet to both front and back (the latter to protect the pickets from friendly fire from the main line 300 yards to the rear). Covered ways connected the main and picket lines, but in case of an attack, Bowen knew his men would have no time to retreat through them; they would have to run back over open ground or be taken prisoner. He had orders for the pickets to fire every ten minutes, even if they had no target. The main line was wide, with headlogs and a deep ditch in front. The men pitched their tents and occupied bombproofs behind the reserve line, 300 yards to the rear of the main position. Bowen's men were on duty for two days, then off for one day. While on duty, half of his regiment remained awake in the main line for half the night, to be relieved by the other half for the rest of the night. This was followed by a twenty-four-hour shift on the picket line, which in turn was followed by a night spent sleeping in the reserve line.[51]

One evening, after placing his men on the picket line, Bowen noticed they were whispering among themselves. Soon firing started on the left, and he hurried about in an effort to determine the cause. His men wanted to know if they should fire also, and Bowen said yes, even though he still had no idea what was happening. Confederate artillery retaliated, nearly hitting Bowen, and then the firing died down for no apparent cause. "Later I learned this alarm was 'a put up job[,]' the boys saying it got so monotonous standing there all night, and they wanted some excitement."[52]

On the line held by the First Division of Hancock's corps, the previous occupants had dug small "gopher holes" in the side of the trench to take shelter from Confederate artillery fire, and the loopholes along the parapet were made of sandbags. Detailed instructions came from corps headquarters concerning sanitary matters in the trenches. "No rubbish whatever will be allowed to be put in the ditches." Hancock also wanted latrines dug and the men "forced to make use of them." His troops cleaned up all the trash and detritus left in the trenches by the previous occupants, and they dug new ditches to drain water from the works.[53]

Even before Hancock's First and Second Divisions replaced the Tenth Corps, Mott's Third Division conducted a small operation designed to move the Rebel picket line farther from Fort Sedgwick. This was Hancock's idea in order to lessen the sharpshooting that took place on this section of the line. Brigade commander Regis de Trobriand supervised the effort, but Lt. Col. George W. Meikel of the 20th Indiana commanded the troops. With his regiment and the 2nd U.S. Sharpshooters, supported by three companies of the 99th Pennsylvania, Meikel was to take the Rebel picket line west of Jerusalem Plank Road. He then had instructions to dig "a new straight line of rifle-pits" from the road west, connecting with the Union picket line located in a nearby woods. The other companies of the 99th Pennsylvania, under Col. Edwin R. Biles, were supposed to take the Rebel picket line east of the road and also dig in.[54]

The Federals moved out at 1:00 A.M. on September 10, each man carrying a pick or shovel as well as his weapon. They captured the picket line, but Meikel was mortally wounded when he exposed himself in an act of bravado. The Confederates struck back two hours later, driving away the 99th Pennsylvania because Biles misunderstood his instructions. Instead of filling in the old Rebel trench and constructing a new one along the edge of a ravine, he extended the picket line into the ravine in a way that exposed it to a flank attack. The Confederates captured thirty of his men, but the 20th Indiana and 2nd U.S. Sharpshooters held firm west of the road, protected by the reversed Confederate trench. The Unionists counterbalanced their loss of forty men by taking ninety Confederate prisoners.[55]

The Federal attack stirred up a hornet's nest as both sides intensified their sharpshooting and artillery fire during the next several days. Even areas adjacent to Fort Sedgwick, such as Confederate Fort Mahone, felt the sting. Griffin's division of the Fifth Corps sent twenty men, armed with telescopic rifles, to help Mott's people at Fort Sedgwick. The men of both sides soon grew tired of dodging bullets and shells, and the pickets arranged temporary truces at night when officers on the main line were less aware of what the pickets were doing.[56]

The shelling of Petersburg had intensified because of the Fourth Offensive in late August, but David Birney suggested it increase still more as a way to lessen the "incessant musket and artillery fire" directed against his lines. Why he thought firing on Petersburg would accomplish this goal is difficult to understand, but the residents endured the pounding as best they could. "Nearly every house had a bomb proof in the yard, or cellar, & the citizens got accustomed to the shells in a surprising way," reported Alexander. He often saw women walking along the streets or sitting on their front porches even though as many as one round every ten minutes fell close by.[57]

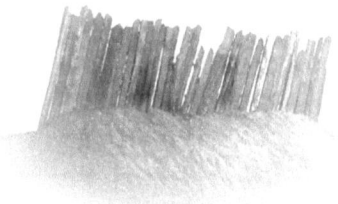

CHAPTER TWELVE

# *The Fifth Offensive*

Grant began to plan his next move as early as September 12, envisioning a strike for the South Side Railroad with another to seal off Wilmington, North Carolina, as a blockade-running port. He was ready to order an offensive by September 27 but postponed the movement against Wilmington. Instead, he wanted a strong effort by Butler's army north of the James River and a similarly strong movement by Meade against the South Side Railroad. Butler might be able to break the Confederate position and perhaps enter Richmond, and Meade could target either the railroad or Petersburg itself. One thing was definite: Grant wanted Meade to dig in and hold any position he took.[1]

The two commanders were free to work out the operational details of their strikes. Meade planned to send two divisions from the Fifth Corps, two from the Ninth Corps, and a cavalry division, about 25,000 men, across Boydton Plank Road as far as the Appomattox River if possible. Butler planned a two-pronged attack with 26,600 men against the 6,000 Confederates north of the James. Birney's Tenth Corps and the black division of the Eighteenth Corps would cross at Deep Bottom and attack New Market Heights from the south, then head up New Market Road to Richmond. The white divisions of Ord's Eighteenth Corps would cross over a new pontoon bridge at Aiken's Landing, attack the Confederate Outer Line defending Richmond where it stretched inland from Chaffin's Bluff, and advance on Richmond along Osborne Turnpike. Butler's plans represented a change in Federal tactics. In bypassing Bailey's Creek, the obstacle that had stymied Hancock's operations twice already, Butler would attack the main defenses of Richmond for the first time in the campaign.[2]

Birney went into action early on the morning of September 29, crossing the pontoon bridge at Deep Bottom and operating west of Bailey's Creek. He began to close with 1,800 Confederates in the New Market Line, contending with slashings, abatis, and chevaux-de-frise. The Rebels were stretched so thin

{ 160 }

that intervals of fifteen feet separated the soldiers in some places. Paine's black division of the Eighteenth Corps launched the first attack, repelled by heavy obstructions and Gregg's Texas Brigade. A few black troops managed to make it onto the parapet but were easily subdued. Not long after this repulse, Gregg received word that Ord's column had attacked the Outer Line and he pulled his men out of the works. Just then, Paine renewed his attack and penetrated the New Market Line.[3]

Gregg's readiness to withdraw indicates the high priority the Confederates placed on the Outer Line. The complex history of this defensive system began when engineer officer William Elzey Harrison constructed a line of fifteen batteries connected by an infantry trench crossing Osborne Turnpike, Varina Road, Mill Road, and New Market Road in June 1862. Batteries No. 7, 8, and 9 were later consolidated, strengthened, and converted into Fort Harrison. A secondary defense line, planned by William Proctor Smith in October and November 1862, started from Harrison's Line at a point between Batteries No. 9 and 10. Heading northwest, it had two big works: the Coles Run Battery (later renamed Fort Johnson) and Smith's Battery. Then in the summer and fall of 1863, the Confederates made an addition to this complex. Harrison's Rear Defense Line started on the James upstream of the river batteries at Chaffin's Bluff and stretched east to Coles Run Battery. It enclosed the bluff area by guarding an approach from the north. At the same time, Jeremy F. Gilmer planned an extension of the Intermediate Line to connect with Chaffin's Bluff. It began where Osborne Turnpike and New Market Road joined at the Intermediate Line and extended south to the Coles Run Battery. A work called Mill Road Battery (later renamed Fort Gregg) was placed just south of that road, while Fort Gilmer appeared north of the road. Finally, the Confederates constructed a Secondary Line on the right wing of Harrison's original 1862 line. It stretched from Fort Harrison to the right, ending at Battery No. 2. This new work was placed some distance behind Harrison's original work in the summer and fall of 1863 to take advantage of more suitable ground and shorten the line of defense.[4]

Ord caught the Confederates by surprise when he approached this complex early on the morning of September 29. The Confederates placed only 800 men near Fort Harrison, and a mere 35 artillerists garrisoned the fort itself. Stannard's division advanced along Varina Road, with Heckman's division in support, a total of 8,000 men. A large open field lay in front of Fort Harrison, but there were few obstructions to hinder a rapid Union advance.[5]

Stannard's men moved quickly for three-quarters of a mile across the open ground but halted 100 yards from the fort, in a spot not covered by the defenders, to catch their breath. They could see a Rebel column coming from the right to reinforce the fort, so officers pushed their men into the ditch. The Fed-

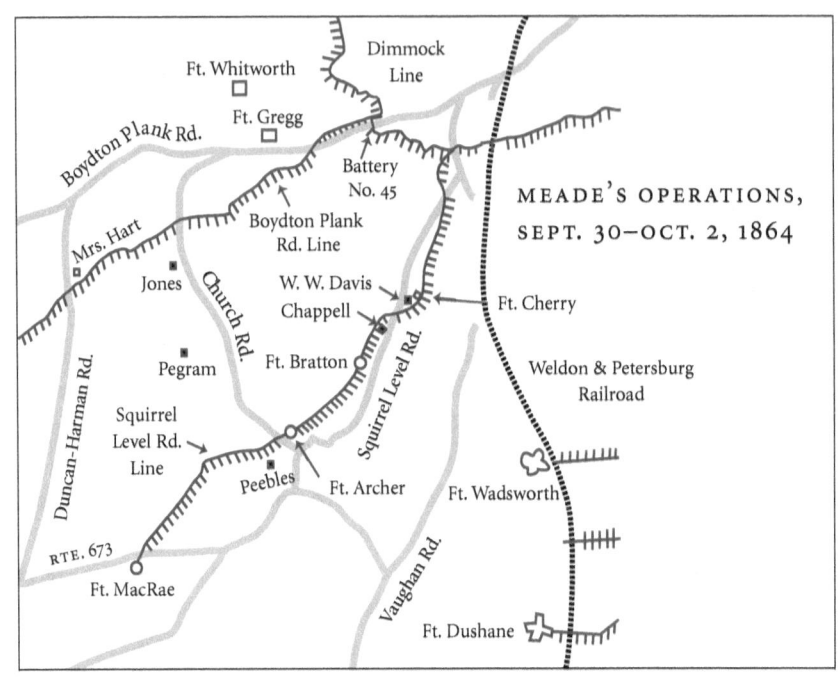

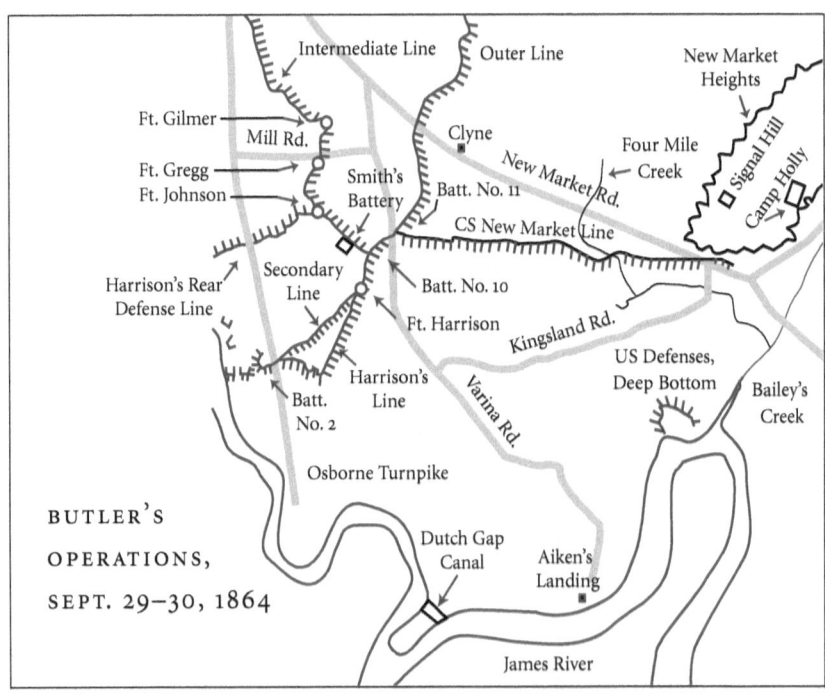

The Fifth Offensive, September 29–October 2, 1864

erals stuck swords and bayonets into the side of the ten-foot-deep ditch to gain a foothold and climb atop the parapet, where scattering Confederate rifle fire greeted them. As soon as there were enough Yankees available, they swarmed into the fort and took it.[6]

Ord's men went on to take Batteries No. 10 and 11. They also captured most of Harrison's old 1862 line to the left of Fort Harrison and most of the new Secondary Line behind it, although the end of both lines at Osborne Turnpike remained in Confederate hands. DuBose's Georgia brigade secured Gilmer's Extension of the Intermediate Line, including Fort Johnson and Fort Gilmer.[7]

A division and a brigade of the Tenth Corps marched up from New Market Heights to attack the Rebel line north of Fort Harrison by midafternoon. Foster's division hit Fort Gilmer first. The work formed a salient in Gilmer's Extension of the Intermediate Line, had a ditch ten feet deep and twelve feet wide, and was fronted by an open, flat area dotted with a few felled trees. There were only two guns in the fort, but elements of DuBose's brigade held it and the adjoining works. Foster's 1,400 men advanced close to the fort but could not cross the ditch. The 5th USCT of the black division in the Eighteenth Corps also advanced but could get no closer than 100 yards from the work.[8]

William Birney's brigade then attacked Fort Gilmer, but Birney sent in his black regiments one at a time, ensuring lack of success. The last to go in, the 7th USCT, managed to get from 140 to 300 men into the ditch, but they could find no way to climb out. Pelted with shells, which were lighted and rolled down the exterior slope of the parapet, they suffered terrible losses. Most of the survivors gave up, but many were killed by their captors in cold blood. A bit later, Jourdan's brigade of Heckman's division attempted but failed to take Fort Gregg.[9]

Grant remained on the north side of the James River all day and was disappointed that Butler failed to capitalize on his success. He had less confidence that Meade could march all the way to the South Side Railroad as a result. His only hope was that Lee would be forced to mass troops before Butler, giving Meade an opening the next day.[10]

Butler's men began to consolidate their gains on the evening of September 29. Col. Edward W. Serrell of the 1st New York Engineers received orders to lay out a line from Fort Harrison to the James River. Two of his subordinate officers were captured by the Rebels while reconnoitering, but they escaped two hours later to report that the area contemplated for the new work was not yet secure. Butler decided to shift the line farther east to avoid the Rebels, but the infantrymen were too tired to accomplish much that night. Serrell also started a parapet across the open gorge of Fort Harrison, which now was the front of the work, facing the Confederates. It consisted of dirt piled on logs, but the men could not complete it by morning. The Federals tore down the Rebel barracks in front of the Union position (to the rear of the Confederate fort) and used the lumber as revetment.[11]

Lee's reaction to the setback was decisive. He shifted nine brigades and seven batteries to the north side of the James, as Grant had hoped, and urged Ewell to use all his available strength to retake the fort. By the afternoon of September 30, there were 16,000 Confederates ready to confront Butler's 21,000 men.[12]

The Federals had made more progress in reversing the works at Fort Harrison by that time. A battery for three guns was started on the left of the new front, positioned to fire along the parapet enclosing the gorge. This was done because Stannard pointed out to Serrell that the ground ascended sharply toward the work. This might allow the Rebels to get close before being detected. The Federals decided to abandon the meager work already expended on the line heading south of Fort Harrison toward the James River and advance the position to the original spot selected for the trench. Apparently patrols had brought word that the Rebels who had captured Serrell's two engineer officers in this area the night before were now gone. Serrell planned to anchor this new line on Cox's Hill, just north of the river, where he would build a battery for seven guns and extend connecting works all the way to Fort Harrison.[13]

The Confederates hoped to smash through the Federal position at the fort. Hoke's entire division, plus Scales's brigade, advanced from the west, while three brigades of Field's division started from Fort Johnson to the north. The plan of attack, concocted by Lee, who personally witnessed the advance, called for Field to begin first and then halt partway to the objective, reform, and link up with Hoke. The plan broke down immediately after Field started at 1:45 P.M. on September 30. One of his brigades failed to stop as arranged, and all three continued to advance at their own pace. Each brigade attacked piecemeal and was ripped apart by rifle and artillery fire. Some Federal units used repeating rifles, and no Rebels got closer than sixty yards from Fort Harrison.[14]

Hoke did no better. Rather than send in his whole force, the Tar Heel commander only advanced Clingman's North Carolina brigade (commanded by Col. Hector M. McKethan) and Colquitt's Georgia brigade. The Tar Heels outpaced the Georgians, reaching a point about seventy yards from the fort. McKethan lost 527 out of 911 men engaged. Total Confederate casualties amounted to 1,200 men, while the Federals suffered 260 losses. They gathered up most of McKethan's regimental flags and close to 300 prisoners by sallying onto the battlefield at dusk.[15]

Meade moved out after Butler began his part of the Fifth Offensive. Lee's plan for defending the area west of Globe Tavern involved pulling two infantry brigades out of the Squirrel Level Road Line and holding them at Battery No.

45, where the Dimmock Line crossed Boydton Plank Road. Dismounted cavalry held the Squirrel Level Road Line to give early warning of a Union movement in the area. The Confederates did not hold the Boydton Plank Road Line at all. Lee hoped that the two brigades at Battery No. 45, with support from the rest of Heth's division and possibly two of Wilcox's brigades, could mount a counterstrike if the Federals advanced in this area.[16]

Warren's Fifth Corps led the way early on the morning of September 30. Griffin's division, in Warren's van, easily captured the Squirrel Level Road Line. Fort Archer fell to a swift infantry attack. It was a "square redoubt of some one hundred feet to the side, with a high parapet nearly finished," according to Charles Wainwright.[17]

While Warren consolidated his hold on the Squirrel Level Road Line, concentrating his men on and near Peebles's Farm, Parke advanced his Ninth Corps toward Boydton Plank Road nearly two miles away. Observers could see stretches of the Boydton Plank Road Line in the distance, "quite a line of red dirt thrown up" but apparently only half constructed, when Parke stopped at Pegram's Farm. Finally, in late afternoon, Parke advanced his units in disjointed fashion onto Jones's Farm, still one mile short of the road.[18]

Then Parke's men were engulfed in a Confederate attack by four brigades—two from Heth and two from Wilcox—that took them by surprise. The Confederates advanced south from the Boydton Plank Road Line along Church Road, smashed or chewed up several of Parke's brigades that had failed to take up a continuous line, and drove the Ninth Corps off Jones's Farm. The Ninth Corps retired to Warren's position on Peebles's Farm by dusk, but the Confederates were unable to push any farther.[19]

The battle of Jones's Farm on September 30 was a completely open field fight. It stopped Meade's advance well short of its ultimate goal, the South Side Railroad, and saved Boydton Plank Road. But the Confederates wanted to reclaim the Squirrel Level Road Line as well. They mounted a counterstrike against the Fifth Corps on October 1, but it ran afoul of Warren's skill as an engineer. Mahone erroneously believed the Union right was in the air, but Warren positioned troops from captured Confederate Fort Bratton to the east to guard against a turning movement. He arrayed the rest of the Fifth Corps along the Squirrel Level Road Line south of Fort Bratton to Fort Archer. From there, the Ninth Corps continued the Union line to the southern edge of Peebles's Farm. Warren's men reversed the Rebel trench all day and night of September 30.[20]

Heth advanced with four brigades straddling Squirrel Level Road against this strong position. They found no vulnerable points, and Heth became reluctant to press home an attack. A misunderstanding of orders sent two regiments of MacRae's North Carolina brigade forward, but they were easily repulsed. As a cold, drizzling rain began to fall, it became apparent that nothing could be accomplished.[21]

"We are at work all along the lines, strengthening them and making roads," reported Warren to Meade's headquarters on October 1. The Fifth Corps leader made it clear that he considered this work more important than continuing the offensive. He could not secure his new position on Peebles's Farm and mount another push toward the South Side Railroad at the same time. But Meade was not satisfied and ordered him to "move forward and attack to-morrow, as soon after daylight as practicable," in conjunction with the Ninth Corps.[22]

What happened was anticlimactic. Meade hoped to distract the Confederates by advancing both the Fifth and Ninth Corps onto Pegram's Farm and then moving Mott's division of the Second Corps northward up Duncan-Harman Road from Fort MacRae to outflank the Rebel right. The two corps easily reoccupied Pegram's Farm, but fears of a sudden counterstrike palsied their movements, allowing the Rebels to rush four brigades into the Boydton Plank Road Line in front of them. Mott found that he faced the extreme right of the Rebel position, with no opportunity to skirt its flank. In the middle of the afternoon, Parke organized a reconnaissance in force, consisting only of 2,100 men out of some 30,000 Federals operating west of the Weldon and Petersburg Railroad, toward Mrs. Hart's house along Duncan-Harman Road. The Federals were hit by enfilade artillery fire from the left and heavy musketry from MacRae's brigade to the front, and they got no closer than fifty yards from the Boydton Plank Road Line. This action ended the Fifth Offensive.[23]

Late that afternoon, the Federals fell back to establish a permanent position. It traversed a portion of Pegram's Farm and curved around to encompass all of Peebles's Farm. The Federals used very little of the Confederate works along the Squirrel Level Road Line, for their position stretched west of those works. From Fort Bratton, the line extended eastward to Fort Wadsworth on the Weldon and Petersburg Railroad.[24]

The Fifth Offensive resulted in significant Union gains on both flanks of the Petersburg-Richmond line. E. P. Alexander thought those gains, however, were limited by Grant's tendency to operate on both flanks at once. If the Federals had massed all their available strength north of the James, he believed, they could have taken Richmond. Meade suffered nearly 3,000 casualties while inflicting only 1,310 on the Confederates near Petersburg. Butler lost 3,350 men compared with Rebel losses of 1,700 north of the James.[25]

## UNION AND CONFEDERATE FORTIFYING AT PETERSBURG

Nathaniel Michler began laying out a line to connect Pegram's Farm with Fort Wadsworth on the morning of October 2. He pinpointed the location of forts

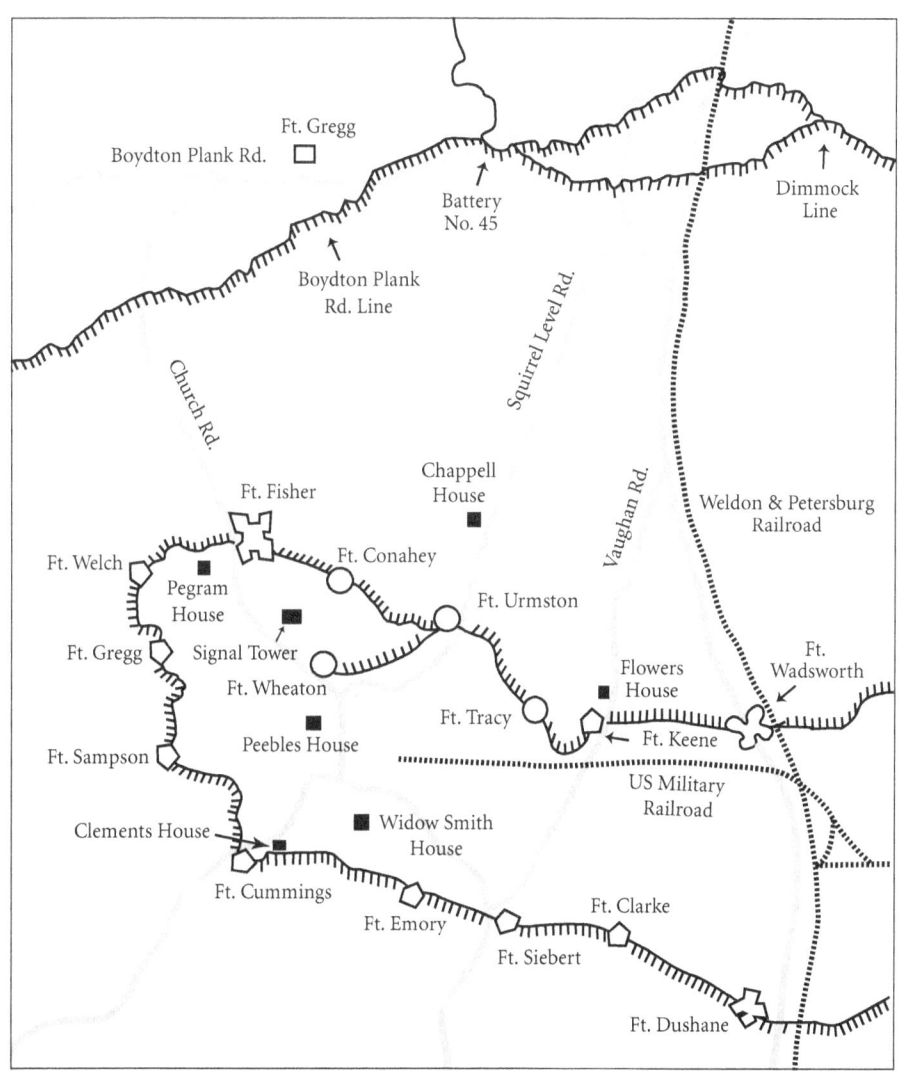

Federal Works West of Weldon and Petersburg Railroad, October 3–26, 1864

and assigned engineer officers to design them. Two companies of the 50th New York Engineers began a major work, later named Fort Welch, near the Pegram House that night. The fort was ready for nine guns (five of them mounted en barbette) by October 5. The New Yorkers, helped by 300 men detailed from the Ninth Corps, put the finishing touches on Fort Welch two days later, with a double row of abatis entirely around it. Other members of the regiment started Fort Keene near the Flowers House, the next work to the west of Fort Wadsworth, on October 3. Fort Urmston began to take shape near the Chappell

*The Fifth Offensive* { 167 }

House on Squirrel Level Road. Fort Conahey, "a queer affair" that "resembled an earthen monitor, or two-story bombproof," was constructed with a casemated battery. Company B, U.S. Engineer Battalion, staked out the fort on October 12 and built a stockade to enclose its gorge by late November.[26]

Meade wanted to extend the south-facing Secondary Line, so Michler scouted the area south of the Pegram House by way of the Clements House and to the junction of Vaughan Road and Church Road. Subordinate engineer officers selected sites for enclosed works—Fort Cummings at Clements's House, Fort Emory near Widow Smith's House, Fort Siebert at the road junction, and Fort Clarke near Forey's House (the latter was the next work west of Fort Dushane).[27]

Meade's men entered another phase of intense work as they concentrated "on fencing in our new property." They found the soil easy to dig and the enemy a long distance away. The works impressed everyone when Meade inspected the new line on October 4. "It is really a handsome sight," thought staff officer Lyman, "to get a view of half a mile of uniform parapet, like this, and see the men's shelter-tents neatly pitched in the pine woods, just in rear, while in front a broad stretch of timber has been 'slashed.' . . . The men work after the manner of bees, each at the duty assigned. The mass throw up earth; the engineer soldiers do the 'revetting,' . . . the engineer sergeants run about with tapes and stakes, measuring busily; and the engineer officers look as wise as possible and superintend." Meade and Parke, both former topographical engineers, shared a professional interest in the work. "'Here is a nice swallow-tail lunette,' says Parke as if introducing a *pati de foie gras*, 'these two faces, you see, look down the two roads of approach, and here is a face that looks into that ravine: nothing could live in that ravine, nothing!'" "'Yes,' replies Father Meade, 'that seems all right; now you want to slash out, about 300 yards further, and get a good field of fire so that the enemy's sharpshooters can't annoy your gunners.'"[28]

Michler declared the line west of the Weldon and Petersburg Railroad essentially finished by October 15. After two weeks of labor, the six-mile line, studded with eleven forts, seemed "for perfection and beauty of finish" unsurpassed by any other fieldworks he had seen. Lydecker began measuring the linear dimensions of each fort and assigning names to them on October 22. The Federals erected an observation tower on Peebles's Farm and built an extension of the Army Line from Warren Station at Globe Tavern to Patrick Station on Peebles's Farm in November.[29]

Even though the Squirrel Level Road Line had fallen on September 30, Lee's tactic of relying on newly constructed works stretching southward from the Dimmock Line had prevented the Federals from achieving a breakthrough. He had no other choice but to continue this policy. While the Yankees dug in on

Pegram's Farm and Peebles's Farm, Heth's division extended the Boydton Plank Road Line from near Duncan-Harman Road down to Hatcher's Run, a distance of about five miles. The Confederates took three weeks to do this, in addition to strengthening the existing works north of Duncan-Harman Road. They were barely finished when Grant launched his Sixth Offensive on October 27.[30]

### UNION FORTIFYING NORTH OF THE JAMES RIVER

On October 1, the day after Lee's attempt to recapture Fort Harrison, Grant recognized that Butler's position north of the James exposed him to a flank attack. Butler found it difficult to select "a tenable line that would have any advantages over our line at Deep Bottom and Dutch Gap," but Grant insisted that he retain all ground won in the Fifth Offensive, as he sent Barnard and Comstock to assist Butler's engineers.[31]

The Confederates felt hamstrung by the results of Butler's attack on September 29. They were forced to devote more strength than usual to their defenses north of the river, reducing their opportunity to assemble a dangerous strike force anywhere else along the Richmond-Petersburg Line.[32]

Butler's engineers worked diligently to consolidate gains made in the Fifth Offensive. Fort Harrison, reversed, strengthened, and renamed Fort Burnham, became the capstone of their defensive system north of the James. Its new name honored Brig. Gen. Hiram Burnham, leader of an Eighteenth Corps brigade who was killed on September 29. The fort demarked the junction of the Eighteenth Corps and Tenth Corps lines, with the former responsible for holding it.[33]

Diggers completed the gorge wall enclosing the rear of the Confederate fort by October 2, making it strong enough to serve as the forward parapet of the new Union fort. Rebel mortar fire killed forty Yankees inside the work on October 2 alone. The Federals strengthened Fort Burnham enough to protect its garrison by October 5. The new occupants continued widening ditches, raising parapets, creating sandbagged loopholes for sharpshooters, and placing abatis. They constructed two traverses inside the fort, each one twenty-four feet wide at the base, eight feet tall, and six feet wide at the top, and added a bombproof to the end of one. Grant personally inspected the fort three times until this refurbishment was mostly completed by October 22.[34]

Butler's engineers built a separate redan 500 yards to the right, where the Confederate line turned northeast, to enfilade an attacker who approached the curtain between the new redan and Fort Burnham. They reversed the Rebel line between the redan (designated Battery No. 11) and Fort Burnham by filling in the Confederate ditch, creating a fire step over it, and using the Rebel trench as their defensive ditch. It was too dangerous to fill in the trench or dig drainage

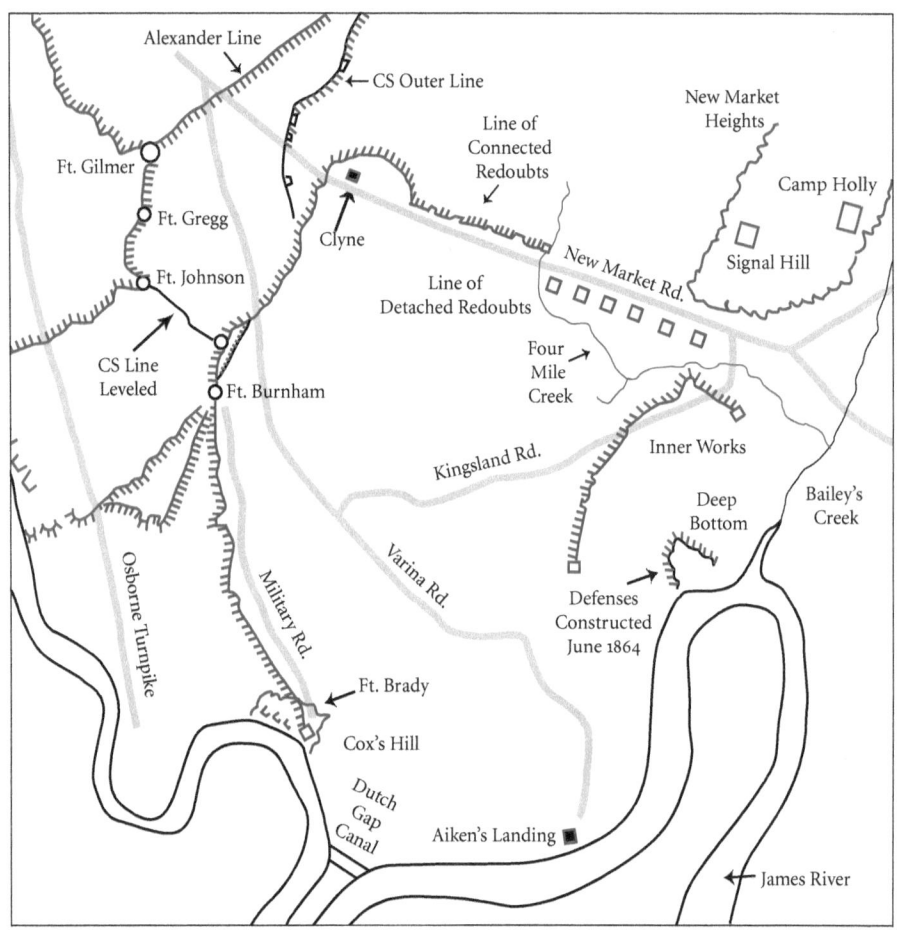

Federal Works North of the James River, October 3–26, 1864

features, so the former Rebel trench soon filled with water. The Federals also leveled 100 yards of the old Confederate line heading northward from this point toward Fort Johnson.[35]

South of Fort Burnham, the new Union line ran close to the captured Confederate position for a while and then veered away from it. The Federals anchored their new line at Cox's Hill, where Fort Brady took shape just upstream from Dutch Gap. Work on this line continued soon after the failed Confederate attempt to retake Fort Harrison on September 30. While infantry details cut and slashed trees and built the parapet, 250 engineer troops perfected the more complex and technical elements. They built four enclosed works on this line, which stretched for more than three miles from Fort Burnham to Cox's Hill. The two northernmost works, square "large redans," as Michie put it, were 800

{ 170 }   *The Fifth Offensive*

TOP Fort Burnham. Depicting the Union-made west face, interior view. (Earl J. Hess)
BOTTOM Fort Brady. (Massachusetts Commandery, Military Order of the Loyal Legion and the U.S. Army Military History Institute)

yards apart and big enough for 200 men. The southernmost work was a "square redoubt" near Fort Brady, and another square redoubt took shape where the line crossed Kingsland Road. In addition to the slashing, Michie placed abatis and telegraph wire entanglements in front of the line. He also built a series of "half-sunken batteries," mounting a handful of 20- and 30-pounder guns along the river, in front of Fort Brady, to fire on Confederate gunboats.[36]

Fort Brady received a lot of attention from the Union engineers. Located less than two miles from the Confederates at Chaffin's Bluff, it lay eighty feet above water level. The Rebels previously had maintained a signal station, some artillery, and incomplete defenses atop Cox's Hill but abandoned all of them on September 29. The view from here was commanding in all directions, and a wide, deep ravine filled with timber intervened between the hill and Chaffin's Bluff. Capt. John L. Suess laid out the fort, and Companies B and H of the 1st New York Engineers began to dig it on October 5, helped by 400 detailed infantrymen. They finished the parapet, which was up to thirty feet wide, in five days. The engineers added an infantry banquette between each of the seventeen artillery platforms, placed two rows of abatis around the fort, and constructed a huge traverse that doubled as a bombproof in the middle of the work. Company C, 1st Connecticut Heavy Artillery, manned the guns, which were moved into the fort by October 12. Finally, the engineers constructed a stockade to cover the gorge, and other troops cut a military road to link Cox's Hill with Fort Burnham. As it approached Fort Brady, this road was sunken as a covered way for 2,300 feet. In places, the covered way was 10 feet wide at the bottom and 13 feet wide at the top, and it provided up to 10 feet of cover for anyone walking in it.[37]

The many guns in Fort Brady ranged from 100-pounder Parrotts, to fire toward the river and Chaffin's Bluff, to field pieces that protected the rear of the fort from an infantry attack. Its magazine had 15 feet of dirt as a roof, and the bombproof-traverse was 90 feet long, 12 feet wide, and 7 feet tall. Photographs taken in March 1865 show that the revetment consisted of horizontal logs extending about 6 feet above the ground, with a 3-foot layer of sandbags on top and an additional 3 feet of earth on top of the sandbags. The engineers cut embrasures halfway down into the log layer and revetted them with gabions and sandbags. They used similar material, with the addition of fascines, in the several water batteries near Fort Brady.[38]

Michie began fortifying the right flank of the Tenth Corps position after the Fifth Offensive, but, for some reason, corps commander Birney ordered a stop to it. Soon after, the Confederates launched a counteroffensive on October 7 to turn and roll up Butler's right flank. The Federal infantry took post behind the Confederate line northeast of Fort Burnham to New Market Road, while Kautz's cavalry division covered Darbytown Road. Field's division advanced against Kautz along that road as Gary's Confederate troopers rode around Kautz's right, forcing the Union cavalry to retire, but Butler's infantry held firm. Pond's brigade, the rightmost unit, continued to face northwest just north of New Market Road. Terry placed Hawley's brigade and Plaisted's brigade at an angle from Pond's right to form a long, refused flank. Hoke attacked Pond's front as Field advanced on Hawley and Plaisted, and both failed to achieve any success. The Federals lost 437 men, while Confederate casualties amounted to 700.[39]

The Confederate attack on October 7 led the Federals to resume fortifying to protect the Tenth Corps flank. Michie laid out a line on October 10, basing it on the old Confederate works up to Clyne's House north of New Market Road. Here he constructed "a strong redoubt fifty yards square" and 400 yards from the road. The line turned east and southeast from the redoubt to roughly follow the position held by Hawley and Plaisted three days earlier. For about one-third of the distance between Clyne's House and Deep Bottom, as far as Four Mile Church, the Tenth Corps line consisted of small, enclosed works connected by infantry parapets with abatis in front. This section was a long refused line to protect the corps flank. But the other two-thirds of the distance to Deep Bottom was shielded by a line of detached works. The first one was located north of New Market Road, but the rest were south of it. This line of detached works ended where Four Mile Creek crossed New Market Road. On the other side of the creek, Michler planned a separate, new line called the Inner Works to protect the crossing of the James River. Both the Inner Works and the refused line from Clyne's House were very strong, but the line of detached works that connected the two was primarily designed to slow down an advancing enemy, not necessarily to stop them, until defending troops could be maneuvered to meet the threat. It was an economical way to deal with defending this long, deep area of newly won ground.[40]

A company of the 1st New York Engineers began digging the Tenth Corps works on October 12, helped by 1,200 infantrymen. They worked so quickly that Michie estimated they accomplished two-thirds of the work in one day, leaving the rest to each Tenth Corps unit assigned to hold the line. The Federals leveled old Confederate works from the square redoubt near the Clyne House for some distance toward the northeast. They finished nearly all the work by the end of October.[41]

Barnard and Comstock laid out the Inner Works as a large, fortified bridgehead to cover Butler's link with the south side of the James River. Company F,

1st New York Engineers, and the 127th USCT began digging the line, which started near the junction of Bailey's Creek and Four Mile Creek and curved west and then south to intersect the James upstream from the mouth of Three Mile Creek. Aiken's Landing, upstream from the left flank of the Inner Works, did not have a separate bridgehead, but it was well within the large enclosed area newly fortified by the Army of the James.[42]

Seven batteries were built along the 3,540 yards of infantry parapet on the Inner Works. Battery No. 1, on the right end, was only fifty yards wide on each side but had embrasures for eight guns. Battery No. 3 was detached forward of the line to command a low area of ground near Four Mile Creek. Its open gorge was in turn commanded by fire from Battery No. 4. Michie used "small pine timber, generally three inches in diameter," for the revetment of the works and assigned sixty men to place abatis along the entire line. Another detail of sixty men slashed timber in front of the position for more than 250 yards. The ditch in front of the Inner Works was from eight to twelve feet wide and six feet deep. The engineers perfected the revetment of embrasures, built infantry banquettes, completed magazines, and enlarged parapets on the line by the end of October.[43]

Michie also planned several works to secure New Market Heights to prevent the Confederates from using the high ground and reaching the Inner Works with artillery fire. He planted a large redoubt with twelve embrasures and two lines of abatis on top of Signal Hill. The Federals slashed a band of timber measuring 500 feet deep and 4,000 feet long around it, not only to create a clear field of fire but to open a view for signal communication between the hill and Camp Holly Redoubt. Michie started the latter work at a prewar militia rendezvous to enclose an area of 3,500 square yards. No fewer than twelve engineer officers and noncommissioned men, plus three infantry companies, worked on it. They cut twenty embrasures in the Camp Holly Redoubt. Michie also put a square redoubt with faces thirty yards long, big enough for two guns and 100 infantrymen, to command a ravine in front of Signal Hill.[44]

The complex task of fortifying Butler's new position north of the James River was essentially finished by November 3, when Michie reported nothing but minor details left to be done. The army now held about 13 miles of trenches north of the river, plus 3½ miles of works across the Bermuda Hundred peninsula. From the Appomattox River to Peebles's Farm, and back again by way of the Secondary Line to the James River, the Federals also held 32 miles of line that was studded with 36 forts and 50 batteries. Altogether, Butler's and Meade's armies filled 48½ miles of earthworks fronting Richmond and Petersburg by mid-October.[45]

## CONFEDERATE FORTIFYING NORTH OF THE JAMES

In the weeks following the Fifth Offensive, the Confederates dug two new defensive lines. Engineer officers laid out the first one on October 1, and the men of Lt. Col. W. M. Elliott's Local Defense Troops from Richmond dug it during the next four days. Soon to be called Elliott's Line, it began on the left at Fort Johnson and ran southwest to the right of the old Secondary Line of 1863. The line terminated at Fort Hoke, a four-sided work with two bombproofs, a large traverse, and an open gorge. There was a pronounced salient on high ground in the middle of this line called Elliott's Salient. To the right, the Confederates refurbished Battery No. 2 of Harrison's Line of 1862 with three embrasured and one barbette artillery positions, renaming it Fort Maury.[46]

Elements of the 1st Confederate Engineers finished the enclosed works along Elliott's Line after October 10. The connecting infantry line consisted only of a parapet, a defensive ditch, and a raised, wooden banquette, but no trench. The Rebels dug a drainage ditch from Fort Johnson at least to Elliott's Salient, running between the line of bombproofs and their winter quarters, with planks stretched over it at intervals for men to cross. Elliott's Salient was bolstered with a large traverse and mortar emplacements but no embrasures for artillery. Some of the bombproofs and banquettes remained unfinished at the time of Lee's evacuation of the Richmond-Petersburg lines.[47]

The rest of Harrison's Line of 1862 and the Secondary Line of 1863, between Fort Burnham and Fort Maury, were in no-man's-land. The Confederates tried to neutralize those works as much as possible by sneaking out during the night to cut down sections of parapet and to rework other sections of it as picket posts. The White Battery remained within their picket lines and could be used as a forward point of defense.[48]

Fort Johnson now lay only 600 yards from the new Union Battery No. 11, just north of Fort Burnham, and there was open, level land between them. Confederate engineers feared the possibility of Union mining, so they dug what probably was the deepest defensive ditch of the Civil War in front of the fort. It eventually descended twenty-seven feet into the ground, with a drain at the bottom to funnel rainwater into Coles Run. In addition, they cut more embrasures into the parapet of the fort and revetted them with gabions. The Confederates leveled W. P. Smith's Line of 1862 for 480 feet toward Battery No. 11 and placed two lines of abatis in front of Fort Johnson. Bombproofs and traverses rounded out the refurbished defenses of the fort.[49]

After the construction of Elliott's Line was well under way, E. P. Alexander had an idea for a new line that would strengthen the Confederate position still

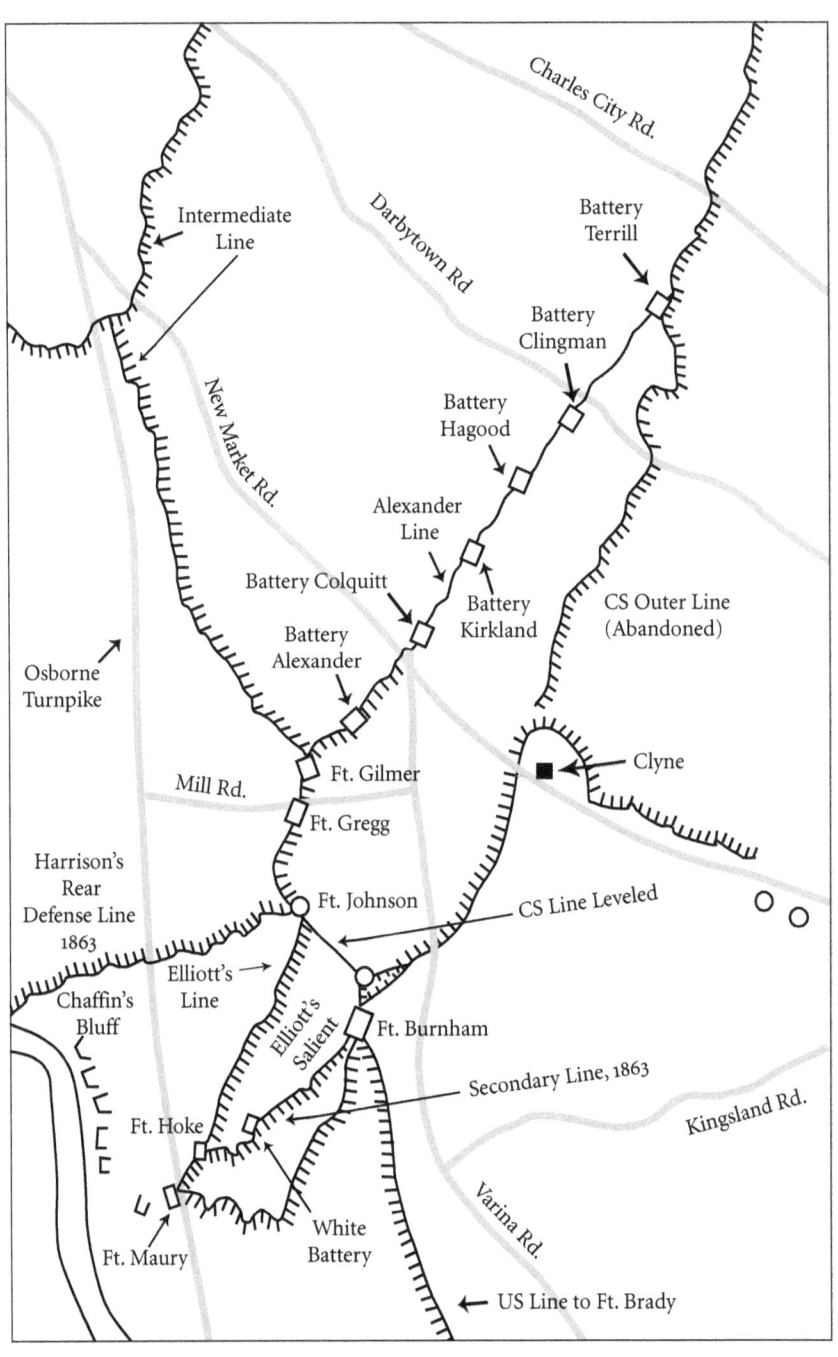

Confederate Works North of the James River, October 3–26, 1864

TOP Wooden banquette at Elliott's Salient. A note on the back of the photograph indicates that Elliott's Salient was also known as Fort Beauregard and that the man in the white shirt stands at the entrance to a bombproof. But it could also be the entrance to the countermine. (National Archives and Records Administration, 77-F-150-73-4) BOTTOM Ditch at Fort Johnson. A note on the back of the photograph indicates that the view looks north along the east face of the fort. (National Archives and Records Administration, 77-F-150-73-6)

Modern view of ditch at Fort Johnson. (Earl J. Hess)

further. He inspected the complex of Rebel fortifications in the area after the failed Confederate attack of October 7 and became frustrated by the lack of a master map. After gathering information about the existing works on October 9, he rode to Richmond and helped Jeremy Gilmer redraw an existing map of the region. This is how he stumbled on the idea to add another line from Fort Gilmer northeastward to a point on the Outer Line of the Richmond defenses north of Darbytown Road. Because this would shorten the defense line and economize on manpower, Lee quickly approved, and engineer officers laid out the position the next day.[50]

The construction of Alexander's Line alarmed the Federals. Butler learned that the Confederates were fortifying near Darbytown Road, and Grant authorized him to conduct a reconnaissance in force to interrupt the work. Butler sent two divisions of the Tenth Corps forward on both sides of Darbytown Road, screened on the right by Kautz, on October 13. They found enough earthworks in their way to cancel the advance along that road, but Kautz reported an unfortified sector just south of Charles City Road. Pond's brigade moved to the area and advanced through thick underbrush, only to discover that "unfinished breastworks" were located farther away than Kautz realized and the area was held by two Confederate brigades. A few of Pond's men managed to get near the newly dug earthworks, but his brigade received fire on three sides and retired. Earlier that day, Grant had urged Butler not to "attack the enemy in his intrenchments," but the word had not filtered down the chain of command in time to cancel Pond's attack. Butler lost 437 troops that day, while the Confederates reported casualties amounting to only 50 men.[51]

The Federal advance on October 13 compelled the Confederates to finish Alexander's Line quickly. Elements of the 1st Confederate Engineers shifted from Chaffin's Bluff on October 18, and Hagood's South Carolina brigade helped them. Law's Alabama Brigade, which had helped to hold the line against Pond on October 13, labored on the section between Darbytown Road and Charles City Road. Work on the entrenchments continued at least until November 1.[52]

The engineers kept Alexander's Line as straight as possible and studded it with redans for field guns only 300 yards apart. The Confederates dug a shallow ditch 2½ feet wide between the gun platforms and the parapet so the gunners could take shelter when not serving their pieces, even though the embrasures were protected by mantlets. This ditch also allowed them to lower their ammunition chests into a protected place and still have easy access to them. Work details cut trees for 600 yards in front of the works and placed abatis and palisades 60 yards in front. Elsewhere, the Rebels dug new works to protect their pickets, who were stationed about 300 yards in front of the line. They dug V-shaped pits about 36 yards apart, with each face 10 feet long and splayed 2 yards at the open end. The two faces were up to 6 feet tall and had banquettes. The infantry established an unfortified vidette line 100 yards in front of the picket line and only 200 yards from the Union videttes.[53]

The Confederates refurbished Fort Gilmer while working on Alexander's Line. Pine logs stacked eleven high formed a new revetment that allowed diggers to raise the parapet. They added eight bombproofs and ten barbette gun emplacements. The Confederates built a new parapet across the gorge, placing a stockade on it and cutting loopholes for muskets every three feet. They also placed several field guns behind the stockade. Fort Gilmer and the line south to at least Fort Johnson were bolstered by a line of stakes planted in front of the abatis. Work details completely rebuilt the line between Fort Gregg and Fort Johnson, which crossed Coles Run with an indented design.[54]

The most innovative feature of this defensive complex was the planting of mines from the northeast corner of Fort Gilmer down to Elliott's Salient, a distance of 2,266 yards. It was the biggest deployment of torpedoes in world history up to that time. In contrast to other deployments at Yorktown and Morris Island, where the torpedoes were scattered, these were systematically placed within the obstructions fronting the works. They constituted not just another layer of defense, but a psychologically potent new direction in the future of field fortification.[55]

Brig. Gen. Gabriel J. Rains, the single most important man in the development of mine technology in America, was responsible for this torpedo field. He had experimented with mines in the Second Seminole War as a captain in the 7th U.S. Infantry and was responsible for planting them at Yorktown in the spring of 1862. They killed and injured many Union soldiers after the Rebels evacuated that town, creating controversy even among Southern commanders who thought their use immoral. Rains served most of the war as superintendent of the Torpedo Bureau in the Confederate War Department, where he was primarily responsible for research and development of underground and underwater explosives. He devoted most of his efforts to placing underwater mines at the entrances to seacoast harbors and in rivers threatened by Union gunboats.[56]

Someone placed a few mines between Fort Gilmer and Elliott's Salient by October 20, but Rains directed the planting of many more beginning about November 13. His men placed 1,298 torpedoes in five days but proceeded at a slower pace, about 100 per day, thereafter. Planted in a line between the abatis and the line of stakes, each one had a bucketlike tin cover to shield it from rain. Anyone stepping on the shield would detonate the fuse. Three feet behind each torpedo, Rains placed "a small red flag on a staff three feet long" so the Confederates would not accidentally stumble on the mine. Rains intended for the flags to be removed at night, and he planted longer streamers to mark paths through the mine belt. He even thought of using lanterns at night with three sides blackened and only one side allowing light through a swatch of red flannel. Rains placed the torpedoes from eighteen inches to five feet apart and laid plank across some of them so that a footfall could explode up to seven devices at one time. One of Rains's operatives, William S. Deupree, lost his life while planting these "infernal machines." Deupree "accidentally fell upon one and was immediately killed in full sight of the foe," who keenly observed what was going on.[57]

One day a group of ladies from Richmond came out to see the torpedoes. They brought a huge dog that was full of spirit, and it ran into the mine belt. Everyone thought it would touch one off; the owner pleaded with the soldiers to shoot it before that happened, but no one had the heart to do so. The dog finally returned unscathed.[58]

Meanwhile, Union intelligence officers received alarming reports that the Rebels were planting torpedoes on all the major roads leading to Richmond. The mines would be detonated by operatives hiding in nearby bushes who could pull cords 400 feet long. Such devices had already been used on Brook Pike north of Richmond earlier in the year. When Sheridan moved toward the capital following his victory at the battle of Yellow Tavern, he lost several men and horses to them on the night of May 11–12.[59]

The Confederates could not match Federal digging on the other side of no-man's-land, but they concluded a respectable amount of fortifying by mid-October. Rebel troops held about nine and a half miles of earthworks from the Appomattox River to Hatcher's Run, plus about three and a half miles of trenches across Bermuda Hundred. They also manned about six and a quarter miles of works north of the James River. All told, Lee's army had dug in along a nearly continuous front of almost twenty miles.

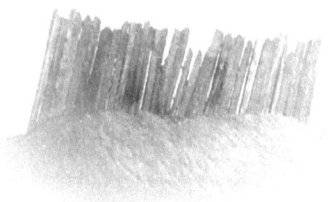

CHAPTER THIRTEEN

# *October and the Sixth Offensive*

Both armies pushed forward with a variety of construction projects along the length of their respective lines in October as the rank and file bundled up to endure colder weather while holding the trenches. The campaign lengthened with no end in sight, but Grant launched one more offensive before winter set in.

## FEDERAL FORTIFYING

A fraise already fronted much of the Union line, and Meade wanted one constructed from the Appomattox River to Fort Stedman as well. Several companies of the 50th New York Engineers and a detail of 1,000 infantrymen, assisted by fifty wagons, concentrated on this work during the daylight hours while a smaller force of 400 men worked at night. Hancock urged his division commanders to make banquettes where they did not exist, while Warren deepened ditches and improved covered ways to more easily haul artillery to the line west of Jerusalem Plank Road. Some of the covered ways had "small bombproof dodging holes in the side walls, like bank swallow nests," according to an observer who also described the regular bombproofs behind the Union line as "huge hemispherical heaps of earth and logs like a New England potato cellar."[1]

## DUTCH GAP CANAL

At Dutch Gap, Butler's men reached the halfway mark of their work on the canal by late September, but progress slowed to a crawl in October due to a collection of Confederate mortars planted little more than 300 yards away. They caused few casualties but unnerved the work crews, and there seemed to be no way to dislodge them. Capt. John L. Suess of the 1st New York Engineers constructed a bombproof with a roof of sandbags and earth to protect the steam pump. He made similar structures for the engine and boiler of the steam dredge, using on average 40 engineers and 250 detailed infantrymen each day.

With such protection, the dredge was able to gouge out 400 cubic feet of earth in twelve hours.[2]

Butler learned that the Confederates forced black prisoners taken during the Fifth Offensive to improve the defenses near Fort Gilmer. In retaliation, he placed Rebel prisoners under fire at Dutch Gap. It took a week for Lee to learn of this and withdraw the African Americans, and Butler withdrew his prisoners as well.[3]

A photograph taken sometime in late October shows that the Federals performed most of the digging by hand, using large two-wheeled carts pulled by teams of horses or mules. They dug down in stages, totaling about fifty feet at this point in the canal, while the steam dredge dug the last few feet down to and below the water level. One can see the "teeth marks" of the dredge shovel in the earth. In addition to their mortars, the Confederates began to construct heavy batteries to fire on the Union gunboats that they expected to steam through the canal when it was finished. The work was frequently interrupted by fire from heavy Union guns, which "frighten us more than hurt us." A postwar photograph of one of these finished Confederate batteries shows it to have a revetment of sandbags; the embrasure was revetted with the same material plus panels of hurdle.[4]

### CITY POINT DEFENSES

The construction of new works to protect City Point from the west was unaccountably delayed. Benham had laid out those works on September 19, but they were far from finished when Grant complained to Meade on October 4. The general-in-chief had wanted simple defenses thrown up quickly to protect the logistical center from a cavalry strike similar to Hampton's Beefsteak Raid. Meade defended himself by noting that he had given Benham the proper instructions: first to build redoubts at the main roads leading to City Point, then to slash trees between the works, and to construct curtains last. Grant supplemented those instructions by informing Benham to finish the work in four days, with parapets no more than four feet thick and curtains consisting of "merely a breast work without exterior ditch." Benham's only defense was that he had too few officers to superintend the work. Grant diverted newly raised regiments from the northern states to contribute labor and serve as a garrison. In addition to these works, Grant wanted Benham to construct defenses at Broadway Landing on the Appomattox and provide a garrison for this important forward base of Abbot's siege train.[5]

Grant's staff officers were satisfied with Benham's progress when they inspected the defenses west of City Point on October 14. When finished twelve days later, they consisted of eight redoubts and nearly four miles of continuous line. The units that garrisoned City Point were so new that they had either cast-off weapons or no guns at all, but ten heavy cannon and fourteen field pieces filled the forts. Photographs of the redoubts show them to be quite impressive, with a narrow but deep and steep-sided defensive ditch. There was a fraise in one section of the ditch, and the abatis in front was well secured to the ground by crotches of limbs. The Inner Line, constructed by Hincks in early May, was located half a mile from the wharf area. It was anchored by an oval-shaped redoubt with ramps leading up to four raised emplacements for field artillery. A large magazine served also to shield the entrance to the fort, and the curtains to either side of the redoubt had ditches. In addition to this Inner Line and the eight redoubts on Benham's Line, there were two other works inside the perimeter at City Point. An emplacement for two field guns pointing toward the river was located only fifty yards east of Grant's cabin, and the other work was placed behind the Bon Accord House near the river bluff.[6]

## CONFEDERATE FORTIFYING

Confederate engineers began to experiment with new ways to strengthen their defenses so as to hold the line with fewer men. They built a dam on Rohoic Creek, which ran parallel to and in front of the Boydton Plank Road Line. Located just downstream from the junction of two branches, it was a large project 300 feet long, 50 feet tall, 100 feet thick at the base, and 30 feet wide at the top. The dam created a large water obstacle in front of this section of the works, stretching half a mile wide and as much as 30 feet deep.[7]

The Rebels thoroughly protected the Howlett Line with abatis and rows of sharpened stakes, placing the latter so close as to make it impossible for a man to squeeze through. They planted another row of stakes on the works in some places.[8]

## MINING

Concerns about enemy mining remained high on both sides of no-man's-land during October. The Confederates resumed work on a countermine where their line crossed both City Point Road and the City Point Railroad. It had been started in early August by a Captain Abercrombie, who dug a long ramp down to its entrance about thirty yards behind the works. Abercrombie then ran it parallel to the railroad for a while before branching off to the right and left. Heavy rain flooded the gallery and caved it in on August 15.[9]

The Confederates began digging out the gallery, but work proceeded slowly. It was not "conducted with proper energy," thought Bushrod Johnson. "The detail is but small, and does not work regularly." Lt. Henry Herbert Harris of Company C, 1st Confederate Engineers, took charge of the project. He ar-

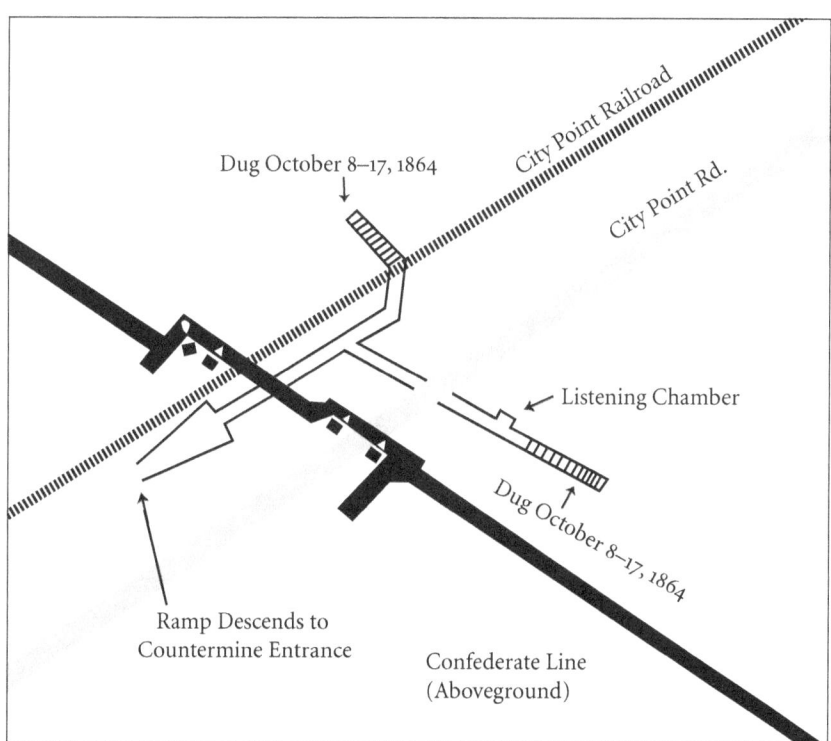

Confederate Countermine at City Point Road, October 1864 (based on sketch in Henry Herbert Harris diary, reproduced in Jackson, *First Regiment Engineer Troops*, 59)

ranged for the services of two sergeants from his company to manage fourteen men from McAfee's North Carolina brigade. The crew started "cleaning out my mine," as Harris put it, and extending the gallery. They rested on Sunday, October 9, but advanced the gallery eight feet the next day. "The great difficulty is to prevent the caving of the coarse sand in which we are working." Harris conducted an accurate measurement of the gallery, but he had too little timber for shoring it. He also became alarmed on October 14 when he heard a pick, horrified that it might signify Union mining, but it turned out to be Rebel troops deepening their trench overhead. After having injected new energy into the project, Harris received orders to take his company north of the James River on October 17, leaving Lt. William G. Williamson in charge of the countermine.[10]

The Federals constantly received reports, all of them unsubstantiated, that the Rebels were advancing mines against their defenses. Meade discounted a rumor that Fort Sedgwick was a target but ordered Michler to "run a gallery in front of . . . its whole length." When Benyaurd investigated, he found the listening shafts full of water, proof that no Confederate miners had dug nearby, and an infantry officer who entered an accessible part of the gallery could hear no signs of digging. Michler discounted the danger to Fort Sedgwick. The distance was too great, over 1,800 feet, and the Union picket line was 600 yards in front of the works. He could detect no signs of a mine, such as air shafts and smoke from ventilation fires. Yet, Michler instructed Benyaud to dig more shafts inside the battery and run listening galleries about fifty feet forward of the work.[11]

Hancock ordered a new line constructed behind both Fort Sedgwick and Battery No. 21, to the rear of the secondary trench that Warren had constructed the previous August. It was to run diagonally across Jerusalem Plank Road from Battery No. 21 to Fort Davis. Men holding the new line could fire at Rebel troops who attempted to pass between Sedgwick and Davis, as well as form a secure rear defense in case the Confederates sprung a mine. But, for some reason, Benyaurd constructed the parapet from the left of Fort Sedgwick directly to Fort Davis. The local commander, Regis de Trobriand, called Benyaurd to task, characterizing his work as "useless" and "objectionable." He compelled the engineer to tear it down and follow Hancock's plan. Benyaurd completed the addition by October 21.[12]

Company A, U.S. Engineer Battalion, began digging the new listening galleries by October 18. They placed them across the front of Fort Sedgwick and Battery No. 21 and were finished by October 29. Rumors continued to fly along the lines. William B. Greene of the 2nd U.S. Sharpshooters reported that Federal counterminers intercepted a Rebel mine and managed to extract all the powder before the enemy could spring it. He wanted to see if it was true and tried to walk into Fort Sedgwick, only to be turned aside by the guards, "so I think there must be something in the story."[13]

Concern for the safety of Fort Stedman rose when Rebel deserters arrived with reports of underground digging on the other side of no-man's-land. Meade assumed this was a defensive effort on the part of the Confederates rather than the preparation of an offensive mine, but engineer officers investigated. Lt. Col. Charles H. Morgan, Hancock's chief of staff, also went into one of the listening galleries at Battery No. 10, just to the right of Stedman, to see if he could hear anything. Morgan detected nothing, even though he was confident of being able to hear sounds "for a distance of nearly twenty yards with great distinctness."[14]

Other than a recommendation by McAfee to dig a gallery from the countermine complex at Colquitt's Salient back toward Poor Creek, there is no indication of any underground Rebel activity in this area. Nevertheless, the Federals performed a great deal of defensive work around Fort Stedman, extending the gallery until it was eighty feet long. They began to dig branches from the gallery as well. Duane decided the countermine was complete by November 20.[15]

Rumors flew north of the James River as well, indicating that Fort Burnham may be the target of Confederate mining. Butler discounted that possibility, noting the ravine that lay between the lines and which had helped to foil Lee's attempt to retake the work on September 30. But the local commander thought he detected signs of Rebel digging, so Butler's engineers sank two countermines at the fort and dug some wells to the southwest to serve as listening posts.[16]

### TRENCH LIFE

October saw a noticeable increase in Confederate desertion as food shortages and Union gains in the Fifth Offensive depressed morale. Lee heard that the Federals detailed "shrewd and sagacious officers" to their picket line to talk Rebels into deserting. They arranged the details during informal truces and staged them under the cover of darkness. He issued a circular on October 20 prohibiting truces and conversations between the lines.[17]

Lee's injunction failed to stop either the truces or desertion. He tried to motivate the rank and file by offering a furlough to anyone who prevented his comrades from leaving. A soldier in Terry's brigade of Pickett's division, identified only as Samuel, nearly got his furlough when he and two other pickets tried to intercept a deserter one night. They ran to within 100 yards of the Union line before giving up the chase. Although he had no stomach for catching deserters, Samuel desperately wanted to go home on leave.[18]

Discipline on the picket line worsened by October. Noncommissioned officers sometimes took pity on the men and allowed them to sleep in their rifle pits, keeping a lookout for the officer of the day. Some men in Wallace's South Carolina brigade developed a code—asking for an ax was a sign that ranking officers were on the way to the picket line and everyone should wake up. Hoke ordered his pickets not only to watch for Union moves but to awaken anyone found sleeping and to keep the works clean by preventing soldiers from relieving themselves in the trenches.[19]

### HOLDING THE LINES

Lt. George D. Bowen of the 12th New Jersey had difficulty adjusting to an unfamiliar section of works near Fort Sedgwick after Gibbon's division replaced units of Mott's division during the Fifth Offensive. The next night, in a pouring rain, Bowen was told to put a man at each bend of the zigzag covered way out to the picket line. While he was doing that, the rest of his picket detail got ahead of him, and Bowen had a very difficult time catching up. He left the trench to make faster time but tripped and fell twice over wire that had been strung six inches high on stakes between the picket line and the fort. Then he became disoriented and waited for half an hour to catch a glimpse of rifle fire, hoping to tell in which direction the Confederates were located. He often heard the zip of bullets nearby but could not tell if the flashes he saw came from Yankee or Rebel guns. Finally, Bowen walked up to the nearest troops and listened to their conversation. Only when satisfied that they were Federals did he reenter the picket line.[20]

A detailed inspection report reveals how the Second Corps disposed of its available manpower from the Appomattox River to a point between Fort Alexander Hays and Fort Howard, including a portion of the Secondary Line to the rear. The division commanders distributed their men into four different parts of the defense system. Miles's First Division stretched 4,667 men from the river to Battery No. 14, placing a total of 1,501 of them as garrisons for ten forts. While keeping a reserve of 1,200 men near the Friend House, Miles also put 260 men on the picket line but only 1,706 along the infantry parapets between the forts. Gibbon's Second Division had only 3,181 men available for duty, with 696 of them holding four forts and 1,300 along the infantry parapet. Gibbon had 600 men on the picket line, but only 585 in reserve. Mott's Third Division was the largest, with 6,025 men. Mott placed 2,000 of them in four forts, manned his infantry parapet with 1,000, beefed up his picket line with 825, and held 2,200 in reserve. As long as the Federals controlled the forts, they could afford to leave light forces in the connecting infantry trenches. In fact, the troops holding the connecting trenches essentially served as a secondary picket line. The Second Corps held a sector nearly six miles long with only 13,873 men. In the open field, a regular battle line would have needed close to 60,000 men to hold that stretch of ground.[21]

North of the James River, Confederate mortar fire continued to harass the garrison of Fort Burnham. One day a projectile landed squarely on a log hut inside the fort and horribly mangled one soldier while a group of men played cards. Daniel W. Sawtelle was curious to see the result. The remnants of the roof were "spattered with blood and pieces of flesh and I saw some ribs or pieces of ribs sticking in the roof." The man had been cut completely in two at the waist. His legs stretched out and the upper part of his body, which appeared untouched, lay at an odd angle compared to the legs. "It was a horrible sight," admitted Sawtelle, "but we were getting so hardened that such sights did not seem to make much impression."[22]

The soldiers of both sides continued to arrange temporary truces whenever they could. Officers usually tried to understand, but they had to draw a line somewhere. Hancock refused to allow his soldiers to raise white flags as a signal for a truce—that was something only officers in high positions had the authority to do. Regis de Trobriand was angry when he discovered that a Rebel picket had been allowed to spend an hour in the Union picket line conversing and perhaps gathering intelligence.[23]

De Trobriand probably was right that these picket truces allowed the enemy to obtain information. Bushrod Johnson possessed a surprisingly accurate view of how the Federals held their line opposite his division, and he proposed offensive action to take advantage of it. Noting that the trenches opposite were thinly held by inferior troops, he suggested a serious attack to capture the entire left wing of the Union position. "I have no doubt that a good line of battle would sweep everything in my front." He had visions of cutting the military railroad and moving west to beyond Jerusalem Plank Road or simply holding a division-length segment of the Union line to force the Yankees to dig a new one farther away.[24]

Johnson's men continued to improve the way they held their own defenses and tried to cut back on communications with the enemy. In Goode's Virginia brigade, about half a mile south of the crater, a remarkable calm prevailed between the lines. None of the pickets fired, allowing men to walk openly or lie in the sunshine. But when Hancock's Federals tried to strike up a conversation with them, the Virginians had "strict orders" not to talk. "Some of our men . . . don't seem to remember who the Yankees are," remarked Fred Fleet of the 26th Virginia, "and that it is highly improper to have anything to do with them."[25]

## THE SIXTH OFFENSIVE

Grant wanted another offensive before fall weather made campaigning too difficult, and he probably also wanted to influence Lincoln's growing chances of reelection to the presidency in November. "Grant is not a mighty genius," Meade reported to a friend, "but he is a good soldier, of great force of character, honest and upright, of pure purposes." Meade noted that Grant's main fault lay in an "unflinching tenacity of purpose, which blinds him to opposition and obstacles." The general-in-chief seemed to have an "almost too confident and sanguine disposition."[26]

Grant reverted in the Sixth Offensive to the old format of moving an undermanned force into little-known territory to accomplish too much, reminiscent of the Second Offensive of June 21–22. He considered other options, but none seemed plausible. Michler, Gillespie, and Benyaurd scouted the area between the point where Meade's right struck the Appomattox and the mouth of Swift Creek, but they could find no practical way to cross the river and interpose a force between Petersburg and Richmond. Grant preferred to keep shifting to the left and he informed Halleck that if he had the Sixth Corps and a cavalry division back from the Shenandoah Valley, he could push all the way to the Appomattox upstream from Petersburg. The Confederate advance that resulted in the battle of Cedar Creek on October 19 delayed that transfer of manpower. Barnard could not see any possibility of success until Grant assembled a mobile column of 40,000 men. "In the present state of military and political affairs," Barnard reasoned, "it is better to do nothing until our forces are much more adequate than they are now to effect decisive results. At present everything is well enough, and Richmond must ultimately fall, unless the course of things is changed by a disaster which would strengthen the hands of the peace and 'cessation' party."[27]

The presidential campaign hovered like a shadow over military operations at Petersburg that fall. Lincoln, representing a continuation of emancipation and unrelenting military pressure against the Confederacy, opposed Democratic candidate George B. McClellan and his party's controversial platform, which called the war a failure and urged a negotiated end to the conflict. Grant rejected Barnard's counsel, preferring to act. "We must keep at them," as Theodore Lyman put it; "that is the only way; no let up, no armistice. They perfectly hate what we are doing now, going a couple of miles and fortifying, then going two more and fortifying again; then making a sudden rush, taking a position and a lot of cannon, and again fortifying *that*. All these moves being a part of what we may call a throttling plan."[28]

The difficulties of pursuing the throttling plan were larger at this stage of the game. It had been a relatively simple matter of shoving large numbers of troops a couple of miles due west from Jerusalem Plank Road in late August, and from the Weldon and Petersburg Railroad in late September, to extend the Union line in stages. Now the Boydton Plank Road Line extended all the way south to Hatcher's Run and blocked short advances. The Federals had to move south, cross the stream well forward of the Rebel earthworks, and head west, trying to turn their right flank. This required a long, sweeping march through poorly mapped territory before the Federals could reach either Boydton Plank Road or the South Side Railroad. Once there, they would be isolated and vulnerable unless they could quickly establish contact with Peebles's Farm by stretching out a line connecting the old position with the new one.

Grant announced on October 20 that Hancock's Second Corps would make the attempt a week later and Butler should demonstrate north of the James River to draw Rebel attention. "I do not want any attack made by you against intrenched and defended positions," he warned Butler, just an attempt to turn the Confederate left flank. Grant also hoped Butler could use his cavalry division to raid the Virginia Central Railroad north of Richmond, essentially duplicating

The Sixth Offensive, October 27, 1864

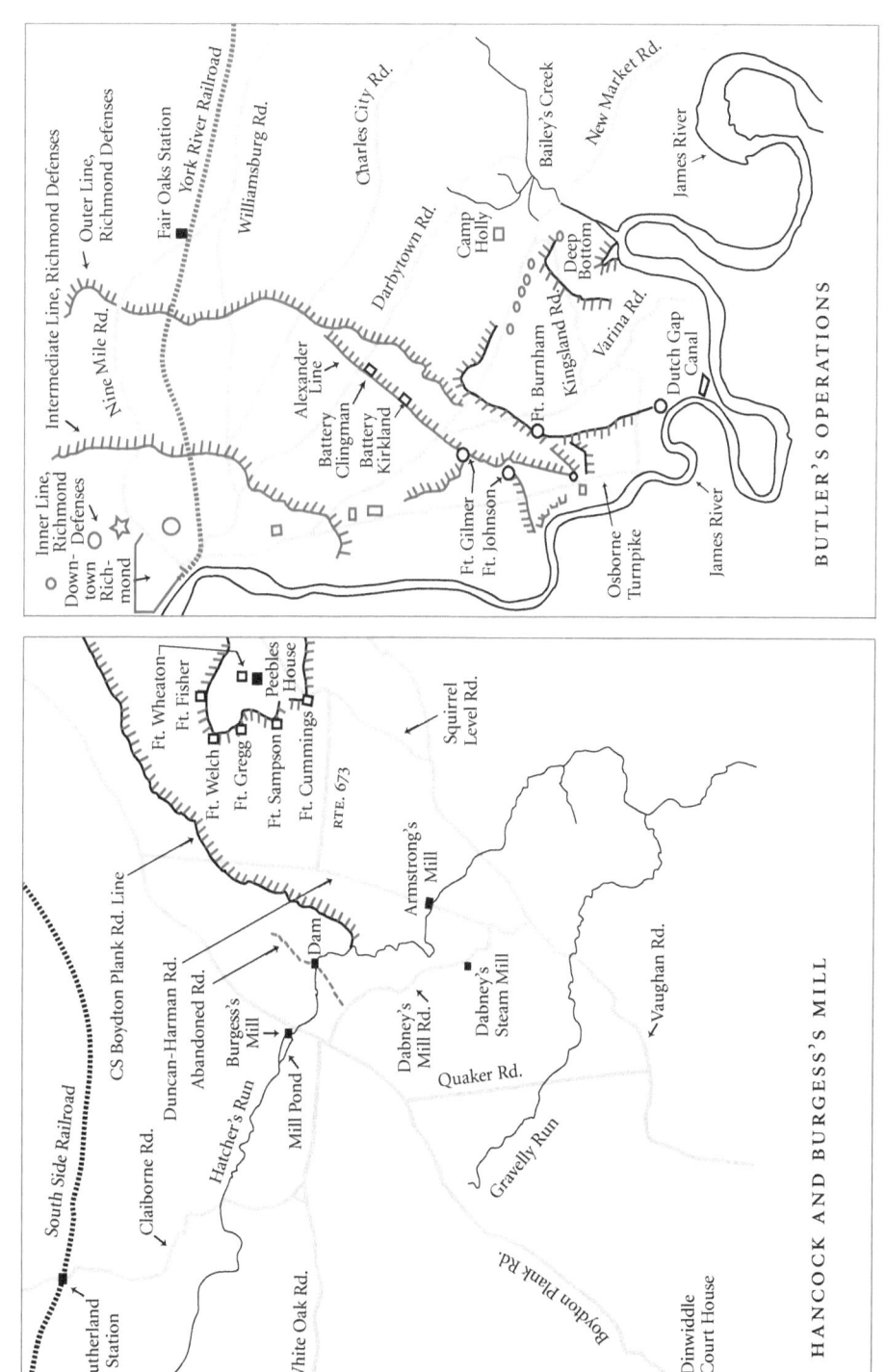

BUTLER'S OPERATIONS

HANCOCK AND BURGESS'S MILL

Hancock's role in the First and Second Deep Bottom engagements of July and August.[29]

Meade organized the details for the offensive. He assembled three mobile columns, with Parke moving Ninth Corps troops west from Peebles's Farm to find a weak spot on the southern end of the Boydton Plank Road Line. Warren would move a column of Fifth Corps troops to Parke's left to help him if he attacked the line or to aid Hancock's Second Corps column as needed. Hancock would move with three days rations, sixty rounds of ammunition, and a minimum of wheeled vehicles along a series of roads around the Confederate right. He was to take possession of the South Side Railroad "and fortify back to [Meade's] present left." Gregg's cavalry division could screen the Second Corps left flank. Meade earmarked a larger proportion of his available manpower for this strike, some 47,000 troops, than for any previous offensive. This was possible because of the Federal policy of building enclosed forts that could be held with minimal garrisons, freeing up more troops for offensive operations.[30]

Hancock started with his Second Division, now led by Brig. Gen. Thomas Egan, and Mott's Third Division early on the morning of October 27. Delayed a bit by trees felled across Vaughan Road, the head of the column reached Hatcher's Run at 6:30 A.M. Smyth's brigade waded the waist-deep water and crawled across tree trunks, losing fifty men in a fight with Rebel cavalry who were protected by an earthwork that had a deep ditch and a slashing in front. Hancock pushed westward on Dabney's Saw Mill Road. The head of his command reached Boydton Plank Road without incident at 10:30 A.M., but the rear did not appear until ninety minutes later. He paused to take stock of the situation. Confederate artillery already fired on him from positions north of Hatcher's Run, but he was in control of the junction of the plank road and the White Oak Road, about a quarter-mile south of the run. The latter road would allow him to strike for the South Side Railroad. His two divisions already were isolated from the rest of Meade's army, and the railroad was yet a long way to the northwest. A message arrived from Meade at 1:00 P.M. ordering him to wait until further instructions.[31]

The two supporting columns could neither divert Confederate attention nor come to Hancock's aid. Parke did not find any place along the Boydton Plank Road Line that seemed vulnerable. He ordered his men to dig in close to the Rebel line for the time being. Ninth Corps pioneers cut a swath ten yards wide through the pine woods, lined up the trunks, and shoveled dirt on them to make a parapet. Parke's men held there until 10:00 A.M. the next day before returning to their former position.[32]

Meade instructed Warren to send help to Hancock, and he selected Crawford's division. It crossed Hatcher's Run at Armstrong's Mill during the late morning and began to advance through a matted jungle along the south bank of the stream, heading directly for the Second Corps position. Hancock sent a staff officer to meet Crawford and arranged his units along Boydton Plank Road south of the run. For reasons that are not clear, neither his subordinate officers nor members of the rank and file bothered to construct defensive works.[33]

Grant and Meade rode to Hancock's position to gauge the situation. They arrived about 1:30 P.M. and waited more than two hours for Crawford to make an appearance, but that officer was delayed by the landscape. Advancing in battle line, his men burrowed through "a real Virginia forrest of the densest discription of small pines and a tangled mass of undergrowth, briars, & weeds," reported a man in the 6th Wisconsin. "We got completely lost & bewildered in this jungle." A small force of seventy-five Rebel skirmishers further slowed Crawford and instilled fear of something more dangerous in his path. Moreover, he had no idea where the south end of the Boydton Plank Road Line was located. His advance essentially ground to a halt nearly opposite the end of the line and still at least a mile from the Second Corps. No longer able to wait, Grant and Meade instructed Hancock to hold his position until noon the next day, in hopes of drawing the Confederates out to fight in the open, and then rode away just before 4:00 P.M.[34]

The Confederates had a meager force positioned near Hancock. Matthew Butler's cavalry division was on White Oak Road to the west, while W. H. F. Lee's cavalry division straddled Boydton Plank Road to the south. The Rebels also had Harris's Mississippi brigade on the plank road north of Hatcher's Run, supported by James Dearing's cavalrymen. The Confederates were eager to come out into the open and take the offensive, and it happened much sooner than anyone expected. William Mahone sent three of his brigades to the area, and Henry Heth decided to add MacRae's North Carolina brigade from his own division to the strike force. Heth took charge of the attack, for he knew a quick and easy way to surprise Hancock by crossing Hatcher's Run on a dam Hampton had earlier built. The Confederates could then use an old, abandoned road to attack Hancock's right flank. Heth dispatched several units to front Hancock along the plank road and instructed all commanders around the Second Corps position to advance after he started his own attack. For reasons that are unclear, only three brigades—MacRae's, King's, and Weisiger's—conducted Heth's assault.[35]

But those brigades surprised the Federals when they crossed the run about 4:30 P.M. They overran a section of artillery, drove away three regiments holding the Union right flank, and then advanced into the hollow center of Hancock's three-sided position. Turning south, the Rebels could see the white-topped wagons of the Second Corps supply train in the distance, but by then the Federals mounted effective counterattacks from the west and north. The Confederates were in danger of being boxed in, and they conducted a fighting retreat across the dam, abandoning the two guns they had earlier taken. The Federals managed to keep the other Rebel units ringing Hancock's position from helping MacRae's, King's, and Weisiger's brigades.[36]

It had been an open field fight, something Grant had wanted with Lee's men. Even though it was a Union victory, Hancock's two divisions were still in a vulnerable position, for there was no sign that Crawford could make contact anytime soon. When he learned of the Rebel attack, Meade authorized Hancock to retreat that night. His troops began to pull out at 10:00 P.M., and the last Federals left the battlefield by 1:00 the next morning. Grant regretted "the necessity of withdrawing," but he understood the "cogency" of Meade's reasoning. "The enemy attacking rather indicates that he has been touched on a weak point," Grant hopefully concluded. In writing to Secretary of War Stanton, Grant downplayed the expectations he and Meade had held for the operation and put the best spin he could on the result. "This reconnaisance, which I had intended for more, points out to me what is to be done."[37]

Meade lost 1,758 men in this aborted strike, while the Confederates suffered 1,300 casualties. Francis Walker, one of Hancock's most trusted staff members, pinpointed the cause of failure. Instead of two divisions, the movement should have been made with two corps. Keeping the bulk of available troops in front of Boydton Plank Road or floundering through the thickets south of Hatcher's Run was a mistake. The Confederates tied these Fifth and Ninth Corps units down and still had several brigades to concentrate against Hancock. Grant should have known this from experience. Even for the comparatively simpler job assigned to Meade in the Fifth Offensive, the Army of the Potomac used two corps to make a lodgment on Peebles's Farm.[38]

Butler's operations on October 27 failed to help Meade. Beginning at 4:00 A.M., the Tenth Corps extended to the right as far as Charles City Road. Then the Eighteenth Corps marched behind it and extended the Union presence as far as Williamsburg Road, the apparent extent of the Confederate left wing. The whole movement was beset by delays, including rain, so that the van of the Eighteenth Corps did not reach the Williamsburg Road until 1:00 P.M. James Longstreet had recovered enough from his Wilderness wound to take charge of troops north of the James River on October 19. He detected the movement and shifted Field's division to Williamsburg Road. Even so, Godfrey Weitzel, who had given up his job as Butler's chief engineer to take command of the Eighteenth Corps, spent two hours scouting the terrain. The head of Field's division reached its position at 3:00 P.M. When Weitzel finally advanced a half-hour later, the Confederates were ready. If Weitzel had gone in before Field's arrival, he would have found only a thin line of dismounted cavalry barring the way.[39]

Weitzel sent in only two of his seven brigades across an open field against the Texas brigade. One Federal unit made it to a point 300 yards short of the Confederate line, while the other managed to close the distance to 150 yards. On his far right, Weitzel also advanced a brigade of black troops along Nine Mile Road against Gary's dismounted cavalrymen. Some of those troops entered the Confederate works and captured two artillery pieces, but a flanking counterattack by Gary's men drove them back and recovered the guns.[40]

Butler ordered Terry's Tenth Corps to press forward and find a vulnerable spot. The Confederate works were incomplete and held by a single rank of troops, each man three to six feet from his comrade, but Terry's men failed to achieve anything. All three divisions conducted a reconnaissance in force north and south of the Darbytown Road, capturing only a few Rebel skirmish pits.[41]

In fact, Butler's move barely interrupted the Confederates as they worked on the Alexander Line. Henry Herbert Harris brought Companies C and G, 1st Confederate Engineers, from the countermine at City Point Road on October 17. He and two other engineer officers inspected the Alexander Line two days later to get their bearings, then moved their camp close to Cornelius Creek the next day. They plunged into the work on October 21, employing 160 black laborers and all of Harris's Company C on a redan called Battery Hagood. While the blacks dug the ninety-foot faces of the work, the white engineer troops worked on the revetment. They cut two embrasures into each face and built additional barbette emplacements. In addition to digging, Harris's men also made up to twenty fascines each day.[42]

Harris began to stake a new line to the rear of Battery Hagood on the morning of October 27, but he was interrupted by heavy skirmish fire. Harris saw his yet-unfinished battery open fire for the first time. Soon he received orders to go 300 yards to the right of Battery Hagood and construct a barbette gun emplacement at Battery Kirkland while Federal skirmishers fired at his men from a distance of only 200 yards. He managed to mount the gun by early afternoon and watched as it opened fire. Then his men went farther to the right, past the left flank of the Tenth Corps, and worked on another barbette gun emplacement at Battery Colquitt or Battery Alexander. This was unique, for engineer troops rarely continued work on a semipermanent earthwork literally under enemy fire.[43]

Grant was disappointed by Butler's lack of results and advised him to stay put overnight, hoping to entice the Confederates to come out of their works and attack. But that never happened, and Butler's men returned to their former positions on October 28. Work continued on the Alexander Line as Harris employed black laborers to finish yet another barbette gun emplacement and stake off the new line to the rear of Battery Hagood. Butler lost 1,603 men on October 27, while Longstreet suffered only 64 casualties.[44]

### TRENCH RAIDS

One of the largest trench raids of the campaign took place on the evening of October 27, although it was not meant to support the Sixth Offensive. The Federals targeted a sore spot, Davidson's Battery, which had dealt so much destruction to the Ninth Corps during the mine attack of July 30. Located 373 yards south of the crater and manned by elements of the 26th, 34th, and 46th Virginia of Goode's brigade, the Yankees called it Fort Crater.[45]

Miles's division of the Second Corps was responsible for the Federal sector opposite Fort Crater; in fact, Miles had been forced to stretch his command to cover everything from the Appomattox River to beyond Jerusalem Plank Road the day before. Lt. Col. St. Clair A. Mulholland's brigade lay opposite the crater sector. His 148th Pennsylvania, which had been armed with Spencer repeaters eleven days earlier, received the assignment to attack Fort Crater with 100 men under Capt. Jeremiah Z. Brown. The men assembled in a hollow behind Fort Morton and then made their way to the picket line one by one, so as not to arouse Confederate suspicion. Brown divided his men into two sections: one was to head straight for the fort and fire across the parapet, while the other was to swerve around the work to the right and enter the gorge. Ten men carried axes to cut through the Confederate obstructions. Once inside the battery, Brown's men were to cheer as a signal for reinforcements to come up.[46]

Advancing a bit after 6:00 P.M. in rain, the Federals appeared to be Rebel pickets coming in after their tour of duty. The division officer of the day therefore gave orders not to fire on them. Other Confederates along the main line saw they were Yankees but assumed they wanted to desert. Soon the strangers were hacking away at the chevaux-de-frise, separating three sections of it. Some Rebels opened a light musketry fire, but Brown's men were upon them before much damage could be done. While one section clambered up and over the parapet, Brown led the other across the curtain and into the rear of the work. Surprised, most of the garrison fled. Brown took thirteen men and four officers prisoner, including Col. Randolph Harrison and Lt. Col. Peyton Wise of the 46th Virginia. He also secured the lone gun in the work.[47]

According to plan, Brown's men cheered mightily for help and prepared to hold the fort. Mulholland ordered up the 26th Michigan as the startled Confederates responded to this unexpected turn of events. While many of Goode's

Virginians had initially abandoned the curtain to north and south of Davidson's Battery, they now regained their composure and reoccupied the works. Twenty minutes passed and there was still no sign of the Michigan regiment, so Brown ordered his men to retire. Leaving the gun but bringing most of their prisoners, they made their way across no-man's-land in small groups to lessen the effect of rifle fire delivered by the waiting Confederates. What happened to the 26th Michigan can only be explained by lack of preparation; Miles did not think Brown's men could take the fort and had not made proper arrangements for support, hoping to risk as few men as possible. The Federals lost seventeen killed or left wounded between the lines, and thirty-three were missing. Brown's men conducted the whole operation superbly, but what the Federals hoped to gain from it is unclear. Nevertheless, Brown received the Medal of Honor in 1896 for his work that day.[48]

Other units of Miles's division were active that evening as well. The 88th New York advanced along Jerusalem Plank Road at 10:00 P.M. and captured about 200 yards of the Rebel picket line. William H. Wallace organized a counterattack with a portion of his brigade, 200 men of the Holcombe Legion and the 18th South Carolina. They sneaked up within thirty yards, then yelled and ran into the captured trench. The Federals were reversing the earthworks when taken by surprise. They fled quickly, leaving behind their entrenching tools and fourteen comrades as prisoners. Confederate losses amounted to one killed, eleven wounded, and eight missing.[49]

Mahone devised a raid on the Union picket line near Fort Sedgwick. By interrogating prisoners, he learned how the Federals changed their reliefs. Dressing some of his sharpshooters in blue, he sent them out at 9:00 P.M. on October 30. They fooled the Yankees long enough to grab a reported 230 prisoners. Mahone's men held a section of the Union picket line all night, then retired at dawn because they had no entrenching tools to reverse the works.[50]

Johnson wanted to retaliate for the attack on Davidson's Battery, and he ordered Wallace to lead the effort after his brigade returned to the crater area. Wallace advanced 200 men of the Holcombe Legion directly in front of the crater on the night of November 5. They carried a good stretch of the Union picket line. To their surprise, the Yankees had dug away the rear bank of the trench so that if unfriendly troops occupied it, they would be easy targets from the main Union position. The Confederates took shelter behind the parapet but were fearfully exposed to a flank fire from the right, where the Federals had reinforced their picket line as far as effective rifle range. Sixty men were sent out with tools to dig some sort of protection, but the conformation of the ground and the angle of Union fire made it impossible. The Rebels withdrew after losing ten men as prisoners to the Yankees.[51]

## BOMBARDING PETERSBURG

Federal shelling of Petersburg decreased almost to the point of cessation by October. One Confederate observer estimated that 20,000 shells had hit the city since mid-June, but the highest count of civilian casualties ran to only four whites and eight blacks killed, mostly in the early weeks of the campaign. A careful survey of physical damage to Petersburg, conducted by Union army officers after the war, listed 625 buildings that were hit by Federal guns.[52]

CHAPTER FOURTEEN

## *November, December, and January*

By the time fall arrived, the earthworks on the Richmond-Petersburg lines had been exposed to rain, heat, and cold for five months. Wooden revetments rotted and parapets eroded. The wooden obstructions in front of the line became targets of human predation as cold infantrymen sought new sources of firewood. Newer construction projects, such as the works built to consolidate gains won in the Fifth Offensive, the Dutch Gap Canal, and the City Point works, were pushed to completion. Digging continued underground as the Confederates completed their elaborate system of countermines. The armies prepared for a winter in the trenches, engaging in raids and enduring sporadic but deadly bursts of artillery and small arms fire.

### FEDERAL CONSTRUCTION

The Federals made division commanders responsible for appointing an officer to oversee the trenches and forward reports to corps headquarters every week. Division leaders also had permission to contact the army's chief engineer directly when they needed assistance.[1]

The reports revealed the same problems all along the lines: parapets were "crumbling down," abatis was "broken up," and rainwater was accumulating in many places. Some artillery emplacements had become "very dilapidated" and needed a thorough overhaul. Scarps as well as parapets were falling down at several forts. Covered ways also eroded, demanding attention.[2]

About ten yards of abatis had been completely removed in front of Fort Clarke, creating a dangerous gap in the obstructions. On other parts of the line, men used the abatis as a refuse pile and threw "brush and other rubbish" on top of it. This weighed down the branches and reduced their effectiveness as an obstruction. Army and corps headquarters ordered the posting of guards who had authority to arrest perpetrators. Similar orders went out to burn huts and other unauthorized structures close to the trench.[3]

Gabion revetment of rear line at Fort Sedgwick. (Library of Congress, LC-DIG-CWPB-02591)

It was not easy to find wood for camp needs because five months of military occupation had almost denuded the area around Petersburg. Nor was it easy to find soldiers interested in working on the fortifications. Details from the Second Corps "affected so much ignorance of the use of tools and showed such a want of interest in the work" that Ira Spaulding used his own men to stockade the gorges of several forts. Now that the lines were relatively quiet, the engineers also fitted magazines with stout doors, hinges, and keys to keep ordnance stores safe. The ground became hard with frost as winter approached, increasing the difficulty of repairing earthen defenses.[4]

The commander of the 7th Rhode Island sent details two miles behind the line to a depot were each man constructed one gabion as his daily quota. The 50th New York Engineers made 456 gabions and 20 sections of chevaux-de-frise in one week. Much of this revetting material went to Fort Sedgwick, where several rows of gabions lined the parapet. An order to enclose the rear of all forts which still had open gorges increased the demand for gabions in early December.[5]

Both north and south of the James River, the Federals completed defenses built on ground they had gained in the Fifth Offensive. The Eighteenth Corps finished the abatis in front of its line by late November, about the time that the

Army of the Potomac finished the line that enclosed Peebles's Farm. Engineers placed wire entanglements and a full row of abatis in front of the line from Fort Fisher to Fort Welch, slashing timber and laying abatis in front of the picket line as well. To observe the enemy, engineers began a tower 130 feet tall near Fort Conahey, completing half of it by late January.[6]

Charles Wainwright thought most of the forts along the line from Fort Wadsworth were relatively simple but strong. Fort Keene had been "very roughly revetted by infantry," according to Ira Spaulding. When members of his 50th New York Engineers stockaded the fort, Spaulding directed them to improve the revetment and raise the height of the parapet.[7]

Fort Conahey caught everyone's attention. With "no recognized geometric form that I ever saw," Wainwright thought it was "complicated enough to make up for all the rest and to afford illustration for a whole course of lectures on engineering." Half of the fort lay on top of high ground and was, in Wainwright's opinion, "an ordinary open work." The other half lay on the descending slope of a ravine and had casemated gun emplacements to fire in several directions along the ravine. The Federals built an infantry parapet atop the casemates, and a loopholed stockade divided the work in two. "This fort has cost more labor than any other," Wainwright concluded, "and is one of the sights to show to strangers. Further than this I doubt the value of its elaborateness."[8]

### DUTCH GAP CANAL

Butler's project at Dutch Gap neared its end after several months of digging. The engineers worked out a plan whereby detailed men could shovel dirt into horse-drawn carts at the forward end of the canal while a steam-powered dredge worked at the other end. The dredge was mounted on a barge that floated on the water let into the canal. The engineers ran a rail line alongside the canal so the dredge could dump muck directly into cars for removal. As soon as the workmen were finished on the forward end, the dredge could then cut through the ledge of blue clay that separated the two halves and allow water to flow through nearly the entire length of the canal. Work progressed smoothly despite Confederate harassment; a mortar shell sunk the dredge, and it had to be replaced by a second machine. This was only one of more than 20,000 rounds the Confederates dropped on and near the canal from August 9, 1864, to January 1, 1865, amounting to an average of 111 rounds each day.[9]

That left only the embankment at the forward end of the canal, which had to be blasted clear to complete the project. Michie planned to dig two galleries twenty-five feet deep into this embankment and spring mines in five powder chambers. The central chamber held 4,000 pounds of powder divided into "four large rubber bags" connected to a watertight box, each bag and the box containing 800 pounds. The four smaller chambers contained tin cans with 125 pounds each. Michie planned to use the Gomez fuse to explode them. The dredge operators gouged out a hole thirty feet deep near the embankment so the dirt and debris from the explosions could fall into it and still leave enough water to float boats through the canal. One of the galleries was rather complex, with several turns and a steep descent to reach the required depth. Michie framed both galleries to prevent cave-ins. The diggers encountered an underground stream, which required constant bailing.[10]

The canal was mostly finished by mid-November, but its completion was delayed several weeks because Union naval commanders were not yet ready to take advantage of it. Butler also was busy planning an expedition against Fort Fisher at the mouth of the Cape Fear River in late December and delayed the blowing of the embankment until he returned. That expedition was a dismal failure, but Butler was present when engineers sprung the mines on January 1. The Gomez fuse did not work as well as expected; the powder mass was too dense and much of it did not burn. The explosion failed to deposit the dirt into the hole gouged out by the dredge; most of it spread out along the length of the canal while part of it fell into the riverbed. The debris created a semicircular ridge in the James River that rose to a height of six feet above the low-water mark. Butler's engineers reported that many more hours of dredge work would be needed to clear the canal, but dredging the ridge from the riverbed would have to wait until after the war, for workers would be exposed to Confederate fire. As a result, the canal was never used for its original purpose. It did, however, offer a peacetime bonus to the region, for the Dutch Gap Canal became the main channel of the James River and shortened travel time for river traffic.[11]

### CITY POINT WORKS

Federal efforts to protect City Point had begun in mid-September, but Benham had few troops to spare from his overworked garrison. He finished the western line, but the approaches from the southeast were not yet covered. Meade's headquarters issued instructions for pushing the work on November 5, but Benham wanted Meade to prioritize the many projects assigned to him. Benham also wanted an opportunity to drill some newly raised regiments assigned to his command. They had been given spades before they were taught how to use rifles or to maneuver in formation. The engineer also received orders to have his command ready for action in early December when the Fifth Corps set out to raid the Weldon and Petersburg Railroad. Nevertheless, he continued to work sporadically on the City Point defenses.[12]

## ROADS

The engineers maintained the road system that fed the troops by laying corduroy. In fact, Michie complained that "this work seems unending." Ira Spaulding divided responsibility among his officers, mapping out a territory for each one. A single company of the 50th New York Engineers constructed 460 yards of corduroy in the covered ways near Fort Sedgwick over the course of three days. A work detail from the Sixth Corps covered its corduroy with three inches of fresh dirt to make a smoother roadbed, while 300 men and fifty teams from the Second Corps corduroyed a long stretch of Squirrel Level Road.[13]

But the foundation of Meade's logistical effort at Petersburg was the Army Line. The railroad served as a trunk line from which roads radiated to various locations along the trenches. Engineers constructed a branch from Hancock Station, east of the Weldon and Petersburg Railroad, to Fort Blaisdell on the Secondary Line near Jerusalem Plank Road. They continued it to Crawford's division of the Fifth Corps for a total of two and a quarter miles from Hancock Station.[14]

## CONFEDERATE CONSTRUCTION

The Confederates also improved their trenches. When the 31st Georgia returned from the Valley campaigns, I. G. Bradwell found impressive works at Gracie's Salient. The parapet stood six feet tall, and the banquette had a layer of "split pine poles" so the men could keep dry. He also found a well-made headlog designed for observation. It consisted of "heavy square headblocks of oak," with a small hole gouged through. The hole was covered on the outside face by a one-inch-thick piece of sheet iron, which also had a small hole drilled through it. Forty feet ahead of the main line, the Rebels built a row of chevaux-de-frise tied together with telegraph wire. Luther Rice Mills returned to duty on November 15 after recovering from a severe wound received on July 30. He took post within 100 yards of the spot where he had been hit and marveled at the alteration of the works. "Everything has changed so much that I do not think I would have recognized the old place."[15]

Between the crater and Jerusalem Plank Road, heavy oak timbers plated with iron served as headlogs. The Confederates drilled loopholes through them, splayed on the inside to give the sharpshooter greater lateral aim. Alexander finished his artillery emplacements north of the James and at Bermuda Hundred in November and December, "putting the fine touches on them," installing loopholes for observation at all the batteries under his charge. Warren Goodale of the 114th New York thought Rebel palisades were better than Yankee obstructions, and they placed them in front of their picket line rather than between the pickets and the main line. North of the James River, local Confederate commanders were concerned with extending the field of fire as much as 1,000 yards, but they warned subordinates not to send ax crews so far out that they precipitated an engagement. On some sections, the Confederates paid less attention to their picket line than to their main defenses. Henry M. Trueheart visited the skirmish line between the crater and Jerusalem Plank Road during a truce and found that its parapet was eroded and the trench had ankle-deep mud and water in it.[16]

W. A. Day of the 49th North Carolina found out how difficult it was to strengthen the obstructions. One night in December he was told to crawl out and count the sections of chevaux-de-frise so engineers could plan how to install a second line of them. The night was so dark that he could hardly see the joints and only guessed that each section was about twelve feet long. Several balls from Union pickets slammed into the obstruction, and a Confederate picket accused him of trying to desert. Day later fell into a pit of shoulder-deep icy water but managed to get out. Day's job was completed, but his captain refused to let him dry and rest. He had to work on the new line of obstructions for several hours before catching the first opportunity to slip off to his bombproof.[17]

The Confederates built dams in front of their main line to use water as an obstruction. A. P. Hill began such a dam on Old Town Run (now called Rohoic Creek or Indian Town Creek), some distance southwest of Battery No. 45. Construction began after the Fifth Offensive, with most work taking place in November and December. Scales's North Carolina brigade finished the dam about Christmastime, and it took two weeks for the pond to fill with rainwater. Shortly after that, heavy rains broke the dam, sending a torrent down Old Town Run into the Appomattox River. The flood uprooted trees and severely damaged an aqueduct that carried the Upper Appomattox Canal across the stream, further damaging the trestle of the South Side Railroad. A smaller dam on Poor Creek, between Colquitt's Salient and Gracie's Salient, remained intact. Sluice gates had been placed at both ends to allow water to flow past and to regulate the size of the pond. The Confederates also built a parapet atop the dam so infantrymen could better defend it.[18]

McGowan's South Carolina brigade provided up to 350 men a day for work details, often sending them two miles from camp. Each Carolinian worked from 8:00 A.M. to 4:00 P.M. every third or fourth day for two months that winter. While some men worked well, others could labor no more than half an hour before poor nutrition and chronic exhaustion had their effect. Then they "would pant and grow faint" and barely finish their shift. The miscellaneous troops in Ewell's department north of the James River could not drill or per-

Gracie's Salient. Note the dam across Poor Creek.
(Library of Congress, LC-DIG-CWPB-03644)

form necessary camp duties because of their "constant and severe labor" on the defenses.[19]

Lee called for 5,000 blacks to work for sixty days, but no more than 2,000 were mobilized. "We know from past experience and observation that negroes impressed for the fortifications are generally badly treated and suffer much," wrote a Virginia slaveowner to the secretary of war. Engineer officer W. G. Turpin denied charges of poor treatment while noting that slaves disliked "to do labor that will thwart the Federals, who they look upon as fighting for their freedom." Hundreds of slave workers ran away from the defenses. "I consequently have not been able to accomplish half I desired," Lee reported to the secretary of war on December 11. He warned that his army could not hold its position for long unless rear lines of defense and transportation facilities received necessary attention. Given how much he had extended his lines, Lee could no longer afford to detail large numbers of troops for such work.[20]

An English engineer officer named Featherstonhaugh visited the Confederate lines in November 1864 and found those works north of the James far stronger than those fronting Petersburg. Part of the reason was that much of the Petersburg line was too close to the Federals to have a ditch in front. Featherstonhaugh was impressed by the use of bombproofs. He found them "sunken, half-sunken, or elevated," according to the lay of the land. The elevated ones often were used as a cavalier behind the main line. The Englishman found a couple of bombproofs built into the parapet. He also noted the Confederate use of torpedoes and dams.[21]

Col. Edward Hastings Ripley, commander of a brigade in the Eighteenth Corps, described Confederate defenses north of the James by referring to "formidable barriers of red earth" and "double and triple rows of [abatis] with torpedoes and 'trip irons' well sprinkled in." Ripley responded to civilian criticism of the lengthy campaign by asserting, "If any insane gent sitting slipshod at home reading the papers, wonders why Grant didn't advance more on Richmond, the 18th Corps would like the job of taking him out on our picket line, and tossing him atop one of their infernal machines to show him exactly why."[22]

## MINING

The process of constructing countermine systems on both sides of the line came to an end by the new year. On the Federal side, a company of the 50th New York Engineers started a new countermine at Fort McGilvery in the first week of November. The soil was so loose that framing had to be erected after digging but a few inches at a time. The men used wheelbarrows to deposit the dirt 400 feet from the entrance. Spaulding considered the listening gallery complete when it reached a length of 140 feet by November 20.[23]

The Second Corps troops holding Fort Sedgwick constantly heard noises or received reports from Rebel deserters that indicated an underground attack. They evacuated the fort on November 17, except for a detail of fourteen men from Company I, 2nd U.S. Sharpshooters. Meanwhile, engineer troops sank three shafts in the ditch of the fort, twenty-two feet deep. They placed "a tight barrel" in the bottom of each shaft and tamped dirt against the sides to create a solid connection between the barrel and the surrounding earth. After breaking open the barrelhead, they placed a string tautly across the top. It was assumed that any digging within sixteen feet of the barrel would cause the string to vibrate. The engineers spent a week doing this work until the regular garrison replaced the Sharpshooters.[24]

The Federals heard more sounds on the night of December 6, and Spaulding sent one of his captains the next day. The officer "spent an hour and twenty minutes in the listening gallery and heard noises which might easily be imagined to proceed from miners at work," but he took no special precautions. A Northern officer was convinced that the Rebels had run a tunnel out from a two-gun battery to their picket line. He also erroneously thought that the Federals had done the same, mistaking the shafts in the ditch of Fort Sedgwick for entrances to this tunnel.[25]

The Confederates were sensitive to reports from deserters. James Stewart of the 8th New York Heavy Artillery told a fanciful tale to Bushrod Johnson on November 21. He claimed that the Federals had constructed a small rail track in an offensive mine aimed at Colquitt's Salient. Stewart "stated that the car could be heard running down grade some time after it started from the entrance to the mine." Johnson wanted an engineer officer to visit the salient and recommend a course of action.[26]

Col. James Jourdan, commander of Fort Burnham, worried that the Confederates had extended a mine under the fort. Weitzel did not believe the story but sent Michie to direct the digging of countermines and authorized him to charge them as soon as possible in case Jourdan was right. Of course, the Confederates were doing no such thing. Michie dug "well holes" on the glacis, just outside the ditch, to serve as listening posts. There was little danger of mining because the Confederates were several hundred yards away with a valley twenty feet deep between the lines.[27]

The only new mine work by the Confederates took place north of the James River. Engineer officers feared that the terrain in front of Elliott's Salient could offer an avenue of underground approach. Company H, 1st Confederate Engineers, and Company H, 2nd Confederate Engineers, moved north of the river early on the morning of December 24. Lt. Carter Nelson Berkeley Minor pushed the listening gallery at Elliott's Salient 425 feet before stopping.[28]

### TRENCH LIFE

The coming of winter caused a lull in active operations but no letup in trench duty. The 31st North Carolina in Clingman's brigade had 159 men available in late November. Seventy-one performed daily guard duty, 30 were on the picket line, 9 stood as sentinels on the works, and 32 guarded prisoners. That left only 17 men to hold the main line assigned to the regiment.[29]

In emergencies, the Confederates stretched their troops to an almost unbelievable extent. Johnson's division covered the entire front from the Appomattox River to the Weldon and Petersburg Railroad during the Hicksford Raid in early December. A more normal allotment of troop strength required Goode's brigade of Johnson's division to cover the line from Rives's Salient, where the Dimmock line crossed Jerusalem Plank Road, to the crater. Longstreet fretted over his meager manpower north of the James River, warning Lee that he could hold only up to the Williamsburg Road. He would have to leave the stretch of trenches between that point and the Nine-Mile Road "entirely neglected" if no more troops could be spared to complete the works.[30]

When he visited Goode's brigade on November 10, Lee suggested that the men dig a secondary line parallel to the main trench "deep enough to hide

[them] from the Yankees," as Fred Fleet put it. A secondary trench would allow the men to get out of trenches dirtied by months of continuous occupation. The Confederates never acted on this idea, which Johnson had advocated months before, because of labor shortages.³¹

Lee's manpower problems eased a bit with the return of troops from the Shenandoah Valley. Kershaw's division of the First Corps left on November 15 and reached Petersburg in a week, taking position north of the James River. Gordon's and Pegram's divisions left Waynesborough on December 8 and traveled by train to Richmond, then filed into the Petersburg trenches. Grimes's division left the Valley on December 14. Ironically, Lee sent Hoke's division away on December 21 when a Union move against Wilmington became apparent.³²

The Federals recalled the Sixth Corps from the Valley as well. Wheaton's division left on December 3, Getty left a bit later, and the whole corps was at Petersburg by December 16. It covered the line from a point just east of Jerusalem Plank Road to Fort Fisher. Many of Wright's men were not happy about their return to "these dirty trenches," as Wilbur Fisk put it. "There is nothing desirable about this place. It is all fighting and no fun." Other Sixth Corps troops were impressed with the extensive obstructions and the strong earthworks that had been built since their departure, and they longed for a Confederate attack to test them.³³

The Federals often shifted corps and divisions along the entrenchments, and commanders had to work out the details. One division of Humphreys's Second Corps relieved two divisions of Parke's Ninth Corps on November 29, so those two divisions could relieve two other divisions of the Second Corps. Humphreys warned Parke that it had to be done at night. He needed to withdraw and replace 2,000 of his men who were standing picket so the movement would not arouse Confederate suspicion. Parke sent staff officers to consult with Second Corps division leaders as to the precise arrangement of troops in the line, and then he moved his headquarters next to Humphreys under cover of darkness, taking over the spot as soon as Humphreys moved his staff and quarters away.³⁴

When finally settled, the Ninth Corps held the line from the Appomattox River to Fort Davis, just west of Jerusalem Plank Road. Ledlie's First Division had earlier been broken up and its units distributed to Potter and Willcox. The black troops were taken away and added to those serving in the Army of the James to form the all-black Twenty-Fifth Corps, while the authorities brigaded newly raised Pennsylvania regiments into a new division commanded by John Hartranft.³⁵

One could see the spires of Petersburg from the roof of the bombproof and

Headquarters bombproof at Fort Sedgwick. Note the gabion, log, and sandbag construction; the chimney; and the wooden door. (Library of Congress, LC-DIG-CWPB-02582)

magazine the Ninth Corps troops constructed after moving into Fort Sedgwick. Made of dirt, timber, gabions, and sandbags, it was sturdy enough to withstand a direct hit from a 64-pounder mortar shell. Officers on duty in the fort did not undress at night and kept shielded lights burning at officers' quarters and at the entrance to the magazine. Gunners manned the artillery twenty-four hours a day. They became used to the constant patter of picket fire and learned to sleep through it, waking up if it stopped.³⁶

Henry Pleasants, who commanded Fort Sedgwick, asked William B. Lapham to open fire and test the range of opposing Rebel artillery. Lapham refused to do so without a written order, so Pleasants supplied one, but the experiment was a mistake. The Confederates responded accurately, pummeling the fort and the infantry camps to its rear. A mortar shell gouged out a hole in the roof of the magazine and tossed a chunk of frozen dirt onto Pleasants's head. When he recovered his senses, Pleasants ordered the firing stopped. The Confederates killed two men, wounded several others, and destroyed some quarters.³⁷

The men lived in "long, barrack-like bomb-proofs" at Fort Sedgwick, "low structures of logs opening to the rear, with frequent doors for easy exit in case of alarm." The roof and chimneys consisted of logs and clay. Rain turned the quarters into "moist and dripping" dens, "making the interior at all times dark

*November, December, and January*

and dismal." Officers had smaller bombproofs, but they were more uncomfortable than the men's. "Rain turned these rat holes into dripping baths," recalled the historian of the 35th Massachusetts, "which continued to drip long after the weather above ground had cleared." The officers preferred to live in tents pitched to the rear of the bombproofs and escape into their underground shelter only when the shelling was heavy.[38]

Elsewhere on the Ninth Corps front, officers made efforts to remove bodies that had been haphazardly interred near the line to a central burial ground. Parke ordered each division to select a lot and fence it in, identifying each burial by name, rank, and unit wherever possible. The old problem of sanitation continued to pester officers. Several brigades of the Ninth Corps did not have proper latrines, "and their ground is in a very filthy condition."[39]

An informal truce on the Ninth Corps front resulted in the capture of a former Confederate general. Roger A. Pryor, who had been born near Petersburg and had crafted a prewar career as lawyer, newspaper editor, and member of the U.S. Congress, had also led a brigade in the Seven Days, at Second Manassas, and at Antietam. Lee and Longstreet lost faith in his abilities and divested him of his units, resulting in his resignation in August 1863. Pryor then enlisted as a private and served as a courier in the 3rd Virginia Cavalry. Federal officers came to believe he visited the Union line at Petersburg under an assumed name and laid a trap for him. Capt. Hollis O. Dudley of the 11th New Hampshire approached the Confederate line on November 27, pretending a desire to exchange newspapers. When Pryor came out to meet him, Dudley grabbed his arm and dragged him back into Union lines. The Confederates protested this action, but Meade kept Pryor, even though he disapproved of Dudley's actions, because of the former general's spying activities. Pryor remained a prisoner of war until near the end of the conflict.[40]

## TRENCH FIGHTING

The frequency, duration, and intensity of picket and artillery firing was influenced by a number of factors, including the presence of black troops. It took a while for the Confederates to learn that Parke's black units had been transferred from the Ninth Corps. When the 36th Massachusetts took position in Fort Sedgwick, Rebel pickets increased the rate of fire on the opposing line. Only when the Federals told them that the blacks were no longer part of their command did the Confederates stop.[41]

At Bermuda Hundred, a normally quiet sector, the picket lines were only forty yards apart in places. The Confederates got along well with Butler's white troops, often trading coffee and newspapers with them. Then black units rotated into line on December 2, and "it enraged our boys," reported a Rebel in the 57th Virginia. The Confederates sent a message across no-man's-land requesting that the blacks be removed, which the Federals ignored. The Confederates suddenly opened fire the next morning, killing several black soldiers who had exposed themselves. The Yankees retaliated with heavy artillery fire for several days before peace was restored on December 6.[42]

There were many other causes for outbreaks of firing, such as an unusual bugle call in the opposing lines that might signal an attack. When Fort Fisher near Wilmington fell in mid-January, the Federals near the crater taunted the men of Ransom's North Carolina brigade, and the Tar Heels opened fire out of frustration. But the crater area had always been the scene of heavy picket and artillery fire. When Henry Trueheart visited the works east of Jerusalem Plank Road, he found men relaxing in the open on both sides of no-man's-land during a truce. Closer to the crater, the truce still held firm, but no one dared to show himself. Closer still to the hole, picket firing continued unabated.[43]

At Gracie's Salient, the pickets were under orders to fire every fifteen minutes, even if there was nothing to shoot at. A lieutenant in the 31st Georgia discovered that a picket had fallen asleep one night, so he ordered the men to fire every five minutes to keep them awake. The Federals took this as a sign of impending trouble and opened a heavy artillery barrage. Some Georgians lost their composure. I. G. Bradwell frantically tried to contact the others on the picket line and found one man crying like a child while huddled in the bottom of his skirmish pit, his endurance broken. Bradwell retired to the main line, his way lit by shell explosions, and found his comrades standing to on the banquette. Everyone endured the tense night to find the Union artillery slackening its fire the next day, but Bradwell thought it never really returned to normal for the rest of the campaign. The lieutenant who had caused all this trouble took up the habit of nudging each picket with the tip of his sword to keep him awake.[44]

One day in November, Lee visited Gracie's Salient and stared at the Union line through field glasses while perched on the banquette. Gracie was afraid for Lee's safety and quietly stood in front of him. "General, you should not expose yourself so much," Lee told him. "If *I* should not, Gen. Lee, why should you, the Commander-in-chief?" Lee merely smiled and walked away. A few weeks later, on December 2, Gracie and several other men near him were killed by a single artillery round while superintending work on the defenses.[45]

Johnson's division, which held the sector nearest Union lines, seemed to waste ammunition, in the eyes of higher authorities. Johnson defended his troops, reporting on December 2 that he detailed 1,100 men every day to fire on the enemy. They expended 20,000 rounds, amounting to an average of 18 rounds per man. Johnson relayed information from Federal deserters that each Union picket received 100 rounds and was told to fire it all during his shift.[46]

Many members of Johnson's division made informal arrangements with the enemy to reduce loss of life. John Forrest Robinson of the 23rd South Carolina recalled that the pickets sometimes agreed to aim high while expending their quota of rounds. If someone happened to plant a ball close to a Yankee, the Federal might call out, "'Say Johnnie dont shoot so low, shoot higher—you might hit one of us.'" Unfortunately, the artillerymen never were a party to such arrangements, and they often fired at targets of opportunity.[47]

Trench raids became fairly common along the line. The sharpshooter battalion of McGowan's South Carolina brigade often nabbed a few prisoners for information, sometimes cooperating with the sharpshooters of Lane's North Carolina brigade to make a bigger sweep. They typically rushed the Federal pickets before dawn and moved up and down the line of skirmish pits, taking prisoners and whatever food and equipment they could find, and returned quickly. The Confederates coordinated one such raid on the Sixth Corps sector with owl hoots and whistles.[48]

Johnson coordinated two trench raids on the night of November 5. Gracie pushed forward three companies of the 41st Alabama to capture thirty-one Federals and advance his picket line without loss. At the same time, Wallace struck the Union picket line for the second time in less than two weeks, capturing 100 yards (twenty pits) and ten men in front of the crater. While there was no attempt to push back the Alabama men on Gracie's front (the Federals thought those pits should have been abandoned anyway), the Yankees fired incessantly at the South Carolinians near the crater. Johnson moved tools up to the captured picket line and his men tried to dig effective cover, but they were forced to give up the ground by dawn. Wallace suffered fourteen killed, forty-one wounded, and forty captured or missing, and he lost most of his entrenching tools.[49]

When Johnson noticed mysterious movements in the Union line and wanted prisoners to interrogate, Capt. John Floyd moved out on the cloudy night of December 20 with 200 members of Wallace's brigade picket reserve. Leaving half of them to reinforce the picket line, Floyd took the rest across no-man's-land. He managed to capture seven pits before he was forced to retire. Floyd captured twenty-eight prisoners and lost only six men in the raid.[50]

MAJOR MOVEMENTS

The beginning of Sherman's March to the Sea on November 15 led Grant to think that Lee might detach some of his men to oppose the movement, and he planned how to take advantage of the reduced Confederate troop strength. Butler could abandon all of his positions north of the James or hold only Deep Bottom and Dutch Gap in order to shift nearly his entire army to the Petersburg line. Meade could then maneuver the Army of the Potomac with twelve days' rations and eighty rounds of ammunition per man to almost any point designated in order to bring the campaign to a quick end. Grant was loath to try such an all-or-nothing endeavor unless the circumstances warranted it. He preferred holding all ground that had been gained and moving with smaller contingents, but Lee had no real opportunity to send troops to Georgia.[51]

Meanwhile, Michie proposed a plan of attack for Butler at Bermuda Hundred. He thought it possible to break the Howlett Line, believing it had a modest parapet and relatively shallow ditch, and establish a new line with its right anchored at Howlett's House and its left extending southwestward to cross the Richmond-Petersburg Turnpike and the Richmond and Petersburg Railroad. The left end of the new line would be refused for flank protection. Michie thought the new position could be fortified in twelve hours. He envisioned a movement to cut communications between Richmond and Petersburg, not a breakthrough accompanied by the capture of either city.[52]

Grant settled for a massive raid to tear up a sizable chunk of the Weldon and Petersburg Railroad. Lee had managed to bypass the break at Globe Tavern by establishing a wagon relay to haul supplies from Stony Creek Station, fifteen miles south of the tavern, by way of Boydton Plank Road and then into Petersburg. The Federals could not stop this until they advanced westward and secured control of the plank road. In the meantime, a large raid could limit the usefulness of the Weldon and Petersburg Railroad. Grant wanted the line torn up at least as far as Hicksford, thirty miles south of the Union position, and ten miles north of the border between Virginia and North Carolina.[53]

The Hicksford Raid was a success with little fighting and few casualties. Meade sent the Fifth Corps and one division of the Second Corps, 22,000 infantrymen accompanied by 4,200 cavalrymen, on December 7. Warren moved quickly enough to get a head start on the Confederates. His cavalry found significant fortifications at Hicksford. The town lay on the south bank of the Meherrin River where three redoubts with connecting infantry lines barred the Federal approach. Another infantry trench lay north of the stream to cover the approach to the railroad bridge. Confederate engineers had also placed abatis and chevaux-de-frise in front of the line on the north side of the river. Two cavalry units advanced against the defenses on December 9 but could make no headway through the obstructions. When Warren arrived, he decided Hicksford was too well defended and turned back without destroying the bridge. The Fifth Corps had already torn up sixteen miles of track and now made haste to return to its winter quarters. Along the way, the men burned buildings at Sussex Court House in retaliation for the murder and mutilation of a dozen stragglers, and they liberated about 100 slaves from local planters. A bitter cold front sailed across the area before Warren reached the Petersburg line, dropping the temperature below freezing and covering the landscape with ice. But the worst danger lay in A. P. Hill's efforts to intercept Warren with a substantial force drawn from his corps. The Federals were saved by the fact that Hill's information lagged several hours behind Warren's movements, and the opponents made no substantial contact before Warren returned to Petersburg on December 12. Confederate engineers repaired the damage to the Weldon and Petersburg Railroad after three months of hard work, due to shortages of material and labor.[54]

CHAPTER FIFTEEN

## *Winter*

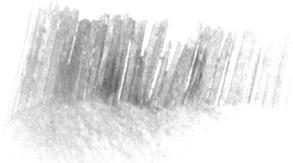

Fred Fleet of the 26th Virginia predicted as early as September 8 that his comrades would suffer shortages of wood and disagreeable living conditions in their underground shelters as cold weather set in. Yet Fleet noted that the French and English endured a winter in the siege lines at Sebastopol ten years before, and for what he called a far less worthy cause than that which animated Civil War soldiers.[1]

Winter offered a taste of bad weather on November 23, when snow fell for the first time that season. This weather front produced temperatures that caused some Confederates to suffer frostbite; others came in from picket duty "crying from cold like children." In fact, many of these same men had no shoes, blankets, or coats. Members of Goode's Virginia brigade endured a horrible night of sleet that so coated their muskets they could not have fired them if the Yankees had advanced. Their suffering "caused many to . . . curse the cause in which they were engaged." Luther Rice Mills of the 26th Virginia agreed that many of his comrades were "generally for *peace on any terms* at the close of a cold, wet night, but after the sun is up and they get warm, they are in their usual spirits." George D. Bowen of the 12th New Jersey noticed the same thing among his Federal comrades. "The cold fatigue and exposure appears to take all the life out of one," he admitted to his diary.[2]

Another cold front passed over Virginia on December 9, during the Hicksford Raid. Sleet fell all that night, coating everything with a solid layer of ice. Fred M. Colston had to ride about in this storm, collecting ammunition for Gordon's Second Corps, and found that the ice had so plastered his coat that he literally had to crawl out from it and thaw the coat by a campfire the next day.[3]

Keeping warm became a constant chore. Warren Goodale of the 11th Massachusetts Light Battery used the parapet of the Ninth Corps trench to break the cold wind, but to the rear there was no such protection. It was sometimes so cold early in the morning that Georgian William Starr Basinger could not dry the water from his beard and hair while washing before it froze on his face. Often the trenches were knee deep with mud or "filled with ice and snow," and the wind seemed to blow constantly from the west. It was impossible to find clothes thick enough to keep the wind from penetrating to the skin. Fortunately, some men could take it all with an air of humor. Sgt. Maj. A. J. Simpson of the 1st Virginia called out work details to construct chevaux-de-frise on cold mornings by yelling, "'Turn out here, men, for shivering and frizzing.'"[4]

Many Confederates relied on outside sources for additional clothing. The Soldier's Relief Association in South Carolina collected boxes of clothes from relatives and delivered them to soldiers at Petersburg. Governor Zebulon B. Vance of North Carolina organized a state effort to forward winter clothes to Tar Heels in Lee's army. He received appeals from mothers for wool, with which they promised to make coats for their sons in the trenches, and he also forwarded ready-made coats to a number of high-ranking officers at Petersburg. A handful of men wore a balaclava, a hood to be pulled down over the head with a V-shaped slit for the eyes and mouth.[5]

### WINTER QUARTERS

The men began to build winter huts as early as the latter part of September, just before the Fifth Offensive. Many Confederate units first dug bombproofs, if they had not already done so, aiming to spend the winter underground. The 49th North Carolina placed its bombproofs in a line about thirty yards behind the trench, each one big enough for a company. They consisted of a hole thirty feet long, twelve feet wide, and seven feet deep, with a wooden frame covered with dirt. Hagood's brigade along the Alexander Line, north of the James River, built cabins of small pine logs in a row a few yards behind the line, with a street between the huts and the trench. Regimental officers lived in huts behind this line, and brigade officers were in huts placed still farther to the rear. Gordon's Second Corps units also constructed huts that were ten by fourteen feet, with a chimney at one end and the door at the other. His men used sticks and clay to fill up the open spaces between logs. Up to a dozen men shared each hut.[6]

Winter quarters appeared at about the same time on the Union side of the Richmond-Petersburg lines. Members of the 190th Pennsylvania constructed their huts five feet tall and seven by nine feet in dimension, using shelter tents as roofs. Lt. George B. Peck Jr. of the 2nd Rhode Island lived in a hut that had a triple thickness of tent for a roof, a dirt floor beaten so hard that it was like cement, and a frame seven feet wide and fifteen feet long. Members of the 14th Connecticut dug a covered way three feet wide and five feet long back from the main trench near Fort Morton, then excavated a square hole at the end of the covered way and placed logs as the roof.[7]

The 2nd Rhode Island built its camp half a mile behind the line, with a wide road between it and the trench. The regiment laid out six streets at right angles to this road, while the huts along the streets were allowed to take any shape or size the owners wanted. The only cross street, on the south side of the camp, was reserved for officers. South of this officer's street, the men constructed a palisade with a gateway and a bridge to cross a drainage ditch. Storage tents, two flagpoles, and an elaborate hut for Col. Elisha Hunt Rhodes completed the military village. As Rhodes put it, the end result was that the "army camp looks like a great city." It was well that the regiment placed its huts so far from the trench, for orders went out in early December that any structures within 100 yards of the main line had to be torn down. The men of Smyth's brigade in the Second Corps demolished and rebuilt nearly all their huts as a result.[8]

The Confederates also allowed a mixture of individual construction and unit-level planning. William Dunlop's sharpshooters constructed their winter quarters in a ravine more than 100 yards behind the line. Dunlop laid it out in a square, with one company of the battalion occupying each of three sides and the officers taking the fourth. The men placed their huts in holes dug into the side of the ravine, with timber revetment to shore up the dirt walls and canvas to serve as roofing.[9]

Many men went to great lengths to domesticate their quarters, making beds of sticks and hay or substituting leafy twigs for mattresses. They ripped boards from hardtack boxes and fashioned them into tables and stools, while nails or wooden pegs driven into log walls became coat hangers. Boards also served as doors, held onto the walls by leather hinges, or less fussy men simply draped gunnysacks across the entrance to their hut. Intact hardtack boxes made good cupboards, and pork barrels or sticks daubed with clay served as chimneys. Decorations included illustrations cut from *Harper's Weekly*, and military equipment hung from available places along the walls.[10]

Everyone, except high-ranking officers, lived in cramped quarters. John Forrest Robinson of the 23rd South Carolina shared a bombproof with seven men. They called it the "'Snoring Saloon'" because one of the roommates had a nostril partially closed by a wound. Worse than this was a problem encountered by I. G. Bradwell of the 31st Georgia. "We were greatly annoyed at night by rats running over us," he reported. "These pests were almost as large as squirrels and were always ready to pounce down on our meager rations if any chance offered." The rats shared winter quarters with the soldiers by digging holes in the dirt walls of the bombproofs.[11]

The bombproofs were safer than huts, but they did not withstand the weather as well. Virginia lay between the frigid north and the semitropical Deep South, and the soldiers at Petersburg experienced sometimes dramatic changes in weather. "Cold snaps, with snow and hail and all the discomforts of a Northern winter, alternated with intervals of mild, sunny days, when it was a delight to be abroad." Such changes in temperature played havoc with living quarters. Water percolated through the roofs of bombproofs and soaked the living arrangements inside. A heavy rain fell January 5–9, flooding hundreds of bombproofs. Some of them were "entirely wrecked" due to cave-ins, and others had to be demolished and rebuilt. Collapsing roofs killed a man in the 24th North Carolina and another in the 56th North Carolina. Even if the bombproofs remained intact, they were miserable places to live in as water continued to drip through the roofs for days after a heavy rain.[12]

Heating arrangements were crucial. Chimneys usually consisted of some makeshift article, such as an empty barrel, or were painstakingly constructed from small sticks and clay. A fortunate group in the 14th Connecticut managed to find enough bricks to make their chimney, while many Federals rigged small stoves from cast-off pieces of metal. Edward King Wightman of the 3rd New York used a camp kettle and a saucepan riveted together, with holes knocked out in appropriate places. A stack of empty tin cans served as the smokestack. "The machine works like a charm," he reported home. The U.S. Engineer Battalion also made stoves from empty tin cans by melting the solder and flattening the tin into sheets. Officers of high rank had enough resources to purchase "little air-tight box stoves" from the sutler. But whether the apparatus was an open fireplace or a jury-rigged stove, it was likely to heat unevenly. As a member of Wallace's South Carolina brigade put it, "You will freeze on one side and bake on the other" and be sorely troubled by the smoke that accumulated in the quarters.[13]

Finding enough fuel for heat became a problem for everyone. One of the first things Longstreet did after taking command north of the James was to issue instructions for his men to practice "as much economy . . . in the consumption of the wood as is consistent with . . . comfort." They were to cut trees in front of the line first, saving those to the rear for later in the winter season. Rationing of wood was common. In the 49th North Carolina, ten sticks of green pine wood and one bushel of coal were allowed for each company per day. The members of McGowan's brigade carried "green pine or swamp wood" on their shoulders for a mile. Richard H. Anderson tried to haul timber to repair bombproofs and revet trenches but could not surmount a number of problems; there were not enough suitable trees within a reasonable distance of the work sites, teams were weak from hunger, and the railroad was overworked. Staff officer Giles Buckner Cooke rode two miles along the wood supply route of Johnson's division to arrange for a steady ration of seventy-seven cords per day for the men. It took him four hours of riding and cajoling numerous support personnel to make all the arrangements for this meager supply.[14]

The Federals experienced wood shortages too, yet there were moments of cooperation for the few trees that remained between the lines. One day after a cold spell, a sergeant in the 36th Massachusetts called out to the Rebels that he intended to cut down a tree halfway between the opposing picket lines. By the time he got there, the Confederates had sent out a squad to do the same thing. They conferred and decided to share the tree rather than fight for it. Since it fell toward the Confederate line, the Rebels took the top half of it and the Yankees took the bottom half.[15]

The quality of rations caused a mutiny of sorts in Clingman's brigade. The commissary sergeant of the 31st North Carolina issued one pound of flour and less than one-third of a pound of bacon to each man in the regiment. Some of the bacon was spoiled, leading more than sixty men to boycott roll call that night. Six men of the 51st North Carolina also participated in the "ration row." Two days later, brigade leader Hector McKethan issued one and a half pounds of turnips and a quarter-pound of cabbage to each man, but he made it clear that this was not done because of their protest; the vegetables had been in the supply pipeline even before the boycott.[16]

Capt. Will Biggs of the 17th North Carolina noted that rations were "most uncomfortably short" as early as November 12. The men ate only two meals a day and often felt hungry after each one. The men of Pickett's division ate all their daily rations in one meal and then went hungry until the next day. Black laborers on the fortifications received the same rations and often prowled around the soldiers' camps at night, looking for food. This is why most black body servants attending Confederate officers were sent home or hired out to other officers who were willing to feed them.[17]

John Forrest Robinson of the 23rd South Carolina looked forward to a promised New Year's dinner with "Visions of roast turkey, pig, cranberry sause, plum pudding, and mince pies." After standing picket all night in a freezing rain, he found only "a strip of fresh fat pig." Greatly disappointed, Robinson fried it with a pone of cornbread. Just before it was ready, a lump of clay fell from his newly made chimney into the pan. Even after he removed most of the dirt, Robinson had to eat his holiday dinner garnished with Virginia mud.[18]

Luther Rice Mills watched as one of his comrades caught a big rat and ate it. "What is it that a dirty soldier won't do?" After more than an inch of snow fell, groups of soldiers roamed the area near their quarters hunting rabbits. Virgil S. Cavin in Scales's brigade pleaded with his relatives for food. "Send me all you can I can't Stay here this a way," he wrote. "I have to work on the brest works and I cant hardly do it for the want of somthing to eat." Cavin included a long list of items and pestered his father until a box of food arrived a month after his request.[19]

Cavin was lucky, for many Confederates never received the packages sent them by loved ones. "There is a regularly organized band of thugs and pickpockets infesting the depot at Petersburg," reported a man in the 11th North Carolina. Packages were particularly vulnerable because overworked shipping agents often could not watch them. Brigade leader George H. Steuart sent armed guards to the depot to pick up all boxes addressed to his men. Battle's Alabama brigade made similar arrangements. Ordnance officer James W. Albright of the 12th Virginia Artillery Battalion found one of his boxes stolen and two others broken into at the depot. He managed to find "the guilty party & gave him a most unmerciful whipping," recovering clothes, food, and brandy.[20]

One-third of a pound of cornbread and three ounces of bacon constituted the normal daily ration of many Confederates. At one point, McGowan's brigade received no meat for a week, and later it received canned beef imported from England through the blockade. Irregular issues of coffee and sugar accompanied a daily ration of tobacco. One bright day, the South Carolinians received a gill of whiskey apiece. "It was amusing, as well as sad, to see the delight of the troops over this drop of comfort."[21]

There were no appreciable food shortages in the Union ranks at Petersburg. Federal soldiers requested food and liquors from home, but as a supplement to an efficient army supply network. The medical director of the Fifth Corps recommended that Warren's men adopt a system of company-level cooking as the most efficient method of serving well-prepared meals laden with fresh vegetables. Thanksgiving was a true feast. Interested citizens gathered 20,000 turkeys at New York City and 4,000 at Philadelphia to be distributed to Meade's Army of the Potomac, Butler's Army of the James, and Sheridan's Army of the Shenandoah. The U.S. Engineer Battalion received barrels filled with turkeys and chickens and "had a grand dinner." A number of infantry regiments in Meade's army received cakes, pies, and fruit in large enough quantities to supply two full meals for each soldier. The entire Army of the James was treated to a Thanksgiving dinner courtesy of many soldiers' aid societies and Delmonico's restaurant in New York City. Even if the food was not free, Union officers could afford to buy turkey and sweet potatoes from the sutler and have their servants cook the fare in sheet iron camp stoves for a special holiday treat.[22]

A shortage of soap complemented the food shortage in Confederate camps. "The neglect of personal cleanliness has occasioned cutaneous diseases to a great extent in many commands," Lee complained. He urged Secretary of War

Seddon to contract with private individuals for its manufacture. Efforts to do so had already yielded little, for contractors wanted high prices and produced little soap.[23]

Lack of soap and a proper diet combined with demanding duty in the trenches to stress Confederate soldiers. Artillery officer Robert Stiles was shocked to see the condition of the Florida troops in Mahone's division, field officers and privates alike. "We could scarcely realize that the unwashed, uncombed, unfed and almost unclad creatures we saw were officers of rank and reputation in the army," he remembered.[24]

Disciplinary problems soon surfaced. The Virginians of Pickett's division had a tendency to stray from the Howlett Line and roam the countryside to the rear, stealing whatever property they could find. Responding to complaints, Lee ordered a thorough inspection of Pickett's command and concluded officers were largely to blame. They failed to set up classes to instruct the men in army regulations (which also would have kept them occupied while not on duty). Lee suggested the troops be kept busy mending their clothing and shoes. "Every man must do all in his power to economise what we have, and make it go as far as possible."[25]

On the Federal side of the trench lines, high-ranking officers tried to keep their men busy with drilling. "Regular recitations in tactics and regulations should now be had," ordered Second Corps commander Andrew A. Humphreys, "and the Articles of War should be frequently read. A systematic effort should be made by division, brigade, and regimental commanders to bring their troops to the highest practicable state of discipline." A recruit in the 99th Pennsylvania of de Trobriand's brigade recorded heavy drilling and almost daily dress parades that winter.[26]

In the Confederate lines, Lee ordered each unit to drill eight times per day, double the number anyone could remember he had ever required before. The men of McGowan's brigade "were worn out in mind and in body, and every effort had become painfully irksome," yet they drilled four times a day in an effort to restore some of their physical tone and optimism.[27]

The waking hours of the Confederate soldier at Petersburg were occupied by loathsome picket duty, day and night, in cold, uncomfortable conditions. William Starr Basinger inspected a segment of picket line north of the James River on the night of December 31, after a day of snow and sleet. He had difficulty picking his way along the narrow path through the abatis and torpedoes, then he found it hard even to find the picket pits because the snow obscured them from view. The pickets had kindled small fires in the bottom of the pits, but the flame could not be seen until one stood next to the hole. Basinger trudged along on his inspection tour, fearful of straying off course and winding up in Union lines; despite the cold, he sweated furiously because of the exertion and returned to his quarters exhausted.[28]

The Federal pickets also built small fires in the bottom of their pits. William Milo Olin had a difficult time keeping a flame going during a twenty-hour period of cold rain that filled the pits with water and caved in the sides. He had to rekindle the fire with green pine wood while standing in nearly knee-deep mud and water. On some parts of the line, picket firing did not cease because of the weather. De Trobriand's men stood in ankle-deep water firing into "a thick fog through which oozes a cold and drenching rain."[29]

While Lee's privates stood picket duty every third or fourth day, his officers did so more often. They stayed awake for twenty-four hours every tour of duty and could "scarcely recover from the effects of this loss of sleep, fatigue, & c, before their services are again demanded." On parts of the line where picket and artillery firing was heavy, the men could hardly move about, "even to the sinks." Daniel W. Sawtelle of the 8th Maine thought that many men who deliberately exposed themselves to enemy fire may have planned to commit suicide to escape the strain of trench life.[30]

Fred Fleet, who was then serving on the staff of Goode's Virginia brigade, left his bombproof one night and observed the eerie calm. "When we look at the thing in the abstract," he pondered, "does it not seem foolish that two nations should sit down and dig, and dig again and sit down for eight long months in front of each other?"[31]

Many of Fleet's comrades were asking themselves the same question as they listened to the growls of their stomachs. "Our army generally is in the lowest spirits I have ever seen it since the commencement of the war," declared R. P. Scarborough of Alabama. Scarborough had never despaired of Confederate victory until early December 1864, when he became convinced that only divine intervention could save the South. Lee's men could hardly live "on what they draw from the government," Scarborough continued. He noted that many soldiers were marrying women in and around Petersburg, "Some for life some for the war and some for one winter only."[32]

John R. Forbes of the 18th Virginia spoke for many when he told his aunt, "I think we are whiped now if we Just only new it." Many soldiers favored peace through a compromise between North and South, and there seemed to be a possibility of that happening in February when Jefferson Davis authorized a delegation to cross the lines at Petersburg and open talks with Union representatives at Hampton Roads. A truce was called, prompting men on both sides to mingle in no-man's-land. They chopped down the few trees that still stood near Fort Sedgwick and shared them, and they exchanged coffee, hardtack, knives, rings, and trinkets made from fuses of exploded shells. Hope reigned supreme for a few hours, but then it was dashed as news arrived that the peace conference had broken up with no result. The Confederate negotiators were not authorized to accept the dissolution of slavery, a prerequisite to any restoration of the Union.[33]

While many of Lee's troops were hopelessly discouraged, others soldiered on despite many signs of trouble besetting the Confederacy. "The Army is in far better spirits than it has been for a month or two past," declared a Tar Heel officer in early March, "and is much more hopeful." Staff officer Edward Cook Barnes argued that all of Lee's men were "for vigorous action and hoot at the idea of the chance of our being subjugated." Whenever there happened to be an extra supply of food available, spirits usually soared. Company commander Henry P. Fortson of the 31st Georgia cheated by reporting more men on duty than he actually had, and he managed to secure respectable rations spiced by the occasional issue of sorghum, apple brandy, and sugar. "I have resolved to fight as long as *Mass Robert* has a corporals guard," declared Fortson, "or until he says give up, he is the man that I shall follow or die in the attempt."[34]

Giles Buckner Cooke spent hours one day inspecting the trenches of Johnson's division. He found the conditions appalling due to several days of almost continuous rain. Mud, water, and inability to build fires made the privates' lives in the works miserable in the extreme, yet Cooke found the troops cheerful. "A great many of the men without blankets, overcoats or shoes endured the awful weather of last night. It is incomprehensible how they can stand so much exposure."[35]

Morale was a delicate thing, strong one day and weak the next, due to any number of factors, and the feelings of one were not necessarily the feelings of all. Anderson's Georgia brigade passed a resolution on February 10, 1865, renewing its pledge to "prosecute the war to the last." A month later, sixty men deserted from the brigade in one night alone.[36]

The majority of officers and men in both armies at Petersburg filled their few idle hours with whatever pastimes they could arrange. Educational lectures became common, while many soldiers made souvenirs of cast-off military items. William P. Hopkins of the 7th Rhode Island made models of mortars out of spent Confederate bullets. One of his creations contained 300 balls and rested on a platform made of 120 more bullets, the whole thing weighing twenty-five pounds and intended as a gift for Rhode Island governor James Y. Smith.[37]

The 50th New York Engineers not only built a model winter camp but constructed an impressive chapel that drew the attention of many observers. It was made of logs squared on three sides, with the rough side exposed on the facade. The engineers constructed a stage twelve feet by twelve feet and a steeple composed of small pine logs. The men staged minstrel shows and listened to lectures, while chaplains held divine services every Sunday. One of Meade's staff officers was married in the engineer chapel. The building was used as a hospital during the final round of fighting at Petersburg, and the engineers placed a tablet at the church before they left the area, donating the chapel to the trustees of the nearby Poplar Spring Church. It stood for many years after the war, and there was some talk of removing the building to Central Park in New York City as a memorial to the engineer regiment.[38]

Some Confederates also built chapels along their line and used them for religious services, classes to reinforce tactics among their officers, and "lectures on different subjects, political and scientific." James A. Graham hoped to teach every man in his 27th North Carolina how to read before the winter was over, "even if I don't have time to teach them any thing more." The regimental band was to travel to North Carolina to give concerts and raise money for the purchase of schoolbooks.[39]

Many of Lee's men devoted a great deal of time recycling spent Union artillery rounds. The Confederate government offered four cents a pound, inspiring hundreds of Rebels to scamper about after every bombardment. "'That is my shell, if she don't bust,'" could be heard during an artillery exchange. One fellow picked up 500 pounds of fragments within 100 yards of his tent, earning twenty dollars in Confederate money.[40]

## DESERTION

As winter progressed, desertion became a more serious problem in Lee's army. The primary cause, everyone agreed, was that "our men do not get anough to eat," with lack of pay often cited as the second compelling reason. "Our men is out of hart again," announced Jesse Hill of the 21st North Carolina, "and a running away like every thing." Those who did not run threatened to do so any day. "Tha say it hant of any use to stay here and be kiled for no thing[;] tha all say we are whiped and tha all no it." Nathan R. Frazier, who joined the 45th North Carolina as a substitute, believed the policy of recruiting black soldiers encouraged desertion. If the Confederate government had instituted the policy early in the war, they "would not of cerd but it will not doo us now[; who] after going through campaign after campaign as we have wants to be found lying ded by the Side of an old rusty ded negro[?] I tell you Brother I don't and it is not only me that dont."[41]

Other factors that contributed to the rise in desertion included distressing letters from home. Many correspondents described home front sufferings and tried to convince the soldiers that it no longer was a disgrace to desert. Lee reported to the secretary of war that civilians in western North Carolina promised their soldiers that the local home guards could never catch all of the deserters who hid in the mountains of that state.[42]

Of course, many men resisted these inducements to desert and still considered it a grave dishonor to be absent from their units without authority. John A. Everett of the 11th Georgia was weary of fighting but still hated the Yankees and intended to continue serving out of pride, "then I can face any man and say to him that I did my duty while in the Noble Armey of Northern Va."[43]

Virgil S. Cavin of the 38th North Carolina toyed with the idea of deserting for many months that winter. "I think I will risk it," he announced on January 26. His comrades left in increasing numbers, but he stayed, unwilling to take the risk after all. "I dont no what To do For the best[;] it wont do to Stay here for wee will bee all kiled." Cavin stuck with his regiment but was captured early in the Appomattox campaign and survived the war.[44]

W. E. Leak of the 22nd South Carolina suffered terribly from hunger and anxiety. He had a wife and children at home, and Sherman's army was burning its way across his home state. Yet he hardly mentioned Sherman; his letters are filled with the grinding poverty of trench life. "It rains, sleets, and snows," he complained. "We have mud in abundance. It is just like living in a hog pen." His daily rations consisted of a tin cup full of cornmeal and some beef, "bone and all." Sitting in picket pits all night, smoking to take his mind off his hunger, Leak often became so famished that he felt ill. The Confederacy's doom was apparent to him, and "peace, peace is all the talk there is." Yet Leak refused to run away, paying with his life for his loyalty to a cause he could no longer trust; he was captured and died at Point Lookout Prison.[45]

For those who decided to take unauthorized leave, a common method was to skip out under cover of darkness while on picket duty and take a short trip across no-man's-land to Union lines. The Florida brigade in Mahone's division suffered an unusually high desertion rate that winter, and about half the men fled to the Federals from picket duty, while the rest deserted from regimental camps and tried to make their way home. Nathan R. Frazier believed that five of his Tar Heel comrades went to Union lines for each one who tried to desert to the rear. Desertions were more frequent on darker, stormy nights. Sometimes men quietly left their pits without their neighbors in line knowing about it, often leaving their guns and accouterments behind. Capt. Gabriel J. Floyd of the 11th Florida suspected a six-man picket post of harboring intentions to desert, so he placed two supposedly reliable men to either side of the pit to watch them. As soon as Floyd retired to his command post, he heard that all six, plus the two sentinels, had left for the Union line. Sometimes pickets saw deserters making their way across no-man's-land and only pretended to stop them, firing their guns into the air.[46]

A Rebel opposite the Sixth Corps line found a novel way to desert. He offered to trade his knife for soap and negotiated with a Federal who came out to bargain. Just as the Unionist was reaching for his soap, the Rebel "looked round behind him to see if any of his companions were looking—and said never mind the soap Yank, I am going where there is plenty of it." He ran for the Federal trench. Confederate pickets yelled out for the Union soldier to lie down as they intended to shoot, but the deserter assured him they were not serious: "they want to come as bad as I do, they'll fire over our heads," and that was exactly what they did.[47]

The Federals encouraged their counterparts to desert at every opportunity. Wright received a request from some Confederates opposite his Sixth Corps line to speak to a mason among the Yankees—they had heard that Grant forced all Rebel deserters into the Union ranks and wanted assurance from someone reliable that it was not true. Meade's headquarters authorized Wright to cooperate. Far from mistreating deserters, Grant worked out a scheme to pay cash for every Confederate rifle they brought with them. Unionists of all ranks easily saw the wisdom of encouraging desertions. Yankee pickets opposite Wallace's brigade often called out, "'Come over Johnnies the doors of Salvation are open now, but they will soon be closed.'"[48]

A conspiracy to desert was uncovered in Wallace's brigade on the night of February 25. Five soldiers were arrested for planning it, but the evidence indicated that as many as sixty men were involved. They apparently were in communication with like-minded soldiers in four North Carolina brigades. Group desertion became a reality by late February, even if this one was broken up. One hundred men of Grimes's division, as well as fifteen soldiers from Johnston's North Carolina brigade of Early's division, decamped on the night of February 26. "These men generally went off in bands," Lee reported, "taking arms and ammunition."[49]

Lee tabulated the number of desertions in his army for the benefit of Secretary of War John C. Breckinridge. From February 15 to February 25, Johnson's division lost 217 deserters, 178 of them to the Union line. The division constituted the bulk of Richard H. Anderson's newly created Fourth Corps. For the same period, Longstreet's First Corps lost 148 deserters, Gordon's Second Corps lost 143, and Hill's Third Corps lost 586 (most of them from Wilcox's division). During this ten-day period, 1,094 Confederates ran away. With statistics added from other time periods, Lee's army lost at least 5,928 deserters between January 10 and March 28, the equivalent of more than a division of troops.[50]

Lee and his subordinates tried to curb this depletion of manpower. If food shortages were the chief cause, then the commissary department had to find more food. Lee believed it was a logistical and administrative problem, for he was certain the home front grew enough crops to feed his men. When rumors filtered into army headquarters that the troops often joked about deserting, Lee issued General Orders No. 8 on March 27, which made it clear that he would not tolerate such talk. He threatened the death penalty for anyone accused of encouraging desertion and required that this order be read several times to each company and regiment. Commanders on all levels employed loyal troops to chase those who fled. The 10th Virginia Cavalry pursued a group of deserters, wearing out its horses and demoralizing the troopers. The only result was that six men who had no motivation to fight anyway were caught and returned to the ranks. After 100 men deserted from Grimes's division on the night of February 26, a "large detachment" of infantrymen was sent to North Carolina to find them and an entire brigade was sent to guard the crossings of the Roanoke River. It seemed to Nathan R. Frazier that "it took one half of hour brigad to gard the othe half to ceep them from going to the yankees."[51]

Perhaps the most significant effort to curb desertion was Lee's amnesty to those who had already left. With the support of Jefferson Davis, it went into effect on February 11, 1865. The amnesty was only the second general order Lee issued after his appointment as general-in-chief of the Confederate armies, and thus it applied to all Rebel deserters, not just to those from the Army of Northern Virginia. If anyone listed as a deserter or absent without leave reported within twenty days of the order's date, they would be fully pardoned for the offense. Lee exempted anyone who had gone on to enlist in the Union army and warned that this would be the last pardon offered by the Confederate government. Some soldiers thought it did a great deal of good. Charles W. Trueheart claimed that thirty-six men out of forty-two who had deserted from the 10th Alabama took advantage of the offer, and "Other reg'ts. of the Brig. are getting back men too." Without readily available statistics to back this up, it is impossible to know whether Trueheart was right, but his claim is not supported in the surviving personal accounts from Lee's army.[52]

Ultimately, all these efforts curbed desertion in only limited ways. The causes of desertion lay in fundamental living conditions in the trenches and could not be improved too much. While reporting yet another set of desertion statistics in the Army of Northern Virginia, more than a month after the proclamation of his amnesty, Lee admitted, "I do not know what can be done to put a stop to it."[53]

There was no similar problem in Union ranks. The Yankees were well fed, their war effort seemed to be surging to an inevitable triumph, and they had enough manpower to rotate units in and out of trench duty. It made little sense for any Federal soldier to desert at Petersburg, but some of them did. Everyone agreed that they were draftees and bounty jumpers, men who would have deserted no matter where the Army of the Potomac and the Army of the James were located. Meade complained of "the frequency and increase of this crime" after a substitute deserted. These men could not expect comfortable living quarters in Rebel hands, but at least they would be out of harm's way and seemed to have been willing to put up with deprivation to save their lives.[54]

I. G. Bradwell of the 31st Georgia was surprised one night to hear a whisper in the darkness of no-man's-land: "'Don't shoot; I am coming in.'" Immediately after, a Yankee jumped into his pit and asked Bradwell to pass the word along to other pickets not to fire as seven more Federals came running into the Confederate line. The authorities paid for the guns they brought over. Bradwell wasted no sympathy on them, noting that they were "unprincipled men and not very dangerous enemies." Bushrod Johnson was happy to see Federal deserters but disappointed that they seemed to know so little of Union troop positions, partly because they were not interested and partly because they tended to desert so soon after arriving on the line that they possessed little information. At least one division in the Army of the James offered a twenty-day furlough to anyone who stopped a deserter, and the Army of the Potomac hung a deserter from the 179th New York. This man confessed to absconding fourteen times and reenlisting under different names to wrap up a hefty sum of money in bounties.[55]

CHAPTER SIXTEEN

# *The Seventh Offensive, February, and March*

A spell of good weather inspired Grant to mount another raid against Lee's supply line along the Weldon and Petersburg Railroad. Gregg's cavalry division would strike out across country to Dinwiddie Court House, a stopover point for the Confederate wagon trains that hauled supplies from Stony Creek Station up Boydton Plank Road. Grant earmarked Warren's Fifth Corps as support, planning to shove it as far south as Stony Creek Station. Humphreys received orders to guard the crossing of Hatcher's Run at Armstrong's Mill, the connecting link between the raiders and the Federal line at Petersburg.[1]

The movement began early on the morning of February 5, and it produced unintended results that caused Grant to change his plans. As Gregg and Warren set out, Humphreys took position on the north side of Hatcher's Run at Armstrong's Mill. Smyth's division established a line northward from the stream along the west side of Duncan-Harman Road for half a mile. Then the Federals continued the line eastward, across the roadbed, to Rocky Branch. Mott's division continued the line on the east side of that brook. A small gap, caused by the stream valley, existed between Smyth and Mott.[2]

The Confederates sent three brigades to drive the Federals away from Armstrong's Mill. Cooke and McComb formed the assaulting force, with MacRae as a reserve. In a poorly conducted offensive, McComb's brigade became disorganized, and many of its members lost their nerve to rush at the partially fortified Federals. Cooke's North Carolina brigade was well in hand and conducted three separate attacks that never got closer than 100 yards from the Union line. Why MacRae's fine Tar Heel brigade never went into action can only be explained by the absence of an overall commander on the field. Most of the pressure fell on McAllister's brigade of Mott's division, the connecting link with Smyth, though Smyth's men delivered some enfilade fire on the attacking Confederates.[3]

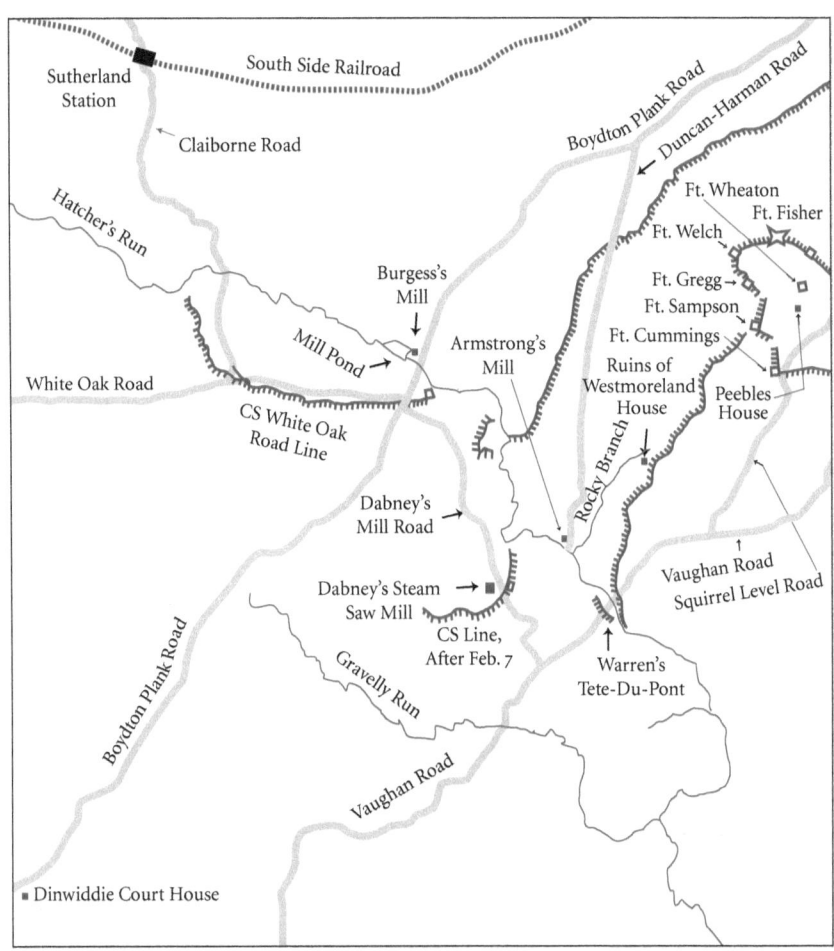

Hatcher's Run, February 5–7, 1865

Grant was encouraged by the Rebel willingness to dash against Humphreys. Gregg made it to Dinwiddie Court House that day, but he captured only eighteen wagons and fifty prisoners, while Warren made scant progress toward Stony Creek Station. Grant decided late on February 5 to scrap his original plan and exploit Humphreys's success north of Hatcher's Run. He hoped to lure more Confederates out of their entrenchments into an open field battle and follow up their repulse by striking westward. Grant contemplated grabbing the South Side Railroad, "or a position from which it can be reached." His order to Meade was very clear: "Change original instructions to give all advantages you can take of the enemys acts."[4]

## THE BATTLE OF HATCHER'S RUN

Meade ordered Warren to give up his march toward Stony Creek Station and assemble where Vaughan Road crossed Hatcher's Run, about one mile downstream, or southeast, of Armstrong's Mill. These two crossings now held prime strategic importance for the Federals. Vaughan Road offered them the shortest route from their Petersburg line westward toward Boydton Plank Road. Duncan-Harman Road ran north and south, the shortest route Confederate attackers could take to intercept the Union advance westward. In effect, if Grant's men could maintain their hold on both crossings, they would have secured their opportunity to head directly toward the remaining Rebel communication routes leading into Petersburg south of the Appomattox. In September, their best opportunity to do that was blunted by the construction of the Confederate Boydton Plank Road Line, but that line did not extend south of Hatcher's Run.[5]

The operation that began on February 5 extended over the next two days as well, for the Confederates were not ready to concede this important advantage. Warren took position at the crossing of Vaughan Road by dawn of February 6. He sent Crawford's division on Dabney's Mill Road, where John Pegram's division of Gordon's Second Corps blocked his way. Outnumbered even when Evans's division came up to help, the Confederates fell back fighting as Crawford pushed westward to Dabney's Saw Mill, where a large pile of sawdust served as a convenient landmark. In fact, the Federals mistook it for a Confederate redoubt. Crawford's men evicted the Confederates from a line of light fieldworks just east of the sawmill, but Evans later counterattacked and reclaimed the ground. Units of Ayres's division joined Crawford and captured the mill and its sawdust pile a second time later that day.

More Confederates came up to even the sides. Mahone's division, led by Joseph Finegan due to Mahone's illness, counterattacked in two lines. Crawford's men were nearly out of ammunition and disorganized by this time; they retreated quickly to a position east of the sawmill where Wheaton's division of the Sixth Corps had arrived to offer support, just as darkness put an end to the spirited slugmatch.[6]

As the action unfolded near Dabney's Saw Mill, Grant cautioned Meade not to go too far: "I would not recommend making any attack against intrenched lines." But he urged Meade to hold on to the crossings of Hatcher's Run to facilitate future moves. His earlier optimism already dulled, Grant tried to husband his strength for several more limited strikes in the future, rather than going for an all-out push toward the South Side Railroad. Other than the sharp action along Dabney's Mill Road, another fight took place along Vaughan Road as Confederate cavalry and infantry advanced northward toward the crossing of Hatcher's Run to test Union defenses. Gregg's cavalry, with some assistance from Warren's infantry, held them at bay.[7]

The spell of good weather that had prompted Grant to initiate the Seventh Offensive ended quickly. Sleet fell even as the Confederates moved troops to attack Humphreys at Armstrong's Mill on February 5. The temperature dropped below freezing on the night of February 6, causing immense suffering for the soldiers bivouacked near Dabney's Saw Mill. Even as the men shivered through the night, Grant instructed Meade to begin fortifying the ground from Peebles's Farm to Armstrong's Mill.[8]

Grant allowed Meade to make one more effort against the Rebels on February 7. Crawford advanced along Dabney's Mill Road at 10:00 A.M. that day and took the Confederate skirmish line fronting their works at the sawmill. Crawford noticed that the skirmishers were more strongly dug in than on the day before, indicating the Rebels intended to hold this position firmly. The weather grew worse and Grant once again cautioned Meade not to waste men, so the army commander ordered Warren to hold Crawford where he was for the time being. Warren had the option of advancing if he saw an opening for success. He waited until midafternoon, then pushed Crawford forward in what amounted to a reconnaissance in force rather than a determined attack. Crawford's men advanced toward the improved Confederate trenches at Dabney's Saw Mill, which had slashing and in some places a ravine in front. The Federals tested the line and then retired as a fierce hailstorm pelted them from above.[9]

This ended Grant's Seventh Offensive at Petersburg. The Federals lost 1,539 men compared with Confederate casualties of about 1,000. Meade had already taken steps to consolidate his new ground before the Federals made their final attempt to capture Dabney's Saw Mill. On the morning of February 6, Michler selected the site of a new line connecting Fort Sampson on the Petersburg line with Armstrong's Mill. Meanwhile, Second Corps troops strengthened their parapets and enlarged the slashing in front of their position at the mill.[10]

"We have extended our lines over four miles more to our left," Grant informed Sheridan, who was still in the Valley. "This brings us no nearer the South side road but will enable us to secure good crossings of Hatchers's run when we do move." The Federals began to dig in on February 7 as engineer officers arrived at various corps headquarters for the work. Troops from the 50th New York Engineers had been busy corduroying roads in the area since February 6, and the U.S. Engineer Battalion had held a section of trench near Fort Howard for three days during the Seventh Offensive.[11]

Engineer officers Harwood, Benyaurd, and Howell supervised the construction of the four-mile line from Fort Sampson. The work was done by the Second Corps while Warren's men fortified the area along Hatcher's Run. Humphreys placed Miles's First Division from Fort Sampson to the ruins of the Westmoreland House, and Mott's Third Division extended the line to the run. The infantrymen built the parapet and cut trees to create a slashing at least 700 yards in front of the works. Corps headquarters issued detailed instructions; Miles and Mott were to establish a strong picket line to protect the diggers and maintain a substantial reserve to repel any attacks. The parapet was to be at least five feet wide at the top. Members of the 4th New York Heavy Artillery supervised the construction of the five batteries along the line, assisted by details of 200 infantrymen at each battery, armed with plenty of shovels, axes, and picks.[12]

The artillery redoubts along the line were ready by February 13, but finishing work continued on them and along the connecting infantry parapet. Humphreys's men continued to cut pine trees for as much as half a mile in front of the line, extending as far as the Union picket line, and some of the trees were fashioned into elaborate abatis 100 yards in front of the main parapet. The rest of the timber was left lying where it fell to form an extensive slashing. Second Corps troops dug a deep ditch in front of the parapet and then began to build new winter quarters 100 feet behind the trench. Orders were issued to ensure that the troops did not take wood from the obstructions to use in campfires or chimneys. Details from the regiments hauled items of comfort or value from the old camps to the men's new lodgings. Finally, Humphreys instructed each division commander to appoint an officer to take charge of the works on his sector and report to the division leader and to the designated engineer officer at army headquarters about any problems that needed attention.[13]

The Fifth Corps assumed responsibility for everything else on the newly occupied ground. Warren pointed out that Armstrong's Mill was not a good place to anchor the new line. High ground along the south side of Hatcher's Run extended from the mill downstream to Vaughan Road; the Confederates could use that ground to threaten Federal use of both crossings. Army headquarters therefore ordered Warren to run the line to Vaughan Road crossing instead of to Armstrong's Mill. Fifth Corps troops began to dig in south of the stream on February 8, working in three-hour shifts. Within five days, Warren's men nearly completed a bridgehead, or tete-du-pont, on the south side of Hatcher's Run to protect the Vaughan Road crossing. Warren used large details of 1,000 men to clear-cut the forest and make extensive slashing in front of his works.[14]

This would be the last continuous extension of the Union line at Petersburg, making a total of fifteen miles of connected infantry and artillery works from Hatcher's Run to the Appomattox River downstream from Petersburg. The new line extended southwest from Fort Sampson for a while, then it curved south toward the Vaughan Road crossing of Hatcher's Run. Interestingly, Meade did not continue the rear-facing Secondary Line that he had constructed all the way from the James River to Peebles's Farm. This demonstrates that the Union high command no longer had much fear of a Confederate strike against their rear. The Rebels had not threatened such a move since September. Moreover, the decision not to extend the Secondary Line also demonstrates that Grant and Meade now had confidence in their grand tactic of conducting offensives with short-term goals, biting and holding one bit of ground after another. In fact, Grant anticipated that Meade could abandon the extension from Fort Sampson to the Vaughan Road crossing in the next offensive, assuming the next move would take the Federals to the South Side Railroad. Grant seemed more secure in his control of events and in eventual Union victory at Petersburg.[15]

The Fifth Corps bore the burden of roadwork to consolidate Federal gains in the Seventh Offensive. Warren employed 2,000 men for three days to corduroy Vaughan Road. The bridge that took the road across Hatcher's Run served adequately until it was washed away by spring rains in early March. Two companies of the 50th New York Engineers then constructed a sturdy span 285 feet long with eleven cribs serving as supports. The bridge bed was eight feet wide to allow two wagons to cross simultaneously, while the cribs and roadbed consisted of heavy timbers raised high enough to withstand all floods.[16]

Finally, to ensure logistical support to this area, the last extension of the Army Line was built from Globe Tavern. It ran south along the old roadbed of the Weldon and Petersburg Railroad for two miles, then headed west for three miles to reach the Cummings House near the junction of Vaughan Road and Squirrel Level Road. The entire length of the military railroad totaled twenty-one miles. As many as fifteen trains per day with up to twenty-three cars behind each engine chugged out of City Point to the far-flung army.[17]

The Confederate response to the Union success in the Seventh Offensive was to extend the Boydton Plank Road Line south of Hatcher's Run, anchoring it on a newly dug redoubt about one mile west of Warren's tete-du-pont near the Vaughan Road crossing. This extension included Dabney's Saw Mill, thus blocking any future Union drive west along that route. But with the crossing of Hatcher's Run firmly in their hands, the Federals could take any number of other roads by curving south and then west. They would have longer routes to take, but each one held more promise of success than crashing through earthworks along Dabney's Mill Road. By mid-March, Federal intelligence officers gathered information about a new earthwork the Confederates built as a reaction to Meade's success at Hatcher's Run. The White Oak Road Line lay south of the run and west of Boydton Plank Road to cover the approaches to the South Side Railroad. It had parapets five feet tall, a deep ditch in front, and several rows of abatis as obstructions. Engineer Maj. Conway Robinson Howard suggested that small protruding salients be built into the connecting infantry line between the artillery batteries so riflemen could better sweep the front. But the line ended at least two miles short of the railroad; Lee obviously was nearing the end of his manpower supply.[18]

### MAINTENANCE AND IMPROVEMENT

In addition to building new works, the Federals also refurbished older defenses. They sought to enlarge and strengthen Fort Fisher by adding bastions, increasing the size of its garrison to 300 men. Engineers added a fraise and placed a wire entanglement in front of the abatis, but they interlaced two additional strands of wire with the branches of the abatis itself. They used most of the fascines and gabions produced in February at the refurbished fort and shipped close to 2,500 feet of lumber to be used in making gun platforms. The engineers finished the fighting positions by late February but continued to work on bombproofs and magazines into late March. Two traverses, each sixty feet long with a magazine eighteen feet long inside them, and a third traverse designed purely for the protection of the gun positions along the western curtain, were nearly finished by March 20.[19]

Henry L. Abbot described a simple but effective cover for his heavy artillerymen. They placed substantial timbers across the trench at fifty-yard intervals, laying one end on top of the parapet and the other on the roof of a bombproof or magazine. Then they placed a layer of railroad iron over it and covered the iron with three feet of dirt. The artillerymen ducked under these splinterproofs whenever the Confederates returned fire.[20]

At Bermuda Hundred, the Army of the James maintained fieldworks that had been built the previous May. Wooden revetment in Battery England was rotting, and the parapet between that work and Batteries Pruyn and Walker needed to be rebuilt. The engineers designed and constructed a new, interior line from Battery Anderson to Battery England, built a new artillery work near Battery Parsons, and emplaced a palisade to enclose the gorge of Battery Marshall.[21]

North of the James, the Federals noted that their opponents were building "splinter-proof huts" along the picket line opposite Fort Burnham. In case these were designed to house sharpshooters who could pave the way for an assault, the 1st New York Engineers strengthened the Union picket line and built loopholes for sharpshooters.[22]

Of equal concern was a constant hail of Confederate mortar fire onto Fort Burnham. Engineer officer William R. King designed casemates for artillery

Casemates at Fort Burnham. (Wisconsin Historical Society, WHI-39030)

that were large and numerous enough to house most of the fort's garrison. They were made of logs and placed mostly below the level of the parapet. Several feet of dirt shielded the log roof, and a firing position for infantry was constructed on the rear of the roof. King wanted to place these casemates along the entire length of Burnham's western front, but he managed to construct only four of them, plus two additional bombproofs, before the campaign ended. The engineers also put a fraise in the scarp and deepened and widened the ditch at Fort Burnham. Three lines of abatis, a line of chevaux-de-frise, and a wire entanglement completed the defenses. The engineers replaced revetting, improved magazines, and drained trenches at Fort Burnham by the end of February.[23]

The engineers added seven magazines and improved the earthworks at all the smaller batteries between Burnham and Fort Brady in March. King devised a cheaper, perhaps more effective way of creating loopholes for sharpshooters along this line. The cost of sandbags had risen due to the army's tremendous demand for them during the Petersburg campaign, so King made loopholes out of lumber. While a sandbag loophole cost about $2.50 (requiring as many as five bags at fifty cents per bag), King estimated that the wood itself cost only ten cents per loophole, and he had a sawmill that could produce lumber for up to 700 loopholes each day. He nailed boards together to form a four-sided funnel, the small end exposed on the outside of the parapet and the whole covered on all four sides by dirt. King admitted that there was a danger from flying splinters caused by return fire; but this arrangement presented a smaller target for Confederate marksmen, and the wood tended to blend in with the color of the dirt and was less visible from a distance.[24]

After the campaign, Federal engineers found that the loopholes the Rebels built opposite Fort Burnham were made of logs up to fourteen inches in diameter, "hewn on two sides, with notches cut in the lower side once in about six feet." They placed them along the crest of the parapet with dirt in front to soften the impact of bullets. The notches were flared toward the inside to allow the sharpshooter greater lateral aim. The Confederates solved the problem of having a wide opening by spiking plates of "thin boiler iron eight or ten inches square" across the opening, with a hole drilled only large enough for the muzzle of a rifle. The Federals found some plates dented by up to twenty bullets, many of which probably would have entered the notch and injured the sharpshooter if not for the iron covering.[25]

Fort Brady was damaged by Confederate gunfire in late January when Rebel gunboats made an aborted attack down the river. King repaired the damage and made an additional gun emplacement below the fort, with parapets thirty feet thick. This sunken water battery was protected by a fraise and accommodated a 100-pounder Parrott rifle. In addition, the Federals removed a bank of earth in front of Fort Brady amounting to 1,500 cubic yards of dirt.[26]

Exposed to months of winter weather, the wooden components of all the fieldworks at Petersburg rapidly deteriorated. The Federals sawed millions of linear feet of lumber (Peter Michie ran three sawmills to produce wood for the Army of the James alone) and shipped it to far-flung positions to replace the revetment of parapets, shore up magazines, and repair wooden gun platforms.[27]

The Confederates also tried to complete parts of their line that were not yet finished. Lee noticed a six-foot gap between one battery emplacement and the end of the connecting infantry line in Heth's division sector. He urged Heth to close the hole and gently chastised him the next time he rode by and saw that Heth had failed to do so.[28]

Longstreet wanted to use black laborers to finish the far left of his line, between Williamsburg Road and Nine Mile Road; but none could be found, and he did not have enough troops to do the work. When Walter H. Stevens complained to Lee about the disposition of Longstreet's picket line, the corps commander admitted that it had the same weakness that afflicted most military positions—it was liable to be captured by a sudden rush of the enemy. But he assured Lee that the picket line was commanded by positions on the main line, demonstrating faith in a flexible system of defense.[29]

Longstreet also placed reliance on strong works fronted by good obstructions, and he urged subordinates to accumulate fireballs that could be ignited to illuminate the area in front of the works in case of a night attack. Longstreet wanted to have "some sensitive shells placed among the abatis," especially opposite Fort Burnham, rigged to explode if the Federals tried to pull it away for an assault. There is no evidence that this was done, but Longstreet suggested that screens of cedar limbs be placed in front of artillery batteries to conceal them from view and urged work on two dams near the Williamsburg Road. The latter became almost an obsession for Longstreet as he tried to push harried engineer officers to use black laborers or white soldiers to increase the size and holding capacity of these dams. He wanted them to be ready for the onset of spring rains in March and urged the engineers to offer extra rations or whiskey to the laborers. Georgia soldier Arthur B. Simms had to move his cabin to let the engineers obtain enough dirt to enlarge one of these dams. It was planned to be 125 feet wide at the base, 25 feet tall, and 25 feet wide at the top, but there is no evidence that either dam was completed before the end of the campaign.[30]

TRENCH WARFARE

The most deadly element of trench life remained the threat of enemy sharpshooters. I. G. Bradwell was convinced that ten times more men were lost to their fire than to enemy artillery, yet the big guns were far more impressive to most observers than the silent killers. A regular evening mortar shelling of Fort Sedgwick provided entertainment of sorts for bored Unionists, as long as the shelling was comparatively light. When it was heavy, they simply took shelter in their bombproofs and waited it out. On March 20 alone, the Confederates dropped 100 mortar rounds into the fort, and another 100 fell just outside, yet no one was injured.[31]

It was common for the artillerymen on both sides to open fire on any unusual movement in the opposing lines. On February 21, some Coehorn mortars in Union Battery No. 15 fired on a Rebel detail repairing abatis near Baxter Road. This sparked an exchange that wounded three Federal gunners and wrecked some ordnance in Battery No. 15. Col. Bryon M. Cutcheon in the Ninth Corps complained that he had no control over the artillery firing, yet his infantrymen suffered far more from it than the gunners. "This firing seems to be directed by no general principle, and is directed at anything and everything, and sometimes apparently nothing, and when over with we stand the same that we did, minus a few good men."[32]

Along the Sixth Corps front, division commander Frank Wheaton issued instructions to brigade commanders and division officers of the day that pickets were not to simply give an alarm and retire on the main position. The picket line was meant to be a forward defense capable of "the most desperate resistance to any line of battle that might be brought against it. Any attacking force less than a line of battle our pickets should destroy with ease."[33]

The Confederates reassigned units along the trench line much more often in the winter months than before. Johnson's division had been in the same trenches since June 15, but it finally moved to a new location in early March, far on the Confederate right, in an attempt to extend the line west of Boydton Plank Road. With the exception of only two nights, Gracie's Alabama brigade had stayed in the same spot continuously from July 9 to March 14.[34]

Troops of Gordon's Second Corps replaced Johnson's division. They asked many questions about that section of the line, "and it would take a big book to hold all the lies told them," recalled an amused Tar Heel. W. A. Day and his comrades were given a few days' rest behind the line, and they rejoiced at the chance to sleep on clean ground and stand completely upright without fear of being shot. "The whole earth is honeycombed by ditches, bomb-proofs, embankments & rifle pits," reported one of Gordon's men. This part of the line was quiet during the day, with Federals often lounging atop their parapets only a couple of hundred yards away. There were strict orders not to communicate with them, and Ellis found it strange to see the Yankees sitting "like a flock of black birds—beckoning, & waving papers, & soliciting some sort of notice, whilst our 'Johnnies,' . . . look on grim & silent as death."[35]

Trench raiding continued to be a part of life along the lines. The sharpshooter battalion of Lane's North Carolina brigade often conducted raids with up to 100 men, and capturing around 15 Unionists was considered a success. Comparatively little mining took place along the lines in February and March, but members of Company A, U.S. Engineer Battalion, were repairing one of the listening shafts at Fort Sedgwick when part of it caved in and several of them had to be rescued.[36]

### SCIENCE, TECHNOLOGY, AND FIELD FORTIFICATIONS

The Petersburg campaign took place during a time when scientists were developing a way to use electricity to spring underground mines. An English military board had concluded in the wake of the Crimean War that electrical devices held the promise of being far more effective than powder trains in touching off mines. In the United States, George W. Beardslee successfully exploded four small mines with Lincoln and Stanton as an audience. Beardslee tried to sell his device to the army following the failed attack at the crater, in which Pleasants barely managed to use a primitive powder train to touch off his mine, but the army for some reason failed to respond.[37]

A careful examination of the mines used to blow up the bulkhead of the

Dutch Gap Canal on January 1 spurred the military to take electricity more seriously. Twelve thousand pounds of powder, two tons more than Pleasants had used, was distributed among five mines, and Michie used a Gomez fuse to touch it off. Often called a safety fuse, it was a distinct improvement over Pleasants's powder train. The Gomez fuse compressed combustible material inside a tube with an outer protective covering. Michie scraped off the covering in several places so the fire could communicate more directly to the powder, then stuck the end of the fuse into the pile of gunpowder and spliced the other end so that all five mines were connected. The explosion failed to burn all the powder, for the accumulation in each mine was too large. Michie thought that an electrical device could have accomplished that goal.[38]

Within days of this finding, Chief Engineer Delafield appointed a board to test Beardslee's Magneto-Electric Battery for exploding mines and torpedoes. Beardslee brought his equipment to West Point and set off small cartridges with it. He channeled the electrical charge through a clock to demonstrate how a mine could be exploded at a specified time. The inventor set off nearly twenty charges simultaneously and convinced the board that his device not only worked but was relatively inexpensive.[39]

Other inventors brought their devices to the army's attention, but they tended to be variations on a common electrical mechanism. Taliaferro P. Shaffner, born in Virginia in 1818, was an expert in mining technology who nearly succeeded in deploying his device along the Petersburg line. Shaffner worked on it in both the United States and Europe before offering his services to Grant free of charge (asking compensation for the materials he had already purchased). Grant was interested and listened to Shaffner's proposal. He allowed the inventor to visit the lines and consult his engineers, who reported favorably on the device, and Stanton facilitated the shipment of materials from Europe through U.S. Customs. On March 28, Shaffner requested fifteen miles of insulated wire for four of his devices, plus 1,000 fuses and some tools. By this time Grant's attention was riveted on the Eighth Offensive; Petersburg was in Union hands six days later, and Shaffner had lost his bid for glory. A year later, his device still unbought and unused, Shaffner appealed to President Andrew Johnson for a commission in the army so he could continue to work on his apparatus. Grant continued to support his efforts, but nothing ever came of them.[40]

Engineers consistently supported electrical devices as the wave of the future in mining technology, but the U.S. Army remained parsimonious. Beardslee went to England and convinced the British army of the utility of his machine, but in America, the army decided to make a similar electrical device of its own rather than buy one from a private inventor.[41]

The Petersburg campaign fostered efforts to find an aerial solution to trench warfare, and the most interesting proposal was pushed forward by Dr. Roderick O. Davidson, a former member of the 11th Mississippi. Davidson was "a man of parts" who dabbled in poetry, music, and science, according to one of his comrades. "Topsy-turvy Yankeedom," went one of his rhymes, "Whence worthless arts and isms come." Davidson apparently thought his proposal for an airship, which he called the Artis Avis, would show the Yankees what Southern science could produce. He developed it after his discharge from the 11th Mississippi, when he received an appointment as a clerk in the Treasury Department in Richmond. Davidson provided enough details about his proposed machine to indicate that he was no scientist, and he pursued funding for his project with the acumen of a P. T. Barnum.[42]

Unable to secure funding from the government, he visited at least eight brigades of Lee's army from December through March 1865, giving speeches about Artis Avis and asking for donations from the soldiers. Davidson explained that his craft was powered by a one-horsepower engine, had wings that were feathered and movable, and had a tail that could be spread out or streamlined to suit the needs of the one-man crew. He modeled it on a real bird, the action of the wings resisting gravity and bringing the craft up, and he claimed it could fly as fast as seventy-five miles per hour. Artis Avis was to carry bombs that could be dropped by touching a release mechanism with the foot. The body of the craft was to be made of straps of iron held together by wire and covered with white oak lumber. Davidson explained to McGowan's troops that he had tested a prototype by securing it to a flatcar and speeding the engine along the railroad. He claimed the Artis Avis was lifted off the flatcar by the wind and flew at the same speed as the train without snapping the connecting rope. If true, this test merely demonstrated that the craft had the proper shape to be affected by the flow of air around it. The crucial element was the power plant, and whether it had enough thrust to get the craft off the ground. Davidson never revealed the answer to that uncertainty even when Col. Asbury Coward of the 5th South Carolina asked him about it.[43]

Davidson's message was clear: "he needed a little more money to make birds enough to destroy Grant's army." The "little more money" amounted to $20,000 for 500 airplanes, and with that, he claimed, the war could be ended in five days. Davidson also stirred up the vision of dropping Greek fire on the major cities of the North, in case breaking the siege of Petersburg did not bring Lincoln's government to the peace table. He also told Benning's brigade that he could sink every Yankee gunboat in the James River.[44]

Soldiers reacted ambivalently to the scheme. "I should as soon look for perpetual motion to be invented as one of Davidson's Birds to rise and fly," commented Arthur B. Simms. Colonel Coward thought him a blatant confidence man, but others held doubts mixed with hope. Marion Hill Fitzpatrick of the 45th Georgia reminded himself that people doubted the viability of the telegraph and the railroad before they were invented. Other soldiers believed in Davidson. "I was very anxious to see that man stampede the Yankee army," asserted a soldier in Benning's Brigade, while another Confederate remembered "the intense excitement and joyous hopes pervading the army that the flying bird would exterminate every Yankee in front of Petersburg." The men contributed what they could. Thomas's brigade pooled $116, while the money collected from three other brigades totaled $697.50. In reporting that DuBose's brigade contributed $127 to Davidson, Arthur B. Simms called it "pretty liberal patronage for a humbug."[45]

The support for Artis Avis among Lee's men was purely emotional, based not on faith in technology but on a desperate longing for the war to end. Thomas R. Evans, a civilian living in Richmond at the time, recalled that Davidson possessed a nonworking prototype. It looked much as the inventor had described it to the soldiers, except it had no engine. Davidson constructed the prototype in a lumberyard at the corner of 7th and Main and allowed visitors to view it. One night, a strong wind broke it all apart, ending his dream of powered flight. This also shattered the hopeless dreams of soldiers who yearned for a deus ex machina to hover over the battlefield and rescue them from the dangers of trench warfare.[46]

The Federals had their version of Roderick O. Davidson, but he was a man of greater technical talents. Edward W. Serrell, the English-born colonel of the 1st New York Engineers, had a checkered career that calls into question his motives for proposing a flying machine. Charges were preferred against him on at least three occasions, mostly for harassing junior officers, disobeying orders, lying about his accomplishments to enhance his reputation, and indulging in "unusual harangues and in extraordinary familiarities" with his men. Serrell was always ready with a plausible explanation for these charges, and he survived all of them.[47]

Serrell proposed making an airplane as early as April 1863, intending it for reconnaissance, but the Engineer Department was not interested. In September 1864 he found a more receptive audience in Benjamin Butler. The army commander responded to Serrell's claim to have found "the method of navigating the air by means of elevating fans." Serrell provided few details; his proposal merely mentioned the use of one set of fans to raise the ship and another to propel it horizontally. Butler put him on detached duty in New York City to work on the machine in November 1864, but Serrell produced nothing except excuses. He reported that "many attempts have been made to find out what was the object of some machinery being built under my direction." After Ord replaced Butler as commander of the Army of the James, he wanted to know what Serrell was doing in New York City, and the colonel claimed to be on recruiting duty. The army severed its connection with this engineer-inventor-conman later that month when it tried to muster him out of service. Serrell quickly offered his resignation so as to make it appear the severance was on his own terms.[48]

While he was on detached service in New York, Serrell turned his gaze back to earth and joined other inventors who proposed making iron shields for the infantry. His idea was to use plates of iron to construct forts in the field that could be quickly assembled and dismantled. Other inventors envisioned erecting such plates atop the parapet of an earthwork, putting them on wheels to be drawn about by horses as movable breastworks, or making them small enough so that individual soldiers could carry them around like medieval shields. One of the more extravagant claims was the assertion by T. G. Boetig of Cincinnati that his "iron field Casemates could be assembled in five seconds."[49]

If airplanes and movable iron breastworks were not the answer to trench warfare at Petersburg, maybe incendiary projectiles could help. The term "Greek fire" was still used in the 1860s to denote any type of burning material that could be delivered on an enemy. Alfred Berney came forward in the spring of 1863 to demonstrate his device to the army, delivering a stream of burning fluid by holding a torch to the nozzle of a hose from which it was pumped. This primitive flamethrower worked when Berney set fire to a pile of wood on a dark night in May 1863. With Lincoln and Stanton watching, he directed the flow of 300 gallons per minute through his apparatus, lighting up the night sky in a brilliant display of engineering and theatrics. Berney's liquid and Greek fire shells developed by Levi Short were used against Charleston in August 1863, but with little success.[50]

Berney improved his equipment and held another demonstration near Dutch Gap for Grant, Meade, Butler, Warren, and Crawford in November 1864. He fired several shells filled with his fluid into bushes and houses after dark and used the flamethrower to pour liquid fire onto a large area of ground. Butler contemplated using the device as a defensive weapon, holding each enclosed work with five men and what Theodore Lyman called a "squirter." Termed a "gadget-minded general" by a modern historian, Butler placed an order with Berney for 1,500 gallons of Greek fire and "eight rotary pumps complete with couplings, hoses, nozzles and other appurtenances." It took Berney three months to fill the order. By the time the equipment arrived in February 1865, Ord had replaced Butler and exhibited no interest in the devices. Meanwhile,

Stanton had become impressed with the incendiary fluid developed by another inventor, Robert L. Fleming of New York City. Fleming had demonstrated his product at West Point in September 1863 and gained the endorsement of the army. Stanton authorized its use against Petersburg in the fall of 1864. Twenty shells filled with Fleming's fluid were fired, but there is no evidence that they caused unusual damage.[51]

CHAPTER SEVENTEEN

## *Fort Stedman and the Eighth Offensive*

Soon after the battle of Hatcher's Run, Grant once again contemplated cavalry raids against Lee's supply lines. John Irvin Gregg's division of Meade's army could tear up the South Side Railroad west of Petersburg and Sheridan could destroy the rails and the canal leading out of the Shenandoah Valley. Both mounted columns could then ride south into North Carolina and join Sherman, who was advancing with 60,000 western veterans to join Grant at Petersburg.[1]

But Grant also explored the possibility of a frontal attack on the Rebel line, encouraging Ord to find "a hole" in the Confederate defenses on Bermuda Hundred. Potter also proposed a Ninth Corps attack along Jerusalem Plank Road to puncture the Rebel line east of Fort Mahone. Ninth Corps brigade leader Napoleon B. McLaughlen proposed a similar plan for attacking from the area around Fort Stedman. Meade concurred with Duane's assessment that the prospects of these plans seemed "very doubtful."[2]

As long as there were no signs that Lee intended to send troops to oppose Sherman, Grant preferred to outflank the Confederate right. Sheridan's cavalry started from Winchester on February 27, 1865, tore some sections of the Virginia Central Railroad and the James River Canal, and reached the White House on the Pamunkey River on March 19. While the troopers rested and refitted, Grant outlined plans for the Eighth Offensive. Sheridan was to add Gregg's former division (soon to be under George Crook) to his force and tear up the South Side Railroad so that it could not be used for three or four days. He had the option of returning or continuing to Sherman in North Carolina. Meade was to support the cavalry strike with all the infantry he could spare, while still holding the extended line of works. Grant hoped to start the operation on March 25.[3]

Delays in preparing Sheridan's cavalry forced Grant to postpone the start of his offensive until March 29, but the essential plan remained intact. Meade would send the Second and Fifth Corps across Hatcher's Run to help the cavalry while the Sixth and Ninth Corps held the Union line at Petersburg. Ord was to bring three infantry divisions and one cavalry division to support the movement, while Weitzel retained enough men to hold the trenches north of the Appomattox. Ord was the first to move; he pulled two white divisions and one black division from the line at Bermuda Hundred and north of the James River on the night of March 24 and sent them to rear areas to rest.[4]

Lee also contemplated the end of the Petersburg campaign. Sherman posed the most immediate threat. His advance through the Carolinas seemed unstoppable, and Lee admitted that he would have to abandon Petersburg and Richmond. Sherman's interruption of Lee's logistical support alone would compel the Rebels to evacuate their trenches as soon as the Yankees neared the Roanoke River. Lee argued that the abandonment of the capital would not necessarily doom the Confederate cause as long as he could maintain the Army of Northern Virginia as an effective field force. To that end, he plotted lines of retreat from both cities as early as February 22.[5]

## FORT STEDMAN

It was clear even by February 22, two weeks following the battle of Hatcher's Run, that Grant was preparing for a push to flank Lee's right as soon as spring weather allowed. Lee waited for "the struggle which must soon commence," but then in late March he listened to a proposal for offensive action brought to him by the commander of the Second Corps. Gordon was intrigued by the possibility of attacking across a narrow point of no-man's-land where only 282 yards separated Colquitt's Salient from Fort Stedman. He believed that by massing the corps and launching it on a surprise attack, he could rupture the first Federal line. Gordon was fully aware that the Yankees had established a second position along high ground occupied by the old Confederate Dimmock Line, reversing some of Dimmock's works. If the Confederates could break this line too, they might open a road to City Point, compelling the Yankees to contract their position in order to save their base of operations.[6]

Gordon envisioned the grand tactical aspects of this offensive, but Lee saw the strategic implications. If he could throw Grant on the defensive and force him to abandon some positions on his left flank, the Confederates might hold the Richmond-Petersburg Lines with minimal force and detach the rest to North Carolina, where they could help Johnston defeat Sherman. If this did not work out as planned, Lee felt he had lost relatively little in the attempt.[7]

Gordon took charge of preparations. It would be only the second Confederate offensive at Petersburg, in contrast to numerous counterattacks in response to Union moves. Battery No. 10, just to the right of Stedman, was 204

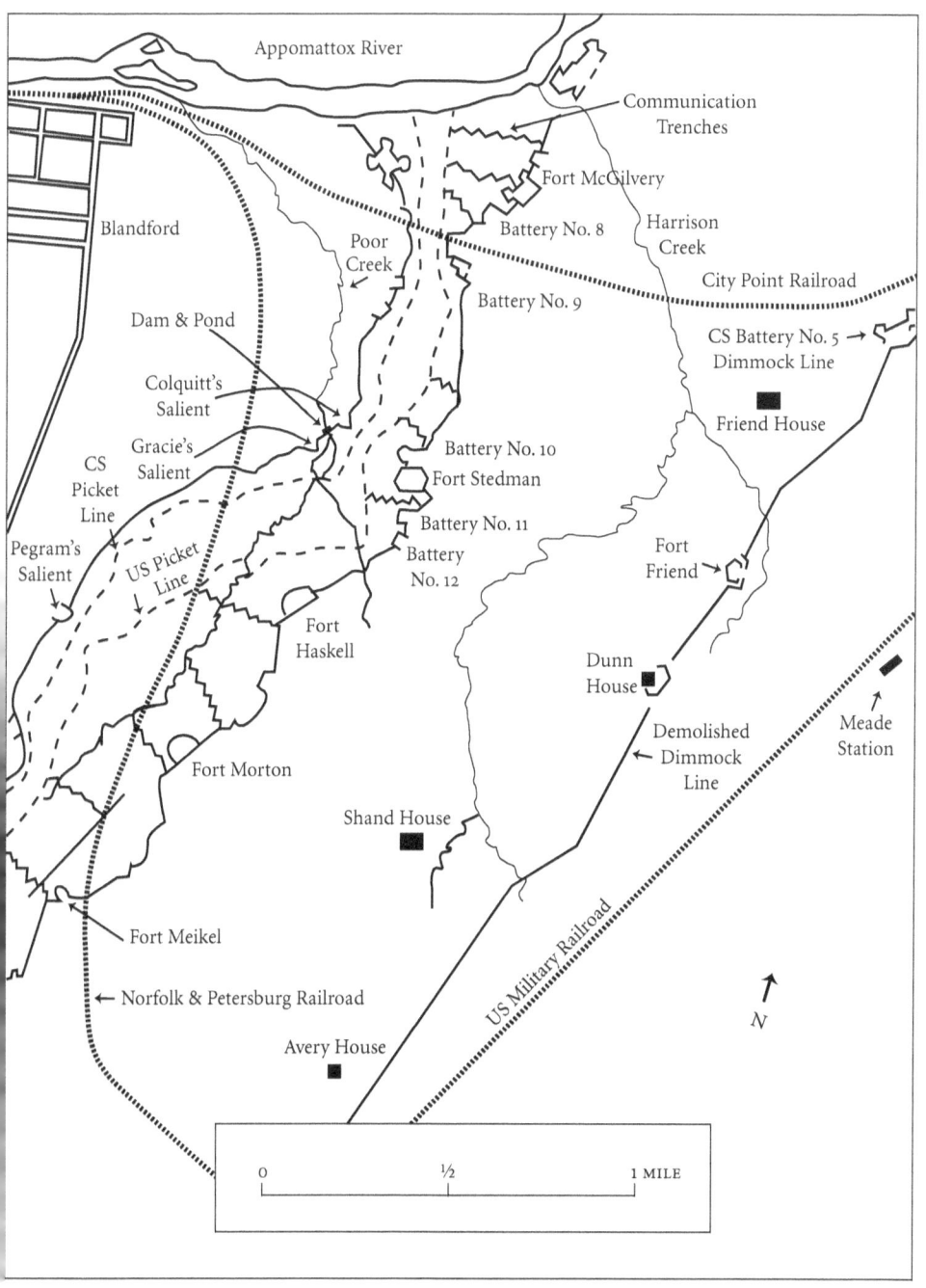

Fort Stedman, March 25, 1865 (based on foldout map in Hodgkins, *Battle of Fort Stedman*)

yards from the main Confederate line, and the picket lines between Stedman and Colquitt's Salient were only 145 yards apart. The Federals had an advanced picket post consisting of a deep trench big enough for half a dozen men located only sixty-eight yards from the Confederate picket line.[8]

The second line behind Fort Stedman came into being when Meade asked Hancock's opinion about holding the existing line while a strike force was sent out to seize Boydton Plank Road in October. Hancock pinpointed Fort Stedman as vulnerable if held too thinly and despaired that no one had yet fortified the slight ridge about one mile to its rear where portions of the Dimmock Line were still intact. This was done sometime later with the construction of Fort Friend and a battery at the Dunn House, securing the area around Fort Stedman.[9]

Parke's Ninth Corps had been responsible for this sector of the Union line since the previous November. Willcox's division stretched from the Appomattox River to Fort Meikel, embracing Fort Stedman, while Potter's division extended from Meikel across Jerusalem Plank Road to Fort Howard. Both divisions covered more than seven miles of trenches, with Willcox responsible for three of those miles. McLaughlen's brigade covered Batteries No. 9, 10, 11, and 12, plus Forts Stedman and Haskell. Parke placed Hartranft's division, consisting of six newly raised Pennsylvania regiments, as a corps reserve. Three of Hartranft's regiments were available to help Willcox.[10]

Fort Stedman, the focus of the coming battle, was not considered a major

{ 248 }   *Fort Stedman and the Eighth Offensive*

Interior of Fort Stedman. (Library of Congress, LC-DIG-CWPB-00540)

work by its defenders. Encompassing about three-quarters of an acre, the fort had no bastions and only four light guns. The parapet was in poor shape; it had never been compacted properly, and winter frost had loosened the soil. No one improved it because the fort was too close to the Confederates to do so safely. The Federals maintained a line of chevaux-de-frise and a line of abatis, while placing an inclined palisade close to the work. Stedman's revetments consisted of logs and fascines, topped by gabions. It had several artillery embrasures, some with wooden mantlets.[11]

The works to either side of Fort Stedman added strength to this sector of the line. To the right, Battery No. 10 lay only about twenty yards from the fort. It was open to the rear but had two field guns and several mortars. The Union line was weak to the right of No. 10, due to a hollow and a patch of low, wet ground. To the left of Stedman, Battery No. 11 lay about 100 yards away. It was later described as "a small ravelin for two guns," but it was connected to Battery No. 12 with a strong curtain. No. 12, located about fifty yards to the left of No. 11, was configured as a square work with six mortars. Fort Haskell, "a strong fortification" mounting four field guns and four mortars, lay to the left of No. 12 and three-eighths of a mile from Fort Stedman.[12]

John C. Tidball, who served as Ninth Corps artillery chief, later wrote that everything from Battery No. 10 to Fort Haskell was, "to all intents and purposes, one work. For ten months it had been growing up under the close and searching fire of the enemy, and had become a labyrinth of bomb-proofs, traverses, gopher holes, huts, and all in every imaginable manner of irregularity. Even those who knew the place well could not find their way about in the dark."[13]

Gordon planned to marshal his legions inside the cramped space of Colquitt's Salient. His three divisions (Evans's, Walker's, and Grimes's) composed the attacking column, with two brigades of Johnson's division in close support. These troops totaled 11,500 men, and Lee made available 8,200 more in case they were needed. This reserve consisted of two brigades of Wilcox's division and all of Pickett's division, although the latter unit was still on its way to the vicinity when the attack began.[14]

Each of Gordon's divisions had to leave its place in the trenches after nightfall on the evening of March 24, move to the rear, reform, and advance back toward the line so that the head of the column pointed in the right direction. Fifty men with axes preceded each division, ready to cut through the lines of Union obstructions. These pioneers were followed by groups of 100 selected men whose job it was to take key targets on the first Federal line. The rest of each division was to follow up and widen the breaches and continue to the second line. Gordon issued white strips of cloth to the advanced groups of 100 men so they would not become victims of friendly fire.[15]

At 3:30 on the morning of March 25, Gordon personally fired three pistol shots as the signal for the attack to begin. It was a complete surprise, although at least one Union picket managed to spread the alarm. The Confederates moved swiftly across the narrow space of no-man's-land, but Capt. J. P. Carson, who led the sharpshooting battalion of Lowe's brigade in Evans's division, recalled that his men received Union rifle fire less than halfway across. The axmen swung away at the obstructions, helped by members of the advance parties.[16]

Gordon's three divisions attacked in three columns very close to each other. One column aimed at the interval between Battery No. 10 and Fort Stedman, quickly taking the small battery and circling around the fort. The second aimed directly at Stedman and lodged for a time in the deep ditch fronting the work. The third column aimed at the interval between Stedman and Battery No. 11, taking the smaller work with the help of some troops from the center column. For a time, the garrison of Fort Stedman held the Rebels at bay by exposing themselves on the parapet and pouring rifle fire into the ditch. They took shelter when the Confederates returned fire, giving the troops lodged in the ditch an opportunity to find a spot on the left flank of the work where the parapet was lower. They quickly moved along the ditch and clambered across just as other Rebels entered the fort through the sally port. It was just becoming light, and the semidarkness added to the confusion that made a prisoner of McLaughlen. He did not know that Stedman had been entered by the enemy and walked into it to encourage the garrison. McLaughlen barked orders to several men before sensing that they were not of his own army, and he was soon taken captive.[17]

The Confederates tried to widen the breach in the Union line but had scant success. To the north, they held Battery No. 10, and the Federals evacuated the curtain between it and the next work; but Battery No. 9 remained in Union control. To the south of Fort Stedman, Battery No. 11 and, soon after, No. 12 fell to the Confederates, but the gray tide stopped at Fort Haskell. Troops from four different regiments were packed in the fort, many loading for those who were closer to the parapet. With the support of Haskell's artillery, they repulsed three separate attacks on the fort.[18]

Gordon opened a gap in the first Union line that was about 1,000 yards long, but he could widen it no farther. Battery No. 9 and Fort Haskell, both enclosed works, became the shoulders of this breach. Henry L. Abbot later argued that this proved the superiority of Union engineering at Petersburg. The Federals relied more heavily on enclosed works, which were capable of independent defense, than did the Confederates, who often left their smaller batteries open to the rear.[19]

Gordon's attack on the second Union line encountered significant delays. Walker needed an hour to get his division past Fort Stedman and form a line to approach the next Union position, because the fort, its curtains, and Batteries No. 10 and 11 served as physical obstacles to the rapid deployment of the troops. Many of the men in Gordon's corps also felt suddenly timid. Capt. R. D. Funkhauser, who commanded the 49th Virginia in Walker's division, tried to lead his troops forward but found only three of them willing to go. The rest took shelter from the steady fire of Union guns under Abbot's command in Batteries No. 4, 5, 8, and 9, as well as the Ninth Corps artillery along the second line.[20]

Walker sent skirmishers forward as he labored to reform his division. They advanced to the lower slope of the ridge whereon the Federal line was located and reported it too strongly held to be taken by a skirmish line. The most important works in this position were Fort Friend and the Dunn House Battery, both reworked batteries of the Confederate Dimmock Line, and both located on prominent rises along the ridge. At slightly less than a mile distant, their guns could deliver fire all over the area occupied by the harried Confederates.[21]

It was up to Hartranft's reserve regiments to repair the breach. The 200th Pennsylvania was camped only one mile from Fort Stedman. It met the Rebels first and repulsed the advanced Confederate skirmishers, with the help of elements of the 57th Massachusetts. Then the Pennsylvania regiment counterattacked in the direction of Fort Stedman but was repulsed. A second advance took the regiment within 100 yards of the fort, but it too was repelled. The

Fort Stedman, 1939. (The Library of Virginia, 1939 World's Fair Photograph Collection, Virginia Room, C1:1/05/06/009)

200th Pennsylvania thereafter reformed with the 209th Pennsylvania and some elements of other Ninth Corps units to block the most direct line of approach to the second Union line.[22]

When Hartranft realized that the units of Willcox's division that had been driven from their positions were forming a semicircular line to contain the Confederates, anchored on Fort Haskell, he reinforced this line with all his regiments as they arrived on the field. By 7:30 A.M., nearly 4,000 Federals stretched from Fort Haskell to Battery No. 9, a distance of about one and a half miles. In the meantime, elements of Willcox's division recaptured Batteries No. 11 and 12.[23]

It was clear by now that Gordon's plan for a breakthrough was hopeless, but retiring would not be easy, as Union artillery rounds "seemed to fall on every square yard of ground, and to sweep over the open space like a hot wind." Walker ordered his division to fall back, covered by the skirmishers, about the time that Hartranft sent his semicircular line forward in a counterattack at 7:45 A.M. Supported by artillery fire, the Union infantry recaptured everything lost that morning.[24]

Far to the west of Fort Stedman, the Federals advanced against the Rebel picket line in reaction to the attack. The initial Sixth Corps effort at 1:00 P.M. failed because it was too small. A second try, involving 2,500 men with three brigades in support, was successful at 3:00 P.M. One supporting brigade made an effort to approach the Confederate main line but was blocked by the inundation along Rohoic Creek. A counterattack by two Georgia regiments temporarily drove some Union soldiers out of their recent capture, but Wright organized a counterstrike at 5:00 P.M. that drove them back. The Second Corps captured a smaller segment of the Confederate skirmish line in the vicinity of the Hatcher's Run battlefield. All the Confederates could do for the moment was establish a new picket line partway between the old one and their main position. Humphreys and Wright lost 1,169 men, and the Confederates lost at least 1,600 in these fights. Casualties in the capture and recapture of Fort Stedman amounted to 2,681 Confederates and 1,044 Federals.[25]

The failure at Fort Stedman wrecked Lee's tenuous plan for dealing with Sherman's approach. Even if Johnston could move fast enough to join Lee at Petersburg without Sherman catching him, that would add no more than 10,000 men to the garrison, while Sherman could add at least 60,000 to Grant's force. If Sherman bypassed Johnston and marched directly for Petersburg, Lee could not strike him en route without being blocked by Meade. Lee now began to think in terms of evacuating Richmond and Petersburg long before Sherman closed on Grant's position.[26]

The Federals were delighted with the results of the fighting on March 25. "It was a great satisfaction to us," crowed William Boston of the 20th Michigan, "for we almost always had to do the charging. We were perfectly willing to change the program." Meade expressed everyone's feelings when he said to Wainwright, "'wish they would try it every day.'"[27]

The Confederates built more works on the farther end of their line, near Boydton Plank Road, as a result of their failure on March 25. William Miller Owen, newly appointed commander of McIntosh's artillery battalion, received orders from the army leader to construct two gun emplacements in front of Fort Gregg that night. He used black laborers and had two pieces in place by dawn. Lee approved of the work but was dissatisfied with a trench that an infantry unit had dug to the left of Owen's guns. The foot soldiers did not have an engineer to guide them, so Lee personally laid out a better line, planting the stakes himself. A few days later, Lee ordered the construction of a larger work to be called Fort Owen on the site of this infantry trench. It was located a quarter-mile south of Fort Gregg near Boydton Plank Road.[28]

Lee insisted that a key point of the Confederate skirmish line lost on March 25, a rise of ground called McIlwaine's Hill, be retaken. The Rebels feared their enemy might use this knoll as an artillery platform to pound the main line. The sharpshooters of four brigades, some 400 men, gathered for the effort. They launched a sudden charge at 5:00 A.M. on March 27. McGowan's and Lane's sharpshooters were in the first line, charged with taking the top of the knoll and then sweeping right and left to enlarge their holding, while Scales's and Thomas's sharpshooters in the second line were to hold the top until Wilcox could send support. The Sixth Corps pickets, taken by surprise, were swept from the knoll. Wright made no effort to retake the hill, but the Confederates evacuated it after nightfall, establishing their new picket line near enough to its top so as to deny the Federals an opportunity to plant batteries. Union casualties in this affair amounted to about 100 men, while Confederate losses were much lighter.[29]

The building of new works on the far right and the recapture of McIlwaine's Hill failed to compensate Lee for his many disadvantages. Modern estimates of Confederate troop strength along the Richmond-Petersburg Lines indicate that the Army of Northern Virginia was stretched to the breaking point. Lee could muster 31,400 men to hold a line twenty-seven and a half miles long. That amounted to 1,140 men per mile. These statistics showcase the importance of heavy field fortifications in Virginia by the last weeks of the Civil War. Lee relied on Longstreet and 10,000 infantry, 1,800 cavalry, and 750 heavy artillerists to hold the works north of the James River. Longstreet's troop density was 1,360 men per mile. Mahone's division of about 4,000 men held the Howlett Line on Bermuda Hundred with the lowest troop density, only 740 per mile. From the Appomattox River to about Lieutenant Run, Gordon's Second Corps covered a bit over four miles of line with about 5,500 men (1,350 men per mile). From Lieutenant Run to Burgess's Mill, Wilcox and Heth held more than eight miles of line with 9,200 men (1,150 men per mile). Beyond Burgess's Mill, Anderson's Fourth Corps and some artillery held the White Oak Road Line as it jutted west. Anderson's 4,800 men banked on the highest troop density anywhere along the Richmond-Petersburg Lines, about 1,600 men per mile.[30]

Two days after the battle of Fort Stedman, Grant, Sherman, and Lincoln met in conference onboard the *River Queen* at City Point. Sherman reported that he could not set out from Goldsboro, North Carolina, before April 10. It would take a couple of weeks beyond that date for his army to be in position to participate in an offensive at Petersburg. Grant did not want to wait so long, and he set wheels into motion that evening to start his planned offensive. Ord's four divisions, which had rested for the past three days, crossed the James as Sheridan moved his cavalry south of the river that night.[31]

### THE EIGHTH OFFENSIVE

Grant wanted Sheridan to move the cavalry via Dinwiddie Court House in an effort to turn the Confederate flank on March 29. Sheridan was not to attack entrenched positions but to attempt to force the occupants into the open, where they could be struck with advantage. If this was not possible, the cavalry was to tear up the South Side Railroad and the Richmond and Danville Railroad, then return to Meade's army or ride southward to join Sherman. Sizable forces of Union infantry were also moving into position to support the cavalry and to exploit any opening that might develop. Grant was ready to convert this cavalry raid into a line-breaking offensive if Lee gave him a chance.[32]

## MARCH 29

Sheridan's three mounted divisions reached Dinwiddie Court House by about 5:00 P.M. on March 29. Warren's Fifth Corps marched southwest on Vaughan Road and then turned onto Quaker Road and headed north. By afternoon, the infantrymen neared Lewis's Farm, only one mile south of Boydton Plank Road. Ord brought his three infantry divisions into play on the morning of March 29. The two white divisions, both belonging to Gibbon's Twenty-Fourth Corps, relieved Humphreys's Second Corps troops in their trenches north of Hatcher's Run, facing the Confederate Boydton Plank Road Line. Humphreys extended the Union line south of Hatcher's Run, straddling Dabney's Mill Road and claiming ground not yet permanently occupied by the Federals. He began to dig a new line of works, his right resting on the stream but in a position so he could support Warren's movement. Meanwhile, the U.S. Engineer Battalion started to corduroy roads between Vaughan Road and Quaker Road to support the new Union presence in the area, as the 50th New York Engineers repaired the necessary bridges.[33]

The Federal movements precipitated a fight between Warren and Anderson. Lee shifted Pickett's entire division to Sutherland Station on the South Side Railroad, about ten miles west of Petersburg and a short distance northwest of Anderson's right flank, to counter the expected turning movement. For the time, Anderson only had Johnson's division to hold the White Oak Road Line, which stretched from Boydton Plank Road just south of Burgess's Mill to the west. Anderson's right flank was due south of Sutherland Station and about four miles east of Five Forks, a major junction that appeared to be the key to Lee's right flank. If Pickett could reach the station, his Virginians might extend Anderson's line and cover Five Forks.[34]

To buy time and determine exactly where the enemy was located, Anderson sent Johnson to reconnoiter in force and drive the Federals away if possible. The division leader led his advance with Wise's Virginia brigade, the remaining three brigades following. Wise ran against Warren's advance at Lewis's Farm, and a short battle ensued. There was no opportunity to dig entrenchments on either side; Lewis's Farm was an open field fight in which neither opponent gained an advantage. Having located the Yankees, Johnson retreated to the

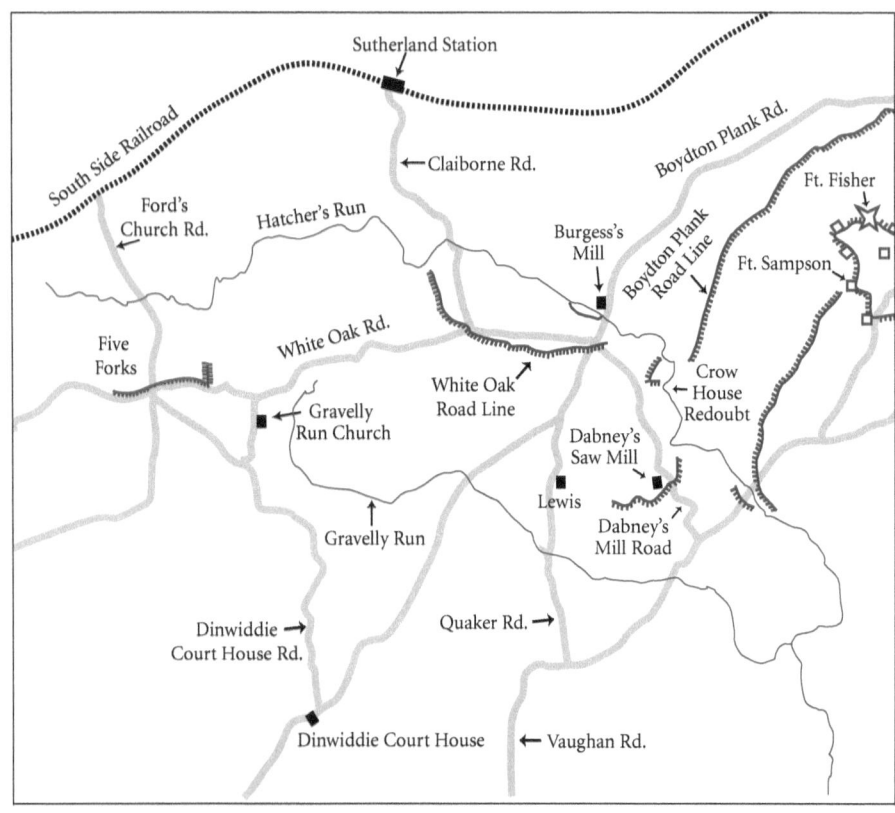

The Eighth Offensive, March 29–April 1, 1865

White Oak Road Line as Warren's men bivouacked near the junction of Boydton Plank Road and Quaker Road.[35]

The fight at Lewis's Farm alerted Lee to the impending danger, and he shifted more troops to the area. McGowan's South Carolina brigade was roused out of the line it had held the past six months and marched in a pouring rain all night. Much of MacRae's North Carolina brigade also shifted west of Burgess's Mill, leaving Lane's North Carolina brigade, McComb's Tennessee brigade, and Thomas's Georgia brigade to stretch ever thinner to cover the vacated sectors along the Boydton Plank Road Line, reducing the troop density to a paltry 888 men per mile. Johnson's probe to Lewis's Farm seemed to indicate that the Confederates were ill prepared to resist a turning movement with the ferocity they had displayed in the earlier phases of the campaign, so Grant decided on the night of March 29 to convert Sheridan's railroad expedition into a major offensive against Lee's right. "I now feel like ending the mat[ter] if it is possible to do so before going back." This decision was taken just as Pickett moved three of his brigades from Sutherland Station to extend Johnson's position along White Oak Road. When McGowan and MacRae got their troops into position, that line was extended farther westward, but it still was not long enough to incorporate Five Forks.[36]

## MARCH 30

Concerned with the security of Five Forks, Lee shifted a large, detached force to the strategic crossroads on March 30. Pickett moved three of his brigades, plus Ransom's and Wallace's brigades of Johnson's division, to the forks. The new position was strengthened by six guns and one cavalry division. It took nearly all day to position his 10,600 men, and then Pickett sent Corse's and Terry's brigades southward as a forward outpost. Lee shifted Scales's brigade from the Boydton Plank Road Line in an effort to lengthen the position along White Oak Road. While Scales held the far left, adjoining Boydton Plank Road, McGowan stretched the right flank farther west along White Oak Road. Still, there was a gap between McGowan and Pickett.[37]

The rain that began on the night of March 29 never really stopped on the 30th, making all movement difficult and disagreeable. Sheridan sent one mounted division northward that divided its strength. One-half of the division skirmished with Corse and Terry south of Five Forks while the other approached the White Oak Road Line. Warren deployed his Fifth Corps before the Confederates who held the latter position with his right adjoining Boydton Plank Road and his left extending to a point south of Claiborne Road. Opposing skirmishers became engaged, pinning the Rebels in their trenches. At the same time, Humphreys's Second Corps wheeled right, pivoting on its connection to Hatcher's Run, in order to close the gap between Warren and Gibbon. The strongest point of the Confederate line opposite Humphreys was the redoubt at the Crow House, located on the south side of the run. In effect, the Federals had turned the corner, laying permanent claim to territory beyond Hatcher's Run and Boydton Plank Road.[38]

When Gibbon had filled the hole vacated by Humphreys, he advanced his troops 400 yards and captured a large section of the Confederate picket line, in order to draw attention from the Second Corps movement. On his left, Turner's division rested its left flank on Hatcher's Run and maintained connection with Humphreys's right flank by using a pontoon bridge constructed by Ord's engineer troops. To Turner's right, Foster's division and then Birney's black division of the Twenty-Fifth Corps extended Gibbon's line, connecting to the left flank of the Sixth Corps. Gibbon tried to entrench his advanced position, but recent rains had made the soil "so spongy that it would not bear the weight of a horse."[39]

By the evening of March 30, Grant thought Sheridan's cavalry could turn the Confederate right if he sent the Fifth Corps to help; he even offered to put it under Sheridan's command. Grant contemplated shifting at least one division of the Second Corps west of Boydton Plank Road to enable Warren to mass his corps south of the junction of White Oak Road and Claiborne Road. He also considered launching concentrated attacks by the Sixth and Ninth Corps against the front of the Petersburg works to support Sheridan. Grant told Meade to tentatively plan for these frontal attacks to take place on April 1, as he expected Lee would further strip his trenches of men in response to Sheridan's moves.[40]

## MARCH 31

On the morning of March 31, Grant's plan for a coordinated cavalry-infantry push to Five Forks was postponed by a Confederate counterattack that caught both Sheridan and Warren by surprise. The result was the battle of the White Oak Road, a seesaw engagement fought mostly without field fortifications, which threatened to derail the entire Eighth Offensive. The Rebel strike was made feasible by the concentration of six infantry brigades along the White Oak Road Line, with five brigades at Five Forks. It was the last time Lee launched a counteroffensive against the Federals at Petersburg.

The White Oak Road Line had evolved into an impressive work. The trees had been cut two to three feet aboveground for about 400 yards in front of the line, the tops pointing toward the south to make an effective slashing. Small branches stuck out from the stumps to further impede movement toward the line. Dunlop established his sharpshooters as a skirmish line in the edge of the pine woods on the far side of this slashing, with "an impenetrable jungle" in his front. Segments of the White Oak Road Line are well preserved today and show the works to have large, thick parapets well placed to sweep the flat land by incorporating shallow angles in the line. The entrenchment crosses White Oak Road and angles back north of it to end near Hatcher's Run.[41]

Lee sent two forces operating in loose coordination with each other to hit the Federals on March 31. Pickett was to advance against Sheridan's cavalry while Johnson was to attack Warren. Since Johnson had already detached two of his brigades to Pickett at Five Forks, he received Eppa Hunton's Virginia brigade as a replacement when this last of Pickett's units finally reached the area. Johnson arranged his own attack plan without consulting corps leader Anderson. McGowan was to lead the offensive by finding and striking Warren's left flank, to be supported by Young M. Moody's Alabama brigade, and Hunton, to his left.[42]

Just as McGowan was pondering where and how to position his troops for the attack, Warren advanced two brigades of Ayres's division to drive the Rebel skirmishers into their main line. This led the three Confederate brigades to advance without regard to a plan, catching the Federals unaware and driving them steadily southward even though Crawford's division tried to help Ayres. Wise's brigade also left the main line but did not participate in the advance. Ayres and Crawford retired to the south bank of Gravelly Run, conducting a fighting retreat. Here Griffin's division and Wainwright's guns provided the muscle to make a stand.[43]

Warren called on Humphreys for help, and two brigades of Miles's division advanced northward, to the west of Boydton Plank Road. They encountered Wise's brigade, which had been waiting for some time for an indication that it should seek out and support the three advancing Confederate units. Wise's Virginians, taken by surprise, managed to stall the Second Corps troops and retire safely to the main line. A bit later, Griffin launched a counterattack across Gravelly Run and drove McGowan, Moody, and Hunton out of a hastily constructed fieldwork, in part because Johnson had become alarmed by the attack on Wise and issued instructions for them to retire from their exposed position. The three brigades took shelter in a modest fieldwork earlier constructed by Ayres's division partway back to the main Confederate line. They were rousted out of this by Chamberlain's brigade of Griffin's division, which found and attacked Hunton's left flank. All three Rebel brigades retreated to the safety of their main line as the Fifth Corps resumed its advanced position. Elements of Warren's corps advanced west of Claiborne Road, interposing between Johnson and Pickett and nearly cutting off communication between the two.[44]

Humphreys tried to do more on March 31. After sending Miles's two brigades to hit Wise, he ordered Mott to advance two regiments east of Boydton Plank Road and west of the Crow House redoubt to distract the Confederates. They endured heavy artillery fire and marched up to the thick slashing fronting the main line before falling back. Another demonstration by two other regiments against Burgess's Mill along the plank road resulted in the capture of part of the Confederate picket line, while yet a third demonstration by skirmishers of William Hays's division penetrated the abatis and silenced some guns in Fort Powell, the work that anchored the junction of the Boydton Plank Road Line and the White Oak Road Line.[45]

Like the Fifth Corps troops, Sheridan also retreated in the face of Pickett's attack but eventually stopped the Confederates in what many historians term the Battle of Dinwiddie Court House. Pickett sent one cavalry division due south to distract the Federals while two mounted divisions and the infantry contingent at Five Forks angled off to the southwest in order to hit the Federal left flank. Active Union patrols alerted Sheridan to the danger, and he deployed six cavalry brigades in an arc to cover both the northern and western approaches to his position. Where Confederate infantry faced Union cavalry, Pickett achieved success, forcing Sheridan to dismantle his defensive posture and conduct a fighting retreat south. By evening, he managed to stop the Confederates about a half-mile north of Dinwiddie Court House. Pickett was now exposed far away from any support, so he retired that night to Five Forks. It had been an open field fight all day.[46]

Instead of a combined arms strike at Five Forks, Grant endured a defensive battle by his cavalry and infantry in two separate but related engagements on March 31. Yet Warren's and Sheridan's ability to repel those attacks saved the Eighth Offensive, and temporary fieldworks played a role in shaping the contour of operations. Grant informed Sheridan on the night of March 31 that he was writing orders for Warren to take his corps southwest and join the cavalry for the projected movement against Five Forks the next day. As planned, Warren was to take orders from Sheridan.[47]

Pickett was under orders from Lee to hold Five Forks at all costs, but he felt scant confidence in his ability to do so. There was still a gap between his position and Johnson's that the Federals could exploit, so Pickett telegraphed Lee for more troops. There were absolutely none to spare. Pickett wanted to abandon the road junction to take up a more defensible position farther north, where the road crossed the northern branch of Hatcher's Run, but this would have allowed the Federals to use Five Forks and gain access to roads that bypassed Pickett altogether and hit the South Side Railroad. He had no alternative but to hold his position at the junction.[48]

## APRIL 1, FIVE FORKS

It took all morning of April 1 for Warren to disengage the Fifth Corps from its position south of White Oak Road and move it toward Sheridan. Ayres's division marched to Dinwiddie Court House to reinforce the cavalry as it pushed northward, following up Pickett's early morning retreat. Crawford and Griffin advanced southwest to threaten Pickett's left flank in case he decided to make a stand before reaching the junction. Moreover, Humphreys now had to move the Second Corps westward to cover most of the ground Warren vacated. This, in turn, compelled Gibbon to extend left to cover some ground Humphreys vacated. Turner's division crossed Hatcher's Run on the pontoon bridge to keep connection with the Second Corps's right.[49]

Pickett gathered five brigades at Five Forks. Ransom's Tar Heels held the left, where the Confederates refused their flank a short distance. Then Wallace's South Carolinians and Steuart's Virginia brigade extended the line westward along White Oak Road to its junction with Ford's Church Road, the center of the forks. Mayo's and Corse's Virginia brigades, with Rooney Lee's cavalry division, held the right wing. Pickett deployed William P. Roberts's cavalry brigade in a thin picket line to cover the gap between Ransom and the right flank of the White Oak Road Line. The rest of Munford's cavalry division spread out along Ford's Church Road north of the junction while Rosser's cavalry division waited north of the branch of Hatcher's Run as a reserve. Pickett's line, which was one and three-quarters miles long, was supported by ten field pieces.[50]

The Confederates found scant fieldworks at Five Forks when they retired to the road junction on the morning of April 1. An officer of Steuart's brigade later recalled that a minor trench had been dug for about 200 yards, which his men improved and lengthened by piling up logs and covering them with dirt. The Confederates also revetted the interior slope of the parapet with logs and scooped out a shallow ditch in front. The refused left flank received quite a bit of attention as well. It extended about 100 yards north of White Oak Road and ended about 60 feet short of a deep ravine. The parapet of the return consisted of small poles with dirt thrown up in front and was much lighter than the parapet on the main line facing south. But the Confederates also revetted the interior slope with logs and made the parapet wide enough to ride a horse on top of it. There are still at least seventeen traverses intact along the return. About ten feet long and placed ten to twenty feet apart, the traverses are attached to the southern two-thirds of the refused line; the rest of the retrenchment simply ends with its left flank in the air.[51]

Federal cavalrymen probed the Rebel position while Warren put the Fifth Corps in place. Only a dismounted brigade of Devin's division managed to penetrate the Confederate line and capture some prisoners, but it was driven out by a counterattack. Devin's men fell back and threw together a log breastwork to hold their position.[52]

Sheridan devised a plan to bring his superior weight to bear on Pickett, outnumbering the 10,000 Confederates with two divisions of cavalry and 12,000 infantry. While Custer's cavalry division feinted against the Rebel right, Warren would engulf the left with a massed attack, and Devin would attack the front at the same time. The difficulty lay in the time necessary to position the infantry just south of the junction of White Oak Road and Gravelly Run Church Road. This seemed the ideal place to stage the advance because Sheridan believed the left flank of Pickett's line lay just north of the junction, and a wide, shallow ravine south of the junction provided cover for Warren to assemble his divisions. He placed Ayres's, the smallest of his three divisions, on the left of Gravelly Run Church Road, Crawford's abreast of him to the right of the road, and Griffin's behind Crawford's. All three divisions were deployed in multiple, compact lines for easier maneuvering; 12,000 men were packed into a formation only 1,000 yards wide. From 1:00 to 4:00 P.M., a reasonable amount of time to perfect such an arrangement, Warren assembled his corps, but Sheridan fumed at the delay. Meanwhile, a sketch depicting the Confederate position as Sheridan believed it to be was widely circulated among division and brigade leaders. No one understood that the refused left flank of Pickett's line was actually 1,000 yards farther west.[53]

Munford's cavalry picked up signs of Warren's massing in the ravine and relayed them to the division commander, but Munford could find no one in authority to pass the warning. Pickett and Fitz Lee were attending a shad bake, an old Virginia tradition at this time of year, one and a quarter miles north of the line. They left Rooney Lee in charge, but Munford could not find him because Lee remained on the far right of the Rebel position.[54]

Warren set out at 4:15 P.M. and soon crossed White Oak Road. A gap between the two wings of the Fifth Corps developed, and it also became apparent that the Confederate line was not where Sheridan had claimed it to be. Ayres was the first to discover the true location of the refused line when his division received enfilade fire from Ransom's brigade. Ayres faced his men left and headed due west, pushing his reserve brigade into the front line to extend his left south of White Oak Road. Sheridan went along with Ayres and helped to steady his men. Ayres crushed the refused segment of Pickett's line in relatively short order, capturing 1,000 men, four guns, and several flags in the process. Then he reformed his division and continued to push westward.[55]

Crawford was moving too fast, and too far along the curve of a large arc toward the northwest, to offer immediate aid to Ayres. Warren scrambled to get his division back into the line of operations, or at least to bring it down on the rear of Pickett's position as soon as possible. Griffin was marching along a more shallow arc and came into action just as Ayres needed help, for the Confederates threw together a new refused line east of the road junction, consisting of Steuart, Wallace, and what was left of Ransom. They managed to assemble some breastworks there as well. Griffin replaced Ayres and pounded the position with two brigades, collapsing Confederate resistance and taking some 1,500 prisoners. Griffin reformed his division and continued pressing west, reaching Ford's Church Road.[56]

About the time that Griffin captured the second refused line, Devin and Custer attacked Pickett's front with two dismounted cavalry brigades. They took huge sections of the entrenchments as Devin sent the 1st U.S. Cavalry in a mounted charge to exploit the advantage. This was one of the few mounted attacks on field fortifications in the war. There could be little possibility of the troopers chasing fleeing Confederates across the countryside, for the area around the junction now became chaotic with mixed regiments and frightened prisoners. Griffin's division bumped into Devin's and Custer's men, forcing the Federals to spend some time sorting out the mess. When they finally did, Devin aligned his whole division facing westward, to Griffin's left, so they could continue the advance on both sides of White Oak Road. Ayres acted as a reserve to the rear.[57]

The shad bake broke up as soon as the sound of firing could be heard, but Crawford's men were within sight of Ford's Church Road as Pickett and others were making their way south, dodging the Federals. Pickett reached the junction just as Griffin took the second refused line. While the Unionists sorted out their confusion around the junction, Pickett established a third refused line west of Ford's Church Road, held by Corse's brigade behind light breastworks. He also positioned Mayo's brigade in a detached position, facing northward to confront Crawford. This arrangement failed to stop the victorious Yankees. Crawford crushed Mayo and went on to drive the Confederates out of their third refused line by dusk, as Rooney Lee covered the Southern retreat to the South Side Railroad.[58]

Five Forks was one of the most crushing defeats suffered by Lee's army in the war, with the loss of up to 4,500 prisoners, thirteen flags, and six guns. Pickett suffered about 600 killed and wounded. Warren's casualties amounted to 633, and Sheridan's cavalry probably suffered less. Most importantly, Lee had lost the screen for his right flank. Sheridan had all but turned that flank with his victory at Five Forks, but it would need further movements and probably more fighting to complete the success the next day. The only sour note on the Union side was that Sheridan unjustly relieved Warren of his corps command immediately after the battle for perceived delays in bringing Crawford into action. Griffin took charge of the corps.[59]

Lee scrambled to make up for this disaster by dispatching Anderson and three brigades from the White Oak Road Line. They left on the evening of April 1 for the South Side Railroad, where Ford's Church Road intersected the tracks. The four brigades left to hold the White Oak Road Line had to extend further to cover the space Anderson vacated. Lee also began to shift Field's division from Longstreet north of the James River down to Petersburg.[60]

CHAPTER EIGHTEEN

# *The Ninth Offensive, April 2*

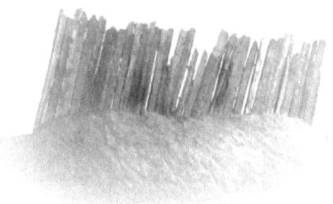

The Eighth Offensive ended with the battle of Five Forks as the scene shifted to the front lines south and west of Petersburg. Grant decided on the night of April 1 to launch two major attacks against the trenches, one of them supported by Gibbon, and with cooperative movements by Sheridan, Griffin, and Humphreys west of Hatcher's Run. The reversion to frontal attacks, rather than completing the turning of Lee's flank, justify calling what happened on April 2 the Ninth Offensive. Whether these attacks were needed or whether it was wiser instead to continue the progress of Sheridan's operations against the flank is an open question. But the attacks on April 2 ended the campaign with a bloody drama on a scale similar to that which had started the campaign in June.

Grant was eager to take advantage of Sheridan's partial turning of Lee's flank. On learning at 1:30 P.M. that Sheridan and Warren had pushed the Confederates to the vicinity of Five Forks, "Grant folded the dispatch, and said 'Then I want Wright and Parke to assault tomorrow morning, at 4 o'clock!'" News of Sheridan's victory at Five Forks reached headquarters at about 8:00 P.M., and Grant "got hasty" to push forward against Lee's front. He telegraphed Ord, "Get your men up and feel the enemy and push him if he shows signs of giving way," following that up with advice not to "fight your way over difficult barriers, against defended lines" but "to see though if the enemy is leaving and if so follow him up." Grant urged that Wright start his attack immediately, but the Sixth Corps commander argued that it would be best to stick to the 4:00 A.M. timetable. "The corps will go in solid," he informed Meade, "and I am sure will make the fur fly." Meade agreed with him, and Wright, according to Lyman, "made, perhaps, the necessary delays." Grant also thought that a massive artillery bombardment might compel the Rebels to give up their trenches that night. He worried that Lee could evacuate those works and mass his army against Sheridan.[1]

At 10:00 P.M. on the night of April 1, 150 Union guns opened fire and kept it up until 1:00 A.M. Grant suggested to Sheridan that he lodge his troops on

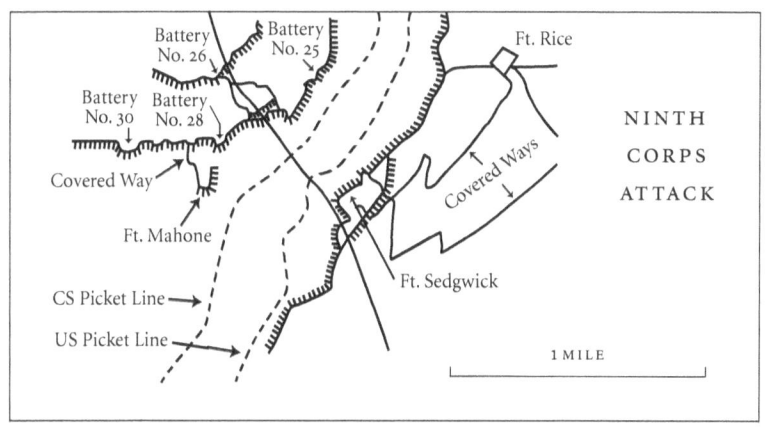

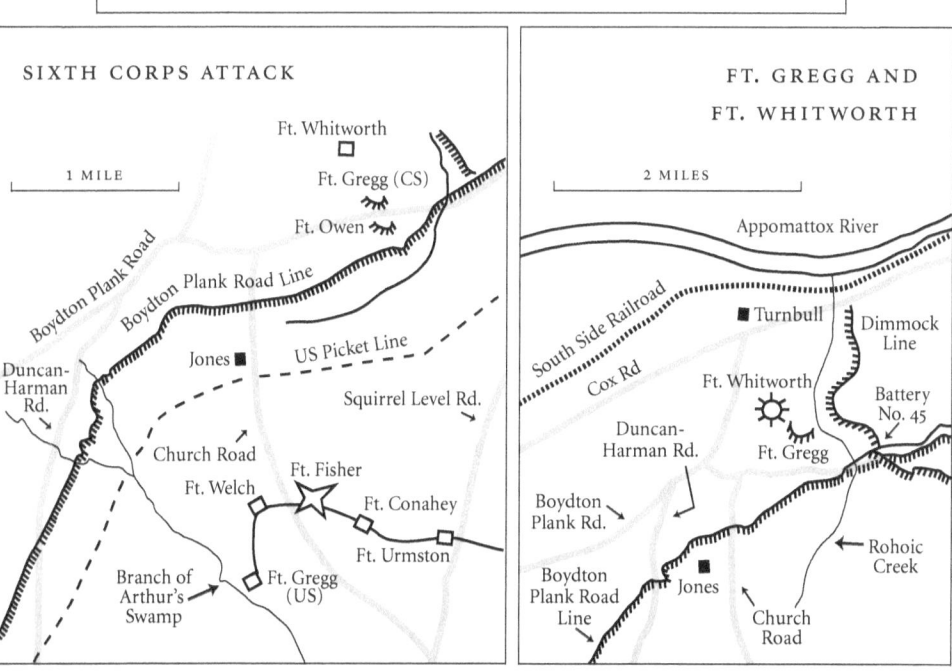

The Ninth Offensive, April 2, 1865 (based on maps in Greene, *Breaking the Backbone of the Rebellion*, 259, 385, 447)

the South Side Railroad on April 2. Sheridan, however, preferred to advance toward Petersburg along White Oak Road, crushing the fortified line by the flank as Humphreys advanced against it from the front.[2]

### NINTH CORPS

Parke's target was the complex of works straddling Jerusalem Plank Road, encompassing six redoubts strengthened from old Dimmock Line origins. Dim-

Artillery emplacements and traverses at Fort Mahone. Taken from atop the parapet at the southern end of the fort, looking north. Note the chevaux-de-frise in the distance, probably placed to block access to the fort from the north. (Library of Congress, LC-DIG-CWPB-02790)

mock's Battery No. 25 lay east of the plank road on the main Confederate line, with No. 26 to its rear on a secondary line. No. 27 straddled the road, while No. 28 lay to the west of the roadway. No. 29 was situated 400 yards forward of the main line and 500 yards west of the plank road. The Confederates had strengthened this work, calling it Fort Mahone, to counter the artillery fire coming from Union Fort Sedgwick about 500 yards away. The soldiers had their own name for Fort Mahone; they called it Fort Damnation in counterpoint to Fort Hell, the Union nickname for Fort Sedgwick. A covered way linked Fort Mahone with the main Confederate line. The Rebels had constructed a strong secondary line east and west of the plank road and about a quarter-mile behind the main line. Two covered ways, one on either side of the road, connected the forward and secondary lines, while chevaux-de-frise and other obstructions lay in front of the main position.³

Gordon reported only 5,500 men available to hold more than six miles of trenches. After posting the necessary pickets, what manpower was left to hold the trench amounted to little more than a skirmish line. The combat effectiveness of all his troops had "rapidly decreased from their physical exhaustion." Bryan Grimes's division of 2,200 men held three and a half miles of work from the crater to Battery No. 45. Battle's Alabama Brigade, led by Edwin L. Hobson,

Federals standing on traverses at Fort Mahone. They are standing on the second and third traverses seen in the previous view (LC-DIG-CWPB-02790). Note the drainage ditch next to the man standing on the ground. (Library of Congress, LC-DIG-CWPB-02610)

straddled Jerusalem Plank Road. To its right, David G. Cowand commanded Grimes's old North Carolina brigade, and William R. Cox's Tar Heel brigade was positioned to Cowand's right. To Hobson's left, east of the road, Edwin A. Nash led a Georgia brigade. After the war, Grimes claimed that he had no more than one man every eight feet along his line.[4]

The Federals advanced at 11:00 P.M. on April 1 to capture Grimes's picket line on both sides of the plank road. The Southern pickets were dug in from 150 to 300 yards in front of their main entrenchment in pits about fifty yards apart. Three men huddled in each pit, protected by a semicircular parapet and a tent fly stretched over the top. Hobson lost half his brigade when the Federals advanced that night.[5]

Parke arrayed eighteen regiments after capturing the Rebel pickets, with Potter to the west of the road and Hartranft to the east. Harriman's brigade of Willcox's division sent three regiments to cover Hartranft's right flank, with the rest deployed to the rear as a reserve. Willcox demonstrated between the crater and the Appomattox River with the rest of his division to divert Confederate attention. Potter planned to lead his division with three companies of the 31st Maine and a party of men supplied with axes to cut through the obstructions. Hartranft also placed axmen in front of his column. Both he and Potter formed

Interior of Fort Mahone. Note the drainage ditch and that the end of the first traverse seen on the right is the second traverse seen in LC-DIG-CWPB-02790. (Library of Congress, LC-DIG-CWPB-02634)

their commands in the open space between the main Union line and the picket line, covered by the darkness.[6]

Parke's men set out at 4:00 A.M., partially covered by mist. Thomas P. Beals halted the three companies of the 31st Maine just before the line of chevaux-de-frise because he outpaced the rest of Potter's division. His men fired into the embrasures of Battery No. 28 until they heard Potter's men yelling; then the pioneers chopped the chevaux-de-frise apart. The van of the division followed Beals but found the ditch in front of No. 28 filled with water. The Federals worked their way around to the connecting curtains west of the battery and clambered across, taking the battery and its tiny garrison. They found the rear of the redoubt open to Confederate artillery fire from the secondary line, so they advanced along the forward line toward Fort Mahone.[7]

Hartranft's division duplicated Potter's success east of Jerusalem Plank Road. The pioneers cut through the obstructions, and the troops swarmed into Battery No. 27. While most Unionists made their way right and left to widen the breach, Miles Clayton Huyette of the 208th Pennsylvania took thirty men and tried to cover the distance to the second Confederate line. Artillery fire forced them back to shelter "in the sunken rear parts of the captured" first line.

To Hartranft's right, Harriman's three regiments took Battery No. 25 with five guns and sixty-eight prisoners.[8]

On Hobson's far left, Cornelius Robinson Jr. led the 3rd Alabama to the right when Hartranft and Harriman hit the line, only to find that the next regiment, the 6th Alabama, had already retreated. Robinson made a stand to contain the enemy. He noted that a particular traverse could be enfiladed by artillery fire from the second line and positioned his regiment in the next traverse to the east. Harriman's Yankees filled the space between the two traverses and tried to pass through a narrow passage under the eastern one, but Robinson's Rebels shot them as they emerged. A short-range duel now ensued as the Alabamans jumped atop traverses and bombproofs to fire down on the Federals. When Robinson's ammunition began to give out, he left a rearguard of six men and pulled the rest of the 3rd Alabama back to the position still held by Nash's brigade. The rear guard followed as soon as the men shot off their last round.[9]

Nash's troops held their ground, shoring up the right flank of the Union breach, but Potter's men widened it west of Jerusalem Plank Road by attacking Fort Mahone. It had been placed forward of the main line to occupy a slight ridge that ran out at a right angle toward the Federal position. Fort Mahone was filled with stout traverses revetted by logs and posts, gabions, and sandbags. The covered way connecting Mahone to the Confederate line had two right angles to lessen the danger of enfilade artillery fire.[10]

Curtin's brigade advanced on Fort Mahone, making its way around the work to enter from the rear as well as across the ditch and over the parapet. The Federals captured three guns and several prisoners inside. But the four Union regiments that piled into the redoubt could not expand much farther west, and they received artillery fire from the second Rebel line as well. Parke's chief engineer tried to direct the troops in refacing the Rebel works to protect against this fire, but there was little they could do.[11]

The Confederates retired west from Fort Mahone to the position of the 53rd North Carolina of Cowand's brigade, between Mahone and Battery No. 30, where a large traverse partway between those two works offered shelter. The Federals advanced to it, but the Rebels jumped on top to fire down on them. Hampden Osborne of the 53rd North Carolina heard a Union officer cry out, "'O for hand grenades and scaling ladders! We would soon clean them out,'" but Cowand's left flank held firm behind the traverse.[12]

Parke's men took Batteries No. 25, 27, 28, and 29 (Fort Mahone) and the curtains connecting these works, but the attack bogged down in the captured trenches. The Federals held only about 500 yards of the Confederate forward line, far from a breakthrough. Grimes positioned two battalions of Virginia Re-

Covered way linking Fort Mahone to Confederate main line. Note the berm and the Federal soldier standing on it in the distance. The muddy, waterlogged roadbed and the angle in the covered way are prominently shown. (Library of Congress, LC-DIG-CWPB-02561)

serves under Fletcher Archer and elements of Cowand's brigade in the second line opposite the breach, and he pulled field guns from Battery No. 30 to the second line to fire into the exposed curtain west of Fort Mahone, compelling the Federals to retire from the traverse where the 53rd North Carolina had held them at bay. Rebel counterattacks led to bitter fighting, traverse to traverse, as the afternoon continued. These traverses often were ten feet tall and twenty feet thick, but both sides jumped on top to fire into the crowded mass on the other side, risking death with each second they tarried.[13]

The Confederate effort played itself out in surges. Grimes's second push took place at 1:00 P.M. and led Parke to call for reinforcements from the Sixth Corps. Some of these new troops simply lay down in front of the captured parapet and fired over the heads of Parke's men inside the Rebel trench. Grimes's third push of the day took place at 3:00 P.M., and it recaptured a portion of Fort Mahone and chunks of Union-occupied trenches east of Jerusalem Plank Road. Charles H. T. Collis's Independent Brigade arrived on the scene and counterattacked to stabilize the situation.[14]

By the time the fighting ended that evening, the Federals controlled about 200 yards of the Rebel forward line and a portion of Fort Mahone. Gordon asked Lee if it was worth trying to recapture the rest. A staff officer informed him that the army would likely pull out of the Petersburg lines that night, so Gordon canceled all plans for continuing the counterattacks. It had been "an awful days fight," as Samuel Beddall of the 48th Pennsylvania put it. Parke lost at least 1,500 troops, but Grimes's casualties are unknown. Hartranft's men strengthened the captured works that night, and Potter's troops used sections of Confederate chevaux-de-frise to construct a bridge across the ditch of Fort Mahone. This allowed them to enter and leave the redoubt without exposing themselves to Confederate fire from the north. Gordon began to pull out of the trenches at 9:00 P.M. according to Lee's timetable for evacuating Petersburg.[15]

SIXTH CORPS

Meade's order to Wright simply stated that the Sixth Corps was to advance at 4:00 A.M. on April 2, heading for Boydton Plank Road. The corps commander was sanguine of success. "If the corps does half as well as I expect we will have broken through the rebel lines fifteen minutes from the word 'go.'"[16]

Wright was so confident because he knew that Lee had stripped the Boydton Plank Road Line. Hill had only four brigades to cover the six miles of works between Battery No. 45 and Hatcher's Run. Moreover, taking the Confederate picket line on March 25 gave an important advantage to the Federals. They could now clearly see the obstructions and the fortifications of the Rebel main line and had ample room to form an assault column in front of their own works.[17]

Lewis Grant, commander of a brigade in Getty's division, was the first to call attention to a ravine that constituted a tributary of Arthur's Swamp and bisected the Confederate line opposite Fort Welch. It was only sixty feet wide but enough of an obstacle so that the Rebels did not dig their trench completely across it. The ravine drained toward the Federal position, widening into a marshy area before it reached the Union picket line. There were many obstacles between the lines, including stumps left over when the Confederates cut trees for firewood. Four rows of abatis were arrayed between the captured Confederate picket line and the main Rebel works, with a fraise set among the array. Hazard Stevens, one of Getty's staff officers, later described the fraise as "a serried row of heavy sharpened stakes set close together." The Federals could see that the ditch in front of the main line was deep and wide, and the headlogs that topped the parapet had loopholes notched into their underside. A further obstacle lay in the scattering of latrines dug in front of the abatis, which would force the Federals to break ranks. But there were flaws in the Confederate defenses. While going to and from the latrines, the Rebels had knocked down a few stakes in the fraise. More importantly, they had created a gap in it and through all the rows of abatis wide enough for a wagon to go out and collect wood. There also was a plank bridge across the ditch and a gap in the parapet for the wagon. The Confederate pickets also used these openings and the plank bridge to go out for their rounds of duty on the skirmish line.[18]

Grant informed Getty, who informed Wright, who brought Meade out to see for himself. The corps and army leaders were not as impressed as the brigade and division commanders, but they consented to preliminary plans for an attack. The greatest advantage Wright possessed was that he could mass 14,000 men to strike a section of Confederate trench that was a little more than one mile wide, defended by only 2,800 Rebels. Lane's North Carolina brigade stood directly in his path, with Thomas's Georgia brigade to the left and part of MacRae's North Carolina brigade to his right. The defects in the Confederate line would play a minor role in the outcome of the attack.[19]

Wright's three divisions formed with each of their brigades arrayed in a column of regiments, all ranks closed in mass to form a dense concentration, and Getty's division was in the lead. Seymour placed his division to Getty's left rear, and Wheaton positioned his division to Getty's right rear. All were to form between the main Union line and the Union picket line under cover of darkness on the night of April 1–2. Garrisons in all the forts along the two-mile sector held by the Sixth Corps were stripped to the minimum; many connecting curtains were abandoned altogether, while the other curtains held only one-tenth of their normal strength. Wright would take only one battery for each division, but at least thirty-five axes were distributed to each brigade so the men could cut through obstructions. If the ditch proved to be too deep, the front regiment of each brigade was to open fire and occupy the attention of the enemy while the rest of the brigade moved to right or left to find a crossing.[20]

The Federals formed in the open country under cover of darkness and the three-hour bombardment Grant unleashed that night. Heavy picket fire erupted, for the gathering host was only 200 yards from the Rebel pickets and 600 yards from the main Confederate position. A number of Federals were hit even before the attack began, including Lewis Grant, who survived a dangerous head wound.[21]

Wright delayed the attack until 4:40 A.M. on April 2 to give the men a bit more daylight. When the Sixth Corps started, it rolled over the Confederates like a tidal wave. The van of Wright's command overran the pickets but received fire from the main Rebel line just before it reached the obstacles. There was no time to wait for the pioneers to cut passages; the infantrymen tore the abatis and the fraise apart with their bare hands, or they found room to squeeze through. Formations dissolved as groups of excited Federals emerged from the obstacle belt, crossed the ditch, and climbed the big parapet. The first man of Getty's division to top the embankment was Capt. Charles G. Gould of the 5th

Vermont, who got there by way of the Confederate picket path and the plank bridge across the ditch. With three other men, Gould engaged the defending Rebels and suffered several bayonet and sword wounds, but he survived.[22]

To Getty's right, Wheaton's division encountered thicker abatis, but Elisha Hunt Rhodes also found a wagon path. He maneuvered his 2nd Rhode Island through it by the flank and reformed a battle line before crossing the main Confederate entrenchment. Rhodes and several of his men managed to jump into the ditch just as Lane's and Thomas's troops opened fire; then they climbed up the exterior slope onto the top, "stepping right among their muskets as they were aimed over the work. It was done so quick that the Rebels had no chance to fire again but dropped their guns and ran." To Getty's left, Seymour's division drove away the Tar Heels of MacRae's brigade.[23]

Within thirty minutes, Wright's corps completely severed the Boydton Plank Road defenses in the most decisive breakthrough of a heavily fortified line in the war. Now, the focus was directed to exploiting that major achievement. Heth still had two and a half brigades, some 1,600 men, holding the line southwest of the Sixth Corps position, so Wright redirected his troops in that direction. Seven brigades were arrayed from the rear of the captured Confederate line as far northwest as the plank road, then they slowly began to move forward. McComb's brigade reformed facing northeast, its right resting on the Boydton Plank Road Line. The Federals captured a redan called Fort Davis, but McComb's sharpshooters counterattacked and retook it. Wright advanced again at 7:00 A.M., and this time he swept everything before him all the way to Hatcher's Run. Meanwhile, what was left of Lane's and Thomas's brigades had retired northeast to the old Dimmock Line defenses that still stood between Wright and the city of Petersburg. More troops arrived to hold this sector—Harris's Mississippi Brigade of 400 veterans—and Longstreet personally showed up to take command. His job was to patch together a force to hold the Dimmock works from the Appomattox River to Battery No. 45. Hill was killed that morning by Sixth Corps troops who ranged widely across the area.[24]

By 9:00 A.M., Wright realized that Humphreys's Second Corps was on the move west of the road and needed no help, so he redirected his command northward to approach Longstreet. The Sixth Corps rested its left on the Appomattox River, but it was up to the Army of the James to extend this line southeast across Boydton Plank Road. Ord had been unable to mount his own attack on the Boydton Plank Road Line because the ground in his front was too marshy, so Grant ordered him to follow the Sixth Corps and support its advance. Ord kept William Birney's division of the Twenty-Fifth Corps in reserve and sent all of Foster's division and most of two brigades from Turner's division to follow Wright. Another brigade, Harris's of Turner's division, advanced directly against the Confederate line southwest of Wright's breakthrough and captured a section of it just as the defenders evacuated. Ord sent engineer Michie to select ground for a defensive line in case of Rebel counterattacks, but Michie took it upon himself to order all of Ord's units forward when he realized the significance of the Sixth Corps achievement. By about 10:00 A.M., both Ord and Wright were forming a line facing northeast, with Ord on the right and Wright on the left. They slowly advanced as 15,000 Federals prepared to test the western defenses of Petersburg.[25]

Wright's attack achieved stunning success with a similar advantage in numbers over the enemy as Parke enjoyed, mainly because Wright had to break only one line of Rebel defenses. The Ninth Corps achieved only partial penetration of a dense system of entrenchments, while the Sixth Corps crushed a single line thinly held. Wright achieved what Grant had wanted since the Second Offensive in late June, reaching the Appomattox River. Even if Lee had decided to hold out along the old Dimmock Line after April 2 rather than evacuate Petersburg, Wright's success would have been a great tactical victory. It severed the South Side Railroad and gave Grant the option of crossing the Appomattox the next day to threaten Lee's communications north of the river.

### FORT GREGG

Lane and Wilcox placed their available troops in Fort Gregg and Fort Whitworth, which had been constructed when the Boydton Plank Road Line was laid out the previous fall. They were located northwest of the plank road and about 1,000 yards in front of the Dimmock Line. Initially, Harris's brigade advanced 400 yards beyond the two forts to meet the approach of Gibbon's Twenty-Fourth Corps. Gibbon deployed on a slight ridge 800 yards from the forts with Foster's division on his right and elements of Turner's division behind as support. One of Turner's brigades deployed left to confront Fort Whitworth. Gibbon sent forward skirmishers, which convinced Harris to retire.[26]

What followed was one of the classic, last-ditch defenses of the Civil War. Badly outnumbered, the Confederate defenders fought to buy time for Longstreet to shore up the Dimmock works and give Lee the option of staying in Petersburg a while longer or withdrawing under cover of night. There were two three-inch rifled guns in Fort Gregg, which was filled with about 200 men of the 12th and 16th Mississippi under Lt. Col. James H. Duncan of the 19th Mississippi. Harris personally commanded the 19th and the 48th Mississippi in Fort Whitworth, which also held four field guns. With accompanying artillerymen and a few troops from Lane's brigade, Gregg was defended by about 350 men; Whitworth, by 200 men. There probably were no more than 1,000

Rebels altogether west of the Dimmock works, including those manning the short section of the Boydton Plank Road Line that adjoined Battery No. 45.[27]

Fort Gregg was a small work with a parapet eight feet thick and raised platforms and embrasures for five guns. It had a banquette for infantry and a ditch fourteen feet wide and six feet deep. Due to recent rains, the ditch was filled with at least two feet of water. The rear was enclosed by a stockade consisting of pine logs up to twenty inches thick and loopholed. Six hundred yards to the north lay Fort Whitworth, which also was known as Fort Baldwin, Fort Anderson, and Fort Alexander. It was a larger work than Fort Gregg, but it had deteriorated over the months. Harris's men had taken wood from the revetment for their campfires while they lived nearby during the winter, and the parapet had eroded. The Confederates meant to dig a curtain between the two but had only managed about thirty yards of it, connecting to the stockade at the rear of Fort Gregg. The 12th Mississippi lined the parapet on the left of Gregg, while the 16th Mississippi covered the right face of the semicircular work.[28]

Gibbon's artillery bombarded the forts while his infantry deployed for the attack, silencing the guns. When the Union troops advanced at about 1:00 P.M., Osborn's and a part of Dandy's brigades led the way, crossing 800 yards of mostly open ground and a marshy swale 200 yards from the fort. The swale disrupted formations, which were further loosened when the Federals started to run as they neared Fort Gregg. Most of the men in the two brigades jumped into the ample ditch of the work, becoming mired in the water and mud. Col. Alvin C. Voris of the 67th Ohio found it waist deep in places, and some of his men actually swam across it. Others stuck their bayonets into the exterior slope of the parapet to serve as a handhold to keep their heads above water.[29]

The rest of Dandy's command and two regiments of Fairchild's brigade soon joined the others, huddling in Fort Gregg's watery ditch, mostly on the southeast and west sides of the work. Potter's brigade and Curtis's brigade of Turner's division also advanced to either side of Foster's men, bringing the total attack force to 4,000 men.[30]

The huddled mass of Federals struggled for up to a half-hour trying to gain entry into the fort as the defenders threw "dirt, stones and various kinds of missiles" across the parapet onto their heads. The Confederates rolled artillery shells down the exterior slope and shot the Yankees who crawled up the parapet and appeared on its top.[31]

It took time for the Federals to work their way around the fort, but they eventually discovered that the short curtain gave them an opportunity to climb onto the fort's parapet more easily. Moreover, the twenty-five Mississippians who defended the stockade were worn down by casualties, allowing the attackers to gain entry from the rear at the same time that the mass of Federals in the ditch managed to crest the parapet. Pvt. Joseph R. Logsden, the regimental color-bearer of the 12th West Virginia, planted his flag atop the parapet, hoping to encourage his comrades to come on, but he was shot and fell back into the ditch. Lt. Joseph Caldwell of Company A tried it too, but he also was shot as the flag fell inside the fort. The West Virginians now rushed into the work to retrieve their colors, becoming the first group of attackers to cross the parapet. Others gouged out footholds in the slope or pushed their comrades up, engaging in a fierce hand-to-hand struggle when they jumped inside the work, although the Confederates had no bayonets.[32]

The entire attack took no more than an hour. Meanwhile, Gibbon sent in Harris's brigade toward Fort Whitworth. The defenders received an order from Wilcox to evacuate just as Harris was about to surround the work, and all but seventy of the Confederates managed to escape.[33]

The defenders of Forts Gregg and Whitworth bought some valuable time. When the Sixth Corps advanced to Gibbon's left at the same time that the Federals started their attack on Fort Gregg, Wright was opposed only by Confederate artillery. Yet he cautiously halted and reformed his command. Confederate staff officer Giles Buckner Cooke directed much of the artillery fire from a position next to Lee's command post at the Turnbull House, also known as Edge Hill, located west of Rohoic Creek in front of the Dimmock Line. The Confederates threw together some breastworks to protect the guns. Field's division arrived on the scene and manned the Dimmock Line, allowing the Confederates to evacuate Edge Hill. Five Sixth Corps brigades advanced to occupy it, digging in east of the Turnbull House that evening.[34]

Archibald K. Jones survived the battle and saw the field in front of Fort Gregg while being led away as a prisoner. "The slaughter was appalling," he later recalled. "The dead were lying two hundred and three hundred yards in front of the fort, and increased in numbers as the fort was neared, until immediately at the fort it was simply fearful. Men shot off the parapet fell back into the ditch, were pitched out behind, and actually lay in heaps." John G. Barnard also viewed the field soon after the end of the engagement and agreed with Jones. "I never saw so many dead in so small a space lying just where they had fallen." Other observers noted the numerous small pits in the exterior slope of the work where Union bullets had penetrated the parapet.[35]

The Federals lost 122 killed and 592 wounded, more than the number of Confederates occupying both forts. They found at least 56 Confederate dead inside Fort Gregg and took 250 prisoners there, in addition to the 70 captured at Fort Whitworth. While some Unionists cleaned up the battlefield, the rest formed a continuous line opposite the Dimmock works that evening, linking the Sixth and Twenty-Fourth Corps positions. Ord was especially eager to lay out and dig protection for the men and artillery. No one knew what to expect the next morning.[36]

### SECOND CORPS

Humphreys planned to attack the Crow House Redoubt on the morning of April 2, but a call from Sheridan for reinforcements the previous evening caused him to cancel those plans. Miles's division marched west during the night of April 1–2 to join Sheridan, and Humphreys planned to await developments. The Confederate works west of Hatcher's Run seemed quite formidable to George Bowen of the 12th New Jersey, who observed that the slashing was so thick "a rabbit could scarce find its way through. . . . It appears doubtful if we can take these works if they are even partially manned."[37]

When he heard of Wright's breakthrough on April 2, Heth ordered his troops to evacuate their works and move north to protect the South Side Railroad. Humphreys advanced two divisions at about the same time, capturing the Rebel picket line at 7:30 A.M. and entering the main line without resistance. By now, Miles was no longer needed at Five Forks, so he made his way back toward White Oak Road, reaching there about 9:00 A.M. Humphreys had intended to advance his entire corps up Claiborne Road, directly toward the South Side Railroad, but orders to send help to Wright reached him. He hurried two divisions east and allowed Miles to advance northward alone.[38]

Heth selected Sutherland Station, about ten miles west of Petersburg on the South Side Railroad, as the concentration point for his troops. Confederate supply trains were already parked there. When told he had to take command of the Third Corps after Hill's death, Heth placed brigade leader John R. Cooke in charge at the station with orders to protect the trains. Elements of Cooke's, MacRae's, Scales's, and McGowan's brigades, amounting to 1,200 men, gathered at the station by late morning. They established a line half a mile long parallel to the railroad and south of Cox Road, with McGowan refusing the Confederate left. An open field 700 yards wide with an easy slope lay in front. The Rebels threw up what William Dunlop called "a slender line of earthworks, hastily constructed of fence rails and what earth could be dug up with bayonets and shoveled with the hands." Cooke was ready for action by 11:00 A.M.[39]

Miles brought up nearly 8,000 troops in four brigades and immediately launched a frontal attack. His lead brigade, Henry J. Madill's, advanced up Claiborne Road against Cooke and Scales and was repulsed. The second attack, led by Clinton MacDougall and Robert Nugent, hit MacRae and McGowan on the

Confederate left at 1:00 P.M. As with the first assault, the defenders opened fire at comparatively long range, about 300 yards, and the Federals were repulsed long before they closed with the position.[40]

Miles now took two hours to prepare his third attempt. He deployed skirmishers and arranged for John Ramsey's brigade to turn Cooke's left, gain the railroad, and crush McGowan. This attack employed Miles's numerical superiority. The Federals started at 4:00 P.M., and within an hour they were on the railroad, compelling the Confederates to beat a hasty retreat. Miles lost 366 men at Sutherland Station. Confederate casualties are not known, but about 600 of Cooke's men became prisoners.[41]

Darkness prevented further exploitation of the Sixth Corps breakthrough. Sheridan's cavalry and the Fifth Corps did little more than occupy the vacated works along White Oak Road after both the Confederates and the Second Corps left the area.[42]

### NORTH OF THE APPOMATTOX RIVER

Along other sectors of the Richmond-Petersburg Line, Federal troops waited anxiously to learn of developments. George L. Hartsuff commanded 5,000 men at Bermuda Hundred, mostly artillerymen acting as infantry. Weitzel held the Union line north of the James River with elements of his Twenty-Fifth Corps, but he was also responsible for supervising the Bermuda Hundred front. Weitzel and some of his subordinates spent the afternoon of April 1 firing different kinds of ordnance at a double row of chevaux-de-frise to see if it could be broken up. This was in anticipation of an order to attack the next day. They found that everything, including chained shot, simply passed through the obstruction.[43]

Weitzel continued to anticipate an order to attack on April 2 and prepared all day for launching a push. When Grant informed him the Confederates might be evacuating the Howlett Line, Weitzel ordered Hartsuff to conduct a reconnaissance to find out. Edward Ferrero advanced a battalion of the 10th New York Heavy Artillery at the head of a column near Redoubt Carpenter. The Federals captured three-quarters of a mile of the Confederate picket line (but only six Rebel troops) and then retreated when they were met by heavy artillery fire, destroying the abatis in front of the Rebel picket posts. Grant did not cancel Weitzel's anticipated attack order until nearly midnight of April 2.[44]

### THE END

"I am now writing from far inside of what was the rebel fortifications this morning but what are ours now," wrote Grant to his wife on the night of April 2. "They are exceedingly strong and I wonder at the sucsess [sic] of our troops carrying them by storm. But they did it and without any great loss." The Federals lost 3,936 men on April 2. Lee's casualties amounted to at least 5,000, most of whom were taken prisoner, but Grant accurately described the results of the day's work. "Altogether this has been one of the greatest victories of the war. Greatest because it is over what the rebels have always regarded as their most invincable [sic] Army and the one used for the defence of their capital. We may have some more hard work but I hope not."[45]

Grant prepared for the worst, a yet-undaunted enemy holed up in the Dimmock Line for a last stand. He guessed that only Gordon's Second Corps held the works around Petersburg but refused to attack it unless there were reliable indications that Gordon was evacuating. Then, a "furious bombardment" to begin at 5:00 a.m., followed by an infantry attack at 6:00 a.m., was in order. At any rate, Grant wanted Sheridan to push the Fifth Corps and his cavalry north of the Appomattox as quickly as possible on April 3. "All we want is to capture or beat the enemy," he informed Sheridan.[46]

CONCLUSION

No one on the Federal side knew for certain what to expect at dawn on April 3. North of the James River, Weitzel's troops carefully moved past the torpedo belt the Confederates had laid down the previous October; numerous red cloths "inserted in split sticks in the ground" marked pathways through the dangerous obstruction. As soon as Weitzel's men entered Richmond, engineer officer King started to lay out and dig a defensive line, probably on the west or south side of the city.[1]

"This Army has now won a most desicive [sic] Victory and followed the enemy," Grant informed Sherman. "This is all that it ever wanted to make it as good an Army as ever fought a battle." Federal losses during the long Petersburg campaign totaled 42,000 men, while Confederate casualties amounted to 28,000. According to a recent estimate, Lee lost 25,000 men, or 40 percent of his strength, due to desertion, combat, and the detachment of several units to other theaters from January 10 through April 2.[2]

The tenor of the Grant-Lee confrontation, which had begun May 4 with the initial move into the Wilderness, had now changed. For the last eleven months it had been characterized by Federal moves that usually resulted in limited, if any, success. Now it was literally a race between the contending armies as Lee engaged in a desperate effort to escape the Army of the Potomac and the Army of the James. Nearly a year of brutal combat had so depleted the Confederacy's best field army that it had to resort to grand tactics unprecedented in its history.

Field fortifications played a role even within the highly fluid nature of operations during the Appomattox campaign. While Lee waited a full day at Amelia Court House, the Federals rushed cavalry and infantry to Jetersville to block his anticipated movement south of that crossroads. Sheridan's troopers and the Fifth Corps were the only Federals digging in at Jetersville on April 4, but the

Second Corps arrived by noon the next day to extend the strong line of earthworks, soon followed by the Sixth Corps. The Union line was about four miles long and flanked by a cavalry division on each wing. Although quickly made, the earthwork remnants that are accessible today show the entrenchment to be strong and imposing. Most of the remnants have a good ditch in front but no trench. The Federals located the line on the top of a gradual slope that provided a good field of fire.[3]

These earthworks altered the course of the campaign. Lee wanted to push southward to join Joseph E. Johnston's forces in North Carolina, but reports that the Federals were too strongly entrenched at Jetersville "seemed to disappoint him greatly." A Virginia artilleryman later recalled that no one who scouted the Federal position could bring back "a single hope of carrying" these works; "they were too grimly strong." Lee decided to move west instead.[4]

Sheridan advanced a cavalry force that attacked Lee's wagon trains near Painesville on April 5. The wagons were guarded by Custis Lee's infantry division and some black Confederate troops. The latter, helped by the engineers, hastily dug earthworks, pulling apart rail fences and piling dirt on top of them. The Federals burned 200 wagons and captured hundreds of white and black prisoners. Lee was able to get a substantial head start on his opponent that day. Not until the early morning of April 6 did the Federals advance from their trenches at Jetersville, only to find the Confederates had gone west.[5]

The Sixth Corps caught up with Lee's rear guard on April 6 and delivered a crushing blow at the battle of Sailor's Creek. The Federals contended with only light breastworks located two-thirds of the way up the western slope of the wide, shallow valley of Little Sailor's Creek, about ten miles west of Jetersville. While the Union center stopped, both flanks pivoted to envelop the Confederate position. Wright captured 3,400 Rebels, including six generals, equivalent to half the men he brought into the action himself.[6]

Elsewhere on April 6, Lee positioned Longstreet's command to block Ord at Rice's Station on the South Side Railroad, about three miles south of the High Bridge crossing of the Appomattox River near Farmville. Longstreet's men constructed "small breastworks of rails" and "cleared the undergrowth of woods" in their front. Gibbon's Twenty-Fourth Corps arrived opposite their position, but darkness prevented an attack.[7]

Both armies passed through Farmville on April 7, but Humphreys pursued so closely that Mahone's division took position at Cumberland Church, three miles north of town, and dug in to protect Lee's supply train. The Rebel position faced north and east and was curved like a fishhook, with the ground sloping up toward them. Mahone's men used their bayonets and hands to dig up enough dirt for a modest parapet. Gordon's Second Corps arrived to extend Mahone's line to the right, and Longstreet extended Gordon's line even farther.[8]

Humphreys found the position "too strong naturally and too well intrenched to admit of a front attack." He tried to outflank Mahone's left but was repulsed, and Barlow's division arrived too late to attempt another flanking movement that day. Humphreys was stymied by one of the last fieldworks constructed by the Army of Northern Virginia. His corps also dug entrenchments that evening to secure its position.[9]

Lee's attempt to escape ended at Appomattox, with his army stretched along the road from the courthouse to New Hope Baptist Church, about four miles east. Sheridan's cavalry held Appomattox Station, two and a half miles to the southwest, and had protected their defensive position just west of the courthouse with rough breastworks. Gordon's Second Corps attacked Sheridan on the morning of April 9 and drove the troopers from their slight works. This last attack by the Army of Northern Virginia pushed three-quarters of a mile, until Gibbon's Twenty-Fourth Corps arrived to block its progress.[10]

At about the same time, Humphreys's Second Corps closed up on Lee's rear position at New Hope Baptist Church, with the Sixth Corps close behind. Capt. A. C. Jones of the 3rd Arkansas reported that his men automatically began to dig in opposite the Federals. At 8:00 A.M., Lee rode by, and then Jones saw a squad of Federal cavalrymen carrying a white flag. His men were busy tearing down a rail fence to get wood for the fieldwork when Jones heard a Yankee officer say, "'Those men had as well quit work.'" This surprised him, but then an order arrived from his own superiors to stop the construction. It was the last trench dug by the Army of Northern Virginia. The line straddled the Richmond-Lynchburg Stage Road, and the accessible remnants show it to have consisted of a trench and parapet, with only intermittent ditching. Literally up to the morning of April 9, field fortifications played a role in the operations of both armies.[11]

THE PETERSBURG CAMPAIGN was the culmination of a long trend toward greater reliance on field fortifications in the eastern theater. From 1861 to 1863, this trend played out in fits and starts as field armies tended to dig in sporadically either before or immediately after a pitched battle. The Peninsula campaign, Chancellorsville, and Mine Run were salient points in this erratic evolution, but with the Wilderness and Spotsylvania, the trend became consistent. Lee relied heavily on extensive and strong field fortifications from Spotsylvania to Cold Harbor as he adopted a defensive strategy in the face of Grant's hammer blows. The Federals responded by digging in to maintain close contact with their enemy and to guard against a sudden counterstrike. At Cold Harbor, after the failure of Grant's June 3 attack, the Federals dug in as close as thirty yards from the Confederate line and attempted to conduct siege approaches (sapping and mining) to cross the last bit of contested ground.

Cold Harbor developed into a potentially long, static confrontation between armies protected by extensive trench systems, but it was curtailed by Grant's decision to cross the James River and strike at Petersburg. The failure of his effort led to the longest campaign of the Civil War, involving the longest and most complex system of field fortifications constructed during the conflict. What caused this evolution toward an unprecedented use of fieldworks? The old interpretation that the use of rifle muskets led to it needs to be reevaluated. Essentially all Union and Confederate infantry regiments were using rifles by mid-1863, months before the battle of Spotsylvania. Also, military operations once again became fluid after the Petersburg campaign ended, with the armies racing westward toward their final confrontation at Appomattox.

The same is true of the western theater, where the Atlanta campaign of May through September 1864 represented the culmination of fortifications use. Operations became very fluid after the fall of Atlanta, with the Confederates invading Union-held Tennessee and most of Sherman's army group heading in the opposite direction to raid through central Georgia to the sea.

If the rifle was the sole, or primary, reason for the heavy use of fieldworks, why did not every campaign of 1864–65 get bogged down in trench stalemate? A vast number of factors, in addition to the type of weaponry used by either army, collectively made up the character of each campaign. The chief difference in the way that the Overland and Petersburg campaigns were conducted in the East and in the way that Sherman conducted the Atlanta campaign in the West was in maintaining continuous contact with the enemy for an extended period of time. This was Grant's innovation; besides the heavy use of temporary fieldworks, it was the only major innovation in grand tactics during the Civil War. Grant pursued his policy of continuous contact from the Wilderness to Petersburg. Lee accepted the challenge and also maintained close contact until the fall of Petersburg on April 2; then he directed his battered army westward in an effort to avoid contact with Grant. In the West, Johnston and John Bell Hood also accepted Sherman's challenge and maintained close contact until the last supply line into Atlanta was cut on September 1.

There was an important connection between continuous contact and the extensive use of fieldworks. Within this context, there is reason to believe that the use of rifle muskets played a role in accentuating the trend toward digging in. With a range that was several hundred yards longer than that of smoothbore muskets, rifles gave sharpshooters much greater scope in a fixed position.

It became more necessary to dig in deeper for protection against sniper and skirmish fire, not to mention artillery and mortar fire, along the Richmond-Petersburg line.

But sharpshooting, skirmishing, and harassing artillery fire were adjuncts to the operations of the battle line; they never substituted for major attacks or flanking movements. The Petersburg campaign would be decided by what the battle line did or failed to do, not by the actions of a handful of snipers armed with modern rifles. Even if there had been no sharpshooters at Petersburg, even if the battle lines were armed only with smoothbores, there is every reason to believe that both armies would have dug in for protection as long as they remained within striking distance of each other.

Historians have long wondered if the trenches were a curse or a blessing for Lee. Trench warfare tied him down, inhibiting the Rebel general from employing offensive tactics that had defeated previous opponents since the Seven Days campaign. Other historians argue that Lee's defensive strategy behind earthworks was wise, for it conserved his strength and exhausted that of his opponent, prolonging the life of his army by several months. The result of Jubal Early's open field campaigning in the Shenandoah Valley tends to support this view.[12]

On the other hand, there is little doubt that the Federals gained more from their use of fortifications than the Confederates gained from their use of earthworks. Grant's men dug, maneuvered, and fought the Rebels out of Petersburg after ten months of persistent effort. They dug more entrenchments than their opponents in order to secure a position very close to the logistical and political center of the Confederate position in Virginia. Lee rarely attempted to attack these earthworks frontally and failed to achieve significant success every time. His only recourse was to prevent Grant from extending the lines westward, succeeding brilliantly in doing so during Grant's Second Offensive. But the Confederates failed to prevent Union extension in the Fourth Offensive and usually failed in doing so thereafter. By September, Federal commanders sensed that the advantage had shifted to their side as they adopted a bite-and-hold tactic, securing their gains with new earthworks. They became a bit more cautious as well; there was less need to risk and dare, for time was on their side, offering an opportunity to minimize casualties as they worked out the new mode of operations with patient determination. This bite-and-hold tactic was possible not primarily because of numerical superiority, but because the Federals intelligently used fortifications to aid their offensive moves, designing and constructing enclosed works capable of self-defense. This allowed them to reduce garrisons and mass troops for another round of pushing west.

Lee's use of fieldworks extended the life of his army by helping it fend off repeated attacks. The Confederates were able to exact heavy losses on attackers and block their movements around the army's flank during the early offensives at Petersburg. But Confederate fortifying began to serve Lee less and less well from September onward. He could not proactively dig works along every line of possible Union advance around his flank, and his engineers continued to rely on heavy belts of obstructions in front of the trenches rather than enclosed works to minimize the number of troops holding the line.

In the end, field fortifications played an enormously important role in determining the outcome of the Petersburg campaign and, with it, the outcome of the Civil War. It is not true that the mere fall of Petersburg would have inevitably led to the fall of Richmond. In mid-June 1864, Beauregard was prepared to retire across the Appomattox River and assume a new defensive position behind Swift Creek if he lost Petersburg to Grant's First Offensive. The Federals would have had to cross the Appomattox to approach this strong position, and Richmond would have still been supplied by two rail lines approaching it from the southwest and the northwest. Even if the Confederates had been forced to evacuate the Swift Creek line, they could have retired into the extensive defenses of Richmond as a last resort. Lee gave up Richmond as well as Petersburg in April 1865 because of what had transpired during the intervening ten months. His army's effectiveness had been reduced by long service in the ditches, the Confederacy had fragmented into ineffectual parts, and, most importantly, Sherman was approaching with at least 60,000 veterans of the western campaigns. If Lee had remained in Petersburg to the bitter end, allowing himself to be invested, then the campaign would have to be considered as a siege operation. But Lee did at Petersburg exactly what he did at Spotsylvania, North Anna, and Cold Harbor: he dug in to protect the line of approach to the capital but left those trenches when necessary to maintain the mobility of his army. Lee often remarked that Grant's relentless drive during the Overland campaign would end up in a siege of Richmond, but he deftly avoided that by evacuating Petersburg. For his part, Grant pinned the Army of Northern Virginia to the ground for ten months at Petersburg, allowing the world around it to crumble without giving Lee an opportunity to salvage anything like victory. He had also given the Army of the Potomac and the Army of the James their opportunity to defeat the South's most effective field army.[13]

APPENDIX ONE

# *Artifacts of War*

Nowhere else during the Civil War were there so many trenches, forts, magazines, bombproofs, covered ways, abatis, slashings, fraises, palisades, and chevaux-de-frise as along the Richmond-Petersburg Line. Orange Judd, editor of the *American Agriculturist*, visited the battlefield in June 1865 and commented that there must have been between 150 and 200 miles of earthworks within 10 miles of Petersburg. A modern accounting places the total length at 127.4 miles. Augustus Buell, a gunner with Battery B, 4th U.S. Artillery, estimated that the Federals alone had close to 35 miles of trenches south of the Appomattox River. A total of forty-one forts studded these works. In many places, confused observers could only identify a bewildering intersection of lines, covered ways, and secondary positions seemingly thrown together at random. "The whole country for miles about seems dug up and shovelled over," remarked an anonymous writer for the Springfield, Massachusetts, *Republican*. It seemed to him that there was "no other purpose than to make as many heaps and as many holes as are possible in a given space."[1]

Moreover, the lengthy stay of about 100,000 soldiers in one spot denuded the vegetation around Petersburg. Earthwork construction accounted for most of it, and the need to collect firewood took care of the rest. By modern estimates, about half of the landscape affected by the campaign consisted of forest in mid-June 1864. By April 1865, only 22 percent of the battlefield still had standing trees. In other words, more than half the timber was cut and used, leading to the deforestation of 4,400 acres of Virginia countryside.[2]

### OBJECTS OF STUDY

On April 3, Meade and Lyman explored the Confederate earthworks only a few hours after Lee's evacuation. Stopping on Cemetery Ridge near the crater, Lyman had trouble taking in the situation. "How changed these entrenchments? Not a soul was there, and the few abandoned tents and cannon gave an additional air of solitude. Upon these parapets, whence the rifle-men have shot at each other, for nine long months, in heat and cold, by day and by night, you might now stand with impunity and overlook miles of deserted breastworks and covered ways! It was a sight only to be appreciated by those who have known the depression of waiting through summer, autumn and winter for so goodly an event!"[3]

Thomas M. Cook, a correspondent for the *New York Herald*, also toured the abandoned earthworks on April 3. He was nearly overwhelmed by "the exhaustion of engineering skill." The landscape was "all dug over. Every manner of earthwork has been thrown up by either army. Corrections of the lines, alterations and changes, have kept the armies busy for a year. It is impossible to describe this vast network of intrenchments from the hasty glance I had while riding over them. The civilian cannot better understand than by conceiving a vast system of sunken roads sufficient for manuevering armies of 100,000 men, without exposing any above level ground."[4]

Grant ordered a complete survey of the Rebel lines on April 12, 1865, entrusting the job to Barnard. All available engineer officers of the Army of the Potomac were assigned to the task. Michler also had to make maps of the battlefields from the Wilderness down to Petersburg and survey the works at Fredericksburg as well.[5]

No officer was more interested in the fieldworks at Petersburg than Henry L. Abbot, commander of the Federal siege train during the campaign. Abbot noted that the Federals normally placed their magazines so they were sheltered as much as possible by the parapet. The entrance was placed toward the rear of the work, and at least six feet of earth covered the timber roof. These magazines typically were six feet wide and six feet deep, with varying lengths. There seldom was room in the works to make the magazine along "the elaborate plans laid down in the text-books." Abbot knew of no instance where such a magazine exploded, although they were often hit.[6]

After examining both lines, Abbot concluded that the Federals used sandbags on top of the parapets to cover their heads, while the Confederates used logs with loopholes cut about every three feet; "but both devices were occasionally employed by each party." Concerning covered ways, Abbot concluded that "absolute protection must be sacrificed to facility in turning the corners with wagons, and especially with siege guns." Sometimes heavy guns overturned while soldiers negotiated them around corners in the covered ways that led to Fort Sedgwick, and Abbot knew that once an officer was crushed to death in this way.[7]

Abbot thought obstructions were most effectively placed only fifty yards in front of the parapet. The second line of obstructions should be placed 100 yards from the works. "Abatis at these distances properly pinned down, with a few telegraph wires twisted around stumps or stakes about a foot above the ground, is almost impassable, and cannot be destroyed with artillery fire, unless by enfilade." Slashings were vulnerable in dry weather, for artillery shells could set them afire. Abbot knew that the Confederates "paid considerable attention to land torpedoes as obstacles against assault, while we neglected them."[8]

While constructing defenses for his siege train park at Broadway Landing, Abbot documented the time and labor involved. The soil consisted of "sandy clay," and the weather was good as troops from the 15th New York Engineers, Company M, 3rd Pennsylvania Artillery, and the 1st Connecticut Heavy Artillery performed a total of 3,000 man-days of work, ten hours per day. Of that number, 2,500 man-days were spent digging and 500 in "cutting and placing 420 yards of pole revetment well anchored with wire, in cutting and planting 600 yards of good abatis, and in slashing several acres of timber in the surrounding ravines." Abbot's parapet was seven feet tall, and his ditch was twelve feet wide and six feet deep. The men moved an average of 6.4 cubic yards of earth each day.[9]

Ira Spaulding tabulated the mountain of supplies and equipment used by his 50th New York Engineers from July 14, 1864, to March 29, 1865. It included 48,872 sandbags, more than 8,000 axes and an equal number of shovels, and more than 2,000 picks. For countermining purposes, the New Yorkers used 28 specialized mining picks. For making the doors to magazines, they acquired 130 strap hinges and 67 padlocks. For connecting sections of obstructions, they used 289 coils of wire and 400 specialized knives for making gabions. Dozens of kegs of nails, spikes, and screws and more than 57,000 linear feet of timber, plank, and boards went into the making of the earthworks. This tabulation does not include materials used by any unit other than the 50th New York Engineers.[10]

Engineer officers often were frustrated by the poor performance of infantrymen detailed to work on the entrenchments. Charles W. Howell bluntly characterized them as "heavy, untrained, shiftless infantry details" and suggested a 600-man pioneer battalion for each division. Ironically, these pioneers would also have been men detailed from the infantry units but dedicated to engineering work, and thus they could be trained on the job to do their tasks. They could have replaced infantrymen who were "slow, careless, and, worse than all, stupidly ignorant of what was required of them, both in throwing up fortifications and in improving roads."[11]

## OBJECTS OF CURIOSITY, COMMERCIALISM, AND REMEMBRANCE

After the war, tourists and veterans streamed to Petersburg to see what had become of the place, and no other landmarks drew so much attention as the remnants of the earthworks. Among the earliest tourists was Orange Judd, who came immediately after the campaign ended. He found fresh burials to the rear of Fort Gregg and bullet holes pockmarking the stockade that enclosed its gorge, all from the heavy battle on April 2. The trees at Fort Stedman were riddled with bullets as well. Black and white residents of Petersburg were already tearing apart abatis along the line to obtain firewood, and local farmers were beginning to level some earthworks to resume farming.[12]

Northern journalist John Townsend Trowbridge visited Petersburg in September 1865. While riding through the Confederate defenses north of the James River, Trowbridge could distinguish between the older, pre-campaign works and the newer ones due to the greatly enlarged size and complexity of those constructed in 1864–65. He also noticed that local inhabitants were using the abatis and wooden revetments for firewood. A helpful civilian gave him tips about how to avoid the torpedo belt as Trowbridge made his way to Fort Burnham to view the casemates.[13]

After crossing the river, Trowbridge rode to the crater. The entrance to Pleasants's gallery was accessible, although half hidden by weeds. Sections of the gallery roof had already caved in, "leaving chasms opening into the mine along its course." Trowbridge also saw the entrance of the countermine dug by the Confederates after July 30, located in the bottom of the crater. The ground around the hole was littered with "bent and rusted bayonets, canteens and fragments of shells." Black and white citizens scoured the landscape for spent bullets, selling them for four cents a pound in Petersburg.[14]

Trowbridge rode through a series of covered ways to visit Fort Sedgwick, passing across "a plain which had been covered with forests before the war, but where not a tree was now standing." Empty huts dotted the area behind the work. Confederate Fort Mahone "was in as perfect condition as when first completed." Trowbridge stepped into its magazine, "a cave with deep dark chambers and walls covered with cold sweat."[15]

Trowbridge was enchanted by the camp of the 50th New York Engineers, "one of the most beautiful villages ever seen." The arched gateway, wooden sidewalks, huts adorned with bedrooms, mantelpieces, and columns were intact. The chapel, the "gem of the place," was magnificent. Only a lone guard stood watch over the encampment. The city of Petersburg, on the other hand, had the appearance of a ghost town. "Tenantless and uninhabitable houses, with broken walls, roofless, or with roofs smashed and torn by missiles, bear silent witness to the havoc of war." Some houses had as many as twenty holes in one wall. Yet there were signs of hope. Trowbridge saw many houses under repair, "bright spots of new bricks in the old walls showing where projectiles had entered."[16]

Local inhabitants began to develop the tourist potential of their battered town almost immediately after the war ended. They sponsored the publication of a booklet titled *A Guide to the Fortifications and Battlefields Around Petersburg*, printed by the local newspaper in 1866. Lazelle and McMullin, a Petersburg photography firm, sold a set of new images taken of the engineer chapel, the forts, and the crater. Much of the narrative in the booklet was written anonymously, but most likely the author was Nathaniel Michler. If so, it is an interesting case of a local Southern community enlisting the aid of a serving Union officer for commercial purposes. Michler noted the caved-in condition of Pleasants's gallery and the fact that bullets could still be found embedded in chevaux-de-frise at some locations, and he reported that the Confederate dam across Rohoic Creek was intact. The signal tower near the winter encampment of the 50th New York Engineers was still strong enough to allow tourists to climb it.[17]

Lazelle and McMullin probably were responsible for a series of photographs taken of the crater from 1865 to 1867. They clearly show the details of this eroded hole, still impressive in its dimensions. The Confederate parapet built immediately to the rear of the crater after July 30 has a postern dug through it, shored up by timber framing, to connect with the depression. Another photograph documents the progress made by landowners in reclaiming their property. The wooden revetment of the parapet along the line north of the crater was gone, and piles of fence rails have been laid out to dry in the sun so they can be reused. By 1867, the land immediately north of the crater was fully under cultivation. The entrance to Pleasants's gallery from the crater was opened for visitors, and a ventilation pipe seems to stick out from the roof of the gallery to allow fresh air into at least the first few yards of the tunnel.[18]

Burnside's attack on July 30 was the most famous battle fought along the Petersburg line. While reclaiming the land around it for agricultural purposes, owner William Griffith kept the crater intact, fenced it off, and charged twenty-five cents admission. He constructed a booth at the entrance where he displayed relics, and later he built the Crater Saloon to sell refreshments. Griffith sometimes allowed veterans, especially ex-Confederates, to enter free of charge. He usually guided the visitors, but sometimes he hired local people to do it for him. Visitors included Longstreet, Heth, Hagood, Alexander, and several Union generals. There were still soldiers buried nearby when Griffith opened his enterprise in 1867, and erosion quickly reduced the size of the hole, but his son continued the tourist trade after Griffith died in 1873.[19]

As the veterans grew older and the bitterness engendered by the war subsided, hundreds of them made their way to Petersburg. Charles W. Owen of the 1st Michigan came to the battlefield in 1893 with his wife. The works were still in good shape, but a "new growth of brush and trees along the old line of works made them look strange and unfamiliar." Ten years later, when Joshua L. Chamberlain visited Petersburg, the new growth had increased in size so that "hedge-like lines of shrubbery" were "running in queer directions not suggested by the natural lay of the land, nor its present uses." Trees and bushes grew thickly on parapets, in ditches, and even on the roofs of bombproofs. Chamberlain noticed in 1903 that most of the Confederate works were already gone, as they were closer to town and often occupied terrain and soil better suited to cultivation.[20]

Chamberlain found the parapet of Fort Sedgwick "well-formed,—high and steep" and its "interior cut up by ridges of traverses protecting from flank fire, and the bottom gashed with the cavernous bomb-proofs making thick cover from the terrific work of great guns and mortars all through the dreary siege." But the fort sported a "thick and dark and somber" growth of trees, as did the well-preserved fortified picket lines between Fort Sedgwick and Fort Mahone. The Confederate works at Rives's Salient, straddling Jerusalem Plank Road, were well preserved too.[21]

Robert A. Reid of the 48th Pennsylvania found nearly the entire Union line from the Appomattox River to Jerusalem Plank Road intact when he visited Petersburg in October 1904. Charles A. Clark, a guide for some seventeen years, took him along the line. The works were leveled only in a few spots; for example, Reid found Fort Morton completely gone, as well as the covered way that connected it to the Norfolk and Petersburg Railroad. He could tell from the darker hue of the soil where the fort had been located. The secondary works to the rear of Fort Morton were intact, as was the 48th Pennsylvania camp, used when the men dug the mine, but pine trees nearly as thick as a man's torso were growing on the works.[22]

Of course, Reid spent a good deal of time at the crater. He walked along the line of the gallery and pointed out the hole used by Pleasants for his ventilation system. The entrance to the gallery in the valley of Poor Creek was closed by dense brush. North and south of the crater, all the Confederate entrenchments were gone, and one of the covered ways used to funnel troops forward on July 30 was gone too. The other was well preserved but filled with a dense growth of brush.[23]

Twenty years later, in the early 1920s, local landowners discovered a unique artifact deep under the ground at Petersburg. Site preparation for two Pennsylvania monuments to be erected near Rives's Salient uncovered the galleries of the Confederate countermine complex at Jerusalem Plank Road. David A. Lyon, who owned the property, immediately developed it for the tourist trade. Soon there was a log cabin at the entrance with a Confederate flag flying over it. A Rebel veteran who visited the site reported that the galleries were fully intact, but the timber framing had rotted and fallen into heaps. He could still see pick marks on the sides and ceilings as well as holes that apparently were meant for drainage inside the galleries. Lyon installed electric lights inside the galleries and rebuilt the framing with boards.[24]

Matthew Venable, who had worked in the Petersburg countermines as a recruit in Company H, 1st Confederate Engineers, also visited the Jerusalem Plank Road site in June 1926. Venable had become a civil engineer in the railroad and coal mining industries after attending the University of Virginia following the war. He also noted the pick marks, "as distinct as if made recently," in "compact brown clay" on the sides of the galleries. He also found intact drill holes in the sides and roofs of the galleries, made with a four-inch auger to determine the depth of the gallery and to provide forward listening holes.[25]

The Union countermine at Fort Sedgwick also came to light in the 1920s. It consisted of a gallery that ran parallel to the Union line, with branches heading toward the Confederate position. It reportedly had a track consisting of wooden sills running for forty feet, probably to haul dirt out of one of the branches as an alternative to the use of wheelbarrows.[26]

Fort Stedman came into the news once again in 1930 when workers employed by the newly created Petersburg National Battlefield discovered the Union countermine there. It reportedly totaled 200 feet in length. They found a shovel, bayonets, rifle parts, a cartridge box, and shoe soles in the gallery. The timbers were well preserved even though the gallery was very muddy. The same workers had uncovered a bombproof at Gracie's Salient the previous year.[27]

David Lyon began to develop the land above the Confederate countermine complex at Jerusalem Plank Road, calling it Pine Gardens Estate, and offered house lots. He promoted the endeavor by circulating a brochure mapping out proposed streets covering the entire area between the Union and Confederate lines east of the road, extending at least as far as Fort Rice. Lyon proposed to preserve the galleries as well as Fort Rice and Fort Sedgwick as parks and tourist attractions. The enterprise never got off the ground, for Lyon started it one month before the stock market crash in 1929. Nevertheless, the countermine galleries remained accessible until the construction of the nearby Walnut Hill Plaza in the 1960s, when the entrance was sealed shut.[28]

The preservation of the Petersburg battlefield shifted from private to public hands by the 1930s. The Griffith family had lost ownership of the crater by 1918, but a local group calling itself the Crater Battlefield Association obtained the site in 1925. This organization constructed a clubhouse near the site of the mine explosion and built an eighteen-hole golf course nearby. The association dug out the Pleasants gallery from the crater toward the Union line in 1926 and opened it for tourists. The organization went bankrupt in 1934, leading to the closure of its golf course. The Petersburg National Military Park acquired the land in 1936, closed the Union gallery, and dismantled the remnants of the golf course.[29]

The crater became the site of remembrance for veterans and interested observers when the first reenactment of the battle took place on November 3, 1903, attended by 430 veterans of Weisiger's brigade. On April 30, 1937, more than 3,000 men participated in another reenactment of the attack, witnessed by 50,000 spectators. This time, the mock battle was staged by U.S. marines, national guardsmen, and cadets of the Virginia Military Institute. Douglas Southall Freeman, who had witnessed the first reenactment as a teenager, gave an address to the assembled crowd, which included four Confederate veterans of the battle.[30]

The Federal government, through the Petersburg National Battlefield (known as the Petersburg National Military Park until the 1960s), laid out the basic components of the battlefield for visitors in different stages of construction as late as the 1970s. This involved building the current visitor center at Battery No. 5 of the Dimmock Line, opening a vista between the location of Fort Morton and the site of the crater, stabilizing erosion inside the crater, and building the current system of roads and walking paths. The park only encompasses a small part of the Petersburg battlefield, mostly sections of the Union and Confederate lines between the Appomattox River and Jerusalem Plank Road, although recent efforts have included the Five Forks battlefield. The latest discovery occurred in 1997 when construction of the New Millennium Studios, a venture by television actors Tim Reid and Daphne Maxwell Reid, revealed the Confederate countermine at Squirrel Level Road. Workers accidentally dug into the gallery and found it filled with water. Subsequent investigation charted the entire length of this long gallery from the former Confederate line out to Dr. Duval's house site.[31]

APPENDIX TWO

# The Richmond-Petersburg Line

The Union and Confederate armies at Petersburg utilized the most complex assortment of field fortifications employed in any campaign of the Civil War. The original Dimmock Line proved inadequate for defending the town, prompting the Confederates to improvise two temporary positions (the Hagood Line and the Harris Line) to stem Federal attacks on June 15–18. The Harris Line became a segment of the permanent Confederate position defending Petersburg. The Confederates also continued to hold about two-thirds of the Dimmock Line, although they heavily altered it to suit their needs.

The Richmond defenses were far stronger and much more extensive than the Dimmock Line, but the Confederates used only a small portion of them during the Petersburg campaign. They heavily modified several miles of the Outer Line, from Chaffin's Bluff inland, to prevent Federal troops from entering Richmond north of the James. A small portion of the Intermediate Line, which neared the Chaffin's Bluff area, also played a part in Rebel defensive arrangements.

Essentially all Union field fortifications along the Richmond-Petersburg Line were new works. The Federals converted a handful of Dimmock Line batteries into Union forts, constituting a secondary line of defense along a limited sector.

## DESIGN AND CONSTRUCTION

Unlike the battlefields of the Overland campaign, which are graced with substantial, well-preserved remnants of fieldworks, the Richmond-Petersburg Line offers spotty examples of extant fortifications. The Confederate salients located between the Appomattox River and Jerusalem Plank Road were filled with dugouts and traverses. Yet only one of these salients, Colquitt's, has any remnants today, and they are so eroded as to be nearly gone.

West of Jerusalem Plank Road, many segments of the works are well preserved. The Federal entrenchments tend to be straight, textbook-style fieldworks. One can understand the way engineer officers, troops, and work details accomplished their job in a standard way, but the individual style of adjustment to the basic work (which can be seen at Spotsylvania, Cold Harbor, and Kennesaw Mountain) is missing.

Earthwork designers had to contend with few terrain abnormalities except while crossing streams and ravines. They usually put traverses in artillery emplacements but not infantry positions. Exterior ditches (in front of the parapet) are common, while trenches (or interior ditches, behind the parapet) are rare. Western troops usually reversed this tendency, more often digging a trench and not a ditch.

## THE DIMMOCK LINE

The original fortification at Petersburg is all but gone today. The few bits and pieces that remain were heavily reworked by Confederate and Union occupants during the campaign. One must rely on photographs, taken mostly in June–July 1864, to document the design and construction of Dimmock's fieldwork.

Matthew Brady exposed an image of Capt. George F. McKnight's 12th New York Light Artillery in Battery No. 8. The unit had occupied the work ever since its capture on the evening of June 15 but left it five days later to participate in the Second Union Offensive, where guns of the battery were captured by Mahone's Confederates. It is a small work open to the rear, and McKnight positioned pieces in front of the curtain to fire over the parapet. There is no ditch in front of the infantry parapet, but one can see where the Federals shoveled dirt from the ground in order to make the parapet higher.[1]

James O'Sullivan exposed an image of the curtain next to Battery No. 11 at the James A. Dunn House, probably on June 20. There is a ditch here that the Federals crossed by piling logs in the bottom and cutting down the banks to make a "ford." They also widened the berm at the foot of the parapet to make a banquette. Unlike Battery No. 8, this section of the Dimmock Line was demolished by mid-July.[2]

## FEDERAL WORKS

The area where Colquitt's Salient faced Fort Stedman is a major stop along the Petersburg National Battlefield tour system. While Fort Stedman is well preserved, appearing as if it had been restored in the 1930s, Union Battery No. 10 is gone. The curtain south of Fort Stedman is well preserved, as are Battery No. 11 and Fort Haskell (Battery No. 12 no longer exists). A large traverse was built inside Fort Haskell that connects to the parapet on the left but not on the right

Right end of main battery at Fort Sedgwick. Battery No. 21 is in the distance; note the corduroy road behind the banquette. The artillery platforms are mostly taken away, but there is still a wooden mantlet and a parados. (Library of Congress, LC-DIG-CWPB-03715)

to allow movement from one half of the work to the other. A well-preserved curtain extends south, skirting the head of several ravines that drain toward the Confederate position at Gracie's Salient. A segment of the infantry line extends forward from Battery No. 13 for about fifty yards, apparently constructed after the building of the main line to take advantage of a slight terrain opportunity. It has at least two traverses to protect infantry positions, twenty yards apart from each other; one is ten feet long and the other is twenty feet long.[3]

The crater is the prime stop for tourists at Petersburg. Much eroded and filled in by nature, it nevertheless has a haunting quality. In fact, other than the 3rd Louisiana Redan at Vicksburg, it is the only Civil War mine crater that is relatively intact. Pleasants's gallery can be traced by the caved-in sections still visible on the surface, and the same is true for the left Confederate countermine gallery. The right countermine gallery has no visible surface signs. The two sections of the crater are still plainly visible. Confederate refortifying efforts after July 30 are also intact. The parapet they constructed along the rear rim of the hole is well preserved, and the Rebel picket line in front, which was fortified in September, can be easily traced.[4]

Nothing is left of the Union line from the crater area to Jerusalem Plank Road. Forts Morton, Rice, Meikel, and Sedgwick are gone. The latter was destroyed during construction of a shopping center after 1961. Several photographs taken immediately after the campaign document the appearance of this section of the Federal works. Battery No. 14 had mortar platforms made of wood, but one of them had an additional layer of brick around the platform, probably to keep the gunners' feet out of the mud. The revetment here consists of logs and posts, but the connecting curtain appears to have no revetment at all.[5]

*Fort Sedgwick*

Fort Sedgwick was among the best-known of the Union forts. It began as a reinforced angle of the infantry line, located just east of Jerusalem Plank Road, with artillery positioned to fire northwest (to the front) and southwest (to the left). The curtain continued from the left flank of the work across the road toward the southwest, and a stockade enclosed the rear of the gun emplacements. The Federals dug one covered way to the fort and another to Battery No. 21 immediately to its right.

Major renovation took place in August and September. Warren dug a new line to the rear of Fort Sedgwick as a fallback position in case the Confederates succeeded in mining the work. It was located about eighty yards to the rear of the flanks of the fort, but 160 yards behind the forward angle. The stockade apparently was taken down at this time as unnecessary, for it does not appear in later maps. The area between the front line and the rear line was converted into living and working space, with bombproofs, wells, stables, and a guardhouse. Shortly after this renovation, Hancock initiated another round of revisions by converting the connecting line that crossed the plank road into a bastion for artillery, infantry, and bombproofs.

Fort Sedgwick had seventeen gun emplacements, nearly every one protected on both flanks by traverses made of two layers of gabions. A combined magazine and headquarters bombproof was located in the center of the fort. To the right, Battery No. 21 held four guns, while Battery No. 20 had ten mortars and two magazines. West of Jerusalem Plank Road, the Western (or Hancock's) artillery bastion had ten gun emplacements facing north and west, and two big and sixteen small bombproofs. In addition, four large and thirteen small bombproofs were spread along the rear line that protected the fort and its nearby batteries. The entire complex, from Battery No. 20 to the Western artillery bastion,

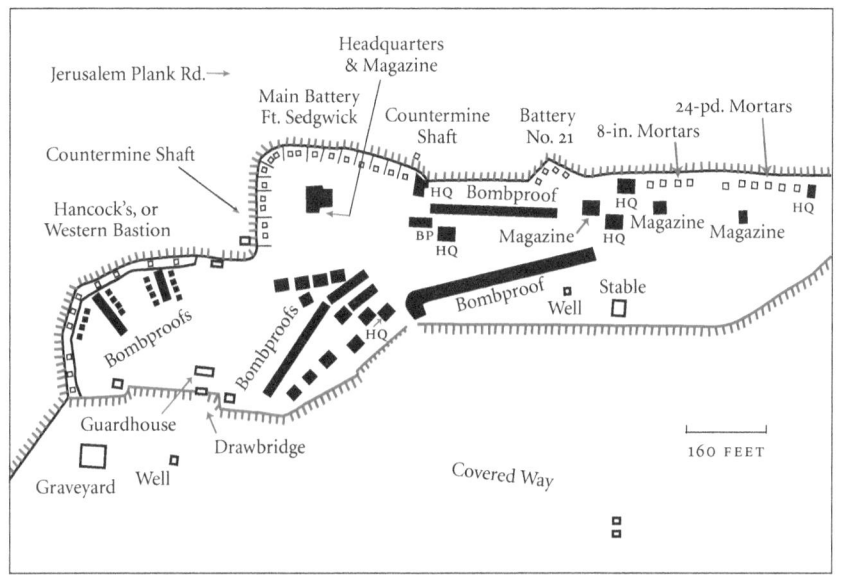

Fort Sedgwick, April 3, 1865 (based on map in Hopkins, *Seventh Regiment Rhode Island*, 231)

was essentially a single, extended work. No wonder that men detailed to nail up a sign for Fort Sedgwick in September put it in the Western bastion, which Regis de Trobriand termed "but an annex" of the real fort.[6]

At least ten photographs taken of the Fort Sedgwick complex superbly document the design and construction of the work. The parapet was revetted mostly with gabions, layers of fascines held together by wire, and sandbags. Well-constructed abatis, which in places crossed the ditch to connect directly with the exterior of the parapet, and nearly solid rows of twenty-foot-long palisades supplement the defenses. The headquarters bombproof was made with heavy timber, sandbags, gabions, and up to ten feet of earth on top. A Confederate picket post near Fort Sedgwick consists of one row of upright gabions placed in a semicircle, with a layer of horizontal gabions on top. Layers of fascines hold the construction together, and sharpshooter loopholes were made of square boxes. Three posts were made this way, all connected by a parapet of earth. Field artist Alfred R. Waud, on the other hand, sketched a Union picket post in the same area that consisted of a short trench with a ramped entrance from the rear and covered with shelter tent halves for protection against the sun.[7]

### West of Jerusalem Plank Road

The Union line from Jerusalem Plank Road westward is much better preserved than the line east of the road. The massive parapets and large extent of Fort Da-

Appendix Two { 299 }

Front of Federal Battery No. 21. This work was located to the right of Fort Sedgwick; note that the abatis crosses the ditch in the foreground and the presence of inclined palisades. (Library of Congress, LC-DIG-CWPB-02618)

Traverses of main battery at Fort Sedgwick. Two men lie on top of a traverse, pretending to be casualties. Note the gabion and fascine construction and the Western Bastion in the distance. The gun platform has not yet been taken up. (Library of Congress, LC-DIG-CWPB-02570)

Bombproofs at Fort Sedgwick. A man holds a bucket to give human dimension to the constructions. (Library of Congress, LC-DIG-CWPB-01335)

vis are impressive, and most of the curtain between Fort Davis and Fort Howard is also preserved. George B. Peck Jr., a recruit in the 2nd Rhode Island, recalled that this curtain was four and a half feet tall but did not have a banquette. The revetment consisted mostly of fascines, and the ditch was little more than "an irregular depression whence earth had been taken as convenient to build the work." The Union picket line was placed 200 yards in front, with a double row of abatis just behind it.[8]

Several of the works from Fort Davis to Fort Wadsworth are intact. A one-gun artillery emplacement 500 yards west of Fort Davis is nothing but a chevron-shaped bulge of the curtain. Battery No. 26 is a circular work located at an angle of the line between Fort Howard and Fort Wadsworth. A deep ditch completely surrounds it, undoubtedly calling for a wooden bridge to allow access into the enclosure. Battery No. 25 is a six-sided work with two raised gun platforms. While Fort Alexander Hays is mostly gone, Fort Howard is a circular work with seven gun emplacements.[9]

Forts Keene and Tracy are gone, but Fort Urmston is preserved. It is a six-sided work; the curtains on each flank connect to its rear wall. Located just west of Squirrel Level Road, nearly on the site of Fort Bratton on the Confederate Squirrel Level Road Line, it has five raised artillery platforms. West of Urmston, Fort Conahey was rectangular in shape, and the high traverse that

Left end of main battery at Fort Sedgwick. This view looks toward the rear line with its gabion revetment. The hole in the parapet is a possible countermine shaft. (Library of Congress, LC-DIG-CWPB-02608)

bisected the work was its most prominent feature. The Federals dug a postern through the traverse to allow access to both halves of the fort. A photograph taken from atop the signal tower at Peebles's Farm indicates that the work had three casemated gun emplacements. Named for Lt. John Conahey of the 118th Pennsylvania, who was killed in the Fifth Offensive, the fort was built half on a slope and half on level ground. Because the slope could have exposed the enclosure to Rebel artillery, the traverse was needed to protect at least half of the fort's interior.[10]

The Federals built a rear line extending southwest from Fort Urmston toward Fort Wheaton. The latter work was located on the site of Confederate Fort Archer, on the Squirrel Level Road Line. The curtain connecting the two works is today well preserved in many accessible places, as is Fort Wheaton itself. It is a rectangular work with artillery emplacements in the corners.[11]

Fort Fisher, the largest earthwork at Petersburg, anchored the Union position in the area of Peebles's Farm and Pegram's Farm. Named for Maj. Otis Fisher, who was killed in the Fifth Offensive, Fort Fisher measured 1,963 linear feet along the parapet and enclosed 2.39 acres of ground. An additional 1.77 acres of ground was dug up as ditches. Extremely well-preserved (likely

Artillery emplacement at Fort Sedgwick. This view is from the left end of the main battery, looking toward the Western Bastion. Note the long traverse inside the Western Bastion, and that the gun platforms have already been taken up. (Library of Congress, LC-DIG-CWPB-02841)

restored in the 1930s), it has nineteen artillery embrasures, a long traverse laid out diagonally across the interior, and four bastions.[12]

A six-gun emplacement lies between Fort Fisher and the next major work to the west, Fort Welch, which is also well preserved. After Welch, the Union curtain curves to the south at nearly a 90-degree angle, continues 200 yards, then makes another 90-degree turn to the left and continues another 30 yards to a swale that is now covered with thick brush. The line crossed this drainage feature and continued to Fort Gregg and Fort Sampson. The latter work, along with Fort Cummings, represented the end of the Union line until the battle of Hatcher's Run in February 1865.[13]

*Secondary Line*

The Federals thought it was important to protect the rear of their long line from the Appomattox River to Fort Sampson by a Secondary Line facing southward to guard against a raid on the army's rear. The Secondary Line resembled a long refused line, extending from the left flank of the main Union position. It could also be termed one wing protecting a huge, entrenched camp. The Federals built this wing in stages as the forward line took shape. Several of the works along the Secondary Line are intact. Fort Patrick Kelly is well preserved, with several raised artillery emplacements in the angles. Fort Stevenson is partially preserved near a cemetery and a pig farm, with artillery emplacements and some ditches intact. Fort Dushane, Fort Emory, and Fort Siebert are on private land and inaccessible. There is little, if anything, left of the curtain connecting the works along the Secondary Line.[14]

### City Point

The defenses of City Point protected Grant's logistical nerve center. The Federals constructed ten works on the western approaches to the wharves; one of them is well preserved. It was not on the main line of eight redoubts, located more than two miles from City Point, but was part of the original defense only half a mile from the wharves. It was a semicircular work with four raised artillery emplacements and a large magazine, and there are twenty to thirty yards of curtain intact on both flanks. Two other, smaller works are located near Grant's Cabin and the wharves.[15]

## CONFEDERATE WORKS

The Confederate line south of the Appomattox River is mostly gone, so we are forced to rely on photographs and contemporary descriptions to gain an understanding of its design and construction.

### Colquitt's Salient

According to one of Hartranft's staff officers, Colquitt's Salient had twenty gun emplacements by March 1865. In front were three rows of chevaux-de-frise, and a covered way twenty feet wide connected the salient to the rear. Nathaniel Michler described the warren of bombproofs just inside the salient: "It is a complete system of burrowing, in imitation of rats and moles; literally living under ground; the impromptu bomb-proofs promiscuously thrown together, no ventilation and no light, damp and cold." Henry L. Abbot also examined the works, calling them "a mere labyrinth of trench, with bombproof cover in every available spot." Rails taken from the Norfolk and Petersburg Railroad were used to build some bombproofs, but smaller shelters predominated. Abbot called them splinterproofs, placed every fifty yards along the trench line by laying fence rails from the top of the parapet back to the top of a convenient traverse. These shelters were six feet wide and had several feet of dirt on top. The Confederates adorned the top of their parapet at the salient with "square hewn log[s] with observation portholes," according to a man in the 57th North Carolina.[16]

### Gracie's Salient

To the right of Colquitt's Salient, Gracie's Salient also had numerous bombproofs behind the line. Photographs taken after the campaign depict a mass of bare mounds of earth. The communication trenches extending from the main line out to the picket line are also visible. There are three tall trees still standing inside the salient and about half a dozen in front of the line. The Confederate dam across Poor Creek at the Salient is well documented by photography and current remnants. Much of it is intact, represented by a ten- to fifteen-foot-tall embankment. An illustration based on a postcampaign photograph clearly shows a parapet constructed on top of the dam, with a log and post revetment. The Confederates built a sluice gate in the center of the dam.[17]

### Confederate Works from Gracie's Salient to Five Forks

West of Gracie's Salient, between Poor Creek and the Norfolk and Petersburg Railroad, there are faint remnants of the Confederate line. About 200 yards east of the track, the Confederates put at least two artillery emplacements at an angle in the curtain, protected by short traverses.[18]

Unfortunately, the complex of Confederate works straddling Jerusalem Plank Road is completely gone, but there are some stretches of works intact and easily accessible west of the road. Battery No. 35, called Fort Walker today, is fairly well preserved east of Wilcox Lake (formed by damming a branch of Lieutenant Creek between Batteries No. 35 and 36). It has four artillery emplacements and thirty yards of connecting infantry trench south of modern South Boulevard. There are also two badly eroded artillery emplacements north of the street. Battery No. 36, today called Battery Pegram, lies west of Wilcox Lake.[19]

Modern Defense Road parallels a forward Confederate line constructed after the start of the campaign. Dimmock dipped his line southward, to the front, to cross the Weldon and Petersburg Railroad and protect the Lead Works, before angling it southward again west of the tracks. Other Confederate engineers thought it was better to continue the line straight across the rail line from Battery No. 39 to Battery No. 45. It shortened the defensive position and kept the Federals farther from Petersburg. Stretches of the curtain for this line, a straight and wide parapet, can be seen along the south side of Defense Road. There are a couple of poorly preserved batteries west of Squirrel Level Road that are merely bulges in the curtain. They have good ditches in front but no traverses to protect the guns. One of these redans has five artillery emplacements. Battery No. 45, today called Fort Lee, is a reinforced salient of the Dimmock Line guarding the point where Boydton Plank Road crossed the entrenchment. It is well preserved with huge parapets, deep ditches, and several artillery emplacements.[20]

Pamplin Historical Park preserves a significant stretch of the Boydton Plank Road Line, although most of the rest of that line from the park to Hatcher's Run is intact on private property. This is the key part of the line held by Lane's North Carolina brigade, which the Sixth Corps breached on April 2. The works cross a swale called Arthur's Swamp, and two small dams the Confederates built to create a water barrier in front of the line are intact. There are several small gaps in the entrenchments to allow wagons to go forward and cut firewood in front of the position, and the Confederates built an artillery redan by angling the line forward to form protection for two guns. There are two dozen picket posts 500 yards in front of the line. They are about ten paces apart and consist of semicircular parapets long enough to shield two or three men. This line was built on March 25, after the Federals captured the original picket line in response to Gordon's attack on Fort Stedman. Remnants of the Union picket line and the original Confederate picket line are intact as well.[21]

The White Oak Road Line is well preserved for at least 300 yards where it crosses Claiborne Road. The artillery emplacements are incorporated into it in simple but effective ways. A short stretch of the original roadbed of White Oak Road is also intact.[22]

*Five Forks*

The Petersburg National Battlefield has recently acquired 1,100 acres of the battlefield at Five Forks, including the remnants of Pickett's refused left flank. Located north of White Oak Road about three-fourths of a mile east of the forks, the retrenchment runs north for about 150 yards and has seventeen traverses ten to twenty feet apart. The traverses are no longer than ten feet. The traverses cover the southern two-thirds of the retrenched line; the northern one-third of it is a small, straight parapet that simply ends with no apparent attempt to protect the left flank of troops holding it. There is virtually nothing left of the Confederate line along the north side of White Oak Road either east or west of the road junction.[23]

### FEDERAL WORKS AT BERMUDA HUNDRED

The line that Butler's Army of the James built on Bermuda Hundred, beginning on May 17, was occupied longer than any other Union fieldwork in the war. It stretched for 6,058 yards from a point on the James River that was one mile downstream from the Howlett House, the left anchor of the opposing Confederate line, to the Appomattox River. Nathaniel Michler described it as

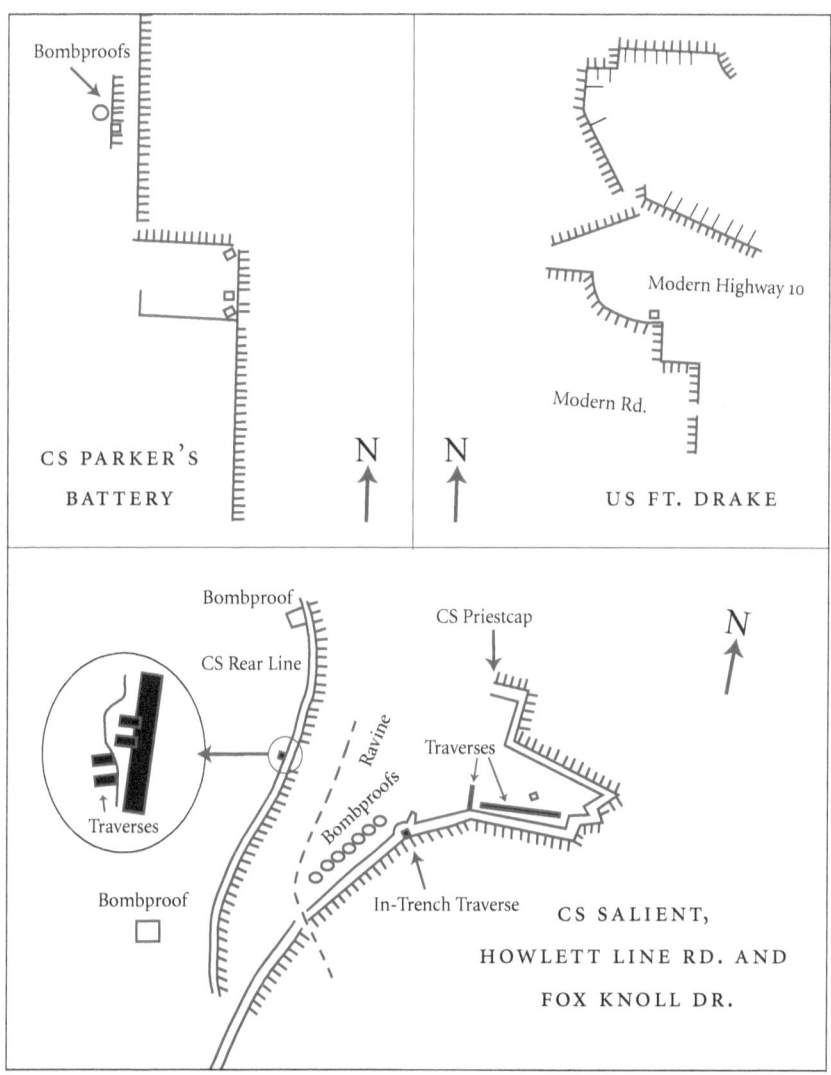

Federal and Confederate Works at Bermuda Hundred, April 3, 1865
(based on field visit, August 1995)

"unusually strong," in part because the landscape was so cut up with ravines that it would have been difficult for the Confederates to mount an attack on more than a quarter of its length at one time. Johnson Hagood described the area as "a wild, thickly wooded country with few clearings, and in many places broken up into short but steep hills." The closest Confederate position to the Union line was 800 yards away.[24]

Photographs taken after the campaign demonstrate the strength of this line.

As at Petersburg, the revetment consisted of a mixture of gabions, sandbags, and logs. The obstructions consisted primarily of well-made abatis, although Redoubt Anderson was fronted by an array of stumps three or four feet tall, the remnants of a grove of small trees. Redoubt Drake had a line of sharpened stakes in front of it.[25]

The best, and most accessible, remnant of the Union line on Bermuda Hundred is a 300-yard stretch near Fort Drake. There is a good portion of the earthwork north of modern Highway 10, with several traverses to protect a complicated angle in the line. The traverses are ten yards apart and six to twelve yards long. There are trenches in this area, but no ditches. South of Highway 10, Fort Drake included traverses that are three yards long to shield a two-gun emplacement in an angle of the line. The emplacements still have large, raised platforms and embrasures.[26]

A 200-yard stretch of Union line is preserved and easily accessible opposite a salient in the Confederate Howlett Line, near the junction of modern Howlett Line Road and Fox Knoll Drive. This remnant stretches from the bottom of a ravine between the lines up to a ridgetop. It is noteworthy because there are small bombproofs about every ten yards along the line. All of them are incorporated into the trench, mostly by digging out a bulge on the enemy side of the trench. Four of these shelters also have well-defined doorways for added protection, created by building a small traverse to partly shield the entrance.[27]

### CONFEDERATE HOWLETT LINE

The Howlett Line protected the vital rail and turnpike link between Richmond and Petersburg from May 17, 1864, until the end of the war. It was longer than, and just as strong as, the Federal earthworks on Bermuda Hundred. Henry L. Abbot was curious to examine it after the campaign ended. He particularly wanted to see what the enemy had done on Chesterfield Heights, near the southern end of the line, for several Confederate batteries positioned there made life precarious in the northern end of the Union line south of the Appomattox River. Federal gunners had been able to return the punishment, and Abbot found on examination that the Rebels endured this by making their artillery embrasures in "an extraordinarily long and narrow shape." One battery containing 4.2-inch siege rifles had a parapet thirty-three feet thick. Its embrasures were two feet wide at the throat and four feet wide at the mouth and were revetted with hurdles. The battery also had stout bombproofs and strong traverses to protect the flanks of each emplacement, with smaller splinterproof shelters scattered everywhere.

Abbot also marveled at a battery built for Whitworth rifles at Chesterfield Heights. The Confederates wisely placed it 400 yards from the edge of the river bluff with a level, plowed field in front. The Federals, on lower ground across the river, could not see the battery, and their rounds landed in the field. They assumed that all the dust kicked up came from the parapet of the Confederate work and were surprised to see it still in good shape after the campaign.[28]

Peter Michie had an opportunity to look at the Howlett Line when the Army of the James briefly held it for a few hours on June 16, and he also conducted a reconnaissance of the Confederate line in September. Michie reported that the "parapet is not formidable, but of the same character as that we now occupy. The ditch is not deep in front of infantry parapets." The position, according to Michie, also had a line of fraise in places and sometimes displayed two lines of abatis.[29]

The Confederates improved their obstructions considerably by April 1865. Abbot reported a line of fraise just outside the work, then an abatis 25 yards out, a palisade at 50 yards, and chevaux-de-frise at 75 yards. Beyond that, at 150 yards in front of the work, was another line of abatis. Five hundred yards out, the Confederates had a fortified picket line with yet another line of abatis in front of it. "We never defended our lines so strongly," Abbot admitted.[30]

Abbot also recorded a "continuous splinter-proof" that was constructed inside the parapet. It consisted of "a heavy framework of logs," the ends of which projected completely through the earth of the parapet to form a fraise sticking out of the exterior slope. The bombproof was capable, he estimated, of covering "one man to every two yards of crest." Abbot noted that the Confederates "often used logs, looped at three feet intervals, on top of the parapet to cover the heads of the infantry." He also found "a strange kind of mantlet," made of wood and with a hinge similar to those found on covers for wells. "It was evidently a very poor device," he reported.[31]

The Howlett Line was anchored on the north at the Howlett Farm, which overlooked the James River at a bend in the stream. Battery Dantzler was the anchor. Originally called Fort Howlett, it was renamed to honor Col. Olin M. Dantzler of the 22nd South Carolina, who was killed in a skirmish near here on June 2. The fort is well preserved in a Chesterfield County park. It held six heavy guns sited to fire down the river. Four of the gun positions are sunken into the earth; three of them have embrasures cut into the natural earth, and a covered way runs perpendicularly just behind all four positions. There are two collapsed bombproofs and a collapsed magazine.[32]

Farther south along the Howlett Line, the position of Parker's Virginia Battery is well preserved too. It was built about May 23 and held continuously throughout the campaign. The remnants are about 175 yards long with a six-foot-tall parapet. It is a simple artillery emplacement at an indentation in the line, with three embrasures, two flank protections, and a ditch in front. The connecting infantry line has a trench, and there are two small dugouts just behind the infantry trench as well.[33]

A salient near the junction of Howlett Line Road and Fox Knoll Drive offers a fine view of an extended remnant of the Confederate line. The remnant embraces about 300 yards of works and has a secondary line to the rear. The parapet is up to six feet tall with a good ditch in front. The salient juts forward atop a prominent hill and is indented. It has at least one position for a field gun, and one side of the salient that faces south has a traverse running just behind the trench to protect the occupants from Union artillery fire from the north. Two angles of the line that stretch south from the salient are protected by traverses, and there is a long line of dugouts, one yard apart from each other, located about ten yards behind the line as it continues south down the slope of a ravine. On the other side of the ravine, the line again angles and is protected by another traverse.

The secondary line that stretches across the base of the salient has a smaller parapet with no ditch and an intermittent trench. There is a large bombproof intact about the center of this secondary line. It was incorporated into the trench by building walls of earth out from the parapet, and there are a couple of traverses to the rear of the trench just to the right of the bombproof as well. The Confederates built a large bombproof on the right of the line, located about twenty yards behind the parapet, and another on the left. Fort Clifton also survives in a county park on the right of the Confederate line.[34]

### FEDERAL WORKS NORTH OF THE JAMES RIVER

The Federal defenses north of the James River were anchored by Fort Burnham, which had been heavily converted from the Confederate Fort Harrison after the Fifth Offensive. A photograph taken after the campaign shows the outside of the Confederate face with its ditch still intact. The new Federal parapet constructed across the gorge of Fort Harrison was smaller than the rest of the work's defenses. The most prominent features of Fort Burnham were the casemates constructed near the end of the campaign. Photographs show that their apertures were revetted with gabions on the side; fascines were placed on top as lintels, and sandbags helped to splay the outer edges of the embrasures. The bombproof at Fort Burnham was a log frame covered with earth. It had a wooden door with either glass or waxed-paper panels on the top half, and the doorway was framed by grain bags filled with dirt.[35]

The Union line from Fort Burnham south to Fort Brady on the James River is well preserved in places. The curtain has a ditch but no trench. While Battery No. 2 is not accessible, Battery No. 3 is a large, well-preserved work with an observation post on top of a large traverse in the center of the front face. Bat-

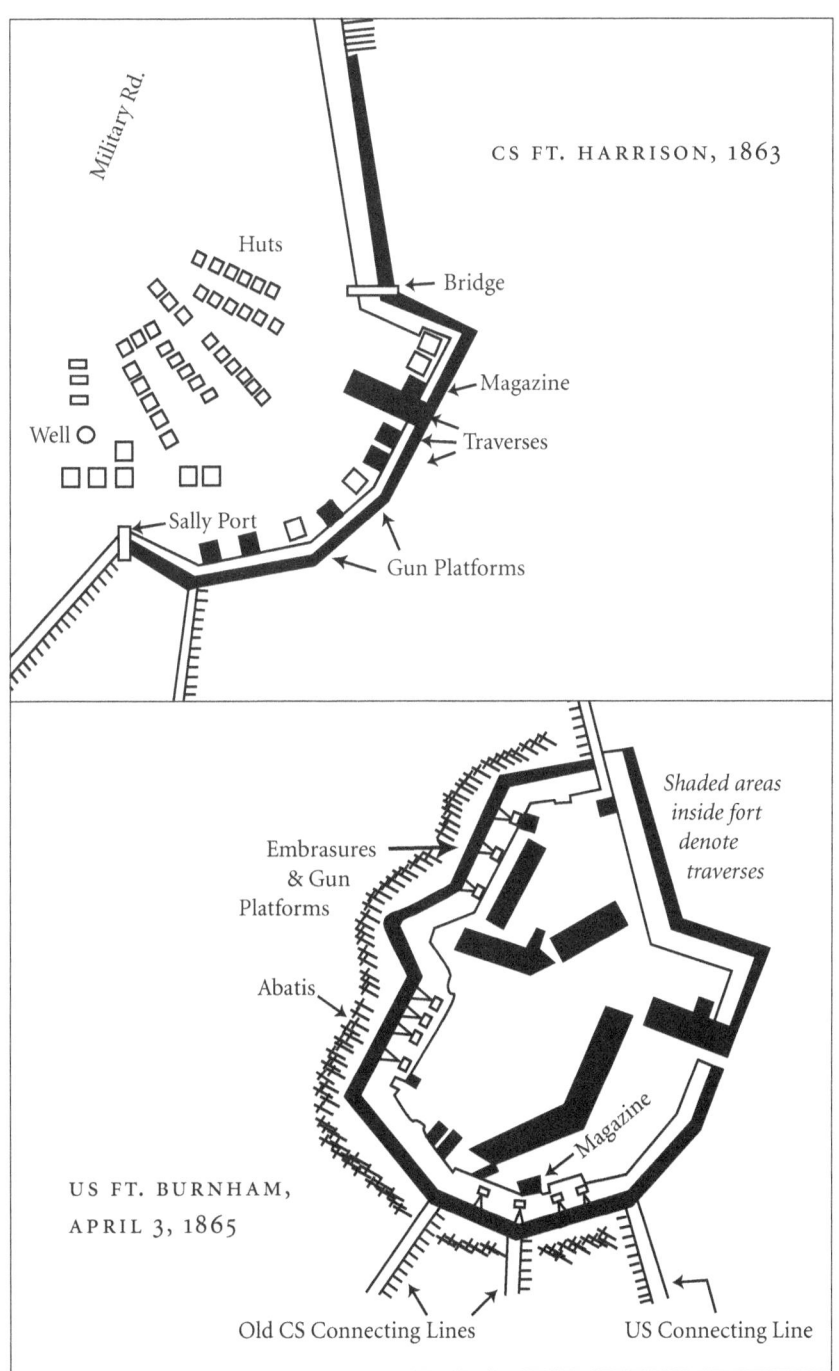

Fort Harrison, 1863, and Fort Burnham, April 3, 1865 (based on maps in Dickinson, "Union and Confederate Engineering Operations at Chaffin's Bluff," 56, 109, RNB)

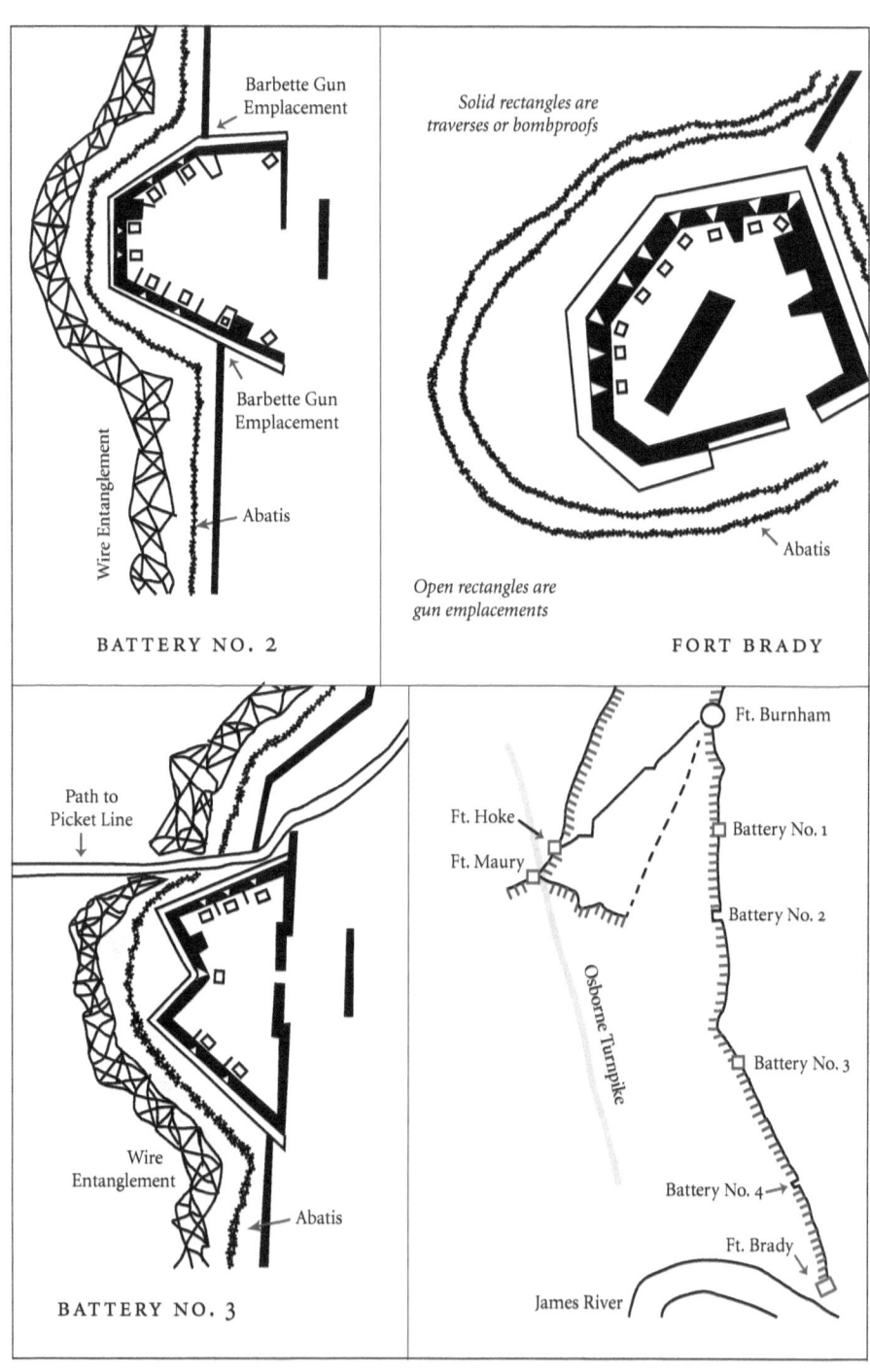

Federal Line from Fort Burnham to Fort Brady, April 3, 1865 (based on maps in Dickinson, "Union and Confederate Engineering Operations at Chaffin's Bluff," 119, 123, 124, RNB)

tery No. 4 covers Kingsland Road with several gun emplacements and a long traverse down the center of the diamond-shaped work. Battery No. 5 consists of a bulge in the curtain with two flanking faces toward the rear to enclose its space.[36]

Fort Brady is also well preserved on Cox's Hill, a high, commanding site to fire on Confederate river traffic. In addition to the emplacements for heavy guns, Fort Brady also has many positions for field artillery pointing inland. The magazine is incorporated into its long traverse, the top of which has since caved in.[37]

### CONFEDERATE WORKS NORTH OF THE JAMES RIVER

Confederate engineers had to scramble to reconstruct effective defenses near Fort Burnham after the Fifth Offensive. Fort Harrison had been the left anchor of a Secondary Line constructed in 1863 behind the original Harrison Line, which had been built in the summer of 1862. The left end of that Secondary Line was abandoned, but the rest was held by the Rebels. Today, much of it exists. Walking from Fort Burnham southwestward, one encounters a small bulge in the line, then a larger bulge designated Battery X, and finally a bigger work named the White Battery before one reaches Fort Hoke. The latter work was enlarged after the Fifth Offensive and given its current name. It has several gun emplacements, embrasures, and traverses and was heavily reconstructed in the 1930s. Farther south from Fort Hoke, Fort Maury was located on the original Harrison Line west of Osborne Turnpike. Engineers heavily reinforced the old Battery No. 2 to make a small but strong work with three embrasures and a bombproof to fire down the turnpike.[38]

Engineers constructed another line to the rear, stretching from Fort Johnson (which was located northwest of Fort Burnham) to a point on the Secondary Line just to the right of Fort Hoke. The major feature in this new line was Elliott's Salient, an angle about one-third of the way along the line from Fort Johnson. A small work termed a pan coupe was located halfway between Fort Johnson and Elliott's Salient, and the curtain along the entire line was adorned with a good ditch, layers of abatis, and torpedoes. Engineers also started a countermine at Elliott's Salient. Photographs taken after the campaign show drainage ditches behind the line and a unique banquette constructed entirely out of wood as a raised platform, due to the presence of low, marshy ground along much of the line.[39]

The Confederates abandoned another line after the Fifth Offensive because of its proximity to the new Federal position at Fort Burnham. Called W. P. Smith's Line and built in October 1862, it stretched southeast from Fort Johnson toward a point to the right of Fort Burnham. Today W. P. Smith's Line is

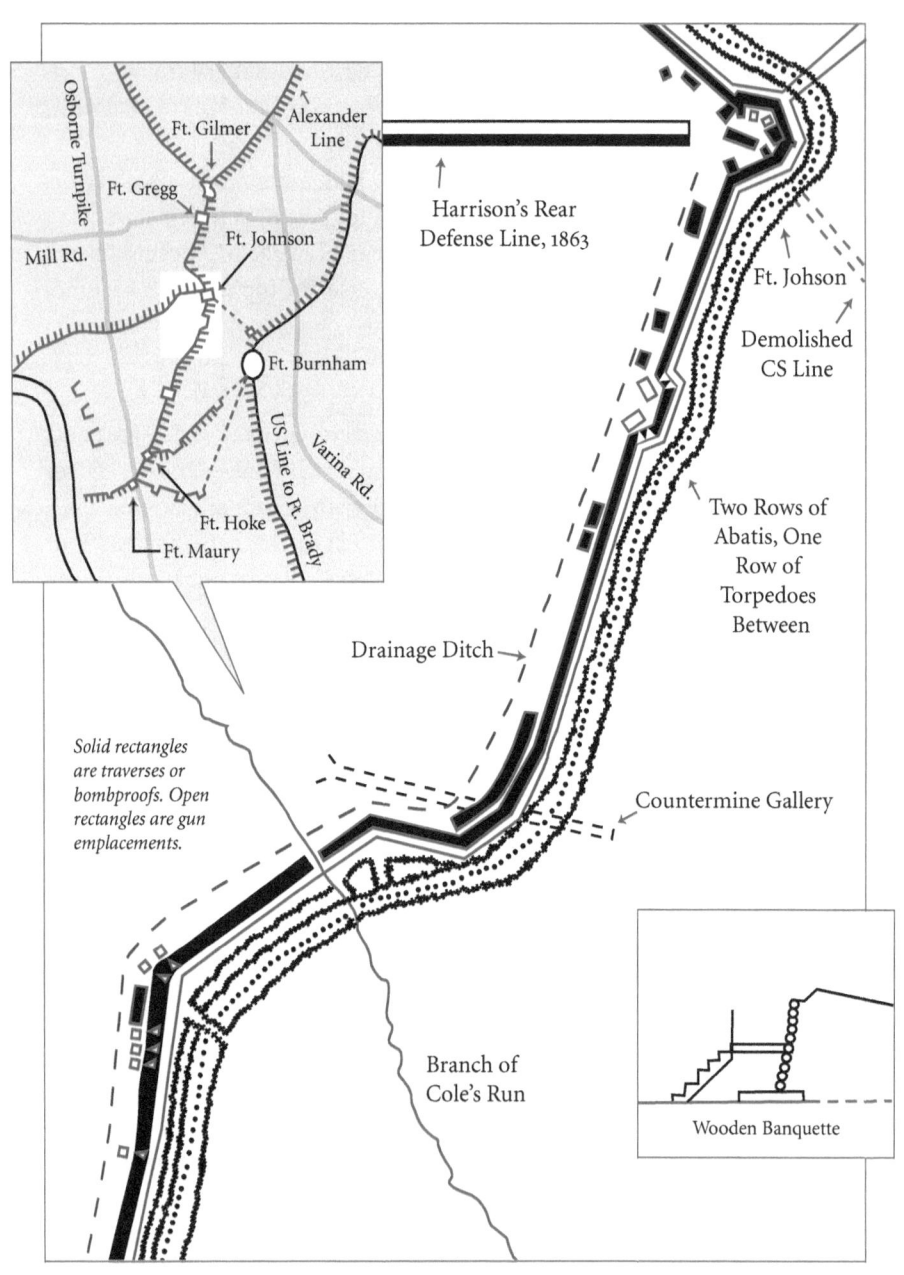

Confederate Line from Fort Maury to New Market Road, April 3, 1865 (based on maps in Dickinson, "Union and Confederate Engineering Operations at Chaffin's Bluff," 93, 94, 101, RNB)

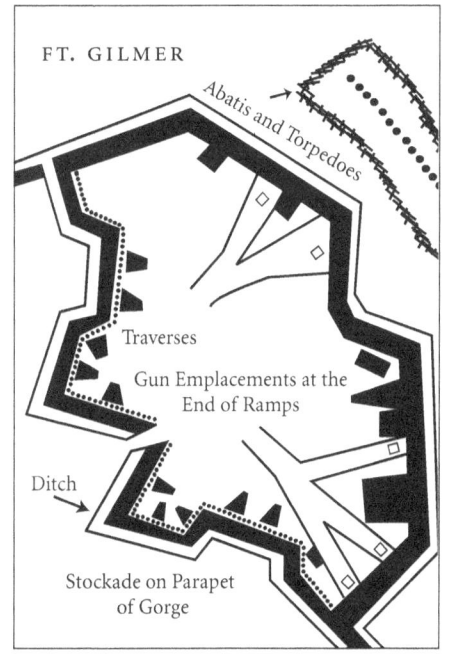
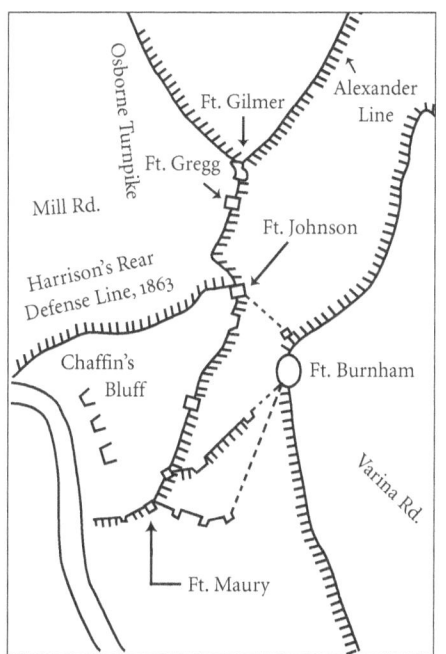
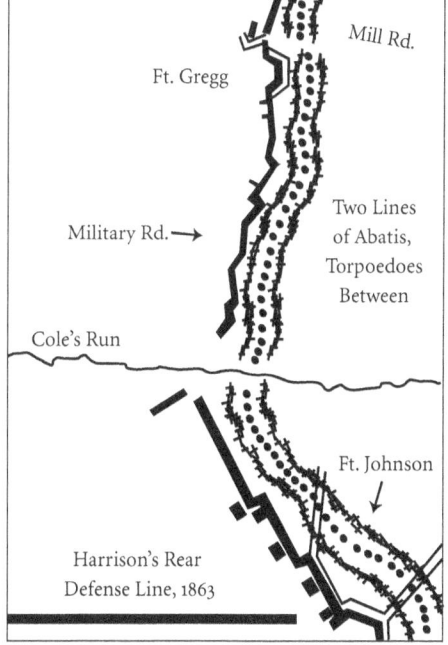

Confederate Line from Fort Johnson to Fort Gilmer, April 3, 1865 (based on maps in Dickinson, "Union and Confederate Engineering Operations at Chaffin's Bluff," 88, 90, 101, RNB)

intact, with a trench but no ditch except in front of one small artillery emplacement.[40]

Fort Johnson itself is a comparatively small work at an angle in the line. It had at least two embrasures, four bombproofs, and a traverse. Its most prominent feature was a ditch twenty-seven feet deep, dug to deter Union mining, which is well preserved today. Postcampaign photographs show that the ditch was dug in two stages, with a small berm visible halfway down the outer slope of the ditch.[41]

North of Fort Johnson and south of Battery Gregg, the curtain crossed Coles Run. This line was heavily reinforced after the Fifth Offensive with several indentations for flanking fire and a heavy cordon of abatis and torpedoes in front. Fort Gregg was a small work covering the approach along Mill Road. Fort Gilmer, a short distance to the north of Fort Gregg, was a large work with an open gorge. A large area of the fort was excavated about four feet deep to obtain dirt for the construction of numerous bombproofs and magazines. The fort had five raised artillery emplacements and some gun positions that were not raised. Engineers constructed ramps to take the field guns up to these raised platforms.[42]

Finally, the last new construction the Confederates started north of the James River following the Fifth Offensive was the brainchild of Edward Porter Alexander. He suggested a new line stretching northeastward from Fort Gilmer across New Market Road and Darbytown Road to serve as a forward line for the Richmond defenses. It was constructed from October 10 through early November 1864 and consisted of a series of small redans for field guns about 300 yards apart. The curtain was generally straight with a banquette and a ditch in front. Some of the Alexander Line is intact. Battery Alexander has six raised artillery emplacements.[43]

CONCLUSION

The sprawling nature of the Richmond-Petersburg Line made its preservation difficult over the decades. The works passed through the hands of many different landowners who had varying degrees of commitment to preserving them. Oversight of preserved remnants today is divided between the Petersburg National Battlefield, the Richmond National Battlefield, the Chesterfield County park system, the privately funded Pamplin Historical Park, and the publicly supported Civil War Preservation Trust. Everyone involved in identifying, preserving, and interpreting the earthworks of the Petersburg campaign deserves a sincere vote of appreciation from scholars and enthusiasts alike.

# NOTES

### ABBREVIATIONS

| | |
|---|---|
| AAS | American Antiquarian Society, Worcester, Mass. |
| ALPL | Abraham Lincoln Presidential Library, Springfield, Ill. |
| AU | Auburn University, Auburn, Ala. |
| BHL-UM | University of Michigan, Bentley Historical Library, Ann Arbor |
| CHS | Chicago Historical Society, Chicago, Ill. |
| CWM | College of William and Mary, Williamsburg, Va. |
| CU | Cornell University, Ithaca, N.Y. |
| DPA | Delaware Public Archives, Dover |
| ECMC-ECU | East Carolina University, East Carolina Manuscript Collection, Greenville, N.C. |
| FSNMP | Fredericksburg and Spotsylvania National Military Park, Fredericksburg, Va. |
| HSSC | Historical Society of Schuylkill County, Pottsville, Pa. |
| IHS | Indiana Historical Society, Indianapolis |
| ISL | Indiana State Library, Indianapolis |
| LC | Library of Congress, Manuscript Division, Washington, D.C. |
| LOV | Library of Virginia, Richmond |
| Mary-HS | Maryland Historical Society, Baltimore |
| Mass-HS | Massachusetts Historical Society, Boston |
| MC | Museum of the Confederacy, Richmond, Va. |
| MCL-DU | Duke University, Medical College Library, Durham, N.C. |
| MDAH | Mississippi Department of Archives and History, Jackson |
| MMF | Moravian Music Foundation, Winston-Salem, N.C. |
| NARA | National Archives and Records Administration, Washington, D.C. |
| NCDAH | North Carolina Division of Archives and History, Raleigh |
| N-YHS | New-York Historical Society, New York, N.Y. |

| | |
|---|---|
| OR | *The War of the Rebellion: A Compilation of the Official Records of the Union and Confederate Armies.* 70 vols. in 128. Washington, D.C.: Government Printing Office, 1880–1901. Unless otherwise noted, all citations are to series 1. |
| OR ATLAS | *The Official Military Atlas of the Civil War.* New York: Fairfax Press, 1983. |
| PEM | Peabody-Essex Museum, Salem, Mass. |
| PNB | Petersburg National Battlefield, Petersburg, Va. |
| RBM-NYPL | New York Public Library, Rare Books and Manuscripts, New York, N.Y. |
| RNB | Richmond National Battlefield, Richmond, Va. |
| SC-EU | Emory University, Special Collections, Atlanta, Ga. |
| SC-SU | Stanford University, Department of Special Collections, Palo Alto, Calif. |
| SC-UNH | University of New Hampshire, Milne Special Collections and Archives, Durham |
| SC-UVA | University of Virginia, Special Collections, Charlottesville |
| SCL-DU | Duke University, Special Collections Library, Durham, N.C. |
| SHC-UNC | University of North Carolina, Southern Historical Collection, Chapel Hill |
| UCB | University of California, Berkeley |
| UGA | University of Georgia, Athens |
| UI | University of Iowa, Iowa City |
| USAMHI | U.S. Army Military History Institute, Carlisle, Pa. |
| VHS | Virginia Historical Society, Richmond |
| VMI | Virginia Military Institute, Lexington |
| WLU | Washington and Lee University, Lexington, Va. |

PREFACE

1  Kitching to Papa, July 6, 1864, in Irving, "More Than Conqueror," 157–58; Griffin to Richmond, July 18, 1864, *OR* 40(3):322; August 5, 1864, Tilton Diary, Mass-HS; August 8–9, 1864, Snook Diary, Mary-HS; Day, "Battle of the Crater," 356; Gallagher, *Fighting for the Confederacy*, 469–70; Michler to Williams, October 20, 1864, *OR* 40(1):291.
2  Sommers, *Richmond Redeemed*, xii; Horn, *Petersburg Campaign*, 219.

CHAPTER ONE

1  "James Chatham Duane," 407–8; Surg. William Edgar certificates, September 26, October 13, 1864, James C. Duane service record, M1064, RG94, NARA; Frank Wagner, "Michler, Nathaniel," 703–4; Michler to Williams, October 20, 1864, *OR* 36(1):295; Meade to Grant, August 29, 1864, *OR* 42(2):565; Meade to Delafield, November 26, 1864, *OR* 42(3):709. The chief engineer of the U.S. Army reported that Duane's "health

has been Seriously injured by the severity of the exposure he has undergone" (Richard Delafield to Meade, February 4, 1865, M1113, RG77, NARA).

2 Record of Events, 15th New York Engineers, *Supplement to the Official Records*, 43(2):210; Spaulding to Duane, August 30, 1864, and June 14, 1865, *OR* 46(1):300, 644, 650.

3 Record of Events, 50th New York Engineers, *Supplement to the Official Records*, 44(2):118, 127, 153–55, 194, 201; Turtle, "History of the Engineer Battalion," 9; Thompson, *Engineer Battalion*, 82, 90–92; Spaulding to Duane, August 30, 1864, *OR* 40(1):299; Duane to Barnard, December 12, 20, 1864, *OR* 42(1):181, 183; Brainerd to Ruggles, February 11, 1865, *OR* 46(2):526.

4 *History of the Thirty-Fifth Regiment*, 241–42, 259; Jones Diary, Gilbert Family Papers, Rhode Island Historical Society, Providence; Potter to Parke, July 2, 1864, Burnside Papers, RG94, NARA.

5 Circular, Second Division, Ninth Corps, October 18, 1864, *OR* 42(3):266–67; Phillips and Parsegian, *Richard and Rhoda*, 47–48.

6 Cullum, *Biographical Register*, 2:812–83; Warner, *Generals in Blue*, 548–49; circular, Department of Virginia and North Carolina, May 20, 1864, and General Orders No. 65, Headquarters, Army of the James, May 20, 1864, *OR* 36(3):32, 34; Weitzel to Barnard, July 5, 1864, *OR* 40(3):20; Delafield to Stanton, October 30, 1865, *OR*, ser. 3, 5:183; "Michie, Peter Smith"; Ord to Grant, March 6, 1865, and Grant to Ord, March 7, 1865, *OR* 46(2):861, 880.

7 Record of Events, 1st New York Engineers, *Supplement to the Official Records*, 42(2):400–401; Michie to Ord, March 9, 1865, *OR* 46(2):906; Michie to Ord, May 12, 1865, *OR* 46(1):1165.

8 Abbot, "Cyrus Ballou Comstock," 218–19; Warner, *Generals in Blue*, 19–20; Special Orders No. 28 and No. 31, Headquarters, Armies of the United States, June 5, 9, 1864, in Simon, *Papers of Ulysses S. Grant*, 11:31n; Special Orders No. 119, Headquarters, Armies of the United States, November 4, 1864, *OR* 42(3):507.

9 Warner, *Generals in Gray*, 282–83; Cooper to Lee, July 20, 1864, and General Orders No. 50, Headquarters, Army of Northern Virginia, July 20, 1864, *OR* 40(3):787, 788.

10 "Stevens, Walter Husted"; muster rolls, Jeremy F. Gilmer to James A. Seddon, December 5, 1862, and Arnold Elzey to Samuel Cooper, March 19, 1864, Walter Husted Stevens service record, M331, roll 236, RG109, NARA; Alfred L. Rives to Alfred M. Barbour, May 21, 1862, M628, RG109, NARA; Minor, "Record of the War," 3:32, Minor Family Papers, SC-UVA; Howard, "Brig. Gen. Walter H. Stevens," 249; Warner, *Generals in Gray*, 292.

11 Louisa Harris Bowie, "Memorial of David B. Harris," and commission as colonel of engineers, October 9, 1863, Harris Papers, SCL-DU; "General David Bullock Harris," 397; Roller, "The Incidents of the Retreat to Appomattox," 13, Roller Papers, SC-UVA; Minor, "Record of the War," 3:45–46, Minor Family Papers, SC-UVA; Krick, *Staff Officers in Gray*, 150.

12 Gilmer to Harris, August 11, 1864, M628, RG109, NARA; Matthew Walton Venable, *Eighty Years After*, 23; Roller, "The Incidents of the Retreat to Appomattox," Roller Papers, SC-UVA; Jackson, *First Regiment Engineer Troops*, 67; muster rolls, J. R. Anderson and W. J. Bailey service records, Company G, 2nd Confederate Engineers,

M258, roll 97, RG109, NARA; Minor, "Record of the War," 3:44, 75, Minor Family Papers, SC-UVA.
13 Jackson, *First Regiment Engineer Troops*, 54–56, 107, 125; Talcott, "Reminiscences," 262, 264; Record of Events, Companies F, I, and K, 1st Confederate Engineers, M258, roll 92, RG109, NARA.
14 Jackson, *First Regiment Engineer Troops*, 66–67; Lee to wife, July 27, 1864, Lee Papers, SC-EU.
15 Charles W. Trueheart to father, December 31, 1864, and to Henry, January 20, February 13, 1865, in Williams, *Rebel Brothers*, 134, 136–37, 140–42.
16 Charles Marshall to Clarke, February 4, 1865, Clarke Papers, VMI.
17 Circular, Headquarters, Army of Northern Virginia, October 20, 1864, Clingman Papers, SHC-UNC.
18 Hicks and Schultz, *Battlefields of the Civil War*, 225.

CHAPTER TWO

1 Martin L. Smith to Sarah, May 29, 1864, Schoff Collection, BHL-UM.
2 Hess, *Field Armies and Fortifications*, 41–43, 99–101, 111–15, 171–73, 237–40.
3 Dickinson, "Union and Confederate Engineering Operations at Chaffin's Bluff," 69, RNB; maps of Henrico County, 1864, RG77, G443, vol. 2, pp. 4–5, NARA.
4 *Montgomery Daily Mail*, May 14, 1864; Alfred L. Rives to Walter H. Stevens, May 2, 1864; to C. C. deNordendorf, June 8, 1864; and to Stevens, May 25, 1864, M628, RG109, NARA.
5 Greene, *Civil War Petersburg*, 4–5, 8.
6 Ibid., 96–98, 105, 108–9, 125, 135, 140, 144, 147, 162; Krick, *Staff Officers in Gray*, 114; Charles H. Dimmock to Robert E. Lee, February 1, 1866, Dimmock Papers, VHS.
7 Livermore, *Days and Events*, 369; Gallagher, *Fighting for the Confederacy*, 421; Howe, *Wasted Valor*, 27; Case, "Personal Recollections," 155; *OR Atlas*, pl. 40, no. 1.
8 Kautz, "Operations South of the James River," 534; Kautz to Davis, June 11, 1864, and Colston to Pearce, June 10, 1864, *OR* 36(2):308–9, 317–18; Gillmore to Butler, June 9, 1864, *OR* 36(3):719–10; Colston, "Repelling the First Assault on Petersburg"; William Glenn Robertson, *Battle of Old Men*, 34–35, 40–48, 60–78; Greene, *Civil War Petersburg*, 176–77, 179–81; manuscript map of Kautz's attack on Petersburg, June 9, 1864, RG77, G160-42, NARA.
9 Colston to Pearce, June 10, 1864, *OR* 36(2):318; Colston, "Repelling the First Assault on Petersburg," 535–36; Beauregard to Bragg, June 9 [10], 1864, *OR* 51(2):998; Beauregard to Bragg, June 9, 1864, *OR* 36(3):886; June 10–11, 1864, Albright Diary, SHC-UNC.
10 Grant to Meade, June 8, 1864, in Simon, *Papers of Ulysses S. Grant*, 11:30–31; Michler to Williams, October 20, 1864; Hancock to assistant adjutant general, Army of the Potomac, September 21, 1865; and Wheaton to Mundee, September 1, 1864, *OR* 36(1):302, 346, 690; Orders, Headquarters, Sixth Corps, June 11, 1864, *OR* 36(3):750; Thompson, *Engineer Battalion*, 67–68; Thienel, *Mr. Lincoln's Bridge Builders*, 166; Clarke Baum to wife, June 11, 1864, Baum Letters, RNB; June 12, 1864, Smith Diary, Mary-HS.
11 Grant to Butler, June 11, 1864, in Simon, *Papers of Ulysses S. Grant*, 11:34–35.

12   Hancock to Assistant Adjutant General, Army of the Potomac, September 21, 1865; Orders, Headquarters, Army of the Potomac, June 11, 1864; and Simms to Goggin, December 1864, *OR* 36(1):346, 748–49, 1065; circular, Headquarters, Second Corps, June 12, 1864, and Orders, Headquarters, Sixth Corps, June 12, 1864, *OR* 36(3):759–60, 764; Howe, *Wasted Valor*, 13, 15–16.
13   Howe, *Wasted Valor*, 17–18; Furguson, *Not War but Murder*, 250.
14   D. H. Hill to Beauregard, [June] 9, 1864, Beauregard Papers, SCL-DU; Howe, *Wasted Valor*, 12–13, 18; William Glenn Robertson, *Back Door to Richmond*, 239.
15   Chisholm diary, June 13, 1864, in Menge and Shimrak, *Civil War Notebook*, 23; Hannum, "Crossing of the James," 229–31.
16   Howe, *Wasted Valor*, 17, 19.
17   Lee to Jefferson Davis, June 14, 1864, in Freeman, *Lee's Dispatches*, 227–32; Thienel, *Mr. Lincoln's Bridge Builders*, 166–79; Howe, *Wasted Valor*, 18–19; Furguson, *Not War but Murder*, 250.
18   Hannum, "Crossing of the James," 230–31, 234–37; Turtle, "History of the Engineer Battalion," 8; Howe, *Wasted Valor*, 16; Nevins, *Diary of Battle*, 420. The site of Wilcox's Landing is accessible today (field visit, March 27, 1997). See also a modern photograph of the site in "Grant and Lee, 1864," 10.
19   Grant to Julia, June 15, 1864, in Simon, *Papers of Ulysses S. Grant*, 11:55; Howe, *Wasted Valor*, 16–17; McAllister to Ellen, June 15, 1864, in James I. Robertson Jr., *Civil War Letters of General Robert McAllister*, 441.
20   Lee to Bragg, June 15, 1864, in Freeman, *Lee's Dispatches*, 235–36; Howe, *Wasted Valor*, 27, 38–40.
21   Longacre, *Army of Amateurs*, 140–41; Howe, *Wasted Valor*, 22, 26.
22   Wise account, n.d., in *Supplement to the Official Records*, 7(1):285; Beauregard, "Four Days of Battle at Petersburg," 540; Howe, *Wasted Valor*, 27.
23   Howe, *Wasted Valor*, 27; field visit to Petersburg, July 7, 1994. Two photographs taken in September 1864 of the Federal mortar Dictator, which was positioned just east of Battery No. 5, offer some insight into this Confederate earthwork. One shows the cleared, open ground in front of the battery, and the other shows the outside face of the parapet. See Frassanito, *Grant and Lee*, 288–89.
24   William Farrar Smith, *From Chattanooga to Petersburg*, 23; Howe, *Wasted Valor*, 28–30.
25   Case, "Personal Recollections," 156–57; Russell diary, June 15, 1864, in Petersburg *Progress-Index*, November 10, 1961, clipping in Russell Papers, SCL-DU; Wise account, n.d., in *Supplement to the Official Records*, 7(1):286; William Farrar Smith, *From Chattanooga to Petersburg*, 23–24; Hincks to Benjamin Butler, July 8, 1891, in Butler, *Butler's Book*, 1083–84; Howe, *Wasted Valor*, 29, 31, 33–35; Horn, *Petersburg Campaign*, 58. Battery No. 5 is well preserved but mostly shows Federal reworking after June 15. The Petersburg National Battlefield visitor center is located here, and one can find a section of well-preserved infantry trench, too. The trench line between No. 5 and 6, Battery No. 6 itself, and the trench line south of No. 6 are all mostly gone. Battery No. 8 was heavily reworked by the Federals into Fort Friend, named after the nearby Friend House, and is well preserved today. Battery No. 9 is virtually gone, but there is a wonderful living history encampment here with reconstructed earthworks,

huts, and a bombproof. There is very little of the Dimmock Line left today because the Federals reworked and used a few batteries and demolished the rest of what lay behind their lines in July 1864. The Confederates incorporated the rest of the Dimmock Line outside Federal reach into what became the Richmond-Petersburg Line. Battery No. 45 to the west of town remains intact, as do some works along modern Defense Road, from Johnson Road to Battery 45.

26 Hagood, "Hagood's Brigade," 397-99; Howe, *Wasted Valor*, 37-38; Wise account, n.d., in *Supplement to the Official Records*, 7(1):286; William M. Thomas, "Slaughter at Petersburg," 224-25.
27 Hincks to Butler, July 8, 1891, in Butler, *Butler's Book*, 1084.
28 Beauregard, "Four Days of Battle at Petersburg," 541; Howe, *Wasted Valor*, 35, 38; Horn, *Petersburg Campaign*, 59.

## CHAPTER THREE

1 Lee to Davis, June 16, 1864, in Freeman, *Lee's Dispatches*, 243-45; Howe, *Wasted Valor*, 43-44, 52.
2 Beauregard, "Four Days of Battle at Petersburg," 541; Howe, *Wasted Valor*, 42-43.
3 Howe, *Wasted Valor*, 58.
4 Grant to Halleck, June 17, 1864, in Simon, *Papers of Ulysses S. Grant*, 11:65; Howe, *Wasted Valor*, 51.
5 Weitzel to Barnard, July 1, 1864, OR 40(1):677; Roe, *Civil War Soldier's Diary*, 220-21.
6 Anderson to Taylor, n.d., 1865, in *Supplement to the Official Records*, 7(1):250; Howe, *Wasted Valor*, 51-52; Gallagher, *Fighting for the Confederacy*, 428; Power, *Lee's Miserables*, 85.
7 Howe, *Wasted Valor*, 58.
8 Ibid., 48-49.
9 Ibid., 44-45; Horn, *Petersburg Campaign*, 60; Gallagher, *Fighting for the Confederacy*, 428.
10 Howe, *Wasted Valor*, 49-51.
11 Wise account, n.d., in *Supplement to the Official Records*, 7(1):286; Howe, *Wasted Valor*, 54, 56.
12 Beauregard, "Four Days of Battle at Petersburg," 541; Hagood, "Hagood's Brigade," 399; Longacre, *Army of Amateurs*, 158-62; Howe, *Wasted Valor*, 53, 55; Horn, *Petersburg Campaign*, 61.
13 Beauregard, "Four Days of Battle at Petersburg," 541; Howe, *Wasted Valor*, 59-60; copy of Confederate map of Petersburg defenses, Union positions June 15-16, RG77, US 393-11, NARA.
14 Beauregard, "Four Days of Battle at Petersburg," 542; Howe, *Wasted Valor*, 58.
15 Bausum, "Personal Reminiscences," 247; Hunt, "Journal of the Siege of Petersburg," 31, Hunt Papers, LC; Gallagher, *Fighting for the Confederacy*, 428; Howe, *Wasted Valor*, 62-69; Horn, *Petersburg Campaign*, 62.
16 Knowles Diary, 124-26, ECMC-ECU; Whitman to mother, June 18, 1864, in Loving, *Civil War Letters*, 122; Larned to sister, June 25, 1864, Larned Papers, LC; June 17, 1864, Noll Diary, BHL-UM; Howe, *Wasted Valor*, 75-79; Horn, *Petersburg Campaign*, 62.

17  Howe, *Wasted Valor*, 79–80, 101–2.
18  Anderson to Taylor, n.d., 1865, in *Supplement to the Official Records*, 7(1):250; Howe, *Wasted Valor*, 72–73, 79–80.
19  John Forrest-Robinson memoirs, 58–63, *Confederate Veteran* Papers, SCL-DU; Elliott, *Southern Soldier Boy*, 23; Howe, *Wasted Valor*, 93–100; Horn, *Petersburg Campaign*, 64.
20  Howe, *Wasted Valor*, 69, 71; Longacre, *Army of Amateurs*, 158–62.
21  Jones to Bernard, May 11, 1891, in Bernard, *War Talks*, 205n; Beauregard, "Four Days of Battle at Petersburg," 542.
22  Beauregard, "Four Days of Battle at Petersburg," 543; Howe, *Wasted Valor*, 108.
23  Hagood, "Hagood's Brigade," 400; Hagood, *Memoirs of the War of Secession*, 280.
24  Pegram to Bernard, August 26, 1892, in Bernard, *War Talks*, 207–8.
25  Hagood, *Memoirs of the War of Secession*, 280; Gallagher, *Fighting for the Confederacy*, 429; Howe, *Wasted Valor*, 107–9; Horn, *Petersburg Campaign*, 63.
26  Robert E. Lee to Jefferson Davis, June 18, 1864, in Freeman, *Lee's Dispatches*, 249; Howe, *Wasted Valor*, 109.
27  Meade to wife, June 21, 1864, in Meade, *Life and Letters*, 2:206; Howe, *Wasted Valor*, 104, 110, 114.
28  McAllister to Ellen and family, June 19, 1864, in James I. Robertson Jr., *Civil War Letters of General Robert McAllister*, 443–44; Bowen, "Diary of Captain George D. Bowen," 197–98; Howe, *Wasted Valor*, 118.
29  Knowles Diary, 128, ECMC-ECU; June 18, 1864, Noll Diary, BHL-UM; Howe, *Wasted Valor*, 120–21.
30  Day, "Life among Bullets," 141; Elliott, *Southern Soldier Boy*, 23–24.
31  Howe, *Wasted Valor*, 122–23.
32  Hagood, "Hagood's Brigade," 400–401; Howe, *Wasted Valor*, 123–24.
33  Charles T. Bowen to friends at home, June 21, 1864, Bowen Letters, PNB; Kitching to Papa, June 21, 1864, in Irving, *"More Than Conqueror,"* 151; Howe, *Wasted Valor*, 125–30; Horn, *Petersburg Campaign*, 66.
34  Nevins, *Diary of Battle*, 425.
35  Hill, "Deeds of Daring," 15–16.
36  Knowles Diary, 128, ECMC-ECU; June 19, 1864, Harris Diary, Harris Papers, RBM-NYPL; Pegram to Bernard, August 26, 1892, in Bernard, *War Talks*, 208; Elliott, *Southern Soldier Boy*, 25; Howe, *Wasted Valor*, 132–33.
37  Bowen, "Diary of Captain George D. Bowen," 198; June 18, 1864, Smyth Diary, DPA.
38  McAllister to Ellen and family, June 9, 1864, in James I. Robertson Jr., *Civil War Letters of General Robert McAllister*, 443–44.
39  Bowen, "Diary of Captain George D. Bowen," 198–99; Howe, *Wasted Valor*, 126, 130–32.
40  Meade to unidentified correspondent, June 24, 1864, in Meade, *Life and Letters*, 2:207.
41  Grant to Meade, June 18, 1864, in Simon, *Papers of Ulysses S. Grant*, 11:78.
42  Nevins, *Diary of Battle*, 425.
43  Wilkeson, *Recollections of a Private Soldier*, 180–81.
44  Bowen, "Diary of Captain George D. Bowen," 199; Pegram to Bernard, August 26,

1892, in Bernard, *War Talks*, 207-8; manuscript map of Petersburg defenses, Federal positions, June 18, 1864, RG77, G443, vol. 1, p. 12, NARA.

45 Beauregard, "Four Days of Battle at Petersburg," 543-44; Gallagher, *Fighting for the Confederacy*, 431-33; Howe, *Wasted Valor*, 133.

46 Beauregard, "Four Days of Battle at Petersburg," 543-44. The battlefield of June 15-18, 1864, has not been preserved. Most of the Dimmock Line involved in that fighting was either leveled or reworked by the Federals. The areas around the Hare House and Elliott's Salient are part of the Petersburg National Battlefield, but, after more than nine months of occupation, they reflect the end rather than the beginning of the Petersburg campaign. None of the houses involved in the fighting of June 15-18 remain. Nothing is left of the Hagood Line, and the Harris Line was so heavily reinforced after June 18 that the few remnants of it today reflect the end of the campaign, too, rather than the fighting of mid-June 1864.

47 Dimmock tried to salvage his reputation as an engineer by soliciting a testimonial from Lee. The general had praised his engineering skill in a letter dated December 5, 1865, and Dimmock, who worked as an architect and civil engineer after the war, wanted to publicize it. But Lee politely refused to have his name used in this manner. See Charles H. Dimmock to Robert E. Lee, January 22, February 1, 1866, Dimmock Papers, VHS.

48 Howe, *Wasted Valor*, 136, 141; Horn, *Petersburg Campaign*, 68.

49 Gibbon, *Personal Recollections*, 229; Theodore Lyman to wife, August 24, 1864, in Agassiz, *Meade's Headquarters*, 224.

50 McNair to father, June 19, 1864, McNair Letters, LOV.

CHAPTER FOUR

1 Grant to Butler, June 20, 1864, and to Meade, June 21, 1864, in Simon, *Papers of Ulysses S. Grant*, 11:91, 101, 103.

2 Nevins, *Diary of Battle*, 427-28; Grant to Halleck, June 24, 1864, in Simon, *Papers of Ulysses S. Grant*, 11:23; Walker, *History of the Second Army Corps*, 544-47, 555-56; Horn, *Petersburg Campaign*, 78-79, 81-83, 85; Trudeau, *Last Citadel*, 62, 64, 68-69, 72-78, 81.

3 Weitzel to Barnard, July 1, August 1, 1864, OR 40(1):677, 680; Maxfield and Brady, *Roster and Statistical Record of Company D*, 36-37; Record of Events, Company F, 1st New York Engineers, *Supplement to the Official Records*, 42(2):466; Lee to Ewell, July 6, 1864, OR 40(3):745; Roe, *Civil War Soldier's Diary*, 222-23.

4 Anderson to Taylor, n.d., 1865, in *Supplement to the Official Records*, 7(1):251; Hagood to Otey, June 26, July 2, 1864, in Hagood, "Hagood's Brigade," 402-6; Henry I. Greer to father, June 28, 1864, Greer and Greer Papers, LC; Horn, *Petersburg Campaign*, 88; Trudeau, *Last Citadel*, 82-83, 85-87.

5 Grant to Meade, June 28, 1864, in Simon, *Papers of Ulysses S. Grant*, 11:144-45; Sumner, *Diary of Cyrus B. Comstock*, 276-77; Warren to Meade, and Meade to Warren, both June 23, 1864, and Barnard memorandum, June 28, 1864, OR 40(2):333, 479.

6 Barnard memorandum, July 2, 1864; Meade to Burnside, Burnside to Meade, and Meade to Hunt and to Duane, all July 3, 1864; and Meade to Grant, July 4, 1864, OR

40(2):584–85, 600, 608–9, 619–20; Grant to Meade, and Meade to Grant, both July 3, 1864, in Simon, *Papers of Ulysses S. Grant*, 11:167–68, 168n; Meade to wife, June 17, 1864, in Meade, *Life and Letters*, 2:205; Hunt, "Journal of the Siege of Petersburg," June 26, 29, July 5–6, 1864, Hunt Papers, LC.

7   Grant to Meade, July 5, 1864, in Simon, *Papers of Ulysses S. Grant*, 11:173; Hunt, "Journal of the Siege of Petersburg," July 5, 1864, Hunt Papers, LC; draft of Duane report, July 10, 1864, Duane Letterbook, SC-UVA; Humphreys to Burnside, and Meade to Grant, both July 7, 1864, OR 40(3):62, 66.

8   Hunt, "Journal of the Siege of Petersburg," July 9–10, 1864, Hunt Papers, LC; Thompson, *Engineer Battalion*, 74; Michler to Williams, October 20, 1864; Hunt and Duane report, July 10, 1864; and Williams to Hunt and Duane, July 11, 1864, OR 40(1):286–87, 292, 294–95. Hunt and Duane worked out all the details of managing siege operations. See draft of orders endorsed by Meade, July 9, 1864, Duane Letterbook, SC-UVA. Apparently, some units in the Fifth Corps began to advance their line with the understanding that they were to begin siege approaches. Col. J. Howard Kitching, who led a brigade in Ayres's division, reported advancing his line 100 yards on the night of July 5 without loss. "There exists considerable rivalry amongst the different divisions and brigades as to which will approach the enemy's lines most rapidly" (Kitching to Papa, July 6, 1864, in Irving, *"More Than Conqueror,"* 157–58).

9   Grant to Meade, July 8, 11, 1864, in Simon, *Papers of Ulysses S. Grant*, 11:193–94, 218; Sumner, *Diary of Cyrus B. Comstock*, 279.

10  Grant, *Personal Memoirs*, 2:606; Richard Delafield to W. H. Pettes, July 19, 1864, M1113, RG77, NARA; Mendell to Duane, July 15, 1864, Duane Letterbook, SC-UVA; Meade to Grant, July 17, 1864, OR 40(3):290.

11  Tilney, *My Life in the Army*, 104; William A. Ketcham to sister, July 7, 1864, Ketcham Papers, IHS; Stevens to mother, July 3, 1864, Stevens Papers, LC; Nevins, *Diary of Battle*, 431.

12  Gallagher, *Fighting for the Confederacy*, 436; July 4, 12, 1864, Smith Diary, Mary-HS.

13  Weitzel to Barnard, August 1, 1864, OR 40(1):680; Bryant, *Diary of Elias A. Bryant*, 170; William A. Ketcham to sister, July 21, 1864, Ketcham Papers, IHS; Johnson journal, July 19–27, 1864, in *Supplement to the Official Records*, 7(1):282–83. Ordnance officer James W. Albright described the Confederate grenades as Ketcham grenades, but he also noted that there were "much larger hand-grenades captured at Plymouth" by Hoke's division in April 1864, which were available at Petersburg. These, however, were "rather too heavy for field practice" (July 26, 1864, Albright Diary, SHC-UNC).

14  "Notes of Genl. Beauregard on W. J. Marrin's Acct. of the explosion of the Federal Mine at Petersburg Va. July 30th 1864," July 17, 1876, Beauregard Papers, ALPL; Michler to Williams, October 20, 1864, and Farquhar quoted in Weitzel to Barnard, July 1, 1864, OR 40(1):291, 679; Abbot, *Siege Artillery*, 130; Duane to Humphreys, July 6, 1864, Duane Letterbook, SC-UVA.

15  Bosbyshell, *48th in the War*, 163; Bosbyshell, "Petersburg Mine," 212; Potter to Parke, June 24, 1864, OR 40(2):396–97; Cavanaugh and Marvel, *Battle of the Crater*, 4; Burnside testimony, report of court of inquiry, OR 40(1):58; Pleasants testimony, in *Report of the Committee on the Conduct of the War*, 126.

16 Pleasants report, August 2, 1864, *OR* 40(1):557; Burnside to Humphreys, July 2, 1864, *OR* 40(2):590; Pleasants testimony, in *Report of the Committee on the Conduct of the War*, 126; Bosbyshell, *48th in the War*, 168.
17 Gould, *Story of the Forty-Eighth*, 271–72; Haas, "Famous 48th," 61; Bosbyshell, *48th in the War*, 168; June 26, 1864, Beddall Diary, Cavanaugh Collection, HSSC; Potter to Van Buren, June 28, 1864, *OR* 40(2):484; Pleasants testimony, in *Report of the Committee on the Conduct of the War*, 126–27; Baird memoirs, 19, BHL-UM.
18 Pleasants testimony, in *Report of the Committee on the Conduct of the War*, 127; Bosbyshell, *48th in the War*, 167–68; "The Petersburg Mine," *National Tribune*, January 17, 1884.
19 Pleasants report, August 2, 1864, *OR* 40(1):557–58.
20 Ibid., 558; Pleasants testimony, in *Report of the Committee on the Conduct of the War*, 126.
21 Burnside to Williams, July 17, 1864, *OR* 40(3):300–301; Bosbyshell, *48th in the War*, 168–69; Pleasants report, August 2, 1864, *OR* 40(1):557.
22 Pleasants report, August 2, 1864, *OR* 40(1):557; Pleasants to Potter, July 20, 1864, *OR* 40(3):354; Pleasants testimony, in *Report of the Committee on the Conduct of the War*, 127.
23 Meade testimony, report of court of inquiry, *OR* 40(1):45; Larry George, "Battle of the Crater," 45–46; Duane testimony, report of court of inquiry, *OR* 40(1):112; Michler to Williams, October 20, 1864, *OR* 40(1):293.
24 Nevins, *Diary of Battle*, 352, 406, 439.
25 Gallagher, *Fighting for the Confederacy*, 432, 442; Powell, "Battle of the Petersburg Crater," 545; Cavanaugh and Marvel, *Battle of the Crater*, 5; Orr, "Archaeology of Trauma," 26; Coit, "Battle of the Crater," 124.
26 Gallagher, *Fighting for the Confederacy*, 442–46.
27 McDonald to Richard H. Anderson, July 4, 1864, McDonald Papers, SCL-DU; July 9, 1864, Smith Diary, Mary-HS; D. Kemper to George W. Randolph, May 4, 1862; Stephen W. Presstman to Randolph, May 2, 1862; Alfred L. Rives to Larkin Smith, May 14, 1862; Jeremy F. Gilmer to Randolph, October 6, 1862; and William Proctor Smith pass, June 20, 1863, Hugh Thomas Douglas service record, M258, roll 93, RG109, NARA.
28 Hugh T. Douglas, "The Petersburg Crater," Petersburg Crater Collection, SC-UVA; E. N. Wise to Daniel, November 14, 1905, Daniel Papers, SC-UVA.
29 Alfred L. Rives to George P. McMurdo, June 23, July 16, 1864, M628, RG109, NARA; special requisition, July 9, 1864, Hugh Thomas Douglas service record, M258, roll 93, RG109, NARA. Spermaceti wax was made by crystallizing sperm whale oil. It did not give off a bad odor when burned and was harder than tallow (which was made of animal fat) or beeswax. Sperm candles did not become soft or bend when exposed to intense atmospheric heat.
30 Hugh T. Douglas, "The Petersburg Crater," Petersburg Crater Collection, SC-UVA.
31 Douglas memorandum, July 15, 1864, *OR* 40(3):776–78.
32 Ibid., 776–77; Douglas to Stevens, July 21, 22, 1864, *OR* 40(3):790–92. Stevens reported that there were two shafts at Colquitt's Salient, but there is no corroborating

evidence for this. See Stevens to D. H. Hill, July 12, 1864, *OR* 40(3):771; Johnson journal, July 20, 1864, in *Supplement to the Official Records*, 7(1):283.
33  Douglas to Stevens, July 25, 1864, *OR* 40(3):801.
34  Weitzel to Barnard, August 1, 1864, *OR* 40(1):680. Federal Battery No. 4 was located near the Jordan House, just south of City Point Railroad, and well to the rear of the main Union line. Battery No. 5 was on the Appomattox River, to the rear of the main Union line. Battery No. 8 was at City Point Railroad on the main Union line. Batteries No. 6 and 7 were between the Appomattox River and City Point Railroad on the main Union line. The Confederates started a countermine along the City Point Road and Railroad at some time before October 1864; it is possible that these Eighteenth Corps countermines were started in response to that project.
35  Grant to Meade, July 25, 1864, *OR* 40(3):438; Grant, *Personal Memoirs*, 2:608.

CHAPTER FIVE

1   James Madison Stone, *Personal Recollections*, 176.
2   Robert A. Guyton to sister, June 26, 1864, Guyton and Heaslet Papers, SCL-DU.
3   Weitzel to Barnard, July 1, 1864, *OR* 40(1):678; Cleveland, "Siege of Petersburg," pt. 1, 86; Livermore, *Days and Events*, 370; *Soldier of Indiana*, 672.
4   McAllister to Ellen and family, June 19, 20, 1864, in James I. Robertson Jr., *Civil War Letters of General Robert McAllister*, 445–47; Carter, *Four Brothers in Blue*, 463; Billings, *History of the Tenth Massachusetts Battery*, 223.
5   Gilreath Reminiscences, ISL.
6   Grant to Meade, July 14, 1864, in Simon, *Papers of Ulysses S. Grant*, 11:247–48; Grant to Meade, July 14, 1864, *OR* 40(3):224; Grant to Meade, July 14, 1864, Duane Letterbook, SC-UVA; Thompson, *Engineer Battalion*, 71; June 23, 1864, Thompson Journal, LC; Michler to Williams, October 20, 1864, *OR* 40(1):293; Lowe, *Meade's Army*, 232.
7   See a series of dispatches in *OR* 40(3):228–33 that detail the process of organizing Second Corps troops to tear down the captured segments of the Dimmock Line. Other sources on this topic include Warren to Meade, and Meade to Warren, both July 14, 1864, and Burnside to Duane, July 15, 1864, *OR* 40(3):237–38, 266; Hancock to Williams, September 24, 1864, *OR* 42(2):994; and July 12–15, 1864, Lyon Diary, SHC-UNC.
8   Stephen Minot Weld to father, July 8, 1864, in Weld, *War Diary and Letters*, 332–33.
9   See exchange of several telegrams between Barnard, Hunt, Benham, Comstock, and Abbot, June 25, 1864, *OR* 40(2):406–7, 422–23; Ledlie to Richmond, July 16, 18, 1864, *OR* 40(3):284, 323; Special Orders No. 18, First Brigade, First Division, Ninth Corps, July 4, 1864, and Special Orders No. 31 and circular, Second Brigade, First Division, Ninth Corps, July 17, 1864, in Special Orders and Circulars, June–September 1864, RG393, NARA; James Madison Stone, *Personal Recollections*, 177; Hartranft to Hutchins, July 21, 1864, *OR* 40(3):373.
10  Sigfried to Richmond, July 25, 1864, and Bartlett to Richmond, July 27, 1864, *OR* 40(3):446, 528–29; Ledlie report, June 30, 1864, Special Orders and Circulars, June–September 1864, RG393, NARA.
11  Willcox to Parke, July 4, 1864, Burnside Papers, RG94, NARA; James Madison Stone,

*Personal Recollections*, 178; Van Den Bossche, "War and Other Reminiscences," 140; Mendell to Duane, August 5, 1864, OR 40(1):302; Thompson, *Engineer Battalion*, 72.

12 *History of Durell's Battery*, 192–93.
13 Benyaurd to Duane, July 14, 1864, Duane Letterbook, SC-UVA; Burnside to Williams, July 14, 15, 1864, and Griffin to Richmond, July 18, 1864, OR 40(3):238, 266, 322; Benyaurd to Duane, July 15, 1864, Duane Letterbook, SC-UVA; Mendell to Duane, August 5, 1864, OR 40(1):302; Thompson, *Engineer Battalion*, 78.
14 Cavanaugh and Marvel, *Battle of the Crater*, 26; *History of the Thirty-Fifth Regiment*, 258–59; Hopkins, *Seventh Regiment Rhode Island*, 196.
15 Mendell to Warren, July 14, 1864, and Warren to Williams, July 18, 1864, OR 40(3):236, 320; Seagrave, *Boy Lieutenant*, 79–81; June 23, July 10, 1864, Hurd Diary, Cavanaugh Collection, HSSC.
16 Warren to Humphreys, July 13, 14, 1864, and Warren to Hancock, July 13, 1864, OR 40(3):213, 234; Humphreys to Warren, July 1, 1864, OR 40(2):569; Charles Wellington Reed journal, July 16, 1864, in Campbell, "Grand Terrible Dramma," 246; Locke to Ayres, July 13, 1864, OR 40(3):215.
17 Spear et al., *Civil War Recollections*, 125–26.
18 Charles E. Davis Jr., *Three Years in the Army*, 373.
19 Mendell to Duane, July 16, 17, 21, 22, 24, 25, 1864, Duane Letterbook, SC-UVA; Carter, *Four Brothers in Blue*, 463; Buell, "The Cannoneer," 241, 254.
20 Buell, "The Cannoneer," 239–42; William R. Ray journal, July 24–26, 1864, in Herdegen and Murphy, *Four Years with the Iron Brigade*, 294–95.
21 Thompson, *Engineer Battalion*, 72–73; Hunt, "Journal of the Siege of Petersburg," 33–34, Hunt Papers, LC; Charles Wellington Reed journal, July 6, 11, 1864; Reed to mother, July 18, 1864; and sketches, in Campbell, "Grand Terrible Dramma," 241–42, 244, 246–47, 251; Kent, *Three Years with Company K*, 302–3; Mendell to Duane, July 14, 5, 1864, Duane Letterbook, SC-UVA.
22 *History of the Fifth Massachusetts Battery*, 873; circular, Headquarters, Fifth Corps, July 6, 1864; Warren to Griffin, July 6, 1864, and Warren to Humphreys, Warren to Mendell, and Mendell to Warren, all July 7, 1864, OR 40(3):43, 65; Thompson, *Engineer Battalion*, 78; Mendell to Duane, July 17, 18, 22, 24, 25, 1864, Duane Letterbook, SC-UVA; Nevins, *Diary of Battle*, 441.
23 July 23–29, 1864, Tilton Diary, Mass-HS; Mendell to Duane, August 5, 1864, OR 40(1):302; July 19, 22, 24, 1864, Lyon Diary, SHC-UNC; Silliker, *Rebel Yell*, 182–83; *History of the Fifth Massachusetts Battery*, 873–74.
24 Michler to Williams, October 20, 1864, and Mendell to Duane, August 5, 1864, OR 40(1):292–93, 301.
25 Warren to Williams, July 15, 16, 1864; Harwood to Warren, July 16, 1864; Warren to Lyle, July 18, 1864; and Warren to Baxter, July 18, 1864, OR 40(3):280, 321–22.
26 Michler to Williams, October 20, 1864, and Mendell to Duane, August 5, 1864, OR 40(1):292–93, 301; Thompson, *Engineer Battalion*, 74, 76, 78.
27 Meade to Grant, July 17, 1864, Burnside Papers, RG94, NARA.
28 Weitzel to Barnard, July 1, 1864, OR 40(1):675; Abbot, *Siege Artillery*, 129.
29 Grant to Butler, June 22, 1864, OR 40(2):320; Abbot, *Siege Artillery*, 135.
30 Mendell to Duane, August 5, 1864, OR 40(1):302.

31  Nevins, *Diary of Battle*, 439; Lapham, "With the Seventh Maine Battery," 149–50, 159–60; Silliker, *Rebel Yell*, 199.
32  Silliker, *Rebel Yell*, 182–83; June 14–23, 1864, Weed Diary, RNB.
33  Mendell to Duane, July 15, 1864, Duane Letterbook, SC-UVA; Richard Delafield to W. H. Pettes, July 14, 1864, M1113, RG77, NARA; circular, Second Corps, July 23, 1864, *OR* 40(3):411.
34  Benham to Humphreys, July 28, 1864, and Humphreys's endorsement, August 1, 1864, *OR* 40(3):559.
35  Robert A. Hutchins to Napoleon B. McLaughlen, November 24, 1864, Special Orders and Circulars, June–September 1864, RG393, NARA; Richard Delafield to W. P. Trowbridge, February 22, 1865; J. D. Kurtz to Trowbridge, February 25, 1865; Delafield to Rufus Ingalls, March 30, 1865; Delafield to Trowbridge, April 27, 1865; and Delafield to Montgomery C. Meigs, June 7, 1865, M1113, RG77, NARA; Lowe, *Meade's Army*, 346.
36  Benham to Humphreys, July 13, 1864, *OR* 40(3):212; Davis and Wiley, *Photographic History*, 2:1103; Spaulding to Duane, August 30, 1864, *OR* 40(1):299; July 8–19, 25, 1864, Snook Diary, Mary-HS.
37  Buell, *"The Cannoneer,"* 241; Davis and Wiley, *Photographic History*, 2:1102; William C. Davis, *Death in the Trenches*, 128.
38  Delafield to Barnard, June 14, 1864, and Barnard's endorsement of June 19 and Hunt's endorsement of June 19; Abbot to Hunt, June 18, 1864; and Abbot to Barnard, June 19, 1864, *OR* 40(2):20–22, 199, 223–24.
39  Abbot, *Siege Artillery*, 133–34; J. D. Kurtz to W. P. Trowbridge, June 15, 1864, and Delafield to Trowbridge, June 21, 1864, M1113, RG77, NARA. See Porter, "Five Forks," 709, for an illustration based on a sketch by Alfred R. Waud depicting a battery in action protected by rope mantlets.
40  J. D. Kurtz to W. P. Trowbridge, June 15, 1864, M1113, and Barnard to Delafield, August 4, 1864, E-18, Letters Received, 1826–1866, box 33, B574, RG77, NARA.
41  Hagood, *Memoirs of the War of Secession*, 280; Gallagher, *Fighting for the Confederacy*, 435.
42  June 26, 28, 30, July 1, 1864, Smith Diary, Mary-HS.
43  June 30, July 2, 6, 10, 11, 1864, ibid.
44  Lee to Anderson, July 4, 1864, *OR* 40(2):713; McDonald to Richard H. Anderson, July 4, 1864, and William Proctor Smith to McDonald, July 7, 1864, McDonald Papers, SCL-DU; Robert A. Guyton to sister, June 26, 1864, Guyton and Heaslet Papers, SCL-DU; J. B. Polley to Nellie, July 6, 1864, in Polley, *Soldier's Letters*, 244; Sorrel to Huger, July 27, 1864, *OR* 40(3):810.
45  Johnson journal, June 29, July 1, 2, 3, 6, 7, 1864, in *Supplement to the Official Records*, 7(1):279–81; Johnson to Brent, June 30, 1864, *OR* 40(2):703–4; Burnside to Williams, July 16, 1864, *OR* 40(3):283; Douglas to Stevens, July 26, 27, 1864, *OR* 40(3):806, 808; "In the Trenches at Petersburg," 23; Day, "Breastworks at Petersburg," 173; Pegram to Bernard, August 26, 1892, in Bernard, *War Talks*, 208.
46  Johnson to Brent, June 30, 1864, *OR* 40(2):703–4; Johnson to Brent, July 19, 1864, *OR* 40(3):783–84.
47  Johnson journal, June 29, July 1, 3, 1864, in *Supplement to the Official Records*, 7(1):279–80; Stevens to Hill, July 12, 1864, *OR* 40(3):771.

48  Alfred L. Rives to Martin L. Smith, June 30, 1864; Rives to George P. Macmurdo, July 16, 1864; Rives to Smith, July 16, 1864; and Rives to Charles H. Dimmock, July 22, 1864, M628, RG109, NARA; Stuart to Mary A. Harper, October 16, 1864, Stuart Papers, SCL-DU; Abbot, *Siege Artillery*, 134; Bliss Reminiscences, 129, USAMHI.

CHAPTER SIX

1  Bryant, *Diary of Elias A. Bryant*, 168; Buell, "The Cannoneer," 254; Buckingham, *All's for the Best*, 113; Will Biggs to Pat, June 27, 1864, Biggs Papers, SCL-DU; J. Warren Pursley to sister, July 15, 1864, Pursley Papers.

2  William A. Ketcham reminiscences, 42–43, Ketcham Papers, IHS; Nevins, *Diary of Battle*, 434; Hopkins, *Seventh Regiment Rhode Island*, 196; James Whitehorne to sister, July 8, 1864, Whitehorne Family Papers, LOV; Chesson, *Journal of a Civil War Surgeon*, 174; June 22, 1864, Snook Diary, Mary-HS; A. M. Stewart, *Camp, March, and Battlefield*, 398–99.

3  Roe, *Civil War Soldier's Diary*, 226; Day, "Breastworks at Petersburg," 174; O. D. Cooke to Colonel, July 20, 1864, Clarke Papers, SHC-UNC; Winne Journal, July 29, 1864, Trent Collection, MCL-DU.

4  Kent, *Three Years with Company K*, 291; Cadwell, *Old Sixth Regiment*, 102–3; Buckingham, *All's for the Best*, 113; Cleveland, "Siege of Petersburg," pt. 1, 93.

5  Hagood, *Memoirs of the War of Secession*, 180; *Lamar Rifles*, 69; Isaac McQueen Auld to mother, July 13, 1864, Auld Letters, Civil War Miscellaneous Collection, USAMHI.

6  *History of the Corn Exchange Regiment*, 489–90; John W. Hudson dispatches, July 25, 26, 1864, Special Orders and Circulars, June–September 1864, RG393, NARA.

7  *History of the Corn Exchange Regiment*, 490; Carter, *Four Brothers in Blue*, 463; Judson, *History of the Eighty-Third Regiment Pennsylvania*, 105; Gilreath Reminiscences, 110, ISL.

8  Carter, *Four Brothers in Blue*, 463; Silliker, *Rebel Yell*, 183; Cleveland, "Siege of Petersburg," pt. 1, 93; Davis and Wiley, *Photographic History*, 2:1106.

9  Pipes Memoir, 48, VHS.

10  Buckingham, *All's for the Best*, 112; *History of the Corn Exchange Regiment*, 489.

11  Winne Journal, July 29, 1864, Trent Collection, MCL-DU; Silliker, *Rebel Yell*, 182; "Dr. A. McDonald's notes upon sanitary experience in the field and at depot hospitals," document 1107, exposures 258–66, United States Sanitary Commission Records, ser. 1, RBM-NYPL.

12  Everett to Ma, July 1, 1864, Everett Papers, SC-EU; G. H. Dorman quoted in Hillhouse, *Heavy Artillery and Light Infantry*, 144–45; J. T. Binford to sister, July 3, 1864, Blanton Papers, SCL-DU; Jeremy F. Gilmer endorsement, July 21, 1864, on Thomas M. R. Talcott telegram, July 10, 1864, and James H. Alexander to Talcott, July 26, 1864, M628, RG109, NARA.

13  Bissell to father, June 24, 1864, in Odcott and Lear, *Civil War Letters of Lewis Bissell*, unpaginated; Aston, *History and Roster*, 19; Washburn, *Complete Military History and Record of the 108th Regiment N.Y. Vols.*, 81; Winne Journal, July 29, 1864, Trent Collection, MCL-DU; Thompson, *Engineer Battalion*, 76; Special Orders No. 48, First Division, Ninth Corps, July 15, 1864, Special Orders and Circulars, June–September 1864, RG393, NARA; Lowe, *Meade's Army*, 228.

14. Wilson W. Fay to W. H. P. Steerer, July 15, 1864; Theodore Gregg to J. P. Gould, July 14, 864; and Frederick Cochrane to Gould, July 15, 1864, Burnside Papers, RG94, NARA; Young to Gould, July 14, 1864, and Bartlett to Richmond, July 27, 1864, *OR* 40(3):239, 529; circular, First Division, Ninth Corps, July 9, 1864, Special Orders and Circulars, June–September 1864, RG393, NARA; Carter, *Four Brothers in Blue*, 462.
15. Small, *Road to Richmond*, 153.
16. Day, "Breastworks at Petersburg," 174.
17. Polley, *Soldier's Letters*, 242–44.
18. Don E. Scott to friend, July 10, 1864, Scott Family Papers, SHC-UNC.
19. Agassiz, *Meade's Headquarters*, 181–82.
20. Lyon to Fisher, July 5, 23, 1864, *OR* 40(3):7–8, 410.
21. Johnson journal, July 11, 15, 1864, in *Supplement to the Official Records*, 7(1):281–82; Small, *Road to Richmond*, 153.
22. Johnson to Goode, July 6, 1864, *OR* 40(3):745–46; William A. Ketcham reminiscences, 59, Ketcham Papers, IHS.
23. Gallagher, *Fighting for the Confederacy*, 435.
24. Gilreath Reminiscences, 110, ISL.
25. Longacre, *From Antietam to Fort Fisher*, 200; Buckingham, *All's for the Best*, 112; circular, First Division, Ninth Corps, July 12, 1864, Special Orders and Circulars, June–September 1864, RG393, NARA; James Madison Stone, *Personal Recollections*, 177–78.
26. Gilreath Reminiscences, 112, ISL; Cleveland, "Siege of Petersburg," pt. 1, 93.
27. Hagood, "Hagood's Brigade," 412.
28. June 14–17, 1864, Weed Diary, RNB; Robert F. Hoke to John M. Otey, June 27, 1864, General Order and Letter Book, Hoke's Division, 1864, Hoke Papers, NCDAH; Henry I. Greer to father, June 28, 1864, Greer and Greer Papers, LC.
29. D. M. Carter to Vance, July 29, 1864, Vance Collection, NCDAH.
30. Power, *Lee's Miserables*, 128–29; Longacre, *From Antietam to Fort Fisher*, 202; Everett to Ma, July 1, 1864, Everett Papers, SC-EU.
31. Johnson to Goode, July 12, 1864, *OR* 40(3):770; Day, "Breastworks at Petersburg," 174; Shaver, *History of the Sixtieth Alabama*, 61.
32. Bowen, "Diary of Captain George D. Bowen," 200; James Mitchell to David, July 17, 1864, Mitchell Letters, PNB; Meade to Grant, July 5, 1864, in Simon, *Papers of Ulysses S. Grant*, 11:175n.
33. Circular, Second Brigade, First Division, Ninth Corps, July 9, 1864, Special Orders and Circulars, June–September 1864, RG393, NARA; Cleveland, "Siege of Petersburg," pt. 1, 93; Buell, *"The Cannoneer,"* 236; Buckingham, *All's for the Best*, 112; Bliss Reminiscences, 146, USAMHI.
34. Judson, *History of the Eighty-Third Regiment Pennsylvania*, 105; Spear et al., *Civil War Recollections*, 128–29; Shaver, *History of the Sixtieth Alabama*, 64.
35. Judson, *History of the Eighty-Third Regiment Pennsylvania*, 104; Clarion Miltmore to mother, June 26, 1864, Miltmore Collection, CHS; Hoole, "Letters of Captain Joab Goodson," pt. 2, 224–25.
36. Buckingham, *All's for the Best*, 112–13.
37. Spear et al., *Civil War Recollections*, 133.
38. Kent, *Three Years with Company K*, 297–98.

39  Hancock to Williams, July 2, 1864, *OR* 40(2):587; Taintor to mother, July 27, 1864, Taintor Papers, SCL-DU.
40  Taintor to mother, July 27, 1864, Taintor Papers, SCL-DU.
41  Loring to Ledlie, July 22, 1864, and Wright to Loring, July 22, 1864, Burnside Papers, RG94, NARA.
42  General Orders No. 97, Eighteenth Corps, July 26, 1864, *OR* 40(3):498.
43  Daniel W. Sawtelle reminiscences, in Buckingham, *All's for the Best*, 113–14; Longacre, *From Antietam to Fort Fisher*, 202; Taintor to mother, July 27, 1864, Taintor Papers, SCL-DU.
44  Lord, "Coehorn Mortar," 18; Hunt, "Journal of the Siege of Petersburg," June 17, 21, 1864, Hunt Papers, LC; Abbot to Balch, July 15, 1864, *OR* 40(3):271; Willcox to Richmond, July 11, 16, 1864, Burnside Papers, RG94, NARA; Grant to Meade, June 23, 1864, in Simon, *Papers of Ulysses S. Grant*, 11:114.
45  Frassanito, *Grant and Lee*, 286–89, 290–91; Bennett, "Grant's Railroad," 16; William C. Davis, *Death in the Trenches*, 138.
46  Moore to McCallum, July 1, 1865, *OR*, ser. 3, 5:70; Bennett, "Grant's Railroad," 14, 16; Horn, *Petersburg Campaign*, 171.
47  Gallagher, *Fighting for the Confederacy*, 441; Hagood, *Memoirs of the War of Secession*, 281.
48  Buckingham, *All's for the Best*, 120–21; G. H. Dorman reminiscences, in Hillhouse, *Heavy Artillery and Light Infantry*, 144.
49  G. H. Dorman reminiscences, in Hillhouse, *Heavy Artillery and Light Infantry*, 144; Longacre, *From Antietam to Fort Fisher*, 201–2; John Malachi Bowden reminiscences, 15, Confederate Miscellany Collection, SC-EU.
50  Trudeau, *Last Citadel*, 91–92; Claiborne, *Seventy-Five Years*, 206–7.
51  Greene, *Civil War Petersburg*, 190, 193, 197–98, 201; Johnson journal, July 8, 10, 1864, in *Supplement to the Official Records*, 7(1):281; *Petersburg Express*, August 1, 1864.
52  Claiborne, *Seventy-Five Years*, 205–6, 240; Shaver, *History of the Sixtieth Alabama*, 60; Blackford, "Memoirs," 451, LOV; Minor, "Record of the War," 3:28, Minor Family Papers, SC-UVA; July 27, 1864, Sale diary, Sale Papers, LOV.

CHAPTER SEVEN

1  Grant, *Personal Memoirs*, 2:608; Sumner, *Diary of Cyrus B. Comstock*, 283.
2  Sumner, *Diary of Cyrus B. Comstock*, 283; Meade to Duane, Duane to Meade, and Meade to Grant, all July 24, 1864, *OR* 40(3):424–25, 427–28; Meade to Duane, and Duane to Meade, July 24, 1864, Duane Letterbook, SC-UVA.
3  Grant to Meade, July 24, 1864, *OR* 40(3):424–26.
4  Mendell to Duane, July 25, 1864, Duane Letterbook, SC-UVA; Grant, *Personal Memoirs*, 2:608.
5  Grant to Meade, July 25, 1864, and Meade to Grant, July 26, 1864, *OR* 40(3):438, 458; Andrew A. Humphreys, *Virginia Campaign*, 250–51; Feis, *Grant's Secret Service*, 256.
6  Grant to Meade, July 25, 1864, *OR* 40(3):437–38; Grant, *Personal Memoirs*, 2:608.
7  Suderow, "Glory Denied," 12–14, 18.
8  Dunlop, *Lee's Sharpshooters*, 131–33; J. F. J. Caldwell, *History of a Brigade of South*

*Carolinians*, 167–68; Lee to Ewell, July 6, 1864, *OR* 40(3):745; Suderow, "War along the James," 14–16, 18.

9   Lee to Ewell, and Kershaw to Ewell, July 24, 1864, and Ewell to Kershaw, [July 27], 1864, *OR* 40(3):796, 811; Dunlop, *Lee's Sharpshooters*, 137; *Story of One Regiment*, 224; Suderow, "Glory Denied," 18–19.

10  Suderow, "Glory Denied," 23; Sommers, *Richmond Redeemed*, 14–15; Horn, *Destruction of the Weldon Railroad*, 10; Cavanaugh and Marvel, *Battle of the Crater*, 31; Walker, *History of the Second Army Corps*, 563.

11  Walker, *History of the Second Army Corps*, 560; Cavanaugh and Marvel, *Battle of the Crater*, 29; Suderow, "Glory Denied," 27.

12  Suderow, "Glory Denied," 22.

13  Ibid., 22–23, 26; Cavanaugh and Marvel, *Battle of the Crater*, 30–32.

14  Walker, *History of the Second Army Corps*, 564–65; Grant to Meade, July 27, 1864, *OR* 40(3):504–5; Suderow, "Glory Denied," 27.

15  Anderson to Taylor, n.d., 1865, in *Supplement to the Official Records*, 7(1):252; Cavanaugh and Marvel, *Battle of the Crater*, 32–34; Suderow, "Glory Denied," 21, 27–29.

16  Grant to Meade, Hancock to Meade, and Grant to Butler, all July 28, 1864, *OR* 40(3):553, 560, 575.

17  Meade to Hancock, Grant to Meade, and Meade to Grant, all July 28, 1864, and Grant to Meade, July 29, 1864, *OR* 40(3):553, 560, 591; Walker, *History of the Second Army Corps*, 565; Gallagher, *Fighting for the Confederacy*, 454.

18  Bowen, "Diary of Captain George D. Bowen," 201.

19  Cavanaugh and Marvel, *Battle of the Crater*, 36, 143–44; Horn, *Petersburg Campaign*, 108.

20  Pleasants report, August 2, 1864, *OR* 40(1):557–58; Burnside to Andrew A. Humphreys, July 26, 1864, *OR* 40(3):476; "Sketch of Mine in front of 2d Div., 9 Corps, near Petersburg, Va.," RG77, Dr. 150–58, NARA.

21  Hugh T. Douglas, "The Petersburg Crater," Petersburg Crater Collection, SC-UVA; Douglas to Stevens, July 28, 1864, *OR* 40(3):813; Edwin N. Wise to Daniel, November 14, 1905, Daniel Papers, SC-UVA; Edwin N. Wise letter, November, 1905, in newspaper clipping, William H. Stewart, "Charge of the Crater," MC.

22  Alfred L. Rives endorsements on Walter H. Stevens's requisitions for candles, July 29, 1864, M628, RG109, NARA; Douglas to Stevens, July 26, 29, 1864, *OR* 40(3):806–7, 816; Hugh T. Douglas, "The Petersburg Crater," Petersburg Crater Collection, SC-UVA; Jackson, *First Regiment Engineer Troops*, 73.

23  Pleasants report, August 2, 1864, *OR* 40(1):557; "Petersburg Mine"; Pleasants testimony, January 13, 1865, in *Report of the Committee on the Conduct of the War*, 128; Powell, "Battle of the Petersburg Crater," 550.

24  Orders, July 29, 1864, Headquarters, Army of the Potomac, *OR* 40(3):596; Burnside testimony, August 12, 1864, report of court of inquiry, *OR* 40(1):71; Chase, *Charge at Day-Break*, 8.

25  Meade testimony, December 20, 1864, in *Report of the Committee on the Conduct of the War*, 39; Scott, *Forgotten Valor*, 555; Weld, *War Diary and Letters*, 354–55; Burnside testimony August 11–12, 1864, and Duane testimony, August 29, 1864, both in report

of court of inquiry, and Hunt to Williams, October 31, 1864, *OR* 40(1):68–69, 74, 77, 280; *OR Atlas*, pl. 64.

26 Pegram letter, August 26, 1892, in Bernard, *War Talks*, 208; LaMotte, "Battle of the Crater"; Sauers, *Civil War Journal of Colonel William J. Bolton*, 226; Andrews, *Sketch of Company K*, 20–21.

27 LaMotte, "Battle of the Crater"; McMaster, "Elliott's Brigade," 10–11; Gallagher, *Fighting for the Confederacy*, 436.

28 William H. Stewart, "Charge of the Crater," 80; Day, "Breastworks at Petersburg," 174; Johnson journal, June 29, July 9, 1864, in *Supplement to the Official Records*, 7(1):279, 281.

29 Johnson journal, June 25, 1864, in *Supplement to the Official Records*, 7(1):279; Eggleston Autobiography, 36–39, VHS; Cavanaugh and Marvel, *Battle of the Crater*, 147–48.

30 Cavanaugh and Marvel, *Battle of the Crater*, 146–48; Thomas F. Rives map of Crater battlefield, 1892, in Bernard, *War Talks*, 229.

31 Thomas F. Rives map of Crater battlefield, 1892, in Bernard, *War Talks*, 229.

32 Burnside to Humphreys, July 26, 1864, *OR* 40(3):476–77; Burnside testimony, August 10, 1864, report of court of inquiry, *OR* 40(1):58–60; Cavanaugh and Marvel, *Battle of the Crater*, 17.

33 Burnside to Williams, August 13, 1864, and Meade testimony, August 8, 1864, report of court of inquiry, *OR* 40(1):524, 46; Burnside testimony, December 17, 1864, and Grant testimony, December 20, 1864, in *Report of the Committee on the Conduct of the War*, 17, 125.

34 Burnside testimony, August 10, 1864, report of court of inquiry, *OR* 40(1):60–61.

35 Warner, *Generals in Blue*, 277; Miller, *North Anna Campaign*, 101, 100–105, 171n; Cavanaugh and Marvel, *Battle of the Crater*, 116.

36 Circular, Headquarters, Ninth Corps, July 29, 1864, in report of court of inquiry, *OR* 40(1):158–59; Anderson, *Fifty-Seventh Regiment of Massachusetts*, 204, 213; Bliss Reminiscences, 130–31, USAMHI; Ledlie to Richmond, August 4, 1864, *OR* 40(1):535; Cavanaugh and Marvel, *Battle of the Crater*, 23, 115; Marvel, *Burnside*, 399–400; Welsh, *Medical Histories of Union Generals*, 200–201.

37 Cavanaugh and Marvel, *Battle of the Crater*, 25, 38.

CHAPTER EIGHT

1 Bosbyshell, *48th in the War*, 169–70; Pleasants report, August 2, 1864, *OR* 40(1):557; Cutcheon, "Twentieth Michigan," 131; Marvel, *Burnside*, 398; Burnside testimony, August 10, 1864, report of court of inquiry, *OR* 40(1):62–63.

2 Pleasants report, August 2, 1864, *OR* 40(1):557; Bosbyshell, *48th in the War*, 169–70; Burnside testimony, December 17, 1864, and Pleasants testimony, January 13, 1865, in *Report of the Committee on the Conduct of the War*, 19, 129.

3 Pleasants report, August 2, 1864, *OR* 40(1):557; Anderson, *Fifty-Seventh Regiment of Massachusetts*, 206; Stevenson, *Account of the Battle of the Mine*, 7; Richards, "Blunder at the Petersburg Mine"; Cutcheon, "Twentieth Michigan," 131–32; Weld, *War Diary and Letters*, 353; July 30, 1864, White Diary, AAS; Weld, "Petersburg Mine," 208.

4 Hugh T. Douglas, "Confederate Countermining in Front of Petersburg," Petersburg

Crater Collection, SC-UVA; William H. Stewart, *Spirit of the South*, 131; Gallagher, *Fighting for the Confederacy*, 456.

5  Pegram letter, August 26, 1892, in Bernard, *War Talks*, 209; Roman, *Military Operations of General Beauregard*, 2:583–84; Johnson to Brent, August 20, 1864, *OR* 40(1):788; Landrum, *History of Spartanburg County*, 556–59; Suderow, "Confederate Casualties at the Crater," 28; Cavanaugh and Marvel, *Battle of the Crater*, 52.

6  Hugh T. Douglas, "The Petersburg Crater," Petersburg Crater Collection, SC-UVA; Edwin N. Wise to Daniel, November 14, 1905, Daniel Papers, SC-UVA.

7  Weld, "Petersburg Mine," 208; Houghton, "In the Crater," 561.

8  Powell, "Battle of the Petersburg Crater," 553.

9  McMaster, "Elliott's Brigade," 21; Potter to Richmond, August 1, 1864, *OR* 40(1):547; Cavanaugh and Marvel, *Battle of the Crater*, 44–46.

10 Powell, "Battle of the Petersburg Crater," 553; Don E. Scott to mother, August 2, 1864, Scott Family Papers, SHC-UNC.

11 Willcox to Richmond, August 6, 1864, and Hartranft to Hutchins, August 5, 1864, *OR* 40(1):574–75, 578–79; Cavanaugh and Marvel, *Battle of the Crater*, 52; Randall Reminiscences, BHL-UM.

12 Meade to Burnside, July 30, 1864, 6:00 A.M.; Burnside to Meade, July 30, 1864; and Harris to division commanders, Ninth Corps, July 30, 1864, *OR* 40(3):658, 666; Marvel, *Burnside*, 401–4.

13 Beaty, "Battle of the Crater," in Hudson, *Sketches and Reminiscences*, 48.

14 Ibid., 49–51, 60; LaMotte, "Battle of the Crater."

15 Robinson, "Artillery in Battle of the Crater," 166; Pendleton to Taylor, February 28, 1865, *OR* 40(1):760.

16 McCabe, "Defence of Petersburg," 289; Mahone, *Battle of the Crater*, 4; Gallagher, *Fighting for the Confederacy*, 464.

17 Andrew A. Humphreys, *Virginia Campaign*, 261–62.

18 Potter to Richmond, August 1, 1864, *OR* 40(1):547–48; Cavanaugh and Marvel, *Battle of the Crater*, 47, 50.

19 Bowley, "The Crater"; Bowley, "Petersburg Mine," 31, 33–34; Van Buren testimony, December 20, 1864, in *Report of the Committee on the Conduct of the War*, 109; McMaster, "Elliott's Brigade," 16–17; Cavanaugh and Marvel, *Battle of the Crater*, 56.

20 Bowley, "Petersburg Mine," 34; Van Buren testimony, December 20, 1864, in *Report of the Committee on the Conduct of the War*, 109; Cavanaugh and Marvel, *Battle of the Crater*, 57.

21 Humphrey to Hutchins, August 4, 1864, *OR* 40(1):586; Wiatt, *26th Virginia Infantry*, 28; Byron Cutcheon autobiography, 283, Cutcheon Papers, BHL-UM; Cavanaugh and Marvel, *Battle of the Crater*, 46, 51.

22 Turner testimony, January 17, 1865, in *Report of the Committee on the Conduct of the War*, 135; Turner to William Russell Jr., August 5, 1864, *OR* 40(1):699; Powell, "Battle of the Petersburg Crater," 560; Cavanaugh and Marvel, *Battle of the Crater*, 53.

23 Meade to Burnside, July 30, 6:00 A.M. and 7:30 A.M., 1864; Burnside to Meade, July 30, 1864; and Harris to division commanders, July 30, 1864, *OR* 40(3):658, 660, 666; Marvel, *Burnside*, 401–4.

24 Cavanaugh and Marvel, *Battle of the Crater*, 24; Marvel, *Burnside*, 403.

25. Chubb testimony, September 1, 1864, and Smith testimony, September 3, 1864, report of court of inquiry, *OR* 40(1):103–4, 119.
26. Bernard, "Battle of the Crater," 6; Bernard, *War Talks*, 334; *History of the Thirty-Fifth Regiment*, 271.
27. Henry Goddard Thomas, "Colored Troops at Petersburg," 564.
28. Bowley, "Petersburg Mine," 34–35; Delevan Bates letter, January n.d., 1891, in Bernard, *War Talks*, 183; Bowley, "The Crater"; Cavanaugh and Marvel, *Battle of the Crater*, 57–58.
29. McMaster, "Elliott's Brigade," 22; McMaster, "Battle of the Crater," 121–22; Cavanaugh and Marvel, *Battle of the Crater*, 85; Forstchen, "28th United States Colored Troops," 129–31.
30. McCabe, "Defence of Petersburg," 289, 289n; William H. Stewart, *Spirit of the South*, 133; William H. Stewart, "Charge of the Crater," 78; Cummings, *Yankee Quaker*, 297; Mahone, *Battle of the Crater*, 5–6.
31. Mahone letter, August 20, 1892, in Bernard, *War Talks*, 214.
32. Bernard, "Battle of the Crater," 6–7; William H. Stewart, *Spirit of the South*, 133; William H. Stewart, "Charge of the Crater," 79–80.
33. David A. Weisiger to B. Perry, April 20, 1896, Weisiger Papers, VHS; Putnam Stith statement, November 1891, in Bernard, *War Talks*, 188; Mahone, *Battle of the Crater*, 7–8; William H. Stewart, *Spirit of the South*, 197; Thomas F. Rives map of Crater battlefield, 1892, in Bernard, *War Talks*, 229.
34. Cavanaugh and Marvel, *Battle of the Crater*, 88–89; Etheredge, "Another Story of the Crater Battle," 205.
35. Cavanaugh and Marvel, *Battle of the Crater*, 89; Bell to Sealy, August 3, 1864, and Carr testimony, September 3, 1864, report of court of inquiry, *OR* 40(1):704, 120–21; Hyde, *History of the One Hundred and Twelfth Regiment N.Y.*, 94–95; Bowley, "Petersburg Mine," 36.
36. Cavanaugh and Marvel, *Battle of the Crater*, 90; Johnson to Brent, August 20, 1864, *OR* 40(1):791; Richard O. Whitehead statement, n.d., in William H. Stewart, "Charge of the Crater," 84–85, MC; Bliss to Peckham, August 2, 1864, *OR* 40(1):550; Cavanaugh and Marvel, *Battle of the Crater*, 89.
37. Etheredge, "Another Story of the Crater Battle," 205; Kenfield, "Captured by Rebels," 233; James E. Phillips to William H. Stewart, sometime after 1900, Phillips Papers, VHS; Cross, "Battle of the Crater"; Bernard, "Battle of the Crater," 15; William H. Stewart, *Spirit of the South*, 135; Mahone, *Battle of the Crater*, 8.
38. Seagrave, *Boy Lieutenant*, 85; Bowley, "Petersburg Mine," 36.
39. Cavanaugh and Marvel, *Battle of the Crater*, 91–93.
40. Meade testimony, August 10, 1864, report of court of inquiry, *OR* 40(1):57; Grant to Halleck, July 30, 1864, *OR* 40(3):636.
41. Burnside testimony, August 10, 1864, report of court of inquiry, and Burnside to Williams, August 13, 1864, *OR* 40(1):64–65, 529; Cavanaugh and Marvel, *Battle of the Crater*, 92–93.
42. Mahone, *Battle of the Crater*, 9; Bernard, "Battle of the Crater," 16; McMaster, "Elliott's Brigade," 23; Mahone letter, August 20, 1892, in Bernard, *War Talks*, 215; Govan and

Livingood, *Haskell Memoirs*, 74–76; Cavanaugh and Marvel, *Battle of the Crater*, 91, 94.

43  Winne Journal, July 30, 1864, Trent Collection, MCL-DU; Powell, "Battle of the Petersburg Crater," 558; Houghton, "In the Crater," 562.

44  Bowley, "The Crater"; Hauptman, *Between Two Fires*, 126; Cavanaugh and Marvel, *Battle of the Crater*, 94.

45  Byron Cutcheon autobiography, 290–91, Cutcheon Papers, BHL-UM; Barrett, "John Frederic Hartranft," 338.

46  McCabe, "Defence of Petersburg," 293; Featherston, "Graphic Account of Battle of Crater," 362; Cavanaugh and Marvel, *Battle of the Crater*, 97; Andrews, *Sketch of Company K*, 23–24; Johnson to Brent, August 20, 1864, OR 40(1):792; Edward Mallet letter, n.d., Raleigh *Daily Confederate*, August 6, 1864.

47  Randall Reminiscences, BHL-UM; Featherston, "Graphic Account of Battle of Crater," 364; William B. Young, "Account of the Battle of the Crater," in Fortin, "Colonel Hilary A. Herbert's History of the Eighth Alabama," 198–99; Featherston, "Battle of the Crater," 297.

48  Scott Memoirs, 26, VHS.

49  Kilmer, "Dash Into the Crater," 776; James Paul Verdery to sister, July 31, 1864, Verdery Papers, SCL-DU; Featherston, "Graphic Account of Battle of Crater," 372–73; William H. Stewart, "Charge of the Crater," 84.

50  Grant to Meade, July 30, 1864 (several telegrams); Meade to Grant, July 30, 1864, 2:15 P.M., 2:20 P.M., and 5:00 P.M.; Ord to Meade, July 30, 1864, 3:00 P.M.; Grant to Butler, July 30, 1864; Meade to Warren, July 30, 1864, 5:00 P.M.; and Hunt to Ord, July 30, 1864, 11:15 P.M., OR 40(3):637–41; 654–55, 675, 687; Abbot to Davis, December 5, 1864, OR 40(1):659–60.

51  Beaty, "Battle of the Crater," in Hudson, *Sketches and Reminiscences*, 60; Featherston, "Battle of the Crater," 298; William H. Stewart, *Spirit of the South*, 140.

52  Whitehead, "Retaking of the Lines," 470; William H. Stewart, "Charge of the Crater," 86; Cross, "Battle of the Crater"; William B. Young, "Account of the Battle of the Crater," in Fortin, "Colonel Hilary A. Herbert's History of the Eighth Alabama," 199–200.

53  Scott Memoirs, 27, VHS; William H. Stewart, "Charge of the Crater," 86.

54  Lee to Seddon, July 30, 1864, 6:30 P.M., OR 40(1):753; Lee to Jefferson Davis, August 1, 1864, in Crist, *Papers of Jefferson Davis*, 10:577; Cavanaugh and Marvel, *Battle of the Crater*, 108; Horn, *Petersburg Campaign*, 118.

55  Willcox to White, July 31, 1864, 8:00 A.M., OR 40(3):708; Bliss Reminiscences, 146, USAMHI; Bernard, "Battle of the Crater," 19–20; William H. Stewart, *Spirit of the South*, 141.

56  Featherston, "Graphic Account of Battle of Crater," 373; Day, "Battle of the Crater," 356; Hall, "Mine Run to Petersburg," 240–41; Rickard, *Services With Colored Troops*, 30; Beaty, "Battle of the Crater," in Hudson, *Sketches and Reminiscences*, 57; Cavanaugh and Marvel, *Battle of the Crater*, 104–5.

57  Grant to Halleck, August 1, 1864, and Grant to Meade, August 1, 1864, 9:30 A.M., in report of court of inquiry, OR 40(1):17, 134; Grant to Meade, July 30, 1864, OR

40(3):638–39; Grant to Ammen, August 18, 1864, in Simon, *Papers of Ulysses S. Grant*, 12:35.

58 Nevins, *Diary of Battle*, 443; Byron Cutcheon autobiography, 322, Cutcheon Papers, BHL-UM; Taylor to Jane, July 31, 1864, Taylor Letters, CWM.

59 Abbot to Davis, December 5, 1864; Monroe to Craig, August 5, 1864; and Piper to Hunt, August 6, 1864, OR 40(1):599–600, 659, 726–27; Cavanaugh and Marvel, *Battle of the Crater*, 146–48.

60 *Richmond Enquirer*, August 3, 1864, reprinted in *New York Herald*, August 7, 1864.

61 Burnside to Williams, August 5, 1864, OR 42(2):58; Grant to Meade, August 13, 1864, in Simon, *Papers of Ulysses S. Grant*, 11:413–14; Welsh, *Medical Histories of Union Generals*, 200–201.

62 Warren testimony, August 29, 1864; Duane testimony, August 29, 1864; Ames testimony, September 2, 1864; and Farquhar testimony, September 5, 1864, report of court of inquiry, OR 40(1):43, 74–75, 78, 109, 122, 127–28; Cavanaugh and Marvel, *Battle of the Crater*, 109–11.

63 Marvel, *Burnside*, 415–16.

CHAPTER NINE

1 Gordon memoirs, 150, 152, WLU; William to Maggie N. Munford, August 7, 1864, Munford-Ellis Family Papers, SCL-DU; Moffett journal, quoted in Hagood, "Hagood's Brigade," 413–44; Wagstaff, "Letters of Thomas Jackson Strayhorn," 330–31.

2 Taintor to mother, August 4, 1864, Taintor Papers, SCL-DU; Chamberlain to Minnie, August 14, 1864, Chamberlain Papers, CU.

3 Herdegen and Murphy, *Four Years with the Iron Brigade*, 300; Lee to Davis, August 9, 1864, in Dowdey and Manarin, *Wartime Papers of R. E. Lee*, 830–31.

4 L. S. Wright to father, mother, and sisters, August 18, 1864, quoted in Jordan, *North Carolina Troops*, 13:580.

5 Inspection report of Pickett's Division, August 13, 1864, 30–31, Confederate Inspection Book, SHC-UNC; Longest to brother, August 4, 1864, Longest Letters, LOV.

6 Maxfield and Brady, *Roster and Statistical Record of Company D*, 47; General Orders No. 99, Headquarters, Eighteenth Corps, August 6, 1864, OR 42(2):72; Bell to wife, August 4, 1864, Bell Papers, SC-UNH.

7 *History of Durell's Battery*, 203; Bearse to mother, August 16, 1864, Bearse Papers, Mass-HS; Johnson to Brent, August 16, 1864, OR 42(1):889; Benjamin Mason to wife, August 16, 1864, Mason Letters, Cavanaugh Collection, HSSC; Johnson journal, August 15, 1864, in *Supplement to the Official Records*, 7(1):461; William Henry Walling to sisters, August 30, 1864, Walling Letters, Civil War Miscellaneous Collection, USAMHI; Daniel W. Sawtelle reminiscences, in Buckingham, *All's for the Best*, 125–28.

8 Day, *True History of Company I*, 86.

9 Power, *Lee's Miserables*, 182–83; Seddon, August 17, 1864, OR 42(2):1182; Ord to wife, August 11, 1864, Ord Papers, SC-SU.

10 August 2, 10, 17, 20–21, 1864, Mullen Diary, MC; Hagood, "Hagood's Brigade," 415.

11 Benjamin Mason to wife, August 16, 1864, Mason Letters, Cavanaugh Collection, HSSC; *History of the Thirty-Fifth Regiment*, 281; Johnson journal, August 1–15, 1864,

in *Supplement to the Official Records*, 7(1):459–62; Gallagher, *Fighting for the Confederacy*, 469–70.

12  Willcox to White, July 31, 8:00 A.M., *OR* 40(3):708; circular, Second Brigade, First Division, Ninth Corps, August 5, 1864, Special Orders and Circulars, June–September 1864, RG393, NARA; Campbell, "Grand Terrible Dramma," 254; August 7, 9, 12, 18, 1864, Snook Diary, Mary-HS; Potter to Richmond, August 8, 1864; Robinson to Richmond, August 11, 1864; and Fisk to Potter, August 11, 1864, *OR* 42(2):92, 119–20; *History of the Thirty-Fifth Regiment*, 281.

13  Record of Events, Company M, 50th New York Engineers, *Supplement to the Official Records*, 44(2):200; Thompson, *Engineer Battalion*, 80–81; *History of Durell's Battery*, 201, 203; *History of the Thirty-Fifth Regiment*, 282.

14  August 3, 1864, Tilton Diary, Mass-HS; Thompson, *Engineer Battalion*, 84; Mervine to Gregory, August 3, 1864, *OR* 42(2):30.

15  Delafield to Stanton, October 30, 1865, *OR*, ser. 3, 5:173; Meade to Grant, August 11, 1864, 11:00 P.M., and Howell to Terry, August 31, 1864, *OR* 42(2):115, 608; J. C. Woodruff to W. P. Trowbridge, August 22, 1864, M1113, RG77, NARA; Roe, *Civil War Soldier's Diary*, 229–30.

16  Valentine, "Transcripts of Letters and Diaries, 1861–1864," 181, Valentine Papers, PEM.

17  Minor, "Record of the War," 3:21–22, Minor Family Papers, SC-UVA; Johnson journal, August 8, 1864, in *Supplement to the Official Records*, 7(1):461; Powell, "Battle of the Petersburg Crater," 557.

18  Gordon memoirs, 149, WLU; Bragg, "Reminiscences of Confederate Service," LOV; Matthew Walton Venable, *Eighty Years After*, 44. Herbert E. Valentine reported that some Eighteenth Corps batteries experimented with firing shell that had very short fuses in an effort to cut Confederate abatis, but he did not indicate whether it worked; see Valentine, "Transcripts of Letters and Diaries, 1861–1864," 185, Valentine Papers, PEM.

19  Pendleton to Stevens and to Walker, August 17, 1864, and Pendleton to Taylor, August 30, 1864, *OR* 42(2):1183–84, 1208.

20  Blackford, "Memoirs," 468, LOV; Blackford, *War Years with Jeb Stuart*, 268–69; Longest to brother, August 4, 1864, Longest Letters, LOV; Wiley, *Norfolk Blues*, 141.

21  Jackson, *First Regiment Engineer Troops*, 78; Krick, *Staff Officers in Gray*, 75.

22  Receipts, August 9, 12, 20, 26, 30, 1864, Edwin Newton Wise service record, 1st Confederate Engineers, M258, roll 96, RG109, NARA; Jackson, *First Regiment Engineer Troops*, 84; receipt, July 28, 1864, Hugh Thomas Douglas service record, M258, roll 93, RG109, NARA.

23  Receipt, August 9, 1864, Edwin Newton Wise service record, 1st Confederate Engineers, M258, roll 96, RG109, NARA; Gilmer to Stevens, August 3, 1864, and Alfred L. Rives to Stevens, August 4, 6, 1864, and to W. H. James, August 7, 1864, M628, RG109, NARA.

24  Receipt, August 12, 26, 1864, Edwin Newton Wise service record, 1st Confederate Engineers, M258, roll 96, RG109, NARA; receipt, July 28, 1864, Hugh Thomas Douglas service record, M258, roll 93, RG109, NARA; Matthew Walton Venable, *Eighty Years After*, 44; Johnson to Brent, August 3, 1864, *OR* 42(1):884; Rives to Stevens, August 5

(two letters), 6, 1864, M628, RG109, NARA; Blackford, *War Years with Jeb Stuart*, 269–70. Pvt. Thomas E. Fowler of Company I, 41st Alabama, enlisted in May 1862. About thirty-five years old, he stood six feet, one inch tall. Taken prisoner at some later point in the war, Fowler took the oath of allegiance at Hart's Island, New York harbor, on June 15, 1865. See Thomas E. Fowler service record, 41st Alabama, M311, RG109, NARA.

25  Douglas to Talcott, and Wise to Douglas, August 2, 1864, *OR* 42(2):1158, 1160; Douglas to Stevens, July 30, 1864, *OR* 40(3):819–20; Hugh T. Douglas, "The Petersburg Crater" and "Confederate Countermining in Front of Petersburg: Experience and Recollection," both in Petersburg Crater Collection, SC-UVA; Wise to Daniel, November 14, 1905, Daniel Papers, SC-UVA; Edwin N. Wise letter, November 1905, in newspaper clipping, William H. Stewart, "Charge of the Crater," MC.

26  Blackford, "Memoirs," 464, LOV.

27  Matthew Walton Venable, *Eighty Years After*, 43; Douglas to Stevens, August 1, 1864, and to Talcott, August 2, 5, 1864, *OR* 42(2):1155, 1158–59, 1163.

28  Gordon memoirs, 147–49, WLU. The exact location of Cooke's Salient is unclear, although Gordon noted that it was south of Pegram's Salient. Presumably it was named after Brig. Gen. John R. Cooke, commander of a North Carolina brigade in Heth's division of Hill's Third Corps, but the exact location of this brigade at any one time on the line is also uncertain. Existing maps show two salients south of Pegram's, one of them the location of Chamberlayne's Battery (formerly Davidson's) just south of Baxter Road, and the other near the Chimneys, where the Harris Line met the old Dimmock Line. Information in the Record of Events for Company G, 1st Confederate Engineers (M258, roll 92, RG109, NARA), pinpoints Davidson's Battery as the location of Cooke's Salient. It also indicates that work on the countermines here began August 4 with three shafts, each 26 feet deep. Galleries extending from those shafts were 61 feet, 68 feet, and 37 feet long. Additionally, "adits," or branches, extended 43 to 50 feet from the galleries. The branches apparently were not connected to each other, and their combined length does not equal Gordon's 1,116 yards. This countermine complex was designated Mine No. 6 and was finished by September 29. It is difficult to know which source to rely on. The second, more southerly salient had a much sharper angle, which would seem to be able to accommodate a long listening gallery such as the one Gordon described. One existing map refers to this angle as Miller's Salient, but the origin of that name is unknown. Capt. John Miller commanded Battery E, 1st North Carolina Artillery, but it is uncertain if that unit occupied this spot. See *OR Atlas*, pl. 64, no. 1, and pl. 79, no. 1.

29  Douglas to Talcott, August 2, 1864, *OR* 42(2):1159–60; Douglas to Stevens, July 31, 1864, *OR* 40(3):821; Matthew Walton Venable, *Eighty Years After*, 21, 44, 47; W. A. Day quoted in "In the Trenches at Petersburg," 23.

30  August 1–2, 1864, Tilton Diary, Mass-HS; Thompson, *Engineer Battalion*, 79; Record of Events, Company M, 50th New York Engineers, *Supplement to the Official Records*, 44(2):199; Warren to Humphreys, August 2, 1864, 2:30 P.M.; Humphreys to Warren, August 2, 1864, 5:15 P.M.; and Meade to Grant, August 3, 1864, 10:00 A.M., *OR* 42(2):19, 26; Chamberlain to Minnie, August 3, 1864, Chamberlain Papers, CU.

31  Thompson, *Engineer Battalion*, 79–80; August 5, 1864, Thompson Journal, LC.

32 Thompson, *Engineer Battalion*, 80.
33 Ord to Burnham, August 2, 1864, 9:00 P.M.; Ord to Meade, August 2, 1864, 11:40 P.M.; Butler to Ord, August 4, 1864, 9:50 P.M.; and Russell to Ames, August 4, 1864, *OR* 42(2):24–25, 50–51; Grant to Ord, August 2, 1864, Ord Papers, UCB; Turtle, "History of the Engineer Battalion," 8–9.
34 Douglas to Stevens, August 1, 1864, and to Talcott, August 2, 1864, *OR* 42(2):1155, 1158; Hugh T. Douglas, "Confederate Countermining in Front of Petersburg: Experience and Recollection," Petersburg Crater Collection, SC-UVA; Cavanaugh and Marvel, *Battle of the Crater*, 107.
35 Douglas to Stevens, August 1, 1864, *OR* 42(2):1155; Hugh T. Douglas, "Confederate Countermining in Front of Petersburg: Experience and Recollection," Petersburg Crater Collection, SC-UVA; Cavanaugh and Marvel, *Battle of the Crater*, 107.
36 Douglas to Talcott, August 2, 5, 1864, *OR* 42(2):1158, 1162–63; receipt, August 4, 1864, Hugh Thomas Douglas service record, M258, roll 93, RG109, NARA. Unfortunately, it is impossible to precisely locate either the Union sap or the Confederate countermine at Gracie's Salient. Existing maps give inconclusive data.
37 Douglas to Talcott, August 5, 1864, *OR* 42(2):1162–63; Hugh T. Douglas, "Confederate Countermining in Front of Petersburg: Experience and Recollection," Petersburg Crater Collection, SC-UVA.
38 Hugh T. Douglas, "Confederate Countermining in Front of Petersburg: Experience and Recollection," Petersburg Crater Collection, SC-UVA; Douglas to Talcott, August 5, 1864, *OR* 42(2):1163; John A. Brady dispatch, August 5, 1864, in *New York Herald*, August 8, 1864; Chesson, *Journal of a Civil War Surgeon*, 188.
39 Ord to Shaffer, August 6, 1864, *OR* 42(1):792–93; Ord to Molly, August 10, 1864, Ord Papers, SC-SU; John A. Brady dispatch, August 5, 1864, in *New York Herald*, August 8, 1864; Meade to Butler, August 5, 1864, 11:30 P.M.; White to Richmond, August 5, 1864, 8:00 P.M.; and Ord to Meade, August 6, 1864, 9:00 A.M., *OR* 42(2):53, 59–60, 71; Tapert, *Brothers' War*, 217–18; John A. Brady dispatch, August 5, 1864, in *New York Herald*, August 8, 1864.
40 Calvin T. Dewese to father, August 1864, Dewese Family Letters, LOV; John A. Brady dispatch, August 6, 1864, in *New York Herald*, August 8, 1864; Ord to Shaffer, August 6, 1864, *OR* 42(1):792–93; Meade to Butler, August 5, 1864, 11:30 P.M.; Ord to Meade, August 6, 1864, 9:00 A.M.; Ord to Shaffer, August 6, 1864; and Crawford to Locke, August 7, 1864, *OR* 42(2):52–53, 71, 79.
41 Beauregard to Cooper, August 6, 1864, *OR* 42(2):1163; Matthew Norris Love to mother, August 6, 1864, Love Letters, PNB; Johnson journal, August 5, 1864, in *Supplement to the Official Records*, 7(1):460; Johnson to Brent, August 6, 1864, *OR* 42(1):885.
42 Charges and Specifications, n.d.; Douglas to Talcott, August 9, 1864; and Douglas to James A. Seddon, August 10, 1864, with endorsements by Talcott, Stevens, Lee, and Gilmer, in Hugh Thomas Douglas service record, M258, roll 93, RG109, NARA; Jackson, *First Regiment Engineer Troops*, 82.
43 Invoices, August 12, 13, 1864, and Talcott to McHenry Howard, September 4, 1864, in Hugh Thomas Douglas service record, M258, roll 93, RG109, NARA; Jackson, *First Regiment Engineer Troops*, 89–90, 93, 101.
44 Receipt, August 26, 1864, Edwin Newton Wise service record, M258, roll 96, RG109,

NARA; Duane, *Manual for Engineer Troops*, 230. Blackford later explained the failure of the August 5 mine as something beyond Douglas's control. He remembered that Talcott discovered that the gallery "had been started at too high a level, and with the necessary ascending grade for drainage it was about to come out of the ground before reaching its destination." It was therefore sprung well short of the saphead. See Blackford, "Memoirs," 463, LOV.

45  Blackford, *War Years with Jeb Stuart*, 262–63; Blackford, "Memoirs," 465–66, LOV.
46  Gallagher, *Fighting for the Confederacy*, 450; Duane, *Manual for Engineer Troops*, 234–37.
47  M. W. Venable, "In the Trenches at Petersburg," 59–60; Blackford, *War Years with Jeb Stuart*, 263.
48  Blackford, "Memoirs," 466, LOV; Jackson, *First Regiment Engineer Troops*, 84.
49  M. W. Venable, "In the Trenches at Petersburg," 59–60.
50  Blackford, "Memoirs," 466–68, LOV; Blackford, *War Years with Jeb Stuart*, 267.
51  Jackson, *First Regiment Engineer Troops*, 87, 90, 92–93. Our only documentation for the Confederate countermine complex at Jerusalem Plank Road comes from the landowners who opened the galleries for tourists and later tried to sell the land above as home lots. Before their enterprise failed, they produced a map of the galleries and took several photographs of them. The map is by Carter R. Bishop and Willie E. Wells and is titled "Confederate Tunnels at Pine Gardens, Prince George County, Virginia, Feb. 23, 1926." Harry Jackson provided a copy of it. Photographs taken in the 1920s show an arched ceiling and walls that were well formed and completely intact. They also show much wooden framing and stairways. Copies of the photographs, including one that shows the entrance, can be found at Petersburg National Battlefield and in the archives of the Petersburg Museums. I believe these photographs show reworking and new wooden framing and stairways undertaken by the landowners in preparation for opening the galleries to tourists in the 1920s. It is difficult to believe that the Civil War structures inside the galleries could have survived more than sixty years underground. It is also difficult to believe that the Confederates would have bothered to cut an arched ceiling and so neatly faced the walls of these galleries. The wood depicted in the photographs has deteriorated a bit, indicating the photographs were taken some time after the tourist development folded. The galleries discovered in the 1920s existed entirely east of Jerusalem Plank Road, but a photograph taken right after the end of the Petersburg campaign purports to show the entrance to a mine located in Fort Mahone. This major Confederate work was constructed a few hundred yards west of the road and south of the main Rebel line, connected to it by a covered way. If this is accurate, then we can assume the countermine complex was much larger, covering an undetermined area west of Jerusalem Plank Road as well. The galleries and branches east of the road were filled in during the 1960s. See Davis and Wiley, *Photographic History*, 2:1104.
52  Bliss to Richmond, August 7, 1864; Warren to Humphreys, August 12, 1864; and Humphreys to Birney, August 27, 1864, OR 42(2):81, 125, 551–52; Silliker, *Rebel Yell*, 192–93; Turtle, "History of the Engineer Battalion," 9. The only detailed information on the Union countermine at Fort Stedman comes from the discovery of the galleries and branches in 1930. See *New York Times* article in clipping from the Petersburg *Progress-*

*Index*, February 1, 1930, PNB; Thompson, *Engineer Battalion*, 82; August 8, 9, 1864, Snook Diary, Mary-HS.
53 Grant to Meade, August 11, 1864, and to Ord, August 25, 1864, *OR* 42(2):114, 511; Grant to Meade, August 11, 1864, in Simon, *Papers of Ulysses S. Grant*, 11:402–3.
54 Butler to Grant, July 28, 1864, *OR* 40(3):570–71; Longacre, *Army of Amateurs*, 193.
55 Michie to Barnard, September 10, 1864, *OR* 42(1):657–58; Delafield to Stanton, October 30, 1865, *OR*, ser. 3, 5:185–87; Longacre, *Army of Amateurs*, 193–94.
56 Cockrell, *Gunner with Stonewall*, 137; Delafield to Stanton, October 30, 1865, *OR*, ser. 3, 5:185–87; Frassanito, *Grant and Lee*, 320–21; Horn, *Destruction of the Weldon Railroad*, 5; Longacre, *Army of Amateurs*, 195.

CHAPTER TEN

1 Grant to Butler, August 12, 1864, and to Meade, August 14, 1864, in Simon, *Papers of Ulysses S. Grant*, 11:405–6, 419.
2 Grant to Butler, August 12, 1864, in Simon, *Papers of Ulysses S. Grant*, 11:406–7; Humphreys to Warren, August 13, 1864, 10:30 P.M., *OR* 42(2):153; Horn, *Destruction of the Weldon Railroad*, 9–10.
3 Suderow, "'Nothing But a Miracle,'" 14; Walker, *History of the Second Army Corps*, 568–69.
4 Suderow, "'Nothing But a Miracle,'" 16; Horn, *Destruction of the Weldon Railroad*, 10; Walker, *History of the Second Army Corps*, 575.
5 Horn, *Destruction of the Weldon Railroad*, 10–11, 15; Walker, *History of the Second Army Corps*, 569–70, 572.
6 Horn, *Destruction of the Weldon Railroad*, 14; Trudeau, *Last Citadel*, 150–52; Suderow, "War along the James," 19; Suderow, "'Nothing But a Miracle,'" 16.
7 Suderow, "'Nothing But a Miracle,'" 16–17, 19–22; Horn, *Destruction of the Weldon Railroad*, 15; Walker, *History of the Second Army Corps*, 572–74; Trudeau, *Last Citadel*, 151–52.
8 Walker, *History of the Second Army Corps*, 575–76; Trudeau, *Last Citadel*, 152–53.
9 Suderow, "'Nothing But a Miracle,'" 22.
10 Ibid., 23; Walker, *History of the Second Army Corps*, 576–77.
11 Suderow, "'Nothing But a Miracle,'" 24.
12 Ibid., 24–25.
13 Ibid., 26; Horn, *Destruction of the Weldon Railroad*, 35–36.
14 Suderow, "'Nothing But a Miracle,'" 27–30; Trudeau, *Last Citadel*, 155–57; Walker, *History of the Second Army Corps*, 576; Horn, *Destruction of the Weldon Railroad*, 40–41, 44.
15 Grant to Meade, August 17, 1864, in Simon, *Papers of Ulysses S. Grant*, 12:21–22.
16 Walker, *History of the Second Army Corps*, 577–79; Trudeau, *Last Citadel*, 158, 160–61; Suderow, "'Nothing But a Miracle,'" 30.
17 Walker, *History of the Second Army Corps*, 579–80; Suderow, "'Nothing But a Miracle,'" 30–31; Trudeau, *Last Citadel*, 164, 170.
18 Suderow, "'Nothing But a Miracle,'" 31; Trudeau, *Last Citadel*, 170.
19 Grant to Meade and to Sherman, both August 18, 1864, in Simon, *Papers of Ulysses S. Grant*, 12:30, 34; Horn, *Destruction of the Weldon Railroad*, 56–57.

20 Horn, *Destruction of the Weldon Railroad*, 54–56.
21 Field visit to Globe Tavern battlefield, July 6, 1994; Bearss, "Battle of the Weldon Railroad," 6, PNB.
22 Horn, *Destruction of the Weldon Railroad*, 57, 59–61; Bearss, "Battle of the Weldon Railroad," 6, PNB.
23 Heth to Palmer, n.d., *Supplement to the Official Records*, 7(1):473; Horn, *Destruction of the Weldon Railroad*, 61–63, 65–66, 68; Small, *Road to Richmond*, 154–55.
24 Grant to Ammen, August 18, 1864, in Simon, *Papers of Ulysses S. Grant*, 12:35–36.
25 Heth to Palmer, n.d., in *Supplement to the Official Records*, 7(1):473; Horn, *Destruction of the Weldon Railroad*, 74, 76–78.
26 Horn, *Destruction of the Weldon Railroad*, 70, 73.
27 Beaudot and Herdegen, *Irishman in the Iron Brigade*, 123; Horn, *Destruction of the Weldon Railroad*, 79.
28 Beaudot and Herdegen, *Irishman in the Iron Brigade*, 125–26; Horn, *Destruction of the Weldon Railroad*, 78–79.
29 Byron Cutcheon autobiography, 345–47, Cutcheon Papers, BHL-UM; August 19, 1864, Crater Diary, UI; *History of the Thirty-Sixth Regiment*, 248; Henry Van Leuvenigh Bird to Maggie, August 20, 1864, Bird Family Papers, VHS; Horn, *Destruction of the Weldon Railroad*, 72, 85–87.
30 Byron Cutcheon autobiography, 348, Cutcheon Papers, BHL-UM; Grant to Hancock, August 19, 1864, 8:00 P.M., and Grant to Hancock and Butler, August 19, 1864, 9:30 P.M., in Simon, *Papers of Ulysses S. Grant*, 12:44–45; Horn, *Destruction of the Weldon Railroad*, 88.
31 Horn, *Destruction of the Weldon Railroad*, 92.
32 Grant to Meade, August 20, 1864, in Simon, *Papers of Ulysses S. Grant*, 12:51–52.
33 Spear et al., *Civil War Recollections*, 141; Bearss, "Battle of the Weldon Railroad," 52, PNB; Horn, *Destruction of the Weldon Railroad*, 93–94.
34 Beaudot and Herdegen, *Irishman in the Iron Brigade*, 123, 128; August 20–21, 1864, Crater Diary, UI.
35 Beaudot and Herdegen, *Irishman in the Iron Brigade*, 123; Warren to Humphreys, August 21, 1864, 5:40 A.M. and 8:30 A.M., OR 42(2):366–67; Grant to Meade, August 21, 1864, 12:45 P.M., in Simon, *Papers of Ulysses S. Grant*, 12:58.
36 Heth to Palmer, n.d., in *Supplement to the Official Records*, 7(1):473–74; Horn, *Destruction of the Weldon Railroad*, 99–101.
37 Beaudot and Herdegen, *Irishman in the Iron Brigade*, 128; Hess, *Lee's Tar Heels*, 244–45.
38 Strayhorn to sister, August 22, 1864, in Wagstaff, "Letters of Thomas Jackson Strayhorn," 332; Day, "Life among Bullets," 216; Byron Cutcheon autobiography, 351, Cutcheon Papers, BHL-UM; Horn, *Destruction of the Weldon Railroad*, 101–3. A color lithograph titled "Battle of the Weldon Rail-Road" depicts the fight of August 21 and shows the Union defenses to have been neatly revetted with boards and posts. It is reproduced in William C. Davis, *Death in the Trenches*, 106–7.
39 Horn, *Destruction of the Weldon Railroad*, 96–99.
40 Harris, *Movements of the Confederate Army*, quoted in Robert G. Evans, *16th Mississippi*, 288; Spear et al., *Civil War Recollections*, 141–42.

41  Hagood, *Memoirs of the War of Secession*, 291–94; Horn, *Destruction of the Weldon Railroad*, 105–7.
42  Hagood, *Memoirs of the War of Secession*, 294–95, 298n; Horn, *Destruction of the Weldon Railroad*, 107. Daley survived Hagood's shot and even asked the former Confederate general for a letter describing the incident so he could apply for a pension in 1879.
43  Nevins, *Diary of Battle*, 456; Peterson to brother, August 22, 1864, Peterson Papers, MMF; Hagood, *Memoirs of the War of Secession*, 300; Horn, *Destruction of the Weldon Railroad*, 111. There apparently is nothing left of the Federal earthworks involved in the battle of Globe Tavern, due to razing during the battle, the construction of a permanent line after the battle, and postwar reclamation.
44  George K. Leet to Rowley, August 23, 1864, Rowley Papers, ALPL.
45  Horn, *Destruction of the Weldon Railroad*, 115, 117; Walker, *History of the Second Army Corps*, 581, 584–85.
46  Britton and Reed, *To My Beloved Wife and Boy at Home*, 245; Murphy, *Civil War Letters*, 200; Horn, *Destruction of the Weldon Railroad*, 117; Horn, *Petersburg Campaign*, 91, 93.
47  Dauchy, "Battle of Ream's Station," 129–30; Bearss, "Battle of Reams' Station," 17–18, PNB; Walker, *History of the Second Army Corps*, 582–83, 591–92; Horn, *Destruction of the Weldon Railroad*, 117–18; field visit to Reams's Station, September 1, 1995.
48  Menge and Shimrak, *Civil War Notebook*, 35; Walker, *History of the Second Army Corps*, 582, 587, 604; Nevins, *Diary of Battle*, 457–58; Horn, *Destruction of the Weldon Railroad*, 118–19. Some important features of the Reams's Station battlefield have altered since 1864. The railroad was removed and rebuilt a couple of miles east of the station after the war. Modern Halifax Road is located on the old railroad bed. When it was widened into a two-lane paved county road, the inner edge of the Union trench was destroyed north of the old Depot Road (modern Stage Road). Yet, much of the parapet is intact, and the angle at the west and north lines is well preserved. South of old Depot Road, there is nothing left of the westward-facing line. Modern Acorn Drive is probably a segment of the 1864 roadbed of Halifax Road. There is a little of the northward-facing line intact, on the far left of the line, but the rest seems to be gone or at least inaccessible. Nothing is left of the southward-facing line hastily constructed by Gibbon's division just before the second Confederate attack (field visit to Reams's Station, September 1, 1995). There is a photograph of the Union works at Reams's Station, taken in the 1930s, a copy of which is at PNB, but it is difficult to tell exactly what part of the works is shown.
49  Gibbon, *Personal Recollections*, 256; Walker, *History of the Second Army Corps*, 585.
50  McGowan to Engelhard, September 1, 1864, in *Supplement to the Official Records*, 7(1):507; Dunlop, *Lee's Sharpshooters*, 190–93; Walker, *History of the Second Army Corps*, 588; Dauchy, "Battle of Ream's Station," 130–31; Beale, *Lieutenant of Cavalry*, 183; Horn, *Destruction of the Weldon Railroad*, 120, 128, 131–32.
51  Walker, *History of the Second Army Corps*, 586, 589–90.
52  Heth to Palmer, n.d., in *Supplement to the Official Records*, 7(1):474–75; Stedman, "Reams Station," 208–9; Hess, *Lee's Tar Heels*, 249; Walker, *History of the Second Army Corps*, 590; Horn, *Destruction of the Weldon Railroad*, 137–38.

53 Dunlop, *Lee's Sharpshooters*, 193–95; Walker, *History of the Second Army Corps*, 589, 592–93; Dauchy, "Battle of Ream's Station," 133; Heth to Palmer, n.d., in *Supplement to the Official Records*, 7(1):475; Horn, *Destruction of the Weldon Railroad*, 133.

54 Dauchy, "Battle of Ream's Station," 134; Heth to Palmer, n.d., in *Supplement to the Official Records*, 7(1):475; August 25, 1864, Mullen Diary, MC; James Gilmer Harris to Edward J. Hale Jr., n.d., and William J. Calais to Hale, August 28, 1864, Lane Papers, AU; Horn, *Destruction of the Weldon Railroad*, 154–55.

55 Hess, *Lee's Tar Heels*, 252–53; Horn, *Destruction of the Weldon Railroad*, 156, 158.

56 Hess, *Lee's Tar Heels*, 253; Horn, *Destruction of the Weldon Railroad*, 158; Stedman, "Reams Station," 210.

57 McGowan to Engelhard, September 1, 1864, in *Supplement to the Official Records*, 7(1):507–8; Horn, *Destruction of the Weldon Railroad*, 127, 162; Gibbon, *Personal Recollections*, 256–57; Bowen, "Diary of Captain George D. Bowen," 206; Dauchy, "Battle of Ream's Station," 129.

58 Raleigh *North Carolina Standard*, September 2, 1864; Samuel Neel Stowe to Edward Joseph Hale Jr., August 28, 1864, Lane Papers, AU; Walker, *History of the Second Army Corps*, 594; Dauchy, "Battle of Ream's Station," 134–35; Curtis to Webster, January 13, 1865, in *Supplement to the Official Records*, 7(1):427–28; Hess, *Lee's Tar Heels*, 154; Horn, *Destruction of the Weldon Railroad*, 158–59, 161.

59 Dauchy, "Battle of Ream's Station," 136–38; Walker, *History of the Second Army Corps*, 595, 597; Horn, *Destruction of the Weldon Railroad*, 164–66.

60 Rogers, "Retaking Railroad at Reams Station," 580; Horn, *Destruction of the Weldon Railroad*, 165. A member of the 12th Virginia in Weisiger's brigade claimed that the Federals had strung wire before their works at Reams's Station that tripped up many Confederates as they closed in on the Yankees, but there is no supporting evidence for this contention. See Henry Van Leuvenigh Bird to Maggie, August 28, 1864, Bird Family Papers, VHS.

61 Beale, *Lieutenant of Cavalry*, 184–85; Gibbon, *Personal Recollections*, 257; Walker, *History of the Second Army Corps*, 596; Horn, *Destruction of the Weldon Railroad*, 166–67, 169, 172.

62 Dauchy, "Battle of Ream's Station," 139; Horn, *Destruction of the Weldon Railroad*, 169–70; Walker, *History of the Second Army Corps*, 598–99.

63 Gibbon, *Personal Recollections*, 259; Sparks, *Inside Lincoln's Army*, 417; Horn, *Destruction of the Weldon Railroad*, 171, 173–74; Walker, *History of the Second Army Corps*, 598–99, 605.

64 Beale, *Lieutenant of Cavalry*, 187; Nevins, *Diary of Battle*, 458; Moffett, *Letters of General James Conner*, 149; Grant to Meade, August 25, 26, 1864, in Simon, *Papers of Ulysses S. Grant*, 12:84, 93.

CHAPTER ELEVEN

1 Warren to Humphreys, August 22, 1864, *OR* 42(2):401–2; Grant to Halleck, August 23, 1864, and Grant to Meade, August 25, 1864, in Simon, *Papers of Ulysses S. Grant*, 12:73, 84–85.

2 Herdegen and Murphy, *Four Years with the Iron Brigade*, 308, 314.

3 Nevins, *Diary of Battle*, 456; Spear et al., *Civil War Recollections*, 143–44.

4 Thompson, *Engineer Battalion*, 82–83; Herdegen and Murphy, *Four Years with the Iron Brigade*, 314; Tilney, *My Life in the Army*, 136; Merryweather to parents, September 7, 1864, Merryweather Papers, CHS; William E. Potter to Thompson, August 26, 1864, Potter Letters, PNB; *Guide to the Fortifications and Battlefields*, 23; Nevins, *Diary of Battle*, 459; Tilney, *My Life in the Army*, 136; Warren to Duane, September 3, 1864, *OR* 42(2):677; Michler to Bowers, September 24, 1864, *OR* 42(1):164; Michler to Bowers, September 17, 1864, *OR* 51(1):275; Delafield to Stanton, October 30, 1865, *OR*, ser. 3, 5:173–74.

5 *History of the Thirty-Sixth Regiment*, 253–54; Byron Cutcheon autobiography, 357, Cutcheon Papers, BHL-UM; Beal to uncle, August 25, 1864, Beal Papers, Mass-HS; John D. Bertolette to N. B. McLaughlen, September 15, 21, 1864, Special Orders and Circulars, June–September 1864, RG393, NARA.

6 Morgan to [Mott], August 29, September 1, 1864; Hancock to Humphreys, and Hancock to Williams, both September 2, 1864, *OR* 42(2):571–72, 635, 661; Michler to Bowers, September 24, 1864, *OR* 42(1):164.

7 Campbell, *"Grand Terrible Dramma,"* 265; Record of Events, Company K, 50th New York Engineers, *Supplement to the Official Records*, 44(2):193–94; Michler to Bowers, September 17, 1864, *OR* 51(1):275; Thompson, *Engineer Battalion*, 81–82, 84.

8 Michler to Parke, August 31, 1864, *OR* 42(2):604; Thompson, *Engineer Battalion*, 84; *OR Atlas*, pl. 67, no. 9; Delafield to Stanton, October 30, 1865, *OR*, ser. 3, 5:174.

9 Humphreys to Gregg, Lockwood to McAllister, Grant to Parke, and Wilson to Mott, all September 4, 1864, *OR* 42(2):682, 686–88, 690.

10 Grant to Parke, Humphreys to Willcox, and Willcox to Humphreys, all September 4, 1864; Humphreys to Hancock, September 5, 1864, *OR* 42(2):682, 689–90, 703; Thompson, *Engineer Battalion*, 84–85; John D. Bertolette to Joseph H. Barnes, September 5, 1864, Special Orders and Circulars, June–September 1864, RG393, NARA.

11 Circular, Headquarters, Second Corps, September 6, 1864; Humphreys to Warren, and Warren to Humphreys, both September 6, 1864, *OR* 42(2):722, 724.

12 Michler to Bowers, September 24, 1864, *OR* 42(1):164; Michler to Bowers, September 17, 1864, *OR* 51(1):274; September 10, 1864, Snook Diary, Mary-HS; *OR Atlas*, pl. 67, no. 9.

13 Herdegen and Murphy, *Four Years with the Iron Brigade*, 310; Michler to Bowers, September 24, 1864, *OR* 42(1):164; Hancock to Humphreys, September 11, 1864, *OR* 42(2):787.

14 Nevins, *Diary of Battle*, 461; William E. Potter to Thompson, August 26, 1864, Potter Letters, PNB; Humphreys to unknown, n.d., in Henry H. Humphreys, *Andrew Atkinson Humphreys*, 250; Tilney, *My Life in the Army*, 36; Buell, *"The Cannoneer,"* 244; Dale E. Floyd, *"Dear Friends at Home,"* 57; Record of Events, Company M, 50th New York Engineers, *Supplement to the Official Records*, 44(2):200; Delafield to Stanton, October 30, 1865, *OR*, ser. 3, 5:174. Maj. Wesley Brainerd worked three companies of the 50th New York Engineers for ten days to drain and lay corduroy on all the covered ways between Fort Sedgwick and the Norfolk and Petersburg Railroad. Lt. Francis Bacon used fifty-five men of the 50th New York Engineers to corduroy the military road linking Jerusalem Plank Road with Warren's headquarters at Globe Tavern. Along one mile of this road, Bacon built four bridges, each from 33 to 145 feet

long. Three of the bridges were 12 feet wide; the fourth was 24 feet wide. See Michler to Bowers, September 17, 1864, *OR* 51(1):275.

15 Humphreys to Morgan, September 3, 1864; Warren to Williams, September 5, 1864; Hancock to Humphreys, September 11, 1864; Special Orders No. 247, Headquarters, Army of the Potomac, September 12, 1864; Hancock to Williams, September 14, 1864; Williams to Parke, September 15, 1864; Humphreys to Gibbon, and Gibbon to Humphreys, both September 16, 1864; circular, Headquarters, Army of the Potomac, September 21, 1864; Hancock to Humphreys, and Humphreys to Hancock, both September 22, 1864, *OR* 42(2):676, 706, 788, 798, 822, 846, 872–73, 954–56, 966; Michler to Bowers, September 17, 1864, *OR* 51(1):276.

16 Meade to Grant, and Grant to Meade, both August 29, 1864, *OR* 42(2):564; Moore to McCallum, July 1, 1865, *OR*, ser. 3, 5:70; Bennett, "Grant's Railroad," 16–18; Horn, *Petersburg Campaign*, 171; Sylvester, "U.S. Military Railroad," 312–13; Grant to Meade, and Meade to Grant, both September 13, 1864, in Simon, *Papers of Ulysses S. Grant*, 12:161, 161n; Trudeau, *Siege of Petersburg*, 29; Nevins, *Diary of Battle*, 461.

17 Grant to Ord, August 30, 1864, in Simon, *Papers of Ulysses S. Grant*, 12:113; Michie to Barnard, September 18, October 10, 1864, *OR* 42(1):659–60; *OR Atlas*, pl. 67, no. 4; Delafield to Stanton, October 30, 1865, *OR*, ser. 3, 5:188.

18 Trudeau, *Last Citadel*, 193, 200.

19 Michler to Bowers, September 24, 1864, and Benham to Williams, November 19, 1864, *OR* 42(1):162–63, 213; Humphreys to Benham, September 19, 1864, and Benham to Humphreys, September 19, 1864. 4:00 P.M., *OR* 42(2):917–19; Michler to Bowers, September 17, 1864, *OR* 51(1):274; *OR Atlas*, pl. 93, no. 1; Thompson, *Engineer Battalion*, 86–87.

20 Thompson, *Engineer Battalion*, 84; Michler to Bowers, September 24, 1864, *OR* 42(1):163; *History of the Fifth Massachusetts Battery*, 919; Edgell to Wilson, September 18, 1864, and Hancock to Benyaurd, September 19, 1864, *OR* 42(2):902, 921.

21 De Trobriand to Hancock, September 22, 1864, *OR* 42(2):970; Thompson, *Engineer Battalion*, 86, 86n; Michler to Bowers, September 24, 1864, *OR* 42(1):163–64; Record of Events, Company M, 50th New York Engineers, *Supplement to the Official Records*, 44(2):200.

22 Hancock to Humphreys, September 11, 1864, *OR* 42(2):787; Michler to Bowers, September 24, 1864, *OR* 42(1):163.

23 James H. Lockwood to Robert McAllister, September 3, 1864, and Humphreys to Hancock, September 5, 14, 1864, *OR* 42(2):676, 703, 822; Michler to Bowers, September 17, 1864, *OR* 51(1):275; William Boston to Aunt Emma, September 10, 1864, Boston Papers, BHL-UM.

24 Billings, *History of the Tenth Massachusetts Battery*, 269–70.

25 Michler to Bowers, September 24, 1864, *OR* 42(1):163–64; Michler to Bowers, September 17, 1864, *OR* 51(1):274–75; Walker and Walker, "Diary of the War," 213.

26 Foster to Smith, September 1, 2, 1864; Terry to Smith, September 7, 1864; and Terry to Graves, September 20, 1864, *OR* 42(2):652, 673, 743, 950; Michie to Barnard, September 18, 1864, *OR* 42(1):659; Michler to Bowers, September 17, 1864, *OR* 51(1):274.

27 Birney to Williams, September 2, 1864; Meade to Grant, and Birney to Williams, both

September 12, 1864; Jackson to Graves, September 20, 1864, *OR* 42(2):672, 795, 802, 949–50.

28  Warren to Humphreys, September 10, 1864, and Hancock to Williams, September 24, 1864, *OR* 42(2):778, 993–94.

29  Wade Hampton to Lee, September 11, 1864, Johnston Family Papers, VHS; Hess, *Lee's Tar Heels*, 258; Sommers, *Richmond Redeemed*, 180; Greene, *Breaking the Backbone of the Rebellion*, 11.

30  Wade Hampton to Samuel R. Johnston, September 23, 1864, Johnston Family Papers, VHS; Sommers, *Richmond Redeemed*, 180, 245–46; Hess, *Lee's Tar Heels*, 258.

31  Sommers, *Richmond Redeemed*, 14–15; copy of Ewell to unknown addressee, November 4, 1864, Richard Stoddert Ewell Letterbook, pp. 15–16, Ewell Papers, SCL-DU.

32  Copy of Ewell to unknown addressee, November 4, 1864, Richard Stoddert Ewell Letterbook, p. 15, Ewell Papers, SCL-DU.

33  Dickinson, "Union and Confederate Engineering Operations at Chaffin's Bluff," 72, RNB; Gallagher, *Fighting for the Confederacy*, 474.

34  Coit, "Battle of the Crater," 128n; Birney to Williams, and A. C. Voris to Adrian Terry, both September 9, 1864, *OR* 42(2):765; Johnson to Brent, September 15, 1864, *OR* 42(1):891–92; Orr, "Archaeology of Trauma," 24–25; Whitney, "Petersburg," unpaginated, PNB; field visit to Petersburg Crater, October 14, 1999.

35  Johnson to Brent, September 24, 1864, *OR* 42(2):1287; C. B. Langley to E. H. Gill, September 15, 1864, Munford-Ellis Family Papers, SCL-DU.

36  Chamberlayne, *Ham Chamberlayne*, 267–68; General Orders, September 30, 1864, Headquarters, Artillery, Army of Northern Virginia, *OR* 42(2):1306–1307; same order in manuscript form in Order Book, June 17, 1862–April 2, 1865, Pendleton Papers, MC.

37  Dowdey and Manarin, *Wartime Papers of R. E. Lee*, 853–54; Lee to Seddon, September 20, 1864, and Special Orders No. 224, Adjutant and Inspector General's Office, September 21, 1864, *OR* 42(2):1260–61, 1268–69.

38  Blackford, "Memoirs," 464–65, LOV; Johnson to Brent, September 26, 1864, *OR* 42(1):896; Minor, "Record of the War," 3:34–35, Minor Family Papers, SC-UVA.

39  George H. Mills, *History of the 16th North Carolina*, 59, 63; Calkins undated memo, PNB; receipts for equipment, September 15, 30, 1864, J. J. Conway and John Bradford service records, 1st Confederate Engineers, M258, roll 92, RG109, NARA; Jackson, *First Regiment Engineer Troops*, 92; *OR atlas*, pl. 40, no. 1; Blackford, "Memoirs," 465, LOV; Hawkins, "Report, Results of Subsurface Investigation," 1–2, 4–5, PNB; Shepley to Butler, November 20, 1864, *OR* 42(3):673. I wish to thank Chris Calkins and Harry L. Jackson for supplying me with information, photographs, and maps of the Confederate countermine at Duval's House.

40  Johnson to Brent, September 16, 1864, *OR* 42(1):892; Meade to Grant, September 11, 1864, in Simon, *Papers of Ulysses S. Grant*, 12:153n; Birney to Williams, September 12, 1864, *OR* 42(2):802.

41  Fleet and Fuller, *Green Mount*, 336–37; Johnson to Brent, September 21, 1864, *OR* 42(1):895.

42  Fleet and Fuller, *Green Mount*, 336; September 3, 1864, Albright Diary, SHC-UNC.

43  Fleet and Fuller, *Green Mount*, 340.

44 Russell diary, September 16, 1864, in clipping of Petersburg *Progress-Index*, November 10, 1961, Russell Papers, SCL-DU.

45 George Breck to editor, n.d., *Rochester Union and Advertiser*, September 4, 1864; Winne Journal, 189–90, Trent Collection, MCL-DU.

46 Circular, Kirkland's Brigade, September 6, 1864, Confederate States of America Archives, Army Units, Army of Northern Virginia, SCL-DU.

47 Johnson to Brent, September 19, 1864, *OR* 42(1):893; Pendleton to Moseley, September 20, 1864, *OR* 42(2):1262–63; same letter is in Pendleton Papers, MC.

48 General Order, Headquarters, Artillery, Army of Northern Virginia, September 21, 1864, Pendleton Papers, MC.

49 Birney to Williams, September 18, 1864, *OR* 42(2):906; Allen, "Civil War Letters," 381.

50 General Orders No. 35, Headquarters, Second Corps, September 24, 1864, *OR* 42(2):996.

51 Bowen, "Diary of Captain George D. Bowen," 209–12.

52 Ibid., 210–11.

53 Lockley to unknown, September 28, 1864, in Pomfret, "Letters of Fred Lockley," 92–93; circular, September 27, 1864, and General Orders No. 36, Headquarters, Second Army Corps, September 27, 1864, *OR* 42(2):634–35, 1054–55.

54 Walker, *History of the Second Army Corps*, 607; Wilson to Mott, September 4, 1862; Special Orders No. 77, First Brigade, Third Division, Second Corps, September 9, 1864; circular, First Brigade, Third Division, Second Corps, September 9, 1864; Hancock to Willcox, September 9, 1864; and Mott to Wilson, September 10, 1864, *OR* 42(2):687, 761–62, 764, 777.

55 Silliker, *Rebel Yell*, 198; Walker, *History of the Second Army Corps*, 607; Horn, *Petersburg Campaign*, 196; Hancock to Humphreys, September 10, 1864, *OR* 42(2):774; Hastings, *Letters from a Sharpshooter*, 254, 255, 257.

56 Wingfield to unknown, n.d., in *Supplement to the Official Records*, 7(1):451; Lockwood to de Trobriand, September 12, 1864, and Hancock to Humphreys, September 11, 1864, *OR* 42(2):779, 787; Silliker, *Rebel Yell*, 199.

57 Greene, *Civil War Petersburg*, 211, 215; Smith to McGilvery, August 29, 1864, and Birney to Williams, September 18, 1864, *OR* 42(2):584, 906; Gallagher, *Fighting for the Confederacy*, 474.

CHAPTER TWELVE

1 Grant to Sherman, September 12, 1864, and Grant to Meade, September 27, 1864, in Simon, *Papers of Ulysses S. Grant*, 12:154, 222–23.

2 Sommers, *Richmond Redeemed*, 5, 7, 17–18, 21, 23, 182.

3 Ibid., 30, 32–38.

4 Dickinson, "Union and Confederate Engineering Operations at Chaffin's Bluff," 5, 7, 9, 11–17, 22–23, 35–55, RNB; Hess, *Field Armies and Fortifications*, 130–32, 238–39.

5 Richard S. Ewell to unknown, November 4, 1864, Richard Stoddert Ewell Letterbook, p. 16, Ewell Papers, SCL-DU; Sommers, *Richmond Redeemed*, 39, 41–45.

6 Clay, "Personal Narrative of the Capture of Fort Harrison," 5–9; Buckingham, *All's for the Best*, 131–32; Sommers, *Richmond Redeemed*, 46.

7   Dickinson, "Union and Confederate Engineering Operations at Chaffin's Bluff," 73, RNB; Sommers, *Richmond Redeemed*, 54–57, 59, 70; Richard S. Ewell to unknown, November 4, 1864, Richard Stoddert Ewell Letterbook, Ewell Papers, SCL-DU.

8   Johnston, "Attack on Fort Gilmer," 442; H. H. Perry, "Assault on Fort Gilmer," 414; September 29, 1864, Scroggs diary, *Civil War Times Illustrated* Collection, USAMHI; Sommers, *Richmond Redeemed*, 76, 82–83, 86.

9   Johnston, "Attack on Fort Gilmer," 442; DuBose to unknown, August 23, 1866, in *Supplement to the Official Records*, 7(1):464; Record of Events, Company K, 7th USCT, in *Supplement to the Official Records*, 77(2):408–9; May, "Fight at Fort Gilmer," 588; Sommers, *Richmond Redeemed*, 88–89, 91–92.

10   Grant to Meade and to Julia, both September 29, 1864, in Simon, *Papers of Ulysses S. Grant*, 12:240–41.

11   Serrell to Read, October 5, 1864, *OR* 42(1):675; Dickinson, "Union and Confederate Engineering Operations at Chaffin's Bluff," 102, 102n, 104–5, RNB; Record of Events, 1st New York Engineers, *Supplement to the Official Records*, 42(2):401.

12   Sommers, *Richmond Redeemed*, 94, 114–15.

13   Serrell to Read, October 5, 1864, *OR* 42(1):675–76; Dickinson, "Union and Confederate Engineering Operations at Chaffin's Bluff," 106–7, RNB; Sommers, *Richmond Redeemed*, 120, 122.

14   Sommers, *Richmond Redeemed*, 134, 136–37, 139–43.

15   Schiller, *Captain's War*, 151; A. M. McKethan to Thomas L. Clingman, October 3, 1864, Burgwyn Papers, NCDAH; memoir, Von Eberstein Papers, ECMC-ECU; Williams to Ma, October 2, 1864, Williams Letters, SHC-UNC; letter by unidentified officer in McKethan's brigade, Raleigh *Daily Confederate*, October 10, 1864; Sommers, *Richmond Redeemed*, 145–48.

16   Sommers, *Richmond Redeemed*, 206–7; Hess, *Lee's Tar Heels*, 261.

17   Nevins, *Diary of Battle*, 466–67; Sommers, *Richmond Redeemed*, 223, 253–55.

18   Nevins, *Diary of Battle*, 467–69; Hess, *Lee's Tar Heels*, 261.

19   Sommers, *Richmond Redeemed*, 288–305; Hess, *Lee's Tar Heels*, 262–63.

20   Heth to Palmer, n.d., in *Supplement to the Official Records*, 7(1):477; Sommers, *Richmond Redeemed*, 309, 315–16, 318; Hess, *Lee's Tar Heels*, 264–65.

21   Sommers, *Richmond Redeemed*, 327, 330, 332, 334–36; Hess, *Lee's Tar Heels*, 266–67.

22   Warren to Humphreys, October 1, 1864, 11:30 A.M., and Humphreys to Warren, October 1, 1864, 7:00 P.M., *OR* 42(3):18–19.

23   Sommers, *Richmond Redeemed*, 359–60, 378–81, 383–84, 388–89, 393–401, 405–6; Hess, *Lee's Tar Heels*, 267–69.

24   Sommers, *Richmond Redeemed*, 408–11.

25   Gallagher, *Fighting for the Confederacy*, 475; Sommers, *Richmond Redeemed*, 176, 416.

26   Michler to Bowers, October 8, 1864, *OR* 42(1):166–67; Delafield to Stanton, October 30, 1865, *OR*, ser. 3, 5:175; John D. Bertolette to N. B. McLaughlen, October 5, 1864, Special Orders and Circulars, June–September 1864, RG393, NARA; Thompson, *Engineer Battalion*, 88, 90–92.

27   Michler to Bowers, October 8, 1864, *OR* 42(1):167–68; Delafield to Stanton, October 30, 1865, *OR*, ser. 3, 5:175; Thompson, *Engineer Battalion*, 88.

28  Agassiz, *Meade's Headquarters*, 238, 240–41, 246–47.
29  Michler to Bowers, October 15, 22, 1864, *OR* 42(1):170, 172, 174; Delafield to Stanton, October 30, 1865, *OR*, ser. 3, 5:175; Thompson, *Engineer Battalion*, 88; Davis and Wiley, *Photographic History*, 2:1111; Bennett, "Grant's Railroad," 18.
30  Heth to Palmer, February 1, 1865, in *Supplement to the Official Records*, 7(1):479; Dunlop, *Lee's Sharpshooters*, 214–15; Hess, *Lee's Tar Heels*, 270.
31  Grant to Butler, October 1, 2, 1864, and Butler to Grant, October 2, 1864, in *Private and Official Correspondence of Gen. Benjamin F. Butler*, 5:208–11.
32  Horn, *Petersburg Campaign*, 157, 168.
33  Dickinson, "Union and Confederate Engineering Operations at Chaffin's Bluff," 106–7, RNB; Sommers, *Richmond Redeemed*, 173.
34  Dickinson, "Union and Confederate Engineering Operations at Chaffin's Bluff," 107–8, 111, RNB; Michie to Barnard, October 10, 25, 31, 1864, *OR* 42(1):663–64, 666.
35  Dickinson, "Union and Confederate Engineering Operations at Chaffin's Bluff," 111–12, RNB.
36  Michie to Barnard, October 25, 31, 1864, and Serrell to Read, October 5, 1864, *OR* 42(1):664, 667, 676; Dickinson, "Union and Confederate Engineering Operations at Chaffin's Bluff," 107, 121–25, RNB.
37  Dickinson, "Union and Confederate Engineering Operations at Chaffin's Bluff," 112–18, RNB; Michie to Barnard, October 25, 1864, and King to Barnard, January 2, 1865, *OR* 42(1):665, 673.
38  Michie to Barnard, October 31, 1864, *OR* 42(1):666; Frassanito, *Grant and Lee*, 317–18; Davis and Wiley, *Photographic History*, 2:1091–92; William C. Davis, *Death in the Trenches*, 134.
39  Polley, "Polley Lost a Foot," 570; Horn, *Petersburg Campaign*, 168–69; Laine and Penny, *Law's Alabama Brigade*, 306. Richard Sommers terms the Confederate attack of October 7 the first battle of the Darbytown Road and considers it part of the Fifth Offensive; see Sommers, *Richmond Redeemed*, 418–19.
40  Dickinson, "Union and Confederate Engineering Operations at Chaffin's Bluff," 106, RNB; Michie to Barnard, October 10, 25, 1864, *OR* 42(1):663–64; *OR Atlas*, pl. 100, no. 2.
41  Michie to Barnard, October 25, 31, 1864, *OR* 42(1):664, 666.
42  Michie to Barnard, October 10, 1864, *OR* 42(1):662; Delafield to Stanton, October 30, 1865, *OR*, ser. 3, 5:189; *OR Atlas*, pl. 67, no. 7; Record of Events, Company F, 1st New York Engineers, *Supplement to the Official Records*, 42(2):467; Sommers, *Richmond Redeemed*, 172, 168.
43  Michie to Barnard, October 10, 25, 31, 1864, *OR* 42(1):663–66; Delafield to Stanton, October 30, 1865, *OR*, ser. 3, 5:189–90.
44  Michie to Barnard, October 25, 31, November 3, 1864, *OR* 42(1):665–67.
45  *Guide to the Fortifications and Battlefields*, 17. Nathaniel Michler probably was the author of this guide to the battlefield around Petersburg, published in 1866.
46  Dickinson, "Union and Confederate Engineering Operations at Chaffin's Bluff," 74–78, RNB; Sommers, *Richmond Redeemed*, 173.
47  Dickinson, "Union and Confederate Engineering Operations at Chaffin's Bluff," 76–

77, 92, 94–95, RNB; Minor, "Record of the War," 3:45, Minor Family Papers, SC-UVA; Jackson, *First Regiment Engineer Troops*, 107.
48 Dickinson, "Union and Confederate Engineering Operations at Chaffin's Bluff," 77, RNB.
49 Ibid., 89, 92.
50 Gallagher, *Fighting for the Confederacy*, 486; Dickinson, "Union and Confederate Engineering Operations at Chaffin's Bluff," 81, RNB.
51 Gallagher, *Fighting for the Confederacy*, 486–87; Butler to Grant, October 13, 1864, in *Private and Official Correspondence of Gen. Benjamin F. Butler*, 5:259; Grant to Butler, October 13, 1864, in Simon, *Papers of Ulysses S. Grant*, vol. 12; Horn, *Petersburg Campaign*, 169–70; Laine and Penny, *Law's Alabama Brigade*, 308–11. Richard Sommers has termed the Union attack on October 13 the second battle of the Darbytown Road and classifies it as part of the Fifth Offensive. See Sommers, *Richmond Redeemed*, 419.
52 Minor, "Record of the War," 3:51, Minor Family Papers, SC-UVA; Hagood, *Memoirs of the War of Secession*, 309; Dickinson, "Union and Confederate Engineering Operations at Chaffin's Bluff," 81, 83, RNB; Laine and Penny, *Law's Alabama Brigade*, 312.
53 Gallagher, *Fighting for the Confederacy*, 486; Hagood, *Memoirs of the War of Secession*, 309–10; Dickinson, "Union and Confederate Engineering Operations at Chaffin's Bluff," 83–85, 99–100, RNB.
54 Dickinson, "Union and Confederate Engineering Operations at Chaffin's Bluff," 86–90, 93, RNB.
55 Ibid., 97–98.
56 Rains, "Torpedoes," 257–59; Hess, *Field Armies and Fortifications*, 87–90.
57 J. V. Bowles to sister, October 20, 1864, Bowles Family Papers, CWM; Rains to Seddon, November 18, 1864, OR 42(3):1219–21; Minor, "Record of the War," 3:58, Minor Family Papers, SC-UVA; Shepley, "Incidents of the Capture of Richmond," 19; Jackson, *First Regiment Engineer Troops*, 107; Dickinson, "Union and Confederate Engineering Operations at Chaffin's Bluff," 97–98, RNB; McEntee to Humphreys, November 13, 1864, and Babcock to Humphreys, November 18, 1864, OR 42(3):613, 645; Sommers, *Richmond Redeemed*, 470, 584; Basinger Reminiscences, 121, UGA. The Federals believed their opponents normally used condemned shells as torpedoes north of the James River. See King, *Torpedoes*, 15.
58 Minor, "Record of the War," 3:60, Minor Family Papers, SC-UVA.
59 McEntee to Bowers, October 20, 1864, OR 42(3):282; Rhea, *To the North Anna River*, 41.

CHAPTER THIRTEEN

1 Circular, Headquarters, Second Corps, October 13, 1864; Michler to Charles Morgan, October 21, 1864; and Warren to Crawford, October 31, 1864, OR 42(3):205, 294, 454; Michler to Bowers, October 22, 29, 1861, OR 42(1):173, 175; reprint of article from Springfield, Mass., *Republican*, in Raleigh *North Carolina Standard*, October 4, 1864.
2 Michie to Barnard, September 18, October 10, 25, November 3, 1864, OR 42(1): 659, 660, 663, 665, 667.

3 Grant to Butler, and Butler to Grant, both October 20, 1864, and General Orders No. 134, Headquarters, Department of Virginia and North Carolina, October 20, 1864, *OR* 42(3):285–86; Frassanito, *Grant and Lee*, 321.
4 Morton to mother, October 16, 1864, Morton Papers, VHS; Frassanito, *Grant and Lee*, 322–23; Davis and Wiley, *Photographic History*, 2:1092.
5 Grant to Meade, October 4, 1864; Meade to Grant, October 5, 1864; Comstock to Benham, October 4, 1864; and Grant to Butler, October 13, 1864, in Simon, *Papers of Ulysses S. Grant*, 12:276, 276n, 277n, 307; Grant to Meade, and Benham to Humphreys, both October 4, 1864, and Humphreys to Benham, October 24, 1864, *OR* 42(3):69, 72, 321.
6 Grant to Meade, October 14, 1864, and Benham to Humphreys, October 20, 25, 1864, *OR* 42(3):225, 284, 342–43; Benham to Humphreys, November 19, 1864, *OR* 42(1):213–14; "Lines of Entrenchment for defense of Camps at City Point, Va.," RG77, Z 407-2, NARA; Trudeau, *Last Citadel*, 287; Prince George Quadrant, U.S. Geological Survey map; Davis and Wiley, *Photographic History*, 2:107–80. The redoubt that anchors the Inner Line of the City Point defenses is well preserved in a city park at Appomattox Street and Fort Street (field visit to City Point, August 1995).
7 Dunlop, *Lee's Sharpshooters*, 219–20; Greene, *Breaking the Backbone of the Rebellion*, 98.
8 Barker to wife, October 27, 1864, Barker Papers, LOV.
9 Humphreys to David B. Birney, August 27, 1864, *OR* 42(2):551–52; Jackson, *First Regiment Engineer Troops*, 103–4. I have not been able to identify Captain Abercrombie or his unit. His name does not appear in the service records of the 1st or 2nd Confederate Engineers, the index of the *Confederate Veteran*, or the index of the *OR*. It is possible he was either an artillery or a staff officer, but there seems to be no way to readily and conclusively identify him.
10 Johnson to Brent, September 24, 1864, *OR* 42(2):1287; Jackson, *First Regiment Engineer Troops*, 106; Daniel, "H. H. Harris' Civil War Diary," pt. 2, 1855–56; October 7–17, 1864, Harris Diary, FSNMP.
11 Grant to Meade, Meade to Grant, and Meade to Hancock, all October 12, 1864, *OR* 42(3):176–77, 179; Michler to Bowers, October 15, 1864, *OR* 42(1):169–70; Hancock to Humphreys, October 12, 1864, and Hancock to Williams, Meade to Grant, and Hancock to Meade, all October 13, 1864, *OR* 42(3):179, 197–98, 204.
12 De Trobriand to Carncross, October 16, 18, 1864, *OR* 42(3):249, 265; Michler to Bowers, October 22, 1864, *OR* 42(1):173.
13 Michler to Bowers, October 22, 29, 1864, *OR* 42(1):173–74; Thompson, *Engineer Battalion*, 90; Hastings, *Letters from a Sharpshooter*, 264–65.
14 Morgan to Miles, October 23, 1864, and Meade to Grant, October 24, 1864, *OR* 42(3):312, 315.
15 Michler to Bowers, October 29, November 7, 1864; Michler to Barnard, November 14, 1864; Duane to Barnard, November 20, 1864; and Johnson to Otey, October 5, 1864, *OR* 42(1):174, 176–77, 179, 899; Thompson, *Engineer Battalion*, 91.
16 Dickinson, "Union and Confederate Engineering Operations at Chaffin's Bluff," 125–26, RNB.
17 Circular, Headquarters, Army of Northern Virginia, October 20, 1864, Confeder-

ate States of America Archives, Army Units, Army of Northern Virginia, SCL-DU; Power, *Lee's Miserables*, 214, 219, 223, 231.

18  Samuel to cousin, October 10, 1864, Kelley Papers, SCL-DU.
19  John Forrest Robinson memoirs, 75–76, *Confederate Veteran* Papers, SCL-DU; J. L. Cross to Hector McKethan, October 23, 1864, Clingman Papers, SHC-UNC.
20  Bowen, "Diary of Captain George D. Bowen," 212-13.
21  Biddle to Humphreys, October 7, 1864, in ibid., 104–5.
22  Buckingham, *All's for the Best*, 140–41.
23  Circular, Headquarters Second Corps, October 6, 1864, and de Trobriand to Finkelmeier, October 21, 1864, *OR* 42(3):93, 296.
24  Johnson to Palmer, October 9, 1864, *OR* 42(3):1143–44.
25  DeWitt Boyd Stone Jr., *Wandering to Glory*, 29; Fleet and Fuller, *Green Mount*, 343.
26  Meade, *Life and Letters*, 2:246.
27  Thompson, *Engineer Battalion*, 90; Grant to Halleck, October 18, 1864, in Simon, *Papers of Ulysses S. Grant*, 12:321; Barnard memorandum, October 15, 1864, *OR* 42(3):233–34.
28  Agassiz, *Meade's Headquarters*, 245–46.
29  Grant to Butler, October 20, 1864, in Simon, *Papers of Ulysses S. Grant*, 12:331.
30  Grant to Meade, October 24, 1864, in ibid., 343–44; Trudeau, *Last Citadel*, 220–23.
31  Walker, *History of the Second Army Corps*, 616–18; Trudeau, *Last Citadel*, 233–34.
32  Phillips and Parsegian, *Richard and Rhoda*, 51; Trudeau, *Last Citadel*, 227, 231; Horn, *Petersburg Campaign*, 177–78; Walker, *History of the Second Army Corps*, 618.
33  Walker, *History of the Second Army Corps*, 619–20; Trudeau, *Last Citadel*, 232; Horn, *Petersburg Campaign*, 178.
34  Reid-Green, *Letters Home*, 98; Walker, *History of the Second Army Corps*, 623–25, 636–37; Trudeau, *Last Citadel*, 242–44; Horn, *Petersburg Campaign*, 181–82.
35  Heth to Palmer, February 1, 1865, in *Supplement to the Official Records*, 7(1):479–82; Trudeau, *Last Citadel*, 236–37, 243, 245–46; Horn, *Petersburg Campaign*, 179.
36  Walker, *History of the Second Army Corps*, 627–31; Horn, *Petersburg Campaign*, 182–84.
37  Walker, *History of the Second Army Corps*, 631–33; Grant to Stanton and to Meade, both October 27, 1864, in Simon, *Papers of Ulysses S. Grant*, 12:351–52, 356–57; Trudeau, *Last Citadel*, 248–50.
38  Walker, *History of the Second Army Corps*, 635–36; Trudeau, *Last Citadel*, 250.
39  Trudeau, *Last Citadel*, 224–25, 229–30, 237–39; Horn, *Petersburg Campaign*, 177, 180.
40  Horn, *Petersburg Campaign*, 180; Trudeau, *Last Citadel*, 239–41.
41  Hagood, *Memoirs of the War of Secession*, 309; Trudeau, *Last Citadel*, 241; Horn, *Petersburg Campaign*, 181.
42  October 17–26, 1864, Harris Diary, FSNMP.
43  October 27, 1864, ibid.; Daniel, "H. H. Harris' Civil War Diary," pt. 2, 1857.
44  Grant to Butler, October 17, 1864, in Simon, *Papers of Ulysses S. Grant*, 12:356; October 28, 1864, Harris Diary, FSNMP; Daniel, "H. H. Harris' Civil War Diary," pt. 2, 1857; Trudeau, *Last Citadel*, 248.
45  Walker, *History of the Second Army Corps*, 637–38; Muffly, *Story of Our Regiment*, 50; Brightman, "Glory Enough," 145.

46 Muffly, *Story of Our Regiment*, 51; Brightman, "Glory Enough," 141–42, 144–46.
47 Johnson to McWillie, October 28, 1864, *OR* 42(1):906; Mackintosh, *"Dear Martha,"* 156; Cutchins, *Famous Command*, 157; Muffly, *Story of Our Regiment*, 51–52; Brightman, "Glory Enough," 146–47, 149. Fred Fleet of the 26th Virginia did not participate in the defense of Fort Crater but reported that the Federals called out "'friends'" as they approached the work. The division officer of the day was not a member of Goode's brigade and was probably unfamiliar with the way Goode handled the rotation of pickets. Fleet also reported that the Federals concealed their Spencer rifles beneath their overcoats to protect them from the rain. See Fleet and Fuller, *Green Mount*, 345–46.
48 Muffly, *Story of Our Regiment*, 52, 56; Brightman, "Glory Enough," 149–50, 152–53, 153n, 155.
49 Walker, *History of the Second Army Corps*, 638; Johnson to McWillie, and Wallace to Foote, both October 28, 1864, *OR* 42(1):906, 933.
50 Anderson to unknown, June 15, 1866, in *Supplement to the Official Records*, 7(1):818–19; Horn, *Petersburg Campaign*, 196.
51 Wallace to Foote, November 6, 1864, *OR* 42(1):933–34.
52 Greene, *Civil War Petersburg*, 3, 221.

CHAPTER FOURTEEN

1 General Orders No. 2, Headquarters, Sixth Corps, January 5, 1865, *OR* 46(2):43.
2 De Trobriand to Finkelmeier, November 6, 1864; Livermore to Carncross, November 14, 1864; and Parke to Williams, and Pennypacker to Lord, both December 3, 1864, *OR* 42(3):535, 617, 789–90, 792; Cutcheon to Hutchins, December 9, 1864, Special Orders and Circulars, June–September, 1864, RG393, NARA; Duane to Barnard, January 23, 1865, *OR* 46(1):157.
3 Duane to Barnard, November 20, 1864, *OR* 42(1):179; General Orders No. 39, Headquarters, 1st Division, Tenth Corps, November 4, 1864; Howell to Duane, December 5, 1864, and Meade's endorsement; Special Orders No. 330, Headquarters, Army of the Potomac, December 6, 1864; and Terry to Jourdan, December 12, 1864, *OR* 42(3):515, 810–11, 822, 983; John D. Bertolette to brigade commanders, November 4, 1864, Special Orders and Circulars, June–September 1864, RG393, NARA; Howell to Duane, January 4, 1865, *OR* 46(2):31.
4 Duane to Barnard, November 20, December 26, 1864, *OR* 42(1):179, 185; Record of Events, Company M, 50th New York Engineers, *Supplement to the Official Records*, 44(2):201–2; Duane to Barnard, January 23, 30, 1865, *OR* 46(1):157, 158.
5 Hopkins, *Seventh Regiment Rhode Island*, 240; Duane to Barnard, January 23, 1865, *OR* 46(1):158; *History of the Thirty-Fifth Regiment*, 321; Humphreys to Duane, December 8, 1864, *OR* 42(3):876.
6 Weitzel to Devens, November 20, 1864, *OR* 42(3):672; Duane to Barnard, November 20, 1864, *OR* 42(1):179; Record of events, Company K, 50th New York Engineers, *Supplement to the Official Records*, 44(2):194; General Orders No. 7, Headquarters, 1st Division, Sixth Corps, January 5, 1865, *OR* 46(2):43; Duane to Barnard, January 23, 1865, *OR* 46(1):157.

7 Duane to Barnard, January 23, 1865, *OR* 46(1):157; Nevins, *Diary of Battle*, 482.
8 Nevins, *Diary of Battle*, 482.
9 Michie to Barnard, November 27, 1864, *OR* 42(1):669-71; Delafield to Stanton, October 30, 1865, *OR*, ser. 3, 5:187.
10 Michie to Barnard, September 10, November 16, 20, December 5, 1864, *OR* 42(1):657-58, 669, 671-72; Delafield to Stanton, October 30, 1865, *OR*, ser. 3, 5:187. For photographs of the Dutch Gap Canal project, see Davis and Wiley, *Photographic History*, 2:1093-96. For plans and illustrations of it, see *OR* 42(1):670 and Grant, "General Grant on the Siege of Petersburg," 575.
11 King to Barnard, January 10, 1865, *OR* 46(1):377; Frassanito, *Grant and Lee*, 321, 323-24; Longacre, *Army of Amateurs*, 259.
12 Humphreys to Benham, November 5, 6, 1864; Benham to Humphreys, November 5, 6, 17, 1864; Williams to Benham, December 9, 1864; and Benham to Williams, December 9, 1864, *OR* 42(3):518-21, 531-32, 634-35, 897.
13 Duane to Barnard, November 20, 1864, January 3, 1865, and Michie to Barnard, December 5, 1864, *OR* 42(1):179, 185, 672; Duane to Barnard, January 23, February 27, 1865, *OR* 46(1):157-58, 162.
14 Moore to McCallum, July 1, 1865, *OR*, ser. 3, 5:71-72; Bennett, "Grant's Railroad," 18; Horn, *Petersburg Campaign*, 172.
15 Bradwell, "In Front of Fort Steadman," 408; Luther Rice Mills, "Letters from the Trenches," 283.
16 Williams, *Rebel Brothers*, 212-13; Gallagher, *Fighting for the Confederacy*, 500; Warren Goodale to children, January 28, 1865, Goodale Papers, Mass-HS; Osman Latrobe to Robert F. Hoke, November 7, 1864, Clingman Papers, SHC-UNC.
17 Day, "Life among Bullets," 217.
18 Jackson, *First Regiment Engineer Troops*, 121-22; George H. Mills, *History of the 16th North Carolina*, 59; Charles W. Trueheart to Henry M. Trueheart, January 29, 1865, in Williams, *Rebel Brothers*, 139-40; Featherstonhaugh, "Notes on the Defences of Petersburg," 194. There are remnants of two dams on one branch of Arthur's Swamp within the confines of Pamplin Historical Park, encompassing a section of the Boydton Plank Road Line, according to director A. Wilson Greene.
19 J. F. J. Caldwell, *History of a Brigade of South Carolinians*, 196; Brown to Chilton, November 5, 1864, *OR* 42(3):1202-3.
20 Lee to Seddon, December 11, 1864, *OR* 42(3):1267; Lacy to Seddon, December 17, 1864, and Turpin endorsement on Vest to Turpin, December 16, 1864, in Berlin, *Freedom*, 727-29.
21 Featherstonhaugh, "Notes on the Defences of Petersburg," 190-91, 193-94.
22 Eisenschiml, *Vermont General*, 269.
23 Michler to Bowers, November 7, 1864; Michler to Barnard, November 14, 1864; and Duane to Barnard, November 20, 1864, *OR* 42(1):176-79.
24 C. A. Stevens, *Berdan's United States Sharpshooters*, 497-98; Lapham, "With the Seventh Maine Battery," 155.
25 Parke to Duane, December 7, 1864, *OR* 42(3):857; Duane to Barnard, December 20, 1864, *OR* 42(1):183; "In the Trenches at Petersburg," 23.

26 Johnson to Shannon, November 21, 1864, *OR* 42(1):914.
27 Weitzel to Terry, November 4, 1864, *OR* 42(3):516; Michie to Barnard, November 16, 1864, *OR* 42(1):669; Delafield to Stanton, October 30, 1865, *OR*, ser. 3, 5:190.
28 Matthew Walton Venable, *Eighty Years After*, 47; M. W. Venable, "In the Trenches at Petersburg," 61; Minor, "Record of the War," 3:77–78, Minor Family Papers, SC-UVA; Jackson, *First Regiment Engineer Troops*, 115; Dickinson, "Union and Confederate Engineering Operations at Chaffin's Bluff," 93, 98–99, RNB. The Confederates constructed countermines at eight locations: Pegram's Salient (July 10 through August); Colquitt's Salient (July 10–August 3); Gracie's Salient (July 22–August 5); Cooke's Salient (July 31 to late September); Jerusalem Plank Road (about August 12 to December); Squirrel Level Road, toward Duval's House (September to about December); City Point Road (early August to late October); Elliott's Salient, north of the James River (late December, finished well before April 3). The Federals constructed countermines at eight locations: Batteries No. 4 and 5 (beginning July 23) and at Batteries No. 6, 7, and 8 (beginning July 25); Battery D, also known as Fort Morton (beginning August 5 or 21, according to differing sources); on the right of Willcox's division line, Ninth Corps (beginning about August 7); Fort Sedgwick (August 1 through November); Fort Stedman (beginning early August); Fort McGilvery (beginning first week of November to November 20); Fort Burnham, north of the James River (beginning second week of November).
29 G. W. Knight to Edward White, November 27, 1864, Clingman Papers, SHC-UNC.
30 Harmon, "Letters of Luther Rice Mills," 305, 306; Longstreet to Lee, December 27, 1864, *OR* 42(3):1324.
31 Fleet and Fuller, *Green Mount*, 346–47.
32 Greene, *Breaking the Backbone of the Rebellion*, 15, 18.
33 Ibid., 37; Rosenblatt and Rosenblatt, *Hard Marching Every Day*, 287; Robert Hunt Rhodes, *All for the Union*, 199, 200, 202.
34 Parke to Humphreys, and Humphreys to Parke, both November 28, 1864, *OR* 42(3):734, 735.
35 *History of the Thirty-Fifth Regiment*, 310; Beals, "In a Charge Near Fort Hell," 106–7.
36 Lapham, "With the Seventh Maine Battery," 151–53.
37 Ibid., 152–53.
38 *History of the Thirty-Fifth Regiment*, 322.
39 C. G. Heffron to C. Rath, November 18, 1864; Special Orders No. 329, Headquarters, Army of the Potomac, December 5, 1864; and extract of report of A. W. Nichols, division officer of the day, December 26, 1864, Special Orders and Circulars, June–September 1864, RG393, NARA.
40 Warner, *Generals in Gray*, 247–48; Parke to Williams, November 28, 1864; Wilcox to Grant, and Williams to Parke, both November 29, 1864; General Orders No. 44, Headquarters, Army of the Potomac, November 30, 1864; and Meade to Wilcox, November 30, 1864, *OR* 42(3):734, 739, 746–47, 752, 753.
41 General Orders No. 297, War Department, Adjutant General's Office, December 3, 1864, *OR* 42(3):791; *History of the Thirty-Sixth Regiment*, 277.
42 Stone to Uncle, December 7, 1864, Stone Letter, VHS; Loehr, *War History*, 54; William

Clifton Harvey journal, December 2–6, 1864, in *Supplement to the Official Records*, 7(1):458.
43   William Clifton Harvey journal, December 2, 1864, in *Supplement to the Official Records*, 7(1):458; DeWitt Boyd Stone Jr., *Wandering to Glory*, 213; Harmon, "Letters of Luther Rice Mills," 286; Williams, *Rebel Brothers*, 212–13.
44   Bradwell, "In Front of Fort Steadman," 408–9.
45   William Miller Owen, *In Camp and Battle*, 356; Anderson to unidentified, June 15, 1866, in *Supplement to the Official Records*, 7(1):819.
46   Johnson to Duncan, December 2, 1864, OR 42(1):918.
47   John Forrest Robinson memoirs, 74–75, *Confederate Veteran* Papers, SCL-DU; *History of the Thirty-Fifth Regiment*, 317–18.
48   J. F. J. Caldwell, *History of a Brigade of South Carolinians*, 195–96; Phillips to father and mother, January 1, 1865, Phillips Letters, Wisconsin Historical Society.
49   Horn, *Petersburg Campaign*, 197; Johnson to McWillie, November 6, 1864, OR 42(1):909–10; Grant to Halleck, Meade to Grant, Hancock to Williams, and Hancock to Humphreys, all November 6, 1864, OR 42(3):528, 529, 532, 533.
50   DeWitt Boyd Stone Jr., *Wandering to Glory*, 211.
51   Grant to Meade, November 5, 1864, OR 42(3):517; Grant to Butler and to Meade, both November 15, 1864, in Simon, *Papers of Ulysses S. Grant*, 12:421, 423; Michie to Barnard, November 21, 1864, OR 42(3):678–79.
52   Michie to Barnard, November 21, 1864, OR 42(3):679.
53   Grant to Meade, December 5, 1864, in Simon, *Papers of Ulysses S. Grant*, 13:64–65.
54   Oakes to J. S. Richardson, December 13, 1864, Oakes Letter, VMI; Jones to mother, December 3, 1864, Jones Papers, ECMC-ECU; Styple, *Our Noble Blood*, 170; Scott, *Forgotten Valor*, 594; Trudeau, *Last Citadel*, 264, 273, 276–77, 279, 283–85.

CHAPTER FIFTEEN

1   Fleet and Fuller, *Green Mount*, 338. For information on the winter spent in the trenches at Sebastopol, see Robins, *Captain Dunscombe's Diary*, 52–102; Bentley, *Russell's Despatches*, 150–73; and Royle, *Crimea*, 295–308.
2   Wingfield to unknown, n.d., in *Supplement to the Official Records*, 7(1):452; Cutchins, *Famous Command*, 157; Luther Rice Mills, "Letters from the Trenches," 284–85; Harmon, "Letters of Luther Rice Mills," 304; Fleet and Fuller, *Green Mount*, 347–48; Minor, "Record of the War," 3:76, Minor Family Papers, SC-UVA; Bowen, "Diary of Captain George D. Bowen," 214–15; Longacre, *Army of Amateurs*, 244.
3   Fred M. Colston to Sallie, December 10, 1864, Munford-Ellis Family Papers, SCL-DU.
4   Goodale to children, January 28, 1865, Goodale Papers, Mass-HS; Basinger Reminiscences, 111, UGA; Robert G. Evans, *16th Mississippi*, 292; Williams, *Rebel Brothers*, 140; Loehr, *War History*, 57.
5   James S. Wingard to Simon, September 9, 1864, Wingard Papers, SCL-DU; Bushrod R. Johnson to Vance, November 19, 1864, and Bettie Whittington to Vance, February 9, 1865, Vance Collection, NCDAH; Scales to Vance, October 19, 1864, Scales Papers, ECMC-ECU; Korn, *Pursuit to Appomattox*, 17.

6 Samuel to Cousin, October 10, 1864, Kelley Papers, SCL-DU; Fleet and Fuller, *Green Mount*, 340; McNair to father, December 2, 1864, McNair Letters, LOV; Hagood, *Memoirs of the War of Secession*, 310; J. W. Bone reminiscence, 40, 42–43, Shuford Collection, NCDAH.
7 *History of the Thirty-Fifth Regiment*, 311; Peck, *Recruit Before Petersburg*, 11–12; McBride, *In the Ranks*, 132; Page, *History of the Fourteenth Regiment*, 325.
8 Nevins, *Diary of Battle*, 484; Peck, *Recruit Before Petersburg*, 13–14; Robert Hunt Rhodes, *All for the Union*, 200; December 7, 1864, Smyth Diary, DPA.
9 Dunlop, *Lee's Sharpshooters*, 234–35.
10 Peck, *Recruit Before Petersburg*, 11–12; Page, *History of the Fourteenth Regiment*, 325; Seymour to brother, November 27, 1864, Seymour Letters, N-YHS; McBride, *In the Ranks*, 132–33; Charles W. Smith, "Lights and Shadows," 433; Robert Hunt Rhodes, *All for the Union*, 202.
11 John Forrest Robinson memoirs, 78, *Confederate Veteran* Papers, SCL-DU; Bradwell, "In Front of Fort Steadman," 409; Bradwell, "On Picket Duty," 303.
12 *History of the Thirty-Fifth Regiment*, 313; Bradwell, "In Front of Fort Steadman," 409; Hopkins, *Seventh Regiment Rhode Island*, 239–40; Pearce, *Diary of Captain Henry A. Chambers*, 240; Fleet and Fuller, *Green Mount*, 353.
13 John Bradley to father, November 8, 1864, Margaret Bradley Willard Papers, SCL-DU; Longacre, *From Antietam to Fort Fisher*, 214; Thompson, *Engineer Battalion*, 91; Tyler, *Recollections of the Civil War*, 319; N. W. Steedman to friend, January 9, 1865, Wingard Papers, SCL-DU.
14 Circular, Headquarters, First Corps, Army of Northern Virginia, October 24, 1864, Clingman Papers, SHC-UNC; Day, "Life among Bullets," 217; Elliott, *Southern Soldier Boy*, 28; Luther Rice Mills, "Letters from the Trenches," 289; J. F. J. Caldwell, *History of a Brigade of South Carolinians*, 197; Anderson to unknown, June 15, 1866, in *Supplement to the Official Records*, 7(1):818; November 23, 1864, Cooke Diary, VHS; General Orders No. 68, Headquarters, Army of Northern Virginia, November 18, 1864, roll 18, Talcott Family Papers, VHS.
15 Nevins, *Diary of Battle*, 482; *History of the Thirty-Sixth Regiment*, 277–78.
16 J. L. Cross to Hector McKethan, October 20, 1864; J. W. Fairfax to McKethan, November 18, 1864; James H. Lippitt to J. H. Taylor, November 26, 1864; B. T. Clark to C. W. Knight, November 27, 1864; C. W. Knight to Edward White, November 25, 27, 1864; and R. S. Gage to McKethan, November 27, 1864, Clingman Papers, SHC-UNC.
17 Will Biggs to Pat, November 12, 1864, Biggs Papers, SCL-DU; Charles Watts to doctor, December 18, 1864, Morris Papers, SCL-DU; S. D. George to John, December 31, 1864, Confederate States of America Archives, Miscellaneous Soldier Letters, SCL-DU.
18 John Forrest Robinson memoirs, 77–78, *Confederate Veteran* Papers, SCL-DU.
19 Jefferson Hedrick to Levina Frank, December 31, 1864, Frank Family Letters, SHC-UNC; Luther Rice Mills, "Letters from the Trenches," 289; Thomas Green Penn to Ma, January 4, 1865, Penn Papers, SCL-DU; Virgil S. Cavin to father, November 25, December 1, 1864; Cavin to brother, December 16, 1864; and Cavin to mother, December 25, 1864, Patterson-Cavin Family Papers, SCL-DU; Power, *Lee's Miserables*, 231, 259.
20 Hoyle to mother, November 12, 1864, Hoyle Papers, SHC-UNC; Barker to wife,

December 9, 1864, Barker Papers, LOV; circular, Headquarters, Battle's Brigade, March 4, 1865, Orders, Rodes's and Battle's Brigades, RG 109, NARA; January 10, 1865, Albright Diary, SHC-UNC.

21 Bradwell, "In Front of Fort Steadman," 409; J. F. J. Caldwell, *History of a Brigade of South Carolinians*, 197.

22 Pierce, "Civil War Letters," 172–73; Winne Journal, 191–94, Trent Collection, MCL-DU; Dana, *Recollections*, 252; Thompson, *Engineer Battalion*, 92; Allen, "Civil War Letters," 383; Longacre, *Army of Amateurs*, 244; Bowen, "Diary of Captain George D. Bowen," 215.

23 Lee to Seddon, January 19, 1865, and endorsements by Seddon, January 26, 1865, and Guerin, February 5, 1865, OR 46(2):1099–1100.

24 Stiles, *Four Years Under Marse Robert*, 311.

25 Walter Harrison to George E. Pickett, November 14, 1864, and Lee to Longstreet, January 19, 1865, Fairfax Papers, VHS.

26 General Orders No. 1, Headquarters, Second Army Corps, January 1, 1865, OR 46(2):6; various entries in December 1864 and January 1865, Bennage Diary, SC-EU.

27 J. F. J. Caldwell, *History of a Brigade of South Carolinians*, 197, 202.

28 Basinger Reminiscences, 121, UGA.

29 Olin to unknown, December 24, 1864, Olin Papers, Mass-HS; Styple, *Our Noble Blood*, 167.

30 Unidentified correspondent to father, March 8, 1865, Briggs Papers, SHC-UNC; Willis M. Parker to Peter Guerrant, December 6, 18, 1864, Guerrant Family Papers, VHS; Buckingham, *All's for the Best*, 121; Gibbon to wife, November 11, 1864, Gibbon Papers, Mary-HS.

31 Fleet and Fuller, *Green Mount*, 353.

32 R. P. Scarborough to cousin, January 31, 1865, Confederate Miscellany Collection, SC-EU.

33 John R. Forbes to aunt, November 30, 1864, Forbes Letters, CWM; Barker to wife, January 12, 1865, Barker Papers, LOV; Lapham, "With the Seventh Maine Battery," 156–57; McPherson, *Battle Cry of Freedom*, 821–24.

34 Unidentified correspondent to father, March 8, 1865, Briggs Papers, SHC-UNC; Edward Cook Barnes to mother, January 12, 1865, and Henry P. Fortson to Mrs. R. A. Barnes, February 27, 1865, Barnes Family Manuscripts, SC-UVA.

35 November 22, 1864, Cooke Diary, VHS.

36 February 10, March 15, 1865, Robert F. Davis Diary, Confederate Miscellany Collection, SC-EU.

37 *History of the Thirty-Fifth Regiment*, 325; Hopkins, *Seventh Regiment Rhode Island*, 239.

38 W. J. George, "Church Built, at Petersburg," 521–22; Korn, *Pursuit to Appomattox*, 22–23; *Guide to the Fortifications and Battlefields*, 18.

39 Bond and Coward, *South Carolinians*, 167; Wagstaff, *James A. Graham Papers*, 201, 205.

40 Luther Rice Mills, "Letters from the Trenches," 305–6; J. William Jones, "Morale of General Lee's Army," 201.

41 Duncan to Finegan, January 21, 1865, and eight officers of 9th Florida to Parker,

January 22, 1865, *OR* 46(2):1144–45, 1148; Hill to companion, February 25, 1865, Hill Papers, ECMC-ECU; Frazier to brother, February 28, 1865, Frazier Papers, ECMC-ECU.

42   Harmon, "Letters of Luther Rice Mills," 307; Lee to secretary of war, February 24, 1865, *OR* 46(2):1254.

43   Everett to Ma, March 16, 1865, Everett Papers, SC-EU.

44   Virgil S. Cavin to father and mother, January 15, 1865; Cavin to brother, January 26, 1865; Cavin to parents, February 18, 1865; Cavin to father, March 2, 1865; and Cavin to father, mother, and brother, March 21, 1865, Patterson-Cavin Family Papers, SCL-DU.

45   W. E. Leak to wife and children, January 30, 1865, Leak Letters, PNB.

46   Lang to Finegan, January 21, 1865, *OR* 46(2):1146–47; Frazier to brother, February 28, 1865, Frazier Papers, ECMC-ECU; Lapham, "With the Seventh Maine Battery," 155–56; Lowry to Fleet, January 19, 1865, *OR* 46(2):1143–44; Justice to Ann, March 15, 1865, Justice Papers, SC-EU; Jesse M. Frank to John Frank, February 22, 1865, Frank Family Letters, SHC-UNC.

47   Rutherford to wife, February 19, 1865, Rutherford Papers, SC-UVA.

48   Wright to Webb, February 18, 1865, and Webb's reply of the same date, *OR* 46(2):587; Grant to Stanton, March 3, 1865, and Stanton's reply of the same date, in Simon, *Papers of Ulysses S. Grant*, 14:88, 88n; John Forrest Robinson memoirs, 76, *Confederate Veteran* Papers, SCL-DU.

49   Johnson to Duncan, February 26, 1865, and Lee to Breckinridge, February 28, 1865, *OR* 46(2):1261, 1265.

50   Lee to Breckinridge, February 28, 1865, *OR* 46(2):1264–65; Longstreet to Walter H. Taylor, March 9, 21, 1865, Longstreet Letterbook, MC; Power, *Lee's Miserables*, 260; Trudeau, *Last Citadel*, 294; Horn, *Petersburg Campaign*, 217.

51   Lee to Seddon, January 27, 1865, *OR* 46(2):1143; General Orders No. 8, Headquarters, Army of Northern Virginia, March 27, 1865, in Dowdey and Manarin, *Wartime Papers of R. E. Lee*, 918; see also General Orders No. 8, *OR* 46(3):1357; Thomas Green Penn to Ma, March 2, 1865, Penn Papers, SCL-DU; Lee to Breckinridge, February 28, 1865, *OR* 46(2):1265; Frazier to brother, February 28, 1865, Frazier Papers, ECMC-ECU.

52   Davis to Lee, February 10, 1865, and General Orders No. 2, Headquarters, Armies of the Confederate States, February 11, 1865, *OR* 46(2):1228–30; Williams, *Rebel Brothers*, 143.

53   Lee to secretary of war, March 27, 1865, *OR* 46(3):1353.

54   Meade to Grant, December 13, 1864, in Simon, *Papers of Ulysses S. Grant*, 13:475.

55   Bradwell, "In Front of Fort Steadman," 409; Johnson to Duncan, February 27, 1865, *OR* 46(2):1264; Longacre, *From Antietam to Fort Fisher*, 215; Hopkins, *Seventh Regiment Rhode Island*, 239.

CHAPTER SIXTEEN

1   Grant to Stanton and to Meade, both February 4, 1865, and Grant to Halleck, February 5, 1865, in Simon, *Papers of Ulysses S. Grant*, 13:361, 365, 370; Trudeau, *Last Citadel*, 312.

2  Bowen, "Diary of Captain George D. Bowen," 216; Horn, *Petersburg Campaign*, 200-201; Trudeau, *Last Citadel*, 312-14.
3  Trudeau, *Last Citadel*, 315-16; Hess, *Lee's Tar Heels*, 284-85.
4  Grant to Halleck and to Meade, both February 5, 1865, in Simon, *Papers of Ulysses S. Grant*, 13:370, 372.
5  Trudeau, *Last Citadel*, 316-17.
6  William H. Stewart, "Hardships of Hatcher's Run," 336; Trudeau, *Last Citadel*, 317-20; Horn, *Petersburg Campaign*, 203, 206.
7  Meade to Grant, February 7, 1865, OR 46(2):447; Grant to Meade, February 6, 1865, in Simon, *Papers of Ulysses S. Grant*, 13:382; Trudeau, *Last Citadel*, 318; Horn, *Petersburg Campaign*, 203.
8  William H. Stewart, "Hardships of Hatcher's Run," 336-37; Grant to Meade, February 7, 1865, in Simon, *Papers of Ulysses S. Grant*, 13:387; Meade to Grant, February 7, 1865, OR 46(2):448; Hess, *Lee's Tar Heels*, 284.
9  Grant to Meade, Meade to Grant, Fred T. Locke to Crawford, and Crawford to [Warren], all February 7, 1865; Meade to Grant, and Warren to Webb, both February 8, 1865, OR 46(2):447-48, 461, 476, 487; Reid-Green, *Letters Home*, 108; Bowen, "Diary of Captain George D. Bowen," 217; Horn, *Petersburg Campaign*, 206; Trudeau, *Last Citadel*, 322-23.
10  Meade to Grant, and Carncross to Smyth and to Mott, all February 7, 1865, OR 46(2):448, 452, 453; Delafield to Stanton, October 30, 1865, OR, ser. 3, 5:178; Horn, *Petersburg Campaign*, 206; Trudeau, *Last Citadel*, 322.
11  Grant to Sheridan, February 8, 1865, in Simon, *Papers of Ulysses S. Grant*, 13:394; circular, Headquarters, Army of the Potomac, February 7, 1865, and Meade to Grant, February 8, 1865, OR 46(2):450, 476; Thompson, *Engineer Battalion*, 94; Duane to Barnard, February 13, 1865, OR 46(1):159-60; Malles, *Bridge Building in Wartime*, 250.
12  Duane to Barnard, February 13, 1865, OR 46(1):159; Thompson, *Engineer Battalion*, 94; circular, Headquarters, Second Corps, February 8, 1865; Carncross to Miles, February 9, 1865; and Carncross to commander of Third Division, Second Corps, February 13, 1865, OR 46(2):483-84, 500, 550.
13  Circular, Headquarters, First Division, Second Corps, February 10, 1865; circular, Headquarters, Third Division, Second Corps, February 11, 1865; Humphreys to Ruggles, February 13, 1865; and Special Orders No. 38, Headquarters, Second Corps, February 14, 1865, OR 46(2):517, 527-28, 549, 556; Fred C. Floyd, *History of the Fortieth (Mozart) Regiment*, 240.
14  Warren to Webb, February 8, 13, 14, 1865, OR 46(2):488, 550, 556; Delafield to Stanton, October 30, 1865, OR, ser. 3, 5:178; McBride, *In the Ranks*, 156.
15  Delafield to Stanton, October 30, 1865, OR, ser. 3, 5:178; *Guide to the Fortifications and Battlefields*, 18; Grant to Meade, February 6, 7, 1865, in Simon, *Papers of Ulysses S. Grant*, 13:382, 387.
16  Warren to Webb, February 9, 11, 1865, OR 46(2):501, 528; Michler to Barnard, March 20, 1865, OR 46(1):162-63; Thienel, *Mr. Lincoln's Bridge Builders*, 232.
17  Moore to McCallum, July 1, 1865, OR, ser. 3, 5:70-73; Duane to Barnard, February 13,

1865, *OR* 46(1):160; Horn, *Petersburg Campaign*, 172; Bennett, "Grant's Railroad," 14, 18–19.

18  Schuyler to Ruggles, March 3, 1865, *OR* 46(2):808; Conway Robinson Howard to James McHenry Howard, March 4, 1865, Howard Papers, VHS.

19  Humphreys to Duane, and Carncross to Miles, both February 1, 1865, and Humphreys to Duane, February 2, 1865, *OR* 46(2):344, 345, 354; Duane to Barnard, February 13, 20, 27, 1865, and Michler to Barnard, March 20, 1865, *OR* 46(1):160, 162, 163; Peck, *Recruit Before Petersburg*, 18.

20  Abbot, *Siege Artillery*, 135.

21  King to Barnard, January 10, 1865, and Michie to Barnard, March 14, 23, 1865, *OR* 46(1):376, 377.

22  King to Barnard, January 18, 1865, *OR* 46(1):377; Vezin to Heckman, January 31, 1865, *OR* 46(2):320.

23  Michie to Barnard, February 13, 21, 27, March 14, 23, 1865, and King to Barnard, February 19, 1865, *OR* 46(1):373–76, 379; *OR Atlas*, pl. 68, no. 8; Dickinson, "Union and Confederate Engineering Operations at Chaffin's Bluff," 127–28, RNB. There is a detailed sketch of the casemates at Fort Burnham in Delafield to Stanton, October 30, 1865, *OR*, ser. 3, 5:191–92.

24  Dickinson, "Union and Confederate Engineering Operations at Chaffin's Bluff," 127–28, RNB; Michie to Barnard, February 27, March 14, 1865, and King to Barnard, February 19, 1865, *OR* 46(1):374–76, 378–79. For a description and sketch of King's board loophole, see Delafield to Stanton, October 30, 1865, *OR*, ser. 3, 5:191–92.

25  Delafield to Stanton, October 30, 1865, *OR*, ser. 3, 5:191.

26  King to Barnard, February 19, 1865, and Michie to Barnard, March 14, 23, 1865, *OR* 46(1):376, 379.

27  Delafield to Stanton, October 30, 1865, *OR*, ser. 3, 5:193; Delafield to W. H. Pettes, February 16, 1865, M1113, RG 77, NARA; King to Barnard, January 10, 25, February 19, 1865, *OR* 46(1):376, 378, 379; Record of Events, Company M, 50th New York Engineers, *Supplement to the Official Records*, 44(2):202.

28  Morrison, *Memoirs of Henry Heth*, 193–94.

29  Longstreet to Lee, February 1, 10, 1865, and Lee to Longstreet, February 9, 1865: *OR* 46(2):1188–89, 1227, 1228. Longstreet to Lee, February 10, 1865, is also in Longstreet Letterbook, MC.

30  Latrobe to Lee, February 18, 1865; Latrobe to Charles W. Field and to Johnston, both March 4, 1865; Latrobe to Alexander, March 8, 9, 1865; and Latrobe to Lee, March 9, 1865, *OR* 46(2):241, 1280, 1281, 1293, 1296, 1297; Longstreet to Benning, February 2, 1865; Longstreet to Lee, March 20, 1865; and Longstreet to Johnston, March 28, 31, 1865, Longstreet Letterbook, MC; Dickinson, "Union and Confederate Engineering Operations at Chaffin's Bluff," 98, 100, RNB; Longstreet to Johnston, March 20, 1865, Johnston Family Papers, VHS; Longstreet to Johnston, March 28, 1865; Latrobe to Alexander, March 30, 1865; and Latrobe to Johnston, March 31, 1865, *OR* 46(3):1360–61, 1368–69; Peacock, "Georgian's View of War," 131.

31  Bradwell, "Holding the Lines at Petersburg," 457; *History of the Thirty-Fifth Regiment*, 323–24; Parke to Webb, and Tidball to Hunt, both February 21, 1865, *OR* 46(2):617.

32  Cutcheon to Lydig, February 22, 1865, *OR* 46(2):645.

33   Clendenin to brigade commanders and division officer of the day, April 1, 1865, *OR* 46(3):426–27; de Trobriand to Whittier, February 28, 1865, *OR* 46(2):730.
34   Johnson journal, March 15, 1865, and Anderson to unknown, June 15, 1866, in *Supplement to the Official Records*, 7(1):744, 819; Shaver, *History of the Sixtieth Alabama*, 61.
35   Day, "Life among Bullets," 218; Richard S. Ellis to brother, March 15, 21, 1865, Munford-Ellis Family Papers, SCL-DU.
36   Greene, *Breaking the Backbone of the Rebellion*, 66–68; Thompson, *Engineer Battalion*, 94.
37   King, *Torpedoes*, 69, 77; Bruce, *Lincoln and the Tools of War*, 226; J. C. Woodruff to G. W. Schramm, August 23, 1864; Woodruff to Edward S. Ritchie, August 26, 1864; and Woodruff to B. C. Pole, August 30, 1864, 1113, RG77, NARA.
38   Delafield to Stanton, October 31, 1865, *OR*, ser. 3, 5:187–88.
39   King, *Torpedoes*, 53–54, 56.
40   Ibid., 18; Grant to Stanton, February 28, 1865; Stanton to Secretary of the Treasury, March 3, 1865; Grant endorsement on report by board of officers, March 22, 1865; Shaffner to Grant, March 28, 1865; Shaffner to Johnson, April 9, 1865; and Grant endorsement, April 10, 1865, in Simon, *Papers of Ulysses S. Grant*, 14:70–71, 71n, 72n, 73n.
41   King, *Torpedoes*, 58, 89.
42   Love, "Company Records," 51.
43   "Confederate Airship," 304–5; Bond and Coward, *South Carolinians*, 168; Lokey, "Battle Near Deep Bottom," 127–28; Peacock, "Georgian's View of War," 132.
44   "Confederate Airship," 305; Peacock, "Georgian's View of War," 132.
45   Lokey, "Battle Near Deep Bottom," 128; Lowe and Hodges, *Letters to Amanda*, 187–88; Doyle, "Flying Bird of 1864," 438; Richmond *Daily Dispatch*, March 7, 1865; Peacock, "Georgian's View of War," 133.
46   Thomas R. Evans, "Tells Story of Flying Machine," 303.
47   Muster rolls, October 1861 through September 1864; Edward W. Serrell to Thomas W. Sherman, December 4, 1861; Serrell to S. H. Pelouze, December 6, 1861; charges and specifications, December 25, 1861, July 29, 1862; Serrell to Henry W. Benham, April 21, 1862; Alfred Sears to James G. Halpine, July 18, 1862; Horatio G. Wright to Serrell, July 7, 1862; Quincy A. Gillmore to Serrell, January 7, 1864; and Edward W. Serrell service record, 1st New York Engineers, RG94, NARA.
48   J. D. Kurtz to Edward W. Serrell, May 8, 1863, M1113, RG77, NARA; Serrell to Benjamin Butler, September 26, 1864; muster rolls, July 1864 through March 1865; copy of Special orders No. 363, Headquarters, Army of the James, November 21, 1864; Serrell to Adjutant General, U.S.A., February 3, March 17, 1865; and Edward W. Serrell service record, 1st New York Engineers, RG94, NARA.
49   J. D. Kurtz to Mr. Towers, July 13, 1863; J. C. Woodruff to Edward Tilghman, Major Ayers to Dexter Hathaway, and J. C. Woodruff to E. H. M. Sugg and to J. H. Reuter, all August 18, 1864; and Richard Delafield to Edward W. Serrell, May 14, 1865, M1113, RG77, NARA; Bruce, *Lincoln and the Tools of War*, 137.
50   Bruce, *Lincoln and the Tools of War*, 229, 237–38, 243–44; Halsted to Foster, January 15, 1865, *OR* 47(2):58.

51 Bruce, *Lincoln and the Tools of War*, 122, 283, 292; Lowe, *Meade's Army*, 300; Halsted to Foster, January 15, 1865, *OR* 47(2):58.

CHAPTER SEVENTEEN

1 Grant to Meade and to Sheridan, both February 20, 1865, in Simon, *Papers of Ulysses S. Grant*, 13:454–55, 457–58.
2 Grant to Ord, February 24, 1865, in ibid., 14:33–34; Duane to Meade, March 3, 1865, and Meade's endorsement, *OR* 46(2):805.
3 Grant to Meade, March 3, 1865; Grant to father, March 19, 1865; and Grant to Sherman, March 22, 1865, in Simon, *Papers of Ulysses S. Grant*, 14:94–95, 187, 202–3.
4 Grant to Meade, March 24, 1865, in ibid., 211–14; Horn, *Petersburg Campaign*, 213.
5 General Orders No. 1, Headquarters, Confederate Army, February 9, 1865; Lee to Longstreet, February 22, 1865; and Lee to Breckinridge, March 9, 1865, *OR* 46(2):1226–27, 1250–51, 1295.
6 Lee to Davis, March 26, 1865, in Freeman, *Lee's Dispatches*, 342–43; Horn, *Petersburg Campaign*, 211–13.
7 Lee to Davis, March 26, 1865, in Freeman, *Lee's Dispatches*, 343–44.
8 Delafield to Stanton, October 30, 1865, *OR*, ser. 3, 5:178; Hodgkins, *Battle of Fort Stedman*, 12; Bradwell, "Fort Steadman and Subsequent Events," 20.
9 Meade to Hancock, October 21, 1864, and Hancock to Meade, October 22, 1864, *OR* 42(3):294, 303.
10 Hodgkins, *Battle of Fort Stedman*, 13–15; Scott, *Forgotten Valor*, 630; March 25, 1864, Boston Diary, Boston Papers, BHL-UM.
11 Hodgkins, *Battle of Fort Stedman*, 10–11, 15–16; Abbot to Delafield, April 25, 1865, *OR* 46(1):173; Carson, "Fort Steadman's Fall," 461; manuscript map showing Federal unit positions from the Appomattox River to the Weldon Railroad, late March 1865, G186-4, Map Collection, RG77, NARA; Davis and Wiley, *Photographic History*, 2:1130–32.
12 Hodgkins, *Battle of Fort Stedman*, 9–11, 15–16; field visit to Fort Stedman, July 7, 1994.
13 Hodgkins, *Battle of Fort Stedman*, 10; Scott, *Forgotten Valor*, 634–35; Kilmer, "Gordon's Attack at Fort Stedman," 581.
14 Trudeau, *Last Citadel*, 335–37.
15 Willie Walker Caldwell, *Stonewall Jim*, 123, 125; Carson, "Fort Steadman's Fall," 461; Hodgkins, *Battle of Fort Stedman*, 23.
16 Willie Walker Caldwell, *Stonewall Jim*, 125; Carson, "Fort Steadman's Fall," 461–62.
17 R. D. Funkhouser account, 133, Musick Collection, USAMHI; Hodgkins, *Battle of Fort Stedman*, 23–26; Carson, "Fort Steadman's Fall," 461–62; Willie Walker Caldwell, *Stonewall Jim*, 126; Kilmer, "Gordon's Attack at Fort Stedman," 580; Abbot to Delafield, April 25, 1865, *OR* 46(1):173.
18 Kilmer, "Gordon's Attack at Fort Stedman," 580–82; Hodgkins, *Battle of Fort Stedman*, 39; John C. Tidball to Orlando B. Willcox, April 30, 1890, and Willcox to Tidball, May 6, 1890, in Scott, *Forgotten Valor*, 628, 630; photograph of Fort Haskell, taken in the late 1930s, in 1939 World's Fair Photograph Collection, LOV.
19 Abbot, *Siege Artillery*, 127; Abbot to Delafield, April 25, 1865, *OR* 46(1):173; Gordon to

Taylor, April 11, 1865, in *Supplement to the Official Records*, 7(1):794–95; Lee to Davis, March 26, 1865, in Freeman, *Lee's Dispatches*, 344–45.

20  R. D. Funkhouser account, 132, Musick Collection, USAMHI; Abbot to Delafield, April 25, 1865, *OR* 46(1):173; Scott, *Forgotten Valor*, 634–35; Case, "Personal Recollections," 163; Willie Walker Caldwell, *Stonewall Jim*, 127.

21  Willie Walker Caldwell, *Stonewall Jim*, 127; Hodgkins, *Battle of Fort Stedman*, 13; Scott, *Forgotten Valor*, 618, 628–29, 633–35.

22  Hartranft, "Recapture of Fort Stedman," 587–88; Scott, *Forgotten Valor*, 630–31.

23  Hartranft, "Recapture of Fort Stedman," 588–89; Hodgkins, *Battle of Fort Stedman*, 41.

24  Willie Walker Caldwell, *Stonewall Jim*, 128; Hartranft, "Recapture of Fort Stedman," 588–89; Scott, *Forgotten Valor*, 631; Hodgkins, *Battle of Fort Stedman*, 43; Horn, *Petersburg Campaign*, 215; Abbot to Delafield, April 25, 1865, *OR* 46(1):173.

25  Stevens to mother, March 26, 1865, Stevens Papers, LC; J. F. J. Caldwell, *History of a Brigade of South Carolinians*, 202–5; Bowen, "Diary of Captain George D. Bowen," 220; Horn, *Petersburg Campaign*, 216; Greene, *Breaking the Backbone of the Rebellion*, 162–69, 174, 181–83; Horn, *Petersburg Campaign*, 214–16.

26  Lee to Davis, March 26, 1865, in Freeman, *Lee's Dispatches*, 345–46.

27  March 25, 1865, Boston Diary, Boston Papers, BHL-UM; Nevins, *Diary of Battle*, 504.

28  William Miller Owen, "Artillery Defenders of Fort Gregg," 66–68; Greene, *Breaking the Backbone of the Rebellion*, 385; Jackson, *First Regiment Engineer Troops*, 130–31.

29  Dunlop, *Lee's Sharpshooters*, 250–54; Greene, *Breaking the Backbone of the Rebellion*, 201–5.

30  Bearss and Calkins, *Battle of Five Forks*, 8–9, 121. Edward Porter Alexander estimated that Lee had available, on average, 1,300 men per mile by late March; see Gallagher, *Fighting for the Confederacy*, 510.

31  Horn, *Petersburg Campaign*, 219–20.

32  Grant to Sheridan, March 28, 1865, in Simon, *Papers of Ulysses S. Grant*, 14:243–44.

33  Spaulding to Duane, June 14, 1865, and Harwood to Clapp, April 19, 1865, *OR* 46(1):642–43, 650; Greene, *Breaking the Backbone of the Rebellion*, 211–12; Horn, *Petersburg Campaign*, 213, 219–20.

34  Greene, *Breaking the Backbone of the Rebellion*, 213–15.

35  Ibid.

36  Bearss and Calkins, *Battle of Five Forks*, 124; Benson, *Berry Benson's Civil War Book*, 180; Greene, *Breaking the Backbone of the Rebellion*, 215–16, 218, 220; Hess, *Lee's Tar Heels*, 290; Grant to Sheridan, March 29, 1865, in Simon, *Papers of Ulysses S. Grant*, 14:253–54.

37  Pickett to Taylor, May 1, 1865, in *Supplement to the Official Records*, 7(1):779–80; Greene, *Breaking the Backbone of the Rebellion*, 220.

38  Greene, *Breaking the Backbone of the Rebellion*, 218, 221, 223.

39  Michie to Ord, May 12, 1865, *OR* 46(1):1165; Delafield to Stanton, October 30, 1865, *OR*, ser. 3, 5:194.

40  Grant to Meade and to Sheridan, both March 30, 1865, in Simon, *Papers of Ulysses S. Grant*, 14:260, 270.

41  Benson, *Berry Benson's Civil War Book*, 180; Dunlop, *Lee's Sharpshooters*, 258–59;

Hunton testimony, June 17, 1880, Warren Court of Inquiry, *Supplement to the Official Records*, 8(1):625; field visit to White Oak Road Line, July 8-9, 1994.
42  Greene, *Breaking the Backbone of the Rebellion*, 226-27.
43  J. F. J. Caldwell, *History of a Brigade of South Carolinians*, 209-12; Greene, *Breaking the Backbone of the Rebellion*, 227-28.
44  J. F. J. Caldwell, *History of a Brigade of South Carolinians*, 212; Hunton testimony, June 17, 1880, Warren Court of Inquiry, *Supplement to the Official Records*, 8(1):625; Bearss and Calkins, *Battle of Five Forks*, 66, 71-72.
45  Bearss and Calkins, *Battle of Five Forks*, 66-68.
46  Pickett to Taylor, May 1, 1865, in *Supplement to the Official Records*, 7(1):780-81; Greene, *Breaking the Backbone of the Rebellion*, 229-33.
47  Grant to Sheridan, March 31, 1865, in Simon, *Papers of Ulysses S. Grant*, 14:289.
48  Pickett to Taylor, May 1, 1865, in *Supplement to the Official Records*, 7(1):781; Bearss and Calkins, *Battle of Five Forks*, 76.
49  Delafield to Stanton, October 30, 1865, *OR*, ser. 3, 5:179; Greene, *Breaking the Backbone of the Rebellion*, 235-38.
50  Greene, *Breaking the Backbone of the Rebellion*, 237-38; Bearss and Calkins, *Battle of Five Forks*, 77-78, 93.
51  Cotton testimony, May 17, 1880; LaMotte testimony, May 25, 1880; Wood testimony, June 1, 1880; and Gilliam testimony, June 29, 1880, Warren Court of Inquiry, *Supplement to the Official Records*, 8(1):239, 374, 486, 681; Birdseye testimony, October 8, 1880, and Gillespie testimony, October 13, 1880, Warren Court of Inquiry, *Supplement to the Official Records*, 9(1):889, 951; manuscript map of battle of Five Forks, G172, Map Collection, RG77, NARA; field visit to Five Forks, July 8-9, 1994.
52  Bearss and Calkins, *Battle of Five Forks*, 84-85.
53  Chamberlain, *Passing of the Armies*, 158-60; Bearss and Calkins, *Battle of Five Forks*, 74, 86-87, 89-92; Greene, *Breaking the Backbone of the Rebellion*, 238-41.
54  Bearss and Calkins, *Battle of Five Forks*, 81-82, 92.
55  Ibid., 92-96.
56  Ibid., 96-101; Greene, *Breaking the Backbone of the Rebellion*, 239.
57  Bearss and Calkins, *Battle of Five Forks*, 104-7.
58  Ibid., 82, 101-4, 107-9; Greene, *Breaking the Backbone of the Rebellion*, 239-41.
59  Bearss and Calkins, *Battle of Five Forks*, 109-10, 113; Greene, *Breaking the Backbone of the Rebellion*, 241.
60  Bearss and Calkins, *Battle of Five Forks*, 111-12; Greene, *Breaking the Backbone of the Rebellion*, 241.

CHAPTER EIGHTEEN

1  Grant to Meade, April 1, 9:05 P.M., and April 1, 1865; Grant to Ord, April 1, 8:55 P.M., and April 1, 1865, in Simon, *Papers of Ulysses S. Grant*, 14:298-99, 302-3; Grant, *Personal Memoirs*, 2:703; Lowe, *Meade's Army*, 356; Wright to Webb, April 1, 1865, *OR* 46(3):422-23; Horn, *Petersburg Campaign*, 240; Porter, "Five Forks," 715-16.
2  Grant to Sheridan, April 1, 1865, and Grant to Meade, April 2, 1865, in Simon, *Papers of Ulysses S. Grant*, 14:306, 313; Greene, *Breaking the Backbone of the Rebellion*, 269-71.
3  Grant to Meade, April 2, 1865, in Simon, *Papers of Ulysses S. Grant*, 14:313; Greene,

*Breaking the Backbone of the Rebellion*, 443, 447; field visit to Jerusalem Plank Road, July 7, 1994.
4  Gordon to Taylor, April 11, 1865, in *Supplement to the Official Records*, 7(1):795; Cowper, *Extracts of Letters*, 104–5, 108–9; Greene, *Breaking the Backbone of the Rebellion*, 443.
5  Grimes to Moore, November 5, 1879, in Cowper, *Extracts of Letters*, 105; Rast, "Fort Mahone and Other Struggles," 355.
6  Circular, Headquarters, Ninth Corps, April 1, 1865, OR 46(3):429; Beals, "In a Charge Near Fort Hell," 107–9; Huyette Reminiscences, 11, N-YHS; Greene, *Breaking the Backbone of the Rebellion*, 445.
7  Thomas M. Cook article in *New York Herald*, reprinted in John Robertson, *Michigan in the War*, 550; Beals, "In a Charge Near Fort Hell," 109–12; Greene, *Breaking the Backbone of the Rebellion*, 446.
8  Huyette Reminiscences, 12–13, N-YHS; Greene, *Breaking the Backbone of the Rebellion*, 447–48.
9  Rast, "Fort Mahone and Other Struggles," 355–56.
10 Osborne, "Struggle for Fort Mahone," 226–27; Frassanito, *Grant and Lee*, 346–48, 351–53, 358, 371.
11 Culver, "Entered and Escaped from Fort Mahone," 368; Phillips to Duane, April 21, 1865, OR 46(1):659; Greene, *Breaking the Backbone of the Rebellion*, 446.
12 Osborne, "Struggle for Fort Mahone," 228–29.
13 Gordon to Taylor, April 11, 1865, in *Supplement to the Official Records*, 7(1):796; Osborne, "Struggle for Fort Mahone," 229; Cowper, *Extracts of Letters*, 105–6; Devereux, "From Petersburg to Appomattox," 258; Greene, *Breaking the Backbone of the Rebellion*, 448.
14 Huyette Reminiscences, 13, N-YHS; Greene, *Breaking the Backbone of the Rebellion*, 448–50.
15 Cowper, *Extracts of Letters*, 108; Gordon to Taylor, April 11, 1865, in *Supplement to the Official Records*, 7(1):796; April 2, 1865, Beddall Diary, Civil War Miscellaneous Collection, USAMHI; Huyette Reminiscences, 14, N-YHS; Grant, *Personal Memoirs*, 2:704; Greene, *Breaking the Backbone of the Rebellion*, 450; *Guide to the Fortifications and Battlefields*, 15.
16 Meade to Wright, and Wright to Webb, both April 1, 1865, OR 46(3):422–23.
17 Hazard Stevens, "Storming of the Lines of Petersburg," 417; L. A. Grant to George W. Getty, January 5, 1884, Stevens Papers, LC; Greene, *Breaking the Backbone of the Rebellion*, 257.
18 Hazard Stevens, "Storming of the Lines of Petersburg," 417–18; L. A. Grant to George W. Getty, December 31, 1883, Stevens Papers, LC; Greene, *Breaking the Backbone of the Rebellion*, 260–61; field visit, July 8, 1994. This section of the Boydton Plank Road Line is exceptionally well preserved and interpreted in the Pamplin Historical Park.
19 Hazard Stevens, "Storming of the Lines of Petersburg," 418–19; L. A. Grant to George W. Getty, December 31, 1883, Stevens Papers, LC; Greene, *Breaking the Backbone of the Rebellion*, 261, 282–83.
20 Orders, Headquarters, Sixth Corps, April 1, 1865; confidential orders, Headquarters, First Division, Sixth Corps, April 1, 1865; and Whittelsey to division commanders

and commander of artillery brigade, April 1, 1865, *OR* 46(3):423–25; Hazard Stevens, "Storming of the Lines of Petersburg," 419–22; Greene, *Breaking the Backbone of the Rebellion*, 265–67, 275–81.

21  Greene, *Breaking the Backbone of the Rebellion*, 271, 273–74.
22  Hazard Stevens, "Storming of the Lines of Petersburg," 423–24; Greene, *Breaking the Backbone of the Rebellion*, 292, 295, 297, 300.
23  Robert Hunt Rhodes, *All for the Union*, 225–26; Greene, *Breaking the Backbone of the Rebellion*, 305–6, 321.
24  Greene, *Breaking the Backbone of the Rebellion*, 324, 352–57, 360.
25  Michie to Ord, May 12, 1865, *OR* 46(1):1165; Greene, *Breaking the Backbone of the Rebellion*, 361–62, 387, 389, 424.
26  Reily, "Fort Gregg," Civil War Miscellaneous Collection, USAMHI; Conerly, "How Fort Gregg Was Defended," 505; Greene, *Breaking the Backbone of the Rebellion*, 364, 384, 391–92.
27  Jones to Nathaniel H. Harris, April 12, 1878, Jones Family Papers, MDAH; A. K. Jones, "Battle of Fort Gregg," 57; Harris, "Defence of Battery Gregg," 477; Reily, "Fort Gregg," Civil War Miscellaneous Collection, USAMHI; Greene, *Breaking the Backbone of the Rebellion*, 386–87.
28  Harris, "Defence of Battery Gregg," 477, 483–84; A. K. Jones, "Battle of Fort Gregg," 58; Wilcox, "Defence of Batteries Gregg and Whitworth," 28; Buckingham, *All's for the Best*, 161–62; Strother, "Battle and Capture of Fort Gregg," 426; Conerly, "How Fort Gregg Was Defended," 505; Greene, *Breaking the Backbone of the Rebellion*, 386, 391, 399. Fort Gregg is well preserved; one can easily observe the raised gun platforms, the ditch and parapet, and the short connecting line to its right. Fort Whitworth is currently used as a recreational facility for a state hospital and is badly eroded due to heavy use of the park facilities (field visit, July 7, 1994).
29  A. K. Jones, "Battle of Fort Gregg," 58; Harris, "Defence of Battery Gregg," 483; Hewitt, *History of the Twelfth West Virginia*, 206; Mushkat, *Citizen-Soldier's Civil War*, 252; Greene, *Breaking the Backbone of the Rebellion*, 393–94.
30  Greene, *Breaking the Backbone of the Rebellion*, 396–99; Longacre, *Army of Amateurs*, 295–96.
31  Conerly, "How Fort Gregg Was Defended," 506; Hewitt, *History of the Twelfth West Virginia*, 207. Capt. Jones of the 12th Mississippi later argued that there were no stones or bricks inside Fort Gregg to be thrown. See Jones to Nathaniel H. Harris, April 12, 1878, Jones Family Papers, MDAH.
32  William Miller Owen, "Artillery Defenders of Fort Gregg," 70; Hewitt, *History of the Twelfth West Virginia*, 207–8; Conerly, "How Fort Gregg Was Defended," 506; Jones to Nathaniel H. Harris, April 12, 1878, Jones Family Papers, MDAH; Greene, *Breaking the Backbone of the Rebellion*, 399–402.
33  Harris, "Defence of Battery Gregg," 478; Greene, *Breaking the Backbone of the Rebellion*, 398, 403–5.
34  April 2, 1865, Cooke Diary, VHS; Longstreet to Taylor, April 11, 1865, in *Supplement to the Official Records*, 7(1):775–76; Greene, *Breaking the Backbone of the Rebellion*, 407–8, 421–29.

35 Jones to Nathaniel H. Harris, April 12, 1878, Jones Family Papers, MDAH; Barnard to wife, April 2, 1865, Barnard Papers, SCL-DU; Buckingham, *All's for the Best*, 161–62.

36 Michie to Ord, May 12, 1865, *OR* 46(1):1166; Greene, *Breaking the Backbone of the Rebellion*, 406. Grant later asserted that the Federals constructed a continuous, fortified line from river to river, above and below Petersburg, on the night of April 2. It is true that the Sixth and Twenty-Fourth Corps dug in continuously from the river to Boydton Plank Road, but the ground between that road and the preexisting Union defenses was not covered. See Grant, *Personal Memoirs*, 2:706.

37 Entry of April 2, 1865, in Bowen, "Diary of Captain George D. Bowen," 221; Greene, *Breaking the Backbone of the Rebellion*, 430.

38 Greene, *Breaking the Backbone of the Rebellion*, 430–33.

39 Heth to Palmer, April 11, 1865, in *Supplement to the Official Records*, 7(1):811; Hess, *Lee's Tar Heels*, 295; Dunlop, *Lee's Sharpshooters*, 274; J. F. J. Caldwell, *History of a Brigade of South Carolinians*, 219; Cooke to unidentified, April 11, 1865, in *Supplement to the Official Records*, 7(1):814; Greene, *Breaking the Backbone of the Rebellion*, 433–34; field visit to Sutherland Station, October 15, 1999.

40 J. F. J. Caldwell, *History of a Brigade of South Carolinians*, 220–21; Hess, *Lee's Tar Heels*, 295; Greene, *Breaking the Backbone of the Rebellion*, 434, 437.

41 J. F. J. Caldwell, *History of a Brigade of South Carolinians*, 222–23; Hess, *Lee's Tar Heels*, 296; Greene, *Breaking the Backbone of the Rebellion*, 438–40.

42 Kellogg to Rawlins, April 2, 1865, in Simon, *Papers of Ulysses S. Grant*, 14:320n–321n.

43 Hartsuff to Ord, October 1865, *OR* 46(1):1170; Shepley, "Incidents of the Capture of Richmond," 19–20.

44 Shepley, "Incidents of the Capture of Richmond," 20–21; Hartsuff to Ord, October 1865, and Ferrero to Howard, April 2, 1865, *OR* 46(1):1170–73.

45 Grant to Julia, April 2, 1865, in Simon, *Papers of Ulysses S. Grant*, 14:330; Greene, *Breaking the Backbone of the Rebellion*, 468; Horn, *Petersburg Campaign*, 246.

46 Grant to Meade and to Sheridan, both April 2, 1865, in Simon, *Papers of Ulysses S. Grant*, 14:315–16, 321.

CONCLUSION

1 Shepley, "Incidents of the Capture of Richmond," 23; Michie to Ord, May 12, 1865, *OR* 46(1):1165; Delafield to Stanton, October 30, 1865, *OR*, ser. 3, 5:193. When Grant and Meade rode into Petersburg on the morning of April 3, a man claiming to be a Confederate engineer told them that Lee "had for some time been at work preparing a strong enclosed intrenchment . . . to fight his final battle there" after evacuating Petersburg. While Meade took the possibility seriously, Grant assumed Lee was too smart to let his army be trapped in a citadel between Petersburg and Richmond. See Grant, *Personal Memoirs*, 2:707–8.

2 Grant to Sherman, April 3, 1865, in Simon, *Papers of Ulysses S. Grant*, 14:339; Trudeau, *Last Citadel*, 419; Horn, *Petersburg Campaign*, 218.

3 Sheridan, "Last Days of the Rebellion," 528; Delafield to Stanton, October 30, 1865,

OR, ser. 3, 5:180; Bowen, "Diary of Captain George D. Bowen," 222; Marvel, *Lee's Last Retreat*, 47–48; Calkins, *From Petersburg to Appomattox*, 24; field visits to Jetersville, September 1, 1995, March 18, 1996.

4 Gallagher, *Fighting for the Confederacy*, 521; Timberlake, "In the Siege of Richmond and After," 412–13; Marvel, *Lee's Last Retreat*, 48–49.

5 Grant to Meade, April 5, 1865, in Simon, *Papers of Ulysses S. Grant*, 14:350; Bowen, "Diary of Captain George D. Bowen," 222; Marvel, *Lee's Last Retreat*, 56–58; Calkins, *Appomattox Campaign*, 87–88, 183–84.

6 Porter, "Five Forks," 721; Marvel, *Lee's Last Retreat*, 78–92. There are no apparent remnants of the Confederate breastworks at Little Sailor's Creek, based on my field visit of September 1, 1995.

7 J. F. J. Caldwell, *History of a Brigade of South Carolinians*, 230; Marvel, *Lee's Last Retreat*, 87.

8 Marvel, *Lee's Last Retreat*, 127–30.

9 Grant, *Personal Memoirs*, 2:723; Humphreys to Webb, April 21, 1865, OR 46(1):684; field visit to Cumberland Presbyterian Church, March 18, 1996; Marvel, *Lee's Last Retreat*, 130–33.

10 Bryan Grimes account, *Supplement to the Official Records*, 7(1):800–802; Cowper, *Extracts of Letters*, 116; Marvel, *Lee's Last Retreat*, 165–68.

11 A. C. Jones, "Third Arkansas Regiment at Appomattox," 314; Marvel, *Lee's Last Retreat*, 158–62; Calkins, *From Petersburg to Appomattox*, 37; field visit to Appomattox, March 18, 1996.

12 Power, *Lee's Miserables*, 315–19.

13 Roman, *Military Operations of General Beauregard*, 2:234–35; Lee to Hill, June 1864, OR 40(2):702–3.

### APPENDIX ONE

1 Mr. Judd, "Visit to a Virginia Battle Field," in *Guide to the Fortifications and Battlefields*, 21; Lowe and Burns, "Using GPS and GIS," 39; Buell, "The Cannoneer," 238; Trudeau, *Last Citadel*, 289; article in Springfield, Mass., *Republican*, reprinted in Raleigh *North Carolina Standard*, October 4, 1864.

2 Lowe and Burns, "Using GPS and GIS," 39.

3 Agassiz, *Meade's Headquarters*, 340–41.

4 Thomas M. Cook article in *New York Herald*, reprinted in John Robertson, *Michigan in the War*, 552.

5 Barnard to Duane, April 12, 1865, OR 46(3):719; Delafield to Stanton, October 30, 1865, OR, ser. 3, 5:182, 195.

6 Abbot to Delafield, April 25, June 3, 1865, OR 46(1):173, 663; Abbot, *Siege Artillery*, 136–37.

7 Abbot, *Siege Artillery*, 132–33, 137.

8 Ibid., 130–31.

9 Ibid., 132n.

10 Spaulding to Duane, June 14, 1865, OR 46(1):649.

11 Howell to Duane, April 19, 1865, OR 46(1):657–58.

12   Mr. Judd, "Visit to a Virginia Battle Field," in *Guide to the Fortifications and Battlefields*, 22, 24, 27; Greene, *Civil War Petersburg*, 271–72.
13   Trowbridge, *Desolate South*, 106, 108.
14   Ibid., 115.
15   Ibid., 115–16.
16   Ibid., 114, 117.
17   Ad for Lazelle and McMullin, in *Guide to the Fortifications and Battlefields*, n.p.; also see 14, 19–20.
18   Davis and Wiley, *Photographic History*, 2:1116, 1118, 1321; Cavanaugh and Marvel, *Battle of the Crater*, 82.
19   Cavanaugh and Marvel, *Battle of the Crater*, 112; Calkins, "History of the Crater Battlefield," 156–57.
20   Charles W. Owen, "Explosion of Mine at Petersburg Described by Comrade C. W. Owen," *National Tribune*, November 1, 1934; Chamberlain, "Reminiscences of Petersburg and Appomattox," 166, 169.
21   Chamberlain, "Reminiscences of Petersburg and Appomattox," 173–74.
22   Robert A. Reid, "Petersburg Crater," *National Tribune*, January 5, 1905.
23   Ibid.
24   "Confederate Trenches at Petersburg," 418–20.
25   Matthew Walton Venable, *Eighty Years After*, 21, 45, 47, 70.
26   "Confederate Trenches at Petersburg," 419.
27   *New York Times*, February 1930, clipping from Petersburg *Progress-Index*, February 1, 1930, PNB.
28   Pine Gardens Estate Auction Broadside, September 12, 1929, PNB; John Pope, "Movie Studio Contractors Unearth Possible Confederate Troop Mine," *Richmond Times-Dispatch*, April 17, 1997.
29   Calkins, "History of the Crater Battlefield," 157.
30   Ibid.
31   Ibid., 158; John Pope, "Movie Studio Contractors Unearth Possible Confederate Troop Mine," *Richmond Times-Dispatch*, April 17, 1997.

APPENDIX TWO

1   Frassanito, *Grant and Lee*, 234, 236–37.
2   Ibid., 238–41; Trudeau, *Siege of Petersburg*, 6. Confederate Battery No. 8 was converted into Union Fort Friend. There is a photograph of it in the 1939 World's Fair Photograph Collection, LOV.
3   Field visit to Petersburg, July 7, 1994.
4   Ibid.; Harry Jackson email to author, April 28, 2004.
5   Davis and Wiley, *Photographic History*, 2:1100, 1109; William C. Davis, *Death in the Trenches*, 130; Trudeau, *Siege of Petersburg*, 29.
6   Map of Fort Sedgwick complex, in Hopkins, *Seventh Regiment Rhode Island*, 231; de Trobriand to Finkelmeier, September 24, 1864, OR 42(2):998.
7   Hopkins, *Seventh Regiment Rhode Island*, 232; William C. Davis, *Death in the Trenches*, 132–33; Trudeau, *Siege of Petersburg*, 22, 32; Frassanito, *Grant and Lee*, 363, 366–68,

375; Davis and Wiley, *Photographic History*, 2:1100–1101, 1105, 1136–37, 1201. The picket post near Fort Sedgwick originally was identified by photographer Thomas C. Roche as a Union position, but Frassanito believes it was a Confederate post. See Frassanito, *Grant and Lee*, 365.

8  Field visit to Petersburg, July 7, 1994; Peck, *Recruit Before Petersburg*, 12–13.
9  Field visit to Petersburg, July 7, 1994.
10 Ibid., July 8, 1994; Davis and Wiley, *Photographic History*, 2:1112.
11 Field visit to Petersburg, July 8, 1994.
12 Ibid. For a good 1930s image of the ditch at Fort Fisher, see 1939 World's Fair Photograph Collection, LOV.
13 Field visit to Petersburg, July 8, 1994.
14 Ibid., July 9, 1994.
15 Field visit to City Point, August 30, 1995.
16 Hodgkins, *Battle of Fort Stedman*, 11–12; *Guide to the Fortifications and Battlefields*, 13; Abbot to Delafield, June 3, 1865, OR 46(1):663; Barrier, "Breaking Grant's Line," 417; Davis and Wiley, *Photographic History*, 2:1108, 1110; Trudeau, *Siege of Petersburg*, 38.
17 Field visit to Petersburg, September 1, 1995; Davis and Wiley, *Photographic History*, 2:1107; Beauregard, "Four Days of Battle at Petersburg," 543.
18 Field visit to Petersburg, September 1, 1995.
19 Ibid., July 7, 1994.
20 Ibid.
21 Ibid., July 8, 1994.
22 Ibid., July 8–9, 1994.
23 Ibid.
24 Michler quoted in Delafield to Stanton, October 30, 1865, OR, ser. 3, 5:183; Hagood, *Memoirs of the War of Secession*, 251.
25 *OR Atlas*, pl. 124. See also an illustration of the Union line at Bermuda Hundred in La Bree, *Confederate Soldier*, 249.
26 Field visit to Bermuda Hundred, August 30, 1995.
27 Ibid. Fort Carpenter and Battery Wilcox, on the northern wing of the Union line, are apparently intact but not easy to access. There is a ten-yard stretch of Union parapet crossing Golf Course Road, near the Bermuda Hundred Golf Course. Forts Wead and Zabriskie are intact, but I did not visit them. Point of Rocks, the southern anchor of the Union line on Bermuda Hundred, has a county park with hiking trails and some faint remnants of Union works that are accessible.
28 Abbot, *Siege Artillery*, 134.
29 Michie to Barnard, November 21, 1864, OR 42(3):679.
30 Abbot to Delafield, June 3, 1865, OR 46(1):664; Abbot, *Siege Artillery*, 130–31.
31 Abbot, *Siege Artillery*, 135–36; Abbot to Delafield, June 3, 1865, OR 46(1):664.
32 *Bermuda Hundred Campaign*, 23; Hagood, *Memoirs of the War of Secession*, 250–51; field visit to Bermuda Hundred, August 30, 1995. Battery Semmes, at Henricus Park, is apparently preserved, but I did not visit it.
33 *Bermuda Hundred Campaign*, 23; field visit to Bermuda Hundred, August 30, 1995.
34 Field visit to Bermuda Hundred, August 30, 1995.
35 Frassanito, *Grant and Lee*, 313; Sommers, *Richmond Redeemed*, 310–11; William C.

Davis, *Death in the Trenches*, 144; Davis and Wiley, *Photographic History*, 2:1125; Dickinson, "Union and Confederate Engineering Operations at Chaffin's Bluff," 56, 109, 110, RNB. Fort Burnham is well preserved (field visit, March 21, 1996).

36 Field visit to Richmond defenses, March 21, 1996; Dickinson, "Union and Confederate Engineering Operations at Chaffin's Bluff," 123-24, RNB.

37 Field visit to Richmond defenses, March 21, 1996; Dickinson, "Union and Confederate Engineering Operations at Chaffin's Bluff," 119-20, RNB; Map of the Environs of Richmond and Petersburg, March 24, 1865, G171, RG77, NARA. I am not aware of any easily accessible remnants of the Tenth Corps defenses north of the James River, those extending northward from Fort Burnham and eastward toward New Market Heights, or the defenses at Deep Bottom.

38 Field visit to Richmond defenses, March 21, 1996; Dickinson, "Union and Confederate Engineering Operations at Chaffin's Bluff," 78, 101, RNB; Hess, *Field Armies and Fortifications*, 237-39. A photograph of Fort Hoke in the 1939 World's Fair Photograph Collection, LOV, depicts a reconstructed embrasure viewed from outside the work, as well as a reconstructed palisade.

39 Dickinson, "Union and Confederate Engineering Operations at Chaffin's Bluff," 93-94, 96, RNB; Sommers, *Richmond Redeemed*, 310-11.

40 Field visit to Richmond defenses, March 21, 1996.

41 Ibid., 1996; Dickinson, "Union and Confederate Engineering Operations at Chaffin's Bluff," 91, RNB; Davis and Wiley, *Photographic History*, 2:1125; Sommers, *Richmond Redeemed*, 310-11.

42 Field visit to Richmond defenses, March 21, 1996; Dickinson, "Union and Confederate Engineering Operations at Chaffin's Bluff," 88, 90, RNB; two photographs of Fort Gilmer, 1939 World's Fair Photograph Collection, LOV.

43 Hagood, *Memoirs of the War of Secession*, 309-10; Dickinson, "Union and Confederate Engineering Operations at Chaffin's Bluff," 82, 84, RNB; field visit to Richmond defenses, March 21, 1996. There is a photograph (image number C1:1/05/05/012) of the Richmond defenses, taken in the 1930s, with specific location unidentified, in 1939 World's Fair Photograph Collection, LOV.

# BIBLIOGRAPHY

## ARCHIVAL SOURCES

Abraham Lincoln Presidential Library,
    Springfield, Illinois
    Pierre G. T. Beauregard Papers
    William R. Rowley Papers
American Antiquarian Society, Worcester,
    Massachusetts
    Henry White Diary
Auburn University, Special Collections,
    Auburn, Alabama
    James Henry Lane Papers
Chicago Historical Society, Chicago,
    Illinois
    Julian Edward Bucklee Collection
    George Merryweather Papers
    Ira Miltmore Collection
College of William and Mary,
    Williamsburg, Virginia
    Bowles Family Papers
    Forbes Letters
    William Taylor Letters
Cornell University, Division of Rare and
    Manuscript Collections, Ithaca,
    New York
    Henry Chamberlain Papers
Delaware Public Archives, Dover
    Thomas A. Smyth Diary
Duke University, Medical Center Library,
    Durham, North Carolina
    Josiah Trent Collection
    Charles Knickerbocker Winne
    Journal
Duke University, Special Collections
    Library, Durham, North Carolina
    John Gross Barnard Papers
    Pierre G. T. Beauregard Papers
    Asa Biggs Papers
    James Blanton Papers
    Samuel Bradbury Papers
    Confederate States of America Archives
        Army Units, Army of Northern
        Virginia
        Miscellaneous Soldier Letters
    *Confederate Veteran* Papers
    Benjamin S. and Richard S.
        Ewell Papers
    Robert A. Guyton and J. B.
        Heaslet Papers
    David B. Harris Papers
    Thomas F. Kelley Papers
    Marshall McDonald Papers
    Beverly Preston Morris Papers
    Munford-Ellis Family Papers
    William H. Noble Papers
    Patterson-Cavin Family Papers
    Green W. Penn Papers

Mary Frances Jane Pursley Papers
Reuben Robertson Papers
William Russell Papers
Mary Eliza (Fleming) Schooler Papers
John Lane Stuart Papers
Henry E. Taintor Papers
Eugene and James Paul Verdery Papers
Margaret Bradley Willard Papers
Simon P. Wingard Papers
East Carolina University, East Carolina Manuscript Collection, Greenville, North Carolina
    Nathan R. Frazier Papers
    Jesse Hill Papers
    Abraham G. Jones Papers
    Francis W. Knowles Diary
    F. M. McMillen Diary
    Alfred M. Scales Papers
    William Henry Von Eberstein Papers
Emory University, Robert W. Woodruff Library, Special Collections, Atlanta, Georgia
    Enos Bennage Diary
    Confederate Miscellany Collection
    John A. Everett Papers
    Benjamin Wesley Justice Papers
    James H. Lee Papers
Fredericksburg and Spotsylvania National Military Park, Fredericksburg, Virginia
    Henry Herbert Harris Diary
    R. S. Robertson Letters
Historical Society of Schuylkill County, Pottsville, Pennsylvania
    Michael A. Cavanaugh Collection
        Samuel Beddall Diary
        Warren H. Hurd Diary
        Benjamin Mason Letters
Indiana Historical Society, Indianapolis
    John Lewis Ketcham Papers
Indiana State Library, Indiana Division, Indianapolis
    Erasmus C. Gilreath Reminiscences
Library of Congress, Manuscript Division, Washington, D.C.

C. B. Comstock Papers
Henry I. Greer and Robert Greer Papers
Henry Jackson Hunt Papers
Daniel Reed Larned Papers
Hazard Stevens Papers
Gilbert Thompson Journal
Library of Virginia, Richmond
    1939 World's Fair Photograph Collection
    Moses Barker Papers
    W. W. Blackford, "Memoirs: First and Last, or Battles in Virginia"
    Robert Richard Bragg, "Reminiscences of Confederate Service, 1861–1865"
    Dewese Family Letters
    Younger Longest Letters
    Enoch Alexander McNair Letters
    John F. Sale Papers
    Whitehorne Family Papers
Maryland Historical Society, Baltimore
    John Gibbon Papers
    Martin L. Smith Diary
    James M. Snook Diary
Massachusetts Historical Society, Boston
    Caleb Hadley Beal Papers
    Edwin Bearse Papers
    Warren Goodale Papers
    William Milo Olin Papers
    William Stowell Tilton Diary
Mississippi Department of Archives and History, Jackson
    Archibald K. Jones Family Papers
Moravian Music Foundation, Winston-Salem, North Carolina
    J. Edward Peterson Papers
Museum of the Confederacy, Richmond, Virginia
    James Longstreet Letterbook, 1865
    Joseph Mullen Jr. Diary
    William N. Pendleton Papers
    William H. Stewart, comp., "The Charge of the Crater: Personal Recollections of Participants in the Charge of the Crater at Petersburg, Va, July 30th, 1864"

National Archives and Records
Administration, Washington, D.C.
RG77 Records of the Office of the Chief
of Engineers
Map Collection
M1113 Letters Sent by the Chief of
Engineers, 1812–1869
RG94 Records of the Adjutant General's
Office
Ambrose E. Burnside Papers
Edward W. Serrell Service Record, 1st
New York Engineers
M1064 Letters Received by the
Commission Branch of the
Adjutant General's Office
RG109 War Department Collection of
Confederate Records
Orders, Rodes's and Battle's Brigades
M258 Compiled Service Records of
Confederate Soldiers Who Served
in Organizations Raised Directly
by the Confederate Government
M311 Compiled Service Records of
Confederate Soldiers Who Served
in Organizations from the State of
Alabama
M331 Compiled Service Records
of Confederate Generals and
Staff Officers and Nonregimental
Enlisted Men
M628 Letters and Telegrams Sent
by the Engineer Bureau of the
Confederate War Department,
1861–1864
RG393 Records of the United States
Army Continental Commands,
1821–1920
Special Orders and Circulars, June–
September 1864 (Second Brigade,
First Division, Ninth Corps), vol.
51/155
New-York Historical Society, New York,
New York
Miles Clayton Huyette Reminiscences
Leverett E. Seymour Letters

New York Public Library, Rare Books
and Manuscripts, New York,
New York
William Hamilton Harris Papers
North Carolina Division of Archives and
History, Raleigh
Henry C. Brown Collection
William H. S. Burgwyn Papers
William Dixon Carr Papers
Robert F. Hoke Papers
Lowry Shuford Collection
Zebulon Baird Vance Collection
Peabody Essex Museum, Salem,
Massachusetts
Herbert E. Valentine Papers
Petersburg Museums, Archives,
Petersburg, Virginia
Photographs Collection
Petersburg National Battlefield,
Petersburg, Virginia
Edwin C. Bearss, "Battle of Reams'
Station"
Edwin C. Bearss, "Battle of the Weldon
Railroad"
Charles T. Bowen Letters
Chris Calkins Memo
Robert D. Dawson Letters
Preston Hawkins, "Report, Results of
Subsurface Investigation," Naeva
Geophysics, Inc., March 24, 1997
W. E. Leak Letters
Matthew Norris Love Letters
James Mitchell Letters
Photographs Collection
Pine Gardens Estate Auction Broadside,
September 12, 1929
William E. Potter Letters
J. Ellis Whitney, "Petersburg: Anatomy
of an Earthwork," *Military
Explorations* (1985) (unpaginated
photocopy)
Rhode Island Historical Society,
Providence
Gilbert Family Papers
Peleg Jones Diary

Richmond National Battlefield,
  Richmond, Virginia
   Clarke Baum Letters
   Clifford Dickinson, "Union and
     Confederate Engineering
     Operations at Chaffin's Bluff/
     Chaffin's Farm, June 1862–April
     3, 1865"
   Marshall J. Smith Reports
   W. S. Weed Diary
Stanford University, Department of
  Special Collections, Palo Alto,
  California
   Edward Otho Cresap Ord Papers
University of California, Bancroft Library,
  Berkeley
   E. O. C. Ord Papers
University of Georgia, Special Collections,
  Athens
   William Starr Basinger Reminiscences
University of Iowa, Special Collections,
  Iowa City
   Lewis Crater Diary
University of Michigan, Bentley Historical
  Library, Ann Arbor
   William Baird Memoirs
   William Boston Papers
   Byron Cutcheon Papers
   Conrad Noll Diary
   William H. Randall Reminiscences
   James S. Schoff Collection
University of New Hampshire, Milne
  Special Collections and Archives,
  Durham
   Louis Bell Papers
University of North Carolina, Southern
  Historical Collection, Chapel Hill
   James W. Albright Diary
   Willis G. Briggs Papers
   William J. Clarke Papers
   Thomas Lanier Clingman Papers
   Confederate Inspection Book
   Frank Family Letters
   Ralph Gorrell Papers
   Lemuel J. Hoyle Papers
   William Gaston Lewis Papers
   Jacob Lyon Diary
   Samuel J. C. Moore Papers
   Scott Family Papers
   Edmund Jones Williams Letters
University of Virginia, Special Collections,
  Charlottesville
   Barnes Family Manuscripts
   John Warwick Daniel Papers
   J. C. Duane Letterbook
   Minor Family Papers
     Carter Nelson Berkeley Minor,
       "Record of the War," 3 vols.
   Petersburg Crater Collection
   John Edwin Roller Papers
   Joseph C. Rutherford Papers
U.S. Army Military History Institute,
  Carlisle, Pennsylvania
   Zenas R. Bliss Reminiscences
   Civil War Miscellaneous Collection
     Isaac McQueen Auld Letters
     Samuel A. Beddall Diary
     John Young Reily, "Fort Gregg,
       Confederates' Desperate Stand or
       the Last Day at Petersburg"
     William Henry Walling Letters
   *Civil War Times Illustrated* Collection
     William A. Clendening Memoir
     Joseph J. Scroggs Diary
   Michael P. Musick Collection
     R. D. Funkhouser Account
U.S. Geological Survey
   Prince George Quadrant Map
Virginia Historical Society, Richmond
   Bird Family Papers
   Giles Buckner Cooke Diary
   Elizabeth Lewis (Selden) Dimmock
     Papers
   Joseph William Eggleston
     Autobiography
   John Walter Fairfax Papers
   Guerrant Family Papers
   Conway Robinson Howard Papers
   Johnston Family Papers
   William Goodridge Morton Papers

Pegram-Johnson-McIntosh Family
  Papers
James Eldred Phillips Papers
David Washington Pipes Memoir
Alfred Lewis Scott Memoirs
Edmund Fitzgerald Stone Letter
Talcott Family Papers
David Addison Weisiger Papers
Virginia Military Institute, Archives,
  Lexington
Robert Alexander Boyd Civil War Notes
  and Diary
John J. Clarke Papers
Benjamin F. Oakes Letter
Washington and Lee University, Special
  Collections, Lexington, Virginia
William Alexander Gordon Memoirs
Wisconsin Historical Society, Madison
William L. Phillips Letters

NEWSPAPERS

Harper's Weekly
Montgomery Daily Mail
National Tribune
New York Herald
New York Times
Petersburg Express
Petersburg Progress-Index
Raleigh Daily Confederate
Raleigh North Carolina
  Standard
Richmond Daily Dispatch
Richmond Enquirer
Richmond Times-Dispatch
Richmond Whig
Rochester Union and
  Advertiser
Springfield, Mass.,
  Republican

BOOKS, ARTICLES, DISSERTATIONS,
ARCHAEOLOGICAL REPORTS, MAPS, AND TOUR GUIDES

Abbot, Henry L. "Cyrus Ballou Comstock." *Professional Memoirs, Corps of Engineers, United States Army and Engineer Department at Large* 8 (1916): 218–22.

———. *Siege Artillery in the Campaigns Against Richmond.* New York: Van Nostrand, 1868.

Agassiz, George R., ed. *Meade's Headquarters, 1863–1865: Letters of Colonel Theodore Lyman from the Wilderness to Appomattox.* Boston: Atlantic Monthly Press, 1922.

Allen, Amory K. "Civil War Letters of Amory K. Allen." *Indiana Magazine of History* 31 (1935): 338–86.

Anderson, John. *The Fifty-Seventh Regiment of Massachusetts Volunteers in the War of the Rebellion.* Boston: E. B. Stillings, 1896.

Andrews, W. J. *Sketch of Company K, 23rd South Carolina Volunteers, In the Civil War, From 1862–1865.* Richmond: Whittet and Shepperson, n.d.

Aston, Howard. *History and Roster of the Fourth and Fifth Independent Battalions and Thirteenth Regiment Ohio Cavalry Volunteers.* Columbus, Ohio: Fred J. Heer, 1902.

Barrett, Eugene A. "John Frederic Hartranft: Life and Services." Pt. 1. *Bulletin of the Historical Society of Montgomery County* 7 (April 1951): 295–378.

Barrier, J. D. "Breaking Grant's Line." *Confederate Veteran* 33 (1925): 417–18.

Bausum, Daniel F. "Personal Reminiscences of Sergeant Daniel F. Bausum, Co. K, 48th Regt., Penna. Vol. Inf., 1861–1865." *Publications of the Historical Society of Schuylkill County* 4 (1914): 240–49.

Beale, G. W. *A Lieutenant of Cavalry in Lee's Army.* Boston: Gorham Press, 1918.

Beals, Thomas P. "In a Charge Near Fort Hell, Petersburg, April 2, 1865." In *War Papers Read Before the Commandery of the State of Maine, Military Order of the Loyal Legion of the United States,* 2:105–15. Portland, Maine: Lefavor-Tower, 1902.

Bearss, Ed, and Chris Calkins. *Battle of Five Forks*. 2nd ed. Lynchburg, Va.: H. E. Howard, 1985.

Beaudot, William J. K., and Lance J. Herdegen, eds. *An Irishman in the Iron Brigade: The Civil War Memoirs of James P. Sullivan, Sergt., Company K, 6th Wisconsin Volunteers*. New York: Fordham University Press, 1993.

Beauregard, G. T. "Four Days of Battle at Petersburg." In *Battles and Leaders of the Civil War*, edited by Robert Underwood Johnson and Clarence Clough Buel, 4:540–44. New York: Thomas Yoseloff, 1956.

Bennett, Gordon C. "Grant's Railroad: Route through Danger." *Civil War Times Illustrated* 22, no. 6 (October 1983): 14–20.

Benson, Susan Williams, ed. *Berry Benson's Civil War Book: Memoirs of a Confederate Scout and Sharpshooter*. Athens: University of Georgia Press, 1992.

Bentley, Nicholas, ed. *Russell's Despatches from the Crimea, 1854–1856*. London: Andre Deutsch, 1966.

Berlin, Ira, ed. *Freedom: A Documentary History of Emancipation, 1861–1867*. Ser. 1, vol. 1. New York: Cambridge University Press, 1987.

*The Bermuda Hundred Campaign in Chesterfield County, Virginia*. Chesterfield, Va.: Chesterfield Office of News and Public Information, 1993.

Bernard, George S. "The Battle of the Crater." *Southern Historical Society Papers* 18 (1890): 3–38.

———, ed. *War Talks of Confederate Veterans*. Petersburg: Fenn and Owen, 1892.

Billings, John D. *The History of the Tenth Massachusetts Battery of Light Artillery in the War of the Rebellion, 1862–1865*. Boston: Hall and Whiting, 1881.

Blackford, W. W. *War Years with Jeb Stuart*. New York: Charles Scribner's Son, 1945.

Bond, Natalie Jenkins, and Osmun Latrobe Coward, eds. *The South Carolinians: Colonel Asbury Coward's Memoirs*. New York: Vantage Press, 1968.

Bosbyshell, Oliver Christian. *The 48th in the War: Being a Narrative of the Campaigns of the 48th Regiment, Infantry, Pennsylvania Veteran Volunteers, During the War of the Rebellion*. Philadelphia: Avil Printing, 1895.

———. "The Petersburg Mine." *The Maine Bugle*, campaign 3, call 3 (July 1896): 211–23.

Bowen, George A., ed. "The Diary of Captain George D. Bowen, 12th Regiment New Jersey Volunteers." *Valley Forge Journal* 2 (1985): 176–231.

Bowley, Freeman S. "The Crater." *National Tribune*, November 6, 1884.

———. "The Petersburg Mine." In *Civil War Papers of the California Commandery and the Oregon Commandery of the Military Order of the Loyal Legion of the United States*. Wilmington, N.C.: Broadfoot, 1995.

Bradwell, I. G. "Fort Steadman and Subsequent Events." *Confederate Veteran* 23 (1915): 20–23.

———. "Holding the Lines at Petersburg." *Confederate Veteran* 28 (1920): 457–59.

———. "In Front of Fort Steadman, 1865." *Confederate Veteran* 25 (1917): 408–9.

———. "On Picket Duty in Front of Fort Stedman." *Confederate Veteran* 38 (1930): 302–7.

Brightman, Austin C., Jr. "Glory Enough: The 148th Pennsylvania Volunteers at Fort Crater." *Civil War Regiments* 2, no. 2 (1992): 141–55.

Britton, Ann Hartwell, and Thomas J. Reed, eds. *To My Beloved Wife and Boy at Home:*

*The Letters and Diaries of Orderly Sergeant John F. L. Hartwell*. Madison, N.J.: Fairleigh Dickinson University Press, 1997.

Bruce, Robert V. *Lincoln and the Tools of War*. Indianapolis: Bobbs-Merrill, 1956.

Bryan, Charles F., Jr., James C. Kelly, and Nelson D. Lankford, eds. *Images from the Storm: Private Robert Knox Sneden*. New York: Free Press, 2001.

Bryant, Elias A. *Diary of Elias A. Bryant of Francestown, N.H.* Concord: Rumford Press, n.d.

Buckingham, Peter H., ed. *All's for the Best: The Civil War Reminiscences and Letters of Daniel W. Sawtelle*. Knoxville: University of Tennessee Press, 2001.

Buell, Augustus. *"The Cannoneer": Recollections of Service in the Army of the Potomac*. Washington, D.C.: National Tribune, 1890.

Butler, Benjamin. *Butler's Book*. Boston: A. M. Thayer, 1892.

Cadwell, Charles K. *The Old Sixth Regiment: Its War Record, 1861-5*. New Haven: Tuttle, Morehouse, and Taylor, 1875.

Caldwell, J. F. J. *The History of a Brigade of South Carolinians Known as "Gregg's," and Subsequently as "McGowan's Brigade."* Philadelphia: King and Baird, 1866.

Caldwell, Willie Walker. *Stonewall Jim: A Biography of General James A. Walker, C.S.A.* Elliston, Va.: Northcross House, 1990.

Calkins, Chris M. *The Appomattox Campaign, March 29-April 9, 1865*. Conshohocken, Pa.: Combined Books, 1997.

———. *From Petersburg to Appomattox: A Tour Guide to the Routes of Lee's Withdrawal and Grant's Pursuit, April 2-9, 1865*. Farmville, Va.: Farmville Herald, 1983.

———. "A History of the Crater Battlefield, 1865-1992." *Civil War Regiments* 2, no. 2 (1992): 156-58.

———. *Thirty-Six Hours before Appomattox, April 6 and 7, 1865*. Farmville, Va.: Farmville Herald, 1989.

Campbell, Eric A., ed., *"A Grand Terrible Dramma": From Gettysburg to Petersburg, The Civil War Letters of Charles Wellington Reed*. New York: Fordham University Press, 2000.

Carson, J. P. "Fort Steadman's Fall." *Confederate Veteran* 22 (1914): 460-62.

Carter, Robert Goldthwaite. *Four Brothers in Blue, or Sunshine and Shadows of the War of the Rebellion*. Norman: University of Oklahoma Press, 1999.

Case, Leverette N. "Personal Recollections of the Siege of Petersburg By a Confederate Officer." In *War Papers Read Before the Commandery of the State of Michigan, Military Order of the Loyal Legion of the United States*, 2:153-66. Detroit: James H. Stone, 1898.

Castel, Albert. *Decision in the West: The Atlanta Campaign of 1864*. Lawrence: University Press of Kansas, 1992.

Cavanaugh, Michael A., and William Marvel. *The Battle of the Crater: "The Horrid Pit," June 25-August 6, 1864*. Lynchburg, Va.: H. E. Howard, 1989.

Chamberlain, Joshua Lawrence. *The Passing of the Armies: An Account of the Final Campaign of the Army of the Potomac, Based upon Personal Reminiscences of the Fifth Army Corps*. Dayton, Ohio: Morningside Bookshop, 1974.

———. "Reminiscences of Petersburg and Appomattox: October, 1903." In *War Papers Read Before the Commandery of the State of Maine*, 3:161-82. Portland: Lefavor-Tower, 1908.

Chamberlayne, C. G., ed. *Ham Chamberlayne—Virginian: Letters and Papers of an Artillery Officer in the War for Southern Independence, 1861-1865*. Richmond, Va.: Dietz Printing, 1932.

Chapman, Sarah Bahnson, ed. *Bright and Gloomy Days: The Civil War Correspondence of Captain Charles Frederic Bahnson, a Moravian Confederate*. Knoxville: University of Tennessee Press, 2003.

Chase, J. J. *The Charge at Day-Break: Scenes and Incidents at the Battle of the Mine Explosion*. Lewiston: Journal, 1875.

Chesson, Michael B., ed. *The Journal of a Civil War Surgeon*. Lincoln: University of Nebraska Press, 2003.

Claiborne, John Herbert. *Seventy-Five Years in Old Virginia*. New York: Neale, 1904.

Clay, Cecil. "A Personal Narrative of the Capture of Fort Harrison." In *Military Order of the Loyal Legion of the United States, Commandery of the District of Columbia, War Papers No. 7*. N.p., ca. 1891.

Cleveland, Edmund J., ed. "The Siege of Petersburg." Pt. 1. *Proceedings of the New Jersey Historical Society* 66 (1948): 76-95.

Cockrell, Monroe F., ed. *Gunner with Stonewall: Reminiscences of William Thomas Poague*. Jackson, Tenn.: McCowat-Mercer, 1957.

Coit, J. C. "The Battle of the Crater, July 30, 1864: Letter from Major J. C. Coit." *Southern Historical Society Papers* 10 (1882): 123-30.

Colston, R. E. "Repelling the First Assault on Petersburg." In *Battles and Leaders of the Civil War*, edited by Robert Underwood Johnson and Clarence Clough Buel, 4:535-37. New York: Thomas Yoseloff, 1956.

Conerly, Buxton R. "How Fort Gregg Was Defended." *Confederate Veteran* 15 (1907): 505-7.

"A Confederate Airship." *Southern Historical Society Papers* 28 (1900): 303-5.

"Confederate Trenches at Petersburg." *Confederate Veteran* 33 (1925): 418-20.

"Confederate Tunnels at Pine Gardens, Prince George County, Virginia, Feb. 23, 1926." Courtesy of Harry Jackson.

Cowper, Pulaski, ed. *Extracts of Letters of Major-General Bryan Grimes, to his Wife*. Wilmington, N.C.: Broadfoot, 1986.

Crist, Lynda Lasswell, ed. *The Papers of Jefferson Davis*. 11 Vols. Baton Rouge: Louisiana State University Press, 1971-2003.

Cross, Thomas H. "Battle of the Crater." *National Tribune*, February 25, 1882.

Cullen, Joseph P. *The Siege of Petersburg*. N.p.: Eastern Acorn Press, 1981.

Cullum, George W. *Biographical Register of the Officers and Graduates of the U.S. Military Academy at West Point, N.Y.* 3 vols. Boston: Houghton Mifflin, 1891.

Culver, F. E. "Entered and Escaped from Fort Mahone." *Confederate Veteran* 18 (1910): 368.

Cummings, Charles M. *Yankee Quaker, Confederate General: The Curious Career of Bushrod Rust Johnson*. Rutherford, N.J.: Fairleigh Dickinson University Press, 1971.

Cutcheon, Byron M. "The Twentieth Michigan Regiment in the Assault on Petersburg, July, 1864." *Historical Collections, Michigan Pioneer and Historical Society* 30 (1905): 127-39.

Cutchins, John A. *A Famous Command: The Richmond Light Infantry Blues*. Richmond, Va.: Garrett and Massie, 1934.
Dana, Charles A. *Recollections of the Civil War with the Leaders at Washington and in the Field in the Sixties*. New York: D. Appleton, 1902.
Daniel, W. Harrison, ed. "H. H. Harris' Civil War Diary (1863-1865)." Pt. 2. *Virginia Baptist Register*, no. 36 (1997): 1840-61.
Dauchy, George K. "The Battle of Ream's Station." In *Military Essays and Recollections: Papers Read Before the Commandery of the State of Illinois, Military Order of the Loyal Legion of the United States*, 3:125-40. Chicago: Dial, 1890.
Davis, Charles E., Jr. *Three Years in the Army: The Story of the Thirteenth Massachusetts Volunteers from July 16, 1861, to August 1, 1864*. Boston: Estes and Lauriat, 1894.
Davis, William C. *Death in the Trenches: Grant at Petersburg*. Alexandria, Va.: Time-Life, 1986.
Davis, William C., and Bell I. Wiley, eds. *Photographic History of the Civil War*. 2 vols. New York: Black Dog and Leventhal, 1994.
Day, W. A. "Battle of the Crater." *Confederate Veteran* 11 (1903): 355-56.
———. "The Breastworks at Petersburg." *Confederate Veteran* 29 (1921): 173-75.
———. "Life among Bullets—The Siege of Petersburg, Va." *Confederate Veteran* 29 (1921): 138-41.
———. *A True History of Company I, 49th Regiment, North Carolina Troops*. Newton, N.C.: Enterprise, 1893.
Delafield, Richard. *Report on the Art of War in Europe in 1854, 1855, and 1856*. Washington, D.C.: George W. Bowman, 1860.
Devereux, Thomas P. "From Petersburg to Appomattox." *Confederate Veteran* 22 (1914): 257-61.
Dowdey, Clifford, and Louis H. Manarin, eds. *The Wartime Papers of R. E. Lee*. Boston: Little, Brown, 1961.
Doyle, J. H. "The Flying Bird of 1864." *Confederate Veteran* 39 (1931): 438.
Duane, J. C. *Manual for Engineer Troops*. New York: Van Nostrand, 1862.
Dunlop, W. S. *Lee's Sharpshooters; or, The Forefront of Battle*. Dayton, Ohio: Morningside Bookshop, 1982.
Eden, R. C. *The Sword and the Gun: A History of the 37th Wis. Volunteer Infantry*. Madison: Atwood and Rublee, 1865.
Eisenschiml, Otto, ed. *Vermont General: The Unusual War Experiences of Edward Hastings Ripley, 1862-1865*. New York: Devin-Adair, 1960.
Elliott, James Carson. *The Southern Soldier Boy: A Thousand Shots for the Confederacy*. Raleigh, N.C.: Edwards and Boughton, [1907].
Etheredge, William H. "Another Story of the Crater Battle." *Southern Historical Society Papers* 37 (1909): 203-7.
Evans, Robert G., ed. *The 16th Mississippi Infantry: Civil War Letters and Reminiscences*. Jackson: University Press of Mississippi, 2002.
Evans, Thomas R. "Tells Story of Flying Machine of Confederacy." *Southern Historical Society Papers* 37 (1909): 302-3.
Featherston, John C. "The Battle of the Crater." *Confederate Veteran* 34 (1926): 296-98.

———. "Graphic Account of Battle of Crater." *Southern Historical Society Papers* 33 (1905): 358–74.
Featherstonhaugh, A. "Notes on the Defences of Petersburg." In *Papers on Subjects Connected With the Duties of the Royal Engineers*, n.s., 14:190–94 (1865).
Feis, William B. *Grant's Secret Service: The Intelligence War from Belmont to Appomattox.* Lincoln: University of Nebraska Press, 2002.
"Field Entrenchments." *Army and Navy Journal*, November 7, 1868, 184–85.
Fleet, Betsy, and John D. P. Fuller, eds. *Green Mount: A Virginia Plantation Family during the Civil War; Being the Journal of Benjamin Robert Fleet and Letters of His Family.* Lexington: University of Kentucky Press, 1962.
Floyd, Dale E., ed. *"Dear Friends at Home . . .": The Letters and Diary of Thomas James Owen, Fiftieth New York Volunteer Engineer Regiment, during the Civil War.* Washington, D.C.: Government Printing Office, 1985.
Floyd, Fred C. *History of the Fortieth (Mozart) Regiment New York Volunteers.* Boston: F. H. Gilson, 1909.
Forstchen, William Robert. "The 28th United States Colored Troops: Indiana's African Americans Go To War, 1863–1865." Ph.D. diss., Purdue University, 1994.
Fortin, Maurice S., ed. "Colonel Hilary A. Herbert's History of the Eighth Alabama Volunteer Regiment, C.S.A." *Alabama Historical Quarterly* 39 (1977): 5–321.
Frassanito, William A. *Grant and Lee: The Virginia Campaigns, 1864–1865.* New York: Charles Scribner's Sons, 1983.
Freeman, Douglas Southall, ed. *Lee's Dispatches: Unpublished Letters of General Robert E. Lee, C.S.A., to Jefferson Davis and the War Department of the Confederate States of America, 1862–1865.* New York: G. P. Putnam's Sons, 1957.
French, Samuel G. *Two Wars: An Autobiography of Gen. Samuel G. French.* Nashville: Confederate Veteran, 1901.
Furgurson, Ernest B. *Not War but Murder: Cold Harbor, 1864.* New York: Alfred A. Knopf, 2000.
Gallagher, Gary W., ed. *Fighting for the Confederacy: The Personal Recollections of General Edward Porter Alexander.* Chapel Hill: University of North Carolina Press, 1989.
"General David Bullock Harris, C.S.A." *Southern Historical Society Papers* 20 (1892): 395–98.
George, Larry. "Battle of the Crater: A Combat Engineer Case Study." *Military Review* 44 (1984): 35–47.
George, W. J. "Church Built, at Petersburg, by Engineers During Civil War." *Professional Memoirs, Corps of Engineers, United States Army and Engineer Department at Large* 4 (1912): 521–22.
Gibbon, John. *Personal Recollections of the Civil War.* New York: G. P. Putnam's Sons, 1928.
Gordon, George H. *A War Diary of Events in the War of the Great Rebellion, 1863–1865.* Boston: James R. Osgood, 1882.
Gould, Joseph. *The Story of the Forty-Eighth: A Record of the Campaigns of the Forty-Eighth Regiment Pennsylvania Veteran Volunteer Infantry.* Philadelphia: Regimental Association, 1908.

Govan, Gilbert E., and James W. Livingood, eds. *The Haskell Memoirs*. New York: G. P. Putnam's Sons, 1960.

Grant, Ulysses. "General Grant on the Siege of Petersburg." In *Battles and Leaders of the Civil War*, edited by Robert Underwood Johnson and Clarence Clough Buel, 4:574-79. New York: Thomas Yoseloff, 1956.

———. *Personal Memoirs of U. S. Grant*. 2 vols. New York: Viking, 1990.

"Grant and Lee, 1864: From the North Anna to the Crossing of the James." *Blue & Gray* 11 (1993): 10-22, 44-46, 50-54, 56-58.

Greene, A. Wilson. *Breaking the Backbone of the Rebellion: The Final Battles of the Petersburg Campaign*. Mason City, Iowa: Savas Publishing, 2000.

———. *Civil War Petersburg: Confederate City in the Crucible of War*. Charlottesville: University of Virginia Press, 2006.

Gregorie, Anne King, ed. "Diary of Captain Joseph Julius Wescoat, 1863-1865." *South Carolina Historical Magazine* 59 (1958): 84-95.

Griffith, Paddy. *Battle Tactics of the Western Front: The British Army's Art of Attack, 1916-18*. New Haven: Yale University Press, 1994.

Gross, Al. "Not Quite Flying Machines." *Civil War Times Illustrated* 13, no. 10 (February 1975): 20-24.

*A Guide to the Fortifications and Battlefields Around Petersburg*. Petersburg: Daily Index Job Print, 1866.

Haas, James F. "The Famous 48th." *Schuylkill County in the Civil War* 7 (1961): 52-62.

Hagerman, Edward. *The American Civil War and the Origins of Modern Warfare: Ideas, Organization, and Field Command*. Bloomington: Indiana University Press, 1988.

Hagood, Johnson. "Hagood's Brigade." *Southern Historical Society Papers* 16 (1888): 395-416.

———. *Memoirs of the War of Secession: From the Original Manuscripts of Johnson Hagood*. Columbia, S.C.: The State Company, 1910.

Hall, H. Seymour. "Mine Run to Petersburg." In *War Talks in Kansas: A Series of Papers Read Before the Kansas Commandery of the Military Order of the Loyal Legion of the United States*, 220-49. Kansas City: Franklin Hudson, 1906.

Hannum, Warren T. "The Crossing of the James River in 1864." *Military Engineer* 15 (May-June 1923): 229-37.

Hardy, John C. "The Final Effort—Last Assault of the Confederates at Petersburg." In *War Papers Read Before the Michigan Commandery of the Military Order of the Loyal Legion of the United States*, 2:217-28. Detroit: James H. Stone, 1898.

Harmon, George D., ed. "Letters of Luther Rice Mills—A Confederate Soldier." *North Carolina Historical Review* 4 (July 1927): 285-310.

Harris, Nathaniel Harrison. "Defence of Battery Gregg." *Southern Historical Society Papers* 8 (1880): 475-88.

———. *Movements of the Confederate Army in Virginia and the Part Taken by the Nineteenth Mississippi Regiment: From the Diary of General Nathaniel H. Harris*. Duncansby, Miss.: W. M. Harris, 1901.

Hartranft, John F. "The Recapture of Fort Stedman." In *Battles and Leaders of the Civil War*, edited by Robert Underwood Johnson and Clarence Clough Buel, 4:584-89. New York: Thomas Yoseloff, 1956.

Hastings, William H., ed. *Letters from a Sharpshooter: The Civil War Letters of Private William B. Greene, Co. G, 2nd United States Sharpshooters (Berdan's), Army of the Potomac, 1861–1865*. Belleville, Wisc.: Historic Publications, 1993.

Hauptman, Lawrence M. *Between Two Fires: American Indians in the Civil War*. New York: Free Press, 1995.

Herdegen, Lance, and Sherry Murphy, eds. *Four Years with the Iron Brigade: The Civil War Journals of William R. Ray, Co. F., Seventh Wisconsin Infantry*. Cambridge, Mass.: DaCapo Press, 2002.

Herek, Raymond J. *These Men Have Seen Hard Service: The First Michigan Sharpshooters in the Civil War*. Detroit: Wayne State University Press, 1998.

Hess, Earl J. *Field Armies and Fortifications in the Civil War: The Eastern Campaigns, 1861–1864*. Chapel Hill: University of North Carolina Press, 2005.

———. *Lee's Tar Heels: The Pettigrew-Kirkland-MacRae Brigade*. Chapel Hill: University of North Carolina Press, 2002.

———. *Trench Warfare under Grant and Lee: Field Fortifications in the Overland Campaign*. Chapel Hill: University of North Carolina Press, 2007.

Hewitt, William. *History of the Twelfth West Virginia Volunteer Infantry: The Part It Took in the War of the Rebellion, 1861–1865*. N.p.: Twelfth West Virginia Infantry Association, ca. 1892.

Hicks, Roger W., and Frances E. Schultz. *Battlefields of the Civil War*. Topsfield, Mass.: Salem House, 1989.

Hill, D. H. "Deeds of Daring—Six Heroes." In *Histories of the Several Regiments and Battalions from North Carolina in the Great War, 1861–'65*, edited by Walter Clark, 5:15–16. Goldsboro, N.C.: Nash Brothers, 1901.

Hillhouse, Don. *Heavy Artillery and Light Infantry: A History of the 1st Florida Special Battalion and 10th Infantry Regiment, C.S.A*. Jacksonville, Fla.: Author, 1992.

*History of Durell's Battery in the Civil War*. Philadelphia: Craig Finley, 1903.

*History of the Corn Exchange Regiment, 118th Pennsylvania Volunteers*. Philadelphia: J. L. Smith, 1888.

*History of the Fifth Massachusetts Battery*. Boston: Luther E. Cowles, 1902.

*History of the Thirty-Fifth Regiment Massachusetts Volunteers, 1862–1865*. Boston: Mills, Knight, 1884.

*History of the Thirty-Sixth Regiment Massachusetts Volunteers, 1862–1865*. Boston: Rockwell and Churchill, 1884.

Hodgkins, William H. *The Battle of Fort Stedman (Petersburg, Virginia), March 25, 1865*. Boston: Privately printed, 1889.

Hoole, W. Stanley, ed. "Letters of Captain Joab Goodson, 1862–1864." Pt. 2. *Alabama Review* 10 (July 1957): 215–31.

Hopkins, William P. *The Seventh Regiment Rhode Island Volunteers in the Civil War, 1862–1865*. Providence: Snow and Farnham, 1903.

Horn, John. *The Destruction of the Weldon Railroad: Deep Bottom, Globe Tavern, and Reams Station, August 14–25, 1864*. Lynchburg, Va.: H. E. Howard, 1991.

———. *The Petersburg Campaign, June 1864–April 1865*. Conshohocken, Pa.: Combined Publishing, 2000.

Houghton, Charles H. "In the Crater." In *Battles and Leaders of the Civil War*, edited by

Robert Underwood Johnson and Clarence Clough Buel, 4:561–62. New York: Thomas Yoseloff, 1956.

Howard, James McH. "Brig. Gen. Walter H. Stevens." *Confederate Veteran* 30 (1922): 249–50.

Howe, Thomas J. *Wasted Valor: June 15-18, 1864*. 2nd ed. Lynchburg, Va.: H. E. Howard, 1988.

Hudson, Joshua Hilary. *Sketches and Reminiscences*. Columbia, S.C.: The State Company, 1903.

Humphreys, Andrew A. *The Virginia Campaign of '64 and '65*. New York: Charles Scribner's Sons, 1883.

Humphreys, Henry H. *Andrew Atkinson Humphreys: A Biography*. Philadelphia: John C. Winston, 1924.

Hyde, William L. *History of the One Hundred and Twelfth Regiment N.Y. Volunteers*. Fredonia, N.Y.: W. McKinstry, 1866.

"In the Trenches at Petersburg." *Confederate Veteran* 34 (1926): 23.

Irving, T. *"More Than Conqueror": Or Memorials of Col. J. Howard Kitching*. New York: Hurd and Houghton, 1873.

Jackson, Harry L. *First Regiment Engineer Troops, P.A.C.S.: Robert E. Lee's Combat Engineers*. Louisa, Va.: R. A. E. Design and Publishing, 1998.

James, Alfred P. "The Battle of the Crater." In *Military Analysis of the Civil War: An Anthology by the Editors of Military Affairs*, 349–66. Millwood, N.Y.: KTO Press, 1977.

"James Chatham Duane." *Professional Memoirs, Corps of Engineers, United States Army and Engineer Department at Large* 4 (1912): 407–8.

Johnston, Charles. "Attack on Fort Gilmer, September 29th, 1864." *Southern Historical Society Papers* 1 (1876): 438–42.

Jones, A. C. "Third Arkansas Regiment at Appomattox." *Confederate Veteran* 23 (1915): 313–15.

Jones, A. K. "The Battle of Fort Gregg." *Southern Historical Society Papers* 31 (1903): 56–60.

Jones, J. William. "The Morale of General Lee's Army." In *The Annals of War*, 191–204. Philadelphia: Philadelphia Times, 1879.

Jordan, Weymouth T., Jr., comp. *North Carolina Troops, 1861-1865: A Roster*. 14 vols. Raleigh, N.C.: Division of Archives and History, 1966–98.

Judson, Amos M. *History of the Eighty-Third Regiment Pennsylvania Volunteers*. Alexandria, Va.: Stonewall House, 1985.

Kautz, August V. "Operations South of the James River." In *Battles and Leaders of the Civil War*, edited by Robert Underwood Johnson and Clarence Clough Buel, 4:533–35. New York: Thomas Yoseloff, 1956.

Kenfield, Frank. "Captured by Rebels: A Vermonter at Petersburg, 1864." *Vermont History* 36 (1968): 230–35.

Kennedy, Frances H., ed. *The Civil War Battlefield Guide*. 2nd ed. Boston: Houghton Mifflin, 1998.

Kent, Arthur A., ed. *Three Years with Company K*. Rutherford, N.J.: Fairleigh Dickinson University Press, 1976.

Kilmer, George L. "The Dash Into the Crater." *Century Magazine* 34 (1887): 774–76.

———. "Gordon's Attack at Fort Stedman." In *Battles and Leaders of the Civil War*, edited by Robert Underwood Johnson and Clarence Clough Buel, 4:579–83. New York: Thomas Yoseloff, 1956.

King, W. R. *Torpedoes: Their Invention and Use, From the First Application to the Art of War to the Present Time*. Washington, D.C.: Government Printing Office, 1866.

Korn, Jerry. *Pursuit to Appomattox: The Last Battles*. Alexandria, Va.: Time-Life, 1987.

Krick, R. E. L. *Staff Officers in Gray: A Biographical Register of the Staff Officers in the Army of Northern Virginia*. Chapel Hill: University of North Carolina Press, 2003.

La Bree, Ben, ed. *The Confederate Soldier in the Civil War*. Paterson, N.J.: Pageant Books, 1959.

Laine, J. Gary, and Morris M. Penny. *Law's Alabama Brigade in the War between the Union and the Confederacy*. Shippensburg, Pa.: White Mane, 1996.

*Lamar Rifles: A History of Company G, Eleventh Mississippi Regiment, C.S.A.* [Roanoke, VA: Stone Print, 1903].

LaMotte, Thomas J. "The Battle of the Crater." *Charleston News and Courier*, May 14, 1899.

Landrum, J. B. O. *History of Spartanburg County*. Atlanta: Franklin, 1900.

Lapham, William B. "With the Seventh Maine Battery." *War Papers Read Before the Commandery of the State of Maine, Military Order of the Loyal Legion of the United States*, 1:145–60. Portland, Maine: Thurston, 1898.

Livermore, Thomas L. *Days and Events, 1860–1866*. Boston: Houghton Mifflin, 1920.

Loehr, Charles T. *War History of the Old First Virginia Infantry Regiment*. Richmond, Va.: William Ellis Jones, 1884.

Lokey, J. W. "The Battle Near Deep Bottom, VA." *Confederate Veteran* 33 (1925): 127–28.

Longacre, Edward G. *Army of Amateurs: General Benjamin F. Butler and the Army of the James, 1863–1865*. Mechanicsburg, Pa.: Stackpole Books, 1997.

———, ed. *From Antietam to Fort Fisher: The Civil War Letters of Edward King Wightman, 1862–1865*. Rutherford, N.J.: Fairleigh Dickinson University Press, 1985.

Lord, Francis A. "A Bayonet for Digging." *Civil War Times Illustrated* 6, no. 2 (May 1967): 37.

———. "The Coehorn Mortar." *Civil War Times Illustrated* 5, no. 5 (August 1966): 18–19.

Love, W. A. "Company Records." *Confederate Veteran* 33 (1925): 50–52.

Loving, Jerome M., ed. *Civil War Letters of George Washington Whitman*. Durham, N.C.: Duke University Press, 1975.

Lowe, David W. "Field Fortifications in the Civil War." *North and South* 4, no. 6 (August 2001): 58–73.

———, ed. *Meade's Army: The Private Notebooks of Lt. Col. Theodore Lyman*. Kent, Ohio: Kent State University Press, 2007.

Lowe, David W., and Bonnie A. Burns. "Using GPS and GIS to Create a Historic Base Map." *CRM* 21, no. 5 (1998): 38–39.

Lowe, Jeffrey C., and Sam Hodges, eds. *Letters to Amanda: The Civil War Letters of Marion Hill Fitzpatrick, Army of Northern Virginia*. Macon, Ga.: Mercer University Press, 1998.

Mackintosh, Robert Harley, Jr., ed. *"Dear Martha . . .": The Confederate War Letters of a Southern Carolina Soldier, Alexander Faulkner Fewell*. Columbia, S.C.: R. L. Bryan, 1976.

Mahone, William. *The Battle of the Crater*. Petersburg: Franklin Press, n.d.
Malles, Ed, ed. *Bridge Building in Wartime: Colonel Wesley Brainerd's Memoirs of the 50th New York Volunteer Engineers*. Knoxville: University of Tennessee Press, 1997.
Marshall, Jeffrey D., ed. *A War of the People: Vermont Civil War Letters*. Hanover, N.H.: University Press of New England, 1999.
Marvel, William. *Burnside*. Chapel Hill: University of North Carolina Press, 1991.
———. *Lee's Last Retreat: The Flight to Appomattox*. Chapel Hill: University of North Carolina Press, 2002.
Maxfield, Albert, and Robert Brady, Jr. *Roster and Statistical Record of Company D, of the Eleventh Regiment Maine Infantry Volunteers*. New York: T. Humphrey, 1890.
May, T. J. "The Fight at Fort Gilmer." *Confederate Veteran* 12 (1904): 587–88.
McBride, R. E. *In the Ranks: From the Wilderness to Appomattox Court-House*. Cincinnati: Walden and Stowe, 1881.
McCabe, W. Gordon. "Defence of Petersburg." *Southern Historical Society Papers* 2 (1876): 257–306.
McClellan, George B. *The Report of Captain George B. McClellan, One of the Officers Sent to the Seat of War in Europe, in 1855 and 1856*. Washington, D.C.: Senate Executive Document No. 1, 35th Congress, Special Session, 1857.
McMaster, F. W. "The Battle of the Crater, July 30, 1864: Letter from Colonel McMaster." *Southern Historical Society Papers* 10 (1882): 119–23.
———. "Elliott's Brigade." Review of *Elliott's Brigade: How It Held the Crater and Saved Petersburg*, by Charles Pinckney Elliot, 9–27. Savannah, Ga: N.p., n.d.
McNeilly, John S. "A Mississippi Brigade in the Last Days of the Confederacy." *Publications of the Mississippi Historical Society* 7 (1903): 33–55.
McPherson, James M. *Battle Cry of Freedom: The Civil War Era*. New York: Oxford University Press, 1988.
Meade, George. *The Life and Letters of George Gordon Meade*. 2 vols. New York: Charles Scribner's Sons, 1913.
Menge, W. Springer, and J. August Shimrak, eds. *The Civil War Notebook of Daniel Chisholm: A Chronicle of Daily Life in the Union Army, 1864-1865*. New York: Ballantine Books, 1989.
"Michie, Peter Smith." *Dictionary of American Biography*, 12:597–98. New York: Charles Scribner's Sons, 1933.
Miller, J. Michael. *The North Anna Campaign: "Even to Hell Itself," May 21-26, 1864*. Lynchburg, Va.: H. E. Howard, 1989.
Mills, George H. *History of the 16th North Carolina (Originally Sixth N.C.) Regiment in the Civil War*. Rutherfordton, N.C.: N.p., 1901.
Mills, Luther Rice. "Letters from the Trenches." *Wake Forest Student* 31 (1911–12): 261–95.
Moffett, Mary C., ed. *Letters of General James Conner, C.S.A.* Columbia, S.C.: R. L. Bryan, 1976.
Moore, J. Staunton. "The Battle of Five Forks." *Confederate Veteran* 16 (1908): 403–4.
Morrison, James L., Jr., ed. *The Memoirs of Henry Heth*. Westport, Conn.: Greenwood, 1974.
Muffly, Joseph Wendel, ed. *The Story of Our Regiment: A History of the 148th Pennsylvania Vols*. Des Moines, Iowa: Kenyon Printing, 1904.

Murphy, Kevin C., ed. *The Civil War Letters of Joseph K. Taylor of the Thirty-Seventh Massachusetts Volunteer Infantry*. Lewiston, N.Y.: Edwin Mellen Press, 1998.

Mushkat, Jerome, ed. *A Citizen-Soldier's Civil War: The Letters of Brevet Major General Alvin C. Voris*. DeKalb: Northern Illinois University Press, 2002.

Nevins, Allan, ed. *A Diary of Battle: The Personal Journals of Colonel Charles S. Wainwright, 1861–1865*. New York: Harcourt, Brace, and World, 1962.

Nosworthy, Brent. *The Bloody Crucible of Courage: Fighting Methods and Combat Experience of the Civil War*. New York: Carroll and Graf, 2003.

Odcott, Mark, and David Lear, eds. *The Civil War Letters of Lewis Bissell*. Washington, D.C.: Field School Educational Foundation Press, 1981.

*The Official Military Atlas of the Civil War*. New York: Fairfax Press, 1983.

Orr, David G. "The Archaeology of Trauma: An Introduction to the Historical Archaeology of the American Civil War." In *Look to the Earth: Historical Archaeology and the American Civil War*, edited by Clarence R. Geier Jr. and Susan E. Winter, 21–35. Knoxville: University of Tennessee Press, 1994.

Osborne, Hampden. "The Struggle for Fort Mahone." *Confederate Veteran* 25 (1917): 226–29.

Owen, Charles W. "Explosion of Mine at Petersburg Described by Comrade C. W. Owen." *National Tribune*, November 1, 1934.

Owen, William Miller. "The Artillery Defenders of Fort Gregg." *Southern Historical Society Papers* 19 (1891): 65–71.

———. *In Camp and Battle with the Washington Artillery of New Orleans*. Boston: Ticknor, 1885.

Page, Charles D. *History of the Fourteenth Regiment, Connecticut Vol. Infantry*. Meriden, Conn.: Horton, 1906.

Peacock, Jane Bonner, ed. "A Georgian's View of War in Virginia." *Atlanta Historical Journal* 23 (1979): 91–136.

Pearce, T. H., ed. *Diary of Captain Henry A. Chambers*. Wendell, N.C.: Broadfoot's Bookmark, 1983.

Peck, George B., Jr. *A Recruit Before Petersburg*. Providence, R.I.: N. Bangs Williams, 1880.

Perry, H. H. "Assault on Fort Gilmer." *Confederate Veteran* 13 (1905): 413–15.

Perry, Milton F. *Infernal Machines: The Story of Confederate Submarine and Mine Warfare*. Baton Rouge: Louisiana State University Press, 1965.

"The Petersburg Mine." *National Tribune*, January 17, 1884.

Phillips, Marion G., and Valerie Phillips Parsegian, eds. *Richard and Rhoda: Letters from the Civil War*. Washington, D.C.: Legation Press, 1981.

Pierce, Francis Edwin. "Civil War Letters of Francis Edwin Pierce of the 108th New York Volunteer Infantry." *Rochester Historical Society Publications* 22 (1944): 150–73.

Polley, J. B. "Polley Lost a Foot—A Furlough." *Confederate Veteran* 5 (1897):569–71.

———. *A Soldier's Letters To Charming Nellie*. New York: Neale, 1908.

Pomfret, John E., ed. "Letters of Fred Lockley, Union Soldier 1864–65." *Huntington Library Quarterly* 16 (1952): 75–112.

Pope, John. "Movie Studio Contractors Unearth Possible Confederate Troop Mine." *Richmond Times-Dispatch*, April 17, 1997.

Porter, Horace. "Five Forks and the Pursuit of Lee." In *Battles and Leaders of the Civil War*, edited by Robert Underwood Johnson and Clarence Clough Buel, 4:708-22. New York: Thomas Yoseloff, 1956.

Powell, William H. "The Battle of the Petersburg Crater." In *Battles and Leaders of the Civil War*, edited by Robert Underwood Johnson and Clarence Clough Buel, 4:545-60. New York: Thomas Yoseloff, 1956.

Power, J. Tracy. *Lee's Miserables: Life in the Army of Northern Virginia from the Wilderness to Appomattox.* Chapel Hill: University of North Carolina Press, 1998.

Powers, George W. *The Story of the Thirty Eighth Regiment of Massachusetts Volunteers.* Cambridge, Mass.: Dakin and Metcalf, 1866.

*Private and Official Correspondence of Gen. Benjamin F. Butler During the Period of the Civil War.* 5 vols. Norwood, Mass.: Plimpton Press, 1917.

Rains, Gabriel J. "Torpedoes." *Southern Historical Society Papers* 3 (1877): 255-60.

Rast, P. J. "Fort Mahone and Other Struggles." *Confederate Veteran* 25 (1917): 355-56.

Reid, Robert A. "Petersburg Crater." *National Tribune*, January 5, 1905.

Reid-Green, Marcia, ed. *Letters Home: Henry Matrau of the Iron Brigade.* Lincoln: University of Nebraska Press, 1993.

*Report of the Committee on the Conduct of the War on the Attack on Petersburg on the 30th Day of July, 1864.* Washington, D.C.: Government Printing Office, 1865.

Rhea, Gordon C. *To the North Anna River: Grant and Lee, May 13-25, 1864.* Baton Rouge: Louisiana State University Press, 2000.

Rhodes, Robert Hunt, ed. *All for the Union: The Civil War Diary and Letters of Elisha Hunt Rhodes.* New York: Orion Books, 1985.

Rhodes, Steven B. "Jeremy Gilmer and the Confederate Engineers." M.A. thesis, Virginia Polytechnic Institute and State University, 1983.

Richards, R. G. "The Blunder at the Petersburg Mine." *National Tribune*, June 18, 1925.

Rickard, James H. *Services With Colored Troops in Burnside's Corps.* Providence: Rhode Island Soldiers and Sailors Historical Society, 1894.

Robertson, James I., Jr., ed. "'The Boy Artillerist': Letters of Colonel William Pegram, C.S.A." *Virginia Magazine of History and Biography* 98 (1990): 221-60.

———. *The Civil War Letters of General Robert McAllister.* New Brunswick, N.J.: Rutgers University Press, 1965.

Robertson, John, comp. *Michigan in the War.* Lansing: W. S. George, 1882.

Robertson, William Glenn. *Back Door to Richmond: The Bermuda Hundred Campaign, April-June 1864.* Newark: University of Delaware Press, 1987.

———. *The Battle of Old Men and Boys, June 9, 1864.* Lynchburg, Va.: H. E. Howard, 1989.

Robins, Colin, ed. *Captain Dunscombe's Diary.* Bowdon, U.K.: Withycut House, 2003.

Robinson, W. P. "Artillery in Battle of the Crater." *Confederate Veteran* 19 (1911): 164-66.

Roe, David D., ed. *A Civil War Soldier's Diary: Valentine C. Randolph, 39th Illinois Regiment.* DeKalb: Northern Illinois University Press, 2006.

Rogers, George T. "Retaking Railroad at Reams Station." *Confederate Veteran* 5 (1897): 580-81.

Roman, Alfred. *The Military Operations of General Beauregard in the War Between the States, 1861 to 1865.* 2 vols. New York: Harper and Brothers, 1884.

Rosenblatt, Emil, and Ruth Rosenblatt, eds. *Hard Marching Every Day: The Civil War Letters of Private Wilbur Fisk, 1861–1865.* Lawrence: University Press of Kansas, 1992.

Roulhac, Thomas R. "The Forty-Ninth N.C., Infantry, C.S.A." *Southern Historical Society Papers* 23 (1895): 58–78.

Royle, Trevor. *Crimea: The Great Crimean War, 1854–1856.* New York: St. Martin's Press, 2000.

Sauers, Richard A., ed. *The Civil War Journal of Colonel William J. Bolton, 51st Pennsylvania, April 20, 1861–August 2, 1865.* Conshohocken, Pa.: Combined Publishing, 2000.

Schiller, Herbert M., ed. *A Captain's War: The Letters and Diaries of William H. S. Burgwyn, 1861–1865.* Shippensburg, Pa: White Mane, 1994.

Schulz, Helen. "The Magnificent Aereon." *Civil War Times Illustrated* 19, no. 8 (December 1980): 26–28.

Scott, Robert Garth, ed. *Forgotten Valor: The Memoirs, Journals, and Civil War Letters of Orlando B. Willcox.* Kent, Ohio: Kent State University Press, 1999.

Seagrave, Pia Seija, ed. *A Boy Lieutenant: Memoirs of Freeman S. Bowley, 30th United States Colored Troops Officer.* Fredericksburg, Va.: Sergeant Kirkland's Museum and Historical Society, 1997.

Shaver, Lewellyn A. *A History of the Sixtieth Alabama Regiment: Gracie's Alabama Brigade.* Montgomery: Barrett and Brown, 1867.

Shepley, George F. "Incidents of the Capture of Richmond." *Atlantic Monthly* 46 (1880), 18–28.

Sheridan, Philip H. "The Last Days of the Rebellion." In *Battles and Leaders of the Civil War,* edited by Peter Cozzens, 6:526–35. Urbana: University of Illinois Press.

Shiman, Philip Lewis. "Engineering Sherman's March: Army Engineers and the Management of Modern War, 1862–1865." Ph.D. diss., Duke University, 1991.

Silliker, Ruth L., ed. *The Rebel Yell and the Yankee Hurrah: The Civil War Journal of a Maine Volunteer.* Camden, Maine: Down East Books, 1985.

Simon, John Y., ed. *The Papers of Ulysses S. Grant.* 28 vols. Carbondale: Southern Illinois University Press, 1967–2005.

Small, Harold A., ed. *The Road to Richmond: The Civil War Memoirs of Major Abner R. Small of the Sixteenth Maine Volunteers.* New York: Fordham University Press, 2000.

Smith, Charles W. "Lights and Shadows." *War Papers Read Before the Indiana Commandery, Military Order of the Loyal Legion of the United States,* 431–50. Indianapolis: Levey Brothers, 1898.

Smith, William Farrar. *From Chattanooga to Petersburg Under Generals Grant and Butler.* Boston: Houghton Mifflin, 1893.

*The Soldier of Indiana in the War for the Union.* Indianapolis: Merrill, 1869.

Sommers, Richard J. *Richmond Redeemed: The Siege at Petersburg.* Garden City, N.Y.: Doubleday, 1981.

Sparks, David S., ed. *Inside Lincoln's Army: The Diary of Marsena Rudolph Patrick, Provost Marshal General, Army of the Potomac.* New York: Thomas Yoseloff, 1964.

Spear, Abbott, et al., eds. *The Civil War Recollections of General Ellis Spear.* Orono: University of Maine Press, 1997.

Stedman, Charles M. "Reams Station." In *Histories of the Several Regiments and*

*Battalions from North Carolina in the Great War, 1861–'65*, edited by Walter Clark, 5:206–12. Goldsboro, N.C.: Nash Brothers, 1901.

Stevens, C. A. *Berdan's United States Sharpshooters in the Army of the Potomac, 1861–1865*. Dayton, Ohio: Morningside Bookshop, 1972.

Stevens, Hazard. "The Storming of the Lines of Petersburg by the Sixth Corps, April 2, 1865." In *The Shenandoah Campaigns of 1862 and 1864 and the Appomattox Campaign 1865: Papers of the Military Historical Society of Massachusetts*, 6:411–35. Boston: Military Historical Society of Massachusetts, 1907.

"Stevens, Walter Husted." *National Cyclopaedia of American Biography*, 12:258–59. New York: James T. White, 1904.

Stevenson, Silas. *Account of the Battle of the Mine, Or Battle of the Crater in Front of Petersburg, VA., July 30th, 1864*. New Castle, Pa.: John A. Leathers, n.d.

Stewart, A. M. *Camp, March, and Battlefield: Or, Three Years and a Half with the Army of the Potomac*. Philadelphia: James B. Rodgers, 1865.

Stewart, William H. "The Charge of the Crater." *Southern Historical Society Papers* 25 (1897): 77–90.

———. "The Hardships of Hatcher's Run." *Confederate Veteran* 19 (1911): 336–37.

———. *The Spirit of the South: Orations, Essays and Lectures*. New York: Neale, 1908.

Stiles, Robert. *Four Years Under Marse Robert*. New York: Neale, 1904.

Stone, DeWitt Boyd, Jr., ed. *Wandering to Glory: Confederate Veterans Remember Evans' Brigade*. Columbia: University of South Carolina Press, 2002.

Stone, James Madison. *Personal Recollections of the Civil War*. Boston: Author, 1918.

*The Story of One Regiment: The Eleventh Maine Volunteers in the War of the Rebellion*. New York: J. J. Little, 1896.

Strother, A. E. "Battle and Capture of Fort Gregg." *Confederate Veteran* 29 (1921): 425–26.

Styple, William B., ed. *Our Noble Blood: The Civil War Letters of Regis de Trobriand, Major-General U.S.V.* Kearny, N.J.: Belle Grove Publishing, 1997.

Suderow, Bryce A. "Confederate Casualties at the Crater." *The Kepi* (June–July 1985): 15–43.

———. "Glory Denied: The First Battle of Deep Bottom, July 27th–29th, 1864." *North and South* 3, no. 7 (September 2000): 17–32.

———. "'Nothing But a Miracle Could Save Us': Second Battle of Deep Bottom, Virginia, August 14–20, 1864." *North and South* 4, no. 2 (January 2001): 12–32.

———. "War along the James." *North and South* 6, no. 3 (April 2003): 12–23.

Sumner, Merlin E., ed. *The Diary of Cyrus B. Comstock*. Dayton, Ohio: Morningside Bookshop, 1987.

*Supplement to the Official Records of the Union and Confederate Armies*. 100 vols. Wilmington, N.C.: Broadfoot, 1995–99.

Sylvester, Robert Bruce. "The U.S. Military Railroad and the Siege of Petersburg." *Civil War History* 10 (1964): 309–16.

Talcott, T. M. R. "Reminiscences of the Confederate Engineer Service." In *The Photographic History of the Civil War*, 5:256–70. New York: Review of Reviews, 1911.

Tapert, Annette, ed. *The Brothers' War: Civil War Letters to Their Loved Ones from the Blue and Gray*. New York: Vintage Books, 1989.

Thienel, Phillip M. *Mr. Lincoln's Bridge Builders: The Right Hand of American Genius.* Shippensburg, Pa.: White Mane, 2000.
Thomas, Henry Goddard. "The Colored Troops at Petersburg." In *Battles and Leaders of the Civil War*, edited by Robert Underwood Johnson and Clarence Clough Buel, 4:563–67. New York: Thomas Yoseloff, 1956.
Thomas, William M. "The Slaughter at Petersburg, June 18, 1864." *Southern Historical Society Papers* 25 (1897): 222–30.
Thompson, Gilbert. *The Engineer Battalion in the Civil War.* Washington, D.C.: Press of the Engineer School, 1910.
Tilney, Robert. *My Life in the Army: Three Years and a Half with the Fifth Army Corps, Army of the Potomac, 1862–1865.* Philadelphia: Ferris and Leach, 1912.
Timberlake, W. L. "In the Siege of Richmond and After." *Confederate Veteran* 29 (1921): 412–14.
Trowbridge, John T. *The Desolate South, 1865–1866.* Freeport, N.Y.: Books for Libraries, 1970.
Trudeau, Noah Andre. *The Last Citadel: Petersburg, Virginia, June 1864–April 1865.* Baton Rouge: Louisiana State University Press, 1991.
———. *The Siege of Petersburg.* N.p.: Eastern National Park and Monument Association, 1995.
Turtle, Thomas. "History of the Engineer Battalion." *Printed Papers of the Essayons Club of the Corps of Engineers* 1 (1868–72): 1–9.
Tyler, Mason Whiting. *Recollections of the Civil War, With Many Original Diary Entries and Letters Written From the Seat of War, and With Annotated References.* New York: G. P. Putnam's Sons, 1912.
Van Den Bossche, Kris, ed. "War and Other Reminiscences." *Rhode Island History* 47, no. 4 (November 1989): 115–47.
Venable, Matthew Walton. *Eighty Years After, Or Grandpa's Story.* Charleston, W.Va.: Hood-Hiserman-Brodhag, 1929.
Venable, M. W. "In the Trenches at Petersburg." *Confederate Veteran* 14 (1906): 178–79.
Wagner, Arthur L. "Hasty Intrenchments in the War of Secession." In *Civil and Mexican Wars, 1861, 1846: Papers of the Military Historical Society of Massachusetts*, 13:127–53. Boston: Military Historical Society of Massachusetts, 1913.
Wagner, Frank. "Michler, Nathaniel." In *The New Handbook of Texas*, 4:703–4. Austin: Texas State Historical Association, 1996.
Wagstaff, Henry M., ed. *The James A. Graham Papers, 1861–1864.* Chapel Hill: University of North Carolina Press, 1928.
———. "Letters of Thomas Jackson Strayhorn." *North Carolina Historical Review* 13 (1936): 311–34.
Walker, Charles N., and Rosemary Walker, eds. "Diary of the War, by Robt. S. Robertson." Pt. 4. *Old Fort News* 28 (1965): 175–232.
Walker, Francis A. *History of the Second Army Corps in the Army of the Potomac.* New York: Charles Scribner's Sons, 1887.
Warner, Ezra J. *Generals in Blue: Lives of the Union Commanders.* Baton Rouge: Louisiana State University Press, 1964.

---. *Generals in Gray: Lives of the Confederate Commanders*. Baton Rouge: Louisiana State University Press, 1959.
*The War of the Rebellion: A Compilation of the Official Records of the Union and Confederate Armies*. 70 vols. in 128. Washington, D.C.: Government Printing Office, 1880-1901.
Washburn, George H. *A Complete Military History and Record of the 108th Regiment N.Y. Vols., From 1862 to 1894*. Rochester, N.Y.: E. R. Andrews, 1894.
Weld, Stephen M. "The Petersburg Mine." In *Papers of the Military Historical Society of Massachusetts*, 5:207-19. Wilmington, N.C.: Broadfoot, 1989.
---. *War Diary and Letters of Stephen Minot Weld, 1861-1865*. Boston: Massachusetts Historical Society, 1979.
Welsh, Jack D. *Medical Histories of Union Generals*. Kent, Ohio: Kent State University Press, 1996.
Whitehead, Richard Owen. "The Retaking of the Lines." In *The Story of American Heroism: Thrilling Narratives of Personal Adventures During the Great Civil War, As Told By the Medal Winners and Roll of Honor Men*. Springfield, Ohio: J. W. Jones, 1897.
Wiatt, Alex L. *26th Virginia Infantry*. Lynchburg, Va.: H. E. Howard, 1984.
Wilcox, Cadmus M. "Defence of Batteries Gregg and Whitworth, and the Evacuation of Petersburg." *Southern Historical Society Papers* 4 (1877): 18-33.
Wiley, Kenneth, ed. *Norfolk Blues: The Civil War Diary of the Norfolk Light Artillery Blues*. Shippensburg, Pa.: Burd Street Press, 1997.
Wilkeson, Frank. *Recollections of a Private Soldier in the Army of the Potomac*. New York: G. P. Putnam's Sons, 1893.
Williams, Edward B., ed. *Rebel Brothers: The Civil War Letters of the Truehearts*. College Station: Texas A&M University Press, 1995.
Wood, Anthony, ed. *Reminiscences of the 35th Ga. Regt. As Seen by a Sharpshooter at the Front*. Conyers, Ga.: THP, n.d.

# INDEX

Abbot, Henry L., 51–52, 58, 103, 235, 288–89, 304, 308–9
Aerial warfare, 240–43
Alabama units
  3rd, 269
  6th, 269
Alexander, E. P., 44, 47, 86, 175, 178
Appomattox campaign, 280–82
Armored breastworks, 243
Artillery, 74–75, 86–87, 92–94, 103, 155–56, 188, 238

Barnard, John G., 4–5, 41, 61, 190, 276
Beauregard, P. G. T., 12–14, 26–27, 36, 44–45
Benham, Henry W., 60, 183
Bermuda Hundred, defenses at, 306–10, 374 (nn. 27, 32)
Biggs, Will, 65, 219
Birney, David B., 159
Blackford, W. W., 111, 113–14, 120–21, 342 (n. 44)
Blacks: as engineer troops, 7; in Fifth Offensive, 161, 163; as laborers on fortifications, 10, 54–57, 123, 153–54, 205, 237; in mine attack, 87–88, 95–96, 98–100, 102–4; as soldiers, 281
Boston, William, 253
Bowden, John Malachi, 76

Bowen, Charles, 32–33
Bowen, George D., 30, 33–35, 157, 187–88, 277
Bowley, Freeman, 99–101
Boydton Plank Road Line, 165–66, 169
Bradwell, I. G., 211, 217, 228
Bridges, 347–48 (n. 14)
Bross, John A., 98–99
Burnside, Ambrose E., 87–89, 96–97, 104–6

Carter, Robert Goldthwaite, 67
Casemates, 236, 364 (n. 23)
Cavin, Virgil S., 219–20, 225
Chaffin's Bluff defenses, 161, 175–81, 313–16
Chamberlayne, John Hampden, 153
Chevaux-de-frise, 60, 64, 111, 200, 204
Chisholm, Daniel, 16–17, 136
City Point defenses, 147, 183–84, 201, 304
Clarke, John J., 7
Clarke, Thomas W., 90
Colston, Raleigh E., 12
Comstock, Cyrus Ballou, 5
Confederate units
  1st Engineers, 6
  2nd Engineers, 6–7
Conner, James, 140
Cook, Thomas M., 288
Corduroy roads, 203, 297, 347 (n. 14)
Covered ways, 53, 55–56, 111, 203, 288

Crater, battle of the. *See* Mine attack at Petersburg

Daley, Dennis B., 134, 345 (n. 42)
Dams, 204–5, 238, 291, 305, 357 (n. 18)
Dauchy, George K., 136
Davidson, Roderick O., 241–42
Day, W. A., 204
Deep Bottom: bridgehead at, 38–40; defenses at, 152, 173–74; first battle of, 79–83; second battle of, 124–29
Desertion, 72, 109, 187, 224–28
Dimmock, Charles H., 11, 36
Dimmock Line at Petersburg, 10–14, 36, 51, 61–62, 265–66, 273–74, 294–96, 322 (n. 25), 324 (n. 46), 327 (n. 7)
Douglas, Hugh Thomas, 47–49, 83–84, 113–15, 118–20
Duane, James Chatham, 1, 17, 42, 44, 318–319 (n. 1)
Dunlop, William, 277
Dutch Gap Canal, 122–23, 182–83, 201–2, 240

Eighth Union Offensive at Petersburg, 254–63
Elliott, Stephen D., 94
Engineers, 1–8
Ewell, Richard S., 152

Farquhar, Francis U., 3, 44–45
Fascines, 60
Field fortifications, xv–xvi; construction of, 50–64, 142–47, 151–53, 166–81, 232–33, 289; dimensions of, 32–33, 57, 63, 172, 179, 302, 306, 308; maintenance and improvement of, 109–11, 147–51, 153–54, 182, 199–201, 235–38; rifle musket and, 283; and soldiers as laborers, 289
Fifth Union Offensive at Petersburg, 160–66, 172–73, 178–79
Fireballs, 24, 238
First Confederate Offensive at Petersburg, 40–41

First Offensive at Petersburg, 18–37
Five Forks, battle of, 260–63
Food, 67–68, 107, 219–20, 224
Fort Brady, 172, 237, 313
Fort Burnham, 169–70, 236, 310–11, 375 (n. 37)
Fort Conahey, 168, 201, 301–2
Fort Davis, 147, 149
Fort Dushane, 144
Fort Fisher, 302–3
Fort Gregg, 274–77, 370 (n. 28)
Fort Harrison, 152, 161–64, 169, 310–11
Fort Johnson, 175, 177–78
Fort Mahone, 266–70, 290
Forts, naming of, 59, 146
Fort Sedgwick, 57, 59, 122, 149, 185–86, 206, 209, 266, 288, 292–93, 297–303
Fort Stedman, 122, 186, 293, 296–97; Confederate attack on, 246–53
Fort Wadsworth, 167
Fourth Union Offensive at Petersburg, 124–41
Fowler, Thomas, 112, 340 (n. 24)
Fuel, 218–19

Gabions, 54, 60, 63, 200
Gibbon, John, 37, 139–40, 257
Gilreath, Erasmus, 71
Glacis, 57
Globe Tavern, battle of, 129–35, 344 (n. 38), 345 (n. 43)
Gomez fuse, 120, 202
Gordon, John B., 246, 250, 270–71
Gordon, William Alexander, 115
Gould, Charles G., 272–73
Gracie, Archibald, 211
Grant, Ulysses S., xiii, 14–15, 17, 23, 35, 100, 189, 104–6, 278–80; and development of grand tactics at Petersburg, 41–45, 49, 78–79, 82–83, 87–88, 103, 124, 128, 132, 135, 141–42, 145, 160, 179, 189–90, 192–93, 195, 212–13, 229–32, 234, 245–46, 256, 264, 274, 371 (n. 1)
Greek fire, 243–44
Greer, Henry, 71

{ 400 } *Index*

Hagood, Johnson, 134–35, 306, 345 (n. 42)
Hagood Line at Petersburg, 19–20, 23, 36, 295, 324 (n. 46)
Haley, John, 67
Hancock, Winfield S., 81–82, 135–36, 140, 145, 149
Hand grenades, 44, 325 (n. 13)
Harris, David Bullock, 6, 28–29
Harris, Henry Herbert, 184–85, 195
Harris Line at Petersburg, 23, 28–29, 36, 61, 63, 295, 324 (n. 46)
Head logs, 55, 203
Hicksford raid, 212–15
Houghton, Charles H., 101
Howell, Charles W., 289
Howlett Line, 21, 23, 308–10
Hunt, Henry J., 42

Illness, 71
Intelligence, 70–71

James River, Union crossing of, 14–18
Johnson, Bushrod R., 63, 153, 156, 184, 189, 211–12
Jones, Archibald K., 276
Jones's Farm, battle of, 165

Leak, W. E., 225
Ledlie, James Hewett, 88–89, 92, 97
Lee, Robert E., xiii, 15–16, 18, 23, 36, 80–81, 164, 168, 211, 226–27, 246, 263, 270–71, 274; and earthwork construction, 62, 207–8, 237
Leet, George K., 135
Lewis's Farm, battle of, 255–56
Livermore, Thomas L., 50
Longstreet, James, 237–38
Loring, Charles G., 93
Lyman, Theodore, 37, 168, 190, 264, 287–88

Mahone, William, 39, 98–99, 102
Maine units
    1st Heavy Artillery, 34
    11th, 81
    20th, 142

Mantlets, 51, 60–61, 64, 297, 309
Massachusetts units
    10th Battery, 50–51
    35th, 3, 54, 97
    56th, 51
McIlwaine's Hill, fight for, 253–54
McNair, Enoch Alexander, 37
Meade, George G., 25, 29–30, 35, 90, 96–97, 100, 104–6, 189, 253; and development of grand tactics at Petersburg, 42, 85, 87–88, 103, 160, 192–93, 264, 371 (n. 1); and engineering, 168
Meikel, George W., 158
Michie, Peter Smith, 4, 16–17, 123, 170
Michigan units
    27th, 93, 96
Michler, Nathaniel, xv, 1–2, 46, 51, 61, 168, 291, 306
Mills, Luther Rice, 219
Mine attack at Petersburg, 41–43, 45–49, 78–79, 83–91, 290–92, 294, 297–98
Mining: Confederate countermine explosion, August 5, 118–20, 342 (n. 44); countermining, 47–49, 83–85, 112–22, 154, 184–87, 206–7, 293–94, 326 (nn. 29–30), 327 (n. 34), 340 (n. 28), 342 (nn. 44, 51–52), 358 (n. 28); at Dutch Gap Canal, 201–2; effect of on morale, 111; use of electricity in, 239–40
Mississippi units
    12th, 134
    16th, 134
Morale, 215, 222–28
Mortars, 75–76
Morton, James St. Clair, 2–3, 26

Native Americans, 102
New York units
    1st Engineers, 4
    12th Battery, 31, 296
    46th, 96
    50th Engineers, 2, 17, 59–60, 144, 200, 223–24, 289–90
    51st, 3

Ninth Union Offensive at Petersburg, 264–79
North Carolina units
    49th, 31, 37, 46, 133
    53rd, 269
    56th, 28, 33

Obstructions, 109–11, 142, 150, 199, 203–4, 233, 272, 278, 289, 309, 339 (n. 18), 346 (n. 60)
Ord, Edward O. C., 118–19
Overland campaign, 282–83

Pamplin Historical Park, 306
Parados, 297
Parke, John G., 168
Petersburg, city of, 10–11, 76–77, 158–59, 198, 290–91
Petersburg campaign, xiii–xv, 12; geography of, 8; impact of field fortifications on, 284–85; length of defenses at, 174, 181, 287; losses in, 37, 83, 91, 103–4, 194, 196, 232, 263, 276, 279–80; segments of, xvii–xxi; siege aspects of, xv, 325 (n. 8)
Petersburg National Battlefield, 294, 306
Phillips, Richard C., 3
Pickett, George, 257, 259–63
Pioneers, 3, 7
Pleasants, Henry, Jr., 41–42, 45, 209
Polley, J. B., 69
Potter, Robert B., 3
Powell, William H., 92
Pryor, Roger A., 210

Railroad at Petersburg, 146, 234
Rains, Gabriel J., 180
Randall, William H., 102
Rats, 217, 219
Ray, William, 142, 145
Reams's Station, battle of, 135–41, 345 (n. 48), 346 (n. 60)
Rhode Island units
    7th, 3, 200

Rhodes, Elisha Hunt, 217, 273
Richmond defenses, 9–10, 295, 375 (n. 43)
Robinson, John Forrest, 219

Sandbags, 51–52, 110
Sanitation, 68, 107–8, 110, 210
Scott, Don E., 92
Secondary Line at Petersburg, 58, 144–45, 168, 234, 303–4
Second Union Offensive at Petersburg, 38–39
Serrell, Edward W., 163, 242–43
Seventh Union Offensive at Petersburg, 229–35
Sharpshooting, 72–73, 138, 236–37, 364 (n. 24)
Shelters, 66–67, 182, 205–6, 209–10, 216–18, 304, 310
Sheridan, Philip H., 255–63
Siege approaches at Petersburg, 42–45, 151
Sixth Union Offensive at Petersburg, 189–96
Skirmishing and picketing, 73–74, 157–58, 179, 196–98, 238–39, 253–54, 299, 301, 374 (n. 7)
Slashing, 142
Smith, Martin Luther, 5, 9, 61
Smith, William F., 20
Snook, James M., 65
Soap, 220–21
Sommers, Richard, 152
South Carolina units
    17th, 94
    22nd, 93
    23rd, 27, 93
    26th, 94
Spaulding, Ira, 2
Squirrel Level Road Line, 151–52, 164–65, 302
Stevens, Hazard, 271
Stevens, Walter Husted, 5, 10
Stewart, William H., 99, 103
Sullivan, James P., 132
Sutherland Station, 277–78

Talcott, Thomas Mann Randolph, 6, 119, 342 (n. 44)
Third Union Offensive at Petersburg, 78–106
Thompson, Gilbert, 117
Tidball, John C., 249–50
Tools, 59–60
Torpedoes, 44, 179–81, 206, 280, 290, 313–16, 353 (n. 57)
Traverses, 66
Trench life at Petersburg, 37, 65–76, 107–9, 150, 154–58, 187, 207–10, 238–39
Trench raids at Petersburg, 196–198, 210–12, 239, 356 (n. 47)
Trowbridge, John Townsend, 290
Truces, 69–70, 104–5, 156, 188–89, 212

United States units
  U.S. Engineer Battalion, 2, 17, 59
  12th Infantry, 33
  43rd USCT, 3

Valentine, Herbert E., 110
Vance, Zebulon B., 216

Venable, Matthew, 121, 293
Verdery, James Paul, 102–3
Vermont units
  5th, 272–73
Virginia units
  Pegram's Battery, 28–29
  26th, 93
  59th, 93

Wainwright, Charles, 35, 136
Walker, Francis, 136
Warren, Gouverneur K., 55, 58, 110, 143–44, 165–66, 213–14, 255–63; and development of grand tactics at Petersburg, 132–33, 141
Weitzel, Godfrey, 4, 278
West Virginia units
  12th, 276
White Oak Road Line, 234–35, 258, 306
Wilkeson, Frank, 35
Wright, Horatio G., 271–74

Young, William B., 102

*Index* { 403 }

www.ingramcontent.com/pod-product-compliance
Lightning Source LLC
Chambersburg PA
CBHW021814300426
44114CB00009BA/169